LECTURES ON PUBLIC ECONOMICS

Economics Handbook Series

Anderson: *National Income Theory and Its Price Theoretic Foundations*
Atkinson and Stiglitz: *Lectures on Public Economics*
Carlson: *Economic Security in the United States*
Chacholiades: *International Monetary Theory and Policy*
Chacholiades: *International Trade Theory and Policy*
Hansen: *A Survey of General Equilibrium Systems*
Hansen: *The American Economy*
Harris: *The Economics of Harvard*
Harris: *Monetary Theory*
Harrod: *The British Economy*
Henderson and Quandt: *Microeconomic Theory: A Mathematical Approach*
Hirsch: *The Economics of State and Local Government*
Hirsch: *Urban Economic Analysis*
Jones: *An Introduction to Modern Theories of Economic Growth*
Kindleberger and Herrick: *Economic Development*
Maddala: *Econometrics*
Nourse: *Regional Economics*
Ott, Ott, and Yoo: *Macroeconomic Theory*
Quirk and Saposnik: *Introduction to General Equilibrium Theory and Welfare Economics*
Taylor: *A History of Economic Thought*
Taylor: *Macro Models for Developing Countries*
Theil, Boot, and Kloek: *Operations Research and Quantitative Economics*
Walton and McKersie: *A Behavioral Theory of Labor Negotiations*

LECTURES ON PUBLIC ECONOMICS

Anthony B. Atkinson

Professor of Economics
London School of Economics

Joseph E. Stiglitz

Professor of Economics
Princeton University

McGraw-Hill Book Company, New York, New York

McGraw-Hill Book (U.K.), Ltd., Maidenhead, England

St. Louis   San Francisco   Auckland   Bogotá
Guatemala   Hamburg   Johannesburg   Lisbon   Madrid   Mexico
Montreal   New Delhi   Panama   Paris   San Juan   São Paulo
Singapore   Sydney   Tokyo   Toronto

LECTURES ON PUBLIC ECONOMICS

1234567890 FGFG 89876543210

British Library Cataloguing in Publication Data

Atkinson, Anthony Barnes
   Lectures on public economics.
   1. Finance, Public
   I. Title II. Stiglitz, Joseph E.
   336   HJ141   79-40854

   ISBN 0-07-084105-5
   ISBN 0-07-084106-3 Pbk

This book was set in Times Roman.
The editor was Bonnie E. Lieberman;
the production supervisor was John Mancia.
Fairfield Graphics was printer and binder.

For Siobhan, Michael, Richard, Sarah, and Charles

CONTENTS

PREFACE

This volume is based on lectures that the authors have given to graduate courses in public economics at (A.B.A.) the University of Essex, Massachusetts Institute of Technology, and University College London, and at (J.E.S.) Yale University and Stanford University. Our first acknowledgement is to the many students who attended these courses and helped us develop the material.

The translation of lectures into the format of a book is always difficult, and in the present case has taken much longer than we envisaged when we embarked on the venture in 1970. In the course of the ten years, we have accumulated many debts to colleagues and friends. Our understanding of the field in general owes a great deal to Peter Diamond, James Mirrlees and Peter Mieszkowski. We have individually benefited from collaboration at different times with Partha Dasgupta, Mervyn King, David Newbery, Agnar Sandmo and Nicholas Stern. Drafts of the Lectures have been circulated widely over a number of years, and we are most appreciative of the comments we have received. We should single out in particular Richard Arnott, who played a key role in the preparation of the penultimate version, and Leif Johansen and Nicholas Rau, who read all the 1977 draft and made most valuable criticisms. In addition, we received helpful comments from the publisher's readers and from: Syed Ahsan, Mike Boskin, David Bradford, Harvey Brazer, Mono Chatterji, Steve Clark, Paul Grout, Jane Hannaway, Claude Henry, Jon Kesselman, Jack Mintz, Robert Moffitt,

Knud Munk, Peter Neary, Janusz Ordover, Mitch Polinsky, Tom Romer and John Whalley. All these people, to whom we are most grateful, have made a great contribution to improving the form of the lectures; they should not however be held in any way responsible for the contents.

Different versions of the manuscript have been typed by a succession of secretaries in Essex, Stanford, Princeton and Oxford, but particular thanks are due to Anne Robinson. She typed both the first full draft and the final version, with remarkably little complaint, as well as attempting on occasion to improve the style. Celia Rhodes of University College London prepared the bibliography and gave editorial help in the last critical weeks. Andrew Best of Curtis Brown, and Julia Maidment and Bonnie Lieberman of McGraw-Hill, provided patient help with the publication. Franklin Allen of Nuffield College, Oxford, was most helpful at proof stage.

We are grateful to those authors and publishers who have given us permission to use material in this book.

Finally, the book is dedicated to our children, in the hope that they have survived the intrusion of this cuckoo into their respective nests.

Anthony B. Atkinson
London
Joseph E. Stiglitz
Princeton

INTRODUCTORY NOTE

This book is intended as a graduate text in the field of public economics. As such, it is more advanced than undergraduate textbooks such as *Public Finance in Theory and Practice* by R. A. and P. B. Musgrave. It assumes a good understanding of modern microeconomics and familiarity with basic calculus. At the same time, it should be emphasized that the book uses no sophisticated mathematics, and that considerable effort has been made to explain the more technical sections. There is nothing in the book that should be beyond the reach of a first-year graduate student, and much of it should be accessible to final-year undergraduates.

In the *Lectures*, we have placed particular stress on recent developments in public economics, aiming to bring together material that is at present scattered in the journal literature. The fields covered include the general equilibrium incidence of taxation, the econometric study of responses to taxes and social security benefits, the optimum design of fiscal policy, debt policy and capital accumulation, and the provision of public goods. In each case we are especially concerned with the development of tools that can be applied to current issues—as aids to "thinking about policy".

In attempting to encompass this range of new developments within the constraints of length imposed by the publishers, we had to face several problems. The first is that we need to refer to a large number of books and articles, drawn from many different fields. The limitations of space have meant however that we cannot provide an exhaustive bibliography of all relevant work. In view of this, we have cited particular sources to demonstrate specific points or to illustrate the kind of work that has been done. We have also included a brief (one-paragraph) guide to reading at the end of Lectures 2–17. Together with the Bibliography at the end of the book (which itself is over 25 pages long), these should provide the reader with an introduction to the literature. In all cases references are given as A. Smith (1776), with the full citation being given in the Bibliography. Where A. Smith published two works in that year, the first is referred to as (1776a), the second as (1776b).

Second, even within the subjects on which we concentrate, we have had to be highly selective in our coverage. As a result, we have been forced to cut out many gems, and we apologize in advance to those whose work has not been adequately treated. This is partially redressed by the addition of Exercises, which are intended both to test the reader's understanding and to extend the scope of material covered. These exercises vary considerably in difficulty and length (one at least can be answered in a single word). We have in some places indicated that the exercise is based on a particular source, which the reader may like to consult (after attempting it).

Third, the range of material covered has meant that it is impossible to maintain the same standard notation throughout the book, let alone use symbols that are clearly mnemonic. Since we are drawing on several different branches of literature, we have to recognize that to use t for time is as natural in growth theory as it is to use t for taxes in public finance. (We have in fact kept t for taxes, with a variety of subscripts, and occasionally resorted to τ or T, while we use u for time.) We have tried to reserve $\bar{X}$ for the mean of X, X' for its derivative (except in diagrams), and $\hat{X}$ for the logarithmic derivative. We have used **X** to denote the vector $(X_1, X_2, \ldots, X_n)$. The reader may detect certain other regularities. There are however symbols that take on different meanings in different Lectures, and all that we can claim is that we have tried to explain carefully the notation employed in each case.

LECTURES ON PUBLIC ECONOMICS

THE ANALYSIS OF POLICY

ONE

INTRODUCTION: PUBLIC ECONOMICS

1-1 INTRODUCTION

These Lectures are concerned with the economics of the public sector. We are all constantly affected by the economic decisions of the government. This is most noticeable in the taxes we pay. Income tax, sales taxes, local taxes, and social security contributions account for a substantial proportion of our income. Owners of capital are affected by taxes on corporate profits, inheritance taxes and capital gains taxes. Almost all of us are at one time or another recipients of income from the government: for example, via social security programmes. A large proportion of workers are paid by the government or produce goods sold to the government. Many children go to schools supported by the government. We enjoy municipal parks, swimming pools, roads and other publicly provided facilities. Many people are concerned about public policy towards the environment or about the conservation of natural resources.

In these Lectures we attempt to describe in a systematic manner the principal consequences of such economic activities by the government and their relation to social objectives. In Part One we examine the effects of various tax and expenditure policies. This "positive" section of the book is concerned with such questions as "Does income taxation discourage work effort or risk-taking?" or "What is the incidence of the corporation tax?". In contrast, in Part Two we present the "normative" theory of public finance, which is an attempt to postulate some simple criteria for government decision-making and to follow through their logical implications. Thus, it deals with such issues as the degree of progression for the income tax, the choice between direct and indirect taxation, the provision of public goods, and pricing rules for public enterprises.

In addressing these questions, we make no attempt to provide a

3

comprehensive coverage. The choice of the title *Lectures on ...* is intended to dispel any impression that the book is an exhaustive account of public economics. The aim of the Lectures is to illustrate the current state of the art, to give some flavour of the strengths and weaknesses of recent developments, and to point to areas where future research is necessary.

The ways in which the book falls short of being comprehensive should be clear from the Table of Contents. Most seriously, no attempt is made to cover stabilization and macroeconomic policy. This is an essential element in any global view of the role of the government, and many issues are dominated by macroeconomic considerations. However, the economics of publishing have changed since the time when Musgrave could devote 210 pages of *The Theory of Public Finance* (1959) to stabilization policy, and there are many excellent treatments in the literature. Our emphasis is therefore on goals other than those of stabilization.

Even with this restriction, the coverage is selective. Some readers will no doubt be horrified or disappointed by the omissions, which include the international aspects of taxation, the economics of property rights, externalities in production, the fiscal problems of economic development, and the administration of taxes and benefits. We hope however they will feel that this selective treatment is justified by the greater depth in which we have been able to discuss the subjects covered. These include, on the taxation side, income and wealth taxes, levies on the transfer of wealth, corporation tax, and indirect taxes. The expenditure side covers the provision of goods and services by central and local governments, and—to a lesser extent—transfer payments. Other subjects included are the national debt and the policy of public enterprises/utilities.

As will be clear from the Lecture titles, the book stresses those subjects in which there has been considerable recent research. This is particularly true of the incidence and design of taxation, which receives rather more emphasis than the expenditure side. The past decade has indeed seen a rapid expansion of the literature, most notably in econometric investigation of the effects of taxation and in theoretical analysis of the optimal design of tax policy.

Finally, we should emphasize the obvious fact that many areas are still unresearched. Despite the long tradition of public finance, and despite the recent influx into the field of economic theorists and econometricians, a great many important issues have yet to be discussed, let alone resolved.

1-2 ROLE OF THE GOVERNMENT

At the beginning of this Lecture we described some of the ways in which the government affects the typical individual. The state, however, has a much more basic role to play in that its first function is to establish and enforce the "rules of the economic game". We are concerned with modern mixed capitalist economies, such as the United States, Canada, Western Europe and Japan, where these rules typically include the legal enforceability of contracts, provisions for bankruptcy, laws defining property rights and liabilities. This basic framework has much to do with how the economy performs, and the other functions of government are very much affected by the kind of ground rules under which the private economy operates. It may indeed be argued that the tax and expenditure activities of the government are of minor significance in relation to its primary function "of preserving and stabilizing the property relations of the capitalist economy" (Gordon, 1972, p. 322). This is not a view we find totally convincing, and we consider that it is still valuable to analyse, as in these Lectures, the impact of fiscal instruments within a given economic system. At the same time, we recognize that it gives only a partial picture of the state's role in modern society, and we return to this below.

Even within the framework of a mixed capitalist economy, the government has a wide range of instruments at its disposal. These Lectures focus on taxation, public spending, and state participation in production (public enterprises/utilities); but in addition the government may make use of direct controls (e.g., rationing, central planning, zoning, licensing), regulation (e.g., of public utilities in the United States, of prices and wages in many countries), legislation controlling firms (e.g., anti-monopoly, pollution, safety) or unions, and monetary and debt policy (and the regulation of monetary institutions). These are areas of state activity that are of actual, or potential, importance. What is more, they overlap considerably with the instruments studied here. Thus, in the case of air pollution caused by automobiles, a government may decide to set minimal standards to be followed in automobile manufacture. It could, however, choose to impose taxes related to the amount of pollution, or to subsidize research into the production of pollution-free automobiles. In the same way, monetary and fiscal policy are closely interrelated.

There may therefore be difficulties in drawing precise demarcation lines. The reader also needs to bear in mind that the effects of the instruments considered may depend on other aspects of government activity. The design of taxation or expenditure may rest critically on the availability of other policies. At the same time, the fiscal instruments on which we concentrate in these Lectures are used in a major way in most modern capitalist economies. (In the Note at the end of this Lecture we provide some background evidence on the importance of different instruments.)

Welfare Economics and Government Intervention

The standard justification of state intervention takes as its starting point the behaviour of the economy in the absence of the government, that is, in the hypothetical situation of a free market economy. From the basic theorems of welfare economics, if this economy is perfectly competitive and there is a full set of markets (conditions discussed in greater detail in Lecture 11), then, assuming that an equilibrium exists, it is Pareto-efficient; i.e., no one can be made better off without someone else being worse off. If it is assumed that social decisions should be based on individual welfare, and that individuals are likely to know better than the government what makes them happy, this creates a presumption that state intervention is not necessary on efficiency grounds. For some, this efficiency argument for decentralization understates the full value of the free market, since they value the right to choose in itself; others believe that there is a relationship between the form of economic organization and political control.

The proposition about the efficiency of competitive equilibrium is used as a reference point to explain the roles of government activity. The first of these is that Pareto efficiency does not ensure that the distribution that emerges from the competitive process is in accord with the prevailing concepts of equity (whatever these may be). One of the primary activities of the government is indeed redistribution. Ideally, this would be achieved through measures that did not destroy the efficiency properties, and much of welfare economics is based on the assumption that non-distortionary ("lump-sum") taxes and transfers can be carried out. For reasons discussed later, such instruments are not typically available in a sufficiently flexible form, and the government has to employ income and wealth taxes, social security benefits related to unemployment or wages, etc. This introduces a trade-off between equity and efficiency which is one of the themes of Part Two of the book.

Second, the economy may not be perfectly competitive. It is the expressed object of anti-trust policy to ensure that firms do not collude or that individual firms do not obtain a sufficiently large share of any market that they can, by restricting their output, increase the price to consumers. But there are some cases where it would be inefficient to have a large number of competing firms. It is widely recognized that in many production processes there is an initial stage of increasing returns to scale. If the point of minimum average costs occurs at so high an output that a single firm would have a significant portion of the market, then, although it might be feasible to divide the firm up into competing units, this would increase costs. Notable examples of such "natural monopolies" are telephones and electricity. In the absence of government intervention, these industries would be likely to be controlled by a few firms, with consequent monopoly power. Accordingly, governments may control such industries directly (as in the United Kingdom) or regulate them (as in the United States).

One central set of economic activities in which the assumption of increasing returns to scale seems to be particularly important is research and development. There may be competition—in the sense of free entry—in these activities, yet a firm that discovers a new product or a new process has a significant effect on the market, even if only temporarily. There is not the perfect competition of the basic theorems of welfare economics, and the resource allocation generated by the market is not in general Pareto-efficient.

Even if the economy were competitive, it may not ensure a Pareto-efficient allocation of resources. The theorem requires that there be a full set of markets for all relevant dates in the future and for all risks. Typically, a full set of futures and insurance markets does not in fact exist. There may be partial substitutes, for example the stock market, but it can be shown that the allocation remains inefficient in many circumstances, and indeed opening additional markets may worsen the allocation (Newbery and Stiglitz, 1979). Similarly, the theorem presupposes perfect information, or that the information that is available is not affected by the actions of individuals. The analysis of markets with imperfect information has only recently begun, but it is already apparent that the welfare economics theorems need to be modified significantly (Stiglitz, 1980). The presence of imperfect information is likely to confer monopoly power. Where competition is maintained an equilibrium may not exist, and when it does exist it may not be Pareto-efficient.

Furthermore, the basic theorem requires that the full equilibrium should be attained. Yet, because of incomplete markets or imperfect information or other reasons, capitalist economies have frequently been characterized by under-utilization of resources (of a kind that creates a strong presumption of inefficiency). Most dramatic of these failures of the market economy are the fluctuations that periodically lead to substantial unemployment. It is now accepted as a responsibility of the government to ensure a low level of unemployment (although views as to what is acceptably "small" may change over time). More generally, the fact that the market economy can lead to such massive under-utilization of resources calls in question the appropriateness of the competitive equilibrium model. It is not obvious that—as some economists have suggested—once the problem of unemployment has been "solved", the classical model of the market economy, with its welfare implications, becomes applicable. It is more reasonable to suppose that the problem of unemployment is only the worst symptom of the failure of the market. There are indeed many other examples that suggest the limited applicability of the competitive equilibrium model: persistent shortage of particular skills, balance of payments disequilibria, regional problems, unanticipated inflation, etc.

Even if the economy is well described by the competitive equilibrium model, the outcome may not be efficient because of externalities. There are innumerable examples where the actions of an individual or firm affect others directly (not through the price system). Because economic agents take into account only the direct effects upon themselves, not the effect on others, the decisions they make are likely not to be "efficient". Air and water pollution are perhaps the most notable examples, and there has been much controversy about the appropriate method of handling these, e.g., regulation, taxes or subsidies.

A particular category of commodities for which the market will not necessarily ensure the correct supply are public goods, of which defence and basic research are conventional examples. These have the characteristic that the consumption of these commodities by one individual need not detract from that available to others. (A more precise characterization is provided in Lecture 16.) Some of these goods are specific to particular locations (e.g., the transmission of radio or television), and are referred to as *local* public goods (see Lecture 17).

Finally, there are what Musgrave (1959) has called "merit wants". This is a category of goods where the state makes a judgement that certain goods are "good" or "bad", and attempts to encourage the former (e.g., education) and discourage the latter (e.g., alcohol). This is different from the arguments concerning externalities and public goods, in that with merit wants, the "public" judgement differs from the private evaluation, rejecting a purely individualistic view of society. This may lead to public spending on merit goods or taxes on "demerit" goods. The ethical basis of such judgements is a question of some dispute, and some writers have tried to bring such objectives within the framework of individualistic judgements, by extending the latter to include views about the nature of society. Thus, a person may have private interest in reducing the tax on tobacco, since cigarettes enter importantly in his private utility function, but recognize in his social judgements that a reduction in cigarette consumption would be desirable.

From this brief discussion, it should be clear that, even if we accept the basic theorem on the efficiency of the competitive economy as a valuable reference point, there remain important reasons for government intervention. These may be summarized under the following headings: (1) distribution, (2) failure of perfect competition, (3) absence of futures and insurance markets, (4) failure to attain full equilibrium, (5) externalities, (6) public goods, and (7) merit wants.

View of the State

The value of the welfare economics theorems as a reference point in explaining the role of the government may be questioned, and we need to consider in more detail what is entailed. First, it is not really being assumed that this hypothetical free market situation could be attained in the absence of the government. There is indeed little reason to believe that the market could function in the way assumed in the "no-government economy": "one description of such a social order, and probably a highly realistic one, would be summarized by the word 'chaos'" (Buchanan, 1970, p. 3). As we argued at the beginning of this section, the state is essential to the functioning of a modern market economy—to prevent such "chaos" developing—by legitimizing property rights, by controlling monetary and financial operations, by regulating entry to economic activities, etc. The fact that the hypothetical "no-government economy" is unrealistic and unsustainable does not by itself make the construction uninteresting. However, the adoption of this reference point does serve to divert attention from the important fact that the state is an integral part of the economic system. This was recognized clearly by classical writers, but is given little prominence in many treatments of public finance, a neglect that has been criticized both by radical economists and by the modern public choice school.

The view of the government as correcting the "failures" of the market economy may also be attacked on the grounds that it commits the functionalist fallacy of assuming that the logical existence of a role for the state can explain why it came into being and behaves as it does. The welfare economics theorems provide a framework within which we can identify potential functions for the state. It is possible that the recognition of these functions (e.g., the supply of public goods) led to the establishment of state provision, and the development of the government role may indeed have been influenced by the rationalizations provided by economists. But they could have been motivated by quite different considerations. Understanding what functions governments have assumed in the past, and why, belongs to the "positive" theory of the state—or to the analysis of governments as institutions, rather than as "enlightened" dictators standing aloof from the economic scene.

The examination of the government as an institution, just like a firm or a household, has to take account of the fact that policies are formulated and executed by individuals, and that they in turn are affected in their actions by rules, customs, incentives, etc. They take decisions on the basis of imperfect information and subject to a variety of constraints. Those who control the government (politicians) and those who administer it (bureaucrats) may well have preferences of their own, which guide their activities and conflict with the welfare of individual citizens. The state may act in the class interests of a section of the population, and decisions reflect the relative power of different interest groups. Tax and expenditure policy may be designed more with a view to electoral success, or the goals of an established bureaucracy, than to social welfare maximization.

The analysis of the behaviour of the state is very relevant in determining the desirability of government action. The fact that the market outcome is inefficient or inequitable does not mean that one can deduce that government intervention will necessarily lead to an improvement. Such a deduction has been compared by Stigler to that of the emperor judging a musical competition between two players, who gave the prize to the second having heard only the first. It has to be shown that there exist policies that will solve, or at least alleviate, the problems, and that the government is both willing and able to implement these policies. For example, it has been argued that, although an omniscient minister of finance might be able to stabilize the economy, the imperfect information at his disposal means that government attempts to stabilize may actually be destabilizing.

The "welfare economic" view of the state is therefore one that must be applied with caution. It provides a useful organizational framework, and in what follows we relate methods of government intervention to the different reasons why competitive equilibrium may fail to exist, to be efficient, or to be equitable. Moreover, for those readers who come to the book with a background in economic theory, seeking an introduction to public economics, the development of the subject from the standard theorems of welfare economics is a natural one. At the same time, this approach does not provide a basis for understanding the full role of the state in influencing the economic system, nor does it explain the behaviour of the government as an institution.

1-3 GUIDE TO THE LECTURES

The aim of the descriptive analysis in Part One is to compare two equilibrium situations: before and after a specified combination of policy changes. From this comparison, we can then draw conclusions about the effects of the policy. Does, for example, the impact of a particular measure correspond to its legislated intent? Is policy X equivalent in its effect to policy Y? What is the effect of policy Z on equilibrium quantities and prices? Thus, we ask about the effect of income taxation on labour supply in Lecture 2, on savings in Lecture 3, and on risk-taking in Lecture 4. Similarly, in Lecture 5 we examine the impact of corporation tax on investment by firms. The effects on product and factor prices are particularly relevant to questions of *incidence*—who bears the burden of taxation and who benefits from government expenditure? Thus, in Lecture 6 we examine the incidence of the corporation profits tax, in terms of the effect on the rate of return (developed further in Lectures 7 and 8). In Lecture 9 we provide an explicit distributional model which can be used to assess the impact of taxation and expenditure on the inequality of incomes.

There are a number of reasons why these "positive" questions are of interest. Some can be directly related to the welfare economic framework. These include the redistributive impact and the effect on private decisions where there are grounds to expect market failure. Thus, if the government feels that the interests of future generations are inadequately taken into consideration, then it may seek tax measures which encourage the accumulation of capital. If the government is concerned with the level of risk taking, it may wish to know whether the income tax discourages people from the choice of adventurous portfolios. In other cases, the effects on certain variables may enter directly into public debate or decision making. For example, people may be concerned with the effect of income tax on work effort *per se*.

The specification of the *combination* of policy changes to be considered is important. We typically think in terms of a single instrument—for example, the income tax—but any policy change must in general involve altering at least two instruments. A rise in the income tax rate must be accompanied by changes in other taxes (to leave revenue unchanged), or in expenditure (to maintain a balanced budget), or in debt/monetary policy. (For an extensive discussion, see Musgrave, 1959, Ch. 10.) The choice of offsetting adjustment in other instruments may well affect the comparison of the equilibria before and after the policy change. For this reason, the analysis is best seen as tracing out the opportunity locus for the economy in policy space: i.e., the consequences for the variables of interest of different combinations of policy instruments. The comparison to which we devote particular attention is that holding constant government expenditure, and debt/monetary policy, so that there is equal revenue. This may be seen as holding "public utility" constant; and is contrasted on occasion with holding private utility constant. (We also consider "balanced growth" incidence, and other concepts discussed later.)

The analysis of a specified policy package may be considered in two stages. First, we investigate the impact on the supply and demand functions, i.e., we ask how the behaviour is affected for given values of the factor and commodity prices. We examine in Lectures 2–4 the response of households and in Lecture 5 that of firms. This provides building blocks for the second stage—the general equilibrium analysis presented in Lectures 6–9. This gives a fuller picture of the effects of policy, allowing for the changes in factor and product prices; this generality is however achieved at the expense of a less rich treatment at the sectoral level. The two levels of analysis are therefore complementary.

After investigating the behaviour of the private economy, we turn to the behaviour of the state. Lectures 10 and 11 serve to bridge the two parts of the book. The former is concerned with the "positive" analysis of the government, seeking to close the system by making the state's decisions endogenous rather than exogenous. Whereas in Lectures 2–9 changes in taxes and expenditure are assumed to come from outside, in Lecture 10 we examine models in which public decisions are influenced by voters, political parties, legislators, and administrators.

Lecture 11 provides an introduction to Part Two. It describes some of the ways in which the objectives of the government have been formulated and the resulting criteria for decision making. The ensuing Lectures apply these criteria to a range of issues in the design of tax and expenditure policy. Lecture 12 is concerned with the structure of indirect taxation. Given that a certain amount of revenue has to be raised by indirect taxes, should the rates be uniform on all goods or differentiated? Lecture 13 asks similar questions about the design of income taxation and the degree of progression. These two aspects are brought together in Lecture 14, on the balance between direct and indirect taxation, which also broadens the analysis to cover the tax treatment of savings and externalities. Lecture 15 deals with public enterprise policy, Lecture 16 with public goods and Lecture 17 with local public goods.

In this normative section, the aim is not to provide definite policy recommendations but rather to examine the structure of arguments. It is a misunderstanding of the purpose of this literature to suppose that it can yield answers such as "the optimal tax rate is 35 per cent". What it tries to do is to examine such statements as "we should not have differential taxes because this distorts consumer choice" and to show that, for example, if by "distortion" is meant causing additional loss of welfare to the individual, then this statement is correct only in certain special circumstances. Similarly, the normative analysis seeks to investigate the sensitivity of the policies chosen to the formulation of objectives (for example, the weight attached to redistribution) and to the instruments available to the government. The intention is to illuminate debate about policy rather than to contribute to the formulation of policy itself. In the final Lecture, 18, we consider a selection of current issues and the ways in which the analysis may be of assistance in thinking about policy.

Theoretical Framework

This book is not intended to be a treatise on pure economic theory (although we have tried to introduce some recent developments—for example, the expenditure function—and notes are appended to certain Lectures for this purpose). At the same time, the theoretical framework is an essential element. In the past, public finance has tended to lag behind best-practice economic theory, and this is still true in certain respects today.

The theoretical framework that has been increasingly adopted in modern public finance is the competitive general equilibrium model set out definitively in Debreu's *Theory of Value* (1959). The model, albeit in highly simplified form, has been widely applied to questions of incidence (as in Lecture 6), and it underlies much of the treatment of normative questions (Part Two). In these Lectures, we have focused on this model because it represents the most fully articulated view of the workings of the modern capitalist economy. We should however emphasize our misgivings about its appropriateness in many circumstances. Recent theoretical work, concerned with non-convexities, imperfect competition and disequilibrium behaviour, has brought out the special nature of many of the results and suggested that the model may not be particularly robust. At a number of points, we have tried to show (e.g., in Lecture 7) how alternative assumptions may affect the conclusions drawn.

The reader should therefore bear in mind throughout the Lectures that the study of public policy can be no more firmly based than the economic theory on which it draws, and that the development of public economics is limited in crucial ways by the shortcomings of competitive equilibrium analysis. Moreover, advances in economic theory may involve discrete changes in the nature of the models employed. Although the mainstream research strategy has been to work sequentially, relaxing one assumption at a time, the alternative theory that emerges may have a totally different form. For example, dropping the assumption of perfect information leads naturally to the consideration of models in which non-convexities and imperfect competition play a crucial role. Thus, the relaxation of one assumption may entail other departures from the *Theory of Value* framework. From a different standpoint, radical economists argue that what is needed is a total reconstruction of economic theory.

Features of the Analysis

Certain themes recur throughout our discussion of different areas of policy and it may be helpful to highlight the most important here.

In the positive analysis of taxation, we stress the dependence of the results on the precise features of the tax system. This is quite obvious to practitioners—and the details of the tax system are covered extensively in many public finance textbooks. There is however a tendency for theoretical analysis to represent taxes in an over-simplified form and thus to miss essential features. A good example is provided by the corporation tax, where the impact depends crucially on the provisions for interest deductibility, for depreciation, and on the relationship between the corporate and personal tax systems. Another example is provided by the complicated budget constraints which result from the interaction of income taxation and social security benefits (see, for instance, Fig. 2.2). In this book we do not seek to go into detail on such things as the US Tax Reduction and Simplification Act, 1977, or to initiate readers into the mysteries of Subsection (1)(b), Schedule 45 of the UK Finance Act, 1975. On the other hand, we have devoted attention to features with considerable economic significance such as the provisions for loss offsets, interest deductibility, the treatment of different types of income, etc.

A second feature of the positive analysis is the emphasis on empirical evidence and the use of econometric techniques. Thus, in Lectures 2–5 we discuss the evidence available from three main sources: interview studies, econometric analysis of observed behaviour, and experiments. Considerable progress has been made in recent years, particularly in the case of the latter two types of evidence. At the same time, the problems in obtaining reliable data and interpreting the results are such that it is at present difficult to draw definitive conclusions. Once again, resolution of issues in public economics depends on progress being made in other fields.

In both positive and normative sections of the book, we emphasize the distributional aspects of public policy. For example, much of the theoretical analysis of income taxation has considered a single representative individual. This provides considerable insight, but does not get to the heart of the purpose of income taxation, which is to distribute a given tax burden according to differences in endowments. At a general equilibrium level, analysis of redistribution involves the construction of models that allow us to predict the effects of policy changes not just on aggregate variables (total wealth) but also on the distribution (the Lorenz curve for wealth). This is inherently more difficult. When it comes to the optimal design of taxation (Lectures 12–14), we argue that differences in endowments are an essential aspect of the formulation, since without such differences the problem is an artificial one.

The normative analysis may be seen as an exercise in the economics of second-best. Suppose that a first-best allocation is not attainable (for example, because the necessary lump-sum taxes for redistribution are precluded). The government has then to design a second-best policy with an eye to balancing equity goals against efficiency losses. This is of course a familiar problem. We do however stress three aspects that have tended to be overlooked. The first is the dependence of the optimal solution on the instruments available to the government—what taxes and expenditure policies are feasible. The nature of the solution may be critically dependent on whether or not a particular form of taxation can be employed. It is essential therefore to consider the information available to the government, the incentives for individuals to reveal information (e.g., about their endowments or about their preferences for public goods), and the constraints on the government's actions (e.g., those imposed by considerations of horizontal equity). The second aspect is the relationship between the solution and differences in objectives. The second-best problems of public economics have provided considerable insight into the implications of different principles, e.g., the precise meaning of horizontal equity, and the extent to which the difference principle of Rawls (1971) is egalitarian. The third aspect is a more technical one: the ill-behaved nature of many of the second-best maximization problems. In contrast to what is commonly assumed in economics, the problems are not necessarily convex; this adds further complexity to an already complicated subject.

In the above we have tried to give some flavour of the approach adopted; in the course of the Lectures, we use the sections headed "Concluding Comments" to underline the main features of the analysis—and indicate the need for further developments.

NOTE: THE PUBLIC SECTOR— STATISTICAL BACKGROUND

This note provides a brief introduction to the quantitative importance of the government sector and of different forms of taxation and expenditure. It is primarily intended for the reader coming new to the subject of public finance, and makes no attempt to go into detail.

Size of the Public Sector

In order to give a quantitative impression of the government budget, we need to deal with a number of definitional questions. First, what do we mean by the "public sector"? For some categories of expenditure, like defence, there is no doubt that they should be included. But many of the activities of the government are very much like private activities. Government enterprises are a case in point; for example, in the United States the Tennessee Valley Authority, the Federal Housing Agency, and the Atomic Energy Authority are all autonomous agencies, and could well be treated as part of the private sector. It depends whether one is concerned with marketed versus non-marketed output or with the extent of government control (or with other criteria). When the extent of coverage has been determined, there remains the question of the appropriate indicator of the magnitude of government activity. For example, when output is marketed, should total sales be included under revenue, and their total outlays under expenditure, or should only the net subsidy be shown as a government expenditure, and the net receipt (if there is a profit) on the revenue side? Should the magnitude of a government loan programme be measured by the values of loans advanced or by the implicit subsidy? Even if the principles of classification criterion are decided, the application is likely to involve ambiguity. If the government sets up a self-financing, independent retirement insurance programme, should this be included in the private sector? If the government regulates a private retirement insurance programme, so that its degree of autonomy is severely limited, should this be treated as in the public sector?

Second, in the case of goods and services provided by the government (e.g., defence or public education) we have to take account of the fact that the value of government expenditure on goods and services is conventionally measured by the value of the inputs rather than the value of outputs. What is measured, in other words, is the market cost of the resources used by the government sector.[1] This is not however fully satisfactory. Whereas for most private goods we can ascertain individuals' relative evaluation of different commodities from the market prices, obtaining a comparable measure of the value of government services is less straightforward. Indeed, some people would assert that for some services (e.g., wars in Southeast Asia) the value is negative.

Third, transfer payments are excluded from national income on the grounds that they are simply a redistribution. If one is concerned with the direct *use* of real resources by the state sector, then transfers should also be excluded from government spending. On the other hand, it may be argued that this underestimates the true scope of government activity and that we should take a measure "gross" of transfers. The difficulty with this is the essential arbitrariness in what one calls a transfer payment. For instance, suppose the government pays a cash benefit with respect to all children. This is recorded as public expenditure. On the other hand, if the government gave a cashable tax credit, only those with tax liabilities less than the child benefit would actually receive money from the government, and the apparent expenditure would be much less than in the previous case. The two systems are, except for paperwork, fully equivalent, yet the size of the government budget looks different.[2] Similar problems are raised by preferential tax treatments and subsidies. If the government subsidizes an industry by not taxing it, revenue is reduced, while if the government provides a cash subsidy, there is an increase in expenditure. (Many economists have argued recently for the explicit accounting of such "tax expenditures".)

The rehearsal of these familiar difficulties shows that there are a number of different ways in which the size of the public sector can be measured (e.g., including or excluding capital items, including or excluding transfer payments), and that there is a substantial element of arbitrariness in any definition. This is the main reason why the figures for the magnitude of public spending as a percentage of gross national product (GNP) quoted in public debate appear to differ so widely.[3] Moreover, the same applies to

[1] There may be exceptions where the government expenditures do not measure the cost of the resources used, for example, then the government obtains services by compulsion as with the military draft, the reason for compulsion being that the wage paid is less than that at which individuals are willing to supply their services. Thus, the defence budget may under-estimate the value of the inputs it uses. More generally, the opportunity cost may depart from the market price, for example, when factors are unemployed.

[2] Similarly, how should we treat interest on the national debt, which is also often excluded as being a "transfer"? There are arguments in favour of excluding it; on the other hand, why should bonds be treated differently from rentals of post offices, which also are transfer payments in this sense?

[3] For example, for the United Kingdom the public sector in 1975 could have been represented as 58 per cent of GNP (at factor prices) or 24 per cent, the former figure including public corporations, capital outlay, debt interest, and transfers, the latter excluding them.

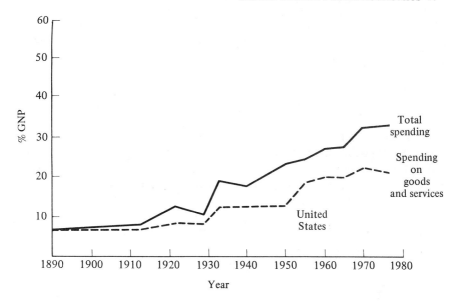

Figure 1-1 Growth of public spending in the United States and United Kingdom. (*Sources:* (a) United States total spending 1890–1950 from Musgrave and Musgrave (1976, Table 6.2). Spending on Goods and Services 1890–1950 from *Long Term Economic Growth*, US Department of Commerce, 1966, basic data. Figures 1950–77 from *Economic Report of the President*, US Government Printing Office, various years. (b) United Kingdom figures 1890–1950 from Peacock and Wiseman (1967, Tables A-6 and A-12). Figures 1950–77 from *National Income and Expenditure*, Central Statistical Office, various years.)

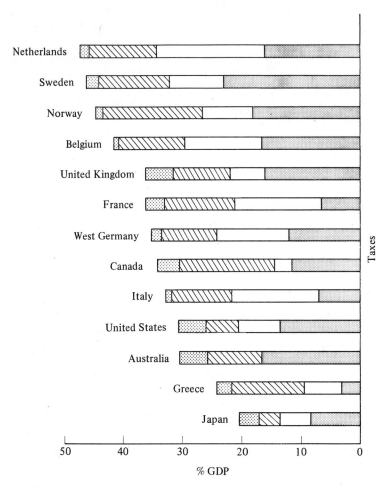

Figure 1-2 Tax revenues in different countries (percentages of GDP at market prices), 1975. (*Source: Revenue Statistics of OECD Member Countries 1965–1975*, OECD, 1977, Tables 3 and 6.)

a measure based on tax revenues, as the examples given earlier (e.g., of the child benefit) indicate.

Any quantitative assessment of the magnitude of the public sector must therefore be regarded with considerable caution, and evidence of the kind given in Figs 1-1 and 1-2 considered with this qualification in mind. These figures show respectively government expenditure proportions in the United States and the United Kingdom since 1890, and the taxation shares (in gross domestic product) for the main OECD countries, as well as a broad breakdown by type of taxes. The basic variables in Fig. 1-1 are total government spending, excluding public corporations, and total spending on goods and services, each expressed as a percentage of GNP at factor cost. (The figures are for selected years and are not designed to show year-by-year changes.)

Given the difficulties described above, only the broadest of conclusions can be drawn, but it is apparent that the magnitude of the state budget is substantial, measured in terms either of total spending (or taxation) or of the absorption of real goods and services. Taking the figures at face value, we can see that the United Kingdom is shown as having had a higher level of spending (relative to GNP) than the United States over the whole of this century. In both countries there has been a large increase over the period in spending as a proportion of GNP. The tax shares in the thirteen OECD countries shown in Fig. 1-2 exhibit a considerable range: from 20 per cent to nearly 50 per cent. Some of the hypotheses that have been advanced to explain the development of the public sector over time and its variation across societies are discussed in Lecture 10.

Structure of Taxation

Problems of definition arise also when we consider the breakdown of expenditure and tax revenue, and any classification involves a degree of judgement in its application. Thus, the distinction between an income tax and a social security tax may not be one of great substance as far as economic effects are concerned, but this involves taking a view about the likely incidence of the taxes. Here we retain the conventional categories, largely derived from administrative practice, and postpone any discussion of their economic significance.

In Table 1-1 we show for the United States the sources of revenue as a percentage of the total in 1977. The table covers federal, state and local levels of government. We have first listed those taxes ("benefit taxes") and charges that are closely linked with particular government services, e.g., highways at the federal level and at the local level, fuel taxes, and charges for the provision of local public services. As we have noted earlier, it is debatable whether we should include "gross" measures of federal receipts or restrict ourselves to the net profit (or loss).

General taxes are divided in Table 1-1 into two categories: taxes on factors and taxes on commodities (outputs). The former may differentiate among different sources of income; commodity taxes may differentiate among different uses. Historically, the major source of revenue at the federal

Table 1-1 United States tax revenues

| | | | Percentage of total revenue in 1977 | | |
			Federal	State and local	Total
	I	Benefit taxes or charges	1.2	3.8	5.0
	II	Individual income tax	26.9	5.1	32.0
	III	Wage taxes (social security)	19.7	3.6	23.3
Factor	IV	Capital taxes			
taxes		Property	—	10.6	10.6
		Profits	10.2	1.7	11.9
	V	Estate taxes	1.2	0.4	1.6
Commodity	VI	Sales taxes	1.7	10.6	12.3
taxes	VII	Customs duties	0.9	—	0.9
		Total*	62.1	37.9	100

Source: Survey of Current Business, US Department of Commerce, July 1978, Tables 3.2 and 3.4.

* Includes certain items not identified above.

level has been the general income tax and this is reflected in the space devoted to the income tax in Lectures 2–4. At the same time, social security wage taxes have increased very substantially in recent years. These special taxes on wages in 1977 exceeded (at the federal level) those on capital (category IV). (The implications of differential factor taxes are discussed in a general equilibrium context in Lectures 6–8.) The most significant tax specifically on capital is the corporation tax. The estate taxes are another type of capital tax—on wealth that is not consumed in the individual's lifetime. The fact that the revenue is a relatively small percentage does not mean that it has no important economic effects (a tax set at prohibitive rates would raise no revenue at all). Like other taxes, they may have strong incentive effects in encouraging certain activities and discouraging others. At the state and local level, the most significant tax in this group is the property tax. The nature of this tax has given rise to considerable debate but we have classified it here as a capital tax.

Taxes on commodities are particularly important for state and local governments, accounting for nearly a third of their revenue. At the federal level, duties on spirits and tobacco are two of the larger commodity taxes; the rationale for this is perhaps that these are "evils" which should be discouraged—the "demerit" goods referred to earlier. Alternatively, there is the view that they impose externalities, e.g., drunken driving, health costs, etc. The tax is then an attempt to bring the private cost into accord with social cost—as discussed in Lecture 14. It is unlikely however that externalities would justify the present tax rates; probably more important is the feeling that alcohol, tobacco and other taxed commodities (e.g., perfume) are luxuries; the fact that the individual can purchase these is a better measure of his true state of wellbeing than just income alone.

The differing tax structure in different countries is illustrated for 1975 in Fig. 1-2. Inter-country comparisons need again to be made with caution, but it appears that taxes on income and profits are more important in the Anglo-Saxon and Scandinavian countries, and social security contributions larger in Belgium, France, Germany, Italy and the Netherlands. Taxes on goods and services are relatively small in both the United States and Japan, and more significant in the EEC countries.

Structure of Expenditure

The classification of expenditure is again a matter where there is considerable scope for judgement. In Table 1-2 we show the percentage of total expenditure accounted for by different programmes in the United

Table 1-2 Public expenditure by type and level of government in United States in 1977

	Percentage of total expenditure	
	Federal	State and local
	%	%
National defence and related	16.5	—
International affairs	0.8	—
Space research and technology	0.6	—
Education and manpower	1.0	17.7
Income maintenance	21.2	6.1
Veterans	3.1	—
Health and hospitals	0.8	3.9
Transportation	1.6	3.7
Commerce (regulation and promotion of business)	—	0.3
Agriculture and rural development	1.4	0.3
Natural resources and environment	0.8	1.2
Housing and community development	0.6	—
Police, prisons and fire	—	3.2
Sewerage and sanitation	—	1.3
Administration and justice	2.5	4.3
Interest	4.7	−1.0
Total*	57.1	42.9

Source: Survey of Current Business, US Department of Commerce, July 1978, Table 3.14.
— denotes less than 0.25 per cent (in some cases no spending under this heading at this level of government).
* Includes other items not listed.

States, where these largely correspond to administrative categories rather than having clear functional significance.

The table is broken down by level of government, and it can be seen that over half of all spending was carried out by the federal administration (spending is allocated to the level responsible for the outlay; a substantial part may be financed by inter-governmental grants). The major items at the federal level are national defence and income maintenance, which together account for some two-thirds of total federal expenditures. The next largest item is debt interest. State and local governments are concerned mainly with education, health, transportation, income maintenance (welfare), and the provision of such local services as police, fire, and sanitation.

The reader may like to consider how the categories of expenditure listed in Table 1-2 can be related to the reasons for government intervention discussed in Section 1-2 and summarized on page 8. In particular, how do different items serve the functions of (1) redistribution, (2) anti-monopoly (regulation and public enterprises), (3) correcting for the absence of futures and insurance markets, (4) eliminating persistent disequilibria, (5) correcting externalities, (6) providing public goods, and (7) merit wants? (N.B. expenditures can perform several functions.)

TWO

HOUSEHOLD DECISIONS, INCOME TAXATION AND LABOUR SUPPLY

2-1 INTRODUCTION

In this and the next two lectures we examine the effect of taxation on decisions made by the household sector. We begin, in this section, by describing the approach to household behaviour underlying the analysis and the kind of effects the tax system may have. The members of a household make an enormous number of decisions during the course of their lifetimes. Some of these decisions are typically uninfluenced by taxation—for example the choice of husband or wife[1]—but many of them are significantly affected by the taxes on income, wealth, and expenditure that are in operation. At the very least, much of public discussion about policy is based on the presumption that taxation is important. Thus, high rates of income taxation are held to discourage work effort, the exemption of capital gains from tax is thought to encourage risk-taking, and it is felt that a switch from income to expenditure taxation would provide a powerful incentive to save.

Framework of Household Decision-Making

Our aim here is to examine the way in which taxation is likely to affect household behaviour, with no judgement at this stage about the desirability

---

1 Although whether a couple marry or not may be affected by the tax laws.

or otherwise of particular taxes. The decisions on which we concentrate are those concerned with:

work effort   —this Lecture

savings
transfer of wealth } —Lecture 3

portfolio composition—Lecture 4

The relationship between these different decisions is set out schematically in Table 2-1. At the beginning of the year, the household has a stock of wealth. This wealth may be held in a variety of different assets—cash, government bonds, equities, etc.—and the household must decide how to allocate its portfolio, a decision on which depends the investment income derived. This portfolio choice is made under uncertainty, being based not only on expected income but also on the risk incurred. The second main decision that affects income is that concerning labour supply: how many hours to work, whether the wife works, whether to retire, etc. The income derived from these sources, together with any amounts received as bequests or gifts during the period, constitute the resources available to the household.

The first decision about the use of resources is how much to save. This is likely to be influenced by a number of factors, including the need to spread consumption over different periods in the household's lifetime, the requirement to build up a reserve against emergencies, and the desire to leave bequests. These are affected not only by tax laws, but also by the public services and transfer payments provided by the government. For instance, if there is a national health service, the need for saving for medical emergencies is less than where medical care is privately paid for and there is limited insurance coverage; the existence of a social security programme may reduce the need for private savings for retirement. The second decision concerns the allocation of the amount that the household plans to consume. How much should the household spend on different commodities? (This is

Table 2-1 Household decision process

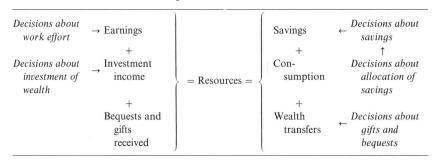

not discussed in any detail in Part One.) Third, there is the decision whether to transfer wealth through gifts (and, ultimately, bequests).

In considering the effects of taxation, there are several points to be borne in mind. First, although the decisions are discussed separately, they are highly interdependent. The decision about the pattern of consumption may be influenced by that about work effort; for example, a tennis racquet is of limited value if the person is working all daylight hours. Savings depend on when a person expects to retire. The choice of portfolio may well be related to the savings decision. In what follows, we take account where possible of the interrelationships, but in some cases making the links must be left to the reader.

In describing the various decisions above, we treated them as taking place within a single period, but this needs to be embedded in a lifetime model of household behaviour. This is most obvious in the case of savings, but dynamic elements are also significant in the case of labour supply (e.g., occupational choice) or in the case of consumption patterns (e.g., purchase of consumer durables). Of particular importance is education. The nature of the school system is largely a public decision, but in almost all Western economies there is some scope for parental choice concerning the provision of education to their children. In any case, considerable learning goes on within the home. The decisions made by parents, and later by individuals themselves, may subsequently affect occupational choice, savings behaviour, and even patterns of consumption. Models of household intertemporal decision making have received considerable attention in recent years. This applies particularly to theories of life-cycle savings, of schooling, and of job search. It is in the nature of such models, however, that the analysis is quite complex—even before we introduce such real-world phenomena as uncertainty and market imperfections. Steering a course between models too simplistic to be a reliable guide and models too complicated to yield useful insights is a difficult task.

This becomes even more the case when we consider other differences between individuals apart from their age. In much of the literature, use is made of the fiction of a "representative" household or individuals. For aggregate analysis this may be sufficient, but it is the essence of many public finance questions that individuals are different. If they were identical, or could be treated as such, then many problems would disappear. Since one of the main aims of the income tax is to distribute the tax burden fairly among differently placed individuals, it makes little sense to confine the analysis to a single, representative individual. One of the important questions concerning any public expenditure is the effect it has on the distribution of income, again a question that is concerned with individual *differences*. Moreover, empirical investigation of the effects of taxation or government expenditure requires that we take explicit account of the source of individual differences—either in aggregating to arrive at macro-relationships or in estimating cross-section models. In what follows, we pay particular attention to the distribution of individuals with differing endowments and tastes.

The Unit of Analysis: Households v. Individuals

For most of this book, we take an individualistic approach. In Part One, concerned with describing the effects of various government policies, we focus primarily on the decisions of the individual; in Part Two we evaluate different policies largely in terms of their effects on the welfare of individuals. The basic objection to this approach is that individuals are members of a large number of groups—the family, town, county, class, club, etc.—and these need to be taken into account in describing the consequences of taxation. Indeed, radical critics of economic theory reject the concept of individuals taking decisions based on preferences and constraints and would replace it by a theory of class relations. At the simplest level, this makes the descriptive analysis of Part One more straightforward, since all we need then do is to examine how each of the major "classes" in society is affected. But at a deeper level, the behaviour of any class is affected by its relationship with others and these are in turn influenced by the fiscal structure. More in the mainstream of economic theory is the assumption that the actions (decisions) of any individual are affected by the actions of others, i.e. that there are "consumption" externalities.

In a rather different way, individuals act collectively through organizations, such as trade unions; and the activities of these organizations clearly affect the equilibrium of the economy. Thus, the effects of a tax, say on labour, may depend critically on the extent to which unions are able to shift the burden of the tax through wage bargaining. Although much of this book concentrates, with misgivings, on the competitive economy, we consider briefly some of the implications of such organizations.

One group that we cannot ignore, at least when concerned with labour supply, is the family. Clearly, the decision of the wife concerning the supply of labour is affected by the income of the husband, and vice-versa. This raises the difficult question of the correct model of family or household decision making. Much of the economics literature treats the family like an individual, maximizing a family welfare function and exhibiting a consistent set of preferences. This is not however necessarily appropriate, since individuals within a family may pursue their own interests. Not only does this lead to different effects of taxation on labour supply and household production, but there may also be significant distributional consequences. An analysis at the level of the household cannot, for example, uncover the effects on the relative position of wives and husbands.

These models have different implications for the effect of any tax on the supply of labour, and this is taken up later. Several observations are, however, pertinent to all of them. First, what we observe is the activity of individuals on the market; we have little opportunity to observe the transactions within the family, but the actions with respect to the market are affected by what goes on within the household. Second, the transactions that actually occur within the household are in part determined by the tax structure. Whether bread is baked in the home or purchased may depend on the taxes on bread and on the labour producing the bread. Third, these decisions are affected not only by the level of taxation, but also by its detailed structure. For instance, whether the income of the wife is aggregated with that of the husband, or whether the incomes of the two are taxed separately, may have an important effect, with a progressive income tax, on the marginal rate of taxation, and hence on labour supply decisions (and even, in certain circumstances, on the decision to get married).

Finally, the distinction between market and non-market transactions raises doubts about the conventional division of the economy into consuming and producing sectors. The literature on household production has stressed the fact that households combine market goods and labour to produce more basic commodities: the household is like a "small factory". The other side of this picture is less emphasized—that the firm is a source not just of income but also of consumption. In Lecture 5 we note that the taxation of companies may affect the balance between remuneration and consumption within the firm (e.g., perquisites of office). (This in turn has implications for the distribution within the household.)

Income, Substitution and Financial Effects

Taxation may be seen as having three effects. Since it must, of necessity, take income away from individuals, it makes them worse off. As a result of being worse off, they behave differently. That is, individuals typically make different decisions when their incomes change. Because they are poorer, they postpone their retirement, they cannot enjoy as much leisure, etc. This is known as the *income effect*.

The second effect arises from the fact that not all activities are taxed, or taxed at the same rate. Taxation diverts economic activity from taxed to untaxed areas, or from areas with higher taxes to areas of lower tax. To a large extent, the analysis of the effects of taxation is a search for those kinds of activities that escape taxation. These include leisure, production within the household sector, and consumption within the firm sector. Each of these can take on several forms, so that more leisure may mean putting in less effort on the job, retiring earlier, working shorter hours, or beginning work later. It should be emphasized that these non-taxed items are not necessarily "loopholes"; they arise fundamentally from costs of observation. For instance, much of "firm consumption" is not taxed because of the difficulty of identifying the consumption element. These attempts to avoid taxes by substituting non-taxed for taxed activities are called the *substitution effects* of the tax.

The final category, about which we shall have relatively little to say, is that of *financial effects*. These arise where the same real activity can correspond to several different forms of payment, which are taxed at different rates. Professionals, by incorporating themselves, can effectively turn ordinary income into capital gains. By providing executives with stock options, firms are able to lower the tax imposed on their managers. The evasion of tax through the cash or "hidden" economy is a similar rearrangement. The tax system may lead therefore to changes in the form of financial organization and the structure of transactions.

In the subsequent analysis, we examine the factors lying behind these various effects on the labour supply decision. They may be offsetting, e.g., the income effect leads to more work, but the substitution effect to less. The total effect may therefore be relatively small. One must however be careful not to conclude that, simply because the tax has little overall effect on labour supply, it is not distortionary. As we show later, distortions are related primarily to the magnitude of the substitution effect, not to the total effect. Although our concern here is with the descriptive analysis, this brings out why the decomposition may be important.

Taxes, Social Security and Labour Supply

Since every tax, whether on income or on expenditure, affects the budget constraint of the individual in one way or another, it may have an impact on labour supply; but in this lecture, we focus attention on lump-sum taxes, wage taxes, proportional income taxes and progressive income taxes.

Lump-sum taxes are defined as those that do not depend on any action of the individual; there is no way that he can change the tax liability. An example would be a poll tax in a country where there is no emigration or immigration. Note that, because individuals are worse off, even lump-sum taxes have an effect on individual behaviour.[2] The impact of a lump-sum tax is however a pure *income effect*, and we say that it is non-distortionary. All other taxes are distortionary, and the nature of the distortion is related to the difference between the effects of the given tax and a comparable (say, in revenue) lump-sum tax. Lump-sum taxes may vary from individual to individual; it is only required that there is nothing the individual can do to change his liability. Thus a poll tax graduated according to rank, in a feudal or caste society, would be a lump-sum tax if ranks were immutable. (Most of the taxes actually employed by governments are not lump sum; and the main role of the concept is as a standard for comparison.)

---

[2] It is sometimes stated in textbooks that lump-sum taxes are those that have *no* effect on behaviour; the correct statement is that they have no *substitution* effect.

A wage tax at rate t_w alters the return per hour that the individual receives; i.e., if w is the before-tax wage, $w(1-t_w)$ is the after-tax wage. The tax liability, T, is then determined by the number of hours that the individual works, L. A wage tax need not be proportional; the rate of taxation may be an increasing (or decreasing) function of the wage.

In contrast, an income tax at rate t_i falls on both wage income and capital income, so that the tax liability is

$$T = t_i(wL+I) \qquad (2\text{-}1)$$

where I is non-wage income. If it is assumed, as in this lecture, that the non-wage income is exogenously given, then the effect of an income tax is equivalent to a proportional wage tax plus a lump-sum tax at rate t_iI.

The tax shown in Eq. (2-1) is proportional, but the income tax typically has a progressive nominal rate structure. The precise definition of progression is an issue on which there is disagreement. Blum and Kalven (1963) argue that the term "progressive" should be confined to cases where the marginal tax rate rises with income. Here, we follow the more conventional usage and call a tax progressive when the *average* tax rate increases with income. The simplest tax with this property is that with a constant marginal rate, t_i, and a guaranteed income G:

$$T = t_i(wL+I-G/t_i) = t_i(wL+I) - G \qquad (2\text{-}2)$$

This may be interpreted as an income tax with an exemption level (G/t_i), so that people with incomes above this pay tax and those below receive a negative tax supplement. Alternatively, it may be viewed as providing a guaranteed minimum income G and then taxing all income at rate t_i. This tax schedule is referred to below as the *linear* income tax.

The nominal tax schedules in force typically do not include the negative tax supplement; they also tend to be piece-wise linear with higher marginal tax rates on higher bands of income. It has moreover to be remembered that the *effective* rates of tax may depart substantially from the *nominal* rates. Within the income tax system, the tax base may be less than fully comprehensive. (This clearly depends on the definition of "income", an issue discussed in a later lecture.) Thus, estimates for the United States, based on the work of Pechman and Okner (1974) and Minarik (1977), show an actual effective rate (on an expanded definition of adjusted gross income) which rises considerably less steeply than the nominal schedule—see Fig. 2-1. The reasons for this divergence include the following: (1) capital gains are taxed at a lower rate; (2) certain forms of income are tax-exempt (e.g., interest on state and local securities); (3) the tax on certain forms of income is deferred (e.g., employers' contributions to pension schemes). These provisions may be defensible; and no conclusions can be drawn from the diagram about the distribution of the tax burden, since we have not considered the question of incidence (e.g., the exemption of state bonds may

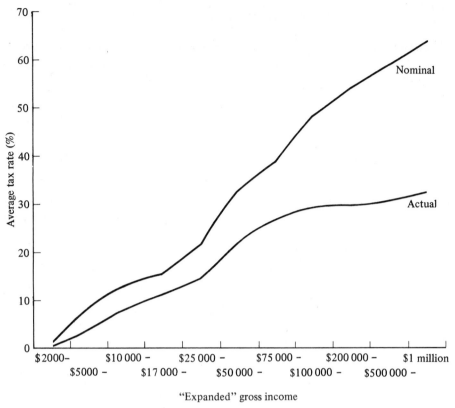

Figure 2-1 Nominal and estimated actual tax rates in the United States 1972. (*Source:* Based on estimates made by Pechman and Okner, 1974.)

be reflected in lower yields). The diagram underlines, however, that ascertaining the actual tax structure is more difficult than it may seem, and that the published tax tables may have only limited relevance.

This conclusion is reinforced when we consider the interaction of the income tax with other aspects of government policy, notably social security programmes. These typically operate what is in effect a parallel income tax system. This works through the contribution side, where social security taxes are commonly proportional to earnings, with an upper limit, and through the benefit side, where social security payments are often related to income. Thus eligibility for welfare benefits may be conditional on income and the amount received may be reduced by a proportion of additional income (e.g. a retirement pension may be reduced if the person has earnings). This may lead to high effective marginal tax rates on those with low incomes—the problem of the "poverty trap". In certain cases, the marginal tax rate may exceed 100 per cent: for example, where entitlement to a given amount of benefit (e.g., Medicaid) depends on income being

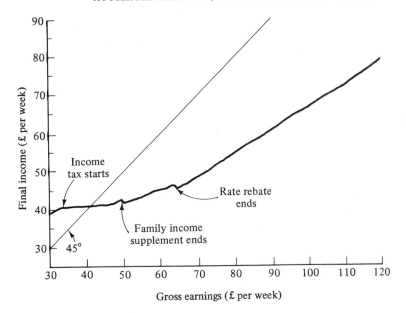

Figure 2-2 Relationship between gross earnings and final income: United Kingdom, April 1978 (couple with 2 children). Final income is the income of the family from earnings and benefits after deduction of tax, social security contributions, net housing costs and work expenses. It is assumed that the children are aged 4 and 6, and that the wife does not work. (*Source:* Based on Chart 6.25 in *Social Trends* 1979, p. 111.)

below a specified level. This is illustrated by Fig. 2-2, which shows the effective final income schedule in the United Kingdom allowing for the interaction of taxation, social security and other forms of government expenditure (particularly housing benefits). For a family claiming all the benefits to which it is entitled, the effective marginal tax rate is very high for a considerable range (the curve is approximately flat).

In what follows, we of necessity treat the tax system in an idealized form; it is important however to remember that the reality that the textbook analysis seeks to capture is more complex than may appear at first sight.

2-2 INCOME TAXATION AND LABOUR SUPPLY

Basic Model of Labour Supply

The analysis in this section concentrates on decisions about hours of work and participation; in the next section we consider other dimensions of labour supply. Variations in hours of work may be considered one of the less important effects of taxation. It is, however, the feature most frequently discussed, and it serves to bring out a number of crucial issues. We also focus here on individual decisions; the behaviour of the household as a unit is taken up later.

The basic model postulates that an individual's labour supply is a function of after-tax wage and after-tax income from other sources. For fixed other income, the labour supply curve is often assumed to be such that, for low wages, an increase in the wage increases labour supply, but for high wages the labour supply curve bends backward. Thus, a wage tax reducing the after-tax wage has the effect of decreasing labour supply at low levels and increasing it higher up the scale. On the other hand, a tax on other income (leaving the after-tax wage unchanged) is normally postulated to increase labour supply. Poorer individuals consume fewer goods and less leisure, but consuming less leisure implies supplying more labour. Hence, the supply curve of labour (regardless of its shape) shifts to the right, i.e., more labour is supplied. An income tax, which reduces the after-tax wage and other income, combines both effects.

To obtain more feeling for the determinants of the sign and magnitude of the effects (e.g., the conditions under which the labour supply curve is backward-bending or positively sloped), we need to derive the labour supply curve. The standard model (Robbins, 1930; Cooper, 1952) treats the individual as maximizing a utility function defined over net income (Y) and leisure, defined to be $L_0 - L$ where L are the hours spent working and L_0 is the total number of available hours. The function $U(Y, L_0 - L)$ is assumed to be quasi-concave (i.e., the indifference curves are convex to the origin), continuously differentiable, and strictly increasing in Y, strictly decreasing in L. In the absence of taxation, the individual budget constraint is

$$Y = wL + I \qquad (2\text{-}3)$$

The individual's choice may be represented geometrically, as shown by the before-tax equilibrium P in Fig. 2-3.[3] It is assumed that there is no constraint from the demand side (restrictions on choice are discussed later). Labour hours chosen vary across individuals with the wage w, with other income I, and with the preferences embodied in U. (To avoid any possible misunderstanding, there is no cardinal significance to U in this Lecture—solely the ordinal properties are relevant.)

Effects of Proportional Taxation

A proportional income tax at rate t_i changes the budget constraint to

$$Y = (wL + I)(1 - t_i) \equiv \omega L + M \qquad (2\text{-}4)$$

---

[3] Algebraically, the solution is obtained by choosing L to maximize $U(wL + I, L)$, which yields as a necessary first-order condition, $U_Y w + U_L = 0$, for an interior solution.

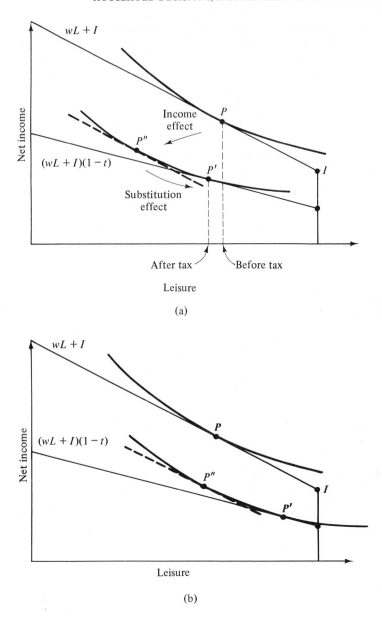

Figure 2-3 Effect of proportional income tax on hours of work: (a) hours of work increase; (b) hours of work decrease.

where ω denotes the after-tax wage rate and M after-tax other income. The effect of the income tax may be considered in two stages. First there is the tax on other income, I. This shifts the budget constraint down, and with the çonventional assumption that leisure is a normal good ($\partial L/\partial M < 0$), increases the supply of labour. Second, there is the effect of a tax on wage income, which is usually decomposed into two parts, a substitution effect and an income effect, according to the Slutsky equation. In the absence of taxation, we have[4]

$$\frac{\partial L}{\partial w} = \left(\frac{\partial L}{\partial w}\right)_{\bar{U}} + L\frac{\partial L}{\partial M} \qquad (2\text{-}5)$$

The first term, referred to as the *compensated* or *Slutsky* term, is the change in labour that would have occurred had lump-sum income changed in such a way as to leave utility unaltered. This is the substitution effect and is always positive. This term is denoted by S (for substitution) in what follows. The second term ($L\partial L/\partial M$) is the income effect, which is the change in labour supply resulting from the fact that, as a result of the increase in wages, individuals are better off.

Combining the two aspects of the income tax, we have

$$\frac{dL}{dt_i} = \frac{\partial L}{\partial \omega}\frac{\partial \omega}{\partial t_i} + \frac{\partial L}{\partial M}\frac{\partial M}{\partial t_i} = -wS - (wL+I)\partial L/\partial M \qquad (2\text{-}6)$$

The term in S is negative; the income effect is positive where leisure is normal. With a wage tax, M would not change and the term in I would not appear; with a lump-sum tax, there would simply be the income effect. (From this point, we concentrate on the income tax, and drop the i subscript.)

Diagrammatically, the two effects are shown in Fig. 2-3. The movement from P to the after-tax equilibrium P' is broken down into two stages: the effect, keeping the wage rate (after tax) constant, of the lowering of utility (P to P''), and the effect of changing the wage rate, at a given level of utility (P'' to P'). As is clear from the Slutsky equation, and from the diagrams, the net effect of income and substitution effects could go either way. Where leisure is a normal good, an income tax may increase or decrease labour supply by an individual.[5] It is possible to identify the characteristics of the indifference map likely to make the income effect dominate the substitution effect, or vice versa, but whether, for any group, one effect dominates the other is an empirical question.

---

[4] The simplest derivation of the Slutsky equation makes use of the expenditure function—see the Note at the end of this lecture.

[5] The possibility that work effort may be increased by taxation is regarded with incredulity by some politicians but is quite meaningful to many survey respondents, e.g., "it's a two-edged sword. High deductions make you want to work more overtime to make up what you lose—but if you get to a certain amount it's not worth working for" (quoted by Brown and Levin, 1974, p. 845).

In order to illustrate the analysis, let us consider the case where the utility function may be written

$$U(Y, L) = u_1(Y) + u_2(L_0 - L) \tag{2-7}$$

Substituting from the budget constraint (2-4), the individual maximizes

$$\chi(L) \equiv u_1(\omega L + M) + u_2(L_0 - L)$$

The first-order condition is (for an interior solution)

$$\chi' = \omega u_1'(Y) - u_2' = 0 \tag{2-8}$$

where the prime (u') denotes the derivative (and u'' the second derivative). Differentiating (2-8) again with respect to ω,

$$(\omega^2 u_1'' + u_2'')\frac{\partial L}{\partial \omega} = -u_1' - \omega L u_1''$$

Rearranging,

$$(\omega u_1'' L + u_2'' L/\omega)\frac{\omega}{L}\frac{\partial L}{\partial \omega} = -u_1'\left[1 - \left(\frac{\omega L}{Y}\right)\left(\frac{-u_1'' Y}{u_1'}\right)\right] \tag{2-9}$$

The second-order conditions ensure that the bracket on the left-hand side is negative (as is χ''). On the right-hand side, we have the term

$$-\frac{u_1'' Y}{u_1'} \equiv \varepsilon_1 \tag{2-10}$$

which is the elasticity of the marginal utility of income.

The elasticity of labour supply with respect to the after-tax wage is positive or negative depending on whether ε_1 times the share of labour in total income is less than or greater than unity. Thus, if $\varepsilon_1 = 1$ (i.e. u_1 is logarithmic) then the labour supply curve slopes upward where there is positive other income $(\omega L < Y)$. This brings out the fact that the Cobb–Douglas utility function:

$$U = a \log Y + (1 - a)\log(L_0 - L) \tag{2-11}$$

has rather special implications for labour supply and may be a misleading example to use.

The effect of the income tax, at rate t, may be seen again from (2-8), which we write out in full as

$$w(1 - t)u_1'[(1 - t)(wL + I)] - u_2' = 0 \tag{2-8'}$$

Differentiating with respect to t,

$$(\omega^2 u_1'' + u_2'')\frac{\partial L}{\partial t} = wu_1'\left[1 - \left(\frac{-u_1'' Y}{u_1'}\right)\right] \tag{2-12}$$

The bracket on the left-hand side is again negative, and the proportional tax leads to a rise in labour supply if the elasticity of marginal utility (ε_1) is greater than unity. In the Cobb–Douglas case, there is no effect.

Exercise 2-1 Consider the utility function defined by

$$U^{1-\varepsilon} = aY^{1-\varepsilon} + (1-a)(L_0 - L)^{1-\varepsilon} \qquad (2\text{-}13a)$$

where a, ε are non-negative parameters. Describe the indifference curves for different values of ε. This utility function is known as the constant elasticity function, since it has a constant elasticity of substitution (defined as the percentage change in the ratio of income to leisure, arising from a percentage change in the wage rate, keeping utility unchanged). Show that it has this property and derive the limiting cases as (1) $\varepsilon \to 1$ and (2) $\varepsilon \to \infty$.
(Hint: the former is the Cobb–Douglas.)

Exercise 2-2 Discuss the special properties of utility functions that have constant marginal utility of leisure

$$U = u(Y) + a(L_0 - L) \qquad (2\text{-}13b)$$

Exercise 2-3 Consider the utility function

$$U = a\log(Y - A) + (1-a)\log(L_0 - L) \qquad (2\text{-}13c)$$

where a, L_0 and A are non-negative parameters. This is a simple version of the linear expenditure system (LES) used in the analysis of commodity demands (Stone, 1954). Show that the labour supply function with an income tax is (for $wL_0 + M > A$)

$$wL = awL_0 - (1-a)\frac{M - A}{1 - t} \qquad (2\text{-}14)$$

where the right-hand side is positive, and zero otherwise.
What does this imply about the effects of taxation?

The Comparison of Taxes and Progressive Taxation

The simplest progressive tax is the linear tax set out in Eq. (2-2), rewritten here with Z denoting pre-tax income

$$Y = Z - T = (1-t)(wL + I) + G \qquad (2\text{-}15)$$

This tax schedule allows the average tax rate to be an increasing function of pre-tax income where $G > 0$, and as noted earlier, this is the sense in which we refer to it as progressive.[6]

By varying t and G, it is possible to trace out the effects of different tax schedules. We can, for example, compare the proportional tax ($t > 0$, $G = 0$) with the lump-sum tax ($t = 0$, $G < 0$). Such comparisons however raise the question of the appropriate basis for comparison. As discussed in Lecture 1, the most commonly adopted criterion is that of equal revenue. In Fig. 2-4 we illustrate the comparison between the proportional and lump-sum tax on this basis. The yield of the tax is given by the distance between the no-tax budget line and the with-tax budget line, so that the revenue with the proportional tax equilibrium at P^I is given by the distance $P^I Q$. A lump-sum tax leaves the after-tax wage rate unchanged ($w = \omega$). The individual's budget constraint with an equal-yield lump-sum tax is a line through P^I parallel to IQ, and the equilibrium is at P^{III}, to the left of P^I. An equal yield lump-sum tax involves a greater supply of labour than the proportional income tax. An alternative basis for comparison is that of taxes giving equal utility to the individual. From Fig. 2-4 it is apparent that both work and revenue are higher with the lump-sum tax (see the point P^{II}).

This analysis may be applied to the case of progressive taxation of the type shown in Eq. (2-15). Where the more progressive tax involves a higher marginal rate, then—for the same revenue yield from the individual—work effort is reduced. This textbook conclusion (e.g., Musgrave, 1959, pp. 241–3) has been questioned in a succession of articles. For instance, Barlow and Sparks (1964) point out that it may be possible for a tax to have both a higher exemption level and a *lower* tax rate (t), and for work effort to be increased. Their example raises a number of issues. As noted by Head (1966), it depends on revenue being a declining function of the tax rate in the proportional tax case, and in this case there exists a lower rate

---

[6] If we seek to go further and compare the *degree* of progression, then matters are more complicated. Musgrave and Thin (1948) define four possible measures of the degree of progression:

1   average rate progression ($dATR/dZ$)
2   marginal rate progression ($dMTR/dZ$)
3   liability progression (MTR/ATR)
4* residual income progression ($(1 - MTR)/(1 - ATR)$)

(* the smaller this measure, the more progressive the tax), where ATR denotes average tax rate and MTR marginal tax rate. Unfortunately, these measures give different answers, even with the simple linear tax (2-15), as the reader can check by taking a series of examples. In seeking a resolution of such conflicts, one has to consider more fundamentally the purposes of measuring the degree of progression and relate it to the measurement of inequality.

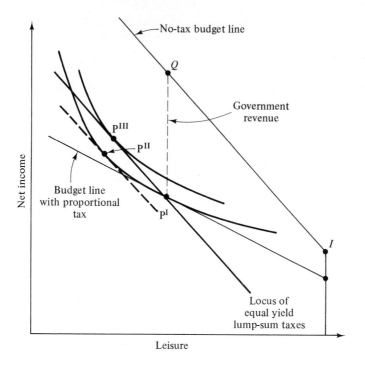

Figure 2-4 Equal-yield lump-sum tax increases hours of work.

proportional tax more stimulating to work effort than the progressive tax.[7] Although it would be natural to conclude that this situation can be ruled out on grounds of its evident inefficiency, we cannot preclude the possibility that it may arise—either because governments are not well-informed, or because several tax authorities are independently setting tax rates.

More fundamentally, the translation of the results to the case of progressive taxation may be criticized on the grounds that analysis of a single individual assumed to pay the same revenue is of little interest in its own right—a point clearly recognized by Musgrave (1959, pp. 243–6). The basic aim of a progressive income tax is to make some individuals better off, and some individuals worse off, than they would have been with a proportional tax. (If all individuals were identical, we would simply impose a uniform lump-sum tax.) The higher tax rate enables the payment of a higher guaranteed minimum. On the other hand, it is important to observe that there may be a limit: at too high tax rates, aggregate labour supply

---

[7] The reader may like to try and prove that, where leisure is a normal good, if we replace one linear tax by another which has a lower marginal tax rate but raises the same revenue, then work effort is increased.
(Hint—draw a diagram similar to Fig. 2-4.)

may be so reduced that the feasible lump-sum subsidy is actually reduced as t increases.

To see this, let us denote the variables for a household by a superscript h (for *household*) and the total number of households by H, and assume that the revenue requirement for other purposes is R_0; then the government revenue constraint is

$$HG = \sum_h t(w^h L^h + I^h) - R_0 \qquad (2\text{-}16)$$

In many empirical analyses, the calculation of the effect of the change in the tax rate on government revenue is made assuming that pre-tax incomes (labour supplies) are fixed; this, however, is likely to be misleading, because people leave the labour force, and because those remaining in the labour force adjust their labour supply.

This may be illustrated by the special case of the LES utility function from which the labour supply function (2-14) can be derived. If for simplicity we set $I^h = 0$, $L_0 = 1$ and $A = 0$, and assume identical taste parameters (a) for all, then the supply function in the case of the linear progressive tax becomes for individual h

$$w^h L^h = aw^h - (1-a)G/(1-t)$$

where

$$w^h > \frac{(1-a)}{a} \frac{G}{1-t} (\equiv w_0) \qquad (2\text{-}14')$$

(L^h is zero otherwise). In the absence of taxation, everyone with a positive wage works, and average income is $a\bar{w}$ (where $\bar{w}$ denotes the mean). With the introduction of taxation, the revenue constraint becomes

$$HG = t \sum_{w^h \geqslant w_0} [aw^h - (1-a)G/(1-t)] - R_0 \qquad (2\text{-}17)$$

This brings out how a calculation based on fixed labour supply may be wide of the mark. A naive estimate of the feasible guarantee based on $ta\bar{w}$ would be in error because (1) people may leave the labour force (so that the sum is over $[w_0, \infty)$ rather than $[0, \infty)$), and (2) the labour supply of those who remain in the labour force may be reduced (the second term). As illustrated in Fig. 2-5, the feasible guarantee falls progressively below the dashed line, and eventually declines. The considerations influencing the optimal choice of tax rate are the subject of Lecture 13.

With simple linear tax schedules, the analysis of the consumer's decision regarding labour supply is a standard problem in the theory of consumers' behaviour. But tax schedules are typically much more complex. There are several important consequences of the kind of tax schedule shown earlier in Fig. 2-2. First, "corner" solutions, where the individual supplies zero labour, appear more likely than they would with, say, the linear tax schedule of

Eq. (2-15). The effect of taxation on the decision not to participate in the labour force is discussed below. Second, the opportunity set may be non-convex. If the individual can vary his hours of work, and if he can borrow and lend, then he may be able to "convexify" by earning, say, £35 one week and £65 the next. Such a response may be a purely financial effect (where the amounts *recorded* vary) or a real effect (e.g., by encouraging risk taking or a preference for seasonal work). (There may be administrative constraints; for example, the assessment period for welfare benefits is typically longer than a week.)

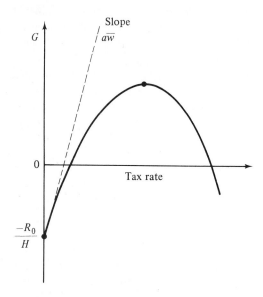

Figure 2-5 Negative income tax: trade-off between guaranteed minimum income and tax rate.

Third, the supply schedule of labour is possibly discontinuous. As an individual's wage rises, he may move discontinuously from supplying zero labour to supplying a large amount of labour, or he may shift discontinuously from one level of hours to another. Finally, the marginal tax rate may be increasing, but in steps, so that the schedule is piece-wise linear. In this case, we may find a clustering of people at the "kinks" in the tax schedule. Individuals with quite different marginal rates of substitution between net income and leisure have the same income. The method of solution may be illustrated by the case where the marginal tax rate jumps from zero to t at a given level of income, say Z_0. We can then identify the utility-maximizing decisions for the two marginal net wages w and $w(1-t)$ and check whether the solutions lie on the permissible segments. If we consider people with different wage rates, but otherwise identical, then there may be a range of w such that gross incomes remain at Z_0, the supply curve of hours being backward-bending at this point.[8]

Exercise 2-4 An income maintenance system is such that a person receives a benefit of 100 per week, which is reduced if the person's income (Z) is above 200 at the rate of 40 per cent (so that benefit in this range is $100 - 0.4\,(Z - 200)$), falling to zero at 450. Draw the after-benefit budget constraint.

Individuals have identical Cobb–Douglas utility functions

$$U = \tfrac{1}{3}\log Y + \tfrac{2}{3}\log (24 - L) \qquad\qquad (2\text{-}18)$$

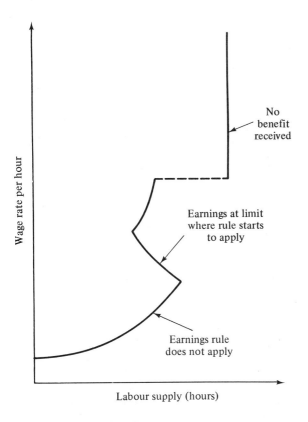

Figure 2-6 Labour supply function where kinked budget constraint.

---

[8] The discussion so far has focused on the non-linearities in the budget constraint arising from the tax system, but there are important non-linearities on the demand side arising from the nature of the work process. Individuals are likely to tire as they work more, so that their marginal productivity declines with increased work; on the other hand, there are likely to be important setup costs in beginning work.

and have no income apart from earnings. Show that the labour supply curve has the general shape sketched in Fig. 2-6. What would happen if the implicit tax rate were 50 per cent rather than 40 per cent?
(Note: this exercise is based on Hanoch and Honig (1978), which the reader may like to consult.)

Exercise 2-5 Consider a population with differing wages but identical utility functions of the form (2-18). The tax schedule has a zero tax for incomes below Z_0, and is proportional at rate t above that point. Derive the observed relationship between the wage and labour supply. What is the effect on labour supply of a change in Z_0 and t? Discuss the errors that would be introduced by using the observed relation with gross wages to predict the effect of changes in the tax system.

Labour Force Participation

So far we have focused on the decision about the *number* of hours to work. In many situations, the individual may have limited control over his hours, and the major decision is whether or not to work. Such decisions may be particularly relevant at the beginning and end of the work career. A person may delay entry to the labour force by remaining at school or in higher education; a person may retire early. These choices are likely to be influenced by taxation, by social security, and by the method of financing of education. Further, if a person is unemployed, he may choose on occasion not to seek employment, or to search less actively for a job, and these decisions may be affected by the system of unemployment compensation and other social security benefits.

The possible effects of taxation may be illustrated by reference to the decision concerning retirement. Leaving on one side the interrelation between work effort and savings (Lecture 3), the same income–leisure analysis can be applied to retirement. If we represent the choice as a simple work–retire dichotomy, where in the latter case the person receives a pension, which is taxable, then an income tax has both income and substitution effects. The extra income from working is reduced; on the other hand, people may not feel able to "afford" to retire. The outcome is therefore indeterminate.[9]

The participation decision may be especially important for secondary workers. This introduces the question of family decision-making. For the

---

[9] The position is further complicated by the earnings rules that are typically associated with the receipt of benefits. Both the United States and the United Kingdom have operated earnings rules that involve effective marginal tax rates of 100 per cent over some range (see Boskin, 1977).

present we assume that the family maximizes an agreed welfare function of the following simple form:

$$U = u_1(Y) + u_2(L_0 - L_1) + u_3(L_0 - L_2) \tag{2-19}$$

where L_1 denotes the hours of the primary worker, L_2 those of the secondary worker, and Y is total family income. With a proportional income tax (and no other income)

$$Y = (1-t)(w_1 L_1 + w_2 L_2) \tag{2-20}$$

The first-order condition for the choice of L_2 is that

$$(1-t)w_2 u_1' \leqslant u_3' \tag{2-21}$$

with $L_2 = 0$ where strict inequality holds.

From this we can see the effect of income taxation on the participation decision. Suppose that in the absence of taxation only the primary worker is in a job and that the hours are assumed fixed. The effect of the tax on the left-hand side of (2-21) may be seen by differentiating with respect to t, taking account of the fact that the u_1' depends on t. The left-hand side of (2-21) increases with t if:

$$-w_2 u_1' - w_2(1-t)w_1 L_1 u_1'' > 0 \tag{2-22}$$

or, dividing by $w_2 u_1'$ and rearranging,

$$\varepsilon_1 > 1 \tag{2-23}$$

where ε_1 is the elasticity of the marginal utility of income (Eq. (2-10)). If the elasticity is greater than unity, individuals who formerly did not participate may be induced to do so by the tax; if the elasticity is less than unity, participation is deterred.

This analysis is incomplete in several respects. We need, for example, to allow for the possibility that incomes are not fully aggregated under the tax law. The wife may enjoy an additional exemption E if she works. The response of hours to taxation must be taken into account. For this purpose, a fuller treatment of the family decision-making process is required, as discussed in the next section.

2-3 BROADER MODELS OF LABOUR SUPPLY

The preceding section employed the standard model of individual consumer behaviour. This may be criticized on a number of grounds, including that it ignores:

1. constraints on individual choice,

2. the enjoyment that many people seem to find in their work,
3. production activities that occur within the household sector and consumption activities within the production sector,
4. the way labour supply decisions are made within a family.

Constraints on Choice

The freedom of the individual to vary his hours of work is circumscribed by the conditions laid down by employers and those negotiated by trade unions. In an extreme case, where the working hours for a particular job are fixed by the employer and the worker cannot change his occupation, then he has no choice. In such a situation we might observe a relationship between L and w, but it would be the employer's offer of hours for different kinds of worker rather than the individual supply curve. (This problem of identification is discussed in Sec. 2-4.)

In reality, the individual is likely to enjoy *some* flexibility. He can decide whether or not to work overtime; he can take a second job; he can move to a job with different hours. As a result, he may be able to choose between a number of different points on the budget line, and the foregoing analysis remains applicable. Moreover, the standard working week may itself be influenced by taxation. Although it may be set by negotiation or legislation, the negotiators and legislators are likely to take some account of the hours individuals want to work, as well as the employers' labour demands. In the long run we should expect that, if taxation led people to want to work longer or shorter hours, this would be reflected in the standard working week. Thus, in a "democratic" union, where the collective decision is taken by majority voting, the outcome will depend on the preferences of the workers, e.g., in certain circumstances the median voter is decisive.[10] This is clearly a highly idealized view of union decision making, but in the long run we should expect individual preferences to have some impact.

Disutility of Work and Choice of Occupation

The assumption that time spent working involves disutility has been questioned:

> most people find some amount of work satisfying for its own sake...customs and moral attitudes exert pressure toward work and against idleness...social credit attaches to "leisure" only when it is taken as evidence of extraordinary pecuniary standing. [Goode, 1949, p. 430]

---

[10] With the linear budget constraint (2-14), utility is a single-peaked function of L, and the median voter is decisive (see the discussion of majority voting in Lecture 10).

Similarly, it may be argued that:

> the controls over work are in fact much more social than economic....A man works to preserve the respect of his wife, children, friends and neighbours, to fulfil the psychological needs induced by the customs and expectations of a life-time and to...replenish the stock of information, cautionary tales and anecdotes which he requires to maintain his participation in the web of social relations. [Townsend, 1968, p. 108]

The earlier analysis can be extended by considering jobs and individual performances as having a wide range of attributes, in addition to the number of hours worked. People may have considerable scope to vary their effort. Some jobs are extremely arduous or unpleasant, or involve a great deal of responsibility; others are relatively undemanding or in pleasant surroundings. Characteristics such as responsibility may be valued positively by some and negatively by others. (This modification makes empirical implementation much more difficult, since dimensions such as effort are notoriously difficult to measure. It is for this reason that most empirical studies have concentrated on hours.)

There is some tendency for jobs with greater non-pecuniary disadvantages to have higher rates of pay in compensation (we are abstracting here from barriers to entry and other important features of the labour market). The individual may be faced therefore with the choice between high earnings–low non-pecuniary benefits ("Management" in Fig. 2-7) and low earnings–high non-pecuniary benefits ("Academic"). It is commonly argued that such choices are influenced by the tax system, and in particular that taxation tends to reduce the supply of people to occupations such as management, where the non-pecuniary disadvantages are relatively high. However, the same analytical apparatus can be applied as before, and there are both income and substitution effects. The tax system may cause people to switch from management to academic life (as illustrated in Fig. 2-7); on the other hand, the income effect of taxation may mean that people no longer feel able to afford the non-pecuniary advantages of the latter.

In considering the impact of taxation, one has to bear in mind the definition of taxable income. The argument just described assumes that all financial returns are taxable, whereas there are a variety of fringe benefits, stock options, etc., that enjoy favourable tax treatment.[11] To this extent, the distinction should be between taxable and non-taxable returns, rather than between pecuniary and non-pecuniary.[12] Indeed, when one allows for consumption within the firm, the reader may question whether the location of the points M and A in Fig. 2-7 is the correct one.

---

[11] Moreover, changes in the tax system may lead to a shift in the "package" offered, so the point M' lies to the southeast of M.

[12] Among untaxed activities must of course be included tax evasion. For a theoretical analysis, see Allingham and Sandmo (1972).

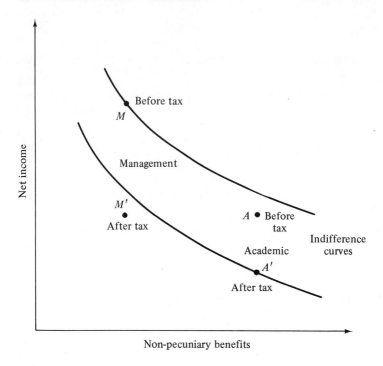

Figure 2-7 Taxation and the choice of occupation.

Household Production

The introduction of household production (Becker, 1965; Lancaster, 1966; and Muth, 1966) is relatively straightforward. Assume that households derive utility from direct consumption of goods (X_2), from leisure, and from household services, C, where the last is produced by household labour, L_1, and goods, X_1:

$$C = C(L_1, X_1) \qquad (2\text{-}24)$$

The household chooses L, L_1, X_1 and X_2 to maximize

$$U(X_2, L_0 - L - L_1, C) \qquad (2\text{-}25)$$

subject to the budget constraint

$$X \equiv X_1 + X_2 = wL \qquad (2\text{-}26)$$

We can then define the *derived* utility function

$$U^*(L, X) = \max_{\{L_1, X_1\}} U[X - X_1, L_0 - L - L_1, C(L_1, X_1)] \qquad (2\text{-}27)$$

This approach, and the implications for taxation, are discussed in Atkinson and Stern (1979), where particular attention is paid to the case where the production function C has fixed coefficients. The introduction of household production affects the interpretation of the consequences of a distortionary tax on market labour; and the likelihood that this distortion is large. Even if consumption and leisure have only limited substitutability, the location of production may be highly substitutable.

Similarly, the model may be modified to allow for the possibility that individuals enjoy consumption benefits through their work. We postulate a utility function of the form

$$U(X_1, L_0 - L - L_1, C(L_1, X_1), L) \qquad (2\text{-}28)$$

where the last argument corresponds to the consumption derived when working L hours (or the enjoyment of work). The formal analysis can be applied as before, although the qualitative conclusions may well be affected. Thus, as individuals become wealthier, it may be possible for them to purchase substitutes for home-produced goods (since there may be a negative marginal utility associated with home work); and for the income effect to increase market labour supply, rather than reduce it. This is the view taken by Scitovsky (1976) and it is illustrated by evidence showing that professionals consistently work more hours than non-professional workers and that their hours have increased over time rather than fallen. If this is the case, then one might expect markedly different effects of taxation on different groups of labour, depending on whether work is "enjoyed" or not.

Family Decision-Making

The model of family behaviour used so far has been that of joint utility maximization, which has been widely employed in both theoretical and empirical (for example, Ashenfelter and Heckman, 1974) literature. This view of the family as a concerted unit is however open to question, and we need to consider the possibly conflicting interests and independent behaviour of family members.

A model at the opposite extreme is that of a couple, with one partner working in the market sector, and the other in the household, which can be thought of as a "trading" economy. Each partner has a utility function, defined over his or her consumption of market-produced goods, household-produced goods, and leisure. Then, a competitive market equilibrium is described by prices and wages at which demand for all goods and labour equals the supply. An income tax is essentially a tax on the production of market-produced goods. This affects the equilibrium terms of trade (the full effects of the tax can be derived from the analysis of Lecture 6). Here we simply note that (1) there are important distributional effects of the tax, in its differential effect on the two partners; and (2) the tax may have an effect not only on the market labour supply (the direct effect) but also on the supply of labour within the household sector, via its effect on the terms of trade. Thus the effective supply, including that of (unobserved) household labour, may be reduced more than the direct effect on observed labour supply.

A number of "mixed" models are also possible, involving some degree of altruism. For instance, one might postulate that individuals share their income equally, but make their decision whether to work individually; in that case, because of the "sharing effect", there will be reduced incentives to work. This analysis is similar to that of labour allocation in co-operative enterprises (Sen, 1966), although the assumptions are less persuasive for the family. Further work needs to be done on methods by which conflicts are resolved, the extent of income- and work-sharing, and other features of family decision-making.

2-4 EMPIRICAL EVIDENCE ON LABOUR SUPPLY

There are three main types of empirical evidence that can be brought to bear on the effect of income taxation on work effort:

1. surveys of attitudes and perceived behaviour,
2. observed labour market behaviour,
3. experimental evidence.

These three approaches are considered in turn. No attempt is made to cover the field exhaustively, not least because there has been a voluminous literature. Instead, we take certain representative studies, examine their strengths and weaknesses, and try to see what can be concluded about the different effects identified in the preceding sections.

Surveys of Attitudes and Perceived Behaviour

Interview studies are designed to obtain information on people's attitudes to taxation and their perceptions as to how it has affected their labour market behaviour. This kind of evidence is essentially qualitative and the conclusions drawn are very much a matter of judgement. In view of this, we concentrate on two representative studies.

In the United States there have been a number of surveys of higher income groups.[13] Of particular interest is that by Holland (1969), who

---

[13] One of the best known is that by Barlow, Brazer and Morgan (1966) of a sample of 957 individuals in the United States with incomes in 1961 of $10000 or higher. They summarize their results by saying that "The picture of the high-income individual emerging from our study is that of a hard-working executive or professional, whose decisions about how much to work are dictated by the demands of his job and by his health, rather than by taxes or other purely pecuniary considerations" (p. 2).

interviewed intensively 125 business executives in 1965–6. In a majority of these interviews he discussed explicitly the response of the executive to a hypothetical lump-sum tax, such that "the individual's inherent capacity to generate income, not his zeal in doing so, would be the determinant of his tax liability" (Holland, 1977, p. 44). The percentages reporting such effects, together with a classification into "harder" and "less hard", are shown in Table 2-2. There is a residual category of "no answer". On this basis it appears that the effect of the income tax, compared with a hypothetical lump-sum tax, is to reduce effort on the primary job but to postpone retirement. There are however very substantial proportions reporting no effects.

Table 2-2 Reported response of executives to taxation—United States

	No effect	Harder	Less hard
Effort on primary job	80	15	1
Vacation	89	8	1
Family members in labour force	88	5	3
"Little ventures" and consulting	70	26	3
Retirement	64	8	24

Source: Holland (1969, Table 1).

This study was directed at a group that may have been likely to be affected by taxation, but that is far from typical of the general population. It is therefore usefully complemented by the interview study in the United Kingdom by Brown and Levin (1974) of the effects on the overtime worked by over 2000 weekly paid employees in 1971. In the first stage of the interview income tax was not mentioned, but it was open to the respondent to bring it up when explaining why he made certain decisions. The interviewer then asked about the effect of taxation, and finally the respondent was asked to agree with one of three statements: (1) Tax has made me work more overtime; (2) Doesn't apply/Neither; (3) Tax has made me work less overtime. The results for all male workers indicate that a very high proportion (74 per cent) claimed to be unaffected, and that the remainder were fairly evenly divided between "more" (15 per cent) and "less" (11 per cent). Brown and Levin then deleted those whose answers seemed implausible or who were unable to vary their overtime hours. The findings for the resulting "highly plausible, unconstrained" group were that the proportion claiming an incentive effect was rather higher (22 per cent), but that the proportion with no effect was still 69 per cent.

These findings, like those of earlier studies such as Break (1957), suggest that for the majority of the workers covered by these studies the effect of income taxation is of secondary importance. Typically between 65 and 80 per cent report that their decisions are not materially influenced and the remainder are split fairly evenly between incentive and disincentive effects. What weight however can be attached to this kind of evidence?

There are clearly a number of major potential difficulties with interview findings. First, there is the accuracy of people's perceptions of their own behaviour, and their ability to convey them in response to survey questions. How far are people able to disentangle the effects of taxation from the many factors that enter into labour supply decisions? Second, there is the honesty with which the respondent answers. His response may be conditioned by "what he believes the questioner expects him to answer, by what he considers it will be in his own best interests that the questioner should be led to believe, or by unconscious selectiveness of memory" (Williams, 1966b, pp. 8–9). In this respect, the studies cited have been careful to avoid emphasizing taxation and have probably minimized the effect. Moreover, if the responses are biased in the direction of exaggerating the effects (taxation gives a perfect opportunity for rationalizing laziness), then this strengthens the conclusions drawn. Nevertheless, evidence from other kinds of survey where the responses can be compared with observed behaviour suggest that there may be marked divergences. When asked, for instance, how they spend their time, people give answers that differ systematically from how outside observers describe the time allocation of the respondent (Hannaway, 1979).

The third difficulty is that of interpretation. Questions can mean different things to different respondents, and their answers can be interpreted in different ways. A good example is provided by the question of Holland about a hypothetical lump-sum tax. In theory, this should have isolated the substitution effect, and all responses should have been either "harder" or "no effect". However, it is clear that a number of the executives interviewed assumed that the average rate would also be lower (see Holland, 1969). Finally, there are the problems of extrapolating from rather special survey samples to the national population and of quantifying the effects based on qualitative questions.

These shortcomings have led to the value of survey evidence being seriously questioned; on the other hand, the other kinds of evidence also have their limitations.

Observed Labour Market Behaviour

The evidence of observed labour market behaviour has been based on both time series and cross-section data. The former, typically showing a secular rise in real wages per hour and fall in average hours of work for men in most countries, has been taken as indicating that the labour supply curve is backward-bending. Conversely, the secular rise in the participation rate of married women has been taken to suggest that their supply curve is upward-sloping.

The cross-section evidence is based on the variation across industries or geographical areas (as in the pioneering study by Douglas, 1934) or on individual data (see, for example, Cain and Watts, 1973). This approach yields broadly similar conclusions. For males of normal working age, the supply curve appears to be backward-bending, with a rather low elasticity (of around -0.1 to -0.2). For women, the supply elasticity appears to be positive and some estimates show it to be quite substantial.

The time series approach is illustrated by the study of Abbott and Ashenfelter (1976) for the United States. They estimate a combined labour supply–consumer demand system (with seven commodity groups) using average *per capita* data for the period 1929–67. For three of the four specifications employed, including the linear expenditure system (LES), they obtain broadly similar results. The supply curve is backward-bending with an elasticity between -0.07 and -0.14. This is further decomposed into income and substitution effects. Writing the elasticity form of the Slutsky equation,

$$\frac{w}{L}\frac{\partial L}{\partial w} = \frac{wS}{L} + w\frac{\partial L}{\partial M} \tag{2-29}$$

the estimated compensated elasticity (wS/L) in the LES case is 0.055 and the income term ($w\partial L/\partial M$) is -0.125, or a total effect of -0.07 (Pencavel, 1979).

The cross-section approach is illustrated in the case of hours of work for men by the estimates of Ashenfelter and Heckman (1973), who use data on 3203 male heads of families from the 1967 Survey of Economic Opportunity. The equation estimated relates differences in hours of work to differences in wages and other income and to a range of personal characteristics. Evaluated at the mean wage and hours, the compensated elasticity is 0.12 and the income term -0.27, implying (Eq. (2-29)) an overall elasticity of -0.15. The findings for married women are rather different. For example, Heckman (1974) used cross-section data for 2100 married white women in 1967 to estimate the labour supply function, allowing for non-participation, and found a substantial positive wage effect. Similar findings are reported by Gronau (1973), Cain and Dooley (1976) and others.[14]

Like the interview studies—although for different reasons—this evidence must be interpreted with care. There is, for example, the fact that this evidence is *indirect*. It does not deal directly with taxation but rather draws inferences from the response to net of tax wages. It is a maintained hypothesis that the effect of income tax operates in the same way as any other reduction in net earnings. It is assumed that the individual responds to a tax increase reducing his marginal net wage from $6 to $5 an hour in

---

[14] Another dimension that has been examined in cross-section studies is that of retirement—see Boskin (1977), Quinn (1977) and Boskin and Hurd (1978).

exactly the way that he would respond to a reduction in his gross earnings that led to the same decline. There are however some reasons (e.g., the prestige associated with gross pay) that may cause the effects to be different. It is therefore important to test this maintained hypothesis on which the validity of the indirect evidence depends.[15]

The estimation of labour supply functions does in fact raise a number of econometric difficulties, including those associated with simultaneous equations, specification bias, sample selection bias, unobservable variables, etc. We simply comment here on a few of the more important problems and on recent attempts to overcome them.

The first major question concerning the econometric work is whether we are correctly identifying the parameters of the supply function. This is most obvious in the case of time series evidence. To begin with, the observations need not all be at equilibrium intersections of the supply and demand curves. Certainly the period covered by Abbott and Ashenfelter, including the Depression, is likely to have included years of disequilibrium; and they themselves suggest that it may be more reasonable to regard workers in these years as being rationed on the labour market. (Techniques for handling such disequilibrium situations have recently been developed.) Even where we confine attention to equilibrium observations, it is quite possible that over a period of 40 years or so the supply curve has shifted. If, for example, changing tastes have led people to value leisure, *ceteris paribus*, more highly, then we may have the situation where the observations are of a backward-bending relationship but the supply curve at any date is upward-sloping. (The effects of some kinds of secular change, such as increased education, could in principle be included, although this has not typically been done.)

Some authors have seen the cross-section approach as one way of escaping from this problem. But there, a similar problem arises: those who are observed, say, to work more and receive lower wages may differ in some systematic way from those who work less and receive higher wages. What we have to do is to specify the characteristics in which individuals differ, and this is rarely considered in detail. An exception is Hall (1975), who considers two models: in the first households differ in their tastes, and in the second they differ in their endowment of hours. This may be illustrated by the LES example used earlier (Exercise 2-3), where the equation for earnings may be written

$$wL = \frac{(1-a)A}{1-t} + awL_0 - (1-a)I \qquad (2\text{-}30)$$

Households differ in observed wages (w) and in other income (I). What

---

[15] One attempt to test this is Rosen (1976a, 1976b). His results, for married women, suggest that there is no significant tax "illusion".

however generates the residual variation? Hall in effect considers a (tastes) and L_0 (endowments) as unobserved sources of variation across individuals. This may be contrasted with the standard approach of simply adding a normally distributed error term to equation (2-30); presumably this is meant to reflect "mistakes" by the individual, although no justification is typically given. The assumption that the "error" term is normally distributed has in fact little rationale, and other assumptions, such as the Beta distribution (Hall, 1975) or the truncated normal (Burtless and Hausman, 1978), might well be more plausible and lead to different results.

In the case of time series, there is the further problem of aggregation across individuals. The equation estimated is typically applied to mean earnings, but the correct functional form depends on the underlying micro-equations and on the distribution of characteristics and endowments (w and I). Under certain assumptions, it is legitimate to follow the standard practice of using the mean wage and mean income variables. For example, with the Eq. (2-30), and the assumption that a and L_0 are identical across individuals, we can aggregate to obtain

$$\overline{wL} = (1-a)\frac{\overline{A}}{1-t} + a\bar{w}L_0 - (1-a)\overline{I} \qquad (2\text{-}31)$$

where bars denote average values. However, this involves strong assumptions and where, for example, the micro-specification is nonlinear in w, we would need to allow for changes over time in the distribution of wages. (This question is discussed, in the context of consumer demand, by Muellbauer, 1975).

The specification just described allowed only for a proportional tax. As the analysis of Section 2-2 made clear, in reality there may be nonlinear budget constraints. The first systematic treatment of this, by Hall (1973), proposed in effect linearizing the budget constraint at the observed point, so that the individual is treated as facing a marginal net wage and an intercept. Brown, Levin and Ulph (1976), whose marginal net wage also took account of the overtime premium, showed that the incorrect average wage procedure may lead to estimates of the substitution effect that are of the "wrong" sign, whereas the sign is correct when the marginal net wage is employed. There is the further difficulty that the marginal net wage and intercept are endogenous, being functions of L. They are therefore correlated with the error term in the equation, resulting in biased estimates of the coefficients. Procedures to deal with this have been developed by Ashworth and Ulph (1977), Burtless and Hausman (1978), and Wales and Woodland (1979).

The key to the use of observed labour supply evidence is the effect of variation in the net wage, and here there may be serious measurement problems. For example, given the available sources, it has typically been necessary to calculate the wage per hour by dividing weekly earnings by hours (in other cases annual hours have been calculated by dividing total earnings by the wage rate). As a result, any measurement error in the hours variable (alternatively the wage rate) means that the independent variable is correlated with the error term in the hours equation and hence that the coefficient estimates are biased (Hall, 1973, pp. 122–3). For this reason a number of authors use an instrumental variable approach, first estimating a "predicted wage" based on personal characteristics.

A related problem is that of missing variables. For example, for those not in the labour force (e.g., married women), we do not have observations on the wage. Equations estimated for those who are in the labour force (the women who do work) will not in general provide unbiased estimates of the labour supply function. Such estimates confound the underlying labour supply parameters with the (non-random) process determining whether a person is in the sample. This "sample selection bias" may also arise where the investigator has to delete observations (e.g., where the employment record is interrupted). Techniques for overcoming this were applied by Heckman in the study of married women referred to earlier and are reviewed in Heckman (1979).

Finally, the ability of this approach to generate useful results depends critically on the availability and quality of the underlying data. One of the major developments of recent years has been the access to rich bodies of micro-data on individuals, and these are likely to continue to be fruitful. At the same time, they are not without problems, and cover only certain dimensions of labour supply. There is a continuing need for the refinement of the basic sources and for evidence on aspects of labour decisions other than hours of work.

Experimental Evidence

Controlled experiments in economics have been fairly rare, but they appear at first sight to offer the solution to some of the difficulties that arise in the interpretation of cross-section and time-series evidence. The problems of the indirect nature of the evidence on the effect of taxation and of identification of the sources of variation in hours seem in theory to be soluble through comparing two samples identical apart from the controlled parameters of the experiment. In this way, the effect of taxation would be directly rather than indirectly measured, and otherwise identical individuals would be confronted with different net wage rates, so that we could observe different points on the same supply curve.

The strengths and weaknesses of the experimental approach have been brought out clearly in the negative income tax experiments carried out in the United States. These studies grew out of concern for the possible adverse effect on work incentives of the negative income tax and a feeling that the extent of such an effect could not be assessed from existing cross-section studies. (The availability and analysis of cross-section data has in fact advanced considerably since then.) As a result the Office of Economic Opportunity funded a $8 million experiment in four New Jersey cities lasting three years and covering some 1200 low-income families. Subsequent experiments were carried out in North Carolina and Iowa (the rural income maintenance experiment), in Gary, Indiana (hometown of one of the authors), in Denver, Colorado, and in Seattle (combined with a manpower programme). A recent review of the experiments is given in Ferber and Hirsch (1978).

In the New Jersey experiment, on which we concentrate here, the sample was limited to those families whose normal income was not more than 150 per cent of the poverty line and that included at least one male eligible for work. Families were assigned on a stratified random basis to either one of eight experimental groups or a control group. In the experimental groups there were different negative income tax programmes, with guaranteed incomes ranging from 50 to 125 per cent of the poverty line and tax rates between 30 and 70 per cent. The experimental and control families were interviewed initially to collect pre-enrolment data, and then every three months.

The results of such an experiment may be presented in a number of ways. Possibly the simplest is to compare the mean weekly hours of work for experimental and control groups both before and during the experiment (Hall, 1975, p. 122), which for white husbands were:

	Experimental group	Control group
Before experiment	$\bar{L}_{X,B} = 34.1$	$\bar{L}_{C,B} = 34.8$
During experiment	$\bar{L}_{X,D} = 31.8$	$\bar{L}_{C,D} = 34.4$

(X denotes experimental, C control group, B denotes before, D during the experiment.)

Following Hall, let us suppose that the experimental selection was random, and that the effect of the experiment was additive. This gives two obvious estimators of the latter effect:

$\bar{L}_{X,D} - \bar{L}_{C,D} = -2.6$ hours (difference between experimental and control groups)

$\bar{L}_{X,D} - \bar{L}_{X,B} = -2.3$ hours (difference between before and during experiment)

These results are rather similar and suggest a significant reduction in labour supply (around 7 per cent).

In the reports of the experiment (Watts and Rees, 1977), a more elaborate regression approach is used. This is more extensive in several respects. First, a range of labour supply variables are considered: labour force participation, employment rate, hours worked, and total earnings. Second, among the explanatory variables were characteristics of the family such as age, education, and family size. These help "control" for any surviving non-random elements in the choice of samples (e.g., because of differential response). Third, the pre-enrolment value of the dependent variable is used as a control variable. Finally, account is taken of the differences in negative tax plans, i.e., the experimental group are not assumed to be homogeneous, as in the simple calculation above. The equations estimated were (schematically):

$$\bar{L}_D = \alpha \bar{L}_B + \text{function of characteristics and treatment variables}$$

The "simple" estimates described in the previous paragraph may be seen as those obtained when differences in family characteristics are ignored and treatment is a zero–one dummy variable.[16]

The results of the New Jersey experiment are summarized in the report as presenting: "a picture of generally small absolute labour supply differentials between the treatment and control groups as a whole. Only among wives, whose mean labour supply is quite small to begin with, are the differentials large in relative terms" (US Department of Health, Education and Welfare (hereafter USDHEW), 1973, p. 21). More concretely, the regression results, including control variables but with no allowance for differential treatment of the experimental group, show a small reduction in hours worked by white husbands (-1.9 hours). For white wives, the reduction in the participation rate is 8 per cent and hours worked, averaged over the whole sample, fall by nearly 2 hours per week (the overall control mean was 4 hours). The regressions, including treatment differentials, show a rather complicated pattern of interactions with income (Watts *et al.*, 1974). We may also note that the report of the Rural Income Maintenance Experiment concluded that the results closely resembled those for New Jersey (USDHEW, 1973).

These experiments have been extremely interesting and they represent a most important innovation. At the same time, there are a number of potential problems with the experimental approach, many of which were recognized clearly by the New Jersey research team (see, for example, Pechman and Timpane, 1975).

First, there are the difficulties associated with any kind of experiment. The celebrated "Hawthorne" effect, according to which mere inclusion in an experiment may change behaviour, is discussed in Orcutt and Orcutt (1968).[17]

---

[16] The two estimates are obtained by setting $\alpha = 0$, yielding $\bar{L}_{X,D} - \bar{L}_{C,D}$ as an estimate of the treatment effect, and $\alpha = 1$, yielding $\bar{L}_{X,D} - \bar{L}_{X,B}$.

[17] In terms of the earlier analysis, this means that $\bar{L}_{X,D} - \bar{L}_{X,B}$ is not an unbiased estimator of the treatment effect; on the other hand, $(\bar{L}_{X,D} - \bar{L}_{X,B}) - (\bar{L}_{C,D} - \bar{L}_{C,B})$ does provide an unbiased estimate.

Second, there is a problem common to many experiments but particularly acute in the case of labour supply, which may involve long-term changes: the extent to which one can predict "permanent" responses from short-term experiments. There are two main consequences (Metcalf, 1973). A temporary income guarantee has a smaller effect on lifetime income than a permanent programme, so that the income effect tends to be understated. On the other hand, the experiment reduces the cost of consuming leisure temporarily—it is a limited period offer—and the substitution effect may therefore be overstated. Metcalf (1974) made tentative estimates of the possible extent of bias, concluding that they are individually potentially substantial but are largely offsetting when measuring the overall response.[18]

Third, the experiments involve by definition only a subgroup of the population, whereas some effects may be exhibited only when the entire population is affected, e.g., where they involve a collective response. Thus, trade union leaders are unlikely to be influenced in their negotiations about standard hours by the fact that a selection of their members are in a (temporary) experiment. The responses may for this reason be understated (Browning, 1971).

Turning to problems that apply more specifically to the particular experiment, there are several that arise from the design of the sample and from the method of analysis (see, for example, Aaron, 1975; and Hall, 1975). Here we refer to two that are closely related to points discussed in the case of cross-section evidence. In the first place the sample was defined by an upper limit on family income. This means that an analysis of earnings and, say, a control variable (such as the tax rate) will lead to biased parameter estimates, since as we near the truncation point the sample is increasingly dominated by families with negative deviations from the supply curve. (The way in which the bias arises may be seen from a diagram with wL ($\equiv Y$) on one axis and w on the other, with the sample cut-off determined by Y.) The analysis by Hausman and Wise of the New Jersey data "revealed large differences between biased least squares estimates and consistent maximum likelihood estimates" (1977, pp. 932–3). Second, there is the response of the family to the budget constraint with which they are faced. In reality, as we have seen, the budget constraint may depart considerably from textbook simplicity. In the experimental context, the position was even more complex. Not only was the negative income tax itself an additional element, but also families could choose whether to participate (see Ashenfelter, 1978). The position was further complicated by the introduction at the time the New Jersey experiment began of a new state welfare programme. The resulting highly complex budget constraint makes it considerably more difficult to draw inferences from the experiment.

---

[18] Further evidence will be available from other experiments which include sub-samples with different durations.

2-5 CONCLUDING COMMENTS

This Lecture has developed several of the themes and illustrated several of the problems that we shall encounter repeatedly in the remainder of the book. In particular, neither economic theory nor empirical evidence can provide a conclusive answer to the effect of income taxation on labour supply. On the other hand, the analysis has provided considerable insight.

We have seen how the tax system diverts economic activity from taxed to non-taxed areas, or from highly taxed to less highly taxed areas, and that the possible diversions take on a large number of different forms. The standard treatment is in terms of the work versus leisure choice, but the same theoretical framework can be applied more broadly to:

market versus home production,
pecuniary versus non-pecuniary returns (consumption within the firm),
taxed versus untaxed pecuniary returns.

In each case, the direction of the impact of taxation is ambiguous, since income and substitution effects tend to work in opposite directions. This means that for many situations empirical evidence is necessary to answer even qualitative questions.

It should be noted that there are some situations where economic theory does yield unambiguous results. There are changes in tax policy such that income and substitution effects work in the same direction, e.g., a negative income tax would increase the income of poor families and reduce their net wage at the margin. Where leisure is a normal good, the negative income tax definitely operates in the direction of reduced work effort. Moreover, the distinction between income and substitution effects is in itself a valuable one. Thus, economists can point out that a lack of change in labour supply is not evidence that there is no distortionary effect; the latter (as we shall see more clearly in Part Two) is related to the substitution effect, and there is no ambiguity about its sign (although there may still be dispute about its magnitude).

The empirical evidence indicates at present only a limited response in terms of the hours worked by men but a more significant effect for women. The latter may have implications for the effects of reforms in the tax treatment of the family (e.g., whether households are taxed as a unit or each individual is taxed separately). The empirical evidence is however limited in its coverage of the groups most likely to be affected and in the dimensions of labour supply recorded. Thus, there is virtually no econometric evidence on the response of doctors, lawyers, and other high earners; and the typical data do not take us very far in understanding such aspects as the degree of effort or ingenuity put into a job or the willingness to accept responsibility.

The precise effects of the tax depend critically on the detailed structure of the tax. Although in a set of lectures of this kind we cannot devote much space to an elaboration of these special provisions and their effects, it is important to bear them in mind. In many texts, the income tax is shown simply as reducing the net wage from w to $w(1-t)$. Here we have seen that a more complex specification is necessary to take account of varying marginal tax rates, of the interaction with social security and other benefits, and of the way in which the tax base is defined. This becomes even more the case when one considers explicitly the process of compliance on the one hand and administration on the other—aspects that need to be incorporated into future work, both theoretical and empirical.

Finally, we should remind the reader of the partial equilibrium nature of the analysis in this Lecture. The changes in labour supply (and in the supply of other factors) that occur as a result of the imposition of the income tax (or a change in the tax structure) will lead to changes in the before-tax wage, and the total effects must be taken into account. These changes make the calculation of equal-yield tax comparisons even more difficult than in the partial equilibrium analysis. For instance, an analysis of the consequences of the enactment of a negative income tax, financed by an increase in the tax rates on middle and higher incomes, must consider not only the effect on the labour supply of the beneficiaries and those who have to pay for the negative income tax, but also the effect of these changes in labour supply on the before-tax wages received by each group.

NOTE ON THE EXPENDITURE FUNCTION

The expenditure function has a number of applications in public economics but is not treated in many textbooks, exceptions to this including Dixit (1976a, p. 33) and Varian (1978, p. 91). We provide therefore a brief, and non-rigorous, introduction, beginning with the case where labour is in fixed supply (that typically treated in the literature).

The *expenditure function* may be defined directly as the minimum level of lump-sum income, M needed to attain a specified level of utility, U_0, when faced with a given vector of consumer prices, $\mathbf{p}$, i.e.,

$$e(\mathbf{p}, U_0) = \min (\mathbf{p} \cdot \mathbf{X}) \quad \text{subject to } U(\mathbf{X}) \geqslant U_0 \qquad \text{(II-1)}$$

It may also be obtained via the *indirect utility function*. This gives the maximum utility achievable at given prices and lump-sum income, M, i.e.

$$V(\mathbf{p}, M) = \max U(\mathbf{X}) \quad \text{subject to } \mathbf{p} \cdot \mathbf{X} \leqslant M \qquad \text{(II-2)}$$

If preferences satisfy local non-satiation, then V is a strictly increasing function of M, and we can invert the indirect utility function to give the expenditure function.

The expenditure function, which is analogous to the cost function used in production theory, has a number of properties, including the following:

1. it is homogeneous of degree 1 in prices ($\mathbf{p}$),
2. it is concave in prices ($\mathbf{p}$),
3. the partial derivative with respect to the jth price equals the compensated demand function for the jth good.

For a fuller statement and derivation from the properties of U (quasi-concavity and local non-satiation), see Diewert (1979) and Varian (1978). The third property is particularly useful, and if we write x_j (lower case) for the compensated demand function, we have

$$x_j(\mathbf{p}, U_0) = \partial e/\partial p_j \qquad \text{(II-3)}$$

From the definitions, it is identically true that the compensated demand at U_0 is the same as the uncompensated demand (capital letters) at income $e(\mathbf{p}, U_0)$.

$$X_j[\mathbf{p}, e(\mathbf{p}, U_0)] \equiv x_j(\mathbf{p}, U_0) \qquad \text{(II-4)}$$

We can differentiate with respect to p_k

$$\frac{\partial X_j}{\partial p_k} + \frac{\partial X_j}{\partial M}\frac{\partial e}{\partial p_k} = \frac{\partial x_j}{\partial p_k}$$

Hence (using (II-3) and (II-4))

$$\frac{\partial X_j}{\partial p_k} = \frac{\partial x_j}{\partial p_k} - X_k\frac{\partial X_j}{\partial M} \qquad \text{(II-5)}$$

This is the Slutsky equation, with the first term being the substitution term. The matrix of second derivatives of the expenditure function is the substitution matrix and negative semi-definiteness follows from the concavity of the expenditure function. Differentiating (II-4) with respect to U_0,

$$\frac{\partial X_j}{\partial M}\frac{\partial e}{\partial U_0} = \frac{\partial x_j}{\partial U_0}$$

So

$$\frac{\partial X_j}{\partial M} = \frac{\partial^2 e/\partial p_j \partial U_0}{\partial e/\partial U_0} \qquad \text{(II-6)}$$

The expenditure function may be extended to allow for variable labour supply, by defining

$$e(w, \mathbf{p}, U_0) = \min\,(\mathbf{p}\cdot\mathbf{X} - wL) \quad \text{subject to } U(\mathbf{X}, L) \geq U_0 \qquad \text{(II-7)}$$

where e now relates to lump-sum income, not total expenditure. This has the properties that the compensated labour supply function (denoted by lower case)

$$l(w, \mathbf{p}, U_0) = -\partial e / \partial w \qquad \text{(II-8)}$$

(the sign being reversed because it is a factor), and the uncompensated supply

$$L[w, \mathbf{p}, e(w, \mathbf{p}, U_0)] = l(w, \mathbf{p}, U_0) \qquad \text{(II-9)}$$

Differentiating with respect to w,

$$\frac{\partial L}{\partial w} + \frac{\partial L}{\partial M} \frac{\partial e}{\partial w} = \frac{\partial l}{\partial w}$$

or

$$\frac{\partial L}{\partial w} = \frac{\partial l}{\partial w} + L \frac{\partial L}{\partial M} \qquad \text{(II-10)}$$

This is the Slutsky equation given in the text (2-5).

For further reading on the dual approach to consumer behaviour, see Diewert (1974, 1978), Gorman (1976) and Varian (1978). The uses in public finance are discussed by Diamond and McFadden (1974).

READING

The basic theory of labour supply is parallel to the analysis of consumer demand presented in most books on microeconomics, e.g., (in increasing order of difficulty) Hicks (1939), Green (1976), Malinvaud (1972) and Varian (1978). It is not however usually discussed very extensively. For a fuller treatment see, among others, Cooper (1952), Diamond (1968)—in connection with a negative income taxation—and Hanoch and Honig (1978), for the effects of nonlinear budget constraints.

The value of survey evidence is assessed in Williams (1966b). The state of evidence based on observed labour market behaviour is well summarized in Cain and Watts (1973), and Godfrey (1975), although there have been substantial developments since then. The New Jersey negative income tax experiment is reviewed in Pechman and Timpane (1975).

THREE

TAXATION, SAVINGS AND DECISIONS OVER TIME

3-1 INTERTEMPORAL DECISIONS AND TAXATION

A crucial determinant of the long-run development of the economy is the saving of individuals and firms, providing funds for investment in new machines and new techniques of production. At the same time, differences in wealth—the result of past savings or the savings of earlier generations—represent a major source of inequality within the economy. It is no wonder then that the question of the effect of tax policy on savings and investment decisions is a central preoccupation of government authorities. Lectures 3–5 are concerned with this subject. This lecture focuses on the *level* of household savings, and Lecture 4 on the *allocation* of savings among different assets (safe and risky). Lecture 5 deals with the behaviour of the firm. The analysis in all three lectures is at a partial equilibrium level, the intention being to provide the building blocks for the general equilibrium treatment in the remainder of Part One.

Before beginning our analysis, we list a few of the policy issues upon which our discussion in this and the next lecture has some bearing.

1. *Consumption tax versus an income tax.* One proposal for reform with a long history is the replacement of the income tax by a tax on consumption expenditure; this can be shown to be equivalent under certain conditions to exempting interest income from tax. Moreover, many countries, while operating an income tax, have moved in the direction of an expenditure tax by exempting certain forms of savings

(e.g., through life insurance policies or pension funds) or exempting the income generated. It is often suggested in popular debate that the expenditure tax leads to a higher level of savings. We discuss the theoretical and the empirical validity of this proposition.

2. *Inheritance taxes.* Most countries impose, in addition to taxes on income, taxes on the transfer of wealth through gifts or bequests. These are intended primarily to reduce the concentration of wealth (an aspect considered in Lecture 9), but may also affect the incentive to save.

3. *Wealth tax.* Some countries impose a tax on the ownership of capital, and in others the introduction of such a tax is under active discussion. How would its effects differ from those of a tax on capital income?

4. *Social security.* State pension schemes have acquired substantial importance, and it has been argued that they have a significant effect on the overall savings rate of the economy.

This list is not meant to be exhaustive but rather to show that some of the central issues of policy debates are concerned in one way or another with the effects of taxation on savings.

The organization of the lecture is parallel to that of Lecture 2. This section discusses various forms of taxation and the different decisions affected by taxation, and other public programmes. Section 3-2 develops the basic intertemporal model, proves a set of equivalence theorems between different kinds of tax structures, and establishes conditions under which, in a simplified model, taxation is likely to discourage or encourage savings. Section 3-3 considers alternative variants on the basic model, while Section 3-4 is devoted to an evaluation of some of the empirical evidence on taxation and the interest elasticity of savings.

Capital Taxes and Savings

There are a variety of types of taxes on capital and the return to capital:

1. taxes on interest income, either at the same rate as other income or at a differential rate (as with the United Kingdom investment income surcharge);

2. taxes on capital gains, that is the increment in the value of a given stock of assets;[1]

3. wealth taxes on the net value of assets owned at a specified date;

4. taxes on the transfer of wealth via gifts or bequests;

5. taxes on real property in the form of houses, land, etc. ("property taxes" in the United States, "rates" in the United Kingdom).

---

[1] Most tax codes distinguish between short-term and long-term capital gains, treating the former like ordinary income but taxing the latter at lower rates.

There is also the tax on corporate profits. It is often considered a tax on "firms" rather than on individuals. However, since corporations are owned by individuals, and profits are eventually distributed to individuals, it can be argued that it is really a tax on a particular form of savings of individuals. We return to this question in Lectures 5 and 6.

As we saw in the previous Lecture, there are typically provisions in the tax code that reduce the effective rate. These include the following.

1. *Depreciation allowances.* The income tax and corporation tax include provisions for the deduction of depreciation. This is necessary to arrive at net income, but the actual allowances frequently fall short of, or exceed, the true economic depreciation. In the same way, the government often provides an incentive for investment via investment credits or cash allowances.
2. *Special treatment of housing.* Most countries tax neither the services of owner-occupied housing (the imputed rent) nor the capital gains on such housing. Since, for many people, housing constitutes their single most important asset, this means that a large fraction of their wealth is exempt from taxation.
3. *Special treatment of life assurance and deferred compensation* (pensions), typically equivalent to an exemption of interest income from tax.
4. *Consumer durables.* No governments tax directly the implicit return associated with consumer durables; the aggregate value of these durables is considerable.
5. *Tax-exempt bonds.* In the United States, the interest on state and local bonds is exempt from interest income taxation.

Although these special provisions are often termed "loopholes" in the tax system, it should be emphasized that there are, for some of them, strong administrative reasons. Suppose, for example, that one wanted to tax the implicit interest income on deferred compensation. How could one treat unfunded pension schemes? One could, for instance, take the present value of the promised pension, e.g., calculate the implied price of the annuity. But the price of an annuity differs for different individuals, depending on their age, sex, occupation, etc. Moreover, the individual has not made a choice to purchase the annuity; it is less liquid than a corresponding cash payment, and should accordingly be treated as less valuable. But how large should the "liquidity allowance" be? Any set of rules devised to handle such problems would typically give rise both to inequities and to distortions.

The fundamental difficulty is the translation from economic concepts to tax legislation. This is well illustrated by the very notion of an "asset". Suppose an individual decides to "incorporate himself", that is form a corporation, the only asset of which is his (future) labour services. If he sells the firm, is he selling an asset or his labour services? The human capital literature treats such future labour services symmetrically with future capital services, but for the tax law the consequences may be quite different. Similarly, we may want to distinguish between labour employed by a firm to repair machines and that employed to build new ones. Such a distinction, although clear-cut in principle, is difficult to couch in legislation or administrative practice.

These special provisions of the tax code alter radically the effective tax rates. Since access to various forms of assets, or their relative attractiveness, may depend critically on a person's income, they have an important effect on the equity of the tax system and the true degree of progressivity. They also may have strong allocative effects.

In the analytical sections of this lecture, we focus mainly on general taxes, not taking account of the kinds of differential treatment illustrated above. We do this with misgivings, since no actual tax base is comprehensive, for the administrative reasons noted, and the reader should bear this qualification in mind.

Finally, the examples we have given of different types of capital accumulation suggest that there are several definitions of "savings" and "consumption". The choice between these depends on the purpose of the analysis. Suppose that we start with consumption. Then, if we are concerned with the extent to which public policy affects the provision for the future, it is the use of resources that is relevant. If taxation leads people to buy a new refrigerator rather than beer to put in the old one, this is postponing consumption just as much as putting money in the bank is. If, on the other hand, we are concerned with the effect of taxation on the macroeconomic equilibrium of the economy, we are likely to be more concerned with *consumer expenditure* than with notional *consumption*. The former corresponds to the standard national accounts concept and includes outlays on durables, while the latter measures the flow of services, including the imputed return on durables (although in empirical applications this treatment is typically not extended to housing). If we turn to income, then the corresponding definition to that of "consumption" would, for example, include the imputed income on durables and the accrual of rights to pensions. This implies a broad definition of savings. On the other hand, if our concern is with the availability of loanable funds, then savings via the acquisition of durables is irrelevant. We would take a narrower definition of savings: the net acquisition of financial assets by households.

Income, Substitution and Financial Effects

As in the case of labour supply, an increase in taxation may have income and substitution effects. Thus a reduction in the after-tax return to capital is equivalent to making future consumption as an aggregate relatively more expensive, and—holding utility constant—tends to increase current consumption. This is the *substitution* effect. The *income*, or *wealth*, effect, as we refer to it here, is slightly more complicated than with labour supply, since a person may be a net demander (i.e. a borrower) rather than a net supplier (a lender). Thus a fall in the after-tax return reduces the income, *ceteris paribus*, of a person who is lending, and the assumption of normality means that present consumption is reduced. On the other hand, for a net borrower, a fall in the after-tax cost of borrowing has a positive wealth effect, and present consumption is raised, assuming normality. It may be noted that we are discussing the effect in terms of present consumption; where the current resources available to the person are unchanged, the effect on savings may be derived directly. (Alternatively, savings may be seen as the "expenditure" on future consumption; a rise in the "price" may or may not reduce expenditure.)

There is therefore no unambiguous outcome. Where consumption is normal, as is assumed throughout this Lecture, and where the person is a net lender, we cannot be sure which effect will dominate. Much of the analysis of Section 3-2 is devoted to elucidating conditions under which the overall direction of the effect can be determined. As before, it is important to remember that the two effects may have different implications. In particular, if they more or less cancel—the overall elasticity is close to zero—it does not follow that we can disregard the effects. As in the case of labour supply, the distortion is not directly related to the overall elasticity, and a zero overall elasticity may still entail substantial welfare costs of taxation. (Although we should note that the welfare economics of intertemporal allocation are less straightforward than in the static model—see Lecture 14.)

It may be argued that savings behaviour, just like hours of work, is subject to considerable constraints and that, since much of personal savings is of a contractual nature, the decisions of households are largely irrelevant. At the same time, there are major items of savings that are non-contractual, and even with pensions there are elements of flexibility—in the longer term if not in the short run. Although individual participation is usually compulsory in a given job, there is some flexibility via the choice of job (which takes us back to the analysis of Lecture 2), and the terms of the contract are likely to reflect in part the preferences of the employees. None the less, we must recognize that pensions are a distinctive asset and are not substitutable for other savings on a one-to-one basis.[2]

The case of pensions also illustrates the *financial* effects of taxation referred to in Lecture 2. The tax system, through its favoured treatment of deferred compensation, provides an incentive for remuneration to be

---

[2] The fact that much wealth is controlled by institutional savers may have important consequences for the pattern of investment in the economy. The relationship between the allocation of these funds among alternative investment opportunities and the "preferences" of the individuals allegedly represented by institutional savers may, at best, be tenuous.

provided in this form. The same obviously applies to the accrual of returns in the form of capital gains. The individual who incorporates himself is converting wage income into capital gain. Moreover, the tax system may have financial effects, influencing the form in which savings occurs, as a result of differential treatment of retained earning and dividends under corporate profits taxation. Individuals pay personal taxes on the income of the corporation in which they own shares only when those returns are distributed in dividends. This, as we see in Lecture 5, encourages firms to retain their earnings, and there is considerable debate as to the extent to which such savings by firms can be viewed as a substitute for or, perhaps more accurately, a part of household savings. The question is sometimes put, can individuals see through the "corporate veil"? Thus, although this chapter is primarily about household savings, the distinction between household and corporate savings is blurred, and we discuss this in Section 3-3.

When different types of assets are taxed differently, there may also be a *capitalization effect*. This arises most clearly in the case of assets in inelastic supply. Then, market equilibrium results in the price of these assets adjusting to the point where the return per dollar invested is the same as on other assets. Consider the following simple example. There are two assets: one-period bonds and land. If we take the rate of interest on bonds as determined exogenously (e.g., as in a small country with an international capital market), then the price of land would reflect the net-of-tax stream of returns, money and imputed, discounted at this interest rate.[3] If the government now announces that land is to be taxed more heavily, relative to bonds, this depresses the price of land, imposing a capital loss on those owning land when the tax is announced, but not affecting the terms on which consumption can be transferred between different periods.[4] There is a capitalization effect, but no continuing effect.

For many assets, the supply is relatively inelastic in the short run but more elastic in the long run. Thus, in the short run there is a large capitalization effect: imposing a tax on the implicit return to owner-occupied housing would depress house prices. In the long run, the supply of housing would decline (so long as the market price was below the replacement cost, no new construction would occur) and the price would rise, until it eventually reached the cost of production. In the extreme case where the long-run supply of housing is completely elastic, there would in the long run be no capitalization effect. More generally, where the long run supply curve of housing is upward-sloping, the allocative effect is the smaller, and the long-run capitalization effect the larger, the smaller the

---

[3] If the price is p, and the returns a permanent constant stream y, then $p = y/r$.

[4] If the differential tax is t^*, the new price is $p^* = y(1-t^*)/r$. Those now purchasing the asset at p^* still receive a yield r on their investment.

elasticity. It may be noted that the return to different assets (with the same degree of risk, etc.) will, if capital is freely mobile, in the long run be equalized whether through the mechanism of the capitalization effect or the allocative effect. For this reason, one cannot ascertain whether a sector is receiving special treatment from an examination of the rate of return.[5]

The capitalization of taxes is an important feature. It means that the effect operates at the time when the market becomes aware of the tax,[6] and that its redistributional effect depends on who owned the asset at that date. It obviously raises issues of equity between similarly placed people (e.g., those who had previously treated land and bonds as perfect substitutes), as well as vertical equity.

Other Public Programmes which Affect Savings

Taxation, though undoubtedly of considerable significance, is not the only public policy that affects savings decisions. How concerned we are about whether a tax on interest income discourages savings depends in part on whether there are other instruments available to the government for offsetting the reduction in savings and on whether public savings can be used as a substitute for private savings. The most important of such policy instruments are (1) social security, (2) debt and monetary policy, and (3) public investment.

Social security performs a number of functions. It provides individuals with income for retirement; it pays benefits to meet needs at particular stages of the life cycle (e.g., child benefits); it covers individuals against the loss of income through sickness or unemployment. As such it is likely to influence the extent of savings for life-cycle and precautionary motives. Thus, if state pensions are viewed as publicly provided annuities, this may affect the private demand for annuities.

Debt and monetary policy are widely viewed as affecting the rate of interest; if that is the case, then the government can use these instruments to increase or decrease savings. To put it another way, if public bonds are substitutes for private capital in personal portfolios, then by increasing the supply of public debt the government can reduce the amount of savings

---

[5] Thus one cannot, for instance, ascertain whether the oil industry has been subjected to special treatment simply by looking at the return to capital in that sector. If there are no barriers to entry, firms will enter the industry or expand their capital stock until the after-tax return is the same as in other industries. The relevant question is what happened immediately after the special provisions were enacted. Did stock prices rise? Note that if the enactment of the special provision was anticipated, then much of the price increase would have occurred prior to, and perhaps long before, the actual date of enactment. This makes testing for the presence of capitalization effects particularly difficult.

[6] Some writers refer to this as the "announcement" effect. This however differs from the traditional use of the term (e.g., Pigou, 1947), and will not be followed here.

available for private capital formation. The extent to which public debt does in fact have this "crowding-out" effect is discussed further in Lecture 8.

Public capital accumulation accounts in many countries for a large fraction of real capital formation, e.g., roads, railways, and public utilities. To the extent that these capital goods can be viewed as ensuring a higher standard of living for future generations, individuals may reduce savings for bequests; to the extent that they are viewed as enabling lower tax rates or higher social security benefits in the future, they may lead to less life-cycle savings.

3-2 THE BASIC INTERTEMPORAL MODEL

In order to provide a simple framework for the analysis, let us assume that the individual expects confidently to live for T years. At age i he receives wage income w_i and consumes C_i. During his life he receives bequests with present value, at the beginning of his life, of I, and he himself makes a bequest B at death.

Of crucial consequence for the intertemporal decisions are the assumptions about the capital market. The standard assumption is that he can borrow or lend as much as he likes at a fixed market rate of interest. This assumption, which we refer to as that of a "perfect capital market",[7] is a strong one; we need to allow for the possibility that lending and borrowing rates may differ, and that the rates may be functions of the amounts borrowed or lent. With the additional assumption, for convenience only, that the market rate of interest is constant over time, the perfect capital market assumption means that the intertemporal budget constraint is (in discrete time):[8]

$$\sum_{i=1}^{T} \frac{w_i}{(1+r)^{i-1}} + I = \sum_{i=1}^{T} \frac{C_i}{(1+r)^{i-1}} + \frac{B}{(1+r)^{T}} \qquad (3\text{-}1)$$

(the generalization to the case where r varies over time is obvious). In other words, the individual's consumption pattern must be such that the present discounted value of consumption plus bequests (right-hand side of Eq. (3-1)) is equal to the present discounted value of his wages plus inheritance (left-hand side).

The critical nature of the perfect capital market assumption may be seen by noting that, if, to take an extreme case, he cannot borrow at all, and

---

[7] This usage is conventional, although, as Stigler (1967) points out, departure from these conditions does not necessarily imply the existence of imperfect competition.

[8] His bequest B is defined as the residue at death, so the budget constraint holds with equality. The bequest is made in period $T+1$.

if his inheritance is received at age K, then there are the additional constraints:

$$\sum_{i=1}^{J} \frac{w_i}{(1+r)^{i-1}} \geqslant \sum_{i=1}^{J} \frac{C_i}{(1+r)^{i-1}} \quad \text{for all } J < K \qquad (3\text{-}2a)$$

$$\sum_{i=1}^{J} \frac{w_i}{(1+r)^{i-1}} + I \geqslant \sum_{i=1}^{J} \frac{C_i}{(1+r)^{i-1}} \quad \begin{array}{c} \text{for all } J \geqslant K \\ (J \leqslant T) \end{array} \qquad (3\text{-}2b)$$

Thus (3-2a) covers the case of the expectant heir constrained to consume in line with his current earnings rather than his future inheritance.

We divide the analysis of taxation into two stages. First, we focus on the effect on the budget constraint. Although this in itself does not determine the effect of taxation, it allows us to show certain *equivalences*, which establish that alternative tax structures have identical effects on the budget constraint for the individual—although not necessarily for the government.

Equivalence Results

The first equivalence that follows immediately from the budget constraint is that *between* a proportional tax t on wages plus all inheritances *and* a proportional tax t' on consumption plus bequests. The effect of the former on the budget constraint is

$$\left[\sum_{1}^{T} \frac{w_i}{(1+r)^{i-1}} + I \right](1-t) = \sum_{1}^{T} \frac{C_i}{(1+r)^{i-1}} + \frac{B}{(1+r)^{T}} \qquad (3\text{-}3a)$$

whereas the latter gives

$$\sum_{1}^{T} \frac{w_i}{(1+r)^{i-1}} + I = \left[\sum_{1}^{T} \frac{C_i}{(1+r)^{i-1}} + \frac{B}{(1+r)^{T}} \right](1+t') \qquad (3\text{-}3b)$$

Comparing (3-3a) and (3-3b), it is clear that the effect on the budget constraint is identical where

$$(1-t) = \frac{1}{1+t'} \qquad (3\text{-}3')$$

The equation (3-3') is in fact the formula for converting from a tax-inclusive basis, typically used for income tax, to a tax-exclusive basis, used for indirect taxes. Thus a wage tax of $\frac{1}{3}$ is equivalent to a consumption tax of 50 per cent. The proportionality of the taxes is obviously important, and the effect of progression is discussed below.

Several features of this equivalence may be noted. First, although the different taxes are equivalent in their effect on the budget constraint, the effect on private *savings* is not identical, since the time paths of tax revenue differ. Thus, suppose a person lives for two periods, receives wage income only in the first, and there is no inheritance: under a wage tax he pays tax only in the first period, but under a consumption tax he pays $C_1(1+t')$ in the first period, $C_2(1+t')$ in the second. Thus, for a given consumption plan (C_1, C_2), he saves more under a consumption tax, so as to pay the tax in the second. The switch from a wage tax to a consumption tax increases, in this case, private savings and reduces government savings (since the receipt of part of the revenue is delayed). If the government can borrow or lend at the same interest rate as individuals, there will in fact be no general equilibrium effects of switching tax regimes: the decrease in public savings precisely offsets the increase in private savings. These conditions are not however necessarily satisfied—see below.

Second, the wage tax, or the equivalent consumption tax, does not affect the trade-off between consumption at different dates for the individual. It has only a *wealth* effect; that is, the effect on savings is only a consequence of the uniform shifting inward of the budget constraint. This in turn has one important corollary: individuals with the same present value of receipts are affected identically, regardless of the timing of their wage income. Later, in the normative discussion of tax systems, we introduce the concept of horizontal equity: "identical" individuals ought to be treated the same. One notion with wide intuitive appeal is that individuals with the same opportunity sets, i.e., facing the same budget constraints, ought to be taxed the same. Thus, the consumption tax (or the equivalent wage tax) is horizontally equitable in comparing individuals with different tastes and patterns of wage incomes—at least in the context of proportional taxes and perfect capital markets.

The implications of capital market constraints are illustrated by the extreme case shown in (3-2) where we can again achieve the same effect by multiplying by either $(1-t)$, on the left-hand side, or $(1+t')$, on the right-hand side. On the other hand, the timing of savings—which does differ under the two taxes—may be important. For example, suppose that there is a "lumpy" investment project available to the individual (e.g., to start a business requires a minimum capital investment). The tax that he has to pay on a wage income is fixed at tw_i, whereas under a consumption tax he can reduce his tax bill by consuming less and thus possibly make the investment feasible. (The lumpy investment is of course a further departure from the perfect capital market assumption.[9])

The nature of the capital market may also affect the general equilibrium equivalence result. Where the government is unable to borrow or lend freely on the same terms as individuals, the fact that the time path of tax payments differs may have real consequences. Some of the consequences are discussed in Lectures 14 and 15.

[9] Capital market constraints also qualify the conclusions drawn about horizontal equity; and, in assessing whether individuals have identical opportunity sets, the capital market imperfections must be taken into account.

Let us now turn to the income tax. From the equivalence discussed above, it follows directly that *a proportional income tax which exempts interest income is equivalent in its effect on the lifetime budget constraint to a proportional consumption and bequest tax.* (It should be noted that the base for the income tax must include inheritances received.) The effect of taxing interest income may be seen from the behaviour of wealth. Let the individual's holding of wealth at the beginning of period j be denoted by A_j (where by definition $A_1 = 0$). The development of wealth-holding is governed by

$$A_{j+1} = (1+r)[A_j + (w_j - C_j) + I_j] \quad j = 1, \ldots, T-1 \tag{3-4a}$$

$$A_{T+1} = (1+r)[A_T + (w_T - C_T) + I_T] = B \tag{3-4b}$$

where I_i denotes inheritances received in period j. From this it is clear that *a proportional tax t_i on interest income is equivalent (for the taxpayer) to a proportional wealth tax (t_W)* where the rates of tax are such that

$$1 - t_W = \frac{1 + r(1 - t_i)}{1 + r} \tag{3-4'}$$

This equivalence only holds of course in this simple one-asset world; in the next Lecture the different implications for risk-taking in a many-asset model are discussed. It should also be noted that, if interest *paid* is deductible, then the equivalence requires that there be a "negative" wealth tax for $A < 0$.

The savings that take place in a period are the increase in the wealth at the end of the period, $A_{j+1}/(1+r)$, over that at the end of the previous period. It can be shown from the instantaneous budget constraint that *a proportional income tax exempting savings is equivalent (for the taxpayer) to a proportional consumption tax.* It is in this context a matter of indifference for the taxpayer whether he is allowed to deduct savings from taxable income or to exclude the interest on that savings; e.g., if a person saves £1 one period, dissaving the next, he postpones his consumption tax and the value of the postponement is rt, the same as the value of exempting interest. Again, the timing of the tax payments may differ, and hence have implications for the government.

Taxes actually levied are typically progressive rather than proportional. This means that we need to take into account the period of assessment. The direct parallel with the proportional tax would be cumulation over the individual's lifetime, so that the tax would be progressive with respect to the square brackets in Eq. (3-3). With, for example, the tax on wage income and inheritances, this means taxing the latter at the marginal rate applicable to earned income, which would be a major departure from present practice. Where there is not lifetime cumulation, and the marginal tax rate varies, either from source to source or period to period, the equivalence results do not go through.

Determinants of Savings

The previous subsection focused on the effect of taxation on the intertemporal budget constraint. To investigate the effect on savings of taxation we have to examine the determinants of the individual's choice of consumption—bequest pattern.

There are several alternative theories, all of which probably play some part in the explanation of savings.

1. *Life-cycle motive.* Where the time profiles of income and desired consumption do not coincide, savings provide the mechanism by which purchasing power available in one period is transferred to an earlier or later date, e.g., saving for retirement, for financing of education, for home purchase.
2. *Precautionary motive.* Individuals may save in order to provide "insurance" against periods in which their incomes are low or their needs (e.g., a medical emergency) are high.
3. *Bequest motive.* Individuals may save in order to provide for their children or other heirs.

We begin with the life-cycle model, which has received a great deal of attention. For this purpose, we take the simplest possible version, where individuals live for only two periods. This is patently unrealistic but serves to isolate the key effects. Moreover, the results can be extended to the more realistic many-period case, at the expense of increased complexity (see, for example, Yaari, 1964, and Tobin, 1967). The other savings motives are taken up in Section 3-3.

Simple Life-Cycle Model

The individual lives for two periods, in the first of which he earns a wage w and in the second he is retired. He saves from his wage income to provide for second period consumption, with a constant lending rate of interest, r. The budget constraint is

$$C_1 + \frac{C_2}{1+r} = w \tag{3-5}$$

and this is illustrated in Fig. 3-1a. The individual allocates consumption to maximize lifetime utility $U(C_1, C_2)$. The indifference curves, and the point chosen, P, are illustrated in the diagram.

The behaviour of the model can be analysed in terms of wealth and substitution effects. The analogy with the treatment of labour supply may be seen most clearly if we observe that $1/(1+r)(\equiv p)$ is just the "price" of consumption in the second period. Then we can write the Slutsky equations:[10]

$$\frac{\partial C_1}{\partial p} = \frac{\partial C_1}{\partial p}\bigg|_{\bar{U}} - C_2 \frac{\partial C_1}{\partial M} \tag{3-6a}$$

$$\uparrow \qquad \uparrow$$

substitution   income
effect   effect

$$\downarrow \qquad \downarrow$$

$$\frac{\partial C_2}{\partial p} = \frac{\partial C_2}{\partial p}\bigg|_{\bar{U}} - C_2 \frac{\partial C_2}{\partial M} \tag{3-6b}$$

where M denotes lifetime wealth (here equal to w). An increase in p (decrease in the rate of interest) leads to an increase in first-period consumption through the substitution effect (in a two-good model the cross-substitution effects are positive), but a decrease through the wealth effect, since the individual is a net lender and therefore worse off (and $\partial C/\partial M > 0$ by assumption). The net effect is therefore ambiguous. On the other hand, for C_2, assuming normality, the wealth and substitution effects both work in the direction of reducing consumption.

In Figs 3-1a and b, the substitution effect of a rise in p is represented by $Q \to P'$, and it can be seen to depend on the curvature of the indifference curve. It is convenient to characterize this in terms of the elasticity of substitution:

$$\sigma \equiv \frac{d\log(C_2/C_1)}{d\log(1+r)}\bigg|_{\bar{U}} \tag{3-7}$$

This is the percentage change in the ratio C_2/C_1 as $(1+r)$, the slope of the budget constraint, changes along the indifference curve. Thus Fig. 3-1a shows a relatively low elasticity, with the ratio C_2/C_1 changing little despite a big change in the slope. The extreme in that direction is the case of zero elasticity, where the indifference curves are L-shaped. Figure 3-1b shows a relatively high elasticity, and the limit is the case where the indifference curves are straight lines.

In this model we can derive a simple expression relating the effect on first-period consumption to the wealth elasticity of consumption and the

---

[10] The derivation of the Slutsky equations is straightforward using the expenditure function—see the "Note" to Lecture 2.

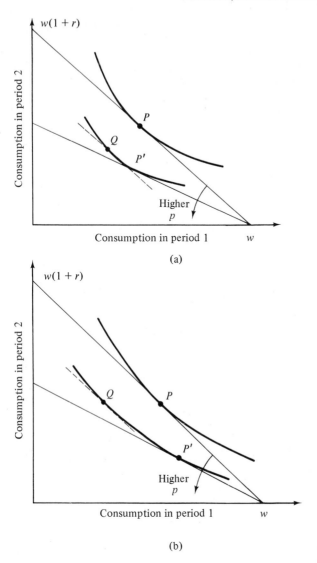

Figure 3-1 Effect of fall in the interest rate on allocation of consumption: (a) low elasticity of substitution; (b) high elasticity of substitution.

elasticity of substitution. Expanding (3-7), and using the definition of $p = 1/(1+r)$,

$$\sigma = \frac{\partial \log C_1}{\partial \log p}\bigg|_{\bar{U}} - \frac{\partial \log C_2}{\partial \log p}\bigg|_{\bar{U}} \qquad (3\text{-}7a)$$

but[11]

$$\frac{\partial C_1}{\partial \log p}\bigg|_{\bar{U}} + p\frac{\partial C_2}{\partial \log p}\bigg|_{\bar{U}} = 0 \tag{3-8}$$

Hence (substituting in 3-7a)

$$\frac{\partial \log C_1}{\partial \log p}\bigg|_{\bar{U}} = \frac{pC_2}{C_1 + pC_2}\sigma \equiv s\sigma \tag{3-9}$$

where s is the savings rate. Substituting into (3-6a)

$$\frac{\partial \log C_1}{\partial \log p} = s(\sigma - \eta) \tag{3-10}$$

where η is the wealth elasticity of first-period consumption $(M/C_1 \cdot \partial C_1/\partial M)$.

Whether savings increase or decrease with the net rate of return depends therefore on the relative magnitude of the elasticity of substitution and the wealth elasticity of consumption. Thus, if the indifference curves are homothetic, so $\eta = 1$, the effect depends simply on whether the elasticity of substitution between consumption early in life and later in life is greater or less than unity. In the Cobb–Douglas case, with $U = a\log C_1 + (1-a)\log C_2$, first-period consumption is independent of the rate of interest, since $\sigma = \eta = 1$. Note that this implies that expenditure on second-period consumption (pC_2) is constant, as we would expect for the Cobb–Douglas function.

Exercise 3-1 The individual utility function U is defined by

$$U^{1-1/\sigma} = C_1^{1-1/\sigma} + C_2^{1-1/\sigma} \tag{3-11}$$

Show that the utility-maximizing choice of consumption plan is

$$C_1 = w/[1 + (1+r)^{\sigma-1}] \tag{3-11a}$$

$$C_2 = (1+r)^{\sigma}C_1 \tag{3-11b}$$

Comment on the properties of this consumption function, and derive the interest elasticity of savings.

---

[11] This makes use of the properties of the substitution terms. Since the substitution term S_{ij} $(=\partial X_i/\partial p_{j\bar{U}})$ equals the second derivative of the expenditure function $\partial^2 e/\partial p_i\partial p_j$ (see "Note" to Lecture 2), it follows that

$$\sum_i p_i S_{ij} = \sum_i p_i \partial^2 e/\partial p_i \partial p_j = 0$$

from the fact that e is homogeneous of degree one in prices.

Exercise 3-2 The utility function U is defined by (where C_0 is a constant)

$$U = a\log(C_1 - C_0) + (1-a)\log(C_2 - C_0)$$

Derive the utility-maximizing choice of consumption plan. This is a simple version of the extended linear expenditure system (Lluch *et al.*, 1977).

We may derive the elasticity of consumption with respect to the *interest rate*

$$\varepsilon \equiv \frac{\partial \log C_1}{\partial \log r} = -\frac{rs}{(1+r)}(\sigma - \eta) \qquad (3\text{-}10a)$$

and the elasticity of *savings* with respect to the interest rate

$$\varepsilon^s \equiv \frac{r}{1+r}(1-s)(\sigma - \eta) \qquad (3\text{-}10b)$$

To illustrate the possible values, let us take $\eta = 1$, $s = \frac{1}{3}$ and $r = \frac{2}{3}$.[12] Then $\sigma = 2$ implies $\varepsilon^s = 0.27$ and $\sigma = 4$ implies $\varepsilon^s = 0.8$. It requires therefore a substantial elasticity of substitution to generate a sizeable positive interest elasticity of savings.

Effects of Taxation

A proportional tax on expenditure, or equivalently a wage tax, shifts the budget constraint inwards to a position parallel to the pre-tax constraint. The tax has a pure wealth effect.

The difference between the expenditure tax and the income tax lies in the taxation of interest income, and it is on this that we concentrate. A proportional tax, t_i, on interest income tilts the budget constraint around the point where no wealth is carried forward (Fig. 3-1), and the effect can be seen from the earlier analysis. The after-tax interest is now $r(1-t_i)$ and hence

$$p = \frac{1}{1+r(1-t_i)} \qquad (3\text{-}12)$$

The "price" of second-period consumption therefore increases with the tax rate, for fixed r.

Combining the tax on interest income with one on wage income at rate t_w, we can see that savings are given by

$$(1-t_w)w - C_1$$

---

[12] It should be noted that the time period is approximately a generation; on the other hand, real rates of return for individuals have not been particularly high over the past generation.

The change in savings in response to changes in t_i and t_w is

$$-wdt_w\left(1 - \frac{\partial C_1}{\partial M}\right) - \frac{\partial C_1}{\partial p}\frac{\partial p}{\partial t_i}dt_i \qquad (3\text{-}13)$$

Let us assume that the relative tax rates are both positive and such that $(1-t_i)/(1-t_w)$ remains unchanged as the tax rates vary. This is clearly satisfied for the income tax $(t_i = t_w)$ and for a particular form of investment income surcharge. Dividing (3-13) by $dt_i/(1-t_i)$, which equals $dt_w/(1-t_w)$, the change in savings in response to an increase in taxation is negative if (noting that $M = w(1-t_w)$)

$$(1-t_w)w\left(1 - \eta\frac{C_1}{M}\right) + s(\sigma - \eta)C_1(1-p) > 0 \qquad (3\text{-}14)$$

where we have substituted (3-10) and used the fact that $\partial p/\partial t_i = rp^2$. Dividing by $w(1-t_w)$, and rearranging

$$s\sigma(1-p) + \frac{1}{1-s} > \eta[1 + s(1-p)] \qquad (3\text{-}15)$$

This shows how the response of savings to the income tax depends on the wealth elasticity of first-period consumption (η), the elasticity of substitution (σ), the savings rate (s), and the price of second-period consumption. Where the utility function is Cobb–Douglas, $\sigma = \eta = 1$, and savings are reduced (for $s > 0$). In the extreme no-substitution case, where $\sigma = 0$, savings could rise, but only if the wealth elasticity of first-period consumption is sufficiently large (greater than the value $1/(1-s^2)$ if $p = 0$). If $\sigma > 0$, the required wealth elasticity would be correspondingly greater. For example, $\sigma = \frac{1}{2}$, $s = \frac{1}{3}$, $p = \frac{3}{5}$, means that savings are reduced unless $\eta \geqslant 1.4$.

The extension of the analysis to the case of a progressive tax is left to the reader. We should however note the implications of the fact that the income tax falls typically on the *money* and not the *real* return to savings. If r denotes the real return, and ρ the rate of inflation, then the price of second-period consumption becomes

$$p = \frac{1}{1 + r(1-t_i) - t_i\rho} \qquad (3\text{-}16)$$

The derivative is now $\partial p/\partial t_i = (r+\rho)p^2$.

For macroeconomic purposes, it is the effect not so much on individual savings as on aggregate savings that is critical. Whenever there is a significant effect on aggregate savings, the assumption of constant wage and interest rates (before tax) is obviously suspect, but the analysis may be seen as concerned with the first-round effects. The full general equilibrium picture is examined in Lecture 8. Suppose all individuals of a given age are identical. Aggregate consumption in the simple model described above is then proportional to

$$\bar{C} = C_1 + C_2/(1+n) \tag{3-17}$$

where n is the rate of growth of the population. Thus

$$d\bar{C} = dC_1 + dC_2/(1+n) \tag{3-18}$$

But we know from the individual budget constraint that

$$dC_1 + pdC_2 = -wdt_w - C_2 \frac{\partial p}{\partial t_i} dt_i \tag{3-18a}$$

Thus, using the definition of p,

$$d\bar{C} = \left[\frac{1}{1+n} - \frac{1}{1+r(1-t_i)}\right] dC_2 - wdt_w - C_2 \frac{\partial p}{\partial t_i} dt_i \tag{3-19}$$

Since $\partial p/\partial t_i > 0$, a tax increase means that the second and third terms on the right-hand side are negative. Moreover, if C_2 is a normal good, the income and substitution effects both mean that higher taxes reduce C_2. It follows that, if the square bracket term is positive, then taxation reduces aggregate consumption. The condition for the square bracket term to be positive is that the after-tax rate of return exceeds the rate of growth.

The effect on aggregate consumption may be illustrated by the constant elasticity utility function (Exercise 3-1). From (3-11a) and (3-11b), aggregate consumption is in this case (with no tax)

$$\bar{C} = w \frac{[1 + (1+r)^\sigma/(1+n)]}{[1 + (1+r)^\sigma/(1+r)]} \tag{3-20}$$

(Where individuals differ in w, but are otherwise identical, we can replace w by the mean $\bar{w}$.) The aggregate propensity to consume out of non-capital income is a function of the rate of interest (equal to unity when $r = n$). This relationship provides a link to the empirical work on aggregate consumption discussed in Section 3-4.

Effect of State Pensions

State pensions are straightforwardly introduced. A government pension g in the second period shifts the budget line up—see Fig. 3-2, where we concentrate on the benefit side, ignoring the contributions necessary to finance it (typically, a tax on wages). The present value of pension benefits enters the consumption function, and where C_1 is a normal good savings declines, as illustrated by the move from P to P'. However, as pointed out by Feldstein (1974a, 1977), there may be important interactions between the savings and retirement decisions. In particular, the existence of state pensions may cause people to retire earlier and hence to increase their savings to cover the longer period of retirement.[13] Aggregate consumption may then be a declining function of the expected pension, allowing for the induced retirement effect.[14]

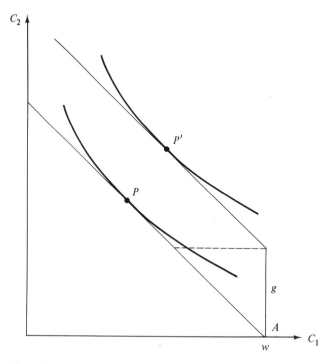

Figure 3-2 Effect of state pension scheme (case of 100 per cent implicit tax shown by dashed line).

In some cases the state pension (or old age assistance) is conditional on the level of current income. Suppose that the full pension is paid only to those with no second-period income from savings and that it is reduced by a proportion of any such income received until the pension is extinguished. The budget constraint for the case where the implicit tax rate is 100 per cent is shown in Fig. 3-2 by the dashed line. If in this 100 per cent tax rate case we consider people with different levels of wage income, otherwise identical, then at low wages there is a corner solution, with no saving and $C_2 = g$. As

---

[13] This is not a necessary consequence of state pensions. It depends on the relationship between pension rights and the age of retirement, and on the fact that the typical system is not actuarially fair (individuals who retire earlier receive a larger "gift" from the state than those who retire later). But clearly, one could design a state pension system with precisely the opposite effect.

[14] We should also consider more generally the interactions between saving and labour supply.

we move to higher wages, there may then be a discontinuity where people jump to the original budget constraint, with no pension being received.

> **Exercise 3-3** The population consists of people identical in all respects except age. In the context of the two-period model of this section, examine the effect of a scheme where a pension g is paid to the second generation financed by a wage tax on the first generation. How do the conclusions depend on whether $r \gtrless n$?

3-3 DEVELOPMENTS OF THE MODEL AND ALTERNATIVE VIEWS

The model described in the previous section brings out some of the key issues but is in need of elaboration. In this section some features of the real world are introduced, including imperfections in the capital market, and alternative motives for saving are examined.

Capital Market Imperfections

The model considered to date does not allow borrowing since the individual has no source of income (apart possibly from the state pension) in the second period. Suppose now that the individual has wage income w_i in period i. This means that the individual could set C_1 greater than w_1 by borrowing, and that a change in r causes the budget constraint to tilt about Q (see Fig. 3-3). The effect of taxation depends on whether interest *paid* can be set against tax. If there is deductibility, taxation of interest income works just like a fall in r, and for those to the right of Q there is a positive wealth effect, tending to increase C_1 (see the dashed line). The Slutsky equations become

$$\frac{\partial C_i}{\partial p} = \frac{\partial C_i}{\partial p}\bigg|_{\bar{U}} - (C_2 - w_2)\frac{\partial C_i}{\partial M} \qquad (3\text{-}21)$$

The income effect depends simply on the difference between consumption and wage income in the second period. Thus, if second-period consumption is roughly equal to w_2, then the substitution effect tends to dominate, and an interest income tax leads to an increase in first-period consumption, and a decrease in savings.

If there is no deductibility, then the budget line becomes kinked—see the heavy line in Fig. 3-3. Those choosing points to the right of Q, such as P'', are unaffected by the tax. This kinked budget constraint also illustrates one of the possible forms of capital market imperfection: where borrowing rates exceed lending rates. The effect of this is likely to be that people cluster at the kink—just as we have seen earlier with labour supply.

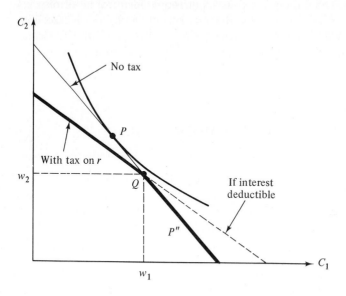

Figure 3-3 Interest income tax and the budget constraint.

Suppose, for example, that individuals differ in their rates of time preference, that the lending and borrowing rates are r_L and r_B, respectively, and that we consider the isoelastic utility function (where δ is the rate of time preference):

$$U^{1-1/\sigma} = C_1^{1-1/\sigma} + \frac{1}{1+\delta} C_2^{1-1/\sigma} \tag{3-11'}$$

so that (parallel to the earlier derivation)

$$\frac{C_2}{C_1} = \left(\frac{1+r}{1+\delta}\right)^\sigma$$

As may be seen from Fig. 3-4, as we consider larger values of δ, the chosen point moves down towards the kink, and there is a critical value, δ_1, where

$$\left(\frac{1+r_L}{1+\delta_1}\right)^\sigma = \frac{w_2}{w_1} \tag{3-22a}$$

There is a further critical value defined by the borrowing rate

$$\left(\frac{1+r_B}{1+\delta_2}\right)^\sigma = \frac{w_2}{w_1} \tag{3-22b}$$

where $\delta_2 > \delta_1$. There is then a range of $\delta_1 \leqslant \delta \leqslant \delta_2$ such that people have zero saving. The implications for taxation are that there are likely to be groups—those at the kink—who do not respond to small changes in t_i. It is of course quite possible that the borrowing rate becomes effectively infinite at some point—where there are constraints on borrowing (see, for example, Jaffee and Russell, 1976, and Stiglitz and Weiss, 1979).

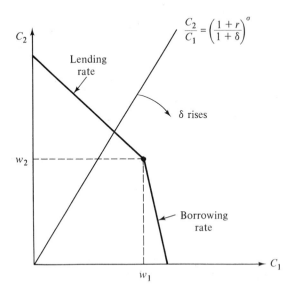

Figure 3-4 Imperfect capital market and different rates of time preference.

Although this Lecture is primarily concerned with savings and not investment, it should be borne in mind that for unincorporated businesses the two are closely linked, particularly in the presence of capital market imperfections.

Precautionary Savings

The life-cycle theory assumes a high degree of foresight and confidence about future events—over what may be a very long period. Thus, the person retiring in the 1980s may have experienced the Depression, the Second World War, the prosperity of the 1950s and 1960s, and then the oil crisis. In retrospect at least, his experience is probably dominated by a sense of uncertainty; and much of his saving may be directed towards more limited goals, e.g., "target" savings for the down payment on a house or for the provision of education for his children. (Note that certain institutional changes, like governmental support for higher education, may have significant effects on savings.)

Many of the contingencies for which individuals will need to have funds cannot be perfectly foreseen. For instance, people may wish to have cash reserves against the possibility of temporary unemployment, accidents, illness. The need for such "precautionary" savings is critically dependent on the availability of insurance; if there is complete unemployment insurance, individuals do not have to save against this contingency. Again, institutional changes may affect aggregate savings.

When part of the motive for saving arises from uncertainty associated with future income or future needs, the effect of taxation on savings may be markedly different from that in the life-cycle model. Assume that a person expects to have a fairly high income next period, so that in the absence of uncertainty he would do no saving; but there is a small chance that he will be unemployed. He therefore sets aside a small amount as "insurance" against this contingency. The interest income tax effectively increases the price of this insurance, and this may induce individuals to purchase less. On the other hand, assume that the person wishes to be sure that, after tax, he has a minimum level of consumption if he is unemployed. His precautionary saving is targeted at providing exactly that amount. Then, to maintain that minimum level of consumption, with an interest income tax, the person must actually increase his savings. Thus, once again we observe an ambiguity in the effect of taxation on savings, but now it depends on the individual's attitude towards the risks he faces.

Exercise 3-4 Assume the individual has a wage of w; but next period he faces a probability π of being unemployed. He maximizes his lifetime expected utility, where the utility function is additive: he chooses C_1 to maximize

$$u(C_1) + E[u(C_2)]$$

where $E(x)$ denotes the expectation of x, and

$$C_2 = w + [1 + r(1-t)](w - C_1) \quad \text{if the individual is employed};$$
$$= [1 + r(1-t)](w - C_1) \quad \text{if the individual is unemployed}$$

(a) Write down the first-order condition for the optimal choice of C_1.
(b) What is the effect of a change in the tax rate on savings?
(c) What is the effect on savings of an unemployment insurance programme?

A fuller analysis of the effects of uncertainty on savings must await the next Lecture, where we discuss individual behaviour under risk. Here we simply note that, not only is there uncertainty about the wages individuals face, and the needs that they may have in the future, but there is also uncertainty about the rate of return on savings. The latter implies that individuals must allocate their savings among assets with conceivably quite different risk properties; and it may not be possible, in general, to separate this portfolio decision from the savings decisions with which we are concerned here.

Bequests and Wealth Transfer Taxation

The model can readily be modified to include inheritance and a straightforward representation of the bequest motive, where the person inherits I in period 1 and leaves B as a bequest in period 2. Initially, let us suppose that the individual derives utility directly from B, so that he maximizes $U(C_1, C_2, B)$ subject to the budget constraint

$$C_1 + pC_2 + p_B B = w + I \qquad (3\text{-}23)$$

where p_B is the price of bequests including any tax on the transfer of wealth (and hence may differ from p).

The effect of wealth transfer taxation may be seen if we treat C_1 and C_2 as a composite commodity, consumption. This is permitted, where p is fixed, by the Hicks composite good theorem (see Liviatan, 1966). Denoting $C_1 + pC_2$ by C, we can draw indifference curves in the (B, C) plane. Where bequests are a normal good, both the income and substitution effects of a change in p_B work in the same direction. Thus a wealth transfer tax, raising the cost of a given net bequest, reduces the level of net bequests. On the other hand, aggregate consumption, C, may be increased or decreased, so that the effect on savings cannot be predicted. As before, if the wealth effect is dominant, then C_1 may be cut, and savings increased, in an effort to restore partially the net value of the estate passed on.

Exercise 3-5 A person has the utility function

$$U = \frac{1}{1-\varepsilon}(C_1^{1-\varepsilon} + C_2^{1-\varepsilon}) + \frac{1}{1-\beta}B^{1-\beta}$$

Examine the effect of a proportional tax on the transfer of wealth and how it depends on whether $\beta \gtrless \varepsilon$. (A continuous-time version of this model is discussed by Atkinson, 1971, and Blinder, 1975.)

The introduction of bequests means that we should consider the pattern of intergenerational transmission. Let superscripts denote generations. From the utility maximization, bequests by generation i as a function of the amount inherited (and w, p, p_B) are:

$$B^i = f(I^i) \qquad (3\text{-}24)$$

The amount received by the next generation depends on the division of estates (and on the pattern of marriage). If estates are equally divided among $(1+n)$ children, then (ignoring marriage)

$$I^{i+1} = \frac{B^i}{1+n} \tag{3-25}$$

This process is illustrated in Fig. 3-5 for two different forms of the function $f(I^i)$. In Fig. 3-5a, the proportion of lifetime wealth spent on bequests falls with the level of wealth, whereas in Fig. 3-5b the reverse is the case (bequests are a "luxury" good). (These are not the only cases which could be drawn.) In Fig. 3-5a, tracing out the dynamic process (arrowed lines) shows that wealth converges to the equilibrium at P. The effect of the wealth transfer tax, in reducing B, is to shift the equilibrium wealth to P', the initial effect (P to P'') being compounded by the reduction in I. In contrast, in Fig. 3-5b all those starting below P_2 converge to P_1; but those above P_2 "escape" to ever-increasing levels of wealth. The effect of the tax is to reduce P_1, and to widen the catchment area (P_2 is increased); there are likely therefore to be discontinuities: those with wealth slightly above P_2' are affected quite differently from those slightly below P_2'. (These conclusions clearly may need to be modified when we allow for general equilibrium effects—and this is taken up again in Lecture 9.)

The formulation of the bequest motive given above is *ad hoc*, and it can be argued that the model should be derived from more basic assumptions about preferences. Thus $U(C_1, C_2, B)$ may capture the position of a person solely concerned with the size of his estate (the prospective entry in the newspaper wills column), but may not allow for the case where bequests are merely an instrument for achieving other objectives, such as increasing the welfare of the children. Meade (1966) has modelled bequest behaviour in terms of parents being concerned that their children achieve a specified consumption level. Becker (1974) and others have suggested that the utility attainable by generation $t+1$ enters the lifetime utility function of generation t.

Such "altruistic" models of bequest behaviour mean that the utility derived from bequests depends on the expected circumstances of succeeding generations. Thus parents have to take a view as to the likely earning capacity of their children. We abstract here from such uncertainty (discussed further in Bevan, 1974, and Stiglitz, 1978b), and assume that the utility derived from the lifetime consumption of generation t may be written as $U^*(C^t)$, where C is the present value of consumption at birth. If parents take account of the welfare of future generations, applying a discount factor $(1+\delta)$, then present consumption is chosen by generation 1 to maximize

$$U^*(C^1) + \frac{1}{1+\delta} U^*(C^2) + \dots + \frac{1}{(1+\delta)^{i-1}} U^*(C^i) + \dots \tag{3-26}$$

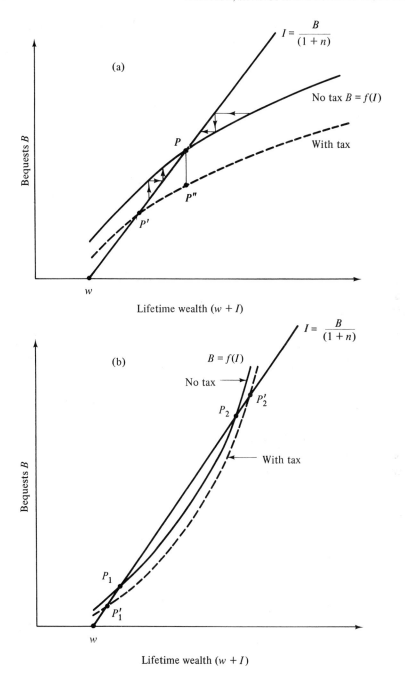

Figure 3-5 Lifetime wealth and bequests: (a) falling proportion spent on bequests; (b) rising proportion spent on bequests.

The value of this maximand, V, may be written as a function of lifetime income, $w + I^1$, of generation 1, and the exogenous income of subsequent generations. The latter is assumed to be constant and equal to w, and the rate of interest is assumed similarly constant. The value V is therefore, if we suppress the constant w, simply a function of I^1 (it is independent of time), and must satisfy the following relationship:[15]

$$V(I^1) = \max_{C^1} \left\{ U^*(C^1) + \frac{1}{1+\delta} V[(w + I^1 - C^1)(1+r)] \right\} \qquad (3\text{-}27)$$

This allows us to see the effect of wealth transfer taxation in an altruistic model of bequests. The choice of C^1 is parallel to that in the two-period model of Section 3-2, and the wealth transfer tax operates in the same way as the interest income tax. The net level of bequests is reduced, but the effect on total savings from bequests depends on the relative strengths of the wealth effect and the substitution effect. In this respect the analysis is similar to the earlier model. On the other hand, this formulation brings out that there is no apparent reason why bequests should necessarily be positive (Shorrocks, 1977),[16] and we need to allow for the fact that negative transfers (children supporting their parents) do not attract "loss offsets" under the tax. The budget constraint is therefore kinked at that point, and there is likely to be a clustering of people at zero bequests. Alternatively, we may impose the constraint $B^t \geq 0$, as in Barro (1974). Individuals for whom the constraint is strictly binding will not respond to small changes in estate taxation.

The altruistic model takes to an extreme the representation of individuals making decisions by utility-maximizing calculus, and can be criticized as making quite unwarranted assumptions about the extent of forward planning. Thus, for many people bequests may be largely the product of chance; with an imperfect annuity market, people may leave substantial estates if they die unexpectedly young. Alternatively, bequests are governed more by class expectations and attitudes, for example, heirs to large fortunes inherit also the desire to preserve — or augment — their inheritance. This brings us more generally to alternative theories of saving.

---

[15] This is the principle of optimality of dynamic programming—see, for example, Intriligator (1971, Ch. 13). In the present case it is derived by noting that the maximum value obtainable from period 2 is $1/(1+\delta)$ times that obtainable from period 1 with the same initial lifetime income. The problem is stationary.

[16] The level of bequests may also be affected by the extent of public capital transferred to future generations, as noted earlier.

Class Savings Models

The life-cycle, and related, theories have been criticized severely by radical economists; for example,

> After struggling with...the intricacies of the housewife's choice between canned peaches and canned pears, the grateful student is one day told that at last he possesses a general theory...to apply the model to intertemporal choice problems, it is merely necessary to substitute "present consumption" for "canned peaches" and "future consumption" for "canned pears".... The student's profound relief...typically prevents him from examining the substantive differences hidden by the formal similarity. [Marglin, 1975, pp. 35–36]

The most important of the substantive differences are the uncertainty referred to earlier, and the fact that choices are not made repeatedly—in contrast to pears versus peaches—so that the assumption of a well-defined, stable preference ordering may be less tenable. Despite, or perhaps because of, the passing on of wisdom from one generation to the next, people may come to regret their intertemporal allocation.

Such criticisms raise a number of issues that we cannot go into here. We need however to note some of the alternative theories that have been advanced and the predictions they yield concerning the effects of taxation. Particularly widespread is the view that—in the face of considerable uncertainty—households determine savings by simple rules of thumb. An example is the proportional savings function in the theory of economic growth. If this proportion is independent of the tax rate, then the analysis is very straightforward; and indeed many consumption functions estimated empirically assume this as part of their specification. Another example is the "class" savings model, or classical savings hypothesis, which has played an important role in the work of Cambridge (UK) growth theorists. In its extreme form, it sees all savings as generated by profit income. This provides an interesting contrast with the aggregate consumption function derived from the life-cycle model in Eq. (3-20), where all saving is out of wage income. The life-cycle and extreme classical assumptions are opposite polar cases—the former attributing capital formation to workers making provision for old age, the latter attributing it to the self-reproduction of capital.

In the more general case, the class savings model allows for a positive, but lower, propensity to save out of wages. The effect of taxation on the savings propensities depends on the underlying model of economic behaviour. As developed by Kaldor, the differential propensities arise because of the corporate sector: "the high savings propensity out of profits...attaches to the nature of business income, and not to the wealth (or other peculiarities) of the individuals who own property" (Kaldor, 1966, p. 310). This raises the issue of the relationship between personal and corporate saving.

Personal Saving and the Corporate Sector

The class savings theory just described assumes in effect that personal and corporate savings are independent. Thus, a change in tax policy that leads companies to retain more causes a rise in aggregate savings. However, it is possible that they are interlinked. Suppose that the acquisition of assets by firms made possible by corporate savings leads to a rise in share values (this need not necessarily happen). The rise in share prices may affect personal savings. In an extreme case, $1 increase in corporate savings leads to $1 increase in share values. The wealth of the shareholders having increased by $1, they reduce their own savings by that amount. Changes in personal savings offset changes in corporate savings on a dollar-for-dollar basis. The retention policies of firms have no influence on aggregate savings.

This extreme case has been referred to as one of "ultra-rationality"; individuals simply regard the corporate sector as an extension of themselves (see, for example, David and Scadding, 1974). They can see through the "corporate veil". For this to be correct requires two assumptions: first, that there are no taxes (e.g., on corporate profits) that make a dollar within the corporate sector different from a dollar in the household sector (much of Lecture 5 is devoted to exploring more precisely the wedges created by tax policy); second, that markets value the capital of the firm perfectly. In the presence of perfect information this might not be an unreasonable hypothesis, but there is a large number of instances where the value of the firm and the value of its capital are markedly different.[17] If the market value of a firm differs from the value of its assets, even temporarily, then corporate saving and household saving will not be fully equivalent.

3-4 EMPIRICAL EVIDENCE—TAXATION AND THE INTEREST ELASTICITY OF SAVINGS

The empirical evidence on savings and consumption behaviour is even more extensive than that on labour supply, not least because the consumption function is an integral part of any macroeconomic forecasting model, whereas labour supply has typically been regarded as less central. At the same time, relatively little of the literature has focused explicitly on taxation, and this alone limits the conclusions that can be drawn.

In order to assess the effect of taxation, we need ideally to be able to answer the following kinds of question: which of the theoretical models described in earlier sections are most consistent with the empirical evidence? With the preferred specification, what is the effect on savings of

---

[17] This is seen most dramatically in the case of closed end mutual funds. These are nothing but firms, the only assets of which are holdings in other, marketed, securities; yet the market value of these firms differs systematically from the market value of the securities that they hold.

taxes and other public policies? Can the impact of these policies be separated into income and substitution effects? In this section we make no attempt to answer these questions. Not only does space not permit, but also there are substantial difficulties. For example, the testing of alternative models, coupled with alternative dynamic specifications (Davidson *et al.*, 1978), involves a number of major methodological issues which would take us too far afield. Instead we try only to indicate the kind of evidence available, to describe a small number of representative studies, and to comment on their implications.

Evidence on Savings Behaviour

In the previous Lecture, we identified three main types of evidence: interview studies, observed labour market behaviour, and experimental findings. The use of experiments is clearly inherently more difficult in the case of savings, given the long-term nature of the decisions, and does not seem likely to provide any more than circumstantial evidence.[18] There have been a number of interview studies of the motives for savings. Among the affluent, the most common objectives found by Barlow, Brazer and Morgan (1966, p. 31) were to provide for retirement, against future emergencies, and for the education of children. This evidence is however difficult to apply to the effect of taxation. Not only are there the general problems with interview evidence referred to in Lecture 2, but in the case of savings it is not easy to separate the influences of different policies, and savings may be highly concentrated in a small group of the population.

The evidence on observed behaviour is that most commonly employed and it is on this that we concentrate. As with estimated labour supply functions, the inferences are typically based on the maintained hypothesis that the effect of, say, taxing interest income is the same as a reduction in the pre-tax interest rate. The response of savings to taxation is inferred—indirectly—from the interest elasticity of savings. The earlier theoretical analysis has shown that this elasticity is ambiguous in sign, and we have therefore to turn to empirical evidence to determine the direction of the effect—let alone the magnitude. This evidence is typically time series of aggregate savings or consumption.[19] Cross-section data have been employed, for example, to analyse the impact of pensions (Munnell, 1976,

---

[18] The (limited) findings of the New Jersey negative income tax experiment with regard to consumption are discussed by Rossi (1975).

[19] The time series studies described here relate to the United States, but those for other countries, like that of Stone (1964) for the United Kingdom, should also be consulted. The variable to be explained is typically either consumer *expenditure*, on a national accounts basis, or *consumption* (allowing for the services, not purchases, of durables). The disposable income data, and hence savings, typically include contributions to pension funds.

and Feldstein and Pellechio, 1977). They could also be used to investigate the interest elasticity, since net interest rates vary across the population, not least because of taxation. The accurate measurement of the net interest rate is however far from easy.

The specification of aggregate time series equations needs considerable care. Ideally, one would like to derive the equations from an explicit theoretical framework, paying particular attention to the aggregation across individuals. This in turn would need to allow for systematic differences between individuals, such as age, for imperfections in the capital market, and for changes in the distribution and composition of assets over time. The work coming closest to this ideal is perhaps that based on the life-cycle formulation, developed by Modigliani. Thus Ando and Modigliani (1963) show how, under a relatively stringent set of conditions, one can aggregate individual consumption relationships to obtain an aggregate function such as

$$C_i = \alpha_{11} + \alpha_{12}w_i + \alpha_{13}w_i^e + \alpha_{14}A_i \qquad (3\text{-}28)$$

where w_i denotes non-property income, w_i^e expected future non-property income, and A_i current assets. (This may be related to Eq. (3-20), where $w^e = w$; the difference being the introduction of A_i.)

Even after making a number of strong assumptions to derive the aggregate relationship, the implementation of such a formulation typically involves compromise. Thus a number of investigators replace w_i by a measure of (permanent) total income, since non-property income is not readily obtained, and additional variables such as unemployment have been introduced. In contrast, other authors do not attempt to relate the specification to individual behaviour. Both approaches are illustrated by the studies described below.

Magnitude of the Interest Elasticity

Relatively few studies have in fact incorporated the interest rate into the consumption relationship. The Ando–Modigliani formulation, for example, was only later extended to allow the parameters to be functions of r (as indicated by Eq. (3-20)). Those that have investigated the effect of the interest rate have produced divergent results. Thus Wright (1967, 1969) estimated an equation similar to (3-28), replacing w by disposable income, for 1929–58, and obtained estimates of the interest elasticity of consumption in the region of -0.02 to -0.03. Converting to a savings elasticity, using the average value of s (cf. Eqs (3-10a) and (3-10b)) gives a figure of around 0.2. In contrast, the later study by Blinder (1975), again based on (3-28) but with allowance for the effect of changes in the distribution of income, found an interest elasticity of consumption for 1949–72 of around -0.003, implying a very low savings elasticity. On the other hand, Boskin (1978), postulating a simple *ad hoc* consumption function, with the interest rate entering semi-logarithmically, found elasticities of saving for 1929–66 in the range 0.3 to 0.6. The "preferred" value of 0.4 was also found in Boskin and Lau (1978).

These differences in results are substantial. Suppose that the effect of interest income taxation is to reduce the net return from 10 to 5 per cent. The predicted reductions in savings with different elasticities are:

Interest elasticity of savings	Reduction in savings (%)
0.05	$3\frac{1}{2}$
0.2	13
0.4	25

There are a number of reasons why the differences in results may arise—apart from the differences in time periods covered. First, there is the definition of the interest rate variable. This should be defined as the expected real after-tax interest rate. Blinder in fact does not allow for taxation, and it may be that the interest rate coefficient is biased downward on this account.[20] There remains however the choice of the appropriate interest rate, and this is far from apparent in a world of capital market imperfections. Second, the results of Wright and Blinder are derived by single-equation methods. Although we have treated savings here in a partial equilibrium fashion, they need to be embedded in a larger model, and account taken of simultaneity. Boskin uses an instrumental variable approach for this purpose, and his comparison of the two sets of estimates indicates that this may account for part of the difference.[21] Third, there is the specification of the basic equations and the interpretation of the coefficients. Thus, Boskin calculates the elasticity with respect to r, holding disposable income constant (this being the other main explanatory variable, together with the unemployment rate), but it is not clear whether this is to be interpreted as a compensated or uncompensated elasticity. Wright (1969), for example, was careful to try to distinguish substitution and wealth effects. This raises the more general question of the correct specification and the explanatory variables that should appear in the equation. These include explicit allowance for demographic and other social changes and for other determinants of personal savings. Particular reference should be made to

[20] The bias may be analysed in the same way as that from using nominal rather than real interest rates (Feldstein, 1970a) and is likely to be downward where pre-tax interest rates and tax rates are positively correlated.

[21] A further difference is that Boskin includes in disposable income the retained earnings of corporations.

the relationship between personal and corporate saving and to the influence of state pensions.

Effects of Corporate Savings and State Pensions

The hypothesis that corporate savings affect personal savings may be tested in two ways. The first assumes that the effect works through stock prices, so that capital gains enter the consumption function. Whether or not they do so has been the subject of controversy (see, for example, Bosworth, 1975). The second method looks directly at retained earnings, to see if they affect consumption. Both approaches are combined by Feldstein (1973a), who starts with an equation for consumer expenditure based on (3-28), again replacing w by disposable income, and adds as explanatory variables the level of retained earnings and accrued capital gains. In the main results for the period 1929–66, the coefficient of capital gains is insignificant, but that of retained earnings is significant and around three-quarters of that on disposable income. This suggests that households see through the corporate veil but not completely—an increase in corporate saving is partly but not fully offset. On the other hand, other writers (e.g. Bhatia, 1979) have found no significant effect.

The effect of state pensions is potentially important, given the size and rapid growth of the value of contingent rights. Feldstein (1974a) has incorporated a variable for state pension wealth into the equations just discussed. Where employment is excluded, and the period of estimation is 1929–71, then the pension wealth variable has a significant and sizeable coefficient. Feldstein calculates that in 1971 the social security wealth (over $2000 billion) reduced saving by about 40 per cent (1974a, p. 920). On the other hand, if the equations are restricted to the postwar period, the coefficient is insignificantly different from zero. This makes it difficult to draw firm conclusions.

The empirical results described are therefore less clear-cut than those on labour supply. There is a wide range of estimates of the interest elasticity of saving; the extent to which corporate savings influence personal savings is open to debate; the findings on pensions are suggestive but not conclusive. A great deal remains to be done on these issues, and on others not discussed, such as the impact of inheritance taxation on savings, and the effects of taxation on different *types* of saving.

3-5 CONCLUDING COMMENTS

As in the previous lecture, the theoretical models do not yield simple predictions. They indicate some of the forces at work, but do not give an unambiguous answer to how taxation affects savings. Thus it is true that a tax on interest income raises the price of future consumption and that this, assuming normality, reduces future consumption. However, savings represent the *expenditure* on such consumption, and here—as in the standard demand model—the effect depends on the relative strength of the substitution and wealth elasticities. This applies both to the simple life-cycle model of Section 3-2 and to the discussions of precautionary and bequest motives in Section 3-3. We have also noted that there may be situations where individuals are unresponsive to taxation (as with capital market constraints) or where planned bequests are zero, or where there is purely an income effect, as with the class savings theories.

In this Lecture we have not attempted to make explicit comparisons between taxes, but the analysis has provided building blocks that can be used for this purpose. Thus the replacement of the (pure) income tax by the (pure) expenditure tax involves in effect a reduction in the tax rate on interest income and a compensating adjustment in the tax on wage income. The consequences may be examined using the models of Section 3-2, modified by the considerations introduced in Section 3-3. The outcome, as far as savings are concerned, depends on the wealth and substitution elasticities. As we have seen from the brief review of the empirical evidence, there is little agreement on the size of the overall elasticity, let alone its decomposition into separate effects.

One of the main motivations for interest in the effect of taxation, and of other public programmes like social security, on aggregate personal savings is a concern with the level of capital accumulation and its contribution to the growth of the economy. These are questions that are dealt with in subsequent Lectures. We should note, however, that there may be other instruments, such as monetary policy, which could be used to offset the deleterious effects (if any) of tax policy on savings. In the long run, the effects of the tax system on the form in which savings occurs may be more important than the effects on the aggregate level of savings. Thus, in the presence of capital market imperfections, with limitations on borrowing, taxes that reduce the after-tax flow of funds to enterprises may restrict their investment. The tax system through its treatment of deferred compensation encourages saving via pension funds. To the extent that these institutions allocate funds differently from the way that individuals would have allocated them themselves, there may be significant effects on the patterns of investment in the economy. The more general question of the effect of taxation on risk-taking is the subject of the next Lecture.

READING

The two-period intertemporal model used in much of the Lecture (the Fisherian model) is treated in microeconomics texts, e.g., Green (1976,

Chs 11 and 12) and Malinvaud (1972, Ch. 10). The continuous time life-cycle model is treated in more depth in Yaari (1964); the incorporation of bequests is discussed there and in Atkinson (1971). An extensive discussion of the effects of taxation on consumption was provided by Hansen (1958). Reviews of empirical work on the effects of taxation on savings are given in Break (1974) and Feldstein (1976a), the latter dealing particularly with the influence of pensions.

FOUR

TAXATION AND RISK-TAKING

4-1 RISK-TAKING AND PORTFOLIO ALLOCATION

Uncertainty is a feature of any economy, and attitudes towards risk-taking are likely to play an important role in determining economic performance. Even in advanced economies, where large corporations seek to reduce uncertainty, the rate at which new products and new techniques are developed still depends crucially on the taking of risks and the availability of finance for risky ventures. This has led in turn to concern that the tax system may discourage risk-taking and the supply of funds to finance it.

Taxation may influence risk-taking at two levels. It may affect portfolio decisions by households (or institutions) and hence the availability of funds; or it may affect the real investment decisions made by businesses and individuals. From the standpoint of the growth of the economy, it is the latter that are directly relevant; however, the influence on financial markets is an important intermediate stage in the process. Most of the (substantial) literature on this subject deals with financial or portfolio decisions, and the analysis here is (with one exception) couched in these terms. At the same time, the real investment side is clearly important. In some cases the results for household portfolio behaviour can readily be translated to the investment policy of firms, and we return to this subject at the end of the lecture.

The principal issue is the effect of taxation on "risk-taking". The interpretation of this concept is not entirely straightforward,[1] and we base much of the analysis on a case where it is clear-cut—where there are only two assets, a safe asset (with a fixed return) and a risky asset. We also make a simple assumption about the individual's objective function, which is taken to be the maximization of the expected utility from terminal wealth. In Section 4-4 we discuss the relationship between this and the savings decisions examined in the previous lecture.

The basic portfolio model is described below. Section 4-2 then presents an analysis of the impact of income and wealth taxation in the two-asset model. Section 4-3 considers the effect of a number of special provisions of the tax code and their economic rationale. Section 4-4 extends the treatment in several directions, including the interaction with savings decisions, and a simple general equilibrium version of the model. The relationship between the theoretical results and observed behaviour is discussed briefly in the concluding section, 4-5.

The taxes considered in this Lecture are principally those on income and wealth, with some references to capital gains taxation. It is these that have attracted most attention in discussions of risk-taking, and there is a widespread popular feeling—not shared by many economists—that the substitution of a wealth tax for income taxation would encourage risk-taking.

Our concern in this Lecture is with the positive question as to whether or not taxes discourage risk-taking; we do not examine the presumption, implicit in much public discussion, that a discouragement would be socially undesirable. The welfare economics of a change in risk-taking raises a number of difficult issues, including the criteria for optimality under uncertainty (e.g., *ex ante* versus *ex post* welfare). At the same time, we need to make the distinction between risk-taking by individuals and firms, or *private* risk-taking, and the total risk-taking in the economy, which we refer to as *social* risk-taking. It is quite possible that a tax may lead to individuals' reducing their risk-taking but to the government's assuming a greater degree of risk, via uncertain tax receipts. Private and social risk-taking may move in opposite directions.

This may be illustrated by a simple case, which also serves as an introduction to the portfolio model with two assets. Suppose that the safe asset yields zero return and that a fraction a of the person's initial wealth A_0 is invested in the risky asset. The individual maximizes the expected utility of terminal wealth, A, which depends on the uncertain return, x, per dollar of the risky asset invested. A is in fact equal to $A_0(1 + ax)$. Denote the value

---

[1] Suppose, for example, there are two risky assets, one of which is riskier in the sense of having a larger variance per dollar invested. Portfolio variance, however, depends on the covariance, and if the returns are negatively correlated a rise in the proportion invested in the riskier asset may *reduce* portfolio variance.

chosen by a^*. Suppose now that the government introduces a proportional income tax, at rate t_i, so that x becomes $x(1-t_i)$, and that this applies for all values, including those where he makes a loss $(x < 0)$. If the individual can increase a to $a^*/(1-t_i)$, then he can secure for himself just the same level of terminal wealth, with each different possible outcome (for x), as he had before.[2] In such a situation, private risk-taking, as measured by the net of tax "risk" $a(1-t_i)$, is unchanged, but social risk-taking is increased—a larger fraction of the portfolio is invested in risky assets.

This example brings out one further factor—that government revenue is uncertain. This introduces the question of the basis for comparison of taxes. It may not be feasible, for example, to secure equal revenue with all possible outcomes. One obvious possibility is to compare taxes with the same expected revenue, and this is particularly appealing where the individual risks are independently distributed. On the other hand, where individual risks are not independent, the government may have preferences concerning the distribution of revenue over different outcomes. Among other things, this draws attention to the need to consider the kind of risky event that we have in mind—whether it is competitive risk, uncertainty surrounding technology, due to cyclical variations, etc., or whether indeed it is "political" risk concerning future changes in tax rates (Ekern, 1971).

Portfolio Model

The basic portfolio model is that sketched above, except that we allow more generally for a non-negative rate of return, r, per dollar of safe asset invested, and that we explore more fully the way in which portfolio decisions depend on the utility function. It is assumed that neither x nor r depends on the amount invested. As described, the individual maximizes expected utility from wealth at the end of the period, where this depends solely on the initial purchase of assets. It is assumed that the utility function is strictly concave, which implies that he is risk-averse, i.e., he prefers a safe wealth of A to a random distribution with mean equal to A (see the note at the end of the Lecture). If we denote by E the expectations operator, then he chooses the proportion a invested in the risky asset to maximize

$$E[U(A)] \equiv \int U\{A_0[1+ax+(1-a)r]\}dF \qquad (4\text{-}1)$$

where $U' > 0$, $U'' < 0$ and $F(x)$ denotes the cumulative probability distribution of x with $x > -1$.

The first-order conditions depend on the constraints on a. Here we assume that he can borrow as well as lend at the sure rate of return but that a is constrained to be non-negative. In other words, he cannot issue risky securities (the extension can readily be made). The first-order conditions for

---

[2] This requires of course that there is no restriction on borrowing.

expected utility maximization are then

$$\frac{\partial}{\partial a} E(U) = E[U' \cdot (x-r)] = 0 \tag{4-2a}$$

or

$$E[U' \cdot (x-r)] < 0 \quad \text{and} \quad a = 0 \tag{4-2b}$$

The assumption that the individual is risk-averse ($U'' < 0$) is sufficient to ensure that the second-order conditions are satisfied. Since U' is independent of x for $a = 0$, we can see from (4-2b) that a corner condition ($a = 0$) occurs if the expected return from the risky asset ($E(x) \equiv \bar{x}$) is less than that from the safe. In what follows we concentrate on the interior solution, assuming $\bar{x} > r$, and a finite degree of risk aversion.

In order to illustrate the working of the model, let us take the quadratic utility function

$$U(A) = bA - A^2/2 \tag{4-3a}$$

where $b > 0$ and $A < b$. This function received considerable attention in the early literature (Tobin, 1958; Markowitz, 1959; and Hicks, 1962). The first-order condition for an interior solution is (from (4-2a))

$$E[(b-A)(x-r)] = 0$$

or

$$E\{[b-A_0(1+r)-aA_0(x-r)](x-r)\} = 0$$

or

$$aA_0 E[(x-r)^2] = [b-A_0(1+r)](\bar{x}-r) \tag{4-4}$$

We can deduce that the demand for risky assets (aA_0) is a linear function of wealth (A_0) and that it is decreasing, since $\bar{x} > r$. The fact that the risky asset is an inferior good is an unattractive and implausible feature of the quadratic utility function (Arrow, 1965).

Utility functions that may be more plausible, but that also yield linear demand functions for assets, are as follows.

Exercise 4-1 Show that for the utility function

$$U = -e^{-bA} \quad \text{where} \quad b > 0$$

the amount invested in the risky asset depends only on the returns and not on the initial level of wealth (A_0).

Exercise 4-2 Show that for the utility function

$$U = A^{1-\varepsilon}/(1-\varepsilon) \quad \text{where} \quad \varepsilon > 0 \quad \text{and} \quad \varepsilon \neq 1$$

the choice of a is independent of A_0, so that the risky asset makes up the same proportion of assets at all wealth levels.

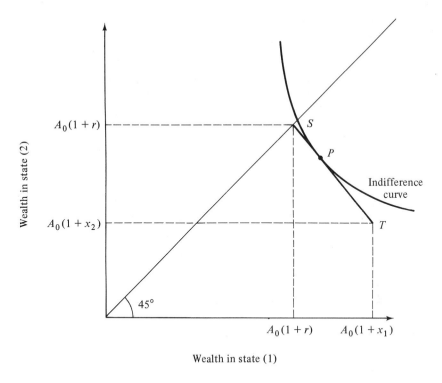

Figure 4-1 Portfolio possibilities where two outcomes to investment (two states of nature).

For much of the analysis we focus on a special case of the model which allows a convenient graphical representation.[3] There are two "states of the world" (outcomes of the investment decision):

State (1). Risky asset yields more than the safe asset: $(x_1 > r)$.
State (2). Risky asset yields less than the safe asset: $(x_2 < r)$.

The individual's opportunity locus is depicted in Fig. 4-1, where his wealth in state (1) is measured along the horizontal axis and his wealth in state (2) on the vertical axis. If all wealth is used to buy the safe asset, he is at the point S on the 45° line, i.e., he obtains the same income in both states of the world. If all wealth is invested in the risky asset, he is at the point T, representing a wealth of $A_0(1+x_1)$ in state (1) and $A_0(1+x_2)$ in state (2). By mixing his portfolio, he can attain any point on the line ST (i.e. $0 \leqslant a \leqslant 1$) or its extension beyond $T(a > 1)$ where he is borrowing. His

---

[3] Another special case which can easily be represented diagrammatically is the mean–variance model. See, for example, Tobin (1958), Richter (1960) and Bierwag and Grove (1967).

expected utility is

$$E(U) = p_1 U\{[(1+r)+a(x_1-r)]A_0\} + p_2 U\{[(1+r)+a(x_2-r)]A_0\} \quad (4\text{-}5)$$

where p_i is the probability of state (i) $(p_1+p_2 = 1)$. The resulting indifference curves (i.e., giving constant expected utility, $E(U) = $ constant) are illustrated in Fig. 4-1. In the case shown, the portfolio choice is P, and a is equal to the ratio of the distance SP to ST.

Wealth and Portfolio Allocation

In the subsequent discussion, certain properties of the portfolio allocation are crucial, particularly the response to an increase in the level of wealth. This moves the budget constraint in a parallel manner—see Fig. 4-2a—and the new point corresponding to a given value of a is found by moving along a ray through the origin. Thus, the new point T', where $a = 1$, lies on the ray through T. The locus of points chosen as wealth changes is called here the wealth–portfolio locus, analogous to the income–consumption curve. If it is a ray through the origin as in Fig. 4-2a, this means that as wealth increases the proportion of total assets allocated to the risky asset remains unchanged. This is the case corresponding to Exercise 4-2. If, on the other hand, the wealth–portfolio locus bends down, the proportion allocated to the risky asset increases with wealth (as in Fig. 4-2b). If all of an increase in wealth goes into the safe asset, there is an equal increment in terminal wealth in the two states of the world. Diagrammatically, this case, which corresponds to Exercise 4-1, gives a wealth–portfolio locus with a slope of $45°$ (Fig. 4-2d). Thus, the wealth–portfolio locus has a slope less than $45°$ if the wealth elasticity of demand for the risky asset is greater than zero.

The wealth–portfolio locus is empirically observable (for example, from cross-section data), and this raises the question of the precise identification of the safe and risky assets. In much of the literature (e.g., Tobin, 1958) they are identified as money and bonds, respectively, in which case the return to the safe asset is zero in cash terms. On the other hand, this does not allow for uncertainty concerning the price level. As long as goods prices are uncertain, all financial assets have some risk, in terms of the consumption which they can generate. Financial assets have in certain periods appeared to be more risky than equities that were thought to provide better "hedges" against inflation.

Even in the absence of inflation, it is not always obvious what is to be treated as the safe asset. For an individual who consumes no housing, the purchase of a house is risky, if the price of houses varies relative to the prices of the commodities he does purchase. For an individual who is planning to consume his wealth one period from now, a one-period bond is safe and a two-period bond (with variability in its capital value) is risky. For an individual planning to consume his wealth two periods from now,

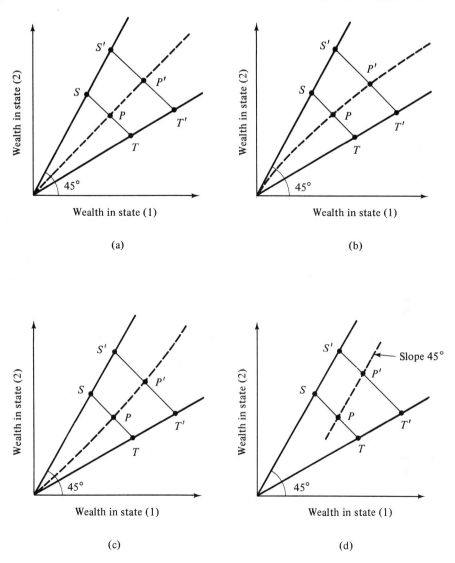

Figure 4-2 Wealth portfolio loci—different cases: (a) wealth elasticity of demand for risky asset = 1 (same portfolio composition at all wealth levels); (b) wealth elasticity of demand for risky asset greater than unity (increasing proportion of wealth allocated to risky asset as wealth rises); (c) wealth elasticity of demand for risky asset greater than zero but less than unity; (d) wealth elasticity of demand for risky asset equals zero.

investing in a one-period bond and then reinvesting is a risky investment strategy; purchasing a two-period bond is safe (Stiglitz, 1970b). Whether a particular asset is risky or not depends not only on the individual's consumption plan, but also on what other assets are available to him. For instance, if the individual holds a large portfolio of equities, and if long-term bonds are negatively correlated with equities, then the bonds provide a kind of insurance; he may be willing to hold long-term bonds even if the expected return were lower than the safe rate of interest. Thus, the application of the model requires a good deal of caution.

4-2 EFFECTS OF TAXATION

Taxation affects both the returns to different assets and the degree of risk. The latter is clearly very important. When losses can be fully offset and taxes are proportional, the government becomes in effect a non-voting partner in the enterprise.[4]

We consider here proportional taxes on wealth (at rate t_w) and income (at rate t_i) with the revenue used to finance government spending, which enters U in an additively separable fashion.[5] The terminal wealth depends on the assumptions made about (1) the extent to which losses may be set against taxation and (2) the tax deductibility of interest paid on borrowing (where $a > 1$). It is assumed initially that there are full loss offsets and full deductibility. The equation for terminal wealth becomes therefore

$$A = (1-t_w)\{1+[r+a(x-r)](1-t_i)\}A_0 \qquad (4\text{-}6)$$

and the first-order condition for an interior solution for expected utility maximization:

$$(1-t_w)(1-t_i)E[U' \cdot (x-r)] = 0 \qquad (4\text{-}7)$$

Since the term $(1-t_w)(1-t_i)$ may be cancelled, this has the same form as (4-2a), and this applies also to (4-2b). On the other hand, this does not imply that a is unaffected by taxation, since the argument of U' is terminal wealth, which depends on t_i and t_w.

In particular we can see at once that $(1-t_w)$ operates just like a reduction in initial wealth. It is equivalent to shifting the budget constraint inwards. Thus, *a proportional wealth tax increases, leaves unchanged, or decreases the proportion of the portfolio allocated to the risky asset as the wealth elasticity of the demand for the risky asset is less than, equal to, or greater than unity.*

---

[4] This aspect was first treated rigorously by Domar and Musgrave (1944), who developed a model of portfolio choice where risk was measured by $\int_{-\infty}^{0} x\,dF$ (the expected value of negative returns) and showed that a proportional tax with full loss offset provisions would *increase* risk-taking. Later, Tobin (1958) reached the same conclusion on the basis of a mean–variance approach to portfolio choice.

[5] i.e., utility is given by $E(U)+\psi(G)$. This is a critical assumption because it means that the choice of a is independent of G—see Section 4-4.

Effect of Income Taxation

The income tax is less straightforward, so that we begin with the special case where the return on the safe asset is zero ($r = 0$). It is then immediate that, if a^* is the solution with $t_i = 0$, then $a = a^*/(1-t_i)$ satisfies the first-order condition. The investment possibilities open to the individual, and expected utility, are unchanged by the tax (moreover, this applies where there are more than two assets). This case is illustrated in Fig. 4-3. If the person holds only the safe asset ($a = 0$), then he is at the same point (S) as before the tax was introduced. The opportunity locus starts therefore from S. A dollar invested in the risky asset rather than the safe asset yields an extra $(x_1)(1-t_i)$ in the good state and an extra $(x_2)(1-t_i)$ in the bad, so that the slope of the locus (ratio of the returns) is unchanged, but the point corresponding to a given value of a is nearer S. Thus the point $a = 1$ moves from T to T'. Since the choice remains, P, the proportion invested in the risky asset must rise to $1/(1-t_i)$ times its previous value (ST' is $(1-t_i)$, the length of ST). Social risk-taking is therefore increased by the tax; on the other hand, if we take $a(1-t_i)$ as a measure of private risk-taking,[6] this is unaltered.

Where the return to the safe asset is strictly positive, the analysis is

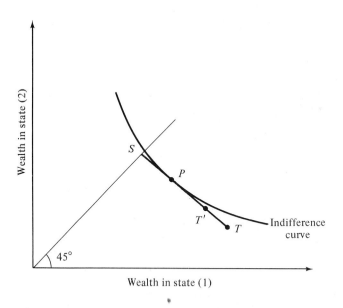

Figure 4-3 Income tax: zero return on safe asset.

[6] The distinction between social and private was introduced by Domar and Musgrave (1944, Section IV). The rationale for the latter may be seen by noting that, for example, the standard deviation of terminal wealth is proportional to $a(1-t_i)$.

more complicated. Differentiating (4-7) with respect to t_i (having set $t_w = 0$ and cancelled the term $(1-t_i)$),

$$E\left(U''(x-r)\left\{(x-r)(1-t_i)\frac{\partial a}{\partial t_i} - [a(x-r)+r]\right\}\right) = 0$$

or

$$\left[(1-t_i)\frac{\partial a}{\partial t_i}\right]E[-U''(x-r)^2] = aE[-U''(x-r)^2] - rE[U''(x-r)] \quad (4\text{-}8)$$

From this we can see at once how the assumption $r = 0$ simplifies the analysis, yielding $(1-t_i)\partial a/\partial t_i = a$, which integrates to give $a(1-t_i) = \text{constant}$. To interpret Eq. (4-8) where $r > 0$, we need two results. The first is that $E[-U''(x-r)^2]$ is strictly positive, which follows from $U'' < 0$ and $x \neq r$ for some x. The second is that the wealth elasticity of the risky asset is positive or negative as $E[U''(x-r)]$ is positive or negative. To see this, let $Z = aA_0$, the demand for the risky asset. Differentiating (4-7) with respect to A_0, again cancelling the term $(1-t_i)$ and setting $t_w = 0$,

$$E(U''(x-r)\{[1+r(1-t_i)] + (1-t_i)(x-r)\partial Z/\partial A_0\}) = 0$$

Rearranging

$$\frac{A_0}{Z}\frac{\partial Z}{\partial A_0} = \frac{E[U''(x-r)]}{E[-U''(x-r)^2]}\frac{[1+r(1-t_i)]}{a(1-t_i)} \quad (4\text{-}9)$$

From the fact that the denominator is strictly positive, it follows that the elasticity has the sign of $E[U''(x-r)]$.

If we apply these results first to the level of private risk-taking, measured by $a(1-t_i)$, then

$$\left[(1-t_i)\frac{\partial a}{\partial t_i} - a\right] = \frac{-rE[U''(x-r)]}{E[-U''(x-r)^2]} \quad (4\text{-}10)$$

It follows that *an income tax decreases (increases) private risk-taking if the wealth elasticity of demand for the risky asset is positive (negative)*. In other words, in the "normal" case, private risk-taking is reduced where $r > 0$. On the other hand, the effect on social risk-taking depends on

$$\frac{(1-t_i)}{a}\frac{\partial a}{\partial t_i} = 1 - \frac{rE[U''(x-r)]}{aE[-U''(x-r)^2]}$$

$$= 1 - \left(\frac{A_0}{Z}\frac{\partial Z}{\partial A_0}\right)\frac{r(1-t_i)}{1+r(1-t_i)} \quad (4\text{-}11)$$

It follows that there exists a critical value of the wealth elasticity of demand for the risky asset (the term in large parentheses on the right-hand side) such that social risk-taking is increased for lower values but decreased for higher values. Suppose, for example, that the tax rate is 50 per cent, and

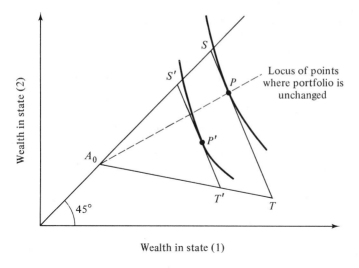

Figure 4-4 Income tax: strictly positive return on safe asset.

that the annual return (r) is 3 per cent; then the critical value of the elasticity is 68. Where the relevant holding period is longer than a year, the critical elasticity may be lower:[7] for example, with $r = 20$ and 100 per cent, it is 11 and 3, respectively. Thus, *unless the wealth elasticity is quite large and/or holding periods quite long, social risk-taking is increased as a result of an income tax.* More generally, *if the wealth elasticity of the demand for the risky asset is less than or equal to unity, then the income tax increases social risk-taking (proportion invested in the risky asset).*

These results can be seen diagrammatically in Fig. 4-4. The terminal wealth of a person investing only in the safe asset is now $A_0[1 + r(1 - t_i)]$, so S moves down the 45° line to S'. On the other hand, the slope of the budget constraint is unchanged, and the new point T' corresponding to $a = 1$ lies on the line joining A_0 to T.[8] The new portfolio choice is P', and the proportion invested in the risky asset is $S'P'/S'T'$. It can be seen from the diagram that this is higher than before the tax was introduced if the wealth–portfolio locus has a slope steeper than that of the line A_0P. A sufficient (but not necessary) condition for a to rise is that the portfolio be a ray through the origin or everywhere be bending up away from this ray, as

[7] This is overlooked, for example, by Mossin when he argues that with "reasonable values of t and r" the value of $\partial a/\partial t_i$ remains positive even with substantial wealth elasticities (1968, p. 78). What values of r are "reasonable" depends on the length of the holding period.

[8] The coordinates of the new point T' are $X = A_0[1 + x_1(1 - t_i)]$ and $Y = A_0[1 + x_2(1 - t_i)]$ respectively. The locus of points with different t_i is given by

$$x_2(X - A_0) = x_1(Y - A_0)$$

Thus it passes through A_0 and has slope (x_2/x_1), which is negative if $x_2 < 0$.

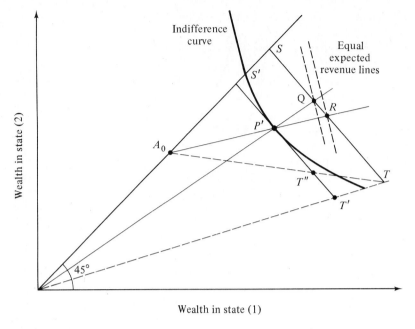

Figure 4-5 Income and wealth taxes leading to equal reduction in expected utility.

in Fig. 4-2c. This is the condition that the wealth elasticity be less than or equal to unity.[9]

Comparison of Wealth and Income Taxation

From the results obtained so far, we can examine the conclusions that can be drawn about the *relative* effects of the two taxes. As already noted, there is the difficulty of choosing the basis for comparison. One comparison of interest is that of taxes that lead to an equal reduction in expected utility (i.e. to the person being on the same indifference curve), and this is shown in Fig. 4-5. Since both income and wealth taxes shift the budget constraint parallel to the no-tax constraint, the person chooses P' in both cases. However, the portfolio allocation is different. The point on the no-tax budget line ST with the same value of a as at P' in the wealth tax case is given by Q (the ray through P'), whereas the point on ST corresponding to the income tax case is R (extension of the line joining A_0 to P'). Since Q is clearly above R, the income tax leads to more (social) risk-taking for a given reduction in utility. What in effect happens is that private risk-taking

---

[9] The effect of anticipated inflation can readily be introduced into this analysis. If the money return becomes $r+\rho$ and $x+\rho$ respectively, the fact that the tax is levied on money income reduces the real return, but the effect is independent of the portfolio choice.

is the same in both situations, but the government is taking more risk in the income tax case so that social risk-taking is higher.

If the government is concerned with the expected revenue, then this may be compared by drawing lines with the slope of the relative probabilities. From the earlier analysis, it may be seen that this equals the downward slope of the indifference curve where wealth in the two states is equal (the 45° line), so that it is greater than that of the budget line where there is an interior solution. Let us assume that the wealth tax is paid on terminal wealth, so that the revenue in the equal expected utility case is represented[10] by the vector $P'Q$. The revenue from the income tax is given by the vector $P'R$. The expected revenue would therefore be equal if the relative probabilities were equal to the slope of the budget line. We have seen however that the relative probabilities are greater, the slope of the equal expected revenue lines being steeper than the budget constraint, so it follows (see dashed lines in Fig. 4-5) that an income tax yields a higher expected revenue than an equal utility wealth tax. The case $r = 0$ is especially straightforward, since the income tax leads to no reduction in expected utility. The expected revenue, however, is positive. For a wealth tax to raise the same expected revenue, the tax rate must be strictly positive, and a necessary and sufficient condition for social risk-taking to be lower (at equal expected revenue) is that the wealth elasticity of demand for the risky asset be greater than unity. (From our earlier analyses, it should be clear that this result is general for the case $r = 0$.) The case where $r > 0$ is left as an exercise to the reader.

Compensated Variations

Readers may have noted a difference in our treatment of risk-taking in this Lecture, and that of labour supply and savings decisions in the preceding Lectures. There, we decomposed the effect of taxation into a substitution and an income effect. The ambiguity in the effect of taxation was due to the fact that the two effects worked in the opposite direction.

The same principle applies in the case of risk-taking. The analysis of the compensated changes is, however, almost trivial in this case. We can show that, if t_i is the tax rate on income and Z $(=aA_0)$ is the demand for the risky asset, then

$$\left.\frac{\partial(1-t_i)Z}{\partial t_i}\right|_{\bar{U}} = -Z + (1-t_i)\left.\frac{\partial Z}{\partial t_i}\right|_{\bar{U}} = 0 \qquad (4\text{-}12)$$

i.e., the compensated effect on private risk-taking is zero. Or more generally, in the case of many assets, *a uniform income tax on all assets, equivalent to a*

---

[10] The vector has two dimensions, representing horizontally the revenue in state (1) and vertically the revenue in state (2).

rise in the price of all assets, compensated for by an increase in wealth which leaves all individuals indifferent, leads all individuals to change their portfolio in such a way as to leave private risk-taking unchanged. To see this, let $A_{00}(t_i)$ be the wealth required to generate the same utility after the tax, and Z^* be the demand in the absence of taxation. Then, if we try

$$A_{00} = A_0 \frac{1+r}{1+r(1-t_i)} \quad \text{and} \quad Z = Z^*/(1-t_i) \quad \text{(4-13)}$$

the terminal wealth in state j after the tax and compensating wealth adjustment is

$$A_{00}[1+r(1-t_i)] + (1-t_i)Z(x_j-r) = A_0(1+r) + Z^*(x_j-r) \quad \text{(4-14)}$$

So that the after-tax wealth in every state of nature is identical to that before the introduction of the tax, with the asset choice Z^*. Using this result, it is easy to show that the portfolio allocation Z is optimal given wealth A_{00}. The effect of the tax with this compensated adjustment in wealth is therefore to keep $Z(1-t_i)$ constant. The same argument applies in the many asset case.

Interpretation of Demand Elasticities

In the preceding chapters we related properties of the utility functions to those of the demand functions. This can be done in the case of risk-taking as well. Two properties of the utility function turn out to be critical:

1. the logarithmic derivative of marginal utility

$$R_A \equiv -U''/U' \quad \text{(4-15a)}$$

often referred to as the measure of *absolute risk aversion*,[11]
2. the elasticity of marginal utility

$$R_R \equiv -U''A/U' \quad \text{(4-15b)}$$

referred to as the measure of *relative risk aversion*.

These are local properties of the utility function, being functions of terminal wealth A. The reader may like to check that the utility function in Exercise 4-1 implies R_A everywhere constant and that in Exercise 4-2 implies R_R everywhere constant. These properties are discussed further in the note at the end of the Lecture.

---

[11] The reason for this terminology is that, for small risks, we can show that the *absolute* amount that the individual would be willing to give up to avoid the risk is proportional to the measure of *absolute* risk aversion. The same applies to the *proportionate* amount and the measure of *relative* risk aversion. (See the note at the end of the Lecture.)

To see the relationship with the demand functions, we may recall from Eq. (4-9) that

$$\frac{\partial Z}{\partial A_0} \gtreqless 0 \quad \text{as} \quad -E[U''(x-r)] \lesseqgtr 0$$

where the latter may be written as

$$E[R_A U'(x-r)] = E[(R_A - R_A^*)U'(x-r)] \lesseqgtr 0 \tag{4-16}$$

where the second step makes use of the first-order condition (we are assuming an interior solution), and we define

$$R_A^* \equiv R_A[A_0(1+r)]$$

(i.e. risk aversion evaluated where $x = r$). Suppose now that the utility function exhibits everywhere strictly decreasing absolute risk aversion, i.e., $\partial R_A/\partial A < 0$. It then follows that if $x > r$, $R_A < R_A^*$ and the expression on the left-hand side of (4-16) is negative. The wealth elasticity of demand is therefore positive. Conversely, if absolute risk aversion is everywhere increasing, the wealth elasticity is negative. (These do not of course exhaust all possible cases, since $\partial R_A/\partial A$ may change sign.)

The relationship with relative risk aversion may be seen from a similar argument. In particular, if relative risk aversion is everywhere decreasing, the wealth elasticity of demand for the risky asset is greater than unity. If relative risk aversion is everywhere increasing, the wealth elasticity is less than unity.

Exercise 4-3 What can be said about R_A and R_R in the four cases of wealth portfolio loci shown in Fig. 4-2?

Finally, we should note that this simple correspondence between the properties of the utility function and those of the demand functions for risky assets is critically dependent on there being only one risky asset (Cass and Stiglitz, 1972, and Hart, 1975). In Section 4-4 we return to the question of generalizing the portfolio model.

Summary

In this section we have examined the effects of wealth and income taxation. The former has a pure wealth effect, reducing the investment in the risky asset in the "normal" case where the wealth elasticity is greater than zero. The income tax has a substitution effect such that the holding of the risky asset is increased so as to keep constant the "private risk" $(Z(1-t_i))$. On the other hand, social risk-taking, measured by the amount invested in the risky asset, is increased. It is therefore quite possible that an income tax may increase the overall level of risk-taking, and in this respect the analysis of this section may be seen as generating counter-examples to the popularly held opinion on this subject. It may however be objected that such counter-examples depend critically on the assumption of full loss offsets and other provisions of the tax system, to which we now turn.

4-3 SPECIAL PROVISIONS OF THE TAX SYSTEM

No Loss Offsets

So far it has been assumed that losses may be set fully against tax; this may not however be the case. To see whether the results depend crucially on the assumption, we now consider the extreme case of no loss offsets: where the return to the risky asset equals $x(1 - t_i)$ if $x \geqslant 0$ and x otherwise. Initially, we contrast the tax and no-tax situations. Later we compare taxes with different degrees of loss offset.

To see the effect of the tax (without loss offset), let us take the special two-state case with the return in the second state negative. A dollar invested in the risky asset now yields an extra $(x_1 - r)(1 - t_i)$ in state (1) and $x_2 - (1 - t_i)r$ in state (2), so that the downward slope of the budget line is

$$\frac{-x_2/(1 - t_i) + r}{x_1 - r}$$

This is steeper; i.e., the absence of the loss offset provision makes the risky asset less attractive at the margin, relative to the no-tax situation. It does not however follow that this kind of income tax will necessarily discourage risk-taking, since there is in addition the wealth effect. This is illustrated by Fig. 4-6 for the case where $r = 0$. The no-tax budget line is ST, the with-tax line is ST'. The move from P to P' may be decomposed into a wealth effect PQ and the movement round the indifference curve QP'. The net result may be seen from the fact that the vertical distance from S to P' in Fig. 4-6 is equal to $(-x_2)aA_0$; in other words, it is an index of the amount invested in the risky asset. Depending on the wealth elasticity of demand, this may decrease or increase, the latter being shown in Fig. 4-6. Even therefore without loss offsets it is possible that social risk-taking may be increased by income taxation.

On the other hand, with sufficiently large tax rates, the demand for risky assets is reduced where there are no loss offsets. To see this, all we have to observe is that for tax rates near 100 per cent, almost the entire portfolio is allocated to the safe asset. This follows because, as the tax rate approaches 100 per cent, the maximum return on the risky asset approaches zero and the expected return becomes negative. Since the indifference curves are convex, the demand curves for the different assets are continuous functions of the tax rate.

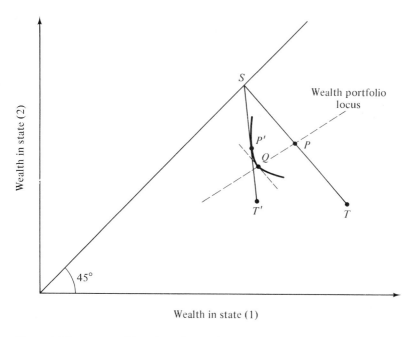

Figure 4-6 Income tax with no loss offset (and zero return on safe asset).

We turn now to the comparison of taxes with and without loss offsets. It seems likely that a reduction in the extent to which losses can be set against tax will reduce risk-taking. The effect does however depend on the basis for comparison. To examine this, let us assume that α of losses can be offset $(0 \leqslant \alpha \leqslant 1)$. Then, if the tax rate is held constant, so that expected revenue falls (and expected utility rises) as α is increased, we can show that $\partial a / \partial \alpha > 0$. Let $\hat{x}(\alpha)$ denote the after-tax return to the risky asset with loss offset provision, α, and $\hat{r}$ the after-tax return to the safe asset, so that terminal wealth is

$$A = A_0[1 + \hat{r} + a(\hat{x} - \hat{r})]$$

and the first-order condition

$$E[U'(\hat{x} - \hat{r})] = 0 \qquad (4\text{-}17)$$

Differentiating with respect to α, and re-arranging,

$$A_0 E[-U''(\hat{x} - \hat{r})^2] \frac{\partial a}{\partial \alpha} = E\left\{ [U' + U''a(\hat{x} - \hat{r})]A_0 \frac{\partial \hat{x}}{\partial \alpha} \right\}$$

Now on the right-hand side $\partial \hat{x} / \partial \alpha$ is strictly positive where $x < 0$ and zero otherwise. It follows that the second term is evaluated only at positive values (where $\partial \hat{x} / \partial \alpha \neq 0$, then $\hat{x} < \hat{r}$ and $U'' < 0$), and that the whole right-hand side is positive. Since the coefficient of $\partial a / \partial \alpha$ is positive, it follows that a is increased.

This conclusion does not however necessarily hold where the tax without loss offsets has a lower tax rate. Suppose, for example, that we compare taxes with equal expected utility. Since the removal of the loss offset provision unambiguously makes individuals worse off in all states in which losses are incurred, it is clear that to compensate the tax rate must be lower.[12] Thus, for any particular portfolio allocation, the pattern of returns is such that there is a larger probability of very small and very large incomes. The new distribution constitutes a *mean utility preserving spread* in the distribution. To analyse the consequences for portfolio allocation, we use a general result of Diamond and Stiglitz (1974). To do this, we note that, since U is by assumption a strictly increasing function of A, and hence of x, we may therefore invert this relationship and write the first-order condition (4-17) as

$$E[\phi(U)] = 0 \quad \text{where} \quad \phi \equiv U'\{A[\hat{x}(U)]\}(\hat{x} - \hat{r}) \tag{4-18}$$

The basic result which can now be used is that an increase in the dispersion of a random variable, keeping the mean constant, increases the expected value of a convex function and decreases that of a concave function. Applying this to the left-hand side of the first-order condition (4-18), the removal of loss offsets leads to an increase in the dispersion of U, and hence to a fall in the expected value where the function ϕ is concave. For the first-order condition to continue to hold, the value of a has then to be reduced.[13] To establish the effect of the loss offset provisions, therefore, all we have to do is to ascertain whether or not ϕ is concave. It is left as an exercise to the reader to explore the relationship between this condition and the properties of absolute and relative risk aversion (and whether they are increasing or decreasing).[14] It can be shown that it is by no means guaranteed that social risk-taking is lower as a result of the (expected utility-preserving) reduction in the loss offset provision (see Diamond and Stiglitz, 1974).

The empirical relevance of the no-loss offset case depends on the form of a country's income tax law, and on the range of an individual's economic activities. Where losses may be set against other forms of income, where losses may be carried forward, and where capital losses may be set against investment income, the full loss offset case may be a reasonable approximation. On the other hand, there are typically restrictions on the

---

[12] Where $r > 0$, expected utility is a strictly decreasing function of t_i. This is left as an exercise to the reader.

[13] Since $(\partial/\partial a)E[U'(\hat{x}-\hat{r})] \sim E[U''(\hat{x}-\hat{r})^2] < 0$, so that lowering a raises the left-hand side of (4-18).

[14] The derivative of ϕ with respect to U is proportional to

$$1 - R_R + R_A \cdot A_0(1+\hat{r})$$

transfer of losses (e.g., capital losses not being eligible for relief on income tax), or where no carry-over is allowed. The no-loss offset case may therefore be more applicable.

A natural question to ask is why tax authorities so commonly impose limitations on the extent to which losses are to be offset. After all, it is exactly in those situations where individuals incur losses that risk-sharing with the government ought to be important. The answer is that it is extremely difficult for the government to distinguish, in many cases, between production and consumption activities. An individual could raise horses because he enjoys raising horses, or he could raise horses as a meaningful economic activity, i.e., for profit. The government would not like to subsidize the former, but might not want to discriminate against the latter as an economic activity. The only way it can distinguish is to require the individual who claims that he is raising the horses for profit to make a profit. If he turns out to be unsuccessful, then he is classified as having embarked on the activity for enjoyment, even if that were not his motive (and even if he hates horses).

Limited Deductibility of Interest

If interest expenses are not deductible, there is a kink in the budget constraint at the point where all of the individual's wealth is invested in the risky asset, i.e., below and to the right of the point T in Fig. 4-1. The effect depends on the balance of the substitution effect, which discourages risk-taking by individuals who previously borrowed, and the wealth effect.

> **Exercise 4-4** Examine the effect of not allowing interest deductibility (but with full loss offsets) and how it depends on the properties of the wealth–portfolio locus.

Again, we can enquire into the reason for this limitation which some (but not all) countries impose; again, we find the answer in limitations on the government's ability to identify the objective of borrowing. For example, a parent could, in principle, give a dollar to his child, and have the child lend the dollar back to the parent; the parent then could pay an arbitrary amount of interest to the child. This is a mechanism by which income from the parent could be transferred to the child; so long as the two have different marginal rates, it is desirable for them to do this. In fact, of course, restrictions are imposed on the rates of interest that could "qualify"; but there is clearly room for considerable discretion in transferring income from one taxpayer to another.

Similarly, the ability to deduct interest enables individuals to take advantage of special provisions of the tax code. For instance, in the United States interest on municipal bonds is tax-exempt. Consider an individual with a 70 per cent marginal tax rate. Assume the borrowing rate is 10 per cent, but the interest rate on municipal bonds is at 7 per cent. He borrows $100. He pays $10 in interest every year, which is tax-deductible, so his "net cost" is $3. He receives $7 in tax-free interest. Thus, for a zero investment, he receives annually $4. Obviously, if he could do this he would demand bonds up to the point where his marginal tax rate falls to 30 per cent. In fact, there are restrictions in that one cannot borrow to buy tax-free bonds, but since funds are fungible, he may be able to borrow for current consumption, and use what he would have spent on current consumption to purchase bonds.

Exemption of Capital Gains

Most countries provide special treatment of capital gains, levying lower rates of tax than on other forms of investment income.[15] In this section we examine the extreme case where there is no tax on capital gains; the extension to the case of partial exemption should be apparent to the reader. The implications depend on the characterization of the two assets. For purposes of illustration we assume that the safe asset yields a return solely in the form of taxable interest, and that the return to the risky asset is entirely capital gains (again the extension to the partial case is immediate). Although this is a caricature, it allows us to examine the frequently made assertion that the special provisions for capital gains encourage investment in risky assets.

Terminal wealth now becomes, with a tax at rate t_i on the safe asset only,

$$A = A_0[1 + ax + (1-a)r(1-t_i)] \tag{4-19}$$

Again, the slope of the budget constraint is altered by the tax, but in contrast to the no-loss offset case it now slopes less steeply. Moreover, it continues to pass through T (since at this point the individual is neither holding the safe asset nor borrowing)—see Fig. 4-7. Suppose now that we consider the indifference curve passing through the new equilibrium P'. Q is the point on this curve with the same slope as the original budget line, and it is clear that we can again distinguish a "wealth" effect (P to Q) and a substitution effect (Q to P'). The latter is in the direction of increased risk-taking. The former depends on the wealth elasticity of demand for the risky asset, but where this is greater than zero it operates to reduce risk-taking. This is illustrated by Fig. 4-7. From (4-19) we can see that the tax, for a given value of a, reduces the wealth in each state of nature by the same

---

[15] A further provision of most tax systems, which also reduces the effective rate, is that the tax is paid only upon realization, rather than accrual. In addition, in some countries assets passed on to heirs escape capital gains tax completely, the heir treating as his "basis" the value of the asset at the time he inherited. Both of these special provisions lead to the problem of people being "locked in" to a given portfolio—see David (1968) and Green and Sheshinski (1978). For an empirical analysis, see Feldstein and Yitzhaki (1978).

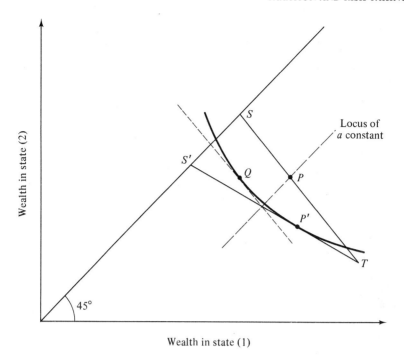

Figure 4-7 Tax on safe asset only (exemption of capital gains).

absolute amount. The locus of points of constant values of a has therefore a slope of 45°—see the dashed line through P in Fig. 4-7. If the wealth elasticity of demand for the risky asset is positive, then the slope of the wealth–portfolio locus is less than 45° (refer back to Fig. 4-2), and Q involves a lower value of a, and hence lower social risk-taking, than at P. As shown, the net effect is for risk-taking to increase (P' is below the dashed line). However, it is quite possible for the tax on the safe asset to reduce risk-taking, counter-intuitive though that may seen. As in other situations, the substitution effect operating in the expected direction may be more than offset by the wealth effect.

The justification sometimes given for the exemption of capital gains, or for their being taxed at a lower rate, is that this provision encourages risk-taking. In this section we have seen that this is not necessarily the case: the outcome depends on the properties of the asset demand functions.

4-4 GENERALIZATION OF RESULTS

Some of the simplifying assumptions made in the preceding two sections were crucial; some were not. The object of this section is to see how robust some of our main results are and how far they can be extended.

Risk and Redistribution

The analysis of the preceding two sections assumed that the proceeds of the tax are spent on a public good, which enters the utility function in a separable way. Thus, the variability in the supply of public goods consequent on the variability of government tax revenue has no effect on risk-taking. In this section we consider the other polar case, to show how our results are dependent on that assumption. We assume that the proceeds of the tax are redistributed to individuals in the form of uniform lump-sum payments. There is in effect a progressive linear tax schedule. Moreover, we assume initially that there is a common risky asset which is purchased by all individuals, i.e., all risks are perfectly correlated. Thus, if all individuals are identical, with identical initial wealth, and if a^* denotes the aggregate portfolio choice, then the *per capita* lump-sum redistribution is (with an income tax at rate t_i)

$$G \equiv t_i[a^*(x-r)+r]A_0 \tag{4-20}$$

and this is a random variable, depending on x. The individual chooses his portfolio to maximize expected utility, derived from terminal wealth, which can now be written:

$$A = A_0\{1+(1-t_i)[r+a(x-r)]\}+G \tag{4-21}$$

For a given a^*, this implies a first-order condition

$$E[U'(x-r)](1-t_i) = 0 \tag{4-22}$$

If we assume that the argument of U' (i.e. terminal wealth) is evaluated at the "equilibrium" value $a^* = a$, then the tax exactly cancels with the lump-sum payment, and it follows that, in this case, the tax has no effect on risk-taking.

This example is rather special in that the outcomes of the risky investment are perfectly correlated for all individuals. Hence, there is no sense in which the government, through taxation, improves the efficiency with which the economy handles risk. Thus, it is not surprising that there is no effect on risk-taking. On the other hand, there are strong reasons to believe that the capability of the market to share and spread risks is limited. Some of these reasons have to do with limited liability laws, i.e., the ability of individuals to default on their loans. Markets for human capital are, as a consequence, notoriously imperfect. The government, with its ability to tax, is not subjected to some of the same limitations as are private lenders. In any case, there appear to be circumstances where the return to different assets which different individuals purchase is imperfectly correlated, where there may be possibilities for risk-sharing effectively through the intermediation of the government, which are not possible through the private market.

Suppose, at the other extreme from the previous example, that the returns are independently distributed; then in the limiting case the lump-sum payment is the expected revenue, evaluated at the equilibrium $a^* = a$:[16]

$$G = t_i[a^*(\bar{x}-r)+r]A_0 \tag{4-23}$$

where $\bar{x}$ is the mean value. The first-order condition for an interior solution is again (4-22), but the argument of the function U' now depends on t_i both directly and via G. Differentiating with respect to t_i,

$$E\{U''(x-r)[x(1-t_i)+t_i\bar{x}-r]\}da = aE[U''(x-r)(x-\bar{x})]dt_i \tag{4-24}$$

where allowance has been made for the effect of the change in a on the level of G. Evaluating at $t_i = 0$, this gives the effect on private risk-taking as being:

$$\frac{1}{a}\frac{da}{dt_i} - 1 = (\bar{x}-r)\frac{E[U''(x-r)]}{E[-U''(x-r)^2]} \tag{4-24a}$$

From the earlier analysis of the properties of the asset demand function (Eq. (4-9)), and the fact that $\bar{x} > r$, the right-hand side is positive where the wealth elasticity of demand for the risky asset is positive.[17] (The reader may like to compare (4-24a) with the earlier expression (4-10) for a proportional tax with the revenue used to finance a public good.)

General Equilibrium

The effects of taxation depend critically on the institutions available within the society for adjusting to risk, and this raises the question of general equilibrium incidence. This subject as a whole is discussed in later Lectures, but since we do not explicitly treat uncertainty we present here a simple case where there is an efficient risk market, the terms of contracts being chosen to provide individuals with the correct incentives.

The model is of "capitalists" who are risk-neutral, and "managers" who are risk-averse. Capitalists provide capital to managers, who employ it in a risky production activity and distribute part of the return to the capitalists. The capitalists cannot monitor the actions of the managers directly; hence, they rely on incentives to ensure that the managers take the actions that maximize returns. We assume that the return per dollar (x) is a function of the effort of managers (L) and risk (θ) in a multiplicative way:

$$x = \theta L^\beta \quad \text{where} \quad E(\theta) = 1 \quad \text{and} \quad 0 < \beta < 1 \tag{4-25}$$

The manager receives α of the return. His expected utility is

$$E[U(\alpha\theta L^\beta)] - v(L) \tag{4-26}$$

---

[16] The progressive tax with fixed lump-sum element is discussed by Ahsan (1974, 1976).

[17] The reader may like to check that expected utility is increased, as a result of the risk-sharing, by this infinitesimal progressive linear tax.

where $v(L)$ is the disutility of supplying effort (and $v' > 0$, $v'' > 0$). We have simplified by assuming that each manager has a unit of capital to manage. Thus, he chooses L so that

$$\alpha \beta L^{\beta-1} E(U'\theta) = v' \qquad (4\text{-}27)$$

The capitalist is risk-neutral, which means that he is only concerned with the expected return per dollar invested (see note at end of Lecture):

$$\bar{x} = (1-\alpha)L^{\beta} \qquad (4\text{-}28)$$

The first-order condition to maximize this return, taking account of the dependence of L on α, may be written (taking logarithms before differentiating)

$$\frac{1}{1-\alpha} = \frac{\beta}{L}\frac{\partial L}{\partial \alpha} \qquad (4\text{-}29)$$

From (4-27), the supply response of managers to changes in α may be calculated. Again taking logarithms,

$$\frac{1}{\alpha}\left[1 + \frac{E(U''\theta^2\alpha L^{\beta})}{E(U'\theta)}\right] = \left[\frac{v''L}{v'} + (1-\beta) - \beta\frac{E(U''\theta^2\alpha L^{\beta})}{E(U'\theta)}\right]\frac{1}{L}\frac{\partial L}{\partial \alpha} \qquad (4\text{-}30)$$

(where the square bracket on the right-hand side is positive by the second-order conditions). Suppose now that managers exhibit constant relative risk aversion, so that

$$\frac{-U''\theta\alpha L^{\beta}}{U'} = R_R \quad \text{constant (less than unity)}$$

and that the function $v(L)$ has constant elasticity, so

$$\frac{v''L}{v'} = \zeta$$

The expression (4-30) then simplifies to

$$\frac{\alpha}{L}\frac{\partial L}{\partial \alpha} = \frac{1-R_R}{\zeta + (1-\beta) + \beta R_R} \qquad (4\text{-}31)$$

Substituting into (4-29) yields, after re-arrangement,

$$\alpha = \frac{\beta(1-R_R)}{1+\zeta} \qquad (4\text{-}32)$$

The optimal contract for the capitalists depends in a simple way on the degree of risk aversion and elasticity of labour supply of the managers.

Now let us impose a proportional income tax with full loss offsets. The return to capitalists is reduced to

$$(1-t_i)(1-\alpha)L^{\beta}$$

but this leaves the first-order condition for the choice of α unaffected. On the other hand, the managers now receive in effect a fraction $\alpha(1-t_i)$ of output, rather than α. Where $R_R < 1$, the managers reduce their labour supply, and the return per dollar to the capitalists falls more than proportionately to $(1-t_i)$. If therefore they face a choice between the risky investment and a safe asset with return $r(1-t_i)$, the latter may now become attractive.[18] The tax will tend to discourage risk-taking—in contrast to the case considered in earlier sections, where the *relative* returns were unchanged by an income tax with full loss offsets. More generally, we may note that the risk-sharing arrangements in the economy may themselves be affected by the treatment of risk by tax authorities.

A Multiperiod Savings Portfolio Allocation Model

In the model analysed to this point, it is terminal wealth, not income or consumption, that enters the utility function. This can be rationalized as viewing the object of savings to be future consumption, if we "idealize" the individual as living for two periods, a work period during which he saves, and a retirement period during which he consumes the proceeds of his savings. On the other hand, we might think of the individual as living for a long time and being therefore concerned primarily with the income that he gets from his investment; in that case, one might think that the appropriate formulation was that where income or return entered directly into the utility function (for instance, Feldstein, 1969). This is not, however, necessarily the case, as the following simple generalization of our earlier model illustrates.

We assume that the individual lives for ever. Again, this is an extreme case; it is chosen for its mathematical simplicity; more realistic cases of individuals living for a large but finite number of periods may be analysed in a similar way. He maximizes the sum of the utility derived from consumption discounted at rate δ. We assume that the utility function has constant elasticity, i.e., is of the form

$$U(C) = \frac{C^{1-\varepsilon}}{1-\varepsilon} \quad \text{where} \quad 0 < \varepsilon \neq 1 \tag{4-33}$$

From the budget constraint, where we have both wealth and income taxes,

$$A_{u+1} = A_u s_u [1 + r(1-t_i) + a(1-t_i)(x-r)](1-t_w) \tag{4-34}$$

where s_u is the fraction of net *wealth* saved at time u (and again $x > -1$), and

$$C_u = (1-s_u)A_u(1-t_w) \tag{4-35}$$

---

[18] Given the assumption of risk neutrality, the investment decision is such that all wealth is invested in the risky asset where its return exceeds $r(1-t_i)$; conversely, where the return is less than $r(1-t_i)$, all wealth is invested in the safe asset.

Let $\chi_u(A_u)$ denote the maximum value of discounted expected utility that the individual can obtain from wealth A_u at time u. Since the individual lives for ever, the discounted value of a given capital at $u+1$ is simply $1/(1+\delta)$ times its value at time u. This simplifies the analysis considerably and means that in writing the objective function we can drop the time subscript from χ and incorporate the discount factor.

The solution to the optimization problem may be seen by applying the principle of optimality, according to which the maximum value $\chi(A_u)$ is given by

$$\chi(A_u) = \max_{s_u} \left\{ U[(1-s_u)A_u(1-t_w)] + \frac{1}{1+\delta} \max_a E\chi(A_{u+1}) \right\} \quad (4\text{-}36)$$

where A_{u+1} is given by (4-34). The level of utility is equal to the utility we get immediately from consumption plus the utility from future consumption; but the latter is just a function of the amount of wealth at the beginning of next period, discounted by $(1+\delta)$. If we knew the function χ, we could immediately infer the optimal value of a and thus the effect of taxation on risk-taking. We need therefore to find a function χ that satisfies (4-36). (Formally, it is a *functional* equation.) Fortunately for the case of constant elasticity utility functions, χ takes on a very simple form. Let us postulate that

$$\chi = \frac{kA^{1-\varepsilon}}{1-\varepsilon}$$

We shall show that there exists a value of the constant k for which (4-36) is identically satisfied. By direct substitution, using the particular form of the utility function (4-33),

$$\frac{kA_u^{1-\varepsilon}}{(1-\varepsilon)} = \max_{s_u} \left(\frac{1}{1-\varepsilon}[(1-s_u)(1-t_w)A_u]^{1-\varepsilon} + \frac{kA_u^{1-\varepsilon}}{1+\delta}\{[s_u(1-t_w)]^{1-\varepsilon}y\} \right)$$

$$(4\text{-}37)$$

where

$$y \equiv \max_a E \left\{ \frac{1}{(1-\varepsilon)}[1+r(1-t_i)+a(1-t_i)(x-r)]^{1-\varepsilon} \right\} \quad (4\text{-}38)$$

From this we can see that if this applies, then the portfolio decision is separable from that about savings, and that a is chosen to maximize the rate of return raised to the power $(1-\varepsilon)$, to take account of risk aversion. The earlier analysis for the one-period model is directly applicable. In particular, wealth taxation leaves the portfolio unchanged (with the isoelastic utility function, the wealth elasticity of demand for the risky asset is unity), and income taxation leads to a rise in social risk-taking.

The value of k, and the optimal savings policy, may be derived from (4-37). Dividing by $A_u^{1-\varepsilon}$, and writing $T = (1-t_w)^{1-\varepsilon}$,

$$\frac{k}{1-\varepsilon} = \max_{s_u} \left[T \frac{(1-s_u)^{1-\varepsilon}}{1-\varepsilon} + \frac{kTy}{1+\delta} s_u^{1-\varepsilon} \right] \qquad (4\text{-}39)$$

The first-order condition for the choice of s_u is (dividing by T)

$$-(1-s_u)^{-\varepsilon} + \left(\frac{ky}{1+\delta} \right) s_u^{-\varepsilon}(1-\varepsilon) = 0$$

Hence, using (4-39)

$$k = T(1-s)^{-\varepsilon} \quad \text{and} \quad s^{\varepsilon} = (1-\varepsilon)Ty/(1+\delta) \qquad (4\text{-}40)$$

This gives a value of k satisfying the equation, and shows that the savings policy depends on the degree of risk aversion (ε), the return on the portfolio (y), the wealth tax (T), and the discount rate.[19]

> **Exercise 4-5** How is the savings rate s in the model just described affected by changes in (1) the wealth tax rate t_w, and (2) the income tax t_i? What happens in the case of the Cobb–Douglas utility function?[20]

The analysis of savings/portfolio decisions given above is intended only to be heuristic; for a more rigorous treatment, the reader is referred to Levhari and Srinivasan (1969), Hakansson (1970), and Rothschild and Stiglitz (1971). The objective of the model is to contrast the two polar cases, where individuals save for an infinite number of periods and where they save for only one period (the case considered in the main part of this Lecture). Remarkably, for the case of constant relative risk aversion (constant elasticity utility function) the portfolio decision is identical in form. In more general cases, there will be interaction between the savings and portfolio decisions—see Sandmo (1969), and Drèze and Modigliani (1972).

More Than One Risky Asset

The basic model used in this Lecture is that of a safe asset and a single risky asset. There are a number of questions that can be raised about this formulation. First, what happens if there is no safe asset? As we have earlier noted, where there is uncertainty surrounding inflation no monetary asset is without risk. However, even if the safe asset is risky, the results obtain so long as the two assets are positively correlated and one is unambiguously more variable than the other (in the sense of Rothschild and Stiglitz, 1970). For example, if the only source of risk is the macroeconomic behaviour of the economy, and both returns react in the same way but one is more sensitive, then the results apply.

---

[19] It may appear from (4-40) that savings are negative where $\varepsilon > 1$; however in that case, y is also negative (see (4-38)).

[20] This is the limiting case of $U = (C^{1-\varepsilon} - 1)/(1-\varepsilon)$ as $\varepsilon \to 1$. This may be seen by applying L'Hôpital's rule (differentiating top and bottom with respect to $(1-\varepsilon)$).

Second, if there exists more than one risky asset, we can, under certain circumstances, divide the problem of portfolio allocation into a two-stage process, as originally suggested by Tobin (1958). The investor decides first on the proportions in which to purchase the risky assets and then on how to divide his total wealth between the safe asset and the "mutual fund" or "unit trust" made up from the risky assets. The conditions under which this "separation" property holds have been investigated by Cass and Stiglitz (1970). They conclude that these conditions are very restrictive. The separation property holds for special utility functions such as those exhibiting constant absolute risk aversion (Exercise 4-1) and constant relative risk aversion (Exercise 4-2), and for special distributions of returns (where all jointly normally distributed). However, the property does not hold for general utility functions and distributions.

This means that where there are several risky assets the applicability of the earlier model is rather limited. We have noted some results that carry over (for example, that concerning the substitution effects) and others are discussed by Cass and Stiglitz (1972). However, important features of the analysis do not apply. In particular, there are no results parallel to those between the measures of risk aversion and the wealth elasticities of demand.

The conclusion that should be drawn is that the two-asset model is valuable as a source of insights and counter-examples, but that not all of the results can be expected to generalize to the many-asset case.

4-5 CONCLUDING COMMENTS

The effect of the tax system on risk-taking has long been the subject of controversy. As was demonstrated in the classic paper of Domar and Musgrave (1944), it is possible that taxation may actually encourage risk-taking, since the government is sharing the risk. Further developments in the theory of portfolio allocation showed how the outcome depends on the properties of the utility function and on the particular features of the tax (e.g., the extent of loss offsets and preferential treatment of capital gains). As in the preceding Lectures, there are both income and substitution effects, although the latter has a particularly straightforward form in the present case (being proportional to the quantity of risky assets purchased).

In further analysis of the portfolio decision, empirical evidence is clearly important, and it has been used to draw inferences about the effects of taxation. Thus, Arrow (1965) concluded from time series evidence on the demand for money in the United States that the wealth elasticity of demand for the risky asset is positive but less than unity (because the elasticity of demand for money is greater than unity). This implies in the two-asset model that both wealth taxation and income taxation increase social risk-taking. In contrast, the cross-section evidence (e.g., Projector and Weiss,

1966) gives a rather different impression, suggesting that the elasticity of demand for the risky asset is greater than unity. There are however considerable difficulties in drawing conclusions from observed portfolios about the risk attitudes of individuals. The identification of "safe" and "risky" assets is far from straightforward, and, as we have seen, the results from the two-asset model do not carry over to the general many-asset case.[21]

The study of the effects of taxation on portfolio behaviour is in some respects at a less advanced stage than the areas of household behaviour discussed in Lectures 2 and 3. On the other hand, the analysis has served to bring out several key features. Of particular importance is the role of the government in risk-sharing. If, for example, the private market provides complete risk-sharing for all but "social risks" (like the business cycle), then the argument that the government can increase risk-sharing through the tax system is less convincing. Indeed, in one extreme case analysed, we showed that there would be no effect at all on risk-taking. Moreover, the risk-sharing arrangements available in the economy may themselves be affected by the tax system. We considered a simple example of the general equilibrium determination of risk-sharing contracts.

In this Lecture we have focused on the case where individuals act to maximize expected utility, and certain limitations ought to be noted. First, individual motivations for undertaking risk may not be described adequately by such a model. This is a subject of longstanding controversy. Second, individual behaviour may be determined more by rules of thumb (perhaps used because of limitations on information—"bounded rationality"). There is considerable evidence of irrationality in portfolio allocation (e.g., individuals at low marginal rates purchasing tax-exempt bonds). In that case, the effect of taxation may be quite different from that analysed in this Lecture; unfortunately, rule of thumb models do not typically give clear predictions about what the effect of taxation would be.

Finally, we should return to the connection between portfolio choice and the real investment decisions of the economy: that if individuals demand more risky assets, then risky projects will find it easier/cheaper to find finance. The linkages are however complex, and several factors need to be taken into account. In several places we have referred to limitations imposed by the capital market, e.g., restrictions on borrowing. Relatively little investment is financed through the issue of new equities. This may be for tax reasons, as we discuss in the next Lecture, or because of imperfections in information or in the capital market. Moreover, the behaviour of the firm under uncertainty is problematic. If there are

---

[21] An analysis of the Projector–Weiss data relating portfolios directly to tax variables has been carried out by Feldstein (1976b). He concludes that the tax effects are important, in that the asset composition varies systematically with the marginal tax rate, although this may reflect a number of different factors.

incomplete markets for risk, there will not in general be unanimity among shareholders; and even if they were to agree on objectives, imperfect information on the part of shareholders may give managers a degree of discretion.

NOTE ON RISK AVERSION

The purpose of this note is to collect together some of the main properties used in the text.

The individual is assumed to maximize expected utility (the discussion of the axiomatic basis for expected utility may be found in, among other places, Arrow, 1965, and Malinvaud, 1972, Ch. 11). The utility of wealth is assumed to be strictly increasing ($U' > 0$), and he is assumed to be risk-averse ($U'' < 0$). The meaning of the latter may be seen if we consider the choice between a certain prospect A_0 and a 50 per cent chance of gaining h or losing h. If he prefers the certain outcome, then

$$U(A_0) > \tfrac{1}{2}U(A_0 - h) + \tfrac{1}{2}U(A_0 + h)$$

or

$$U(A_0) - U(A_0 - h) > U(A_0 + h) - U(A_0)$$

In contrast, if $U'' = 0$ he is indifferent between the certain and risky outcomes and is said to be *risk-neutral*. In this latter case he maximizes expected wealth.

Intuitively, the more concave the utility function, the more risk-averse the individual. This may be formalized in terms of the *risk premium* that the individual is willing to pay to avoid the uncertain prospect. Let us define Π as the premium he is just willing to pay to avoid the risk associated with an investment that yields $A_0 + z$, where z has mean zero and variance σ^2.

$$U(A_0 - \Pi) = E[U(A_0 + z)]$$

Taking a Taylor expansion of both sides, we have

$$U(A_0 - \Pi) \simeq U(A_0) - U'(A_0) \cdot \Pi + \text{higher-order terms}$$

and

$$E[U(A_0 + z)] \simeq U(A_0) + U'(A_0) \cdot E(z) + \frac{U''(A_0)}{2} E(z^2) + \text{higher-order terms}$$

Since $E(z) = 0$, we can approximate[22]

$$U'(A_0)\Pi = -U''(A_0)\frac{\sigma^2}{2}$$

---

[22] For a rigorous treatment, see Pratt (1964). For a discussion of the limits on the validity of the Taylor expansion, see Loistl (1976).

or

$$\Pi = \frac{-U''(A_0)}{U'(A_0)} \frac{\sigma^2}{2} = R_A \frac{\sigma^2}{2}$$

In other words, the individual is indifferent between an uncertain wealth with mean A_0 and arbitrarily small variance σ^2 and a certain wealth $A_0 - R_A\sigma^2/2$.

By a similar process, we may define the proportionate risk premium, R_R.

Both R_A and R_R are in general functions of A_0.

READING

The behaviour of the household under uncertainty is discussed by Green (1976, Chs 13–15), Malinvaud (1972, Ch. 11) and Varian (1978). The reader may find it useful to consult Arrow (1965) and Tobin (1958). The discussion of the effects of taxation draws on Mossin (1968) and Stiglitz (1969c), as well as the valuable survey by Roberts (1971).

FIVE

TAXATION AND THE FIRM

5-1 TAXES AND THE FIRM

In this Lecture, we consider the effects of taxation on decision-making by the firm. Again, we are focusing at this stage on partial equilibrium effects; i.e., it is assumed that the prices paid by the firm are unaffected by the imposition of the tax. Thus, in considering the imposition of, say, a payroll tax, we assume that it increases the costs of labour to the firm; in reality, it may lower the wage received by the worker. Such general equilibrium repercussions are taken up in Lectures 6–8.

This first section of the Lecture describes some of the various taxes imposed on firms. The main part of the Lecture concentrates on the corporate profits tax, about which there has been a great deal of controversy. We begin in Section 5-2 with an analysis of the effect on the cost of capital to the firm, and the determination of financial policy. How does the impact of the tax depend on the provisions for the deductibility of interest? How is it related to the preferential treatment given to capital gains under the personal tax system? The implications for decisions about real variables, notably investment, are then explored. Section 5-3 examines the links between investment and the cost of capital under differing assumptions about depreciation, and the method of finance in a model where capital is freely variable. Section 5-4 widens the discussion to allow for imperfect competition, alternative objectives of the firm, costs of adjustment and the role of expectations. Finally, Section 5-5 reviews some of the empirical evidence on taxation and investment.

Types of Taxes

There are many different types of tax that are, or have been, imposed on firms.

(1) Taxes on individual factors The most common kind of tax on labour is a *payroll tax*, usually levied as a fixed percentage of the wage bill. In the United States, the social security tax is a payroll tax, and similar taxes are in force in many countries. The converse of a payroll tax is where the government provides *wage subsidies*. Subsidies may also be paid at the margin, i.e., in respect of *increases* in employment. The *corporate profits tax* is sometimes viewed as a tax on the return to capital in the corporate sector. If there are constant returns to scale, and hence no "pure profits", and if interest is not deductible, then it seems clear that the corporate profits tax ought to be viewed this way. On the other hand, the interest deductibility provisions typically in force may mean that the tax falls primarily on pure profits, not on the return to capital. This is an issue we discuss. Also, just as there are wage subsidies, there are subsidies for investment: investment tax credits or grants (actually, for durable capital goods they are analogous to marginal employment subsidies).

Taxes on factors may be general taxes or confined to particular forms of input or to particular activities. Thus, payments to bondholders are generally exempt from corporate profits tax, and returns in the form of an increase in the value of an asset (capital gains) are treated differently from other returns. Factor taxes may be confined to one sector of the economy, as with the Selective Employment Tax in Britain, levied on the services sector (with a subsidy to manufacturing). The corporate profits tax treats differentially the return to capital in the corporate and non-corporate sectors. This has clear general equilibrium implications, discussed in Lecture 6.

(2) Taxes on total output or total input One tax widely discussed in recent years is the *value added* tax (VAT), i.e., a proportionate tax on the value added by the firm. The consequences depend on the definition of the tax base. On an *income* base, value added is defined as wage payments plus the return to capital (net of depreciation), so it is equivalent to a uniform payroll tax plus an equal rate profits tax (with depreciation provisions but no deductibility of interest). The other variants of VAT are the *product* base, where there is no depreciation provision, and the *consumption* base, where all purchases of capital goods are deducted. The latter is equivalent to a uniform payroll tax plus an equal rate profits tax with free depreciation. In contrast, *production and turnover taxes* are levied on the value of gross *output* of a firm.

In considering the effects of different taxes, the impact on the degree of integration in the economy needs to be considered. Thus, gross turnover taxes may provide an incentive for vertical integration. The same may apply where there are differing present discounted values of tax payments depending on the timing of transactions (for discussion in connection with the value added tax, see Shoup, 1969).

Effects of Taxes

Suppose that a firm is profit-maximizing and competitive, facing fixed factor prices **w** for the vector of labour inputs (**L**) and **r** for capital inputs (**K**), and a fixed output price p (for simplicity we consider a single-product firm). If the firm's production function is $F(\mathbf{K}, \mathbf{L})$, then it chooses **K** and **L** to maximize profits, which at a given date are

$$\Pi = pF(\mathbf{K}, \mathbf{L}) - \mathbf{w} \cdot \mathbf{L} - \mathbf{r} \cdot \mathbf{K} \tag{5-1}$$

where we assume F to be twice differentiable and concave.

The consequences of a tax may be separated into an output effect and a factor substitution effect. The former depends on whether the tax is universal (i.e., on all firms) or partial, and on the competitive nature of the market. A proper analysis of the output effect requires a general equilibrium analysis of the kind presented in the next Lecture.

Here we concentrate principally on the factor substitution effect. If we treat capital and labour as aggregates, then from the first-order conditions for profit-maximization

$$\begin{aligned} p\partial F/\partial K &= r \\ p\partial F/\partial L &= w \end{aligned} \tag{5-1a}$$

For a given output, a rise in r relative to w leads to a less capital-intensive technique (moving round the isoquant). By taking labour and capital as aggregates, we are of course ignoring some important effects. For instance, a fixed tax per worker increases the cost of unskilled labour relative to that of skilled (assuming no change in wages) and provides an incentive to substitute skilled for unskilled. A regressive payroll tax, such as the social security tax, has a similar effect. In the case of capital, taxation may affect the choice of durability. The analysis of these effects is left to the reader.

Our analysis will concentrate on the corporate profits tax. It is commonly argued that this raises the relative cost of capital, w being deductible but not capital costs. To the extent that this is true, it leads to less capital being employed for a given output—in this sense it is biased against investment. The key issue is therefore what happens to the cost of capital as the corporation tax is increased. This depends in turn on the financial policy of the firm—the mix between debt and equity—and we therefore begin in Section 5-2 with the financing decision.

The formulation above assumed that the firm could vary capital and labour inputs at will. In practice, there are limitations on the flexibility of input choice. Thus, many models have treated capital as a stock variable, with the rate of change in this stock (via investment) being the decision variable. (The same may apply to employment.) We may then ask how the level of investment is affected by taxation. Is it discouraged by the corporate profits tax? How far is the effect offset by investment grants or tax credits? It is important to observe that it is not just current tax rates that are relevant but also *expectations* of tax rates. An anticipated increase in the tax credit may result in firms postponing investment until the increased tax credit becomes effective; an anticipated decrease in the tax credit may result in firms undertaking investment earlier than otherwise. Thus it is not only the level of investment that may be affected but also the timing. These, and other real-world considerations, are taken up in Section 5-4.

Rationale for Corporate Taxation

Before analysing the effects of corporate profits taxation, it is natural to ask why such a tax is levied. Although this is in part a normative issue, and might therefore be more properly discussed in Part Two, there is a close relationship between the answer to this question and one's view of the way in which the corporate profits tax affects the firm.

If one starts from the position that a firm is no more than a way in which individuals own assets, then a tax on the income of the firm is simply a tax on the income of those individuals who own the firm. It is, in other words, a tax on a specific class of assets and/or factors. If these assets (factors) can shift costlessly from the corporate to the non-corporate sectors, then the consequences of the tax are felt throughout the economy. The after-tax returns will be the same in the corporate and non-corporate sectors.

If this view is correct, it is hard to see the justification for a separate corporate profits tax. It may be that it is an efficient method of collection—a form of withholding tax. In this case, the tax that corporations pay should be imputed to the individuals who own the firm (just as the income that the firm receives should be imputed to the owners). Even if individuals cannot see through the corporate veil (see Lecture 3), the tax authorities should be able to, and the corporate and personal tax systems should be fully integrated.

The alternative view sees corporate activity as different in some essential way, so that there is no *a priori* reason why corporate income should be taxed at the same rate as other income. One argument is that corporate status conveys certain privileges, in particular that of limited liability, and the tax is a levy on the resulting benefits. Another is that the tax falls primarily on pure profits and hence is less distortionary than taxes on other kinds of income. Perhaps most important in political terms is the belief, held by many taxpayers, that it is borne by corporations rather than individuals—and is therefore relatively "painless".

There is therefore a variety of views, based on particular beliefs about the incidence of the tax. One of the objectives of this and the next Lectures is to assess the extent to which these beliefs are valid.

5-2 CORPORATION TAX AND THE COST OF CAPITAL

The crucial role of financial policy when considering the effects of the corporate profits tax is well illustrated by the "Marshallian" view of the tax as falling on pure profits. For simplicity, let us treat labour (L) and capital (K) as aggregates and assume that capital can be freely varied. The Marshallian view, as represented for example by the arguments made before the Colwyn Committee in Britain in the 1920s, is that a profits tax did not affect output in either the short or the long run. The reasoning is that the tax was levied (at rate t_c) on profits, so the firm receives net:

$$\Pi = (1 - t_c)[pF(K, L) - wL - rK] \tag{5-2}$$

The first-order condition for the choice of K is $pF_K = r$, and this is unaffected by the tax. In the short run, the profit-maximizing behaviour of firms in the industry is unaffected. In the longer run, entry and exit are determined by the marginal firm, which by definition is making zero pure profit, so that long-run output is unchanged. The tax falls on pure profits, or the return to entrepreneurship.

This analysis depends however on the assumption that the tax base excludes the cost of capital (rK), so that it falls only on pure profits, a point that was brought out by Robertson (1927). The definition of the tax base is indeed the key issue. As in the case of personal income taxation, the translation of the theoretical concept of profits into fiscal legislation is far from straightforward. There are difficulties surrounding items such as depreciation, depletion, inventory accumulation, capital gains and losses, and intercorporate dividends. We make no pretence here at dealing with the detailed provisions of the corporate tax law. However, there are certain key features that profoundly affect the nature of the corporation tax. Chief among these are the deductibility of interest and the treatment of depreciation.

In this section we examine the significance of interest deductibility for financial policy and the implications of the method of financing for the behaviour of the firm.

Financial Structure

The analysis focuses on the fundamental financial identity of the firm. We can identify the following receipts of the firm at time u:

1. *gross profits*, i.e., the value of output minus the cost of variable inputs (labour),

$$\Pi_u = p_u F_u - w_u L_u \qquad (5\text{-}3)$$

2. *new bond issues* (where B_u denotes bonds outstanding at the beginning of the period)

$$B_{u+1} - B_u \qquad (5\text{-}4a)$$

3. *new equity issues* (where θ_u denotes the equity at the beginning of the period),

$$\theta_{u+1} - \theta_u \qquad (5\text{-}4b)$$

and we can identify the following disbursements:

1. dividends, D_u,
2. interest payments to bond-holders, rB_u,
3. investment, I_u.

The fundamental relationship is that revenues equal disbursements in period u:

$$\Pi_u + B_{u+1} - B_u + \theta_{u+1} - \theta_u = D_u + I_u + rB_u \qquad (5\text{-}5)$$

We can define retained earnings as

$$RE_u = \Pi_u - rB_u - D_u \qquad (5\text{-}6)$$

i.e., profits not distributed as interest or dividends. It follows that

$$I_u = RE_u + (B_{u+1} - B_u) + (\theta_{u+1} - \theta_u) \qquad (5\text{-}7)$$

i.e., investment is financed by retained earnings, borrowing or new issues.

For the present, we take Π_u and I_u as fixed and consider variations in the financial decisions. It should be noted that the basic accounting identity implies that at least two of the financial variables have to be changed at a time. Moreover, they are linked over time: for example, an increase in bonds today implies increased interest payments in the future.

In the absence of taxation, the net financial flow from the corporation to the personal sector is:

$$Y_u \equiv D_u + rB_u - (B_{u+1} - B_u) - (\theta_{u+1} - \theta_u) \qquad (5\text{-}8)$$

and from (5-5) we can see that this is equal to $\Pi_u - I_u$. In other words, the net flow is determined by the real variables and does not depend at all on the financial structure. This is the basis for the Modigliani–Miller theorem: *in the absence of taxation (and bankruptcy), corporate financial policy is irrelevant and has no effect on the value of the firm.* This was originally proved, under quite special assumptions by Modigliani and Miller (1958); it is extended to a more general model in Stiglitz (1969a, 1974a).

We now introduce the tax system, with the following provisions:

1. corporate profits are taxed at the rate t_c,
2. interest payments by corporations are deductible,
3. interest payments by individuals are deductible at the personal tax rate, t_p,
4. dividends and interest received are taxable at the rate t_p,
5. capital gains are taxable at an effective rate $t_g < t_p$.[1]

This corporate tax is often referred to as "classical", and involves a simple tax on corporate profits, with no "credit" being given to shareholders for the corporation tax paid. It may be seen as a tax on incorporation, with the shareholders being liable for personal taxation on dividends and capital gains. Numerous variations are possible. In some countries an attempt is made to integrate the personal and corporate tax structures, the individual receiving credit for the imputed corporation tax paid on his behalf. (Different tax systems are discussed in detail in King, 1977.) In some countries interest payments by individuals are not deductible; in others there have been proposals to tax capital gains at the same rate as dividends.

With this tax system, the corporate tax liability is $t_c(\Pi_u - rB_u)$, and the financial identity becomes

$$\Pi_u(1 - t_c) + (B_{u+1} - B_u) + (\theta_{u+1} - \theta_u) = D_u + I_u + r(1 - t_c)B_u \qquad (5\text{-}5')$$

For the personal sector, there is liability to income tax and capital gains tax,[2] so that the net financial flow after tax is

$$Y_u = (D_u + rB_u)(1 - t_p) - (B_{u+1} - B_u) - (\theta_{u+1} - \theta_u)$$
$$-\text{capital gains tax liability} \qquad (5\text{-}8')$$

Taxation and Financial Policy

The way we analyse the effect of taxation on the financial structure of the firm is to use what is sometimes called a perturbation argument. We assume that the economy is in equilibrium, and then consider a feasible perturbation to the financial policy of the firm, examining its effect on the consumption possibilities of the individuals owning the firm. For most of the analysis, we aggregate and consider a "representative" member of the personal sector who owns the shares of the firm. We also assume that tax

---

[1] The effective rate takes account of such factors as the postponement of the tax liability where gains are taxable on realization; in this case the tax rate is endogenous, depending on individual decisions about transactions, but for simplicity we treat it here as a constant, so that it is effectively a reduced rate on accruals.

[2] In reality, a substantial proportion of shares is held by tax-exempt institutions, and this important feature of the capital market needs to be borne in mind.

rates are constant over time, and are correctly anticipated. The implications of expectations regarding changes in tax rates are discussed in later sections.

The first perturbation we consider is a re-arrangement in the means by which funds are transmitted to the personal sector. Suppose that the firm reduces both D_u and $(\theta_{u+1} - \theta_u)$ by \$1. The former "costs" the personal sector $\$(1 - t_p)$; the effect of the latter depends on the capital gains tax, and can be seen to be a gain of $\$(1 - t_g)$. Since $t_g < t_p$, this represents a net gain to shareholders, and bondholders are no worse off. This brings us immediately to one of the key puzzles of corporate financial policy—why, with the tax system described, do firms pay dividends? Where the tax rate on capital gains is less than that on dividends, it is clearly better to buy back shares (generating capital gains) than to pay dividends.

Several explanations have been given for the fact that firms regularly pay dividends. The first is that dividends serve as a signal concerning the "real" value of the firm. Thus if dividends are reduced, potential purchasers of the shares believe that it may be because the firm is in bad financial straits, i.e., is unable to pay out dividends. This is not however very persuasive, since buying back shares could serve as an equally effective signal. More important are the legal restrictions on the buying back of shares and the fact that some tax codes treat such repurchases as equivalent to paying dividends. Thus, in the United Kingdom a company can buy back its own shares only by obtaining a special court order. In the United States the redemption of shares may be regarded by the Internal Revenue as a dividend.[3]

For the reasons just described, a corporation may not seek to repurchase shares, but there are a number of actions the firm can undertake that, at least in a perfect capital market, are essentially equivalent. Assume, for instance, that the firm was planning to issue a \$X dividend. Instead, the firm acquires a firm with a value of \$X. This is a purely financial transaction—nothing real is involved. The personal sector receives from the corporate sector the \$X it would have received with a dividend. The "original" company is now worth \$X more than it would have been had the dividend been distributed, and there is thus a contingent capital gains liability, but at rate t_g rather than the dividend rate. That the two actions—paying dividends and having the firm buy another firm—are fully equivalent is obvious if the same individual owns both firms. But even if different individuals own the different firms the two actions are equivalent,

---

[3] Another argument put forward for not retaining earnings, in spite of the tax advantages, is that the market undervalues investments within the corporate sector. Thus, a dollar invested in a corporation increases the value of the corporation by less than one dollar. In this case, even with unfavourable tax treatment, individuals might prefer having the funds distributed as dividends. But if firms are undervalued, a firm seeking to acquire real assets would always buy another firm, rather than new machines on the market. This could not be sustained in equilibrium.

provided there exists another firm with the same risk characteristics as the firm making the acquisition. (Otherwise, the risk opportunities available to individuals may be changed.) Individuals simply re-adjust their portfolios.[4]

The fact that a substantial fraction of the profits of the corporate sector is distributed as dividends cannot therefore readily be explained within this framework. In what follows, we simply assume $\theta_{u+1} - \theta_u \geqslant 0$, so that any payments to shareholders must take the form of dividends. Firms are also restricted from being under-capitalized; there are cases where tax authorities have disallowed the tax deductibility of interest payments, but these have mainly again been closely held firms. Because of bankruptcy considerations, most firms that are widely held do not seem to attempt to increase the debt equity ratio to the point where tax authorities might impose constraints.

We consider now a perturbation of financial policy such that the firm increases dividends by \$1 in period 1, financed by borrowing, with the interest and repayment of the principal being met in period 2 by a reduction in dividends. From the financial identity for the firm, (5-5'), we can see that the reduction in dividends in period 2 is $1 + r(1 - t_c)$. The implications for the net flow to the personal sector depend on the capital gains tax liability. If, initially, we assume that t_g is zero, then the change is

	Shareholders	Bondholders
Period 1	$+(1-t_p)$	-1
	dividend	lending
Period 2	$-(1-t_p)[1+r(1-t_c)]$	$+1+r(1-t_p)$
	dividend	repayment interest

The effect on the individual depends on his rate of discount, or the opportunity cost of funds, which we write as $r(1-\tau)$. If he reduces his borrowing on receiving $(1-t_p)$ dividends, or if he increases his lending, then $\tau = t_p$; if he increases his savings in a tax-exempt medium (e.g., pension fund), then $\tau = 0$. For the shareholder the increase in borrowing is desirable where

$$(1-t_p)[1+r(1-\tau)] \geqslant (1-t_p)[1+r(1-t_c)] \qquad (5\text{-}9)$$

The condition is simply therefore that $t_c \geqslant \tau$. Essentially, the individual is substituting corporate borrowing for personal borrowing; since interest is deductible, whether this is desirable depends on where the tax savings are greatest. Where $\tau = 0$, corporate borrowing clearly dominates, but where

---

[4] In the United States, for closely held corporations, tax authorities do restrict purely financial acquisitions and, to some extent, non-financial acquisitions (there may be restrictions on excessive retentions used to finance the firm going into other activities). But it is not clear how effective these restrictions are.

$\tau = t_p$ this is more problematic, and with the typical levels of corporation tax (around 50 per cent) it is quite possible that this is less than the marginal tax rate of the "representative" shareholder.[5]

Let us suppose for the present that $t_c < \tau = t_p$. The shareholder therefore favours a reduction in corporate borrowing and dividend payments. How far should this process be carried? It may be noted that the condition for optimal financial policy is independent of the quantities: if $t_c \neq \tau$, then (5-9) can never hold with equality. This is in contrast to the models of earlier Lectures where there were typically interior solutions. In the present case a corner solution is likely to obtain. To see this, let us go back to the financial identity (5-5'), and write the net financial transfer to shareholders as

$$\chi_u = D_u - (\theta_{u+1} - \theta_u) \tag{5-10}$$

By assumption, $D_u \geqslant 0$ and $\theta_{u+1} - \theta_u \geqslant 0$, and it is clear that at least one is zero (otherwise the firm could reduce both dividends and new issues and reduce taxes paid). If we consider variations in B_{u+1}, holding debt in all other periods constant, then this generates the locus (obtained by taking the corporate financial identity for two successive periods and eliminating B_{u+1}):

$$\chi_{u+1} + [1 + r(1 - t_c)]\chi_u = (1 - t_c)\{\Pi_{u+1} + [1 + r(1 - t_c)]\Pi_u\}$$
$$+ B_{u+2} - [1 + r(1 - t_c)]^2 B_u - I_{u+1} - [1 + r(1 - t_c)]I_u \tag{5-10'}$$

which is shown in Fig. 5-1 (which relates to the case where the right-hand side is positive). By successively reducing borrowing, the firm can reach the point P where $\chi_u = 0$.

Would the firm want to go further and make new issues, thus making χ_u negative? The effect of this may be seen to be:

	Shareholders	Bondholders
Period 1	-1	$+1$
	new issue	reduced lending
Period 2	$(1-t_p)[1+r(1-t_c)]$	$-1-r(1-t_p)$
	increased dividend	reduced receipts

This would be beneficial for shareholders if:

$$(1 - t_p)[1 + r(1 - t_c)] > 1 + r(1 - \tau) \tag{5-11}$$

and with $\tau = t_p$ this is clearly not satisfied. In contrast to reducing

---

[5] For bondholders the increased loans are attractive where $\tau = t_p$ but not for $\tau < t_p$. This raises the question of the capital market equilibrium. The existence of institutional lenders is significant here.

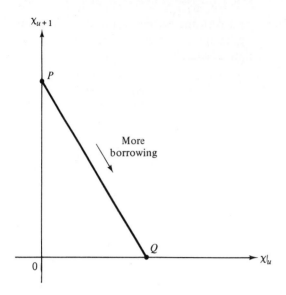

Figure 5-1 Choice of financial policy.

dividends, there are no tax savings on increasing new issues. Where $t_c < t_p$ we have therefore a corner solution at P, with dividends being deferred as far as possible.

Where $t_c > \tau$, a policy of increasing borrowing is desirable and this can be continued until point Q, where $\chi_{u+1} = 0$. Going further would mean that new issues would have to be made to finance the debt repayment. In that case, condition (5-9) would become

$$(1 - t_p)[1 + r(1 - \tau)] \geqslant 1 + r(1 - t_c) \qquad (5\text{-}9')$$

since the new issues do not attract tax relief like a reduction in dividends. It is possible that for sufficiently low personal tax rates this is satisfied and we would have an "all-debt" firm.

A fuller treatment of financial policy, and its extension to many periods, is provided by Stiglitz (1973), but it appears likely with the assumptions made that the firm will be at a corner solution. The most reasonable assumption is perhaps $t_c < \tau = t_p$, and this is the central case on which we focus later. In this situation, the firm reduces dividends to zero or, more plausibly, an "acceptable" minimum. Where investment exceeds retained earnings, any increase is financed by borrowing. (As may be seen from (5-10'), a rise in I_u shifts the locus in Fig. 5-1 in towards the origin and P moves down the vertical axis.) Where investment is less than retained earnings, any increase in I_u reduces the rate at which debt is being paid off (hence has the same opportunity cost). In contrast, at Q a rise in I_u leads to a reduction in D_u: investment is financed by retained earnings.

This description of the firm's financial policy does not seem totally inconsistent with observed behaviour. For established firms, new issues are relatively unimportant; firms do not typically seek to recapitalize as all-equity concerns; on the other hand, they do not appear to move in the direction of reducing the equity element by borrowing in excess of what is required for investment. At the same time, there are a number of features of the model that warrant comment.

Capital Gains and Market Value

A crucial role was played in the preceding argument by the assumption that capital gains are taxed at a lower rate than dividends; indeed, we set $t_g = 0$. To examine this, we need a model of the determination of the stock market value of the firm—and this also provides an alternative way of deriving the results given above in the absence of uncertainty. The model used here starts from the basic capital market equilibrium condition that in period u the dividends received plus the capital appreciation must equal the opportunity cost of owning the firm, where the latter is $r(1-\tau)$. Treating the firm as a single holding, the condition on net of tax returns is that:

$$(1-t_p)D_u + (1-t_g)(\Psi_{u+1} - \Psi_u) = r(1-\tau)\Psi_u \qquad (5\text{-}12)$$

where Ψ_u is the stock market value of the firm. This can be re-arranged:

$$\Psi_{u+1} - \left[1 + \frac{r(1-\tau)}{1-t_g}\right]\Psi_u = \frac{-(1-t_p)}{1-t_g}D_u \qquad (5\text{-}13)$$

Solving this difference equation

$$\Psi_0 = \left(\frac{1-t_p}{1-t_g}\right)\sum_{i=0}^{\infty}\frac{D_i}{\left[1 + \dfrac{r(1-\tau)}{1-t_g}\right]^{i+1}} \qquad (5\text{-}14)$$

(where it is assumed that this sum converges). The stock market value is equal therefore to the present value of dividends discounted at a rate that depends on the opportunity cost of capital and on the tax treatment of capital gains. If capital gains are taxed at the same rate as other income $(t_g = t_p)$, and if $\tau = t_p$, the stock market value is the same—for a given stream of dividends—as in the no tax case.

> **Exercise 5-1** The valuation formula (5-14) is based on the assumption that capital gains are taxed on accrual (albeit at a lower effective rate). Recalculate Ψ_0 assuming that the capital gains tax is imposed only at the end of S periods. For any given S, what is the relation between the accrual and realization taxes which have the same effect on market value?

The effect of a switch from retained earnings to borrowing (dividends + \$1 in period 1, $-\$[1+r(1-t_c)]$ in period 2) may now be examined. From (5-14) this raises the value of the firm where

$$1 + \frac{r(1-\tau)}{1-t_g} > 1 + r(1-t_c)$$

which may be re-written as

$$(1-t_g)(1-t_c) < (1-\tau) \tag{5-15a}$$

or

$$\tau < t_c + (1-t_c)t_g \tag{5-15b}$$

The right-hand side is the total tax burden on equity return taken as capital gain (corporate profits tax plus capital gains tax on the remainder). This brings out the key role played by the tax treatment of capital gains. If gains were taxed at the same rate as other income ($t_g = t_p$), then this inequality would clearly hold, if $\tau = t_p$, and borrowing would be desirable. At the other extreme, with $t_g = 0$, the condition is $\tau < t_c$, as before. In general the situation is in between, although the effective rate on accrued gains is rather low, so that we are in practice close to the case analysed earlier. Allowance for capital gains tax liability probably does not alter the qualitative conclusions drawn.[6]

Qualifications to Analysis

The analysis so far has assumed that the corporation tax is of the "classic" type; there are however alternative versions which are, or have been, in force. For example, the United Kingdom has employed the "imputation" system, where shareholders receive some credit for the tax paid by the company: distributed profits are regarded as having paid tax at a rate t_m. This means that the total payment D is treated as equivalent to a grossed-up amount $D/(1-t_m)$ on which the taxpayer is then taxed at a rate $(t_p - t_m)$. The treatment of this case is left as an exercise to the reader.

Exercise 5-2 Show that with the imputation system, the condition (5-15) for the choice between borrowing and retained earnings is unchanged but that it pays the firm to issue new shares to pay higher dividends if

$$1 - t_g < 1 - \frac{t_p - t_m}{1 - t_m} = \frac{1 - t_p}{1 - t_m} \tag{5-16}$$

---

[6] The same applies to the comparison of new issues and borrowing (King, 1977, p. 96).

and that it pays to issue shares to reduce indebtedness if (with $\tau = t_p$)

$$t_c < t_m \tag{5-17}$$

(see King, 1977, Ch. 4).

These results are summarized in Fig. 5-2, which shows the regimes for different values of the relative tax treatment of capital gains, $(1 - t_g)/(1 - t_p)$. The symbol $<$ denotes "inferior to". The switch from the classic system $(t_m = 0)$ to imputation may make a substantial difference. In particular, new issues may now become attractive. The results are particularly relevant to discussions about the integration of corporate and personal taxation, and the reader should consider the conditions under which fiscal policy would be neutral with regard to method of finance.

In the absence of integration, the optimal financial policy depends on the relative rates of personal and corporate taxation. This leads us to the question of differences in the position of individual shareholders. What

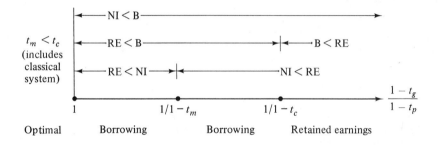

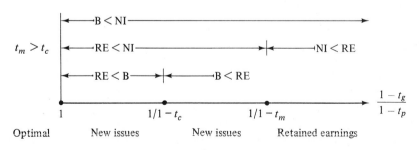

Figure 5-2 Company financial policy and tax regimes. "$<$" denotes "inferior to"; NI, new issues; RE, retained earnings; B, borrowing. This diagram is constructed using inequalities (5-15), (5-16), and (5-17) and assuming $\tau = t_p$.

happens if we abandon the fiction of a "representative shareholder"? Where all individuals lie within the tax bracket for which a particular policy is optimal, then the analysis continues to apply. On the other hand, where there are differences that cross critical boundaries, such as $t_c = t_p$, then we have to consider the possibilities for "tax arbitrage". We can in fact show that, if there are any all-equity firms, there will never be an all-debt firm. To see this, consider a firm yielding a (safe) return of r^*, owned by an individual at a low tax bracket, so that the firm pursues an all-debt policy. Assume the firm costs \$1. Suppose now that a wealthy individual instead borrows the \$1 offering a (safe) return (perhaps slightly in excess) of r^*, and uses the \$1 to make exactly the same investment. He then sells the firm to another wealthy individual (of the next generation) at the value of the assets, which have grown to $1 + r^*(1 - t_c)$. The net return to the wealthy person (with no investment of his own) is

$$r^*[(1 - t_g)(1 - t_c) - (1 - t_p)]$$

This is positive (and hence advantageous to him) precisely in the conditions (e.g., (5-15a)) that we saw above would lead a firm to pursue an all-equity policy. Hence, there is a tax arbitrage possibility between low and high marginal tax rate individuals, and there cannot exist all-debt firms in an economy in which there are all-equity firms.

5-3 TAXATION AND INVESTMENT

We turn now to the real, as opposed to financial, decisions made by the firm. In the context of a competitive firm, maximizing its stock market value at given prices for output and inputs, we examine the impact of taxation on the supply of output, and particularly on the capital employed. The mechanism by which taxes affect investment is the cost of capital discussed in the previous section, and this therefore depends on the financial policy. However, we need first to discuss the provisions for depreciation.

Depreciation

An asset will generate a gross stream of returns, from which depreciation has to be deducted to calculate the net return. Most tax systems make some provision for depreciation when calculating tax profits. In assessing their relative generosity, a useful benchmark is that of "true economic depreciation" (Samuelson, 1964a), which is the replacement cost of physical wear and tear. (At this point we assume that all prices are constant over time; the effect of inflation is discussed later in the section.) This depreciation provision is neutral with respect to investment decisions, as is illustrated by the following simple model. Suppose that an asset generates a stream of returns Π_u, the corporate tax rate is t, and the discount rate is $r(1-t)$. With depreciation allowances δ_u at time u, the value of the asset at time u^* is:[7]

$$\Psi = \int_{u^*}^{\infty} [\Pi_u(1-t)+t\delta_u]\, e^{-r(1-t)(u-u^*)}\, du \qquad (5\text{-}18)$$

Differentiating with respect to u^* to give the time derivative,

$$\dot{\Psi} = r(1-t)\Psi - (1-t)\Pi_u - t\delta_u \qquad (5\text{-}19)$$

This is the change in value of the asset, and true economic depreciation is by definition equal to $(-\dot{\Psi})$. Re-arranging, with δ_u at the true economic level,

$$\delta_u = \Pi_u - r\Psi$$

and

$$\dot{\Psi} = r\Psi - \Pi_u \qquad (5\text{-}20)$$

The differential equation is therefore unaffected by the tax. Since the boundary condition, where $\Psi = 0$ at the point of scrapping, is also unaffected, it follows that the tax is—with true economic depreciation—neutral. (The role of the assumption that the discount rate is $r(1-t)$ is discussed below.)

If there were perfect markets for all used assets, there would be no difficulty in calculating true economic depreciation; but used capital goods markets are notoriously imperfect. As a result the government typically employs rule of thumb depreciation formulae; for example:

1. a fraction of the expenditure is allowed each period (straight-line depreciation);
2. a fraction of the written-down value (declining balance) is allowed;
3. a fraction of the expenditure that declines linearly over the lifetime (sum of the digits) is allowed;[8]
4. a whole or part of the value may be written off at once (free depreciation or investment tax credit).

Such formulae do not typically ensure true economic depreciation. Whether they are more or less generous depends in general on the relationship between the "true life" and that used for tax purposes. (Free depreciation is an exception, since this is always more generous for a durable asset.) Consider the case of straight-line depreciation over Γ years of an asset costing C which generates an infinite stream of returns $\Pi_0 e^{-\gamma u}$

---

[7] We assume throughout that taxable profits are sufficient to cover the depreciation allowances or that there are full loss offsets.

[8] i.e., for an asset with a life of 10 years, the amount written off is $10/55, 9/55, 8/55, \ldots, 1/55$.

from time zero. Let us assume that in the absence of taxation the project is on the margin of acceptance, i.e.,

$$C = \Psi_0 = \int_0^\infty \Pi_0 \, e^{-(r+\gamma)u} \, du = \frac{\Pi_0}{r+\gamma} \tag{5-21}$$

The introduction of a tax at rate t, with the discount rate becoming $r(1-t)$, and true economic depreciation, leaves the value unchanged. In contrast with straight-line depreciation,

$$\Psi_0^* = (1-t) \int_0^\infty \Pi_0 \, e^{-[r(1-t)+\gamma]u} \, du + t \int_0^\Gamma (C/\Gamma) e^{-r(1-t)u} \, du$$

$$= \frac{\Pi_0(1-t)}{r(1-t)+\gamma} + tC \cdot (DA) \tag{5-22}$$

where DA denotes the value of depreciation allowances per dollar. Re-arranging,

$$\Psi_0^* = \frac{\Pi_0}{r+\gamma} + tC \left[DA - \frac{\gamma}{\gamma + r(1-t)} \right] \tag{5-23}$$

where we have substituted from (5-21). The straight-line depreciation is therefore greater or less than true economic depreciation, according as

$$DA = \frac{1}{\Gamma} \int_0^\Gamma e^{-r(1-t)u} \, du \gtrless \frac{\gamma}{\gamma + r(1-t)} \tag{5-24}$$

There exists a critical Γ such that this holds with equality;[9] for shorter "tax lives" the straight-line depreciation gives more generous allowances.

The case of declining balance is more straightforward. Suppose that there is an allowance $\delta C \, e^{-\delta u}$ at date u. This gives (again using (5-21))

$$\Psi_0^{**} = \frac{\Pi_0}{r+\gamma} + tC \left\{ \int_0^\infty \delta e^{-[\delta + r(1-t)]u} \, du - \frac{\gamma}{\gamma + r(1-t)} \right\} \tag{5-25}$$

It is clear that the term in braces is zero if $\delta = \gamma$ and this case corresponds to true economic depreciation. It is positive (negative) if $\delta > \gamma (\delta < \gamma)$. In what follows we concentrate particularly on this relatively simple form of depreciation and on free depreciation.

Exercise 5-3 Suppose that a firm can depreciate on a declining balance formula at a fixed rate δ and then switch (at a date it chooses) to straight-line depreciation with a life Γ. What is the condition for this to be equivalent to true economic depreciation in the model described above?

---

[9] To see that the left-hand side is a declining function of Γ, change variables by substituting $Z = u/\Gamma$. The existence of a critical value follows from the fact that the left-hand side is unity when $\Gamma = 0$ and tends to zero as $\Gamma \to \infty$.

Bond-Financed Investment

In the previous section we identified as a central case that in which investment was financed *at the margin* by borrowing. Where investment exceeds retained earnings, the additional capital is borrowed; where retained earnings exceed investment, the surplus is used to reduce indebtedness. We begin therefore with this case, where the cost of capital at the margin is $r(1-t_c)$, interest being assumed deductible under corporation tax. Again, it is assumed throughout this section that taxes are expected to remain at their current levels—an important assumption, as we show in Section 5-4.

We assume that the firm is choosing capital inputs (K) and labour inputs (L) to maximize its profits, and that there are no costs to varying factor inputs—costs of adjustment are discussed in the next section. Suppose that we consider a variation in the firm's policy for K, such that the firm has an extra unit of capital in period 1, but no changes in subsequent periods. In other words, investment is increased by one unit and then reduced by one unit in the next period. If we assume that the price of capital goods is unity, this involves borrowing an extra \$1 for one period. In the absence of taxation, the change in profits is positive if

$$p\, \partial F/\partial K > r + \gamma$$

where γ is the true economic rate of depreciation. Let us now introduce taxation, with true economic depreciation (we discuss alternatives below). The change in profits is positive if

$$(1-t_c)p\, \partial F/\partial K > r(1-t_c) + \gamma - t_c\gamma$$

Profit maximization therefore requires (since the terms in $(1-t_c)$ cancel) that

$$p\, \partial F/\partial K = r + \gamma \tag{5-26}$$

(there is a corresponding first-order condition for L that we do not discuss). If the tax system allows true economic depreciation, and there is full interest deductibility, the condition for optimality is not explicitly affected by taxation (the possibility of a general equilibrium effect via r is not considered in this Lecture). In this sense, the tax system may be said to be "neutral"; in other words, for a constant value of r, the first-order conditions are unchanged by the tax.

These findings need to be modified when there is free depreciation. Suppose that the firm can write off at once the entire investment. This effectively reduces the price of capital goods from 1 to $(1-t_c)$, since there is an immediate tax saving of t_c. On the other hand, suppose that only a fraction ζ of interest is deductible. The first-order condition becomes

$$(1-t_c)p\, \partial F/\partial K = r(1-\zeta t_c)(1-t_c) + \gamma(1-t_c) \tag{5-27}$$

or

$$p \, \partial F / \partial K = r(1 - \zeta t_c) + \gamma \qquad (5\text{-}28)$$

From this we can see that free depreciation, coupled with no interest deductibility, also leaves the first-order condition unaffected. In the usual case where interest is deductible, then free depreciation reduces the right-hand side below the no-tax value. In this sense, taxation actually "encourages" investment. Moreover, the effect can be quite marked. Suppose $r = 16$ per cent, $\gamma = 15$ per cent and $\zeta = 1$, $t_c = 50$ per cent. Then the reduction in the cost of capital (right-hand side of (5-28)) is from 31 to 23 per cent. Put the other way round, if interest is not deductible, then true economic depreciation is not neutral and free depreciation is necessary to secure neutrality (it is not a "bribe"). Finally, we may note that the effect of free depreciation is to convert the tax into one on pure profits; hence the non-distortionary result is the traditional Marshallian one. At the same time, *intra-marginal* effects differ from those of the tax with interest deductibility and true economic depreciation.

Free economic depreciation is an extreme form of accelerated depreciation, and there are many intermediate cases. It is possible for example that the firm is allowed to write off a fraction δ of its capital that is greater than the true economic depreciation. In allowing for this, it is necessary to take account of the fact that the depreciated value declines faster than physical capital (Boadway and Bruce, 1979). Thus, the benefit from a higher initial allowance has to be set against the lower depreciation allowances later. Free depreciation is an extreme case of this, where no subsequent depreciation is possible.

Finance by Retained Earnings

We now examine the implications of taxation for investment where it is financed by retained earnings. It is assumed that a fraction ϕ of the investment can be depreciated freely (i.e., written off at once), and that the remaining $(1 - \phi)$ attracts true economic depreciation.

We again consider a variation of one unit in the capital stock in period 1. The shareholder has therefore to finance $(1 - \phi t_c)$ of the investment (the ϕt_c term representing the free depreciation—i.e., investment financed by the government as a sleeping partner). Financing by retained earnings for one period means that the shareholder is forgoing dividends for one period, in exchange for an increase in the second period. As in the previous section, we treat the opportunity cost as $r(1 - \tau)$, where $\tau = t_p$ if the alternative uses of funds are taxable at the personal rate (or the investment is financed by borrowing in tax-deductible form). The first-order condition is then

$$p \, \partial F / \partial K = \frac{r(1 - \tau)(1 - \phi t_c)}{1 - t_c} + \gamma \qquad (5\text{-}29)$$

(The reader should check that this can be obtained by the perturbation argument used before.)

The effect of taxation depends on whether

$$(1-\tau)\frac{(1-\phi t_c)}{1-t_c} \gtrless 1 \tag{5-30}$$

Thus, with equity financing, the condition turns on the extent of free depreciation and on the opportunity cost. If $\tau = 0$, then the cost of capital is raised if $\phi < 1$, but taxation is offset completely where $\phi = 1$. This may be contrasted with the case of debt finance with interest deductibility, where free depreciation goes "too far". Alternatively, we can look at the relation between τ and t_c. If $\phi = 0$, then the condition is $t_c \gtrless \tau$.

Exercise 5-4

1. Under what conditions is $r(1-\tau)$ the correct cost of capital for an all-equity firm?
2. How does the above analysis need to be modified if there is not true economic depreciation ($\delta \neq \gamma$)?

From this analysis it is apparent that taxation may either raise or lower the cost of capital. This is illustrated by the special cases shown in Table 5-1. Thus, with $t_c = 50$ per cent, the net cost of capital might be doubled or halved. Consequently, the effect on capital employed could go either way.

Table 5-1 Financial policy and cost of capital (net of depreciation)

	True economic depreciation ($\phi = 0$, $\delta = \gamma$)	Free depreciation ($\phi = 1$)
Debt finance: interest deductible	r	$r(1-t_c)$
interest not deductible	$\dfrac{r}{1-t_c}$	r
Retained earnings	$\dfrac{r}{1-t_c}(1-\tau)$	$r(1-\tau)$

Implications of Inflation

In the analysis to this point we have not taken explicit account of inflation. We now assume that there is a constant (anticipated) rate of inflation ρ, so that all prices rise by a factor $(1+\rho)$ each period. Suppose that, as before, the firm increases its investment in period 1 by one unit, with an offsetting reduction of one unit of physical investment in the next. The reduction in investment *expenditure* in period 2 is now $(1+\rho)$, since capital goods have become more expensive; on the other hand, the cost of replacement investment has risen. The effect on the profitability condition for investment financed by borrowing, in the absence of taxation, is (King, 1977, Ch. 8)

$$p\,\partial F/\partial K \gtrless (1+r)-(1+\rho)+\gamma(1+\rho) \qquad (5\text{-}31)$$

The first-order condition is therefore

$$p\,\partial F/\partial K = r-\rho+\gamma(1+\rho) \qquad (5\text{-}32)$$

Inflation affects the investment in two ways: first, the relevant rate of interest is now the real rate $(r-\rho)$; second, the depreciation provision must be made at current, not historic, cost.

The effects of taxation depend on the treatment of interest payments and of depreciation. Typically (in the late 1970s), the tax system is not indexed with respect to borrowing, so that the nominal interest is tax-deductible; on the other hand, there has been considerable debate about changing the depreciation provisions to allow for the effects of inflation. (For discussion of inflation accounting and taxation, see, for example, Aaron, 1976, and Kay, 1977.) If the depreciation allowances allow full replacement cost $(\delta = \gamma(1+\rho))$, then an additional unit of investment in period 1, offset by a corresponding reduction in the next, increases profits if

$$\left[p\frac{\partial F}{\partial K} - \gamma(1+\rho)\right](1-t_c)-(r-\rho)+t_c i^* > 0 \qquad (5\text{-}33)$$

where i^* denotes the interest payments that can be set against tax. From this, the first-order condition is

$$p\frac{\partial F}{\partial K} = (r-\rho)+\gamma(1+\rho) + \frac{t_c}{1-t_c}(r-\rho-i^*) \qquad (5\text{-}33a)$$

If all interest is tax deductible $(i^* = r)$, then the right-hand side is reduced by taxation. In order to achieve neutrality, only *real* interest payments should be deductible (King, 1977, p. 242)—a factor often neglected in public debate.

> **Exercise 5-5** Suppose nominal interest is fully deductible; is there a depreciation formula that would ensure neutrality? (Consideration needs to be given to the difference between the written-down and actual capital stocks.)

Summing Up

In this section we have examined the impact of taxation on the effective cost of capital in different financial regimes. Where investment is financed at the *margin* (the marginal nature is critical) by bond finance, the provision of true economic depreciation means that the first-order conditions for investment are unaffected by taxation (the cost of capital is unchanged). In this sense the tax is neutral. This neutrality can also be achieved by free depreciation with no interest deductibility. Other situations may lead the cost of capital to rise or fall as a result of taxation.

One feature brought out by the analysis is the key role played by the detailed provisions of the tax law, with respect to such aspects as depreciation, interest deductibility and allowance for inflation. There is no such thing as *the* corporation tax, and its effects may differ substantially across countries, or from year to year, depending on these provisions. Moreover, its impact depends on the interaction with personal taxation, via the financing decision. These features have important implications for the empirical studies reviewed in Section 5-5. Before coming to this, however, we need to take a wider view of the determinants of investment.

5-4 A WIDER VIEW OF INVESTMENT

The model described so far has assumed a competitive firm, maximizing profits or stock market value, making decisions about the choice of capital–labour ratio on the basis of the current cost of capital. There is no room for market imperfections, for departures from profit/value maximization, for the irreversibility of investment, for expectations regarding future prices or tax rates. In this section we describe some of the ways in which the analysis can be developed. This treatment is brief, not least because progress in formulating more realistic investment models has to date been limited.

Market Imperfections

At one level the extension of the analysis to the case of a firm that acts imperfectly competitively in the product market is straightforward. If we assume that the firm acts as though it faces a downward-sloping demand curve, then the marginal value product of capital is simply replaced by the marginal *revenue* product. The considerations concerning the cost of capital apply as before. Thus, we can handle pure monopoly or large group monopolistic competition (discussed in greater detail in Lecture 7). Where however we seek to extend the model to oligopolistic interdependence, there is no simple extension that can be made. In the absence of any widely accepted theory of firm behaviour, it is impossible to make any definite predictions about the impact of taxation on investment. Thus it is possible that, in small-group imperfect competition, capacity may be an important strategic decision; there may be tacit collusion limiting capacity (it has the merit that any breach would be "visible" to rivals). Investment may be determined with a view to preventing entry (see, for example, Spence, 1977, and Dixit, 1979). This gives a different view of the investment process.

Risk, Imperfect Information and Imperfect Capital Markets

We have not explicitly discussed the role of risk and uncertainty. The analysis of the financial structure of the firm does not require that there be no uncertainty, and the Modigliani–Miller theorem is not dependent on this. The original demonstration (Modigliani and Miller, 1958) allowed for risk classes, and this has been extended to much more general conditions (Stiglitz, 1969a). What is however critical is that there be no bankruptcy.

The assumption of no bankruptcy, and the corollary that individuals can issue unlimited risk-free bonds at a specified rate of interest, is clearly unrealistic. It means, for example, that a person with zero assets can invest unlimited amounts in a firm that everyone else believes with certainty is going to yield zero profits. When we allow for bankruptcy, then bonds become risky assets, and the risk depends on the amount borrowed. The capital market becomes therefore inherently imperfect. If the receipts expected by the lender are less than those expected by the borrower, because of differential information or beliefs, and the discrepancy increases as the firm borrows more, this may lead—in the absence of taxation—to an interior optimal debt equity ratio (Stiglitz, 1972 and Feldstein, Green and Sheshinski, 1977).

These effects on financial policy have important implications for the determination of investment; and the financial and real decisions are now even more closely related than before. The cost of capital may depend on the scale of the firm. The level of investment may be determined not just by the cost of capital but also by the availability of finance. (This provides a natural link to the theories that regard investment as a function of corporate cash flow.) The corporate profits tax may affect investment, even if it is neutral with respect to the cost of capital. Moreover, there is quite possibly a differential impact: "old" firms, for which profits exceed desired investment, may be relatively little affected, but new firms with limited access to the capital market, and for which desired investment is constrained by cash flow, may have their investment reduced.

The existence of uncertainty raises in a serious way the question of the objectives pursued by the firm. Even in a world of certainty, shareholders may have different marginal tax rates and hence different preferred policies. When there are differing views about the future and attitudes to risk, the problem of securing unanimity is likely to be even more severe. The recent literature (e.g. Grossman and Stiglitz, 1977) has indeed shown that it is difficult to formulate a satisfactory model of firm behaviour where shareholders have divergent interests or beliefs. Except in rather special circumstances (see, for example, Ekern and Wilson, 1974), there is no unanimous agreement on the maximand of the firm, and conventional assumptions such as that of stock market value maximization do not apply. Divergent interests may in turn explain some of the "puzzles" of corporate behaviour, such as dividend policy.

Managerial Models of the Firm

The problem of specifying the objective of the firm has been discussed in more general terms in the extensive writing on managerial models of firm behaviour.

A simple illustration of this approach is provided by the sales maximization model of Baumol. He assumes that the manager running a large corporation has some latitude to pursue his own interests, and that his objective is maximizing the scale of the enterprise: "once his profits exceed some vaguely defined minimum level, he is prepared to sacrifice further increases in profits if he can thereby obtain larger revenue" (Baumol, 1958, p. 187). This is formalized as maximizing revenue subject to a minimum profit constraint. If revenue can always be increased by extra promotion outlay, then the constraint is binding at the firm's optimum, since otherwise the "surplus" profits could be spent on, say, advertising and hence could raise revenue. The effect of taxation then depends on the form of the profit constraint; and it is in this respect unfortunate that it is "vaguely defined". Either a gross or a net profit constraint could be postulated; there may also be constraints on dividends or other financial flows that make the timing of profits critical.

An alternative approach is that of Williamson (1964), where managers aim to maximize a utility function defined over staff expenditures (an indicator of power or status), managerial emoluments, and profit in excess of a minimum requirement. The trade-offs envisaged by Williamson may be seen, at least in part, as between consumption *within* the firm, e.g., via staff expenditures, and consumption *outside* the firm (salary). In this respect there is a parallel with the discussion of labour supply in Lecture 2. The implications for the desired level of capital depend again on the form of the profit constraint.

The notion of managerial discretion has been developed in a dynamic context by Marris (1964) and others. In the starkest form, these involve managers aiming to maximize their own utility, derived principally from the rate of growth achieved, subject to a take-over constraint. The latter requires that the stock market value does not fall below some specified fraction of the value of the real assets. To the extent that this allows latitude to the managers, they choose a higher level of investment than would maximize the stock market value (for a given initial scale). The effects of the profits tax in this model are discussed by Solow (1971).

In these models, uncertainty is not treated explicitly, but it is clear that a key role in explaining the existence of managerial discretion is played by the differential information available to shareholders and managers. Thus, in the simple model discussed in the previous Lecture, capitalists could not observe the effort put in by managers, and had to resort to an incentive scheme. (We discuss similar costs of supervision in the context of bureaucracies in Lecture 10.) We can in fact view the relationship between managers and shareholders as a problem of indirect control in the presence of imperfect information. The shareholders attempt to design an incentive structure that leads managers in pursuing their own interests to take account of the concerns of the shareholders. But because the indirect control mechanism is not perfect, there will not be a complete coincidence. At the same time, there is an alternative option open to shareholders—that of selling the shares, possibly to a take-over bidder. (For discussion of the consequences of take-overs, see Stiglitz, 1972, and Hart, 1977).

Costs of Adjustment

In the previous section it has been assumed that the capital stock could be freely adjusted, but it is more realistic to allow for constraints on the firm's flexibility. The opposite assumption that investment is totally irreversible may be too extreme in that second-hand markets for capital goods do exist, but it may be closer to reality than the assumption of complete reversibility.

It is equally possible that there are costs of adjusting capital upwards, and there has been a substantial literature (e.g., Eisner and Strotz, 1963, Lucas, 1967) on the optimal investment policy when there is a cost of investment function $C(I)$. Much of this has assumed that the function is increasing and strictly convex ($C' > 0$, $C'' > 0$ for $I \geqslant 0$). A variety of reasons have been given for an increasing marginal cost of investment ($C'' > 0$), including rising costs of purchase of new equipment and internal costs of adjusting to a larger scale. These are not fully convincing, since there are factors, such as indivisibilities, that work in the opposite direction;[10] and the case of a concave or linear function ($C'' \leqslant 0$) has been examined by Rothschild (1971). He shows that this leads to the concentration of a firm's response in a single period, in contrast to spreading its reaction over several periods (as with a convex function).

The cost of adjustment models focus attention on a key issue—the timing of investment and the role of expectations. What is derived from these models is not just an optimal level of capital but also the time path of adjustment. Thus, where the current prices are expected to continue to rule, a firm may choose a steady path of investment, approaching its goal gradually so as to reduce the costs of adjustment (where $C'' > 0$). On the

---

[10] There is also some ambiguity as to whether the costs relate to gross investment (as with costs of purchasing) or net investment (as with internal expansion).

other hand, if it expects the price of capital to fall (e.g., because of an investment tax credit), it may delay investment to take advantage of the more favourable tax treatment later—and we turn now to this aspect.

Expectations about Policy

Expectations about changing prices or tax policy are important even without the cost of adjustment assumption. Thus, the earlier analysis of Section 5-3 was based on firms having static expectations, and it needs to be modified where changes are anticipated. Suppose, for example, that there is free depreciation on a proportion ϕ of investment, true economic depreciation on the remainder, and that a fraction ζ of interest is tax-deductible. The difference is that the firm expects confidently that the extent of free depreciation will change to ϕ^* next period (all other tax parameters and prices remaining constant). The effect on profits is positive if (using the same perturbation argument as before) with bond finance

$$p\,\partial F/\partial K(1-t_c) > (1-\phi t_c)[1+r(1-\zeta t_c)]-t_c\gamma(1-\phi)$$
$$+\gamma(1-\phi^*t_c)-(1-\phi^*t_c) \quad (5\text{-}34)$$

The last term is the saving on one unit of physical investment in the next period and it, like the depreciation, costs $(1-\phi^*t_c)$ per unit. Re-arranging, the first-order condition is

$$p\frac{\partial F}{\partial K} = \frac{r(1-\zeta t_c)(1-\phi t_c)}{1-t_c} + \gamma + \frac{(1-\gamma)(\phi^*-\phi)t_c}{1-t_c} \quad (5\text{-}35)$$

The first conclusion that may be drawn is that, where tax parameters are expected to change, the neutrality results derived earlier no longer hold. Thus, the combination of free depreciation ($\phi = 1$) and no interest deductibility ($\zeta = 0$) does not ensure that the first-order condition is independent of t_c if firms expect ϕ to change ($\phi^* \neq \phi$). The expectation of a fall in the investment allowance reduces the cost of capital, and the effect may be quite significant. Suppose that the firm expects ϕ to fall from 50 to 40 per cent; then with $t_c = 50$ per cent, $\gamma = 0.15$, this is equivalent to a reduction in the cost of capital of 8.5 percentage points.

In general terms, the consequence of changes in tax policy that are expected to be short-lived is that, prior to the introduction of, say, a subsidy, investment will fall sharply; and shortly before its removal it will rise sharply, falling immediately after to below the level that would otherwise have obtained. There may therefore be significant effects of a temporary tax policy outside the period of operation (acting in the opposite direction to that intended). The anticipation of policies is particularly likely to be important where the passing of legislation is a drawn-out process. In the United States, congressional approval of tax changes may be very much delayed; for example, the Revenue Act 1962, which introduced a 7 per cent investment tax credit, took 18 months.

The government needs therefore to take account of the expectations of firms when considering the impact of tax policy. Moreover, expectations themselves may well be influenced by policy, a point emphasized by Lucas (1976). Suppose that we begin with the situation described above, where a fall in ϕ is expected. If we set $r = 16$ per cent, $\zeta = 1$, then the cost of capital is $(\frac{3}{4} \times 16 + 15 - 8\frac{1}{2})$ per cent $= 18\frac{1}{2}$ per cent. If the government does indeed cut ϕ to 40 per cent, then with static expectations ($\phi^* = \phi$) the cost of capital rises to $(\frac{4}{5} \times 16 + 15)$ per cent $= 27.8$ per cent. However, if this cut in ϕ is expected to be temporary, so $\phi^* = 0.5$, the rise is even more marked—to over 35 per cent. Taking account of induced changes in expectations may therefore be of considerable significance, which considerably complicates the interpretation of the effects of past policy (see Section 5-5).

Central to any treatment of expectations is some understanding of how they are formed. Empirically, there has been considerable experimentation with different expectation formation models for variables such as the rate of inflation. The success to date is rather limited, and there is every reason to expect the modelling of expectations regarding policy parameters to be even more complex. This clearly poses serious difficulties for the design of short-term policy—a problem that of course applies much more generally than just to the corporation tax.

5-5 EMPIRICAL INVESTIGATION OF TAXATION AND INVESTMENT

The empirical study of the effects of taxation on company behaviour has been one of the most active areas of applied research in public finance. There has, for example, been considerable work on the influence of the corporation tax on company financial policy. Has corporate dividend behaviour been influenced by fiscal legislation? (For references to this literature, see Brittain, 1966, Feldstein, 1970b, and King, 1977.) In this section we focus however on the real decisions of the firm, and particularly the impact of taxation on investment. This not only serves to illustrate the problems that arise, but is also of considerable intrinsic interest. On the other hand, one of the main conclusions of the earlier sections is that, in the presence of taxation, the financial and real decisions cannot be completely separated; indeed, one of the major problems with the empirical work concerns the specification of the true marginal cost of capital after tax.

The main evidence has been based on observed investment behaviour. This may relate to firms, where there have been a number of time series studies of investment by individual firms, to industries, or to economy-wide aggregates. There is indeed a long tradition in the econometric study of investment, dating from early attempts to estimate accelerator models, but we concentrate here on the work of Jorgenson and associates (originating with Jorgenson, 1963). These studies, although controversial, are particularly relevant since they provide an explicit treatment of the effects of taxation, and since they have been the reference point for much of the subsequent literature.

Econometric Studies of Investment Behaviour

The main feature of Jorgenson's approach is that the desired capital stock that enters the estimated equations is related directly to the theory of optimal firm behaviour, in the absence of uncertainty and costs of adjustment. The key element of the model is the cost of capital, c, which we have discussed in earlier sections. Thus, we have equations of the form

$$p\, \partial F/\partial K = ra_1(\mathbf{t}) + \gamma a_2(\mathbf{t}) \equiv c \tag{5-36}$$

where a_1, a_2 are functions of the tax rates ($\mathbf{t}$ being a vector representing different dimensions of the tax system). Referring back to Section 5-3, we can see, for example, that this would correspond to Eq. (5-29) if $a_2 = 1$ and $a_1 = (1-\tau)(1-\phi t_e)/(1-t_c)$. To this Jorgenson adds the important assumptions about the technology that the elasticity of substitution and the degree of returns to scale are equal to unity:

$$F(K,L) = AK^\alpha L^{1-\alpha} \tag{5-37}$$

It follows that (where F denotes output)

$$\partial F/\partial K = \alpha F/K$$

and hence, from (5-36), the desired capital stock is related to output by

$$K^* = \alpha pF/c \tag{5-38}$$

Having specified the optimal capital stock in this way, Jorgenson then arrives at the relationship to be estimated by taking account of the backlog of uncompleted projects and of replacement investment.

The model has been estimated using a variety of types of data in the United States. Hall and Jorgenson (1967), on whose study we focus, estimate equations for total investment in manufacturing and non-farm non-manufacturing, distinguishing between equipment and structures, using time series evidence for the period 1931–63 (excluding 1942–49).

The effect of tax policy works through c and hence K^*. From the estimated coefficients, Hall and Jorgenson (1967, 1971) calculate how effective tax changes have been in the United States. For example, they show that adoption of accelerated depreciation allowances following the 1954 legislation reduced the cost of capital by some 9 per cent and estimate that a substantial increase in investment was induced, attributing 17.5 per cent of net investment in manufacturing equipment over the period 1954–70 to this change in depreciation allowances. The cut in corporation tax from 52 to 48 per cent in 1964 is estimated to have *increased* the cost of capital by about 1 per cent (as a result of the depreciation provisions being in excess of true economic depreciation), and this caused a small reduction in investment (for a given level of output). The overall conclusion they reach is that "tax policy can be highly effective in changing the level and timing of investment expenditures" (Hall and Jorgenson, 1971, p. 59).

This empirical work has been the subject of considerable debate, and we can distinguish several lines of criticism. The first concerns the treatment of output. A number of authors (for example, Brechling, 1975) have taken issue with the fact that this is treated as exogenous in the estimation of the investment equation. In part this is a theoretical argument, based on the observation that output is a decision variable for the competitive firm. It is objected that Jorgenson's model is closer to the accelerator than to neoclassical theory, which yields factor demands as functions of the *prices* of factors and outputs. Jorgenson's reply to this is that the investment relationship should be viewed as giving investment *conditional* on output. This may be legitimate as an empirical procedure, with the relationship being just one structural equation in a set of simultaneous equations, and Jorgenson does state explicitly that the estimates show the impact of changes in policy holding constant the level of output (Hall and Jorgenson, 1969, p. 394). On the other hand, the interpretation of the results is then rather difficult, and one cannot draw straightforward conclusions about the effect of a change in tax policy.

The recognition that the investment relationship is part of a simultaneous system draws attention to the consequent econometric difficulties. The theoretical framework shows that the equation for desired capital must at the firm level be seen in conjunction with that for desired labour;[11] at an aggregate level, investment enters as an important determinant of output. The extent of the simultaneous equations bias introduced is hard to assess, and there are obstacles to the use of the most obvious methods to avoid this problem (see Hall, 1977, pp. 82–4).

A third set of objections relates to the treatment of lags. The theoretical formulation takes no account of lags in adjustment, and their incorporation into the estimating equation is essentially without theoretical justification. This is one of the reasons for the development of the theory of investment based on costs of adjustment which we have described briefly above (for discussion of attempts at its empirical implementation, see Brechling, 1975).

---

[11] It is perhaps puzzling that the Jorgenson model, which emphasizes factor substitution, does not include the cost of labour. This enters via the demand for labour equation—not estimated by Jorgenson. For estimates of joint factor demand equations, see Nadiri and Rosen (1969) and Coen and Hickman (1970).

Fourth, a number of authors have questioned Jorgenson's treatment of technology. For example, Eisner and Nadiri (1968) consider a more general production relationship not based on the Cobb–Douglas, which allows the elasticity of K^* with respect to output and p/c to differ from unity, and they argue that the elasticity with respect to p/c is significantly less than 1. This implies a smaller response to tax changes. Jorgenson has replied with a spirited defence of the Cobb–Douglas assumption (1972). A rather different development, which also allows the elasticities with respect to output and prices to differ, is that of models of limited *ex post* substitutability ("putty-clay") by Bischoff (1969, 1971) and others.

Treatment of Tax Policy

The final objections concern the treatment of tax policy. As we have seen, taxation, depreciation allowances, etc., affect the cost of capital (c) and hence the desired capital stock. It is a maintained hypothesis that a change in taxation has the same effect as a change in other variables that enter the cost of capital (e.g., the interest rate), but ideally we should test this hypothesis. There are in fact good reasons to expect taxation to have a different effect. It may for example take time for new tax measures to have an impact on business decision-making. Fisher refers to the case of the slow take-up by businessmen of the accelerated depreciation allowances made possible in 1954 (one of the examples taken above), and notes that attempts to use estimated investment equations "would have been dead wrong, because the effects of tax policy were not the same as the effects of differently inspired movements in the same variables of the same magnitude as theoretically would have been induced by the tax change" (Fisher, 1971, p. 246).[12]

The second objection to Jorgenson's treatment of tax policy is that it is assumed that firms have static expectations with respect to tax policy. Investment is assumed to be planned on the basis that current tax rates and depreciation provisions will rule forever. This is patently unrealistic. Investment tax credits may be expected to be temporary, or higher allowances may be expected in the future (as during the 1966 suspension of the investment tax credit in the United States). As we have seen, these may lead to anticipatory behaviour—investment may not correspond to the

---

[12] In the United Kingdom, Feldstein and Flemming (1971) have tested a more general version of the Jorgenson model, allowing separately for the different components of the cost of capital (and with an elasticity of substitution, σ, which may differ from unity):

$$K^* = Q[\alpha(r+\gamma)^{\beta_1}(1-t_c)^{-\beta_2}(1-DA)^{\beta_3}]^{\sigma}$$

where DA is the discounted value of depreciation allowances. They also allow for the availability of internal funds by introducing the dividend payout ratio, which in turn is influenced by the relative tax treatment of dividends and retained earnings. The results suggest that the different components of the cost of capital do have different effects.

long-run desired capital stock. The quantitative importance of these factors may be very substantial. It is therefore possible that the effective cost of capital has changed much more dramatically than assumed in Jorgenson's calculations, and that the response to a given percentage change is less than predicted. More generally, the effect of policy can be estimated only with an explicit treatment of the formation of expectations.

Third, there is the precise form in which the tax parameters are introduced. As we have seen, the cost of capital depends on the method of finance, and on the interaction between personal and corporate tax systems. Moreover, it is the cost of capital at the margin that is relevant, and not the average cost of capital. There are difficulties in implementing this empirically, and comparison of the formulae typically used in empirical work with those derived above shows that they coincide only under certain assumptions. Examination of this is left as an exercise to the reader.

> **Exercise 5-6** Under what conditions do the formulae employed by Hall and Jorgenson (e.g., 1967, Eq. 6, or 1971, Eq. 2.12) correspond to those derived in Section 5-3?

Summing Up

We have discussed the Jorgenson analysis of investment at some length because it is a pioneering attempt to base empirical work on an explicit theoretical framework. Moreover, it suggests that tax policy has a powerful impact. It seems however premature to accept this as definitely established. As we have seen, there are considerable difficulties in making the transition from the theoretical model to the empirical work, including the specification of the production function and of the lag structure, the incorporation of the tax variables, and the econometric problems. The assumption that firms have static expectations with respect to tax policy simplifies the analysis but may give a misleading impression where firms anticipate changes in tax rates and investment allowances. There are moreover criticisms that may be levelled against the theoretical framework itself—that it takes inadequate account of rigidities in the capital stock, of imperfect competition, of the process of firm decision-making and of behaviour under uncertainty. The empirical analysis of the effects of tax policy on investment has made substantial progress, but—as in other areas—improved ability to predict the effects of fiscal measures depends on improved understanding of key economic relationships.

5-6 CONCLUDING COMMENTS

We have seen in this Lecture that the effects of taxation on the level and timing of investment may be considerably more complex than is often portrayed (or assumed in econometric studies). The corporation tax itself can take on a variety of guises, depending critically on the provisions for interest deductibility and depreciation. Tax policy affects the capital structure of the firm and hence the marginal cost of capital. In this, the interaction with the personal tax system is particularly significant, depending on the relative tax rates on capital gains, interest and corporate profits.

Perhaps as important as the impact on the level of investment is that on its *pattern*, which we have not discussed. Tax provisions may affect decisions about the durability of capital goods. Different firms are likely to be differentially affected. Where the capital market is imperfect, and the availability of finance a constraint on investment, firms at different stages of development or with different risk characteristics may respond in a variety of ways not captured by the models we have discussed.

There are a number of ways in which the analysis needs to be extended to take account of these complexities. In the Lectures that follow, we shall, however, work with a simplified version of the effects of the corporation tax—this being the cost of moving to a general equilibrium framework.

READING

In emphasizing the financial structure of the firm, the Lecture goes outside the topics typically covered in textbooks on the theory of the firm. The treatment of the effect of taxation draws heavily on Stiglitz (1973, 1976a) and King (1974, 1977). A good survey of both theory and empirical evidence is given by Nickell (1978). The econometric analysis of investment is covered in the collection of readings by Helliwell (1976), whose introduction is most useful.

SIX

TAX INCIDENCE—SIMPLE COMPETITIVE EQUILIBRIUM MODEL

6-1 INTRODUCTION: TAX INCIDENCE

One of the most valuable insights that economic analysis has provided in public finance is that the person who effectively *pays* a tax is not necessarily the person upon whom the tax is levied. To determine the true *incidence* of a tax or a public project is one of the most difficult, and most important, tasks of public economics.

In principle, the analysis of the incidence of a tax is a straightforward matter. We calculate the general equilibrium of the economy before the change in taxation or expenditure, and we recalculate the equilibrium afterwards; the *changes* provide a description of the incidence of the tax. We can say whose income has gone up or down and by how much, and what prices have changed. In almost all situations, the real incomes of individuals other than those upon whom the tax is levied will change. Quite often, the change in real income of those upon whom the tax is levied is smaller than the magnitude of the tax. We say then that the tax has been *shifted* to others within the economy.

Since a calculation of what happens to every single individual in the economy is obviously too complicated, public policy analysis focuses on the incidence on different *groups* in the economy. The identification of these groups is, of course, a critical question. Among the distinctions that have played a major role in earlier discussions of incidence are the following.

1 Producers, consumers and suppliers of factors In the case of a tax on the production of a commodity, we can distinguish between the effect on the profits of the producer, on the incomes of those who supply factors or intermediate products, and on the consumers of the product. To the extent that the price of the product rises, we say that the tax has been shifted *forward* to consumers, since their real income is, other things equal, reduced. If the price of factors (intermediate goods) is reduced as a result of a decrease in demand, then we say that the tax is shifted *backwards*.

2 Functional distribution: labour and capital The effect of tax may be broken down into that on the main factors of production. Thus, we may examine the effect on the relative demands for capital and labour (the two factors considered here) and, taking account of the supply responses, on the wage and rate of return (rental price) to capital.

3 Personal distribution The effect of taxes or government expenditure may be investigated with respect to the position of individuals at different points on the income scale. Does the public provision of higher education mainly benefit middle- and upper-income groups? What is the incidence of free food stamps on different income groups?

4 Regional incidence A tax or expenditure programme may have different effects in different regions. For example, agricultural price support policies may have a beneficial effect on the producing regions, a negative effect on consuming regions. The same question may be asked on a wider scale concerning *international* incidence. Which countries benefit or lose if the United States changes its tax treatment of foreign investment?

5 Intergenerational incidence Taxes or spending may have a different impact on different generations. A particular expenditure programme may impose costs on the current generation but provide benefits to those alive in the twenty-first century. Conversely, it is often suggested that resort to debt financing may allow governments to shift the burden on to future generations.

In this and the next two Lectures we concentrate primarily on the incidence on factors. This is not only intrinsically of interest but also provides an important ingredient for the analysis of the personal distribution in Lecture 9. We do however consider some of the other dimensions of incidence; for example, in Lecture 8 we refer to the impact on different generations.

The study of the incidence of taxation is complicated by the fact that usually we cannot or do not disturb the economy in only one way. If we increase one tax, we must typically decrease another tax, or increase public expenditure or adjust the government debt policy. The incidence thus depends on the "package" of policies. In the analysis we try to focus attention on the tax or expenditure in question by "neutralizing" the other effects. Thus, in examining the corporate profits tax, we assume that the proceeds of the tax are redistributed back to individuals. If we were to analyse incidence within a macroeconomic model with unemployment, we might consider a set of policies that kept national income at the same level. Later, we analyse tax incidence within a growth model where we take policies that leave the balanced growth path (the aggregate capital labour ratio) unchanged. In all cases, it is crucial to be explicit as to what exactly is being compared.

Tax Incidence: Partial Equilibrium

Much of the public finance literature of the first 60 years of this century was based on partial equilibrium analysis, drawing more on Marshall than on the classical economists, whose treatment of tax incidence was firmly rooted in a general equilibrium view of the world. To illustrate the partial equilibrium approach, and its limitations, we take a simple example.

Suppose that we have a crop, say grapes, produced on land that cannot be employed for any other purpose and using labour, denoted by L, that is in perfectly elastic supply at a wage w. If $F(L)$ is the production function (where $F' > 0$, $F'' < 0$), then in competitive equilibrium

$$pF' = w \qquad (6\text{-}1)$$

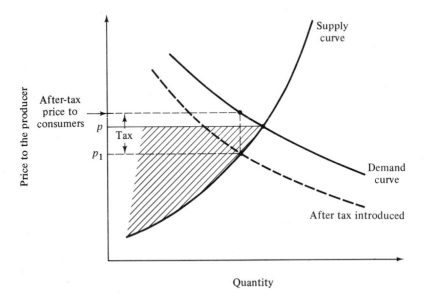

Figure 6-1 Partial equilibrium analysis of taxation.

where p is the price of output. This generates the supply curve (inverting the production function to obtain L as a function of F) shown in Fig. 6-1, and there is a demand curve of the usual shape. The intersection gives the market equilibrium. It is easy to show that the shaded area, between the supply curve and the market price, represents the rents received by the owners of the land.

Now, if a tax is imposed on the consumption of grapes, the new equilibrium is given by the producer price p_1. Notice that land rents are decreased: some of the tax is borne by landowners. Moreover, the after-tax price has risen: some of the tax is borne by consumers. Since the workers have the option of working for a wage w elsewhere, there is no reduction in the wage. The tax is therefore borne by the landowners and the consumers, and the division depends on the elasticities of demand and supply (the latter depending in turn on the nature of the production function). If, for instance, grapes are produced by land alone, so that the supply is completely inelastic, the entire cost of the tax is borne by landowners. There is the same outcome if there exists a perfect substitute to grapes (not produced using land) so that the demand curve is horizontal.

This analysis is perfectly valid with the assumptions made, and it provides considerable insight. The assumptions do however rule out some of the important effects. Thus, the factor supplies are taken to be either totally elastic or totally inelastic. These extreme assumptions may be reasonable when considering a tax on an activity that is "small" in relation to the economy as a whole, but they are clearly inappropriate for many taxes. In general, the response of the taxed sector affects the return to the different factors, and the equilibrating adjustments in, say, the wage will have second-round effects in all sectors of the economy. We have therefore to "go behind" the partial equilibrium supply curve to the underlying factor demands and supplies.

Similarly, on the demand side the shift away from grapes has an effect on other sectors, and this in turn induces changes in factor demands. The reduced demand for labour in the grape industry may be offset by an increased demand resulting from the switch of consumer expenditure from grapes to chocolate. Indeed, if chocolate is more labour-intensive, the overall demand for labour may rise. Finally, we have to allow for the interaction of supply and demand elements; the changes in factor incomes may lead to a shift in the pattern of demand. Thus, the demand for grapes may be a function of the incomes of landowners and workers—which is not allowed for explicitly in the partial equilibrium construction.

These considerations led to increasing dissatisfaction with the partial equilibrium treatment. The single most important step forward in applying a general equilibrium approach to public finance questions came with Harberger's adaptation of the two-sector competitive equilibrium model in his analysis of the incidence of corporation tax (1962). This model, which provides the focus for this Lecture, is described in detail in the next section; first we provide an intuitive account of the main features.

General Equilibrium Analysis of Corporation Tax: Introduction

In the previous Lecture, we investigated the effect of the corporate profits tax on the choice of factor intensity. Much of the analysis turned on whether the tax raised the cost of capital to the firm, and we saw that this depended on, among other things, the tax deductibility of interest payments and the depreciation provisions. Thus, if we write the cost of capital to the firm as rT, where T is a function of t_c, it is conceivable that $T(t_c) < 1$. In what follows we assume that $T(t_c) > 1$ for $t_c > 0$, where $T - 1$ represents the "effective" proportionate increase in the cost of capital,[1] but the opposite case can be seen by appropriately reversing the conclusions. We assume throughout that there is true economic depreciation, and output is expressed net of depreciation.

The effect of the rise in the cost of capital from r to rT is for the firm to adopt a less capital-intensive technique at any level of output. If we assume constant returns to scale, as we do in this Lecture, then the supply curve is horizontal and is shifted up by the tax. The extent of the upward shift depends on the significance of capital costs in the total; obviously if no capital is employed, then at the margin there is no effect.

At this point we have to consider the relation of the taxed sector to the rest of the economy. The feature emphasized by Harberger is that the tax falls only on the corporate sector. There is a substantial part of the economy (e.g., agriculture, supply of rental housing, professions) where most activity is unincorporated. The effect of the rise in price in the corporate sector is to switch demand towards the non-corporate outputs.

In the factor market we have therefore two effects. The first is the reduction in the demand for capital and increase in demand for labour, per unit of output in the corporate sector. The second is the change in demands for factors resulting from the switch of output from the corporate to the non-corporate sector. The second of these effects may either reduce further the demand for capital or work in an offsetting direction (if the non-corporate sector is more capital-intensive). The resulting changes in factor demands are assumed to be equilibrated by variations in the factor prices.

The change in factor prices, r and w, leads to changes in factor intensities in both sectors, and induces changes in factor supplies. It may also lead to variation in the pattern of demand as a result of differential income effects. Thus, if those receiving capital income have a higher propensity to consume the product of the corporate sector, a reduction in r

---

[1] The reader may like to relate T to the parameters of the tax system, as for example in Eqs (5-28) and (5-29) in the previous Lecture.

causes a further shift in demand away from that sector. If a new equilibrium is established (the dynamic process of adjustment is clearly crucial), then the resulting r and w provide a guide to the changes in money incomes as a result of the tax. (A full welfare analysis must take account of changes in factors supplied and of changes in relative product prices.)

The primary purpose of this Lecture is to make precise the stages of the process described above and to derive explicit conditions for the factor prices to rise or fall.

6-2 STATIC TWO-SECTOR MODEL

The model employed is that widely applied in international trade theory (see Caves and Jones, 1973) and in the two-sector growth literature (Uzawa, 1961; Solow, 1961). We concentrate in this Lecture on the static, or "momentary", equilibrium with fixed capital and labour. The latter assumption means that we are abstracting from the variation in factor supplies that have been the particular concern of earlier Lectures (particularly Lectures 2 and 3). The general equilibrium effect of variable factor supply is examined in following Lectures. The present model assumes however that factors are mobile between sectors. In this sense it is neither a short-run nor a long-run model; and the assumptions are probably better seen as a useful analytical device, separating the different issues, than as corresponding to any actual time period. (The consequences of alternative assumptions about factor mobility are discussed in Section 6-4.)

Basic Model

The essential features may be summarized as follows. There are two perfectly competitive industries which produce two goods in quantities X and Y under conditions of constant returns to scale. They use two factors of production, capital and labour, which are fixed in supply, at K_0 and L_0 respectively, fully mobile between sectors, and fully employed.[2] The prices of the two goods are denoted by p_X and p_Y, the wage rate by w, and the rate of return (rental price of capital) by r. In the version described in this section there are no taxes.

The production side of the economy is best approached via the cost function (for a brief outline of the properties of this function, see the Note at the end of the Lecture). The cost functions may be written, since there are

---

[2] We are not therefore considering the possibility of an equilibrium where one factor is in excess supply even at a zero price. We also assume both goods are produced in strictly positive quantities.

constant returns, as

$$C_X = c_X(r, w)X$$
$$C_Y = c_Y(r, w)Y \tag{6-2}$$

so that c_i is both average and marginal cost in sector i. The partial derivatives with respect to r are written as c_{KX}, c_{KY}, and those with respect to w as c_{LX}, c_{LY}. Since the factor demands are obtained by differentiating with respect to the factor prices (see Note), the demand for factors in sector L_i, K_i are

$$L_X = c_{LX} X, \quad L_Y = c_{LY} Y$$
$$K_X = c_{KX} X, \quad K_Y = c_{KY} Y \tag{6-3}$$

The full employment condition may therefore be written

$$c_{LX} X + c_{LY} Y = L_0$$
$$c_{KX} X + c_{KY} Y = K_0 \tag{6-4}$$

The c_{ij} may be seen as input coefficients per unit of output, but it should be noted that they depend on r and w—see below.

The assumption of competition means that the prices are equal to marginal cost:

$$p_X = c_X(r, w) \tag{6-5a}$$
$$p_Y = c_Y(r, w) \tag{6-5b}$$

On the demand side it is assumed that aggregate demands are generated by the maximization of a single utility function subject to an aggregate budget constraint. The utility function is assumed to be continuous, strictly quasi-concave and locally non-satiated; the expenditure function is therefore homogeneous of degree one, concave and continuously differentiable in positive prices. At certain points we assume that the utility function is homothetic, which means that the ratio of the demands is independent of income (i.e., income elasticities are unity). In the general case we write the (uncompensated) demand functions as

$$X = X(p_X, p_Y, M) \quad \text{and} \quad Y = Y(p_X, p_Y, M) \tag{6-6}$$

where M denotes income $(wL_0 + rK_0)$ for the economy as a whole. The compensated demand functions are given by (using lower-case letters for the compensated demands):

$$x = \frac{\partial e(p_X, p_Y, U)}{\partial p_X}$$

$$y = \frac{\partial e(p_X, p_Y, U)}{\partial p_Y} \tag{6-6a}$$

Taking account of the fact that c_{ij} are functions of w and r, we have in

Eqs (6-4), (6-5) and (6-6) a full description of the general equilibrium system. There are six unknowns (X, Y, p_X, p_Y, r and w) and six equations. By Walras' law, one of the equations is redundant,[3] but it is clear that we can solve the equations only for relative prices. The cost function is homogeneous of degree one in factor prices, and the factor demands and commodity demands are homogeneous of degree zero. We can therefore take one of the goods or factors as a *numeraire*.

Three basic questions concerning general equilibrium are the *existence* of a solution, whether it is *unique*, and whether it is *stable* under a specified process of adjustment. In the present case, existence of an equilibrium follows from the standard theorems (for example, see Arrow and Hahn, 1971, for a statement of the theorems and the conditions). Uniqueness is a consequence of the assumption that demands are generated by maximizing a common utility function (and hence satisfy the Weak Axiom of Revealed Preference). This assumption is, as we have noted, restrictive, and with quite realistic alternatives uniqueness is no longer guaranteed. An explicit example of non-uniqueness in a model with two classes of consumer is given in Section 6-5. Finally, the stability of equilibrium depends on the adjustment process. In Section 6-4 we examine a "Marshallian" process, where factors move between sectors in response to differences in returns, and give conditions for local stability.

Perturbations of the Economy

We are particularly interested in the response of the economy to exogenous variations in the parameters (e.g., tax rates). One could approach this by totally differentiating the general equilibrium system and solving for the derivatives. Such a mechanical approach would however provide little insight. Instead we follow the approach, first set out by Jones (1965), of considering the different elements of the process, characterized by the "equations of change". Thus, we relate changes in relative demands to changes in the ratio of product prices (Eq. (6-9)). On the supply side, we relate changes in quantities to changes in relative factor prices (w/r) in Eq. (6-16), and relate changes in relative product prices to changes in the factor price ratio (Eq. (6-11)). These latter two relationships yield a general equilibrium "supply curve".

For this purpose, we introduce the notation $\hat{X}$ to denote the proportionate change dX/X. On the demand side, total differentiation of

---

[3] The consumer budget constraint requires that

$$p_X X + p_Y Y = wL_0 + rK_0$$
$$= (wc_{LX} + rc_{KX})X + (wc_{LY} + rc_{KY})Y$$

from (6-4). Using the fact that c_X is homogeneous of degree one, the right-hand side is $c_X X + c_Y Y$. It follows that (6-5a) implies (6-5b), i.e., the latter is redundant.

the compensated demand functions yields

$$\hat{X} = \hat{x} = \varepsilon_{XX}\hat{p}_X + \varepsilon_{XY}\hat{p}_Y + \eta_X \frac{dU}{M} e_u$$

$$\hat{Y} = \hat{y} = \varepsilon_{YX}\hat{p}_X + \varepsilon_{YY}\hat{p}_Y + \eta_Y \frac{dU}{M} e_u \qquad (6\text{-}7)$$

where we have used the properties of the expenditure function (see Note to Lecture 2) and have used ε_{ij} to denote the compensated elasticity and η_i the income elasticity. It follows that

$$\eta_Y \hat{X} - \eta_X \hat{Y} = (\eta_Y \varepsilon_{XX} - \eta_X \varepsilon_{YX})\hat{p}_X - (\eta_X \varepsilon_{YY} - \eta_Y \varepsilon_{XY})\hat{p}_Y \qquad (6\text{-}8)$$

Making use of the property that $\varepsilon_{ij} = -\varepsilon_{ii}$,[4] this reduces to

$$= (\eta_Y \varepsilon_{XX} + \eta_X \varepsilon_{YY})(\hat{p}_X - \hat{p}_Y)$$

$$\equiv -\sigma_D(\hat{p}_X - \hat{p}_Y) \qquad (6\text{-}9)$$

We assume that $\sigma_D > 0$, a sufficient condition for which is that neither good be inferior, which at this level of aggregation seems not an unreasonable assumption. The special case of homotheticity (i.e. $\eta_X = \eta_Y = 1$) gives $\sigma_D = -(\varepsilon_{XX} + \varepsilon_{YY})$, which is the aggregate elasticity of substitution in demands.

Turning to the supply side, differentiation of the price equations gives

$$\hat{p}_X = \frac{wc_{LX}}{c_X}\hat{w} + \frac{rc_{KX}}{c_X}\hat{r} \qquad (6\text{-}10a)$$

$$\hat{p}_Y = \frac{wc_{LY}}{c_Y}\hat{w} + \frac{rc_{KY}}{c_Y}\hat{r} \qquad (6\text{-}10b)$$

We now use the notation:

$$\theta_{Li} = \frac{wc_{Li}}{c_i} \quad \text{factor share of labour in industry } i$$

$$\theta_{Ki} = \frac{rc_{Ki}}{c_i} \quad \text{factor share of capital in industry } i$$

(so $\theta_{Li} + \theta_{Ki} = 1$). The change in relative prices is therefore

$$\hat{p}_X - \hat{p}_Y = (\theta_{LX} - \theta_{LY})\hat{w} - (\theta_{KY} - \theta_{KX})\hat{r}$$

$$= \theta^*(\hat{w} - \hat{r}) \qquad (6\text{-}11)$$

---

[4] This follows from the fact that the compensated demands are zero degree homogeneous in prices:

$$p_X e_{XX} + p_Y e_{XY} = 0$$

where[5]

$$\theta^* \equiv \theta_{LX} - \theta_{LY} = \theta_{KY} - \theta_{KX} \tag{6-12}$$

θ^* is a measure of factor intensity, based on shares in value added. As one would expect, if X is relatively labour-intensive ($\theta_{LX} > \theta_{LY}$) then a rise in w/r causes a rise in its relative price (p_X/p_Y).

The changes in factor intensities may be seen from the fact that

$$\hat{c}_{LX} = \frac{wc_{LLX}}{c_{LX}}\hat{w} + \frac{rc_{LKX}}{c_{LX}}\hat{r} \tag{6-13}$$

From the fact that c_{LX} is homogeneous of degree zero in factor prices,

$$wc_{LLX} + rc_{LKX} = 0 \quad \text{and} \quad wc_{KLX} + rc_{KKX} = 0$$

Hence

$$\hat{c}_{LX} = -\left(\frac{rc_{KX}}{c_X}\right)\left(\frac{-wc_{LLX}c_X}{rc_{LX}c_{KX}}\right)(\hat{w} - \hat{r})$$

$$\equiv -\theta_{KX}\sigma_X(\hat{w} - \hat{r}) \tag{6-14a}$$

where σ_X is the elasticity of substitution.[6] Corresponding expressions may be obtained:

$$\hat{c}_{LY} = -\theta_{KY}\sigma_Y(\hat{w} - \hat{r}) \tag{6-14b}$$

$$\hat{c}_{KX} = \theta_{LX}\sigma_X(\hat{w} - \hat{r}) \tag{6-14c}$$

$$\hat{c}_{KY} = \theta_{LY}\sigma_Y(\hat{w} - \hat{r}) \tag{6-14d}$$

From the fact that factor supplies are fixed, differentiating (6-4) gives for labour

$$c_{LX}X(\hat{c}_{LX} + \hat{X}) + c_{LY}Y(\hat{c}_{LY} + \hat{Y}) = 0$$

Denoting the share of the labour force in X and Y by λ_{LX} and λ_{LY}, respectively (so $\lambda_{LX} = c_{LX}X/L_0$), and using (6-14), we derive

$$\lambda_{LX}\hat{X} + \lambda_{LY}\hat{Y} = (\hat{w} - \hat{r})(\lambda_{LX}\theta_{KX}\sigma_X + \lambda_{LY}\theta_{KY}\sigma_Y) \tag{6-15a}$$

[5] θ^* is the determinant

$$\begin{vmatrix} \theta_{LX} & \theta_{KX} \\ \theta_{LY} & \theta_{KY} \end{vmatrix}$$

This can be expanded as

$$\theta_{LX}(1 - \theta_{LY}) - \theta_{LY}(1 - \theta_{LX}) = \theta_{LX} - \theta_{LY}$$

(using the adding up property of θ_{ij}). The other equivalence follows similarly.

[6] To see the relationship between σ_X and the more usual definition via the production function, we may note that the latter is

$$-\frac{d\log(K/L)}{d\log(r/w)} = \frac{d\log K}{d\log(w/r)} - \frac{d\log L}{d\log(w/r)}$$

Substituting from (6-14a) and (6-14c), the right-hand side is $\sigma_X(\theta_{LX} + \theta_{KX}) = \sigma_X$.

The corresponding equation for the capital market is

$$\lambda_{KX}\hat{X} + \lambda_{KY}\hat{Y} = -(\hat{w}-\hat{r})(\lambda_{KX}\theta_{LX}\sigma_X + \lambda_{KY}\theta_{LY}\sigma_Y) \qquad (6\text{-}15\text{b})$$

Subtracting (6-15b) from (6-15a), we obtain

$$\lambda^*(\hat{X}-\hat{Y}) = (\hat{w}-\hat{r})[\sigma_X(\theta_{KX}\lambda_{LX}+\theta_{LX}\lambda_{KX})+\sigma_Y(\theta_{KY}\lambda_{LY}+\theta_{LY}\lambda_{KY})]$$
$$\equiv (\hat{w}-\hat{r})(a_X\sigma_X + a_Y\sigma_Y) \qquad (6\text{-}16)$$

where[7]

$$\lambda^* \equiv \lambda_{LX} - \lambda_{KX} = \lambda_{KY} - \lambda_{LY} \qquad (6\text{-}12\text{a})$$

The term λ^* is again a reflection of relative factor intensities, defined in terms of physical inputs rather than factor shares. As we would expect, if X is relatively labour-intensive ($\lambda^* > 0$), then a rise in the output of X relative to Y is associated with a rise in the wage relative to the rate of profit.

Geometric Illustration

In the case where demands are homothetic ($\eta_X = \eta_Y = 1$), the three equations (6-9), (6-11) and (6-16) may be solved for the effect of a (as yet unspecified) perturbation on the relative outputs (X/Y), relative product prices (p_X/p_Y) and factor price ratio (r/w). The solution may be illustrated in a four-quadrant diagram, as in Fig. 6-2.[8] The top right-hand quadrant shows the demand relationship. From (6-9), X/Y falls as p_X/p_Y rises, with the slope depending on the magnitude of the compensated own price elasticities. The top left-hand quadrant relates (X/Y) to (w/r), using Eq. (6-16). The slope here depends on the sign of λ^*. In Fig. 6-2 we have assumed $\lambda^* > 0$, i.e., the X sector is relatively labour-intensive. The curve therefore has (X/Y) rising with (w/r), with a slope that is greater the larger are the elasticities of substitution. The bottom right quadrant relates (p_X/p_Y) to (w/r), using Eq. (6-11). This depends on θ^*. We may, however, show that $\lambda^* \geqslant 0$ implies $\theta^* \geqslant 0$ (in the absence of taxes or other distortions), and vice-versa.[9] This result, which may cease to hold where there are distor-

---

[7] λ^* is the determinant

$$\begin{vmatrix} \lambda_{LX} & \lambda_{LY} \\ \lambda_{KX} & \lambda_{KY} \end{vmatrix}$$

It may be expanded as

$$\lambda_{LX}(1-\lambda_{KX}) - \lambda_{KX}(1-\lambda_{LX}) = \lambda_{LX} - \lambda_{KX}$$

using the condition that $\lambda_{iX} + \lambda_{iY} = 1$.

[8] A four-quadrant diagram is also employed by McLure (1974), but it should be noted that he assumes that labour is immobile between sectors.

[9] $\theta^* = \theta_{LX}\theta_{KY} - \theta_{LY}\theta_{KX}$ (see earlier footnote), so $\theta^* \geqslant 0$ implies $c_{LX}c_{KY} \geqslant c_{LY}c_{KX}$, which implies $\lambda_{LX}\lambda_{KY} \geqslant \lambda_{LY}\lambda_{KX}$ or $\lambda^* \geqslant 0$ and vice versa.

tions and/or taxes, means that the two measures of labour intensity—in terms of values and physical quantities—coincide.

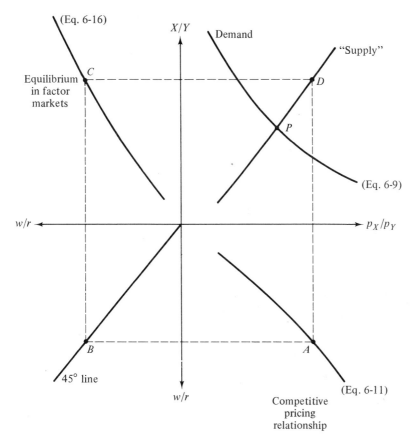

Figure 6-2 Geometric illustration of general equilibrium (X-sector labour-intensive).

Combining the pricing and supply relationships, we can construct a "supply curve" in the top right quadrant. This involves mapping from (p_X/p_Y) in the bottom right quadrant to (w/r) in the top left, via the 45° line, and hence to (X/Y). (See the sequence labelled $ABCD$ in Fig. 6-2.) The slope of this supply curve depends on the elasticities of substitution and the factor intensities. There is, as we have seen, a unique intersection at P.

By reducing the analysis to Fig. 6-2, we may appear to have gone back to the simple supply and demand framework. However, the analysis has brought out clearly the various factors lying "behind" the supply curve, and these are useful when we examine the comparative statics of the model. This is illustrated by the case of the corporation tax examined by Harberger and to which we turn in the next section.

> **Exercise 6-1** Draw the diagram corresponding to Fig. 6-2 with the assumption $\lambda^* < 0$. Does the "supply" curve have the same slope as in Fig. 6-2?

Elaboration of the Model

The version of the model illustrated in Fig. 6-2 may be seen as a basic formulation which is elaborated as the analysis proceeds in this and the next two Lectures. It may however be useful to the reader to summarize at this stage the main ways in which the assumptions are relaxed.

Assumptions about demand The geometric version and the analysis of Section 6-3 assume that demands are generated by a single homothetic utility function. In Section 6-4 we relax the assumption of homothetic demands; in Section 6-5 we allow for two classes of consumer with different tastes and endowments of labour and capital.

Assumptions about factor mobility The assumption of free factor mobility between sectors is relaxed in Section 6-4, where we allow for one factor being immobile and for a dynamic adjustment process in the factor market.

Assumption of full employment In this Lecture full employment is assumed, but in Section 7-5 below we examine the way in which unemployment can be taken into account and the incidence of taxation where markets do not clear.

Assumption of fixed factor supplies Throughout this Lecture, it is assumed that there is no addition to capital or change in total labour supply. In Lecture 8 we consider the long-run development of the economy where there is accumulation of capital. (Variation in labour supply can readily be introduced—and this extension is left to the reader.)

Assumption of perfect competition In Section 7-2 of the next Lecture we examine the consequences of market imperfections and pure monopoly; in Section 7-3 we present an explicit model of monopolistic competition.

The reader who finds the assumptions of the present model unpalatable should therefore see it as a foundation for later—more realistic—variations.

6-3 INCIDENCE OF CORPORATION TAX

In this section we use the model to examine the effect of a corporate profits tax, which is assumed to raise the cost of capital from r to rT in the corporate sector (taken to be X). The analysis is presented in a somewhat different way from that of Harberger (1962), but we retain his simplifying assumptions that (1) the corporation tax is introduced at an infinitesimal level into a world with no other taxes, (2) the proceeds are returned to consumers as a lump-sum subsidy, and (3) the demands are homothetic. These are clearly unrealistic, but allow us to explore some of the implications in a simple way.

The likely general equilibrium effects of the corporate tax have been sketched in Section 6-1 and are shown in more detail in Fig. 6-3. There are basically two effects (this distinction was originally made by Mieszkowski, 1967). The first is the *factor substitution effect*, which depends on the scope for substituting labour for capital in the taxed sector. If $\sigma_X > 0$, this tends

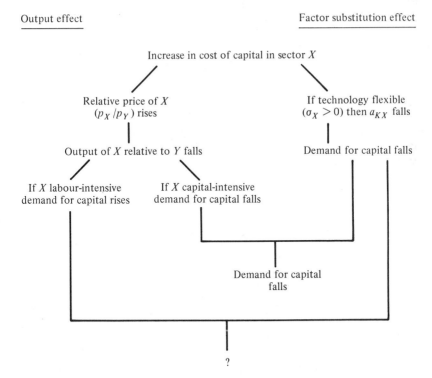

Figure 6-3 Effect of corporation tax on the demand for capital.

to reduce the overall demand for capital. If $\sigma_X = 0$, the full impact is via the second, *output*, effect. To this extent the tax is like a selective excise tax on the product X, and the pattern of demand shifts towards Y. The consequences for factor demands depend on the relative factor intensities. If X is capital-intensive, then a shift away reduces the demand for capital and reinforces the factor substitution effect. If X is labour-intensive, then it works the other way; and the net effect depends on the relative strength of the two effects. If, for example, $\sigma_X = 0$, then the demand for capital rises where X is labour-intensive.

Algebraic Treatment

In order to make this more precise, let us go back to the model of the previous section and change the cost of capital in sector X from r to rT_{KX}. We confine attention to an infinitesimal tax, so that all differentials are evaluated at $T_{KX} = 1$. The assumptions made about the use of revenue mean that the demand side is unaffected, the income effect being cancelled out by the lump-sum return of revenue when evaluated at $T_{KX} = 1$. With the assumption of homotheticity,

$$\hat{X} - \hat{Y} = -\sigma_D(\hat{p}_X - \hat{p}_Y) \tag{6-9'}$$

On the supply side,

$$\hat{c}_{LX} = -\theta_{KX}\sigma_X(\hat{w} - \hat{r}) + \theta_{KX}\sigma_X \hat{T}_{KX} \tag{6-14a'}$$

$$\hat{c}_{KX} = \theta_{LX}\sigma_X(\hat{w} - \hat{r}) - \theta_{LX}\sigma_X \hat{T}_{KX} \tag{6-14c'}$$

(the conditions for sector Y are unchanged). As a consequence, we have an additional term:

$$-\lambda_{LX}\theta_{KX}\sigma_X \hat{T}_{KX}$$

on the right-hand side of (6-15a), and a term

$$+\lambda_{KX}\theta_{LX}\sigma_X \hat{T}_{KX}$$

on the right-hand side of (6-15b). The derived equation (6-16) is modified therefore to

$$\lambda^*(\hat{X} - \hat{Y}) = (\hat{w} - \hat{r})(a_X\sigma_X + a_Y\sigma_Y) - a_X\sigma_X \hat{T}_{KX} \tag{6-16'}$$

Finally, the price equation becomes

$$\hat{p}_X - \hat{p}_Y = \theta^*(\hat{w} - \hat{r}) + \theta_{KX} \hat{T}_{KX} \tag{6-11'}$$

This shows that the relative price of the corporate sector rises, for constant w/r, to an extent that depends on the share of capital in value added.

In this model, people have identical demand curves, and incidence can be measured by the factor price ratio (w/r). If we combine (6-9') and (6-11'),

$$\hat{X} - \hat{Y} = -\sigma_D\theta^*(\hat{w} - \hat{r}) - \sigma_D\theta_{KX} \hat{T}_{KX}$$

Hence, from (6-16')

$$(\hat{w}-\hat{r})(\sigma_D\theta^*\lambda^* + a_X\sigma_X + a_Y\sigma_Y) = a_X\sigma_X\hat{T}_{KX} - \sigma_D\lambda^*\theta_{KX}\hat{T}_{KX} \quad (6\text{-}17)$$

The coefficient of $(\hat{w}-\hat{r})$, denoted by D, is positive, since a_i, $\sigma_i \geq 0$ and we have seen that θ^* and λ^* have the same sign. D is referred to as "the aggregate elasticity of substitution" by Jones (1965); for the interpretation in terms of the relationship between aggregate factor demands and factor prices, see the later analysis. It may be noted that $D > 0$ is the condition for the demand curve in Fig. 6-2 to have a steeper downward slope than the "supply" curve (in fact $\lambda^*\theta^* > 0$ means that the supply curve cannot slope downwards).

The right-hand side of Eq. (6-17) consists, as the intuitive argument suggested, of two terms. The first is non-negative and is the factor substitution term (note that it depends on σ_X); the second is the output effect, depending on the elasticity of demand (σ_D) and the factor intensity condition $(\lambda^* \gtrless 0)$. We can draw at once certain conclusions about the effect of the corporation tax on the relative return to the two factors:

1. a sufficient condition for the net rate of profit on capital to fall relative to wages is that the corporate sector be capital-intensive $(\lambda^* < 0)$;
2. it is possible that the net rate of profit rises relative to wages, and a sufficient set of conditions for this to happen is that the corporate sector be labour-intensive $(\lambda^* > 0)$ and have fixed coefficients of production $(\sigma_X = 0)$;
3. where the corporate sector is labour-intensive it is, other things equal, more likely that the profit rate rises relative to wages (a) the smaller the elasticity of substitution in the corporate sector, (b) the larger the elasticity of demand (σ_D), and (c) the greater the difference in factor intensities.

Geometric Treatment

Graphically, the qualitative results may be seen from the four-quadrant diagram. Figure 6-4a shows the case where the corporate sector is relatively labour-intensive (as in Fig. 6-2); Fig. 6-4b relates to the case where $\lambda^* < 0$.

The effect of the tax may be seen from Eq. (6-11') to shift the curve in the bottom right quadrant out to the right (p_X/p_Y rises for given w/r). In the top left quadrant, the curve shifts outward to the left (w/r rises for given X/Y). The implications depend on λ^*, θ^*. Where these are positive, the supply curve definitely moves down, and the relative price of the corporate sector output is increased by the tax. The balance of demand (X/Y) shifts in the direction of the non-corporate sector. On the other hand, the effect on w/r could go either way, and it is possible—as shown in Fig. 6-4a—that w/r falls. Where $\lambda^*, \theta^* < 0$, it is possible that the supply curve shifts up, causing the relative price of the corporate sector output to fall, and hence X/Y to rise (as shown in Fig. 6-4b), but w/r is definitely increased in this case.

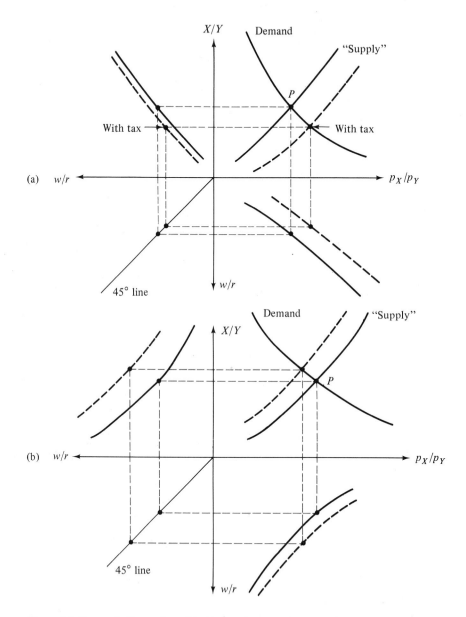

Figure 6-4 Geometric illustration of incidence of corporation tax: (a) λ^*, $\theta^* > 0$: corporate sector relatively labour-intensive; (b) λ^*, $\theta^* < 0$: corporate sector relatively capital-intensive.

Harberger's Analysis

Harberger provides an expression equivalent to (6-17) for the change in the rate of profit induced by the tax.[10] Taking the wage as fixed ($\hat{w} = 0$), Harberger defines the following "benchmark" situations.

1. $\hat{r} = 0$, where "labour and capital [bear] the tax in proportion to their initial contributions to the national income". In this case, there is no change in the factor price ratio and the condition for it to happen is (from (6-17))

$$\sigma_D = \frac{(\theta_{KX}\lambda_{LX} + \theta_{LX}\lambda_{KX})\sigma_X}{\theta_{KX}(\lambda_{LX} - \lambda_{KX})} \tag{6-18}$$

so necessary conditions are $\lambda^* > 0$ and $\sigma_D > \sigma_X$.[11]

2. $\hat{r} = -(K_X/K_0)\hat{T}_{KX}$, where "capital bears the entire tax", in the sense that the change in after-tax capital income is equal to the tax revenue; i.e.,

$$\frac{d}{dT_{KX}}(rK_0) = -\frac{d}{dT_{KX}}[(T_{KX} - 1)rK_X]$$

evaluated at $T_{KX} = 1$. By substituting in (6-17), it may be seen that this is implied by $\sigma_X = \sigma_Y = \sigma_D = 1$. One special case where this holds is therefore that of Cobb–Douglas production and demand functions.

Harberger gives a range of illustrative calculations for the United States, based on substituting plausible values for the parameters. For this purpose he distinguishes between agriculture, real estate, and miscellaneous repair services as the non-corporate sector, and the remainder as the corporate sector. To estimate the parameters involved Harberger made a number of strong assumptions, and these are described in his article (1962). The values for some of the key parameters are (his Set II):[12]

$$\lambda_{LX} = \tfrac{10}{11}, \quad \lambda_{KX} = \tfrac{2}{3}, \quad \lambda^* = \tfrac{8}{33}$$
$$\theta_{KX} = \tfrac{1}{6}, \quad \theta_{KY} = \tfrac{1}{2}, \quad \theta^* = \tfrac{1}{3}$$

Substituting into (6-17), with $\hat{w} = 0$

$$(-\hat{r}) = \frac{140\sigma_X - 8\sigma_D}{16\sigma_D + 140\sigma_X + 42\sigma_Y}\hat{T}_{KX} \tag{6-19}$$

---

[10] In his derivation, Harberger (1962) normalizes all prices at unity at the point $T_{KX} = 1$. This normalization is the reason why certain expressions may appear to have the wrong dimensions.

[11] Since the top of the right-hand side may be written as

$$\theta_{KX}\lambda_{LX} + (1 - \theta_{KX})\lambda_{KX} > \theta_{KX}(\lambda_{LX} - \lambda_{KX})$$

[12] This set is based on calculations of the hypothetical no-tax situation on the assumption of Cobb–Douglas functions; he also gives an alternative set based on the observed values with the tax.

Harberger starts with the Cobb–Douglas case, where we have seen that capital bears the full burden:

$$(-\hat{r}/\hat{T}_{KX}) = \tfrac{132}{198} = \tfrac{2}{3} = \lambda_{KX}$$

He then considers a range of variations in the elasticities σ_X, σ_Y and σ_D. On the basis of these calculations, he forms the view that:

> it is hard to avoid the conclusion that plausible alternative sets of assumptions about the relevant elasticities all yield results in which capital bears very close to 100 per cent of the tax burden. The most plausible assumptions imply that capital bears more than the full burden of the tax. [Harberger, 1962, pp. 234–5.]

Exercise 6-2 Examine the sensitivity of $(-\hat{r}/\hat{T}_{KX})$ to the different parameters. What would you consider "plausible" values? What qualifications limit the conclusions that can be drawn regarding the incidence of the corporation tax?

The Harberger analysis provides considerable insight into the different factors at work, but it is premature to draw the firm conclusion quoted above. Even accepting the basic framework of the model (e.g., perfect competition and fixed factor supplies), there are a number of reasons why the treatment may be misleading. The assumption that there are no other taxes in existence is clearly questionable in this empirical application. The effective rate of corporation tax, in terms of its impact on the marginal cost of capital, may be considerably less than the nominal rate (and may indeed be negative), but it cannot necessarily be treated as infinitesimal. The assumptions about the demand side must be relaxed. A more systematic approach needs to be adopted to the estimation of the key parameters and to the numerical calculations. These aspects are taken up in Sections 6-4–6-6.

6-4 GENERAL TAX INCIDENCE

This section gives a more general treatment (allowing for the existence of other taxes and for a non-infinitesimal level of the corporation tax) and examines the dynamics of adjustment. Clearly, the existence of other taxes is an important feature of the real world, and the results of the previous section—based on an infinitesimal corporate tax in an otherwise tax-free world—cannot be applied directly. As we shall show, the change in the results arises from the existence of taxes *combined with* a non-homothetic utility function. The dynamics of adjustment are of interest both in their own right and because the stability conditions may have implications for the comparative static analysis. Consideration of the dynamic process also leads one to question certain features of the model.

Equivalence of Taxes

The range of taxes is now extended to include partial factor taxes in each sector so that the gross payments to factors are:

$$rT_{Kj}, \quad j = X, Y$$
$$wT_{Lj}, \quad j = X, Y$$

and to selective excise taxes, so that consumer prices are:

$$q_j = p_j T_j, \quad j = X, Y$$

(The revenue is again assumed to be returned to the consumers in lump-sum form.) If we consider the impact of these taxes on the three key equations of the preceding section, we can see that the demand curve ((6-9) in the non-homothetic case) does not include taxation explicitly if it is defined in terms of the consumer prices q_j:[13]

$$\eta_Y \hat{X} - \eta_X \hat{Y} = -\sigma_D(\hat{q}_X - \hat{q}_Y) \tag{6-9''}$$

The equation for consumer prices becomes

$$\hat{q}_X - \hat{q}_Y = \theta^*(\hat{w} - \hat{r}) + (\hat{T}_X - \hat{T}_Y) + \theta_{LX}\hat{T}_{LX} - \theta_{LY}\hat{T}_{LY} + \theta_{KX}\hat{T}_{KX} - \theta_{KY}\hat{T}_{KY}$$
$$\equiv \theta^*(\hat{w} - \hat{r}) + (\hat{T}_X^* - \hat{T}_Y^*) \tag{6-11''}$$

and Eq. (6-16) becomes

$$\lambda^*(\hat{X} - \hat{Y}) = (\hat{w} - \hat{r})(a_X \sigma_X + a_Y \sigma_Y) + a_X \sigma_X(\hat{T}_{LX} - \hat{T}_{KX})$$
$$+ a_Y \sigma_Y(\hat{T}_{LY} - \hat{T}_{KY}) \tag{6-16''}$$

The first point that can be seen from this more general set of equations concerns the *equivalence of taxes*. The equivalence of taxes that might appear initially to have different incidence has long been recognized. Musgrave (1959, pp. 348–55) provides a clear account under assumptions similar to those made here, as well as noting the qualifications necessary in a more realistic setting. The main results are summarized in Table 6-1 (based on Break, 1974, and McLure, 1975).

Table 6-1 Equivalence of taxes

T_{KX}	and	T_{LX}	=	T_X
and		and		and
T_{KY}		T_{LY}	=	T_Y
=		=		
T_K	and	T_L	=	T

Note: T_i and $T_j = T_k$ means that a tax on i and j at the same rate is equivalent to a tax on k.

---

[13] Adjustments in lump-sum income, as revenue is returned, via $\hat{M}$ have been eliminated.

The first proposition is that—in this model—a tax on capital and labour income at the same rate ($T_K = T_L$) (i.e., a general income tax) is equivalent to a tax on both products at the same rate. (This is the equivalence in a static model between a general expenditure tax and a uniform rate VAT.) From the equations above, it can be seen that this has no effect on relative prices or relative factor returns. Second, a tax on both factors in the same industry at the same rate (e.g., $T_{LX} = T_{KX}$) has no substitution effect (the terms cancel in (6-16″)) and is equivalent to an excise tax. Since $\theta_{LX} + \theta_{KX} = 1$, it is equivalent to a selective excise at the same rate (see (6-11″)). Third, a tax on capital in both sectors at the same rate ($T_{KX} = T_{KY}$) is simply a tax on a fixed factor. As a result of these equivalences, it is only necessary to examine three of the taxes set out above (although the three must be independent) in addition to the effect of a general tax T. For example, suppose that in addition to T_{KX} we know the effect of T_X and T_K; then the effects of T_{KY} and T_{LX} follow immediately by subtraction.

Exercise 6-3 Examine in the case of homothetic demands the effect of an excise tax in sector X on the relative consumer prices of the two goods. How do the results compare with those obtained from a partial equilibrium model?

Effect of Corporation Tax

From this point, we concentrate on the effect of a change in the corporation tax ($\hat{T}_{KX}$), but the existence of other taxes is taken into account. Thus, in equations (6-11″) and (6-16″) we set $\hat{T}_{ij} = 0$ for $ij \neq KX$, but the terms θ_{ij}, λ_{ij}, etc., are functions of the other tax rates. This may have important implications. In particular, as Jones (1971a), Magee (1971) and others have pointed out, the ranking according to physical factor intensity (λ^*) may depart from that according to value (θ^*) where there are factor market distortions or taxes. Thus λ^* has the sign of $c_{LX} c_{KY} - c_{LY} c_{KX}$ (from the definition of λ^*). On the other hand θ^* has the sign of $\theta_{LX} \theta_{KY} - \theta_{LY} \theta_{KX}$ where θ_{ij} are the gross shares:

$$\theta_{LX} = \frac{wT_{LX} c_{LX}}{p_X}, \quad \theta_{LY} = \frac{wT_{LY} c_{LY}}{p_Y}$$

$$\theta_{KX} = \frac{rT_{KX} c_{KX}}{p_X}, \quad \theta_{KY} = \frac{rT_{KY} c_{KY}}{p_Y}$$

So, re-arranging, λ^* has the sign of

$$\frac{p_X p_Y}{wr} \left(\frac{\theta_{LX}}{T_{LX}} \frac{\theta_{KY}}{T_{KY}} - \frac{\theta_{LY}}{T_{LY}} \frac{\theta_{KX}}{T_{KX}} \right) \qquad (6\text{-}20)$$

Where $T_{LX}/T_{LY} = T_{KX}/T_{KY}$, as with an equal rate factor tax in each sector, this is guaranteed to have the same sign as θ^*, but otherwise it need not hold.

The three basic equations contain in effect four unknowns ($\hat{X}$, $\hat{Y}$, $\hat{q}_X - \hat{q}_Y$, and $\hat{w} - \hat{r}$) in the non-homothetic case. We therefore adopt a slightly different method of solution (based on Neary, 1978), making explicit the conditions for factor supply. Differentiating the full employment condition $L_X + L_Y = L_0$,

$$\hat{L}_X(L_X/L_0) + \hat{L}_Y(L_Y/L_0) = 0$$

or

$$\lambda_{LX}\hat{L}_X + \lambda_{LY}\hat{L}_Y = 0 \qquad (6\text{-}21a)$$

and similarly

$$\lambda_{KX}\hat{K}_X + \lambda_{KY}\hat{K}_Y = 0 \qquad (6\text{-}21b)$$

Moreover, from (6-14)

$$\hat{K}_X - \hat{L}_X = \hat{c}_{KX} - \hat{c}_{LX} = \sigma_X(\hat{w} - \hat{r} - \hat{T}_{KX}) \qquad (6\text{-}21c)$$

(using $\theta_{KX} + \theta_{LX} = 1$) and

$$\hat{K}_Y - \hat{L}_Y = \hat{c}_{KY} - \hat{c}_{LY} = \sigma_Y(\hat{w} - \hat{r}) \qquad (6\text{-}21d)$$

Finally, from the production function,

$$\hat{X} = \theta_{LX}\hat{L}_X + \theta_{KX}\hat{K}_X \qquad (6\text{-}22a)$$

$$\hat{Y} = \theta_{LY}\hat{L}_Y + \theta_{KY}\hat{K}_Y \qquad (6\text{-}22b)$$

(N.B. θ_{ij} are the gross shares.) The equations (6-21) allow us to solve for $\hat{K}_i$, $\hat{L}_i$ and hence for $\hat{X}$, $\hat{Y}$ from (6-22). In particular,

$$\lambda^*\hat{L}_X = \lambda_{LY}(\lambda_{KX}\sigma_X + \lambda_{KY}\sigma_Y)(\hat{w} - \hat{r}) - \lambda_{LY}\lambda_{KX}\sigma_X\hat{T}_{KX}$$
$$\lambda^*\hat{L}_Y = -\lambda_{LX}(\lambda_{KX}\sigma_X + \lambda_{KY}\sigma_Y)(\hat{w} - \hat{r}) + \lambda_{LX}\lambda_{KX}\sigma_X\hat{T}_{KX} \qquad (6\text{-}23)$$

Since

$$\hat{X} = \theta_{KX}(\hat{K}_X - \hat{L}_X) + \hat{L}_X$$

we have from (6-21c) and (6-23)

$$\lambda^*\hat{X} = (\hat{w} - \hat{r})[\theta_{KX}\sigma_X\lambda^* + \lambda_{LY}(\lambda_{KX}\sigma_X + \lambda_{KY}\sigma_Y)]$$
$$- \lambda_{LY}\lambda_{KX}\sigma_X\hat{T}_{KX} - \sigma_X\theta_{KX}\hat{T}_{KX}\lambda^*$$

and similarly

$$\lambda^*\hat{Y} = (\hat{w} - \hat{r})[\theta_{KY}\sigma_Y\lambda^* - \lambda_{LX}(\lambda_{KX}\sigma_X + \lambda_{KY}\sigma_Y)] + \lambda_{LX}\lambda_{KX}\sigma_X\hat{T}_{KX} \qquad (6\text{-}24)$$

Substituting into (6-9'') and using (6-11''), we obtain an expression of the form

$$(\hat{w} - \hat{r})D^* = -\sigma_D \lambda^* \theta_{KX} \hat{T}_{KX}$$
$$+ \sigma_X [\lambda_{KX}(\lambda_{LY}\eta_Y + \lambda_{LX}\eta_X) + \lambda^* \theta_{KX}\eta_Y] \hat{T}_{KX} \qquad (6\text{-}25)$$

where $D^* > 0$ is the condition for local stability if the adjustment mechanism involves factors moving between sectors in response to differences in factor prices. It is assumed here that this holds.

The expression on the right-hand side of (6-25) may again be divided into an output and a factor substitution effect. The former (the term containing σ_D) works as before, with the direction depending on the *physical* factor intensity (λ^*). The factor substitution term is that containing σ_X, and may be rewritten (using the definition of a_X), as

$$\sigma_X \{a_X + \lambda_{KX}[\lambda_{LY}(\eta_Y - 1) + \lambda_{LX}(\eta_X - 1)] + \theta_{KX}(\eta_Y - 1)(\lambda_{LX} - \lambda_{KX})\} \qquad (6\text{-}26)$$
$$\equiv \sigma_X(a_X + \zeta) \qquad (6\text{-}27)$$

Comparing with the factor substitution term in (6-17), it can be seen that the difference is that $\zeta \neq 0$. From the individual budget constraint,

$$(\eta_X - 1)b_X + (\eta_Y - 1)(1 - b_X) = 0 \qquad (6\text{-}28)$$

where b_X, b_Y are the shares in total expenditure ($b_X = q_X X / M$). Substituting and re-arranging,[14]

$$-\zeta = \frac{(\eta_Y - 1)}{b_X}(\lambda_{LX}\lambda_{KX} - b_X a_X)$$
$$= a_X(\eta_Y - 1)\left[\left(\frac{M}{rK_0 T_{KX} + wL_0 T_{LX}}\right)\left(\frac{p_X}{q_X}\right) - 1\right] \qquad (6\text{-}29)$$

From this we can derive at once one important result: it is the simultaneous relaxation of the assumptions *both* of a homothetic utility function *and* of zero taxes that leads to changes in the results. Either $\eta_Y = 1$ or $T_{ij} = T_j = 1$ is sufficient for ζ to be zero. Thus, if there are no taxes in the X sector, then $M = rK_0 + wL_0$, and if there is no excise tax, then $p_X = q_X$. If however there are such taxes and the utility function is non-homothetic, then the earlier conclusions need to be modified.

To see which way the factor ζ tends to change the conclusions, we may note that the square bracket in (6-29) is an indicator of the tax burden on the X sector. If there is an excise in sector X, then $q_X > p_X$; if the weighted average of factor taxes is positive, then the other term is also less than one. For example, if we are considering a non-infinitesimal corporate tax with

---

[14] The second step uses the definitions for a_X, b_X, θ_{ij}, and λ_{ij} and cancels terms.

$T_{KX} > 1$ but $T_{ij} = T_j = 0$ otherwise, then the square bracket is negative.[15] We have therefore the following possibilities for the sign of ζ:

	Sector X overall tax burden	
	Less	Greater
X income elasticity		
>1 (hence $\eta_Y < 1$)	positive	negative
<1 (hence $\eta_Y > 1$)	negative	positive

Going back to (6-27), we can see that the factor substitution effect is, other things equal, strengthened in the diagonal cases (ζ positive) and weakened in the off-diagonal cases.

These results are to some extent intuitive. The introduction of an infinitesimal tax into a world with already existing taxes imposes a non-infinitesimal excess burden and has an income effect on demand (i.e., the real income loss exceeds the revenue returned as a lump-sum subsidy to consumers). This additional effect influences relative commodity demands (and hence $\hat{w} - \hat{r}$) only in the non-homothetic case. It is therefore the interaction of the two aspects that is relevant. What is less clear intuitively is the relationship between income elasticities and relative tax rates revealed in the previous paragraph. This illustrates the value of a formal algebraic analysis.

Factor Mobility and Dynamic Stability

Up to now, we have assumed, following Harberger, that capital and labour are fully mobile between sectors, but we consider briefly alternative assumptions about factor mobility and their relation to the stability of the equilibrium. (The case of imperfect factor mobility is discussed in McLure, 1969, 1970, 1971, where he interprets the model as applying to two regions of the economy.) For simplicity, we revert to the assumption of homothetic demands, the extension being left as an exercise to the reader.

A variety of assumptions could be made about the behaviour of the model out of equilibrium. Here we take a "Marshallian" rather than a "Walrasian" view, with quantities adjusting slowly (via movement of factors) and prices adjusting instantaneously. Thus, at any moment there are fixed amounts of each factor in each sector (L_X, L_Y, K_X and K_Y are fixed), which determines outputs X and Y (from the production function). Commodity prices are assumed to secure instantaneous equilibrium in the goods market, so p_X/p_Y is determined. When the economy is out of

---

[15] This case is examined in Krauss (1972) and Ballentine and Eris (1975).

equilibrium, the value marginal product of a factor is not necessarily equalized in the two sectors; and the dynamics of the economy are assumed to be such that factors move towards the sector with the higher return.

The conditions that must hold at any instant are therefore the production functions, the demand relation, and the full employment of factors. Differentiating these conditions, any adjustment of the factors must be such that

$$\hat{X} = \theta_{LX}\hat{L}_X + \theta_{KX}\hat{K}_X \tag{6-22a}$$

$$\hat{Y} = \theta_{LY}\hat{L}_Y + \theta_{KY}\hat{K}_Y \tag{6-22b}$$

$$\hat{X} - \hat{Y} = -\sigma_D(\hat{p}_X - \hat{p}_Y) \tag{6-9'}$$

(where excise taxes are assumed fixed), and must satisfy the full employment conditions (6-21). Using the latter, to eliminate $\hat{L}_Y$, $\hat{K}_Y$, we have at every instant

$$\frac{A_K\hat{K}_X}{\lambda_{KY}} + \frac{A_L\hat{L}_X}{\lambda_{LY}} = -\sigma_D(\hat{p}_X - \hat{p}_Y) \tag{6-30}$$

where

$$A_K = \theta_{KX}\lambda_{KY} + \theta_{KY}\lambda_{KX} > 0$$
$$A_L = \theta_{LX}\lambda_{LY} + \theta_{LY}\lambda_{LX} > 0$$

Now let us denote the value marginal product of capital in sector i by r_i. Differentiating,[16]

$$\hat{K}_X - \hat{L}_X = \frac{-\sigma_X}{\theta_{LX}}(\hat{r}_X - \hat{p}_X) - \frac{\sigma_X}{\theta_{LX}}\hat{T}_{KX}$$

$$\hat{K}_Y - \hat{L}_Y = \frac{-\sigma_Y}{\theta_{LY}}(\hat{r}_Y - \hat{p}_Y) \tag{6-31}$$

where we have assumed that only the corporate tax may change. In (6-30), (6-31) and the full employment conditions (6-21), we have five equations in the eight unknowns ($\hat{K}_i$, $\hat{L}_i$, $\hat{p}_i$, $\hat{r}_i$ for $i = X, Y$). However, the choice of *numeraire* is open, and the dynamic adjustment equation determines two of the factor changes, so the system is completely described. (The wage rates, w_X and w_Y, can be determined from the price equation.)

Let us first examine the case where one factor is immobile. The more plausible case is perhaps that capital is sector-specific (this is treated in an international trade context in Mussa, 1974). The impact of the corporate profits tax is then straightforward—it reduces the net return to capital in that sector and has no other effect (the assumptions that allow us to ignore

---

[16] If the production function is $g(k)$ per worker, where k is the capital–labour ratio, then the value marginal product in X is $p_X g'(k_X) = r_X$. Differentiating logarithmically, $(g''k_X/g')\hat{k}_X = \hat{r}_X - \hat{p}_X$. We then use the definition of the elasticity of substitution.

demand effects are clearly important here).[17] The opposite case of labour immobile, capital freely mobile has been studied by McLure (cf. 1974). In this situation we can solve for the equilibrium by setting $\hat{L}_X = \hat{L}_Y = 0$, $r_X = r_Y$, and choosing a *numeraire* ($\hat{p}_Y = 0$). After re-arrangement

$$\hat{K}_X\left[\lambda_{KY}\theta_{LX} + \left(\frac{\sigma_X}{\sigma_Y}\right)\lambda_{KX}\theta_{LY} + A_K\left(\frac{\sigma_X}{\sigma_D}\right)\right] = -\sigma_X\lambda_{KY}\hat{T}_{KX} \quad (6\text{-}32)$$

As is to be expected, the tax on capital in X leads to a fall in the capital employed if there is any margin for substitution ($\sigma_X > 0$); the relative price of X rises and the rental to capital (relative to p_Y) falls.

The stability of the equilibrium may be examined first in the case of labour immobile. Suppose we set $\hat{L}_X = \hat{L}_Y = 0$, $\hat{p}_Y = 0$ as before, but allow for $r_X \neq r_Y$, and consider the process of adjustment for fixed values of the parameters (i.e., $\hat{T}_{KX} = 0$). Solving for

$$\hat{r}_X - \hat{r}_Y = -\frac{1}{\lambda_{KY}}\left(\frac{\lambda_{KY}\theta_{LX}}{\sigma_X} + \frac{\lambda_{KX}\theta_{LY}}{\sigma_Y} + \frac{A_K}{\sigma_D}\right)\hat{K}_X$$

$$\equiv -\frac{1}{\lambda_{KY}}A_K^*\hat{K}_X \quad (6\text{-}33)$$

Since A_K^* is positive, it follows that an increase in K_X locally reduces the differential (i.e., evaluating locally at $r_X = r_Y$). So if the dynamic process is such that K_X increases (decreases) as $r_X - r_Y > 0$ (<0), then this is locally stable.

If we return to the case where both factors are mobile, then the stability analysis, like the comparative statics results, is more complex. We now have L varying, so that the analogue of (6-33) is

$$\hat{r}_X - \hat{r}_Y = (A_L^*/\lambda_{LY})\hat{L}_X - (A_K^*/\lambda_{KY})\hat{K}_X \quad (6\text{-}34a)$$

where

$$A_L^* = \left(\frac{\lambda_{LY}\theta_{LX}}{\sigma_X} + \frac{\lambda_{LX}\theta_{LY}}{\sigma_Y} - \frac{A_L}{\sigma_D}\right)$$

Moreover, using the expression for the value marginal product of labour, we can obtain a comparable equation for the wages:[18]

$$(\hat{w}_X - \hat{w}_Y) = (A_K^{**}/\lambda_{KY})\hat{K}_X - (A_L^{**}/\lambda_{LY})\hat{L}_X \quad (6\text{-}34b)$$

---

[17] The symmetric case of a tax on labour when it is immobile may be seen from (6-30), (6-31) and (6-21b). The equilibrium is closed by setting $r_X = r_Y$ and $L_X = L_{X0}$, and it may be noted that a change in T_{LX} would not appear in these equations ((6-31) depends on the cost of capital alone).

[18] Using the same notation as in fn. 16, $p_X(g - k_X g') = w_X$. Differentiating logarithmically, $(-k_X g'')/(g - k_X g')\hat{k}_X = \hat{w}_X - \hat{p}_X$. Using the definition of the elasticity of substitution, this gives an expression analogous to (6-31).

where

$$A_K^{**} = \left(\frac{\lambda_{KY}\theta_{KX}}{\sigma_X} + \frac{\lambda_{KX}\theta_{KY}}{\sigma_Y} - \frac{A_K}{\sigma_D} \right)$$

$$A_L^{**} = \left(\frac{\lambda_{LY}\theta_{KX}}{\sigma_X} + \frac{\lambda_{LX}\theta_{KY}}{\sigma_Y} + \frac{A_L}{\sigma_D} \right)$$

We may illustrate the dynamic behaviour in a box diagram (as in Neary, 1978). In Fig. 6-5, we draw the loci $r_X = r_Y$ and $w_X = w_Y$. Where A_L^*, $A_K^{**} > 0$ these slope upwards, as may be seen from (6-34a and b). Moreover, if we move off the locus $r_X = r_Y$ in the direction of increasing K_X, then $r_X < r_Y$, since $A_K^* > 0$ (this is the analogue of the stability analysis where L immobile). If therefore the dynamic process involves K_X falling when $r_X < r_Y$, then the arrows above the $r_X = r_Y$ locus point downward. By a similar argument, the arrows to the right of $w_X = w_Y$ point to the left (since $a_L^{**} > 0$). It follows that, as drawn, the equilibrium at P is locally stable. On the other hand, if the curves had cut the other way (the slope of $r_X = r_Y$ being steeper), then the equilibrium would be locally unstable (it is a saddlepoint). The condition for the curves to cut in the way shown is that:[19]

$$\frac{A_L^{**}}{A_K^{**}} > \frac{A_L^*}{A_K^*} \tag{6-35}$$

Substituting from the definitions of A_i^*, A_i^{**}, this can be shown, after considerable re-arrangement, to require

$$\sigma_D \lambda^* \theta^* + a_X \sigma_X + a_Y \sigma_Y > 0 \tag{6-36}$$

This in turn corresponds to the coefficient D in the analysis of Section 6-3 (see Eq. (6-17)). Note that these are *local* results.

Exercise 6-4 Show that the condition (6-35) is both necessary and sufficient for the local stability of the process described in the text, drawing the phase diagrams (like Fig. 6-5) for the different possible cases (note that $A_K^*, A_L^{**} > 0$ always).

The importance of the stability analysis is that, conditional on a specified adjustment process, we can rule out certain situations. Thus, where the initial equilibrium is locally stable, the expression D must be positive. In

---

[19]

$$\left. \frac{dK_X}{dL_X} \right|_{\hat{r}_X = \hat{r}_Y} = \frac{\lambda_{KY}}{\lambda_{LY}} \frac{A_L^*}{A_K^*} \frac{K_X}{L_X}$$

$$\left. \frac{dK_X}{dL_X} \right|_{\hat{w}_X = \hat{w}_Y} = \frac{\lambda_{KY}}{\lambda_{LY}} \frac{A_L^{**}}{A_K^{**}} \frac{K_X}{L_X}$$

The terms cancel when evaluating at the same point in (L_X, K_X) space.

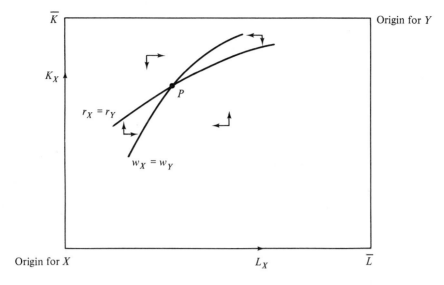

Figure 6-5 Stability of factor adjustment process in locality of P.

the absence of initial taxes or distortions, this does not add anything, since we have seen that $\lambda^*\theta^* \geqslant 0$ (and $\sigma_i \geqslant 0$). However, if there are initial distortions, it is possible that λ^*, θ^* have different signs. This affects the interpretation of the results, but what condition (6-36) tells us is that if the reversal ($\lambda^*\theta^* < 0$) is sufficient to reverse the sign of D, then the resulting equilibrium is locally unstable. In the analysis of locally stable equilibria, we can therefore concentrate on the case where the coefficient of $(\hat{w}-\hat{r})$ is positive.

6-5 INCIDENCE IN A TWO-CLASS ECONOMY

In this section, we relax the assumption that demands are generated by an aggregate utility function and allow for the effect of changes in the distribution of income on the pattern of demand in a two-class model. There are several reasons why these changes are of interest. First, the demand responses are clearly an important part of general equilibrium incidence and we need to take account of differing endowments and preferences (the significance of this has been brought out by Meade, 1955, Mieszkowski, 1967, and Diamond, 1978). Second, they are relevant to the distributional incidence of taxation, and the results are later used in Lecture 9. Finally, they provide a straightforward illustration of the problems caused by multiple equilibria, and it is with this that we begin.

Multiple Equilibria

Multiple equilibria are sometimes viewed as curiosa, but quite strong assumptions are required to ensure uniqueness.[20] In order to illustrate how multiple equilibria arise, and some of their implications, we begin with a simple example which abstracts from the production side. This example, due to Shapley and Shubik (1977), is of a pure exchange economy where there are two classes of individual, denoted by 1 and 2, consuming two goods, X and Y, with utility functions

$$U^1 = X - 100(e^{-Y/10})$$
$$U^2 = Y - 110(e^{-X/10}) \qquad (6\text{-}37)$$

and they have endowments of $40X$, $50Y$, respectively. If the relative price of Y is denoted by p, their budget constraints are

$$X_1 + pY_1 = 40, \quad X_2 + pY_2 = 50p \qquad (6\text{-}38)$$

The demand function for type 1 is derived from utility maximization (omitting constants)

$$\max - pY_1 - 100e^{-Y_1/10}$$

giving a first-order condition

$$10e^{-Y_1/10} = p \quad \text{or} \quad p \geqslant 10 \text{ and } Y_1 = 0$$

The demand function is therefore

$$Y_1 = 10 \log_e(10/p) \quad \text{for} \quad 0 \leqslant p \leqslant 10 \text{ (otherwise zero)} \qquad (6\text{-}39a)$$

It is a declining function of p, and is plotted upside down in Fig. 6-6 (see right-hand scale). The demand function for type 2 is derived similarly

$$Y_2 = 50 - (10/p)\log_e(11p) \quad \text{for} \quad p \geqslant \tfrac{1}{11} \text{ (otherwise } Y_2 = 50) \qquad (6\text{-}39b)$$

This is U-shaped, with the rising portion corresponding to the range where the income effect of a rise in p (via increased value of endowments) offsets the direct price effect. Thus, there may be multiple equilibria, and, as shown in Fig. 6-6, there are in fact three: E_1, E_2 and E_3.[21]

The existence of multiple equilibria means that care must be exercised when carrying out comparative statics exercises. Suppose, for example, that

---

[20] As we noted earlier, in the no-tax, no-distortion economy, the assumption that the demands are generated by a common utility function is sufficient. This does not, however, necessarily carry over to an economy with taxes or distortions, so that the problem may have arisen in the previous section. (See Foster and Sonnenschein, 1970, for examples of non-uniqueness with a single consumer.)

[21] The local stability properties of these equilibria depend on the adjustment process. Under the Walrasian assumption that the price increases (falls) when there is excess demand (supply), E_1 and E_3 are locally stable.

a tax is levied on the market sale of good Y, so that for type 1 (who are the only net purchasers) the price now becomes pT. The revenue is used to finance government expenditure assumed to enter utility functions additively. The demand function for type 1 is now

$$Y_1 = 10 \log_e(10/pT)$$

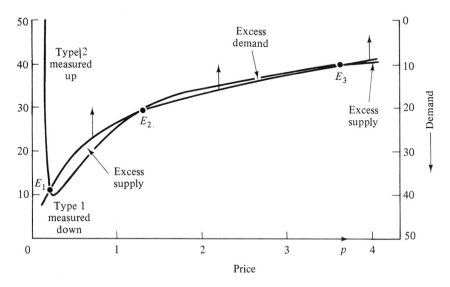

Figure 6-6 Example of multiple equilibria.

and the curve shifts up (see arrows in Fig. 6-6). If the economy had initially been at E_1, then we would observe a movement up the type 2 demand curve, with p falling but not by enough to offset the tax, so Y_1 falls. On the other hand, if the economy had been at E_3, small changes in T may lead to a new equilibrium close to E_3, with p falling by more than enough to offset the effect of the tax, and Y_1 rising. For a sufficiently large T, however, the equilibria E_2 and E_3 cease to exist and the economy "jumps" to the (now unique) equilibrium on the downward-sloping part of type 2's demand curve. There may therefore be discontinuities in the response to tax changes.[22]

---

[22] "Regular" economies, where the set of equilibria depends continuously on the economy, have recently been intensively studied by general equilibrium theorists. For a survey of the field, at a relatively non-technical level, see Debreu (1976), which contains a useful bibliography. See also Balasko (1978).

Two-Class Model with Production

The pure exchange example highlights the key role of differences in tastes (differing utility functions) and in endowments. The same features are now treated more generally in the two-sector model of production. For simplicity, we continue to consider two classes of individuals. This model has been widely used in the literature on economic growth and international trade, and "is sufficiently rich in possibilities to be worth examining, for it captures in a crude way many of the two-way distinctions that strike us as interesting and relevant—rich and poor, capitalists and workers, urban and rural dwellers, etc." (Mirrlees, 1975, pp. 27–8).

The two classes are assumed to differ in their endowments and demand functions. Individuals of type i have a total endowment K_i of capital and L_i of labour, which generate an income $rK_i + wL_i$ ($\equiv M_i$). An extreme case is the "classical" model where the two groups are workers ($K_1 = 0$, $L_1 = L_0$) and capitalists ($K_2 = K_0$, $L_2 = 0$). For simplicity, we assume that the utility functions are homothetic, so that the total demand functions for the two groups may be written as[23]

$$p_X X_i = s_i(p_Y/p_X)M_i$$
$$p_Y Y_i = [1 - s_i(p_Y/p_X)]M_i \qquad (6\text{-}40)$$

where we allow $s_1 \neq s_2$. The polar case is where $s_1 = 1$, $s_2 = 0$, as in the extreme "classical" savings model (where workers purchase only the consumption good, and capitalists only the capital good).

In this model there is again no guarantee that the competitive equilibrium is unique, as is illustrated by the literature on the momentary equilibrium of two-sector growth models (see, for example, Hahn, 1965, and Dixit, 1976b). The comparative static analysis that follows should therefore be interpreted as applying to local variations about a particular (locally stable) equilibrium. On this basis, we can modify the earlier treatment. In particular, the demand equations now yield

$$\hat{p}_X + \hat{X} = \left(\frac{\varepsilon_1 X_1}{X} + \frac{\varepsilon_2 X_2}{X}\right)(p_Y\hat{/}p_X) + \frac{X_1}{X}\hat{M}_1 + \frac{X_2}{X}\hat{M}_2$$

$$\hat{p}_Y + \hat{Y} = -\left(\frac{\varepsilon_1^* Y_1}{Y} + \frac{\varepsilon_2^* Y_2}{Y}\right)(p_Y\hat{/}p_X) + \frac{Y_1}{Y}\hat{M}_1 + \frac{Y_2}{Y}\hat{M}_2 \qquad (6\text{-}41)$$

---

[23] The fact that the utility function is homothetic means that the expenditure function may be written

$$e = p_X g(p_Y/p_X)\phi(U)$$

where we have made use of the fact that e is homogeneous of degree one. The demand functions follow directly.

where ε_i denotes the elasticity of s_i, and ε_i^* denotes the elasticity of $(1-s_i)$, with respect to (p_Y/p_X). Subtracting, and redefining σ_D

$$\hat{X} - \hat{Y} = -\sigma_D(\hat{p}_X - \hat{p}_Y) + \left(\frac{X_1}{X} - \frac{Y_1}{Y}\right)(\hat{M}_1 - \hat{M}_2) \qquad (6\text{-}42)$$

where we have made use of the fact that

$$\frac{X_1}{X} - \frac{Y_1}{Y} = \frac{X_1 + X_2}{X} - \frac{Y_1 + Y_2}{Y} + \frac{Y_2}{Y} - \frac{X_2}{X} = \frac{Y_2}{Y} - \frac{X_2}{X}$$

Moreover, by substituting from the demand equations (6-40), it may be seen that $X_1/X \gtrless Y_1/Y$ according as $s_1 \gtrless s_2$.

The income effect depends on the relative endowments. Let us denote by κ_i the share of capital income in the total income of group i. Then:

$$\hat{M}_1 - \hat{M}_2 = (\kappa_1 - \kappa_2)(\hat{r} - \hat{w}) \qquad (6\text{-}43)$$

Combining this with (6-42), we can see that distributional effects change the structure of the results to the extent that there are differences in the relative importance of different types of income ($\kappa_1 \neq \kappa_2$) *and* there are different marginal propensities to consume ($s_1 \neq s_2$). (See Mieszkowski, 1967, for discussion of the case where $\kappa_1 = 1$, $\kappa_2 = 0$.)

Where demand functions differ, we need to consider incidence in terms of the effect not only on factor prices but also on commodity prices. From the indirect utility function,

$$dV_i = \alpha_i dM_i - \alpha_i X_i dp_X - \alpha_i Y_i dp_Y$$

where α denotes the marginal utility of income. Or

$$\frac{1}{\alpha_i M_i} dV_i = \hat{M}_i - \frac{p_X X_i}{M_i}\hat{p}_X - \frac{p_Y Y_i}{M_i}\hat{p}_Y$$

$$= \kappa_i \hat{r} + (1 - \kappa_i)\hat{w} - s_i\hat{p}_X - (1 - s_i)\hat{p}_Y \qquad (6\text{-}44)$$

If this is taken as a measure of the relative effect on the two groups (it is the percentage change in lump-sum income required to keep V unchanged), then the difference is

$$(\kappa_1 - \kappa_2)(\hat{r} - \hat{w}) - (s_1 - s_2)(\hat{p}_X - \hat{p}_Y) \qquad (6\text{-}45)$$

The distribution of income is affected by changes in relative factor prices to the extent that $\kappa_1 \neq \kappa_2$ and by changes in relative product prices if tastes differ ($s_1 \neq s_2$). It is these latter effects that were ignored in the previous section. Suppose for example that there is a corporation tax on the X sector and that this sector is relatively labour-intensive. If the net rate of profit falls, this worsens the relative position of the "capitalist" group more dependent on capital income ($\kappa_1 > \kappa_2$). On the other hand, if the relative price p_X/p_Y rises, and if the capitalists spend a larger fraction of their income on the output of the non-corporate sector $(s_1 < s_2)$, this tends to redress their relative position.

> **Exercise 6-5** Solve the general equilibrium system for the effect of an infinitesimal corporate profits tax in the two-class model (i.e., using (6-42) and (6-43)). Under what conditions does the group with the higher value of κ gain according to the criterion described above?

6-6 NUMERICAL APPLICATIONS OF THE MODEL

In the previous two sections we have relaxed some of the assumptions of the original Harberger model, allowing in particular for non-infinitesimal taxes and initial distortions, for immobility of factors, and for differences in demand patterns. In this section we examine some of the steps that have been taken to implement the model empirically—to make more realistic computations of the general equilibrium effect of taxation than the numerical exercises of Harberger described in Section 6-3.

Computation of Equilibria

The basic method is to compute the general equilibrium of the economy with and without the tax, and to compare the results. Thus, in the case of the corporate profits tax (all other taxes zero), we have the conditions for equilibrium:

$$c_{LX}(rT_{KX}, w)X + c_{LY}(r, w)Y = L_0$$
$$c_{KX}(rT_{KX}, w)X + c_{KY}(r, w)Y = K_0 \tag{6-4'}$$

and

$$X = X[c_X(rT_{KX}, w), c_Y(r, w), rK_0 + wL_0]$$
$$Y = Y[c_X(rT_{KX}, w), c_Y(r, w), rK_0 + wL_0] \tag{6-6'}$$

where we have eliminated the product prices using (6-5). One of these equations is redundant, but we can in principle solve the remainder for the quantities and the factor price ratio. The resulting solutions are functions of T_{KX} and we can then compare $r(T_{KX})$ with $r(1)$, this being a global comparison rather than a differential approximation for small tax rates.

The computation of equilibria is in principle straightforward, but the provision of a general and practicable method of solution has turned out to be quite difficult. Various methods have been tried. Irving Fisher devised a mechanical and hydraulic analogue machine, intended to calculate equilibrium prices.[24] Frank Graham used a tedious process of trial and error to solve numerical models of world trade. The postwar development of nonlinear multi-sector models led to the employment of iterative methods of the Newton type (see, for example, Johansen, 1960). Such methods appeared to work relatively well in practice but did not guarantee a general solution or that convergence could be achieved where little was known about likely initial values. In recent years, a more general approach to the development of computational algorithms has been developed, exploiting the relationship with fixed-point methods used to prove the existence of equilibrium,[25] based particularly on the work of Kuhn (e.g., 1968), Scarf (1967) and Scarf and Hansen (1973). The underlying method is described in a relatively non-technical manner in Scarf (1969).

Computation of General Equilibrium with Taxes

The application of these computational techniques to general equilibrium with taxes is well illustrated by the calculations of Shoven and Whalley (1972) for the United States. On the production side, the elasticities of substitution are assumed constant, and the endowments are those in Harberger (1962).[26] On the demand side, there are assumed to be two classes of consumers with constant propensities to purchase the two goods (i.e., a unitary price elasticity). The parameters are not econometrically estimated, but are based on a range of plausible values consistent with the aggregate data. Thus, Shoven and Whalley consider six combinations of σ_X, σ_Y, with the distributional and scale parameters being chosen to correspond to the observed factor shares in the observed equilibrium (the same values as Harberger). The first group of consumers (the "rich") is assumed to receive 23 per cent of labour income and 40 per cent of capital income respectively, and to spend a slightly larger fraction of their income on the output of the corporate sector ($\frac{7}{8}$ against $\frac{49}{59}$).

Shoven and Whalley compare two situations. In the initial ("distortionary") situation, capital income in the X sector is taxed at a rate of 168 per cent and that in the Y sector at 45 per cent.[27] In the second

---

[24] The machine is described in *Mathematical Investigations in the Theory of Value and Prices*, published in 1892, and two versions were actually constructed, consisting of canisters connected by an elaborate system of rods, hinges, and tubes filled with water (Scarf, 1967, p. 207).

[25] Any computational technique guaranteed to converge to a solution is equivalent to a proof of existence.

[26] As Shoven (1976) later pointed out, the Harberger figures are in error—see below. Shoven and Whalley also consider the case of a variable labour supply, which is not discussed here.

[27] These are based on the observed average rates of tax; it is clearly debatable how far these rates of tax are actually applicable when calculating the cost of capital at the margin. (There are also the errors referred to in the previous footnote.)

("non-distortionary") situation, capital is taxed at a flat rate of 45 per cent
in both sectors. It may be noted that these tax rates are defined on a tax-
exclusive basis (i.e., as a percentage of net income), and that a rate of 168
per cent corresponds to 62 per cent on a tax-inclusive basis. The revenue is
assumed to be redistributed to consumers in proportion to capital. The
wage is taken as fixed at unity, and in the initial situation all other prices
are normalized at unity. With the elimination of the tax distortion, the
prices change to

$$p_X = 0.95, \quad p_Y = 1.23 \quad \text{and} \quad r = 1.43$$

In other words, the price of the corporate product is reduced relative to that
of the non-corporate sector, and the net return to capital rises relative to the
wage. The extent to which capital bears the burden of the tax may be
measured by the change in r expressed as a fraction of T_{KX}:

$$\text{Capital share of burden} \equiv \frac{[r(1) - r(T_{KX})]K_0}{\text{revenue}}$$

This is the analogue of the measure used by Harberger for the infinitesimal
case. In the present case it is

$$\frac{(1.43 - 1.0)38}{\text{revenue}} = 0.996$$

According to this, capital bears almost all of the burden. This is not perhaps
surprising, since the production and demand functions are Cobb–Douglas,
and the demand patterns for the two classes are very similar. We are
therefore close to the case considered analytically (for infinitesimal taxes) in
Section 6-3.

Shoven and Whalley present a more complete set of results; however,
the later paper by Shoven (1976) points out that errors in the original
Harberger calculations mean that their results need recomputation. We
therefore give in Table 6-2 the computations of Shoven (1976). The results
show the rate of return relative to the non-distortionary (uniform tax)
situation and capital's share of the burden, as measured above. There are
different assumptions about the elasticities of substitution and the consumer
demand elasticities, and the findings agree qualitatively with those of
Harberger. A reduction in the elasticity of substitution in the non-corporate
sector (σ_Y) tends to increase the burden borne by capital (compare case 1
and case 3), although it should be noted that the rate of return is itself little
changed. A reduction in the elasticity in the corporate sector (σ_X) tends to
reduce the burden; on the other hand, a reduction in the elasticity of
demand (from 1.0 to 0.5) works in the opposite direction. It is difficult to

Table 6-2 Calculations of corporate tax incidence for the United States

Case*	2-sector model Consumer demand elasticities 1.0		0.5		12-sector model Consumer demand elasticities 1.0		0.5	
	Return to capital†	Capital share of burden	Return to capital†	Capital share of burden	Return to capital†	Capital share of burden	Return to capital†	Capital share of burden
1. $\sigma_X = 1.0$ $\sigma_Y = 1.0$	0.77	1.0	0.75	1.18	0.77	1.0	0.75	1.17
2. $\sigma_X = 1.0$ $\sigma_Y = 0.5$	0.75	1.17	0.73	1.45	—	—	—	—
3. $\sigma_X = 1.0$ $\sigma_Y = 0.25$	0.74	1.28	0.71	1.62	—	—	—	—
4. $\sigma_X = 0.75$ $\sigma_Y = 0.25$	0.76	1.05	0.73	1.41	0.77	1.04	0.73	1.37
5. $\sigma_X = 0.5$ $\sigma_Y = 0.25$	0.81	0.75	0.76	1.10	—	—	—	—
6. $\sigma_X = 0.25$ $\sigma_Y = 0.25$	0.89	0.33	0.83	0.62	0.88	0.39	0.83	0.62

Source: Shoven (1976, Tables 4 and 6, rounded).
* In the 12-sector model, σ_Y refers to the non-corporate sector (agriculture, real estate and crude oil, and gas), σ_X refers to the corporate sector (mining, construction, manufacturing, lumber, petroleum, trade, transportation, communication, and public utilities, services).
† Relative to no-distortion situation.

draw definite conclusions without narrowing further the range within which the parameters can vary, and this requires a more thoroughgoing attempt to estimate econometrically the underlying model. At the same time, it appears that the results on incidence in general agree with those obtained using the local approximation. The same applies with the more elaborate 12-sector model, some of the results for which are shown in the right-hand part of the table.[28]

In the case just described, the results are in broad agreement with those reached by cruder methods. That this is not always the case is illustrated by the calculations by Shoven and Whalley (1977) of equal yield taxes. They consider the particular instance of replacing the present differential taxes on capital by a uniform tax on all sectors,[29] using a model estimated for the United Kingdom. The initial tax rates, on net of tax income, varied from 17 to 141 per cent. As the authors note, a "back-of-the-envelope" calculation is commonly made in practice, based on dividing the foregone revenue by the base for the new tax at the initial equilibrium—in other words, ignoring any general equilibrium repercussions. This back-of-the-envelope method gave an equal yield replacement tax rate of 82 per cent. If one allows for the general equilibrium effects, then the equal real yield tax rate is 90–100 per cent (depending on the price index used). There is therefore an error in the crude calculation of up to a quarter.

The computation of the general equilibrium effects of taxation is likely to become more widespread, and larger models, with more detailed disaggregations of production and demand, are being constructed: see, for example, Fullerton, Shoven and Whalley (1978) for the United States, and Whalley and Piggott (1977) for the United Kingdom. No doubt in the future this work will be more closely integrated with the econometric estimation of the parameters of the model, and there will be convergence with the approaches adopted in macroeconomic modelling. (The procedure by which parameters have been derived to date has largely been concerned with replicating the observed equilibrium, rather than with estimation according to customary econometric methods.)

[28] The same approach has been used by Whalley (1975) to provide a general equilibrium assessment of the 1973 tax reform in the United Kingdom, including the introduction of the value added tax and the abolition of the selective employment tax (SET) and purchase tax. Of particular interest is the discussion of SET. This was a tax on the use of labour in one sector (services) and a subsidy on labour in another (manufacturing). However, the impact of rates (local property tax) is also greater in the service sector, since it is relatively intensive in its use of buildings. The removal of SET therefore eased the distortion across sectors in the price of labour but intensified the distortion within the service sector. This illustrates the need to take account of other taxes when evaluating a particular tax change.

[29] There is no guarantee, of course, that such an equal-yield tax rate exists. It should also be noted that there is no guarantee that an equilibrium located by the algorithm is unique (see Whalley, 1977, p. 1858, for discussion of this).

6-7 CONCLUDING COMMENTS

The simple competitive general equilibrium model described in this Lecture has been widely used in public economics. Thus, Brittain (1972), in his analysis of the incidence of the social security tax, employs the Harberger framework. After arguing that a general tax on labour is borne by labour (as is the case with the assumptions made earlier), he asks whether incomplete coverage of the working population would undermine this result. Noting that the case of a payroll tax in one ("covered") sector is parallel to the Harberger analysis of the corporation tax, he uses a simple Cobb–Douglas version to make the point that the burden of the tax is shared with the uncovered sector, and is in fact entirely borne by labour.[30] A rather different sectoral classification is applied by Boskin (1975a), who distinguishes between *market* and *household* economic activity. It is typically assumed that a uniform tax on all market sector activities is neutral with respect to resource allocation, but this ignores the effect on household production. In practice, the latter is taxed at a much lower rate, and an over-allocation of labour to the home may be induced. Boskin reinterprets the Harberger model in this way, with capital and labour assumed to be mobile between the two sectors (home and market). Taking account of income tax, property tax, corporation tax, social security tax and indirect taxes, he calculates, on the basis of his "preferred" values of the elasticities of substitution and demand, that the rise in the price of market output relative to household output induced by differential taxation is around 30 per cent.

These applications, together with that to corporate profits taxation on which we have concentrated, demonstrate that the Harberger model has provided a valuable—and yet simple—framework within which general equilibrium effects can be analysed. At the same time, the assumptions of the model are highly restrictive and the attempts at empirical implementation reveal all too clearly their heroic nature. First, the model is one of perfect competition, whereas this is patently unrealistic for the corporate sector. Harberger himself included a section on monopoly, and the extension of the model, at least in the direction of monopolistic competition, is important. Second, it has been assumed that markets clear, whereas the world is characterized by disequilibrium in goods and—particularly—factor markets. Third, the model is static and no account is taken of changing total factor supplies. In the Lectures that follow we consider some of the ways in which these shortcomings may be remedied.

---

[30] This particular conclusion depends (as our analysis makes clear) on the special assumptions; and, more generally, the assumption of a fixed labour supply is questionable in this particular application.

NOTE ON THE COST FUNCTION

The cost function is analogous to the expenditure function (see Note to Lecture 2), and is defined as

$$C(\mathbf{w}, X) = \min_{\mathbf{L}} (\mathbf{w} \cdot \mathbf{L}) \quad \text{subject to} \quad F(\mathbf{L}) = X$$

where we have used the vector $\mathbf{L}$ to denote factor inputs, $\mathbf{w}$ to denote their prices, and $F(\mathbf{L})$ to denote the production function. (For fixed factor prices, the cost function corresponds to the textbook cost curve.)

The cost function is dual to the production function in the sense that either can, under certain conditions, provide a complete specification of the technology. Thus, if the production function $F(\mathbf{L})$ is continuous, increasing and quasi-concave, then it may be shown that there exists a cost function C which is continuous, increasing, concave in $\mathbf{w}$, and linearly homogeneous in $\mathbf{w}$. Conversely, if C has these properties, then it can be shown that there is a corresponding production function (for a precise statement, see Varian, 1978, Ch. 1, or Diewert, 1979). The fact that C is concave may be seen graphically from considering a variation in one factor price (w_1). Suppose that the minimum cost at factor prices $\mathbf{w}^*$ is achieved by L^*. If w_1 varies from w_1^*, then the firm can clearly do no worse than a cost of

$$w_1 L_1^* + \sum_{2}^{n} w_i^* L_i^*$$

which is shown by a straight line (the reader should check by drawing the diagram).

It is assumed here that C is twice differentiable. In that case:

$$\left. \frac{\partial C}{\partial w_i} \right|_{\mathbf{w}^*} = L_i(\mathbf{w}^*, X)$$

i.e., the derivative with respect to the ith factor price gives the demand for that factor, conditional on $\mathbf{w}^*$ and X. (This is clearly analogous to the property of the expenditure function.) The factor demands are homogeneous of degree 0 with respect to $\mathbf{w}$. The derivative with respect to X gives marginal cost.

In the text we assume that the production function exhibits constant returns to scale, which implies that the cost function has the special form

$$C = c(\mathbf{w})X$$

It follows that marginal cost is $c(\mathbf{w})$, and that factor demands are given by

$$L_i = c_i \cdot X$$

READING

The two-sector model is set out compactly in Jones (1965, 1971a; see also Caves and Jones, 1973). The original Harberger article (1962) may possibly be more easily understood after reading the surveys of subsequent literature by Mieszkowski (1969) and McLure (1975). The more general treatment of Section 6-4 draws on Vandendorpe and Friedlaender (1976) and Neary (1976). For a brief introduction to the computation of general equilibrium prices, see Scarf (1969).

SEVEN

TAX INCIDENCE: DEPARTURES FROM THE STANDARD MODEL

7-1 INTRODUCTION

The importance of general equilibrium analysis arises from the complex interrelations between the variables in an economic system. The immediate first-round effects are often offset by subsequent adjustments; and to know the full impact of a tax, one needs to trace through all its consequences. This is no easy task, as we have already seen. Not only must one formulate a model of the entire economy, but one must be able to calculate the effect of a change in some parameter, say a tax rate, on the whole system. As a result, the general equilibrium analysis of tax incidence has, for the most part, been limited to the competitive equilibrium framework described in Lecture 7. It has typically been assumed that firms act perfectly competitively and that all markets clear.

The need to relax the assumptions of perfect competition, and that the economy has attained equilibrium, is apparent. The difficulty lies in providing an adequate theoretical framework to analyse the incidence of taxation under imperfect competition and in the presence of disequilibrium. In recent years, steps have been made to provide a general equilibrium treatment of imperfect competition, but even with relatively straightforward assumptions about strategic behaviour there remain serious obstacles. There has been a substantial literature on macroeconomic disequilibrium, but there is considerable disagreement about the appropriateness of different models. It is not therefore possible at present for the public finance economist to appeal to a generally accepted body of theory. It follows that the alternative models presented in this Lecture should not necessarily be regarded either as fully satisfactory or as exhausting those that could be advanced.

In this Lecture we consider three main departures from the model of Lecture 6. The first is the existence of market imperfections. In Section 7-2 we start with distortions in the factor market, where returns are not equalized in the two sectors of the economy (for example, because of a union "premium" in the corporate sector) and then go on to a monopoly mark-up pricing policy. How do such distortions modify the conclusions reached in the previous Lecture about the incidence of the corporation tax? Section 7-3 gives a more explicit treatment of imperfectly competitive behaviour, presenting a model of monopolistic competition and analysing the effect of the tax on the scale of firms. The second departure is concerned with more realistic assumptions about production. Section 7-4 examines the implications of the taxation of intermediate goods, allowing for the interdependence of industries (via the input–output table), and describes a simple hierarchical model of production. Finally, in Section 7-5, we consider the case where markets do not necessarily clear and the incidence of taxation in the presence of unemployment.

The aim of this Lecture is to incorporate some of the important real-world features which are patently missing from the model of Lecture 6. We have set about this task by seeking to extend the earlier analysis, and much of the discussion takes the form of modifying the earlier general equilibrium equations. It may be argued that a more "root and branch" approach has to be adopted, and we have considerable sympathy with this view (see Lecture 1). Again, the limitation is the lack of the necessary theoretical framework. There is as yet no "radical" theory sufficiently articulated in the areas needed to examine the incidence of taxes and expenditure. The Lecture should be read bearing in mind this qualification. The analysis needs to be developed, for example in the treatment of uncertainty, information, and market power, and these factors may have quite far-reaching implications for the way in which we view the general equilibrium of the economy.

7-2 MARKET IMPERFECTIONS

In this section we start from the two-sector (X and Y), fixed-factor (K and L) model of Lecture 6, and examine the implications of market imperfections. For concreteness, we focus on the corporation tax, which has been taken as the main application of the analysis. Suppose that the government increases the tax on capital in the corporate sector (T_{KX}), and that we are interested in the response of the wage–rental ratio (w/r). How do the conclusions need to be modified when there are departures from the assumptions of perfect competition? In analysing this, we retain in this section the simplifying assumptions about production (there are assumed to be constant returns to scale and no intermediate goods). We assume throughout that demands are generated by a single aggregate utility function and that tax revenue is returned to consumers in lump-sum form.

Distortions in the Factor Market

The first situation considered is that where there are distortions in the factor market, so that the returns are not equalized in the two sectors. This is not necessarily the most important form of market imperfection, but it is a relatively simple case to examine initially. The example we take for purposes of illustration is a wage differential:

$$w_X = \zeta w, \quad w_Y = w \tag{7-1}$$

This case has been discussed at length, especially in the literature on international trade (see for example Jones, 1971a, and Magee, 1976), and has been treated as representing the effects of unionization by Johnson and Mieszkowski (1970). On this basis, the union is able to secure a premium in the X sector (if $\zeta > 1$) or Y sector ($\zeta < 1$). It should be noted that the relationship between such a differential and the ultimate goals of the union is not discussed (a point to which we return briefly), and that the premium is taken as exogenous.

The effect of the wage differential may be seen from the general equilibrium equations set out in Lecture 6, modified for the possibility that $w_X \neq w_Y$. The full employment conditions are (where c_{ij} denotes the input of factor i into industry j):

$$c_{LX}(r, w_X)X + c_{LY}(r, w_Y)Y = L_0$$
$$c_{KX}(r, w_X)X + c_{KY}(r, w_Y)Y = K_0 \tag{7-2}$$

The product prices are equal to marginal costs:

$$p_X = c_X(r, w_X)$$
$$p_Y = c_Y(r, w_Y) \tag{7-3}$$

Finally, demands are given by

$$X = X(p_X, p_Y, M)$$
$$Y = Y(p_X, p_Y, M) \tag{7-4}$$

One of these is again redundant by Walras' law. From the five equations, and the factor market equations (7-1), we can solve for X, Y and four out of the five prices (p_X, p_Y, r, w_X, w_Y), the other being the *numeraire*.

This model can be used to examine the consequences of *changes* in the differential, ζ. Our primary concern here however is with the implications of the *existence* of ζ ($\neq 1$) for the comparative static results with respect to the *change in taxation* ($\hat{T}_{KX}$). The position is parallel with that in Section 6-4, where the existence of other taxes was seen to affect the response to T_{KX}, and we can draw on that analysis.

To obtain the comparative static results, we totally differentiate the general equilibrium conditions, deriving the "equations of change" (see pages 167–70):

$$\eta_Y \hat{X} - \eta_X \hat{Y} = -\sigma_D \hat{p}_X - \hat{p}_Y) \tag{7-5}$$

where η_i denotes the income elasticities (with $\eta_Y = \eta_X = 1$ in the homothetic case) and σ_D is the aggregate demand elasticity;

$$\hat{p}_X - \hat{p}_Y = \theta^*(\hat{w} - \hat{r}) + \theta_{KX} \hat{T}_{KX} \tag{7-6}$$

where θ_{ij} denotes the share of factor i in the value of the jth output, and θ^* is the determinant;

$$\lambda^*(\hat{X} - \hat{Y}) = (a_X \sigma_X + a_Y \sigma_Y)(\hat{w} - \hat{r}) - a_X \sigma_X \hat{T}_{KX} \tag{7-7}$$

where λ_{ij} is the fraction of factor i in sector j, λ^* is the determinant, σ_X, σ_Y the elasticities of substitution, and

$$a_i = \lambda_{Li} \theta_{Ki} + \lambda_{Ki} \theta_{Li} \tag{7-8}$$

It is clear that the premium is equivalent as far as factor prices are concerned to a tax on labour in the X sector (for simplicity we take $\zeta \geqslant 1$); on the demand side the effects are also equivalent with the simplifying assumptions being made here. From the analysis of Section 6-4 we can deduce that it is the conjunction of the distortion with non-unitary income elasticities that is especially important. Applying the results obtained there (Eq. (6-29)), we can see how $T_{LX} = \zeta > 1$ influences the effect of the corporation tax, modifying the size of the factor substitution effect as the income elasticity of demand for the corporate product is greater (less) than unity.

In the case where there are unitary income elasticities, the existence of the distortion does not add extra terms to the expression for the change in the wage–rental ratio (w/r), but it does affect their interpretation. From (7-5)–(7-7), with $\eta_X = \eta_Y = 1$, we can solve for

$$(\hat{w} - \hat{r})(\sigma_D \theta^* \lambda^* + a_X \sigma_X + a_Y \sigma_Y) = a_X \sigma_X \hat{T}_{KX} - \sigma_D \lambda^* \theta_{KX} \hat{T}_{KX} \tag{7-9}$$

This is identical in form to the equation with $\zeta = 1$ (see Eq. (6-17)), but the implications may be rather different. As we saw in Lecture 6, distortions may lead the ranking of sectors according to physical capital intensity (λ^*) to differ from that according to factor shares (θ^*). From Eq. (6-20), λ^* may be seen in the present case to have the sign of

$$\theta_{LX} \theta_{KY} - \theta_{LY} \theta_{KX}(\zeta/T_{KX}) = \theta^* + \theta_{LY} \theta_{KX}(1 - \zeta/T_{KX}) \tag{7-10}$$

To see the implications, let us take the example where the production functions are Cobb–Douglas, so that θ^* is constant, and where the corporate sector is relatively labour-intensive in terms of value $(\theta^* > 0)$. We are considering the effect of increasing an already existing corporate tax $(T_{KX} > 1)$. In the absence of the distortion, it is clear from (7-10) that $\lambda^* > 0$. Hence going back to (7-9), we can see that the factor substitution effect (first term on right-hand side) and output effect (second term) work in opposite directions. If the elasticity of demand is sufficiently large relative to the elasticity of substitution in X, then it is possible that (w/r) falls—the net return to capital is relatively increased by the tax. On the other hand, the differential ζ tends to reduce the right-hand side of (7-10), and there is clearly a value

$$\zeta/T_{KX} = \frac{\theta_{LX}\theta_{KY}}{\theta_{LY}\theta_{KX}} = \frac{\theta_{LX}'/(1-\theta_{LX})}{\theta_{LY}/(1-\theta_{LY})} \tag{7-11}$$

(greater than 1) such that $\lambda^* = 0$. The physical factor intensities are in this situation equal, and the output effect is zero. With this level of distortion, it is not possible for a rise in the corporate tax to reduce (w/r), and this illustrates how the *existence* of market imperfections may significantly affect the incidence of taxation.[1]

The effect of the presence of the distortion is shown in Fig. 7-1, which is the upper part of the four-quadrant diagram used in the previous Lecture. The "supply" curve is constructed from the relationship between X/Y and w/r shown in the left-hand part of the diagram and that between w/r and p_X/p_Y (not shown). In Fig. 7-1a, we have the no-distortion case with a small tax, and θ^*, $\lambda^* > 0$. It is possible, as shown, for the output effect to outweigh the substitution effect. We have transferred the demand curve to the left-hand part (via the lower two quadrants, not shown) to illustrate the two effects. Figure 7-1b shows the case where the union premium is such that (7-11) is satisfied and $\lambda^* = 0$. The supply curve is vertical. The effect of the tax is to raise w/r (see left-hand part) and p_X/p_Y.

Exercise 7-1 In a box diagram for labour and capital, draw the loci $r_X = r_Y$ and $w_X = \zeta w_Y$ (see Section 6-4). How do changes in ζ affect the equilibrium? Now examine the effect of an increase in T_{KX} for a given level of distortion. (Hint: use a large sheet of paper.)

From this analysis, one can see whether it is possible for tax policy to be employed to offset the existence of market imperfections. Suppose that the differential ζ is immutable. If the government then levies a tax on the

---

[1] It may be checked that the condition for local stability, under the adjustment process described in Section 6-4, is satisfied where $\lambda^* = 0$, provided that one of σ_X/σ_D, σ_Y/σ_D is strictly positive (see Neary, 1978).

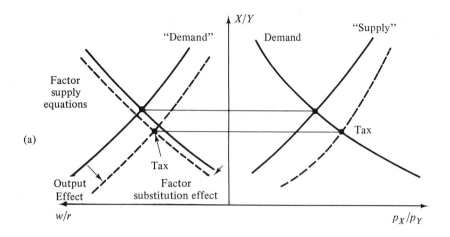

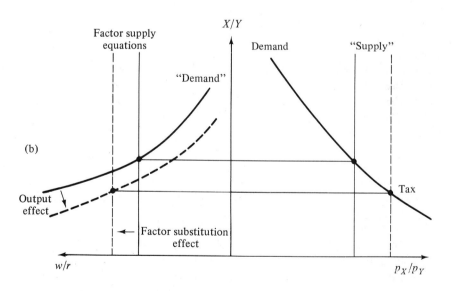

Figure 7-1 Effect of presence of distortion on response to corporation tax: (a) no distortion; (b) with distortion such that $\lambda^* = 0$.

use of capital in the X sector at the same rate ($T_{KX} = \zeta$), this means that the choice of factor intensity in that sector is the same as if the factor prices were w and r. On the other hand, the relative price of product X is higher. However, if the government levies a tax on the output of Y at the same rate, this means that the conditions of the no-tax equilibrium have been reproduced. (In effect, this uses the equivalences set out in Table 6-1.)

The wage differential (ζ) has been treated as representing the effects of unionization, but this does not seem a particularly satisfactory way of investigating union behaviour. In particular, there is no clear relationship between the level of the differential and the objectives of the union (whether, for example, it is in the interests of the union members to achieve a higher premium). A more fruitful approach to this particular distortion seems to be by considering the restriction of factor movement that lies behind the establishment of a differential. The power of the union then arises from the ability to limit entry. In the extreme case, there is no mobility of labour at all (as in Jones, 1971b), and the implications of such immobility for the incidence of the corporation tax have been examined in Section 6-4, where we saw that $\sigma_X > 0$ implies that the return to capital definitely falls (relative to p_Y) as a result of the tax. Again, this demonstrates how market imperfections may change the conclusions.

Monopoly Power

From imperfection in the factor market, we turn to imperfection in the product market. As remarked earlier, to treat the corporate sector as acting perfectly competitively is a particularly unsatisfactory assumption. We now explore some of the implications of monopoly in sector X, while continuing to assume perfect competition in the non-corporate sector.

In his original paper, Harberger (1962) included a brief discussion of monopoly, based on the assumption that the corporate sector is characterized by constant mark-up pricing.

$$p_X = (1+m)c_X(rT_{KX}, w) \tag{7-12}$$

(where we now assume $\zeta = 1$). The mark-up acts in this respect like an excise tax T_X, and the fact that the monopoly profit accrues to entrepreneurs, rather than as revenue to the government, does not make any difference in view of the assumption about the demand side. However, as has been noted by several writers (e.g., Ballentine and Eris, 1975), it is not legitimate to apply formulae derived for infinitesimal changes from a no-tax, no-distortion position. The existence of a mark-up $m > 0$ has to be taken into account when considering the response to a corporate tax.

The situation is simplified if the utility function is homothetic, and that assumption is made in what follows. In this case, as we have seen earlier, the form of the equations of change ($\hat{w} - \hat{r}$ in terms of $\hat{T}_{KX}$) is not affected. Nor, in the case of a monopoly mark-up, is there any reversal of sign between θ^* and λ^*, since T_X does not enter (6-20). We have however to be careful about the interpretation. In particular, the factor shares θ_{ij} refer to shares in the *cost* of output, not to factor shares in the *value* of output. Thus, the observed factor share, denoted by a superscript o, in the value of output including monopoly profit is

$$\theta^o_{LX} = \frac{\theta_{LX}}{1+m} \quad \theta^o_{KX} = \frac{\theta_{KX}+m}{1+m} \tag{7-13}$$

If therefore we examine the effect of the tax, T_{KX}, on the rental of capital, the expression for the change in (w/r) becomes (from Eq. (7-9)):

$$(\hat{w}-\hat{r})(\sigma_D\theta^{*o}\lambda^* + a^o_X\sigma_X + a_Y\sigma_Y + \chi) = \sigma_X a^o_X \hat{T}_{KX}$$
$$-\sigma_D\lambda^*\theta^o_{KX}\hat{T}_{KX} + \chi\hat{T}_{KX} \tag{7-14}$$

where

$$\chi = m\lambda^*\theta^o_{LX}(\sigma_D-\sigma_X)$$

and θ^{*o}, a^o_X denote the values evaluated at the observed values. This means that in evaluating the magnitude of the substitution effect and the output effect at the observed factor shares, the existence of the monopoly mark-up needs to be taken into account. The direction of the correction depends on whether the demand elasticity, σ_D, is greater or less than the elasticity of factor substitution in the corporate sector.

The corporation tax has so far been treated as a tax on the rental of capital only, but in assessing its incidence the effect on monopoly profit must also be considered. If it falls also on monopoly profits, the total yield of the tax is $(T_{KX}-1)(rK_X + mp_X X)$. With the simple constant mark-up pricing supposed, the tax on monopoly profit makes no difference. This might well be modified if we made alternative, and possibly more realistic, assumptions. On the production side, the mark-up may be determined to achieve a post-tax target (as has been assumed in some versions of the cost-plus pricing rule); and in this case the price, and hence the output, of the corporate sector would be affected. Alternatively, if the monopoly profit is supposed to be the return to entrepreneurship or innovation, and these qualities are elastically supplied, output may again be affected. (On the demand side, if the pattern of demand is affected by the distribution of income, there may again be shifting of a tax on monopoly profits.)

The representation of market power in terms of a simple mark-up pricing rule is crude and has not been related explicitly to the objectives of the firm. Under certain assumptions, such pricing behaviour could be derived from the behaviour of a single profit-maximizing monopolist facing a constant elasticity demand curve, with elasticity greater than unity.[2] It does not however seem particularly realistic to view the corporate sector as a single gigantic monopolist. As it is put by Harberger,

> [the mark-up] is kept down to modest size by the existence of many independent firms within the corporate sector; by the availability, elsewhere in the corporate sector, of reasonably close substitutes for the products of any one firm; and by the perennial threat of new entry into any field in which the monopoly mark-up is large. [1962, p. 239]

In the next section, we present a model of imperfect competition (based on Dixit and Stiglitz, 1977) which incorporates some of these features.

7-3 MONOPOLISTIC COMPETITION

The model described in this section is simple but captures the fact that, although there are strong competitive elements within the economy, virtually every firm in the corporate sector has some degree of monopoly power. The same may also apply to the non-corporate sector; however, we treat its output (Y) here as being produced under perfect competition. The model is one of monopolistic competition, in which each firm has a declining cost curve, although constant marginal cost. The scale of the firm, and hence the number of firms, depends on the relative importance of fixed costs, whereas prices depend on marginal costs and the degree of competition. The imposition of taxes in this model is relevant to the effect not just on prices but also on industrial structure.

Model of Monopolistic Competition

The source of a firm's monopoly power in this model is located in differences in demands—the firms in the corporate sector have differentiated products—and we begin with the demand side. As before, we assume that demands are generated by an aggregate utility function, which we write as $U(\Gamma(X_i), Y)$ where X_i is the output of the ith firm. In other words, U is separable in Y and Γ, where the latter is a sub-utility function of the products of the corporate sector. The sub-utility function is assumed to have the constant elasticity form

$$\Gamma^\rho = \sum_i X_i^\rho \qquad (7\text{-}15)$$

---

[2] From the condition marginal revenue equals marginal cost,

$$p_X(1 - 1/\varepsilon_X) = c_X$$

where ε_X is the elasticity of demand or $m = 1/(\varepsilon_X - 1)$.

It is assumed that $0 < \rho \leqslant 1$, which means that the function is concave and that $X_i = 0$ is a possible solution. The parameter ρ is an indicator of the degree of substitutability $(1/(1-\rho)$ is the elasticity of substitution between any two products), or of the preference for variety. Thus where $\rho = 1$, the goods are perfect substitutes, but where $\rho < 1$, diversity is valued.

In order to give relatively uncomplicated results, we take the special case where U has the Cobb–Douglas form; i.e.,

$$U = (1-\delta)\log Y + \delta \log \Gamma \tag{7-16}$$

Denoting by p_i the price charged by the ith firm, the consumer's budget constraint is

$$p_Y Y + \sum_i p_i X_i = M \tag{7-17}$$

where M denotes total income. The demand equations may be derived directly from the utility maximization conditions:

$$U_Y = \frac{(1-\delta)}{Y} = \alpha p_Y$$

$$U_i = \frac{\delta}{\Gamma}\frac{\partial \Gamma}{\partial X_i} = \delta X_i^{\rho-1}\Gamma^{-\rho} = \alpha p_i$$

and the budget constraint, which (substituting) gives $\alpha = 1/M$. So

$$Y = \frac{(1-\delta)M}{p_Y}, \quad X_i = \left(\frac{\delta M}{p_i \Gamma^\rho}\right)^{1/(1-\rho)} \tag{7-18}$$

On the supply side, firms maximize profits and entry occurs until the marginal firm can only just break even. We assume that all firms have identical cost conditions and, given the symmetry in the utility function, all firms in the industry have the same level of output. We have therefore to determine the number of firms, denoted by n, and the level of output per firm, denoted by $\bar{X}$, so $n\bar{X} = X$, where X is total output. In view of the symmetry, and the break-even condition, there are zero pure profits, so that income, M, does not include an element of pure profits (as opposed to the rental of capital).

The profit-maximizing policy involves setting marginal revenue equal to marginal cost. From the demand condition (7-18),

$$-\frac{p_i}{X_i}\frac{\partial X_i}{\partial p_i} = \frac{1}{1-\rho} + \frac{\rho}{1-\rho}\frac{p_i}{\Gamma}\frac{\partial \Gamma}{\partial p_i} \tag{7-19}$$

Moreover,

$$(\Gamma^\rho)\left(\frac{p_i}{\Gamma}\frac{\partial \Gamma}{\partial p_i}\right) = \sum_{j \neq i}\left(\frac{p_i}{X_j}\frac{\partial X_j}{\partial p_i}\right)X_j^\rho + X_i^\rho\left(\frac{p_i}{X_i}\frac{\partial X_i}{\partial p_i}\right) \tag{7-20}$$

At this point, we have to make assumptions about the strategic behaviour of firms. In particular, we assume that firms act in a Cournot–Nash fashion, taking their competitors' outputs as fixed; i.e., $\partial X_j/\partial p_i = 0$ for $i \neq j$. Second, we have to ask whether firms take account of the indirect influence, via Γ, of the change in their own output (i.e., the second term on the right-hand side of (7-20)). In Dixit and Stiglitz (1977) this effect is ignored, but here we allow a more general treatment, introducing a parameter γ, so that $\gamma = 1$ implies that the effect is taken into account and $\gamma = 0$ that it is ignored.

Given the symmetry of the equilibrium, $\Gamma^\rho = nX_i^\rho$. Substituting into (7-19) and denoting the elasticity by ε, we have

$$\varepsilon = \frac{1 - (\gamma\varepsilon\rho/n)}{1 - \rho} \tag{7-19a}$$

or

$$\varepsilon = \frac{1}{1 - \rho(1 - \gamma/n)} \tag{7-19b}$$

If $\gamma = 0$, the elasticity is $1/(1-\rho)$; where $\gamma = 1$, the elasticity increases with the number of firms and approaches $1/(1-\rho)$ as n tends to infinity. In Chamberlinian terminology, this is the elasticity of the dd curve, i.e., the curve relating the demand for each product type to its own price with all other prices held constant. Where all prices move together, which is the Chamberlinian DD curve, the elasticity is unitary.

On the cost side, we depart from the earlier assumption of constant returns to scale. Each firm has a declining cost curve, based on a fixed cost, C_0, and a constant marginal cost, c_X. The equality of marginal revenue and marginal cost requires therefore that the price set by all firms is given by

$$\rho(1 - \gamma/n)p_X = c_X \tag{7-21}$$

The second condition for equilibrium is that firms enter until the next potential entrant would make a loss. If n is sufficiently large that 1 is a small increment, we can assume that the marginal firm is exactly breaking even:

$$(p_X - c_X)\bar{X} = C_0 \tag{7-22}$$

where $\bar{X}$ is determined from the demand curve

$$p_X n\bar{X} = \delta M \tag{7-23}$$

The three equations (7-21)–(7-23) determine the market equilibrium, giving for specified values of c_X, C_0, and M the equilibrium number of active firms:

$$n\frac{C_0}{\delta M} - \frac{\gamma\rho}{n} = 1 - \rho \tag{7-24}$$

The number of firms is larger, the smaller fixed costs (C_0) relative to the total sales (δM), the greater the preference for variety ($1-\rho$), and the more account taken of the indirect effect (γ). The larger the number of firms, the smaller the mark-up over marginal costs (for fixed ρ and c_X). In the Dixit–Stiglitz (1977) case, with $\gamma = 0$ the price is simply c_X/ρ, and the scale of each firm is $[\rho/(1-\rho)]C_0/c_X$. This case is illustrated in Fig. 7-2, where it may be checked that the excess of revenue over variable costs (the shaded area) is equal to the fixed cost C_0, and that a rise in C_0 would shift the equilibrium horizontally.

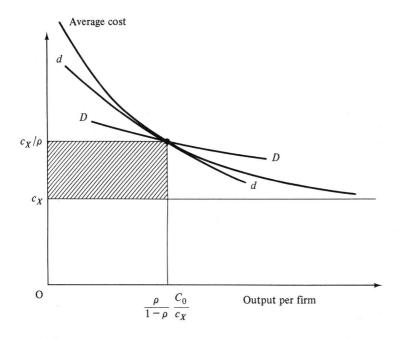

Figure 7-2 Behaviour of monopolistically competitive firm.

General Equilibrium

We now embed this model of monopolistic competition in the general equilibrium framework, allowing for the dependence of the costs c_X and C_0 on the factor prices. For the marginal cost of the corporate sector, we write c_{LX} and c_{KX} as the marginal input requirements of labour and capital, and C_{L0} and C_{K0} as the respective fixed inputs per firm. The assumptions about the non-corporate sector are as before, so that the factor market equilibrium conditions are

$$c_{LX} X + n C_{L0} + c_{LY} Y = L_0 \qquad (7\text{-}25a)$$
$$c_{KX} X + n C_{K0} + c_{KY} Y = K_0 \qquad (7\text{-}25b)$$

(where $X = n\bar{X}$). The conditions for pricing are (7-21) and, for the non-corporate sector,

$$p_Y = c_Y(w, r) \qquad (7\text{-}26)$$

and for demands we have (7-23) and

$$p_Y Y = (1 - \delta)M \qquad (7\text{-}27)$$

where $M = wL_0 + rK_0$.

In contrast to the earlier situation, there are seven unknowns $(X, Y, p_X, p_Y, w, r$ and $n)$, of which one is determined by the choice of *numeraire*. We have seven equations, (7-21)–(7-23), (7-25a and b), (7-26), and (7-27), of which one is redundant. Given that an equilibrium exists, it can be found by solving these equations.[3]

We are particularly interested in the comparative statics, and for this purpose we write down the equations of change. The demand equation is straightforward:

$$\hat{X} - \hat{Y} = -(\hat{p}_X - \hat{p}_Y) \qquad (7\text{-}28)$$

(Because of the special utility function assumed, $\sigma_D = 1$.) Differentiating the pricing equations, and letting θ_{iX} denote the share in *marginal* costs,

$$\hat{p}_X - \hat{p}_Y = \theta^*(\hat{w} - \hat{r}) - \frac{\gamma}{n - \gamma}\hat{n} \qquad (7\text{-}29)$$

Differentiating the factor market equations (7-25),

$$0 = \lambda_{KY}\hat{Y} + \lambda_{KX}\hat{X} + \lambda_{KY}\hat{c}_{KY} + \lambda_{KX}\hat{c}_{KX} + \lambda_{K0}\hat{n} + \lambda_{K0}\hat{C}_{K0} \qquad (7\text{-}30a)$$
$$0 = \lambda_{LY}\hat{Y} + \lambda_{LX}\hat{X} + \lambda_{LY}\hat{c}_{LY} + \lambda_{LX}\hat{c}_{LX} + \lambda_{L0}\hat{n} + \lambda_{L0}\hat{C}_{L0} \qquad (7\text{-}30b)$$

where λ_{L0}, λ_{K0} denote the proportion of total labour and capital used as fixed cost inputs (and λ_{LX}, λ_{KX} those in variable inputs). Defining σ_0 as the elasticity of substitution in fixed costs, and θ_{i0} as the shares in fixed costs

$$\hat{C}_{L0} = -\theta_{K0}\sigma_0(\hat{w} - \hat{r})$$
$$\hat{C}_{K0} = \theta_{L0}\sigma_0(\hat{w} - \hat{r}) \qquad (7\text{-}31)$$

---

[3] Existence can easily be demonstrated in the simple model under consideration here, but it cannot in general be taken for granted in models of monopolistic competition. As pointed out by Roberts and Sonnenschein (1977), the reaction curves may not be convex-valued, and hence the continuity properties necessary for standard existence arguments may be lacking (although there may exist equilibria in mixed strategies).

Substituting from this and the corresponding conditions for $\hat{c}_{iX}$ and $\hat{c}_{iY}$ (see Eq. (6-14)), and subtracting (7-30a) from (7-30b),

$$\hat{X}(\lambda_{LX}-\lambda_{KX})-\hat{Y}(\lambda_{KY}-\lambda_{LY})+\hat{n}(\lambda_{L0}-\lambda_{K0}) = (\hat{w}-\hat{r})(a_X\sigma_X+a_Y\sigma_Y+a_0\sigma_0) \quad (7\text{-}32)$$

where a_0 is defined as $\lambda_{K0}\theta_{L0}+\lambda_{L0}\theta_{K0}$. Suppose that we now define $\lambda^{**} = \lambda_{KY}-\lambda_{LY}$ as a measure of the capital intensity of the Y sector relative to the X sector as a whole. Equation (7-32) may then be re-arranged as (using $X = n\bar{X}$)

$$\lambda^{**}(\hat{X}-\hat{Y}) = (\hat{w}-\hat{r})(a_X\sigma_X+a_Y\sigma_Y+a_0\sigma_0)+(\lambda_{L0}-\lambda_{K0})\hat{\bar{X}} \quad (7\text{-}33)$$

Finally, from the break-even condition in the X sector, substituting for p_X and differentiating,

$$\hat{\bar{X}} = \Delta(\hat{w}-\hat{r}) + \frac{\gamma\hat{n}}{(n-\gamma)[1-\rho(1-\gamma/n)]} \quad (7\text{-}34)$$

Where $\Delta \equiv \theta_{L0}-\theta_{LX}$ is a measure of the relative factor intensities in fixed and variable costs.

The model is easiest to analyse where $\gamma = 0$ (i.e., the firm ignores the indirect effect) and we concentrate on this case. The behaviour of (X/Y), (w/r) and $\bar{X}$ is then governed by equations (7-28) and (7-29), eliminating (p_X/p_Y), (7-33) and (7-34). What in effect is new is the introduction of the terms in $\hat{\bar{X}}$. These depend, as might be expected, on the relative factor intensity of fixed and variable costs in the monopolistically competitive sector via Δ and $(\lambda_{L0}-\lambda_{K0})$. Where $\Delta < 0$, then fixed costs are relatively capital-intensive (in terms of factor shares), and a rise in (w/r) reduces the size of the representative firm (from (7-34) with $\gamma = 0$). This is the case shown in Fig. 7-3, where we also assume $\lambda_{L0} < \lambda_{K0}$ (and $\theta^* > 0$, $\lambda^{**} > 0$). The dashed lines show the effect of the corporate profits tax, to which we now turn.

Impact of Corporate Profits Tax

We now consider the effect of a tax at rate T_{KX} on the use of capital in the X sector, affecting both marginal and fixed costs, taking for simplicity the case $\gamma = 0$. The effect on the three key equations is:

$$\hat{X}-\hat{Y} = -\theta^*(\hat{w}-\hat{r})-\theta_{KX}\hat{T}_{KX} \quad (7\text{-}35)$$

$$\lambda^{**}(\hat{X}-\hat{Y}) = (\hat{w}-\hat{r})(a_X\sigma_X+a_Y\sigma_Y+a_0\sigma_0)+(\lambda_{L0}-\lambda_{K0})\hat{\bar{X}}$$
$$-(a_X\sigma_X+a_0\sigma_0)\hat{T}_{KX} \quad (7\text{-}33')$$

$$\hat{\bar{X}} = \Delta(\hat{w}-\hat{r}-\hat{T}_{KX}) \quad (7\text{-}36)$$

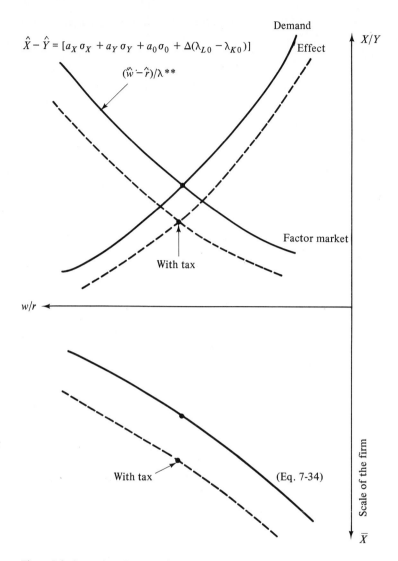

$$\hat{X} - \hat{Y} = [a_X \sigma_X + a_Y \sigma_Y + a_0 \sigma_0 + \Delta(\lambda_{L0} - \lambda_{K0})]$$

Figure 7-3 General equilibrium effect on scale of the firm.

The differences from the competitive case may be seen from these relationships. First, the pricing policy (where $\gamma = 0$) involves a constant mark-up on costs, and the tax on fixed costs does not enter. The analysis is parallel to that in the previous section. Second, there are now two elements to costs in the corporate sector. If there were no fixed costs, then we should have the output effect (term in Eq. (7-35)) and the factor substitution effect (term in Eq. (7-33′)) as before. As it is, fixed costs influence the outcome, through the additional factor substitution effect (7-33′), which depends on the degree of substitutability in fixed costs, and through the effect on the scale of the firm. The latter depends in turn on the capital intensity of fixed costs relative to variable costs (Δ) and relative to the rest of the economy as a whole ($\lambda_{L0} - \lambda_{K0}$). If fixed costs are relatively capital-intensive in both senses, then the first-round effect is for the size of the firm to be increased (see dashed lines in Fig. 7-3) and this reinforces the substitution effect. If the output effect is still strong enough to outweigh the latter effect, then w/r falls, and in the final equilibrium, $\bar{X}$ is still higher. Where w/r rises, this tends to offset the first-round effect.

In order to illustrate the analysis, let us take the extreme case where fixed costs are all capital, and marginal costs all labour (so that $\Delta = -1$ and $\lambda_{L0} = 0$). For a specified factor price ratio (w/r), marginal cost is unaffected by the corporate tax and hence there is no change in price ($\theta_{KX} = 0$ in (7-35)). On the other hand, fixed costs are increased proportionately by T_{KX} and the average cost curve shifts upward—see Fig. 7-4. The new curve is shown by the dashed line; and at the previous

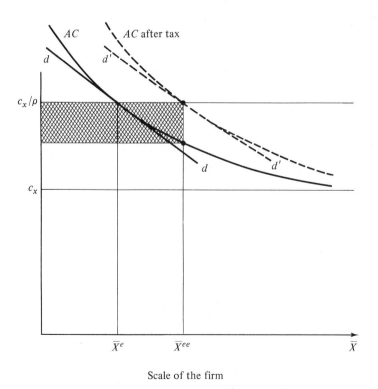

Scale of the firm

Figure 7-4 Effect of corporation tax on monopolistically competitive firm: the shaded area represents the tax revenue.

equilibrium output, $\bar{X}^e$, firms are either making less than the normal rate of profit (if the tax is levied on quasi-rents generated by existing capital) or are finding that replacement investment (if the tax is levied on the purchase of capital equipment) is not profitable. This leads to exit from the industry (total output X is unchanged since the product price is unchanged) until the new dd curve (denoted by $d'd'$) is tangent to the average cost curve at the new equilibrium output level, $\bar{X}^{ee}$. Corporation tax, by increasing the fixed costs, in effect raises the entry barriers to the industry. This does not lead directly to higher prices, but the burden has in part been passed on to the consumer in reduced variety.[4]

This account has so far been in partial equilibrium terms. The increase in $\bar{X}$, and reduction in n for a given output, leads to a reduced demand for capital (see the term in (7-33′)), and this necessitates equilibrating adjustments in w/r. The direction of change now depends on the considerations discussed earlier, except that any change in (w/r) feeds back to $\bar{X}$. It may be seen however that $\lambda^{**} > 0$ means that w/r must rise (where the coefficient of (w/r) is positive), since there is no demand effect in this special case (see Fig. 7-3).

The general solution for the effect on (w/r) and on $\bar{X}$ may be written:

$$(\hat{w} - \hat{r})D = [a_X \sigma_X + a_0 \sigma_0 + \Delta(\lambda_{L0} - \lambda_{K0}) - \theta_{KX} \lambda^{**}]\hat{T}_{KX} \qquad (7\text{-}37)$$

$$\hat{\bar{X}}D = -\Delta(a_Y \sigma_Y + \theta_{KY} \lambda^{**})\hat{T}_{KX} \qquad (7\text{-}38)$$

where the coefficient D is assumed positive and the definition of D is analogous to that in Lecture 6. Of especial interest is the effect on the scale of the firm. Where the parenthetical term in (7-38) is positive (sufficient conditions for which are that $\lambda^{**} > 0$ or $\sigma_Y \geqslant 1$), the gross factor price of capital in the corporate sector rises (w/rT_{KX} falls), and this increases the equilibrium firm size where fixed costs are relatively capital-intensive ($\Delta < 0$). If these conditions hold, and they seem quite plausible, then the corporation tax leads to increased scale, and in this sense increases industrial concentration.

The model of monopolistic competition presented here incorporates only certain features of imperfect competition, and the assumptions on which it is based are very special. This applies for example to the demand side, where the choice of functional forms is more than merely a matter of algebraic convenience (see Dixit and Stiglitz, 1977). On the other hand, the model does provide certain insights, such as those concerning the effects of taxation on the scale of firms, in a fully articulated general equilibrium framework. Moreover, the assumptions about strategic behaviour do not seem—within the terms of reference of the model—to be totally

---

[4] This may be seen from the sub-utility function, where (from (7-15)) $\Gamma = n^{1/\rho}\bar{X} = Xn^{1/\rho - 1}$ and hence is an increasing function of n for a given output.

unreasonable. What the model does not set out to capture, but which is clearly most important, is the small group interdependence of oligopolistic competition. This requires us to take a substantial step beyond the Cournot–Nash assumption to more sophisticated strategies, allowing for collusive behaviour.

> **Exercise 7-2** Consider the dynamic adjustment process which might reasonably be postulated for the monopolistic competition model, paying especial attention to entry and exit. Examine the conditions for local stability and discuss their implications for the comparative static results.

7-4 STRUCTURE OF PRODUCTION

The assumptions made so far about the input–output relations of the economy have been simplistic in the extreme. Each sector has been assumed to produce its final output using only capital and labour. A lot of the debate about tax incidence is however concerned with the inter-industry structure. This applies particularly to indirect taxes and value-added taxation, where significance is attached to the taxation of intermediate goods and the relationship between different stages of production (manufacturing, wholesaling, retailing, etc.).

Input–Output Relations and Taxation of Intermediate Goods

In this section we explore some of the implications of input–output relationships and of different stages of production. Initially, we assume that there is only one basic factor, labour, with perfect competition and constant returns to scale in production. The pricing relation is

$$p_X = c_X(w, p_X, p_Y)$$
$$p_Y = c_Y(w, p_X, p_Y) \tag{7-39}$$

where the cost function has been extended to allow for the fact that X and Y are now used as intermediate goods. From these equations we can solve for the prices p_X and p_Y as functions of the wage, which we take to be fixed at unity.[5]

Suppose now that the government levies an *ad valorem* sales tax on all sales (to final and intermediate users) of the good X. This would clearly provide an incentive for transactions in the X good to be internal to the

---

[5] The fact that we can solve for the prices independently of demand is an example of the non-substitution theorem—see below.

industry (vertical integration) rather than market sales, but to the extent that this does not happen, the after-tax prices q_X, q_Y are given by

$$q_X = T_X c_X(w, q_X, q_Y)$$
$$q_Y = c_Y(w, q_X, q_Y) \qquad (7\text{-}40)$$

Differentiating logarithmically,

$$\hat{q}_X = \left(\frac{c_{XX} q_X}{c_X}\right)\hat{q}_X + \left(\frac{c_{YX} q_Y}{c_X}\right)\hat{q}_Y + \hat{T}_X$$

$$\hat{q}_Y = \left(\frac{c_{XY} q_X}{c_Y}\right)\hat{q}_X + \left(\frac{c_{YY} q_Y}{c_Y}\right)\hat{q}_Y \qquad (7\text{-}41)$$

Using θ_{Xi} to denote the share of intermediate good X in the cost of production of i (similarly θ_{Yi}), we can solve

$$\hat{q}_X D = (1 - \theta_{YY})\hat{T}_X$$
$$\hat{q}_Y D = \theta_{XY} \hat{T}_X \qquad (7\text{-}42)$$

where

$$D \equiv (1 - \theta_{XX})(1 - \theta_{YY}) - \theta_{XY}\theta_{YX}$$

which is strictly positive where labour is used in both industries.

It follows that both final prices are increased by the tax, the extent of the feedback to the price of Y depending on the importance of X in its production (θ_{XY}). What happens to relative prices? This depends on whether $1 - \theta_{YY} \gtrless \theta_{XY}$, but from the definition of θ_{ij}, $1 - \theta_{YY} = \theta_{XY} + \theta_{LY}$, so where labour is employed in sector Y, the relative price of the taxed good must increase. The indirect effect of the tax via θ_{XY} cannot therefore in this case reverse the effect on relative prices.[6]

> **Exercise 7-3** Suppose that the government imposes an arbitrary set of taxes and subsidies on the final sale of goods X and Y and on their use as intermediate inputs (the latter denoted by T_{XY}, T_{XX}, etc.). How does the existence of these taxes and subsidies affect the comparative static analysis of the effects of (1) an *ad valorem* and (2) a specific tax on all sales of good X?

The model described above provides a simple illustration of the effect of input–output relations and the need to allow for the indirect effects. Even if

---

[6] A general version of this result for n goods is proved in Metzler (1951). That the price changes are all positive follows from the Hawkins–Simon condition that the economy be productive, i.e., that the production of one unit of a good does not require more than one unit in inputs, either direct or indirect. Metzler shows that the price of the taxed good rises by more than that of untaxed goods.

the relative price effect is preserved, the quantitative impact may be quite different. Thus, in assessing the impact of an excise on gasoline, both as intermediate and final product, it is necessary to allow for all the indirect effects. The direct effect discouraging people from driving to the beach may be counteracted if the cost of producing garden swimming pools is increased; the direct effect on the cost of oil-fired central heating may be substantially offset if electricity prices rise. These lessons have been absorbed in the international trade literature, in the form of the concept of "effective protection"; but in the field of public finance they have received less attention.

To see the implications of corporation tax, T_{KX}, we now treat the commodity inputs as circulating capital, on which there is a required rate of profit r. The pricing equations then become

$$
\begin{aligned}
p_X &= c_X[w, p_X(1+rT_{KX}), p_Y(1+rT_{KX})] \\
p_Y &= c_Y[w, p_X(1+r), p_Y(1+r)]
\end{aligned}
\tag{7-43}
$$

As before, we take the wage as unity, and the key element is the determination of r. Suppose that r is fixed (for example by the balanced growth conditions—see the next Lecture). The non-substitution theorem then applies, and prices are again determined independently of demand conditions. The effect of the corporation tax is like that of an excise tax, and the considerations we have just discussed apply with equal force. The tendency of the tax to increase the relative price of the corporate sector is muted by the input–output interactions (see Metcalfe and Steedman, 1971, for further discussion of this model).

Hierarchical Production Model

The analysis so far has treated the technology of the different sectors in a symmetric fashion, but the hierarchical structure is important. This applies particularly to discussions of retail versus manufacturer's sales taxes (see for example Friedlaender, 1967). Here we present a simple hierarchical model which also relaxes the assumptions of constant returns to scale and perfect competition, although we revert to the assumption of a single factor, labour, which is taken as the *numeraire*.

The assumptions about technology and about the form of imperfect competition are in fact based on those of Section 7-3. Both manufacturers and retailers are assumed to act as monopolistic competitors, charging mark-ups m^m, m^r, respectively, on marginal cost. Both sectors have a fixed labour cost C_0^m, C_0^r, respectively, per establishment, and constant marginal cost. The technology is hierarchical, with the manufacturer producing his output using labour alone (c^m per unit) and the retailer—the second stage—using in fixed proportions purchases from the manufacturing sector and labour (c^r per unit).

The equilibrium of this model may be seen straightforwardly. With labour as the *numeraire*, the cost curve of a single manufacturing establishment is $C_0^m + c^m X^m$ where X^m is the output of the establishment. With free entry, this must equal revenue. Since the manufacturer's price, p^m, is a mark-up on marginal cost, the break-even condition is

$$p^m X^m = (1 + m^m) c^m X^m = C_0^m + c^m X^m \tag{7-44}$$

It follows that the size of the firm is given by

$$X^m = C_0^m / (c^m m^m) \tag{7-45}$$

In the retail sector, the cost is

$$C_0^r + (c^r + p^m) X^r \tag{7-46}$$

where X^r is the output per establishment. With free entry, this must again equal the revenue. The retailer's price, p^r, is a mark-up on marginal cost, so

$$p^r X^r = (1 + m^r)(c^r + p^m) X^r = C_0^r + (c^r + p^m) X^r \tag{7-47}$$

The equilibrium size of the retail establishment is therefore

$$X^r = \frac{C_0^r}{m^r [c^r + (1 + m^m) c^m]} \tag{7-48}$$

The conditions for equilibrium in the intermediate good market are that

$$n^m X^m = n^r X^r \equiv X \tag{7-49}$$

where n^m, n^r are the number of manufacturing and retailing firms, respectively. In the labour market, the condition is

$$n^m C_0^m + n^r C_0^r + (c^m + c^r) X = L_0 \tag{7-50}$$

The general equilibrium of the economy involves solving these three equations for X, n^m and n^r, where we substitute for X^m and X^r from (7-45) and (7-48). The solution is:

$$X = \frac{L_0}{(1 + m^r)[c^r + c^m(1 + m^m)]}$$

$$n^m = \frac{c^m m^m X}{C_0^m} \quad \text{and} \quad n^r = \frac{m^r [c^r + (1 + m^m) c^m] X}{C_0^r} \tag{7-51}$$

As in the monopolistic competition model of Section 7-3, the scale of the firm is determined by the relationship between fixed and variable costs. For given costs and mark-ups, the number of firms expands proportionately to output. A decrease in the mark-up in the retail sector leads, other things equal, to a rise in scale in this sector and a fall in the number of establishments (n^r is proportional to $m^r / (1 + m^r)$).

Impact of Taxation

In order to illustrate the effects of taxation, let us suppose that the government imposes a tax on labour employed in the retail sector, so that C_0^r and c^r become $C_0^r T$ and $c^r T$, respectively. This is like the selective employment tax operated at one time in the United Kingdom.[7] This has no effect on the manufacturer's price, which is determined solely by c^m, but leads to a rise in the retail price. If we assume that the input coefficients and mark-ups are unchanged, then the break-even condition in the retail sector becomes

$$p^r X^r = (1 + m^r)(c^r T + p^m)X^r = C_0^r T + (c^r T + p^m)X^r$$

or

$$X^r = \frac{C_0^r T}{m^r[c^r T + (1 + m^m)c^m]} \tag{7-52}$$

Assuming that the government returns the proceeds of the tax in lump-sum form, the condition for equilibrium in the labour market is unchanged, and the new equilibrium is

$$X = \frac{L_0}{c^r(1 + m^r) + c^m(1 + m^m)(1 + m^r/T)}$$

$$n^r = \left(\frac{m^r}{C_0^r}\right)[c^r + (1 + m^m)c^m/T]X \tag{7-51'}$$

(the scale of firms in the manufacturing sector is unaltered). For a given output, the number of retailing establishments tends to fall (X^r is increased) as a result of the tax. To secure equilibrium, output and the number of manufacturing firms have to increase. The tax has the effect of reducing the overhead component of retailing and thus increasing total output. If there were to be a reduction in the mark-up, then this would further reinforce the effect.

> **Exercise 7-4** In the context of this model, examine the effect of a manufacturer's *ad valorem* sales tax. What conclusions can be drawn about the "pyramiding" of taxes? How does the tax compare with a value added tax? (See Friedlaender, 1967.)

The models described in this section have been rather special in their assumptions, and could be elaborated in several respects. They serve none the less to illustrate the way in which the structure of production may

---

[7] A tax imposed from 1966 to 1973 on labour in the service industries (with a subsidy being paid to manufacturing). The brainchild of Lord Kaldor, it generated a great deal of controversy, and employment for one of the authors, who worked on the inquiry into the effects of the tax under Professor W. B. Reddaway (1970).

influence the incidence of taxation in a simple general equilibrium framework. It is clear that any empirical application, developing along the lines described in Lecture 6, should take account of the input–output structure, and the nature of firm behaviour at different stages of production.

7-5 NON-MARKET-CLEARING

The general equilibrium analysis of tax incidence has to date been undertaken largely independently of the literature on macroeconomics. Thus, competitive equilibrium models, with all markets clearing, have been used to investigate the incidence of different taxes, whereas a quite separate literature, using aggregate demand/monetary models, has examined the implications of taxes for the level of employment and the rate of inflation. In other areas of economics, this gap has been narrowed, a notable example being the integration of relative price effects and income–expenditure determination in international economics; but in public finance the separation has persisted much longer.[8] This section considers some of the issues that arise when examining the incidence of taxation in a model where markets do not necessarily clear, focusing particularly on unemployment.

Wage Rigidity and Unemployment

In order to examine the implications for tax incidence, we need to specify a theory of involuntary unemployment, and here there is considerable disagreement. A large number of models have been put forward in recent years, described variously as "Keynesian", "disequilibrium" and "non-Walrasian". It is not our intention here to debate the merits of these models, or their relation to the *General Theory*. Nor do we make any claims for the realism of the particular models discussed. The intention is to illustrate how the conclusions regarding tax incidence may need to be modified when markets do not clear.

In this spirit we take a model that has not been particularly studied in the literature but that remains close to the discussion of earlier sections. We introduce the notion of wage rigidity, represented by the wage bearing a fixed relationship with the product prices:

$$w = v_X p_X + v_Y p_Y \tag{7-53}$$

---

[8] In this respect public economics has been slow to absorb the lessons of James Meade's *Balance of Payments* (1951). In contrast, his *Trade and Welfare* (1955) has directly and indirectly had a very considerable influence on recent public finance. However, note should be made of work in the Keynesian tradition. An early example is Kalecki (1937); more recent references include Asimakopoulos and Burbidge (1974) and Eatwell (1971).

where v_i are fixed weights (say, in a retail price index). If we take good Y as the *numeraire*, and there is a mark-up m_i in sector i, then the price equations, with constant returns to scale, are

$$p_X = (1+m_X)(c_{LX}w+c_{KX}rT_{KX})$$
$$1 = (1+m_Y)(c_{LY}w+c_{KY}r) \tag{7-54}$$

The price system of the economy is self-contained: from (7-53) and (7-54) we can determine w, r, and p_X. In this sense we are in a "fix-price" world (Hicks, 1965), and changes in quantities do not feed back to prices. (It does not of course imply that prices are necessarily constant over time.) This means that we can solve directly for the effect of the corporate profits tax on prices. Differentiating,

$$\hat{w} = \left(\frac{v_X p_X}{v_X p_X + v_Y p_Y}\right)\hat{p}_X \equiv \beta(p_X)\hat{p}_X \tag{7-55a}$$

$$\hat{p}_X = \theta_{KX}(\hat{r}+\hat{T}_{KX})+\theta_{LX}\hat{w} \tag{7-55b}$$

$$0 = \theta_{KY}\hat{r}+\theta_{LY}\hat{w} \tag{7-55c}$$

Hence

$$(\hat{w}-\hat{r}) = (-\hat{r})/\theta_{LY}$$

and

$$\hat{r}[(1-\beta)\theta_{KY}+\beta\theta_{KX}] = -\beta\theta_{KX}\theta_{LY}\hat{T}_{KX} \tag{7-56}$$

The extent of shifting depends on the weight of the two products in the price index to which wages are linked. In the extreme case $\beta = 0$, where the wage is rigid in terms of the non-corporate sector output, the corporation tax has no effect on the after-tax return and in this sense is fully shifted. In this case, $\hat{w} = 0$ and $\hat{p}_X = \theta_{KX}\hat{T}_{KX}$. At the other extreme, $\beta = 1$, the rate of return falls and the wage rises, relative to the *numeraire*; at the same time p_X and the gross rate of return still both rise. The rise in price is given by $\hat{p}_X = \theta_{KY}\hat{T}_{KX}$ and is therefore greater (smaller) than where $\beta = 0$ according as the corporate sector is more labour (capital) intensive.

Taxation and the Level of Employment

The effects of the tax are not however limited to the price system, and of particular interest is the effect on employment. This depends on the demand side. The recent literature on macroeconomics has emphasized the effect of rationing on one market (e.g., labour) on decisions in other markets. Consumers maximize utility subject to possible quantity constraints. In the present case, this may be illustrated by the assumption that the "representative" consumer chooses his supply of labour L^S to maximize

$U(X, Y, L^S)$ subject to $p_X X + p_Y Y = wL^S + rK_0$, the supply of capital being taken as fixed. If however the desired labour supply exceeds that demanded, L^D, the consumer is rationed on this market and utility is maximized subject to the constraint $L^S = L^D$ (the process of rationing is assumed to be such that each worker is employed for the same fraction of the desired L^S). (For a clear discussion, in a public finance context, see Dixit, 1976c.)

Where there is unemployment (labour supply rationed), the demand side may be represented by the "partial" expenditure function $e(p_X, p_Y, L^D, U)$, with the consumer's behaviour being determined by

$$e(p_X, p_Y, L^D, U) = wL^D + rK_0 \qquad (7\text{-}57)$$

$$X = e_X \qquad (7\text{-}58)$$

where e_X denotes the derivative with respect to p_X. The former gives, on the right-hand side, the income received, and the latter uses the standard properties of the expenditure function. To see the effect of an easing of the rationing constraint, differentiate totally:

$$e_L \, dL^D + e_U \, dU = w dL^D$$
$$dX = e_{XL} \, dL^D + e_{XU} \, dU$$

so

$$\frac{dX}{dL^D} = e_{XL} + (w - e_L) e_{XU} / e_U \qquad (7\text{-}59)$$

A rise in employment has therefore a "substitution" effect (via e_{XL}) and an income effect, where the latter depends on $(w - e_L)$. Where the consumer is rationed, this is positive, i.e., he would like to work more.

The demand functions may therefore be written $X(p_X, L^D, w, r)$, $Y(p_X, L^D, w, r)$ where we have taken account of the fact that Y is the *numeraire* and that utility depends on w, r and L^D. In writing them this way we have assumed that labour is rationed on the supply side, i.e., that in the factor market

$$c_{KX} X + c_{KY} Y = K_0 \qquad (7\text{-}60)$$

$$c_{LX} X + c_{LY} Y = L^D < L^S \qquad (7\text{-}61)$$

In other words, at the factor prices ruling, the demand for factors is such that the constraint on capital is binding but not the constraint on labour (we do not go into the dynamic adjustment process by which this rationed equilibrium has been reached). This is only one of the possible equilibrium situations. Whether the economy is in an unemployment regime or another regime will depend on the particular values of the parameters.

Let us now consider the effect of the corporation tax. Assuming that the equilibrium condition (7-60) continues to hold, we can derive, using the same approach as before, the change in employment:

$$\hat{L}^D = a_X \sigma_X \hat{T}_{KX} + \lambda^* (\hat{X} - \hat{Y}) - (a_X \sigma_X + a_Y \sigma_Y)(\hat{w} - \hat{r}) \qquad (7\text{-}62)$$

From this we can see that the effect of the corporation tax on employment operates in three ways:

1. a direct effect on the use of labour in the corporate sector, which depends on the elasticity of substitution (σ_X);
2. a demand effect, which depends on the relative labour intensities: if the corporate sector is relatively labour-intensive, then a relative rise in its output implies an expansion of employment;
3. if $\beta > 0$ there is a further effect, since (w/r) rises and hence there is a substitution against labour in both sectors.

In the case of the demand effect, it depends on the price elasticities as before, but also on the substitution effects (via e_{XL} and e_{YL}) and the income effects (see Eq. (7-59)).

The effect of a corporation tax, raising the cost of capital in one sector, depends therefore on the elasticities of substitution, on the factor intensities, and on the reactions of the rationed consumer. As in the full employment models considered earlier, the direct impact may be more than offset by the indirect, general equilibrium, effects—for example, if the demand response is biased towards capital-intensive industries. It may be noted that, in evaluating the welfare consequences of a change in the tax rate, we need to take account of the effects on employment. Whereas in the full employment model the indirect utility function depended only on the prices $V(p_X, p_Y, r, w)$, it now has to incorporate the quantity constraint $L^S \leqslant L^D$. Where the individual is unable to sell all the labour he wishes, an expansion of employment contributes *ceteris paribus* to an increase in welfare.

The model is clearly unsatisfactory in a number of respects; for example, the absence of investment, the failure to allow for the fact that the incidence of unemployment is not spread evenly and of its consequent distributional effects, and the assumption that prices are rigid but quantities are perfectly flexible. Where consumers are rationed on the labour (or any other) market, the formation of expectations takes on additional significance. Current behaviour depends not just on current and expected prices, but also on the quantity constraints that people expect to face in the future. The public finance model needs to be developed in these respects, drawing on the recent developments in macroeconomics. The purpose of this section has simply been to indicate how non-market-clearing can be handled.

> **Exercise 7-5** Examine the effect, in the model described above, of an increase in government expenditure on good X. How does the expansion of employment depend on the various parameters of the model?

7-6 CONCLUDING COMMENTS

The conclusions of this Lecture are perhaps concerned more with developments in economic theory than with the incidence of taxation, and we have emphasized throughout the Lectures that the study of taxation can be no more soundly based than the models that are employed (explicitly or implicitly). This is well illustrated by the subjects covered in this Lecture. Among the areas where further development is needed before the analysis can be taken further are the objectives of unions (Section 7-2), oligopolistic behaviour (Section 7-3), and satisfactory models of macroeconomic disequilibrium (Section 7-5).

This emphasis on economic theory is important, since many of the controversies concerning economic policy arise from disagreements about the appropriate model of the economy. Does the assumption of a perfectly competitive economy at full employment provide a good basis for the analysis of the incidence of taxation? The answer to that question depends in part on how sensitive the results are to the specification of the model, and one can view this Lecture as being directed towards throwing light on this issue.

At a rather general level, the analysis has borne out the earlier lessons. The theoretical tools that we developed in the preceding Lecture have been shown to be extremely versatile; they enabled us to analyse easily the incidence of taxation in a variety of economies exhibiting different kinds of imperfections. Moreover, the results have reinforced the belief that the general equilibrium effects are potentially important and can be safely ignored only in special circumstances (this, we shall see, is even more true in the long-run models explored in the next Lecture).

At the same time, the detailed results have, in some cases, proved to be quite sensitive to the specification of the model; and the models have introduced considerations (such as the effect on the scale of firms) that were absent from the simple competitive equilibrium treatment. The development of the theoretical framework remains therefore of high priority.

READING

It is difficult to provide any general reading for this Lecture. Reference should however be made to the literature on macroeconomic disequilibrium, where the recent contributions include Barro and Grossman (1976), Malinvaud (1977) and the papers in Harcourt (1977). For valuable surveys of temporary equilibrium theory, see Bliss (1975) and Grandmont (1977).

EIGHT

TAXATION AND DEBT IN A GROWING ECONOMY

8-1 INTRODUCTION

One of the major concerns about the tax system is whether it discourages or encourages the growth of the economy. Although the belief in growth as a value in itself, or as the remedy for the ills of society, which seemed to be prevalent in the early 1960s has given way to a more sceptical attitude, it seems clear that an understanding of the long-run consequences of tax and expenditure policy is essential. We are concerned particularly with two basic questions:

1. How do adjustments in the rate of capital accumulation alter the results on the incidence of taxation derived in the previous Lectures?
2. How does the tax system—and other governmental policies, including the social security system—affect the long-run pattern of growth in the economy?

   To answer these questions, we have to formulate a theory of the determinants of growth. In Section 8-2, we outline the one-sector equilibrium growth model that has been used in most treatments of the dynamic effects of taxation. The application of this model to the question of incidence is discussed in Section 8-3. We then turn to a model where the motives for capital accumulation are set explicitly in terms of the life-cycle savings theory treated in Lecture 3, and compare it with alternative approaches (Section 8-4). The implications for one major question of dynamic incidence—the burden of the national debt—are developed in Section 8-5.

227

Nature of Growth Theory

Before embarking on the exposition of the theoretical model itself, it may be helpful to consider briefly the nature of the theory of economic growth, how it should be interpreted, and some of the sources of controversy.

A substantial part of the literature has been concerned with the properties of *steady-state* or *balanced* growth. This is a situation where the rate of growth (by which we shall always mean the proportionate growth) of all relevant magnitudes remains constant over time. Thus capital, labour, output, and total consumption all grow at constant rates (in the most straightforward case these rates are equal). Where such steady-state paths exist, then we can examine how they are influenced by changes in the parameters.

What however is the relation of steady-state paths to the behaviour of the economy? Suppose that we begin with the competitive model of Lecture 6, where the full employment equilibrium of the economy is determined (we assume for the moment uniquely) for given levels of capital and labour. The changes over time in capital and labour then govern the *equilibrium path* followed. The question we now have to ask is whether the equilibrium path converges to a steady state. Suppose, for example, that the labour force grows exogenously at a constant exponential rate, n. (This assumption is made throughout the analysis.)[1] The rate of growth of capital depends however on the level of savings (on the equilibrium path, planned savings are equal to planned investment); and whether or not there is convergence to steady state rests on the properties of the savings function.

Examination of the behaviour of equilibrium paths in simple models suggests that convergence to a steady state may or may not be assured. Moreover, the time required for the economy to approach the vicinity of a steady state may be quite long—longer than it may reasonably be expected that the parameters remain unchanged. In this sense the steady state may be a poor approximation, and we should study the full equilibrium path. The position is further complicated when we allow for *disequilibrium behaviour*. As we have seen in Lecture 7, equilibrium in the factor or output markets may not be achieved, and we have to examine in the context of a fully specified disequilibrium model whether the economy converges to an equilibrium path, which in turn may or may not be tending to a steady state. It is quite possible that the economy may converge to a steady state not characterized by equilibrium, e.g., where capital and the labour force are growing at the same rate, but there is a constant level of unemployment.

The significance to be attached to steady-state and equilibrium paths has been much debated, and indeed the whole subject of growth theory is

---

[1] The model may be extended to allow the rate of population growth to depend on *per capita* income or other variables—see Solow (1956) and Hahn and Matthews (1964, Section I.6).

surrounded by controversy. In part this is concerned with the omission of key features of reality, such as uncertainty, the role of expectations, and market imperfections, which have been discussed to some extent in earlier Lectures. In part it is directed at particular features of the standard treatment—notably the assumption of an aggregate production function. In the main part of these Lectures, we work with the "orthodox" Solow (1956) model, in which malleable capital is used to produce a single output according to an aggregate production function, with a higher ratio of capital to labour being associated with a lower competitive rate of profit. Thus, in Section 8-3 we compare steady-state economies with different tax rates, and use the aggregate production function to relate the differences in capital–labour ratios, k, to differences in rates of profit, r.

Now this steady-state comparison is a good example of a case where the criticisms of the orthodox model are well taken. The relationship between k and r is one that cannot be guaranteed to hold when we allow for the heterogeneity of capital, as the debate on "reswitching" has brought out (see for example Bliss, 1975, and Harcourt, 1972). Thus, the findings are not ones for which generality can be claimed.

This important qualification, together with the points made earlier about the status of equilibrium paths, needs to be remembered when interpreting the results. It is none the less consistent with the purposes of the analysis. We are not seeking to provide a definitive, exhaustive account of the effects of policy; rather, we are using the models as a source of insights and as vehicles for illustrating mechanisms that may not otherwise be apparent. For example, we show that a tax on investment income may, in the malleable capital model, be shifted via a rise in the gross rate of return, with its redistributive potential being consequently reduced. This conclusion may not remain universally true when we allow for heterogeneous capital; none the less, the *possibility* remains that shifting may take place—and we need to check when considering policy proposals the likelihood of this actually happening. It is in this spirit that we use the orthodox model.[2]

Taxation and Balanced Growth Incidence

In analysing the impact of taxation on steady-state and equilibrium paths, there are several effects that are of particular interest: (1) on the *rate of growth* in the long run; (2) on the *level* of *per capital* income and consumption; (3) on the distribution of income *among factors*; and (4) on the distribution of income *among individuals*. We shall be considering the first three in this Lecture, paying particular attention to the case of a tax on capital income. The last aspect is discussed in Lecture 9.

---

[2] We commend to the reader the advice of Mirrlees that one "can entertain a model and use it without being committed to it" (1973, p. xii).

As in the static model, the basis for comparison is of critical importance, and the question may be posed in several ways. We can, for example, examine the consequences of increasing a particular tax, with the proceeds being spent on current government expenditure, which does not affect savings decisions, there being no other change in government policy. On the other hand, just as in the case of short-run macro-policy we consider offsetting changes which keep the level of aggregate demand unchanged, so in the long-run growth context we may want to compare situations where the aggregate capital–labour ratio is unchanged. The government has instruments, particularly monetary and debt policy, with which it can offset the aggregate effects of taxes. In a sense, as we argue later, debt policy provides a lump-sum redistribution between different generations; within limits, any depressing effect on savings caused by tax policy can be offset in a non-distortionary manner. An alternative notion of incidence to use in this context is therefore what we call *balanced growth path incidence*, where the rate of interest is kept constant by debt policy. Even though the government is undertaking compensatory actions to keep the interest rate constant, this does not mean that the tax-cum-monetary policy change has no effect (as we shall see).

8-2 AN AGGREGATE MODEL OF EQUILIBRIUM GROWTH

In this section, we describe the one-sector equilibrium growth model in the absence of taxation.[3]

Assumptions of the Model

The production side is assumed to be represented by an aggregate production function relating output, Y, to total (malleable) capital, K, and labour, L:

$$Y = F(K, L) \tag{8-1}$$

where F is a twice differentiable increasing concave function, homogeneous of degree one. Initially we assume no technical progress. The homogeneity (constant returns to scale) assumption means that the production function may be written in the intensive form:

$$Y = Lf(k) \tag{8-2}$$

---

[3] The model is that of Solow (1956). For further discussion and references, see Hahn and Matthews (1964), Solow (1970), Jones (1975), Dixit (1976b), and Stiglitz and Uzawa (1969). For a more mathematical treatment, see Burmeister and Dobell (1970) and Wan (1971).

where $k = K/L$ is the capital–labour ratio and the assumptions described above mean that $f' \geqslant 0, f'' < 0$. If in addition we require that

$$f'(0) = \infty, \quad f'(\infty) = 0 \tag{8-3}$$

the production function is said to satisfy the Inada (1963) conditions, but we do not necessarily want to impose these restrictions. The output may be defined as either gross output, or output net of depreciation.

The supply of labour is assumed to be a fixed fraction of the total population, to be exogenously determined, and to grow exponentially at rate n:

$$L = L_0 e^{nu} \tag{8-4}$$

or

$$\dot{L}/L = n \tag{8-4'}$$

where u denotes time, and $\dot{L}$ the derivative with respect to time. The case of an elastic labour supply, where the labour services supplied per person change with the wage rate, is treated by Feldstein (1974b). He shows that the labour supply response has no effect on the steady-state wage and interest rate (with constant returns these depend not on the absolute size of the labour force but only on its rate of growth).

At each moment capital is also inelastically supplied; over time its growth depends on savings and on depreciation. The gross savings rate out of output Y is assumed to depend on the capital–labour ratio (the nature of this dependence is discussed below), and we take the simple case of a proportionate rate of depreciation, γ, often referred to as "radioactive decay". This means that

$$\dot{K} = s(k)Y - \gamma K \tag{8-5}$$

or

$$\dot{K}/K = \frac{s(k)f(k)}{k} - \gamma \tag{8-5'}$$

On an equilibrium path it is assumed that both capital and labour are fully employed. From the production and factor supply equations, we obtain the basic growth equation. Differentiating (8-1),

$$\dot{Y}/Y = \left(\frac{F_L L}{Y}\right)\frac{\dot{L}}{L} + \left(\frac{F_K K}{Y}\right)\frac{\dot{K}}{K} \tag{8-6}$$

i.e., the weighted average of the growth rates of labour and capital. If we write g_x for the proportional growth rate of variable x, and let

$$\alpha = \frac{F_L L}{Y}, \quad 1 - \alpha = \frac{F_K K}{Y} \tag{8-7}$$

we have (using (8-4′))

$$g_Y = \alpha n + (1-\alpha)g_K \qquad (8\text{-}8)$$

and if we let $y(= Y/L)$ denote output *per capita*,

$$g_y = g_Y - g_L = (1-\alpha)(g_K - n) = (1-\alpha)g_k \qquad (8\text{-}9)$$

(this needs to be modified where there is technical progress—see below).

These relationships are purely technological, and do not assume anything about the degree of competition. With perfect competition, factor payments are equal to the value of marginal products:[4]

(wage) $\qquad w = \partial Y/\partial L = f(k) - kf'(k) \qquad$ (8-10a)

(interest rate) $\; r = \partial Y/\partial K = f'(k) \qquad$ (8-10b)

(With perfect competition, α is equal to the competitive share of labour.) The state of the economy is then completely described by the capital–labour ratio.

Dynamic Behaviour of the Model

The first question we need to ask is whether there is a steady-state solution. This requires that capital and labour grow at the same rate; i.e., $g_Y = g_K = g_L = n$ and $g_k = 0$. From (8-4′) and (8-5′),

$$g_k = \frac{s(k)f(k) - (n+\gamma)k}{k} \equiv \frac{\phi(k)}{k} \qquad (8\text{-}11)$$

Balanced growth requires that gross saving per worker just offsets depreciation and the capital-widening necessary to allow for the growth of the labour force. There is no capital-deepening. The simplest case is where $s(k)$ is a constant, s. The existence of a steady-state solution depends then on the extent of possible variation in the output–capital ratio, i.e., whether for all values of s, n, and γ there exists a k such that

$$\frac{f(k)}{k} = \frac{(n+\gamma)}{s} \qquad (8\text{-}12)$$

It is sufficient for the existence of a solution that the production function satisfies the Inada conditions and that $f(0) = 0$. This is shown in Fig. 8-1a. There is a unique value of k, denoted by k^*, such that (8-12) holds. On the other hand, neither uniqueness nor existence is guaranteed in more general cases. Suppose that $f(0) < 0$, which seems a possible situation. In this case we may have either no steady state (Fig. 8-1b) or two steady states (Fig. 8-1c).

From the diagrams we can readily trace the full dynamic path of the

---

[4] A constant degree of monopoly could straightforwardly be introduced.

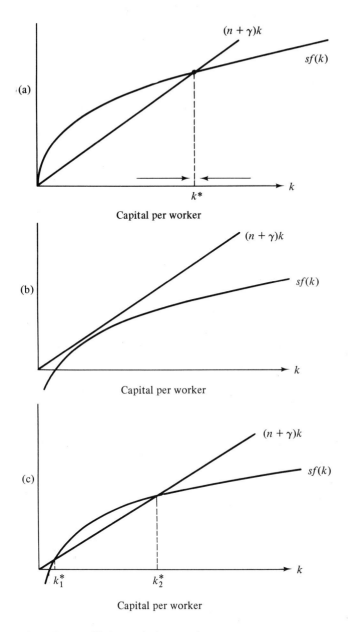

Figure 8-1 Equilibrium paths in a growing economy.

economy, and examine whether equilibrium paths converge to a steady state. Suppose that the initial capital stock is k_0 and $k_0 < k^*$ in Fig. 8-1a. This means that $sf > (n+\gamma)k$ and hence $\dot{k} > 0$. The economy follows a path with rising capital per man (see arrow), and approaches asymptotically $k = k^*$. Conversely, if $k_0 > k^*$, the economy approaches k^* from above. There is therefore a globally stable long-run equilibrium at k^*. In the more complicated case of Fig. 8-1c, the equilibrium k_2^* is *locally* stable in that there is an interval around it such that the economy tends to converge; but it is not globally stable. The final outcome depends on the initial capital stock: if $k_0 > k_1^*$, the economy converges to k_2^*; if $k_0 < k_1^*$, k tends to zero.[5]

The model may be seen as describing the dynamic development of a simple general equilibrium system of the kind discussed in Lecture 6. At the same time, the structure of the model is considerably less rich. On the production side we have in effect collapsed the two sectors into one. This allows us to by-pass a number of problems that have been discussed in the literature on two-sector models, including the uniqueness of momentary equilibrium (see, e.g., Dixit, 1976b, Ch. 6). Uniqueness is typically assumed, but is by no means guaranteed, as we have seen in Lecture 6. On the demand side, we may treat the two goods as corresponding to investment and consumption goods (identical in production). We have not however given a very careful treatment of the allocation of demand—the savings decision—and we turn now to this, and to two other features of the model that need elaboration.

Savings Behaviour

Starting from a disequilibrium perspective, the accumulation of capital depends on the specification of *ex ante* investment and savings functions and the mechanism by which they are brought into equilibrium (this being the kernel of the instability problem posed by the Harrod model). The study of equilibrium growth paths, on the other hand, takes as given that investment and full employment savings are equal, and proceeds typically by analysing development over time in terms of the behaviour of savings. This procedure, which is that adopted in the model described above, is quite legitimate; it does however underline the limitations of confining attention to equilibrium paths. The equilibrium assumption allows us in effect to abstract from the determinants of investment—and the role of uncertainty, expectations, "animal spirits", etc.—but at the cost of assuming that disequilibrium phenomena are unimportant for the purpose at hand or are transitory. Since the mechanism by which equilibrium is attained is not in general specified (although see Tobin, 1955, Solow, 1956, and Meade, 1961), it is a heroic assumption.

---

[5] The condition for local stability at k^* of the equation (see (8-11)) $\dot{k} = \phi(k)$ is that $\phi'(k^*) < 0$.

Within the confines of an equilibrium model, the specification of the savings function needs careful consideration. In much of the literature, savings are assumed to be based on rules of thumb. The proportional savings case is an instance of this. Another common assumption is that of "classical" savings, where there are different propensities to save by type of income or class. In the former (Kaldor, 1955) version there is a propensity to save s_r out of profits and s_w out of wages. In the latter (Pasinetti, 1962) version the differential savings propensities are associated with capitalists and workers. The foundation for the Kaldor view has been discussed in Lecture 3, where we brought out its relationship with the company sector and the extent to which individuals see through the corporate veil. (The underlying assumptions about corporate financing—and the relationship with the considerations discussed in Lecture 5—are an aspect in need of more elaboration.)

Where the savings relationship is of the classical (Kaldorian) type, the condition for steady growth becomes

$$s(k)f(k) = s_r(1-\alpha)f(k) + s_w\alpha f(k) = (n+\gamma)k \qquad (8\text{-}13)$$

In the extreme case where there is no saving out of wages,

$$s_r(1-\alpha)f = (n+\gamma)k \quad \text{or} \quad s_r r = n+\gamma \qquad (8\text{-}14)$$

The steady-state rate of return is given by the rate of growth and the propensity to save; indeed, where all profits are saved, the rate of return (net of depreciation) equals the rate of growth.

A quite different approach to the specification of savings is based on household utility maximization (as discussed at some length in Lecture 3). In general, the rigorous derivation of a savings function by this route is likely to be complex, but in Section 8-4 we consider a simple two-period life-cycle model illustrative of this line of argument.

Technical Progress and Natural Resources

The easiest way to introduce technical progress is to assume that factors become more effective over time, e.g., that one worker can do the work that two did a decade ago. Where this *factor-augmenting* technical progress is going on at constant exponential rates, the production function may be written[6]

$$Y = F(e^{\kappa u}K, e^{\lambda u}L) \qquad (8\text{-}15)$$

where κ denotes the rate of capital augmentation and λ the rate of labour augmentation. Differentiating logarithmically,

$$g_Y = \alpha(n+\lambda) + (1-\alpha)(g_K+\kappa) \qquad (8\text{-}16)$$

---

[6] We are taking here a macroeconomic view of technical change and as such may be ignoring important microeconomic aspects. For one example as to how the factor-augmenting approach may be misleading, see Atkinson and Stiglitz (1969).

It can however be shown (see, e.g., Dixit, 1976b, p. 74) that steady growth with strictly positive factor shares is not possible unless technical progress can be written in a purely labour-augmenting form.

The next step is to make technical progress endogenous to the model. Both the direction and the rate of technical advance are likely to be influenced by economic variables, including taxation and government expenditure. The *direction* of technical change has been explored in a series of papers initiated by the work of Kennedy (1964), von Weizsäcker (1966) and Samuelson (1965). They assume that there is a trade-off between labour-augmenting and capital-augmenting technical progress, and that firms maximize the instantaneous rate of unit cost reduction (i.e., firms are myopic, or are able to appropriate returns for only one instant). This "innovation possibility frontier" captures the notion of choice but leaves open a number of questions, notably the determination of its shape and location, which must in part result from the deliberate allocation of resources to research and development. This can be thought of as an investment—an expenditure today for which there is hoped to be a return in future years in the form of a lowering in the costs of production (for a process invention). Since raising the rate of interest lowers the present discounted value of returns, a higher rate of interest would tend to be associated with a lower rate of technical progress: we would have $\lambda(k)$ with $\lambda' > 0$. A rather different view of endogenous technical advance sees it as the product of experience or "learning by doing" (Arrow, 1962). Where the stock of past experience is proxied by the stock of capital, the effect operates like increasing returns to scale.[7]

Finally, if there exists a finite supply of an exhaustible, non-renewable natural resource, then the rate at which it is depleted affects the rate of growth of the economy; but the rate at which it is exhausted depends on (and influences) the rate of interest. Comparing steady states, a high savings rate is associated with low interest rates and low rates of resource depletion, and hence with higher growth rates than economies with lower savings rates (Stiglitz, 1974c). The introduction of a second asset means that we have to take account of the capital market equilibrium condition: the return from holding stocks of the natural resource must equal the return to physical capital. With this extension, the convergence of the equilibrium paths to the steady state becomes problematic (Hahn, 1966). Moreover, since the return to holding the natural resource is the increase in its relative price, it depends crucially on the way in which expectations are formed.

In what follows we remain within the confines of the basic model with exogenous labour-augmenting technical progress and no natural resources.

---

[7] We do not go here into the vintage/embodiment aspects of technical progress, nor their interrelation with the technical progress function in the work of Kaldor (see Kaldor and Mirrlees, 1962).

The reader should however bear in mind the way in which the analysis may be changed by these factors. In particular, the long-run rate of growth of output may no longer simply be determined by the growth of effective labour. Where the rate of technical advance, or the rate of depletion, is endogenous, then it may be possible permanently to raise or lower the rate of growth through tax or other measures.

8-3 GROWTH AND TAXATION

We now examine the effects of taxation in the basic model outlined earlier. A variety of taxes is considered, although the simplified structure of the model reduces the effective range of instruments. Since labour is supplied inelastically, a wage tax and a lump-sum tax on earners are equivalent; since all assets are assumed to earn the same rate of return, a tax on capital and a tax on the income from capital are equivalent.

It is assumed that technical progress is purely labour-augmenting. If we write k for the ratio of capital to labour measured in efficiency units (i.e., capital per effective man), then the basic equation governing growth over time (the analogue of (8-11)) is

$$\dot{k} = s(k)f(k) - (n + \gamma + \lambda)k \tag{8-17}$$

The rate of technical progress is assumed to be determined exogenously, which means that the steady-state rate of growth of output is unaffected by taxation (it is equal to $n + \lambda$).[8]

Government policy may however affect the level of capital, and output, per man. Suppose, for example, that taxation reduces $s(k)$. As shown in Fig. 8-2, this leads the steady-state, capital–labour ratio to fall from k^* to k^{**} (the steady state is assumed unique). The long-run *per capita* income is therefore lower. Whether the before-tax competitive share of labour is increased or decreased depends on whether the elasticity of substitution between capital and labour is greater or less than unity. What happens under perfect competition to the after-tax distribution of income may therefore be ambiguous.

Incidence of Capital Taxation

In order to explore this more fully, we focus on a tax on capital at rate t_c, assuming initially that the proceeds are used for current government expenditure. The tax influences the dynamic behaviour of the economy via the savings function and we write $s(k, t_c)$.

---

[8] Output grows at rate $n + \lambda$, so output per head grows at λ; similarly, capital per worker rises at rate λ (to keep the capital–*effective* labour ratio constant).

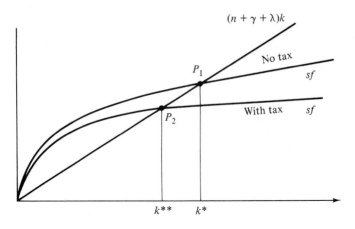

Capital per effective man

Figure 8-2 Taxation and equilibrium growth.

The impact on the steady-state growth path, assuming one exists, may be seen by differentiating the condition $\dot{k} = 0$ with respect to t_c:

$$(sf' + s_k f - v)\frac{dk}{dt_c} = -s_t f \tag{8-18}$$

where $v \equiv n + \gamma + \lambda$ and s_t denotes the derivative with respect to t_c. Where the steady-state path is locally stable, the coefficient of dk/dt_c is negative, and k rises (falls) if s_t is positive (negative)—as indicated by Fig. 8-2. Suppose s_t is negative. The fall in k leads to a rise in the gross return to capital and a fall in the wage; to this extent the tax is "shifted". Is it possible for the *net* return to capital to rise? Writing r for the net return,

$$r = (1 - t_c)f'(k) \tag{8-19}$$

and

$$\frac{dr}{dt_c} = (1 - t_c)f''\frac{dk}{dt_c} - f' \tag{8-20}$$

Using the definition of the elasticity of substitution $(\sigma \equiv f'(f - kf')/(-kff''))$,

$$\frac{dr}{dt_c} = -f'\left[1 - \frac{(1 - t_c)(-s_t)(f - kf')}{(v - sf' - s_k f)k\sigma}\right] \tag{8-21}$$

This depends on the strength of the response of savings $(-s_t)$ as well as on the characteristics of the steady state. In order to make further progress, we need to specify the savings process.

Turning to special forms of the savings function, we can see that the effect is straightforward in the case of the extreme classical savings function (with no saving out of wages). Then

$$s_r(1 - t_c)f'k = s_r rk = vk \qquad (8\text{-}22)$$

i.e., the net return is unchanged and the tax is fully shifted. When the capital stock has adjusted to its new steady-state level, the rise in the gross rate of return is just enough to offset the tax, and it is the wage rate that is reduced. This provides a striking example of how the long-run incidence may differ from that in the short-run.

In the more general classical savings case, with $s_w > 0$, the steady growth condition is

$$sf(k) = s_r rk + s_w \alpha f = vk \qquad (8\text{-}23)$$

This can be re-arranged to give (using $r = (1 - t_c)f'$)

$$r = \cfrac{v}{s_r + s_w \left(\cfrac{\alpha}{1 - \alpha}\right)(1 - t_c)^{-1}} \qquad (8\text{-}24)$$

Thus in the Cobb–Douglas case, with $\alpha = \frac{2}{3}$ and $s_r = 0.5$, $s_w = 0.125$, a 50 per cent tax causes the net return to fall by only a quarter. There is therefore a considerable degree of shifting.

Exercise 8-1 Analyse the incidence of a capital tax in a model where there are two classes of individuals with different savings propensities. The capitalist class receives no wage income and saves a fraction s_r; the working class receives all wage income and capital income proportionate to its capital, and saves a fraction s_w. How do the results with this Pasinetti model compare with those from the Kaldor version described above? (See Pasinetti, 1962, Meade and Hahn, 1965, Samuelson and Modigliani, 1966.)

Exercise 8-2 Examine the savings behaviour where accumulation is governed by an infinitely lived "representative" individual, who maximizes an additive utility function of *per capita* consumption at each date, discounted at a fixed pure rate of time preference, but weighted by the population alive at each date. (Assume no technical progress.) Show that this leads to the same behaviour in steady state as the extreme classical assumption. (See Stiglitz, 1970a.)

A Redistributive Capital Tax

If the tax on capital leads to a fall in k, this means that part of the burden of the government expenditure is being shifted. Suppose now we consider an explicitly redistributive tax, with the proceeds $T(=t_c f'k)$ *per capita* being used to finance a lump-sum transfer to workers. Is it possible that this too will be shifted so that the redistributive goal is not achieved?

The effect on the level of savings may in the classical savings case be represented simply by T:

$$sf(k) \equiv s_r[(1-\alpha)f - T] + s_w(\alpha f + T) \tag{8-25}$$

Differentiating the condition for steady growth,[9] and using $\bar{s}$ to denote the weighted average savings rate $(\bar{s} \equiv s_w \alpha + s_r(1-\alpha))$,

$$[\bar{s}f' + (s_w - s_r)\alpha'f - v]\frac{dk}{dT} = s_r - s_w \tag{8-26}$$

or

$$D\frac{dk}{dT} = s_r - s_w \tag{8-27}$$

where the steady state is locally stable, D is negative, and the tax plus transfer lowers the capital–labour ratio (since $s_r > s_w$).[10]

The gross wage falls. Differentiating the net income of wage-earners with respect to T,

$$\frac{d(\alpha f + T)}{dT} = 1 + (\alpha'f + \alpha f')\frac{dk}{dT} \tag{8-28}$$

$$\frac{d(\alpha f + T)}{dT} = \frac{\bar{s}f' - v + (s_r - s_w)\alpha f'}{D}$$

$$= \frac{s_r f' - v}{D} \tag{8-29}$$

(using the definition of $\bar{s}$). Now for small taxes (i.e., evaluating at $T = 0$), the steady growth condition means that, if $s_w > 0$, then $s_r f' < v$ and local stability implies $D < 0$. An increase in the net income of the wage-earners is therefore assured. On the other hand, the effective transfer from \$1 tax may be considerably less than \$1. Taking the Cobb–Douglas example, with $\alpha = \frac{2}{3}$, $s_r = 2s_w$, the right-hand side of (8-29) equals 0.75; if $s_r = 4s_w$, the ratio falls to 0.5. The effective transfer may therefore be a lot smaller than the nominal tax, particularly when there is a large difference between s_r and s_w. In the extreme case where $s_w = 0$, the steady growth condition is

[9] The derivative is taken with respect to the total transfer T, rather than the tax rate. The reader may like to work out the corresponding results for t_c, and to check whether the total transfer T is everywhere increasing in t_c.

[10] Although we have assumed that savings rates are constant, the extension to non-constant savings rates is straightforward (see Feldstein, 1974c).

$s_r f' = v$, and the effective transfer (evaluated at $T = 0$) is zero. The redistributive policy is in this case quite powerless.[11]

Balanced Growth Incidence

We now consider the concept of balanced growth incidence, where changes in taxation are accompanied by offsetting adjustments in monetary policy to hold constant the capital–labour ratio. First, we need to introduce the monetary instruments. Money or government bonds provide alternative stores of value, a means by which individuals can hold their savings. On the other hand, the introduction of money causes the complication that changes in the price of money relative to real capital affect individuals' incomes (capital gains should be included in disposable income) and savings (the increase in the value of an individual's assets is, in effect, savings). Moreover, the distribution of money (say in the form of transfer payments) increases individuals' incomes. In the subsequent analysis, we sidestep these issues and assume that the government only issues short-term bonds paying the going rate of interest. From the individual's point of view, bonds and equities are assumed to be perfect substitutes. Thus, the price of bonds (relative to capital or consumption goods) remains fixed (say at unity).

If we denote total government bonds by B, bonds *per capita* by b, and use T_c to denote the total tax paid on capital income (including bond interest) measured per worker, the classical savings model yields the capital market equilibrium condition

$$s_r[(1-\alpha)f + rb - T_c] + s_w(\alpha f + T) = \frac{\dot{K} + \dot{B}}{L} \tag{8-30}$$

For simplicity, we ignore depreciation and technical progress, so

$$g_k = g_K - n = [s_w \alpha + s_r(1-\alpha)]\frac{f}{k} - n + \underline{\frac{(s_w T - s_r T_c)}{k} + s_r \frac{rb}{k} - \frac{\dot{B}}{K}} \tag{8-31}$$

If the development of capital accumulation (k) is to be unaffected, we require that the sum of the underlined terms be zero. The government budget constraint is

$$\frac{\dot{B}}{K} = \frac{T - T_c}{k} + \frac{rb}{k} \tag{8-32}$$

---

[11] This can also be the case with $s_w > 0$ if the Kaldor savings assumptions are replaced by the Pasinetti version with the differential propensities attached to individuals rather than sources of income—see Exercise 8-1.

so that we must have

$$(T - T_c) + rb = (s_w T - s_r T_c) + s_r rb$$

or

$$T(1 - s_w) = (1 - s_r)(T_c - rb) \tag{8-33}$$

Moreover, in steady state $\dot{b} = 0$, so $\dot{B} = nB$ and from (8-32)

$$(r - n)b = (T_c - T) \tag{8-34}$$

Combining these, the steady-state transfer is

$$T = \left[\frac{n(1 - s_r)}{n(1 - s_w) - r(s_r - s_w)} \right] T_c \tag{8-35}$$

Using the condition $g_k = 0$, the denominator may be shown to be proportional to $s_w(f - nk)$, which in steady state is strictly positive for $s_w > 0$. Where there is saving out of wages a positive transfer is possible; and balanced growth incidence implies an improvement in the income of the wage-earning class. (In the extreme classical savings model, with $s_w = 0$, there is no way in which debt policy can be used to offset the effect of T_c.)

Summary

In the model used in this section, the steady-state rate of growth is determined exogenously by population increase and technical progress. The analysis has therefore concentrated on the effect on the capital–labour ratio and on competitive factor returns. In particular, we have shown examples where a tax on capital income may be shifted completely, and have demonstrated that in less extreme cases the effective redistribution may be very much reduced in the long run as a result of adjustments in the capital stock. Where the model is extended, these results need to be modified. Suppose, for example, the rate of technical progress is a function of expenditure on research. Such expenditure, and hence the long-run rate of growth, may well be affected by capital taxation.[12] Alternatively, in a model with natural resources, a tax on capital income may affect the capital market equilibrium (see Exercise 8-3).

> **Exercise 8-3** In the context of the model with natural resources described in Stiglitz (1974c), examine the effect of a capital tax on the return to physical capital (i.e., exempting the capital gains on natural resources), taking different assumptions about the way in which expectations are formed.

[12] The effect of, say, the corporation tax on research and development expenditure depends on whether there is special tax treatment and on the method of financing, as in the case of physical investment discussed in Lecture 5.

8-4 TAXATION IN A LIFE-CYCLE MODEL

The assumptions made about savings in the previous sections were either entirely *ad hoc* (the proportional savings assumption) or based on the class savings hypothesis. The latter may provide a good approximation to actual savings behaviour, but in this section we consider for purposes of contrast the rather different approach based on individual life-cycle savings decisions, discussed at some length in Lecture 3. We take a discrete time model where the individual lives for two periods, working in the first, using savings from the first to provide for retirement, and there are no bequests. This is the Samuelson (1958a) consumption loan model, applied to public finance questions by Diamond (1965).

Model of Life-Cycle Savings

As in Lecture 3, the individual consumes c_1 in period 1, and c_2 in period 2, of his life, and he faces the budget constraint

$$c_2 = (w - c_1)(1 + r) \qquad (8\text{-}36)$$

We need to identify carefully the different generations. For the generation born in period u, the relevant wage is w_u and the relevant rate of return r_{u+1}. We can therefore write $c_1(w_u, r_{u+1})$ or *per capita* savings (assets) as

$$A_u(w_u, r_{u+1}) \equiv w_u - c_1(w_u, r_{u+1}) \qquad (8\text{-}37)$$

All individuals are assumed identical, and there are (at this stage) no bonds. For simplicity, we ignore depreciation and technical progress. The total capital available in period $u+1$ is therefore the savings of the preceding generation of workers:[13]

$$K_{u+1} = A_u(w_u, r_{u+1})L_u$$

or (since the population is assumed to grow at rate $(1+n)$),

$$k_{u+1} = \frac{A_u(w_u, r_{u+1})}{1+n} \qquad (8\text{-}38)$$

It may be noted that savings depend on expectations concerning the interest rate in the next period.

We begin by describing the steady-state behaviour. From (8-37) and (8-38)

$$c_1 = w - (1+n)k \qquad (8\text{-}39a)$$

---

[13] The form of this condition may appear slightly strange, since the *stock* of capital is equal to savings. The latter are however gross savings of "new" savers, and there is (partially) offsetting dissaving by the retired generation. It is for this reason that the steady growth condition below has savings equal to $(1+n)k$ rather than nk.

and

$$c_2 = (1+r)(1+n)k \qquad (8\text{-}39\text{b})$$

and by varying k we can trace out the possible steady-state consumption levels. The curve has slope

$$\frac{dc_2}{dc_1} = \frac{\partial c_2/\partial k}{\partial c_1/\partial k} = \frac{(1+n)[(1+r)-(-kf'')]}{-kf''-(1+n)}$$

which may be re-arranged using the definition of the elasticity of substitution:

$$-\frac{dc_2}{dc_1} = \frac{1+r-\alpha r/\sigma}{1-(\alpha r/\sigma)/(1+n)} \qquad (8\text{-}40)$$

The curve need not be downward-sloping. Where, for example,

$$1+n < \alpha r/\sigma < 1+r \qquad (8\text{-}41)$$

the curve slopes upwards. Moreover, the downward slope is greater or less than $(1+r)$ according as r is greater or less than n. In particular, the point G is the "golden rule" steady state with $r = n$, and slope equal to $(1+r)$. In Fig. 8-3 we show for purposes of illustration the Cobb–Douglas case. As we move up the curve, k rises and r falls, until the latter reaches $(1+n)/\alpha$ and

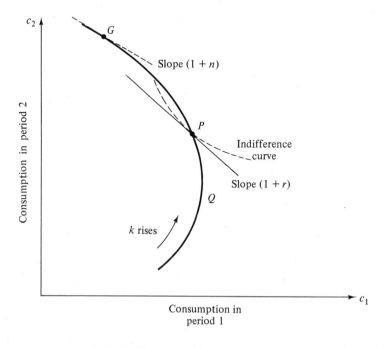

Figure 8-3 Equilibrium in life-cycle model.

the slope is vertical at point Q.[14] Beyond this, further increases in k cause r to fall; it reaches n at G.

In the competitive equilibrium, the individual's marginal rate of substitution between c_1 and c_2 must equal $(1+r)$. Through each point on the $c_1 c_2$ curve in Fig. 8-3 we can draw a line with slope $(1+r)$, noting that r falls as we move up the curve. For a competitive equilibrium, this line must be tangent to the individual's indifference curve. It may happen that the indifference curve is tangent to the $c_1 c_2$ frontier at G (the golden rule), but in general we would expect to find a situation such as P in Fig. 8-3 where $r \neq n$ (as drawn $r > n$). Re-arranging (8-38), we have in steady-state

$$r = \frac{rk}{w}\frac{1+n}{s} = \frac{1-\alpha}{\alpha}\frac{1+n}{s} \qquad (8\text{-}42)$$

where s is the propensity to save (A/w). This may give values of r greater or less than n (Diamond, 1965, p. 1135).

Whether such a steady state is locally stable depends on the assumptions made concerning expectations. Suppose that the expected rate of return is written as $\pi(k_{u+1}, k_u)$. Differentiating (8-38),

$$\frac{dk_{u+1}}{dk_u}\left(1+n-A_r\frac{\partial\pi}{\partial k_{u+1}}\right) = A_w\frac{\partial w}{\partial k_u} + A_r\frac{\partial\pi}{\partial k_u}$$

For local stability we require $dk_{u+1}/dk_u < 1$. If individuals have perfect foresight, then $\pi = r(k_{u+1})$, and it is necessary that, evaluated at the steady state (the coefficient of dk_{u+1}/dk_u is assumed positive (see Diamond, 1965, p. 1132))

$$1+n-A_r\frac{\partial r}{\partial k} - A_w\frac{\partial w}{\partial k} > 0 \qquad (8\text{-}43)$$

(Question for the reader: what difference would it make if individuals have static expectations so that $\pi = r(k_u)$?)

Incidence of Taxation

We now introduce the tax on capital income examined before, together with lump-sum transfers T_1 and T_2 to the two generations (workers and retired, respectively). The individual budget constraint is then:

$$c_1 + \frac{c_2}{1+r} = w + T_1 + \frac{T_2}{1+r} \qquad (8\text{-}44)$$

where $r = (1-t_c)f'(k)$, and the $c_1 c_2$ frontier is given by

$$c_1 = w - (1+n)k + T_1$$
$$c_2 = [1+f'(1-t_c)](1+n)k + T_2 \qquad (8\text{-}45)$$

---

[14] It should be noted that α is constant in the Cobb–Douglas case, and that the unit of time is a generation (so $r > 1$ is quite possible).

Suppose first we consider the case where the revenue from the capital tax is used to pay a lump-sum transfer to the older generation; i.e., $T_2 = t_c f'(1+n)k$. From (8-45), it may be seen that, for given k, the tax terms cancel, so that the frontier is unchanged. On the other hand, the after-tax interest rate corresponding to a given k is reduced by the tax, so that the previous equilibrium no longer holds. To see what may happen, consider the case of a Cobb–Douglas production function, as illustrated in Fig. 8-4 (the same figure as before, with the pre-tax equilibrium at P). For given k, the after-tax return falls, so that the slope of the budget line rotates to the dashed line. Fairly weak conditions are sufficient to rule out a rise in k as a result of the tax. Suppose that the new equilibrium were at P'. At that point $f'(k)$ is less than $f'(k_P)$, and the budget line is made flatter by the tax. The indifference curve through P' must therefore have a slope less than at P. A sufficient condition to rule this out is, for example, that consumption is a normal good.

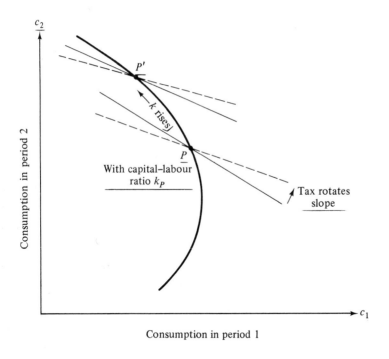

Figure 8-4 Capital income tax in life-cycle model.

The effect of the tax may be explored more fully by using the steady-state condition:

$$(1+n)k = A(w, r, T_1, T_2) \tag{8-46}$$

where w is a function of k and r is a function of t_c and k. Differentiating totally,

$$dk\left(1+n-A_w\frac{\partial w}{\partial k}-A_r\frac{\partial r}{\partial k}\right)=\frac{\partial A}{\partial T_1}dT_1+\frac{\partial A}{\partial T_2}dT_2-A_r f'dt_c \quad (8\text{-}47)$$

If the local stability condition (8-43) holds, the coefficient of dk is positive. In order to see the implications of the right-hand side, we make use of the notation introduced in Lecture 3:

$$\frac{\partial A}{\partial T_1}=\frac{\partial A}{\partial w}=1-\frac{\partial c_1}{\partial M}=1-(1-s)\eta \quad (8\text{-}48)$$

where M denotes the first-period present value of income (wealth) including transfers, η is the elasticity of c_1 with respect to M, and we are evaluating at $T_2=0$. Similarly,

$$\frac{\partial A}{\partial T_2}=-(1-s)\eta p \quad \text{where} \quad p=\frac{1}{1+r} \quad (8\text{-}49)$$

$$\frac{\partial A}{\partial r}=pc_1\frac{\partial \log c_1}{\partial \log p}=pc_1 s(\sigma_D-\eta) \quad (8\text{-}50)$$

where the second step in (8-50) makes use of Eq. (3-10) in Lecture 3, and σ_D is the elasticity of substitution in *consumption* between c_1 and c_2.

We consider first the case where the proceeds of the interest tax finance a lump-sum transfer to the older generation (as in Fig. 8-4), evaluating at $t_c=T_2=0$. The revenue condition implies

$$dT_2=k(1+n)f'dt_c \quad (8\text{-}51)$$

Substituting into the right-hand side of (8-47), and using (8-49) and (8-50), it may be seen to be proportional to $-\sigma_D dt_c$. The local stability condition (8-43) implies therefore that the capital–labour ratio is reduced where there is a strictly positive elasticity of substitution between c_1 and c_2.

Where the revenue is given in lump-sum form to the first generation, the results are different. Again taking an infinitesimal tax, from the revenue constraint,

$$dT_1=f'kdt_c \quad (8\text{-}52)$$

and the right-hand side of (8-47) is proportional to (using (8-48) and (8-50))

$$(\eta-\sigma_D)\frac{1+n}{1+r}+\frac{s}{1-s}+(1-\eta) \quad (8\text{-}53)$$

If, for example, the utility function is of the Cobb–Douglas form ($\sigma_D=\eta=1$), this is clearly positive. The tax on capital, used to make a transfer to the younger generation, raises k (where the local stability condition (8-43) holds). In contrast to the redistributive capital tax considered in Section 8-3, the indirect effects reinforce the transfer. This may appear somewhat surprising. However, the life-cycle savings model is the polar opposite case from pure classical savings. There, the capitalist class had the larger savings propensity, and a transfer to wage-earners reduced the rate of accumulation. Here, the wage-earning generation are the only savers, and a transfer to this generation raises savings.

Balanced Growth Incidence

As in the previous section, we may introduce government bonds and examine the case where monetary policy offsets the effects of taxation on the capital–labour ratio. With the introduction of debt per worker b, the steady-state growth condition becomes

$$(1+n)(k+b) = A(w, r, T_1, T_2) \tag{8-54}$$

In steady state, the level of bonds per worker is constant, so that the new issue of debt each period is nb per worker (i.e., to allow for the population growth). This must equal the government deficit after allowing for interest payments; i.e., per worker

$$nb = T_1 + \frac{T_2}{1+n} - t_c(k+b)f' + rb \tag{8-55}$$

(where tax is paid on debt interest). This may be rewritten as

$$t_c(k+b)f' - T_1 - \frac{T_2}{1+r} = (r-n)\left[b + \frac{T_2}{(1+n)(1+r)}\right] \tag{8-56}$$

First, we may note that consumption plans are determined by the present value of lump-sum transfers $(T_1 + T_2/(1+r))$. On the other hand, savings equal $w + T_1 - c_1$. Suppose therefore that we reduce T_2 by dT_2 while increasing T_1 by $dT_2/(1+r)$, so that the present value is unchanged. Total savings per retired person then rise by $dT_2/(1+r)$. This is equivalent in terms of the effect on the total physical capital stock to *reducing b* by $dT_2/[(1+n)(1+r)]$, and we can see from (8-56) that such a reduction would have an equivalent effect on the government budget constraint.[15] We can see therefore that in this model government debt is equivalent to a fall in T_1 accompanied by a rise in T_2 so as to leave the present value of lump-sum tax payments unchanged (Diamond, 1973b, p. 222, and Bierwag, Grove and Khang, 1969). This bears out our earlier statement that debt policy is equivalent to lump-sum redistribution between generations. It has in turn important implications for the question of the burden of the national debt discussed in the next section.

---

[15] To see this, consider an increase of $b (= dT_2/[(1+n)(1+r)])$, in addition to the lump-sum transfers. The square bracket on the right-hand side of (8-56) is unchanged overall. On the left-hand side, the total $k+b$ is unchanged, as is the present value of lump-sum transfers.

Exercise 8-4 How would the above analysis change if the government issued bonds which were *tax exempt*?

If we now differentiate the steady-state growth condition (8-54), and the government revenue constraint, evaluating at $b = T_1 = T_2 = t_c = 0$, we obtain:

$$dk\left(1+n-A_w\frac{\partial w}{\partial k} - A_r\frac{\partial r}{\partial k}\right) = \frac{\partial A}{\partial T_1}dT_1 + \frac{\partial A}{\partial T_2}dT_2$$

$$- A_r f'dt_c - (1+n)db \quad (8\text{-}57)$$

and

$$(k+b)f'dt_c - dT_1 - \frac{1}{1+r}dT_2 = (r-n) \times \left[db + \frac{1}{(1+n)(1+r)}dT_2\right] \quad (8\text{-}58)$$

Balanced growth incidence requires that $dk = 0$, and from these equations it is possible to examine the effect of different combinations of taxes, taking account of the equivalence set out in the preceding paragraph.

Exercise 8-5 Examine the balanced growth incidence of a capital tax used to pay a lump-sum transfer to the working generation (where $T_2 = 0$). What is the relationship between the size of the transfer and the revenue raised?

Different Views of the Accumulation Process

In this section we have examined the view that savings decisions are based on the utility-maximizing calculations of households planning to spread consumption over their lifetimes. As we have noted, this is at the opposite pole from the extreme classical view that wage-earners save little, and that the primary source of accumulation is saving out of profits. This polarity of views may be represented in terms of the differential propensities s_r and s_w. Going back to the analysis of Section 8-3 (Eq. (8-23)), we can see that the proportional savings function provides a benchmark case. If one assumes that the dominant motive is accumulation out of profits, then $s_r > s_w$ and the shifting of the profits tax reduces the effective redistribution. On the other hand, if one assumes that the main source of savings is through wage-earners making provision for retirement, then $s_w > s_r$, and the indirect responses (via increased k) reinforce the effect of the transfer.

8-5 BURDEN OF THE NATIONAL DEBT

The question whether financing government expenditure by borrowing rather than taxation imposes a greater burden on future generations has given rise to a great deal of confusion among laymen and, at a more esoteric, if not more useful, level, among economists. Popular misconceptions often stem from assuming that the national debt is analogous with private debt, which is true for *external* government debt but not for *internal* debt:

> A nation owing money to other nations ... *is* impoverished or burdened in the same way as a man who owes money to other men. But this does not hold for national debt which is owed by the nation to citizens of the *same* nation.... "We owe it to ourselves". [Lerner, 1948, p. 256]

Given this essential difference between internal government and private debt, in what sense can the burden be shifted through internal debt finance? The answer clearly depends on what is meant by "burden" and how the existence of debt affects the behaviour of the economy.

Debt, Aggregate Consumption and Capital Formation

The first definition of burden is that of a reduction in aggregate consumption, a definition that underlies the "Keynesian" view which gained currency in the 1940s and 1950s.[16] According to this, in a closed economy with full employment, the resources used for government expenditure must be drawn from other current uses of resources. As it is put by Samuelson, "To fight a war now we must hurl present day munitions at the enemy, not dollar bills, and not future goods and services." A closed economy cannot dispose of more goods and services than it is currently producing, and the reduction in resources available for current non-government use is independent of the method of finance. If debt rather than tax finance is adopted, then future taxpayers have to pay interest on the debt, but this is purely a transfer payment.

The assumptions made in the Keynesian argument may however be questioned. There *are* ways in which current decisions affect future output: for example, by reducing the stock of natural resources, via a lower rate of technical advance, and by decreasing the stock of capital. In what follows we focus on the last of these—the possibility that debt finance may shift the burden by passing on a reduced capital stock—but the reader may like to consider the other two aspects.

That a switch from tax to debt finance may affect the rate of capital formation has been argued by Modigliani (1961) in the context of a simple life-cycle model. Each person consumes all his income over his lifetime.

---

[16] Although this view is frequently referred to as "Keynesian", it has a much longer history. Thus, in 1920 Viner referred to the fact that "the cost of the war for a country which does not borrow from abroad must be borne from current income" (1920, p. 47). It was Keynes, however, who popularized this position and was influential in its being accepted by governments, particularly in the Second World War.

With a stationary population and technology, there is a constant level of aggregate assets, A, although there is continuous reshuffling of ownership from dissavers (such as retired persons) to savers. Initially, there is no government debt, so that total real capital, K, equals A. At time u there is an increment in government expenditure dG. If financed by debt, savings are unaffected but the debt displaces private capital in household portfolios and this reduction in the stock of private capital is permanent. On the other hand, if the expenditure is financed by taxation, it reduces the lifetime income of all those alive at u. They spread this reduction in consumption over their lifetime, so that total savings fall initially by sdG (where $0 < s < 1$). As time passes, private capital increases, and by the time the last person alive at u has died, K has returned to its original value. There is therefore a different pattern of aggregate consumption with the two methods of finance, and output is permanently reduced by the debt policy.

This model provides considerable insight, but is not complete. No allowance is made for the changes in factor prices consequent on the fall in capital; nor is any account taken of the financing of the debt interest. In order to explore this more fully, we begin with an explicit general equilibrium model, but based on simple assumptions about savings. The model is in fact that set out in Section 8-3 when examining balanced growth incidence. From the equations given there (ignoring depreciation and technical progress),

$$kg_k = [s_w \alpha + s_r(1-\alpha)]f - nk + s_w T - s_r T_c + s_r rb - \dot{B}/L \qquad (8\text{-}31')$$

and the government budget constraint

$$\dot{B}/L = T - T_c + rb \qquad (8\text{-}32')$$

where T_c is the tax levied on capital, T the lump-sum transfer to wage-earners.

We begin by considering the steady-state conditions: $g_k = 0$ and $\dot{B} = nB$. In contrast to the balanced growth incidence analysis, we now allow k to vary and we are interested in how it responds to changes in the level of debt, with the taxes being adjusted to secure budget balance. What we are in effect considering are the implications of debt resulting from earlier decisions about financing. At some distant date in the past, the government chose to use debt rather than taxation; the consequences of the tax reduction have died away, but the debt (constant in *per capita* terms) remains. Does this impose a burden in terms of the capital–labour ratio being lower? From the condition $\dot{B} = nB$ and $(8\text{-}32')$,

$$T = T_c - (r-n)b \qquad (8\text{-}59)$$

Hence $g_k = 0$ implies

$$nk = [s_w \alpha + s_r(1-\alpha)]f - (s_r - s_w)(T_c - rb) - nb(1-s_w) \qquad (8\text{-}60)$$

In the proportional savings case, $s_r = s_w = s$, $b > 0$ implies a lower steady-state capital–labour ratio than $b = 0$, but k is not a monotonic function of b (Phelps and Shell, 1969). This is shown in Fig. 8-5. With debt b_1 there are two possible steady states, k_1^* at P_1, and k_1^{**} at Q_1; if the level of debt is increased, then k^* falls but k^{**} rises. On the other hand, if the government holds b constant, then the behaviour of the equilibrium path is such that the equilibria P_1 and P_2 are locally stable, but Q_1 and Q_2 are locally unstable.[17]

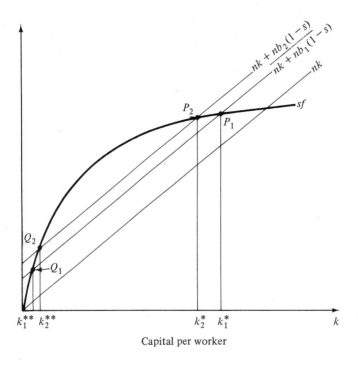

Figure 8-5 National debt and equilibrium growth.

The diagram shows the global comparison of different levels of debt, but how does this relate to Modigliani's marginal change in b? Differentiating (8-60), setting $s_r = s_w = s$,

$$(sf' - n)\frac{dk}{db} = n(1 - s) \tag{8-61}$$

[17] The behaviour of k is governed by (from (8-31'))

$$\dot{k} = sf - nb(1 - s) - nk$$

The condition for local stability is that $sf' < n$, which is not satisfied at Q_1 or Q_2.

A dollar of debt displaces at the margin a dollar of private capital (the case taken by Modigliani) if and only if $f' = n$. If the capital stock is below the golden rule level ($f' > n$), then where $sf' < n$, the reduction in the capital stock is greater than Modigliani argued. This arises because we are taking account of the fact that the interest payments ($f'b$) exceed the new debt issued (nb). (Phelps and Shell, 1969, show that this, basically an envelope result, holds in a much wider class of steady-state models.)

In the case of classical savings ($s_r > s_w$), the steady-state condition also includes the term $-(s_r - s_w)(T_c - rb)$, and this brings out a significant point. One cannot discuss the effect of the national debt without specifying the other accompanying adjustments in fiscal policy. The impact of debt depends on the nature of the taxes employed. Suppose first that $T = 0$, so that the excess of interest over new debt is financed by a capital tax. Equation (8-60) may then be re-arranged so that the underlined term is $-(1 - s_r)nb$. The effect works as before, with s_r replacing s. On the other hand, with $T_c = 0$, the underlined term in (8-60) becomes

$$-(1 - s_r)nb + (s_r - s_w)(r - n)b$$

In this case, the taxes necessary to finance the debt ($(r - n)b$) have the effect of transferring income from those with a lower propensity to save (s_w) to the capitalist classes. The taxes employed have therefore an impact on savings, and this may (where r is large relative to n, or s_r close to 1) reverse the direction of the effect of debt.

The lesson to be drawn is that the impact of debt depends on the other instruments open to the government, a point that is brought out even more clearly in the life-cycle model.

National Debt in the Life-Cycle Model

In the steady-state analysis of the life-cycle model in the previous section, we showed that an increase in debt is equivalent to a lump-sum transfer to the retired financed by a lump-sum tax on the younger generation. This means that any effects of the government debt may be neutralized by the appropriate combination of lump-sum taxes and transfers. The existence of the debt can only be said to be a "burden" if the government is constrained in its use of lump-sum taxes. The burden of the debt is indeed a misnomer, since the burden arises only because of the existence of constraints on tax policy.

In order to see what such a constraint might mean, we assume that the lump-sum transfers have to be employed in fixed proportions ($dT_2 = \psi dT_1$), and that there is no capital tax. From (8-57) and (8-58), we have (evaluating for infinitesimal taxes and debt),

$$\left(1 + n - A_w \frac{\partial w}{\partial k} - A_r \frac{\partial r}{\partial k}\right) \frac{dk}{db} = -\left(\frac{\partial A}{\partial T_1} + \psi \frac{\partial A}{\partial T_2}\right)\left(-\frac{dT_1}{db}\right) - (1 + n) \quad (8\text{-}57')$$

and

$$\left(1 + \frac{\psi}{1+n}\right)\left(-\frac{dT_1}{db}\right) = r - n \qquad (8\text{-}58')$$

where the coefficient of dk/db, denoted by D, is positive for local stability (under condition (8-43)). From this, we can see how the Modigliani analysis is modified in this more complicated model. In effect he took account of the terms $1+n$ on each side of (8-57'), which imply $dk/db = -1$. This ignores the change in factor prices induced by the change in k (other terms in the coefficient of dk/db) and the taxes necessary to finance the debt (positive where $r > n$). From the earlier analysis, the effect of the taxes via the first parenthetical term on the right-hand side of (8-57') depends on

$$[1 - (1-s)\eta] \gtrless \frac{\psi(1-s)\eta}{1+r} \qquad (8\text{-}62)$$

where we have used (8-48) and (8-49). Thus, where all taxes are levied on the first generation ($\psi = 0$), as assumed by Diamond (1965), the above-mentioned term is positive where c_2 is normal,[18] and the tax effect reinforces the reduction in k (for $D > 0$). On the other hand, where all taxes are raised from the older generation, that term is negative, and the effect reversed. This demonstrates once again the sensitivity of the conclusions to the choice of taxes to make up the rest of the package. Finally, it should be emphasized that the constraint $dT_2 = \Psi dT_1$ is an artificial one; the main purpose of introducing it is to bring out the consequences of the assumptions made in different studies.

The life-cycle model provides a convenient vehicle to discuss the alternative notion of the "burden" of the debt being the reduction in lifetime utility. Thus, Bowen, Davis and Kopf (1960) define "the real burden of a public debt to a generation as the total consumption of private goods foregone *during the lifetime* of that generation" (p. 702). This they consider "a more accurate representation of the everyday notion of burden [and] a more sensible concept for deciding if the real cost of a certain project can or cannot be postponed to future generations". In terms of the model considered above, the change in the steady-state lifetime utility is given by the indirect utility function $V(w, r, T_1, T_2)$. The calculation of the effect, making use of the fact that $\partial V/\partial r = (\partial V/\partial w)[A/(1+r)]$, is left as an exercise.

Exercise 8-6 In the case $\psi = 0$, show that dV/db, evaluated at

---

[18] $$(1-s)\eta = \frac{c_1}{M} \times \frac{M}{c_1}\frac{\partial c_1}{\partial M} = \frac{\partial c_1}{\partial M}, \quad \text{so} \quad \frac{\partial c_1}{\partial M} < 1$$

ensures that the left-hand side is positive.

$b = T_1 = 0$, is proportional to

$$-(r-n)\left(1 + \frac{(-kf'')\{1+n+(r-n)[1-(1-s)\eta]\}}{(1+r)D}\right) \qquad (8\text{-}63)$$

How is the expression altered if $\psi > 0$? (See Diamond, 1965.)

From (8-63), we can see that, with $\psi = 0$, the existence of debt lowers steady-state utility where $r > n$ and the local stability condition ($D > 0$) holds. It should be noted that this reduction in utility is not caused by deadweight loss associated with taxation. As has been argued by Meade (1958), and others, the taxes necessary to finance the debt may have an excess burden. Here, however, we have assumed that the taxes are lump-sum, so that this is not the source of the utility loss. Indeed, it can be seen that, where $r > n$ in the no-tax equilibrium, then steady-state utility could be raised by setting $b < 0$ (or equivalent variations in lump-sum taxes). The no-tax situation is not a first-best benchmark, since it may not correspond to a desired intertemporal distribution—and this may provide grounds for government intervention. Moreover, when considering the intertemporal distribution, it is necessary to look beyond simply the changes in steady-state utility.[19]

Debt and Bequests

The analysis described above has been criticized for treating debt and taxation asymmetrically. Individuals are assumed to take account of current taxes but ignore the future tax liabilities created by the issuing of debt: "society fools itself into consuming more, thinking that possession of government paper provides for its future" (Tobin, 1965, p. 681). This has led to the argument that there is no essential difference between debt and tax finance.

This position has been called "classical" or "Ricardian", on the grounds that it goes back to Ricardo's discussion of the capitalization of the tax burden of financing debt:

[He] argued that the fully rational individual should be indifferent as between paying an extraordinary tax of $2000 once-and-for-all and paying an annual tax of $100 in perpetuity, assuming an interest rate of 5 per cent.... [If] the government borrows $2000 and commits taxpayers to finance interest payments of $100 annually, the

[19] In order to make any welfare judgement we clearly need to consider the whole path. With debt finance of a given expenditure at u, if the interest rate rises to equilibrate the capital market, then those in the second generation at u may actually have an increase in utility (since r rises and w is unaffected, having been earned in the preceding period). The next generation however face a lower wage and in addition have to finance the interest on the debt. The level of lifetime utility then declines with each generation until the steady-state is attained (assuming that the process is stable).

individual...will fully capitalise the future tax payments when the debt is created, and he will write down the capital value of the income-earning assets which he owns by the present value of these future tax payments. [Buchanan, 1960, p. 52]

If all individuals are infinitely-lived, and if the capital market is perfect, then this is correct. Total taxes payable at time u are $rB_u - \dot{B}$, and the present value at interest rate r is given by (discounted to time 0)

$$\int_0^\infty (rB_u - \dot{B})e^{-ru}du$$

Integrating by parts, this equals

$$B_0 - \lim_{u \to \infty} (B_u e^{-ru})$$

Provided that in the limit the last term tends to zero (as with $B_u = be^{nu}$ and $n < r$), then the present value of taxes equals the initial bond issue.

The case where individuals have finite lives, but are linked across generations by bequests, has been studied by Barro (1974). He shows that, where there is an interior solution for the amount of bequest or gift across generations, then the Ricardian result holds for small variations in debt. Where debt finance is used, each generation takes account of the reduction in subsequent utilities caused by the taxes necessary to finance the debt, and increases its bequest. Providing there is an interior solution for intergenerational transfers (which may be made in either direction), the general equilibrium of the economy is unaffected by tax and debt policy. (This is an application at the economy level of the Modigliani–Miller theorem, discussed in Lecture 5.)

The assumptions underlying this argument are strong, as was indeed recognized in Ricardo's discussion. First, there may be an absence of altruism from parent to child; perhaps more importantly, there may be an absence of altruism from child to parent. Thus, one generation may be able to redistribute towards itself from succeeding generations only by coercion (government policy). Second, there is uncertainty about survival, private risk of "extinction" being greater than the social risk. Third, even if there is perfect symmetry in the utility function between antecedents and descendants and no uncertainty, there still may be constraints on the private transfer of income (wealth) among generations. These constraints arise from the non-existence of a perfect annuity market and the non-existence of perfect rental and mortgage markets.[20] The consequence of this (and the unpredictable timing of death) is that individuals may leave more to their heirs than they would have left had there been perfect markets.

---

[20] See Rothschild and Stiglitz (1976) for an analysis of why, with imperfect information, annuity markets are likely to be intrinsically imperfect.

Accordingly, if the government varies its debt policy to increase the tax burden on future generations, this will not necessarily be fully offset by changes in bequests.

The extension of the life-cycle model to take account of bequests is obviously important, as are the incorporation of uncertainty and market imperfections. It is however an open question whether the infinite family plan implied by the Barro model is a better guide to the effects of debt than the shorter horizon model used earlier. It may well be that different representations of savings behaviour are necessary for different groups in the population. Indeed, the model needs to be extended to take account of differences between individuals in wealth. The *distribution* of the burden of the national debt may be as important as its aggregate impact.

8-6 CONCLUDING COMMENTS

This Lecture has had two primary objectives. The first has been to show that the long-run incidence of taxation, or other government measures, might be markedly different from the short-run incidence. In assessing the impact of policy, one must remember that what seems fixed and unalterable can in the long-run be adjusted—as the designers of the window tax discovered.

In this Lecture we have illustrated this by reference to the taxation of capital income and the impact of the national debt. In the case of the capital tax, the long-run incidence is critically determined by how the tax affects aggregate savings, and this in turn depends on the particular assumptions concerning the determinants of savings within the economy. For instance, if a constant fraction of profits (and none of wages) are saved, or if the savings behaviour of the economy can be described in terms of an infinitely-lived representative individual (with an additive utility function and a fixed rate of pure time preference), then in the long run the after-tax rate of return is determined independently of the tax rate. In contrast, if saving is seen as the outcome of lifetime utility maximization, with workers saving for old age and passing on no bequests, then the results may be quite different. The conclusions may depend sensitively on one's view of the accumulation process.

The effects of the national debt, and similarly of social security schemes (transferring resources between the two generations), are equally governed by the savings behaviour. Whether the existence of government debt diverts savings and leads to a reduction in real capital accumulation depends, for example, on whether people take a long-term view of the liabilities of succeeding generations and adjust bequest behaviour. The impact on the steady-state capital stock, and level of utility, depends on the quantity of capital accumulated in the no-tax–no-debt situation—whether in the absence of government intervention there is a desired intertemporal distribution.

The second purpose of the Lecture has been to bring out the need to consider a complete "package" of tax changes. Thus, a tax on capital income may reduce saving and lead to a rise in the gross rate of return; on the other hand, it may be possible by the use of other taxes and/or monetary policy to offset the effects (as seen in the discussion of balanced growth incidence). How far debt finance reduces the capital stock inherited by future generations depends on the choice of taxes; and the use of terms such as the "burden of the debt" obscures the fact that debt policy is only one of a package of instruments for attaining a desirable intertemporal distribution.

The models employed in this Lecture have provided a useful framework to illustrate some of the long-run effects of taxation and debt policy on the rate of capital accumulation, and its consequences for the general equilibrium of the economy. At the same time, they provide only a limited basis for understanding the determinants of the long-run rate of growth, particularly technical progress and entrepreneurial activity. The assumption that the rate of technical advance is exogenous has meant that tax policy affected only the steady-state levels of the capital–labour ratio, wages, etc. In a fuller analysis, we should consider how taxation may discourage—or encourage—the long-term *rate of growth* of the economy.

READING

There are a number of excellent textbooks on the theory of economic growth, including Solow (1970), Jones (1975), Dixit (1976b), Burmeister and Dobell (1970), and Wan (1971). The life-cycle model is based on Diamond (1965, 1970). A convenient source of different views on the national debt is the collection of readings edited by Ferguson (1964), reviewed by Tobin (1965).

NINE

DISTRIBUTIONAL EFFECT OF TAXATION AND PUBLIC EXPENDITURE

9-1 TAXATION, SPENDING AND REDISTRIBUTION

In previous Lectures we have examined the incidence of taxation by factors or classes—we have asked whether a tax is borne by those receiving capital income or those with wages. The subject of this Lecture is the distribution among individuals. How does fiscal policy affect the inequality of incomes? Does the benefit from public spending go mainly to those with low incomes, and who bears the tax burden? These are questions that have long been of concern. As long ago as 1869, W. S. Jevons prepared a memorandum for the British Treasury, estimating that the tax rate was 10.1 per cent for a family with expenditure of £40 per annum compared with 9.0 per cent for a family with £500 (Roseveare, 1973).

In this Lecture we examine some of the present-day distributional issues. These include the incidence of the tax system, the allocation of the benefits from public spending, the dynamic impact of policy (allowing for its effect on accumulation of capital), and the extent of intergenerational redistribution. This examination raises a number of issues, both conceptual and empirical. Although it is obvious that tax and expenditure policies affect individuals differently, measuring the extent of the differences is much less straightforward. If we are concerned with the variation in taxation and benefits according to "ability to pay", then there are a number of difficulties in the choice of index to measure this. Even an ideal concept of income or consumption does not necessarily represent differences in opportunity sets; and when we allow for the deviation of observable income, or consumption, from the ideal measure, the problems become still more severe. These aspects are discussed further in this introductory section.

In order to assess the redistributive impact of a particular policy, a comparison has to be made between the situation with the tax or expenditure in existence and that without, and this introduces a second major class of issues. In the simple framework described at the end of this section, individuals are assumed to have fixed endowments of capital and earning capacity, and the wage and rate of return are assumed exogenously determined. This however only gives the first-round effect. The tax or expenditure is likely to lead to changes in endowments and may well affect the general equilibrium of the economy. Thus a tax on capital income may have second-round effects on the accumulation of both physical and human capital.

The *incidence* of taxation has been discussed in earlier Lectures; here we incorporate the main considerations—in simplified form—into two distributional models (Section 9-2). The models allow for accumulation, inheritance, the transmission of earning capacity, and the role of chance or "luck". As such, they do not include all the varied elements that influence the distribution of income, but we have supplemented the formal algebra by a qualitative account of the most significant mechanisms that remain to be incorporated. The models are used in Section 9-3 to explore the effects of public policy, where particular attention is paid to taxation and to its indirect—and possibly disequalizing—effects.

The final class of issues arises when we seek to implement the model empirically. The observed data on income, wealth, etc., do not correspond accurately to the theoretical constructs; the empirical procedures have to rely on proxy measures; assumptions have to be made about the extent to which people benefit from different public programmes and about incidence. In Section 9-4 we describe briefly the main results on the redistributional effect of the government budget in the United States and comment on the difficulties in their interpretation, focusing particularly on the question of incidence.

Concepts of Ability to Pay

In theory it is typically assumed that we are concerned with the distribution of taxes and benefits among individuals according to their ability to pay (the normative basis for this is not discussed here—see Lecture 11); in empirical work, this is typically taken to mean measured money income. There is a considerable distance between these two concepts.

The widely accepted "ideal" or "comprehensive" definition of income is that of Haig and Simons:[1]

> Personal income may be defined as the algebraic sum of (1) the market value of rights exercised in consumption and (2) the change in the value of the store of property rights between the beginning and end of the period in question. [Simons, 1938, p. 50]

[1] As noted by Goode (1977), the definition should more properly be referred to as the Schanz–Haig–Simons, or indeed the Davidson–Schanz–Haig–Simons, measure.

It is however apparent that differences in comprehensive income measured in this way do not necessarily correspond to differences in ability to pay, defined in terms of opportunity sets. People with identical opportunity sets make different decisions, because of differences in tastes, and as a consequence have different measured incomes. Thus, everyone may have the same wage rate, w, per hour and the same unearned income, M, but there may be differences in the tastes for leisure leading to differences in hours worked, L. As a result, measured income $Y = wL + M$ may vary—even though all individuals have the same endowments and market opportunities. Conversely, people may have different opportunity sets but the same measured income. Suppose that the labour supply function has the form $L = E^* w^{-1}$. Earned income is then the same for all ($= E^*$), even though those with higher w clearly have superior opportunity sets. This has led to suggestions that we should consider "full" income, which includes the imputed value of leisure income (Becker, 1965, and Musgrave, 1976). If $(L_0 - L)$ is the amount of leisure, then full income would be $wL_0 + M$. It would reflect the differences in options open to people, being less (more) unequally distributed than money income according as the rich work harder (less hard) than the poor. On the other hand, this poses problems both in the definition of a measure of inequality defined over full income[2] and in its implementation.

The case of leisure is an example of the general issue of "observability" which we have discussed at a number of points in these Lectures. There are items that augment opportunities—and may well come under the Haig–Simons rubric—but are intrinsically unobservable because they do not correspond to market transactions. Two clear examples are capital gains that have accrued but have not yet been realized and production for home consumption. These generate income according to the comprehensive definition, but are not typically included in measured income. Similarly, there are benefits from government expenditure. Cash transfers are clearly part of comprehensive income, but so in principle is the benefit derived from outlays by the state on goods and services. The imputation of such benefits raises a number of issues, including the correct identification of the beneficiaries.

The second question concerns the treatment of uncertainty. Two people may have identical opportunity sets *ex ante* but have different *ex post* outcomes. Our feelings about this depend on the concept of equity. If we are concerned with *ex ante* possibilities, then actual incomes may not be a good guide. The fact that a wealth tax bore heavily on someone who turned out to lose all his capital would not on an *ex ante* basis be regarded as indicating a regressive impact, but in terms of measured income (allowing

---

[2] For discussion of the relationship between measures of inequality based on observed income and those taking account of variations in labour supply, see Allingham (1972), Stiglitz (1976a) and Ulph (1978).

for the loss) it might appear that way.[3] Conversely, if we are concerned about *ex post* outcomes, we would not be happy about treating the person as receiving the average, or actuarial, benefit from government spending (e.g., on health), and would want to try to measure the actual provision in relation to need.

This leads on to a third aspect—the redistributive effect over a person's lifetime, rather than just in the current period. It can be argued that we are interested not in transitory variations in income week by week, or year by year, but in normal or permanent income (Friedman, 1957). Similarly, a lot of government expenditure is designed to transfer income between different stages in the life cycle. This has led to proposals that the redistributive impact be assessed in terms of *lifetime* income. Assuming that there is a perfect capital market, so that the individual can borrow or lend freely at an interest rate r (about which he has confident expectations),[4] a person's expected lifetime discounted income is measured by

$$\chi(0) = \int_0^\infty (W_u + M_u) P_u e^{-ru} \, du \qquad (9\text{-}1)$$

where W_u and M_u are expected wage income and capital receipts at time u, and P_u denotes the survival probability. The capital receipts refer to bequests and gifts received, not to investment income (which is taken into account in the discounting). On this basis we would assess the impact of, say, a state pension plan in terms of the present value of contributions relative to the present value of pensions over the lifetime, and the answers are likely to be considerably different from the pattern of redistribution in terms of current incomes.

From the individual's lifetime budget constraint, it follows that the present value of receipts is equal to the present value of expenditure (leaving aside for the moment the effect of uncertainty). This has been used to support proposals to move from income to expenditure taxation. Thus, at the end of a person's life, Q, we must have

$$\int_0^Q (W_u + M_u) e^{-ru} \, du = \int_0^Q (C_u + g_u) e^{-ru} \, du \qquad (9\text{-}2)$$

where C_u denotes consumption and g_u wealth transferred (including any final bequest or debts). A proportional tax levied at each date on consumption plus wealth transfers would therefore have the same base as a tax on lifetime income;[5] and the same would not be true of a tax on current

---

[3] The *ex post* Haig–Simons measure may be contrasted in this respect with the *ex ante* measure of Hicks (1939, Ch. XIV).

[4] For simplicity, a constant r is taken.

[5] With a non-proportional tax, the issue of averaging would arise. See the classic discussion in Vickrey (1947) and, for recent references, Goode (1964, 2nd edn 1976).

income ($W_u + M_u + rA_u$), where A denotes assets held. (See the discussion of the equivalence of taxes in Lecture 3.)

The expenditure base defined above includes wealth transferred, but it has sometimes been argued that the base should include only consumption, which would be equivalent to entering only receipts net of transfers on the left-hand side of (9-2), as one would if one treated the dynasty as an integrated unit. This alternative version is referred to below as a lifetime *consumption* base.

From the lifetime budget constraint, one can see the equivalence of an expenditure base and lifetime receipts; it is important however to note that the timing is different, and hence any taxes levied will be liable at different dates. Suppose a person has an increase in W_u, but expects this to be later offset by a reduction, so that C_u is not changed. With an expenditure base tax liability is unchanged, but with a receipts base the tax liability is brought forward (although with the same present value).

This highlights the key role played by the perfect capital market assumption. In reality, individuals may not be able to borrow and lend freely at a given interest rate. There may be a gap between borrowing and lending rates, and quantitative restrictions on borrowing. In an extreme case, a person may be quite unable to borrow. There may be differences in interest rates between individuals; indeed, this may be an important way in which endowments differ. In these circumstances it is not possible to summarize a person's opportunity set by the measure of expected lifetime income. We have to consider explicitly the flow of receipts and the market opportunities, and no simple indicator is likely to be appropriate.[6]

Unit of Analysis

In empirical work, the unit of analysis is typically taken as the nuclear family or household, and the distribution based on all such units in existence at a particular date. On the other hand, the lifetime approach seems more relevant to *individuals*. A person may belong to several different families during his life, and it makes little sense to regard him as changing identity on leaving or entering a nuclear family. Moreover, the family unit obscures transfers between husband and wife, between parents and children. Does the tax system discriminate against women? Does the benefit from education accrue to parents or children? (Calculation of income, allowing for intra-family transfers and the imputation of taxes and benefits, clearly poses substantial problems in practice.)

---

[6] See, for example, the analysis of Polinsky (1974). He assumes that people are unable to borrow and demonstrates circumstances in which the tax structure preferred by the individual is progressive (in effect, allowing taxes to be deferred to later periods when the borrowing constraint is not binding).

This leads on to a further point. In addition to the overall distributional impact of policy, we may be concerned with the effect on particular *groups* of individuals. Thus, we may ask whether the expenditure system benefits particular regions, ethnic groups, or types of household (e.g., those with large families). The extent to which we aggregate individual units in this way depends of course on the purpose at hand.

Once the unit of analysis has been identified, we need to define the population. This is relatively clear-cut when examining current redistribution, but with a lifetime approach we need to consider the issue of *intergenerational* distribution. Typically, discussion of lifetime income focuses on the experience of a particular generation (an age cohort born, for example, in a certain decade). This has the advantage of being manageable, but it ignores the very substantial redistribution between generations. Thus, it is relevant that those retiring shortly after a state pension scheme begins may be subsidized by younger generations. Conversely, the octogenarians of today, whose prime earning period coincided with the Depression, may be financing through indirect taxes the education of the eight-year-olds who will enjoy the fruits of the twenty-first century!

Finally, the definition of the unit is relevant to the allowance to be made for differing circumstances or needs. We are typically concerned not with income *per se* but with income in relation to the needs of the individual or family. The identification of these needs and the allowance that should be made is a normative issue, but we may want to deduct items from the definition of income (e.g., for the expenses associated with illness or disability) or to calculate income per equivalent person (e.g., allowing for differing family size or age). For further discussion of these issues, see Atkinson (1975b).

A Simple Framework

We now describe a simple framework intended to link some of the conceptual aspects discussed above to the theoretical and empirical sections that follow. To this end, we introduce the following notation. Individual i in the generation that started life u years ago has lifetime capital receipts (discounted to his birth) of I_u^i and lifetime earning capacity N_u^i. With a constant wage rate, w his lifetime income is

$$\chi_u^i = I_u^i + w N_u^i \tag{9-3}$$

The mean for all individuals in the generation is given by

$$\bar{\chi}_u = \bar{I}_u + w \bar{N}_u \tag{9-4}$$

and the variance by

$$\text{var}\,[\chi_u] = \text{var}\,[I_u] + w^2\,\text{var}\,[N_u] + 2w\,\text{cov}\,[I_u, N_u] \tag{9-5}$$

where var $[X]$ denotes the variance, and cov $[X, Y]$ the covariance. If we introduce the notation V_X for the coefficient of variation of $X(=\sqrt{\text{var}(X)}/\bar{X})$ and corr $[X, Y]$ for the coefficient of correlation between X and Y, then

$$V_{\chi_u}^2 = (1-\alpha)^2 V_{I_u}^2 + \alpha^2 V_{N_u}^2 + 2\alpha(1-\alpha)V_{I_u}V_{N_u}\,\text{corr}\,[I_u, N_u] \qquad (9\text{-}6)$$

where $\alpha \equiv w\bar{N}_u/\bar{\chi}_u$. In other words, the dispersion of lifetime income depends on the inequality in endowments, the correlation between them, and the shares of wages and capital in total income.[7]

The coefficient of variation is quite commonly taken as a measure of the degree of inequality. Although such summary measures need to be treated with caution (see Lecture 11), and the coefficient of variation has particular shortcomings (it is especially sensitive to changes in high incomes), we can use it for purposes of illustration. $V_{\chi_u}^2$ then measures the inequality of lifetime income among those in generation u. If we further take account of intergenerational differences, then the coefficient of variation over all generations, denoted by V_χ^2, is the weighted sum of individual $V_{\chi_u}^2$ plus the coefficient of variation obtained if everyone had the mean income of their generation (the "between-generations" inequality).

The measure V_χ^2 takes the lifetime approach to its logical conclusion; at the other extreme, the empirical studies are based on aggregation over generations, but in this case taking current income, not lifetime income. This departs from the measure based on lifetime incomes, on account of systematic life-cycle factors and of transitory variation in incomes. Similarly, analysis of public policy will be different to the extent that government actions alter the life-cycle pattern of income (e.g., via pensions) or modify short-term fluctuations (e.g., via unemployment insurance). These aspects of the use of a current income measure are taken up again in Section 9-4 when we discuss the empirical evidence; in the theoretical sections we concentrate on the lifetime measure.

A preliminary view of the effect of taxation may be seen from Eq. (9-6). Where endowments and factor returns are fixed, the effect of a change in taxation depends on the relative importance of capital and earned income, on the dispersion of these two components and on the extent to which a high capital endowment is correlated with high earning capacity. Suppose, for example, that a redistributive tax on inheritance reduces V_I^2, while leaving $\bar{I}_u$ unchanged (as might happen if the tax proceeds were used to finance a negative capital tax). This can be seen to reduce the coefficient of variation of lifetime income where (dropping the u subscript)

$$V_I > \frac{\alpha}{1-\alpha}(-\text{corr}\,[I, N])V_N \qquad (9\text{-}7)$$

---

[7] The measure of income, χ_u, is best interpreted as an *ex ante* indicator; *ex post*, there is likely to be a random term reflecting chance, etc.

Where capital and labour endowments are positively correlated, or independent (corr $= 0$), this is clearly satisfied.

More generally, suppose that the government imposes taxes t_i and t_w on inherited capital and wage income respectively, and makes a uniform lump-sum payment, G, to everyone, so that net lifetime income becomes

$$Y^i \equiv (1-t_i)I^i + w(1-t_w)N^i + G \tag{9-8}$$

with moments

$$\bar{Y} = (1-t_i)\bar{I} + w(1-t_w)\bar{N} + G$$

$$\operatorname{var}[Y] = (1-t_i)^2 \left\{ \operatorname{var}[I] + w^2 \left(\frac{1-t_w}{1-t_i} \right)^2 \operatorname{var}[N] \right.$$

$$\left. + 2w \left(\frac{1-t_w}{1-t_i} \right) \operatorname{cov}[I,N] \right\} \tag{9-9}$$

Hence

$$V_Y^2 = (1-t_i)^2 (\bar{\chi}/\bar{Y})^2 \left[(1-\alpha)^2 V_I^2 + \alpha^2 \left(\frac{1-t_w}{1-t_i} \right)^2 V_N^2 \right.$$

$$\left. + 2\alpha(1-\alpha) \left(\frac{1-t_w}{1-t_i} \right) V_I V_N \operatorname{corr}[I,N] \right] \tag{9-10}$$

where α refers to pre-tax income, and $\bar{\chi}$ is mean pre-tax income.

This expression yields some straightforward results. For example, a proportional income tax with no grant ($t_i = t_w = t$, $G = 0$) has no effect on the relative degree of inequality ($\bar{Y} = (1-t)\bar{\chi}$), and the squared $(1-t)$ terms cancel. A purely redistributive tax leaves $\bar{Y} = \bar{\chi}$, so that where there is a straight income tax ($t_i = t_w = t$), the coefficient of variation is reduced by a factor $(1-t)$. Where t_i, t_w differ, the impact depends on the relative contribution of the different factors. Suppose, for example, that endowments are uncorrelated. The government levies a capital tax with the proceeds being used to subsidize wages, so that $\bar{Y} = \bar{\chi}$ and $dt_i/dt_w = -\alpha/(1-\alpha)$. Differentiating the variance of Y and evaluating at $t_i = t_w = 0$, this policy can be seen to reduce the coefficient of variation if

$$V_I^2 < V_N^2 > \frac{\alpha}{1-\alpha} \tag{9-11}$$

For example, if V_I were twice V_N, inequality would decline as a result of the redistributive tax on capital as long as the share of capital in total income exceeded 20 per cent. If the endowments are positively correlated, and the share of capital is less than 50 per cent, the inequality-reducing effect is larger.

Exercise 9-1 Calculate the formula corresponding to (9-11) when endowments are correlated, and examine for likely values of the parameters the effect of the redistributive tax. How do the results change if one evaluates at $t_i > 0$?

In this framework, inequality in lifetime income arises basically from differences in endowments. Individuals inherit from their parents, or others, different amounts of capital, both material and human, and different earning abilities and aptitudes. In the next section, we examine how the inheritance process works in an explicit intergenerational model and the role of such factors as family size, marriage and the division of estates.

9-2 MODELLING THE DISTRIBUTION OF INCOME

To assess the impact of the tax system on the distribution of income and wealth, we require a theory of the determination of the income and wealth distribution. Let us begin by assuming factor prices are given. Then each person's income can be related to three broad categories of factors:

1. *Endowments.* Ability, gifts of "human capital" from parents, gifts of wealth: these determine the individual's *opportunity set.*
2. *Tastes.* The individual makes decisions about how much to work, how much to save, how to invest his savings (in safe versus risky prospects, etc.). These decisions reflect his "tastes", in terms of attitudes towards leisure, saving, risk-taking, etc. These attitudes may be moulded by parental influence (and hence positively—or negatively—correlated across generations) and may be influenced by the social climate.
3. *Luck.* The outcomes of the decisions of the individual are stochastic, so that two individuals who have the same opportunity set and the same tastes, and thus make the same decisions, may still have different incomes. Some people work for a firm that goes bankrupt; some people invest early in Rank Xerox.

Public policy affects each aspect of this income–wealth-generating mechanism. In earlier Lectures we saw how taxation can change before- and after-tax incomes of different factors, how the opportunity sets of individuals are affected, and how this influences the decisions they make. These decisions in turn may alter the endowments of the next generation. The effects may be cumulative—or offsetting.

We present below two explicit models of the development of the distribution from one generation to the next, and of the factors influencing lifetime inequality. The formal models concentrate on differences in endowments, which are endogenous, and on the role of random factors. We try to indicate qualitatively however the possible influence of differences in tastes.

The Transmission of Wealth

We consider first the extent of accumulation for bequests and then its division among the next generations (these decisions may of course be interdependent). There are many motives for passing on wealth (we refer to bequests but include under this gifts *inter vivos*). First, bequests may be unintended. Given that annuity markets are imperfect, people may leave substantial estates even though they have no altruistic feelings towards their heirs. This is especially likely with assets that in practice are indivisible. These "unplanned" bequests introduce a random element into the relationship.

Second, bequests may arise because parents wish to share their lifetime wealth, including their own inheritance, with their children. The most common treatment of the bequest motive is to assume that bequests enter the lifetime utility function (e.g., Yaari, 1964, 1965). The level of bequests then depends on the nature of preferences; for example, whether bequests are a "luxury" good (Atkinson, 1971). In the special case where the life-time utility function is homothetic, bequests are proportional to lifetime wealth:

$$B_u^i = s_1(r)(I_u^i + wN_u^i) \qquad (9\text{-}12)$$

where r and w are assumed constant throughout the lifetime. As before, we use the notation X_u^i to denote the value of a variable for individual i in generation u, where a generation is assumed to last one period and there is no overlapping of generations. The second parenthetical expression on the right-hand side of (9-12) may be thought of as *ex ante* expected lifetime income. If we allow for a stochastic element in lifetime income, then individuals may respond rather differently, having for example a lower propensity to consume out of windfall or "entrepreneurial" gains.

The motives for bequests have been discussed in Lecture 3, where we noted that the formulation underlying (9-12) provides no explanation as to why bequests enter the utility function. If individuals are concerned about the welfare of their children, and possibly other descendants, then the level of bequests will typically take account of the expected income of future generations (see for example Meade, 1966; Becker, 1974; Stiglitz, 1978b, and Shorrocks, 1979). This approach allows in particular for bequests resulting from expected wage differences between parent and child. If there is regression towards the mean (see below), an individual with high earnings may expect to have children with a lower earning capacity, and hence share his own higher earnings by making bequests. (An obvious example of this phenomenon is where parents make special provision for children who are handicapped.)

These different elements may be brought together in the following generalization of (9-12):[8]

$$B_u^i = s_1(r)(I_u^i + wN_u^i) + s_2(r)w(\bar{N}_{u+1} - N_{u+1}^i) + s_3(r)\beta_u^i \qquad (9\text{-}13)$$

where r is the (exogenous) constant rate of interest. The second term allows for a "forward-looking" bequest relationship, taking account of the earnings of the next generation (assumed to be known). The third term represents the effects of random chance, both via "unintended" bequests (in an imperfect annuity market) and via saving out of the uncertain element of lifetime income. The variable β_u^i is assumed to be distributed independently of I and N (and of other random terms), and across generations, with constant mean and variance.

The total bequest is divided among the heirs to give the inheritance of the next generation (we assume that all wealth passes linearly one generation at a time). This part of the process depends on the inheritance rules governing the division of estates and their interaction with family size. If we consider I_{u+1}^i as representing the combined wealth of the husband and wife in the next generation, then the pattern of marriage may also be very significant.

The unequal division of the estate among children can result in considerable inequality. Suppose, for example, that each family has $(1+n)$ boys and $(1+n)$ girls, and that only the eldest son inherits (primogeniture). The eldest son of the eldest son of the eldest son, etc., will have considerable wealth, whereas the second born has $I^i = 0$ in all families. If promogeniture involves the wealth passing to the eldest *child*, then the process of concentration is intensified, since some heiresses marry heirs.

Where wealth is divided among both male and female heirs, the pattern of marriage is relevant. Suppose, for example, that the family divides its wealth in fractions ζ to boys and $(1-\zeta)$ to girls. The distribution in the next generation depends on the correlation between the wealth of husbands and wives. Where marriage is "random", the division $(0 < \zeta < 1)$ is equalizing. However, in the extreme case of "class marriage", where the wealth of husbands and wives is perfectly correlated, then the distribution is independent of ζ. It is in fact just like each boy marrying his own sister: no averaging of estates takes place.

The fact that the number of children is itself a random variable introduces a further stochastic element into the wealth–income generating process. Moreover, family size may be a function of capital or income.

In the main model we make one particular set of assumptions: that there is equal division among sons (alternatively class marriage) and that

---

[8] The linearity assumed in (9-13) is a convenient simplifying assumption, but should be relaxed in any development of the model.

family size is fixed (at $1+n$). We also consider an "alternative model" where there is primogeniture (and again fixed family size); this is discussed later.

With equal division, the wealth inherited by the next generation is

$$I^i_{u+1} = \frac{1}{1+n} B^i_u \qquad (9\text{-}14)$$

It should however be remembered that the process by which wealth is divided may be considerably influenced by public policy. Legislation restricting freedom of bequest is found in a number of countries. Taxation may be designed to encourage the division of estates. Education policy may affect the degree of assortative mating. Family size may be influenced by policies that affect the cost of children (e.g., child benefits or tax deductibility of education expenses).

Determination of Earnings Capacity

The wage that an individual receives is determined by his inherited ability, his human capital and the extent to which he can get his abilities recognized. Inherited ability, in turn, is related to that of his parents. In the formal model, we follow the history of a family through, say, the male line, but this is only for convenience.

In the transmission of ability, we assume that there is "regression towards the mean": children of above-average parents have abilities that are above average, but less so than their parents. There are several reasons for this "regression towards the mean"; it could be based on a genetic process, or it could be because a father (mother) who is above the mean in ability marries on average someone who is less able than he (she), and so the child, reflecting the ability of both parents, is less able than the father (mother). If the latter is the case, the speed of "regression towards the mean" depends, to some extent, on mating patterns. The more that marriage is based on *ability* (the more likely able individuals are to marry other able individuals), the slower is the process of regression towards the mean.

The amount of human capital that an individual acquires depends on both public and private decisions. The nature of state education is clearly important. The private decisions are likely to be influenced by the level of parental wealth, which allows spending on private education (transmission of human wealth in this way may be encouraged by the taxation of material inheritance).

Actual earnings are related only imprecisely to the productivity of the individual, given imperfect information and other real-world features of the labour market.[9] Thus, one of the functions of parents sending their children to élite schools is for them to be identified as more able. This *screening* function of education is distinct from the human capital function. The access of individuals to jobs is also likely to be affected by parental earnings and wealth. Thus entry to certain occupations may be influenced by parental occupation (e.g., medical school), and an important role may be played by "contacts" and the family social network.

The different mechanisms are represented in simplified form by the relationship

$$N_u^i = a_1 N_{u-1}^i + a_2 (B_{u-1}^i - \bar{B}_{u-1}) + v_u^i \tag{9-15}$$

where $0 < a_1 < 1$. The first term represents the genetic transmission; the second the advantage provided by parental wealth (relative to the mean); v_u^i is the stochastic term distributed independently of N, B (and β), and across generations, with constant mean and variance.[10]

Behaviour of the Model

We examine here the behaviour of the model for fixed factor prices. It is governed by the difference equations (from (9-13), (9-14) and (9-15)),

$$B_u^i = \frac{s_1}{1+n} B_{u-1}^i + s_1 w N_u^i + s_2 w (\bar{N}_{u+1} - N_{u+1}^i) + s_3 \beta_u^i \tag{9-16}$$

$$N_u^i = a_1 N_{u-1}^i + a_2 (B_{u-1}^i - \bar{B}_{u-1}) + v_u^i \tag{9-15}$$

It is assumed that the random terms, β_u^i and v_u^i, are independent across individuals, and that the population is sufficiently large that we can replace sample moments by the corresponding population moments, in this way moving from a stochastic to a distributional model. This assumption is not necessarily an appropriate one, and we might, for example, expect the random terms to be correlated across individuals (e.g., reflecting the state of the economy). The working of the model is set out schematically in Fig. 9-1.

The mean values are then governed by

$$\bar{B}_u = \frac{s_1}{(1+n)} \bar{B}_{u-1} + s_1 w \bar{N}_u + s_3 \bar{\beta} \tag{9-17a}$$

$$\bar{N}_u = a_1 \bar{N}_{u-1} + \bar{v} \tag{9-17b}$$

[9] The two are related, however, to the extent that the identification of individuals' abilities affects their assignment to various jobs (based on comparative advantage), and this in turn affects their productivity. For a more extensive discussion of the screening function of education, see Stiglitz (1975a).

[10] It would have been preferable to allow the random term to be related to capital; for instance, if part of the stochastic term arises from variability in the return to capital.

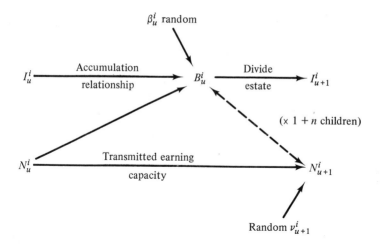

Figure 9-1 Intergenerational model.

The assumption $0 < a_1 < 1$ ensures convergence of earnings capacity to $\bar{N}(=\bar{v}/(1-a_1))$. The condition that the mean lifetime wealth converges is that $s_1 < 1+n$, which requires in effect that the intrinsic growth of capital $(s_1 - 1)$ should be less than the growth of population. This condition is assumed to hold (its relation to the general equilibrium of the economy is discussed below). The mean values converge therefore to

$$\bar{N} = \frac{\bar{v}}{1-a_1}, \quad \bar{B} = \frac{s_1 w\bar{N} + s_3\bar{\beta}}{1 - s_1/(1+n)}$$

and the relative shares in lifetime income are

$$\frac{\bar{B}/(1+n)}{w\bar{N}} = \frac{s_1 + s_3\bar{\beta}(1-a_1)/w\bar{v}}{1+n-s_1} \tag{9-18}$$

i.e., it depends on the intrinsic growth of capital, the rate of population growth, and the relative means of the random terms in the two equations. A policy that affects only the distribution of after-tax wages and not its mean (e.g., a redistributive wage tax) will leave the capital stock unchanged. Other policies that influence savings rates or redistribute income from capital to labour will in general change $\bar{B}$. This will be important in the subsequent discussion, since when $\bar{B}$ changes the change in the coefficient of variation will not be the same as the change in the variance.

Our main concern is with the distribution of wealth and consumption. For simplicity we focus on the male line; i.e., we do not allow for the fact that, as the model stands, women have neither wealth nor income. This should not be taken at face value; our "individuals" might better be thought of as neuter, reproducing themselves unaided. The behaviour of the distribution is characterized in terms of the second moments. These are more complicated, and to illustrate the analysis we concentrate on the simplified case where $s_2 = 0$ (i.e., bequests are not influenced by future earning capacity) and $a_2 = 0$ (i.e., N represents "raw" earning capacity, and there is no influence via parental wealth).[11] In other words, the relationship represented by the dashed line in Fig. 9-1 is left out of account.

We proceed by first setting out the difference equations for the variables B_u^i and N_u^i in this case. From these, we can derive (using the assumptions about the random terms) the difference equations for the second moments (variances and covariance), and then solve for the steady-state values to which they converge. From these, the distribution of lifetime consumption can be obtained, and we can see how it depends on the parameters of the model.

The difference equations for the basic variables are:

$$(B_u^i - \bar{B}_u) = a_3(B_{u-1}^i - \bar{B}_{u-1}) + a_1 a_4(N_{u-1}^i - \bar{N}_{u-1})$$
$$+ a_4(v_u^i - \bar{v}) + s_3(\beta_u^i - \bar{\beta}) \quad (9\text{-}19a)$$

$$(N_u^i - \bar{N}_u) = a_1(N_{u-1}^i - \bar{N}_{u-1}) + (v_u^i - \bar{v}) \quad (9\text{-}19b)$$

where $a_3 = s_1/(1+n)$ and $a_4 = s_1 w$. From these we can calculate, using the assumptions about the random terms, that the second moments are given by:

$$\text{var}[B_u] = a_3^2 \text{var}[B_{u-1}] + a_1^2 a_4^2 \text{var}[N_{u-1}] + a_4^2 \text{var}[v]$$
$$+ s_3^2 \text{var}[\beta] + 2a_1 a_3 a_4 \text{cov}[B_{u-1}, N_{u-1}] \quad (9\text{-}20a)$$

$$\text{var}[N_u] = a_1^2 \text{var}[N_{u-1}] + \text{var}[v] \quad (9\text{-}20b)$$

$$\text{cov}[B_u, N_u] = a_1 a_3 \text{cov}[B_{u-1}, N_{u-1}] + a_1^2 a_4 \text{var}[N_{u-1}] + a_4 \text{var}[v] \quad (9\text{-}20c)$$

From (9-20b) it is clear that $0 < a_1 < 1$ ensures that the variance of earnings capacity converges to

$$\text{var}[N] = \frac{\text{var}[v]}{1 - a_1^2} \quad (9\text{-}21a)$$

Similarly $0 < a_3 < 1$ (i.e., $s_1 < 1+n$) implies that the covariance converges to

$$\text{cov}[B, N] = \frac{a_4 \text{var}[N]}{1 - a_1 a_3} \quad (9\text{-}21b)$$

---

[11] B can be taken as including human capital.

Finally, the same conditions ensure that the variance of B converges:[12]

$$\text{var}[B] = \frac{1}{1-a_3^2}\left[s_3^2\,\text{var}\,[\beta] + \left(\frac{1+a_1a_3}{1-a_1a_3}\right)a_4^2\,\text{var}\,[N]\right] \qquad (9\text{-}21c)$$

In this simplified version of the model, the equilibrium variance of wage income is that associated with the random component, and this also feeds into the variance of wealth. Since $a_3 = s_1/(1+n)$, the variance of B is larger, the closer the intrinsic growth rate of capital (s_1-1) is to the rate of population growth. It also increases with the extent of inheritance of earning capacity (a_1) and with the variance of the random term.

From these moments of the distribution, we can calculate the inequality of lifetime income or consumption, as measured by the coefficient of variation. Taking lifetime consumption, this is defined as

$$C_u^i = wN_u^i + \frac{1}{1+n}B_{u-1}^i + \beta_u^i - \frac{B_u^i}{1+r} \qquad (9\text{-}22)$$

where the last term represents the present value of wealth passed on (r being taken here as the interest rate per generation). Hence

$$C_u^i = w\left(1 - \frac{s_1}{1+r}\right)(a_1N_{u-1}^i + v_u^i) + \frac{1}{1+n}\left(1 - \frac{s_1}{1+r}\right)B_{u-1}^i$$

$$+ \left(1 - \frac{s_3}{1+r}\right)\beta_u^i \qquad (9\text{-}22')$$

In equilibrium,

$$\bar{C} = \left(1 - \frac{s_1}{1+r}\right)\left(w\bar{N} + \frac{\bar{B}}{1+n} + a_5\bar{\beta}\right) \qquad (9\text{-}23)$$

where

$$a_5 \equiv \frac{1 - s_3/(1+r)}{1 - s_1/(1+r)}$$

and the variance is given by

$$\text{var}[C] = \left(1 - \frac{s_1}{1+r}\right)^2\left[w^2\,\text{var}\,[N] + \left(\frac{1}{1+n}\right)^2\text{var}\,[B]\right.$$

$$\left. + a_5^2\,\text{var}[\beta] + \frac{2wa_1}{1+n}\text{cov}[B, N]\right] \qquad (9\text{-}24)$$

The coefficient of variation of consumption is therefore, substituting for $\bar{B}$

---

[12] The difference equation may be written as $\mathbf{x}_u = Z\mathbf{x}_{u-1}$ where $\mathbf{x}$ denotes the vector (var$[B]$, var$[N]$, cov$[B, N]$). The condition for stability is that the characteristic roots of Z are less than unity in absolute value, and this is clearly satisfied given $0 < a_1 < 1$, and $0 < a_3 < 1$. See Samuelson (1947, Appendix B).

and cov $[B, N]$,

$$
V_{\bar{C}}^2 = \frac{w^2 \left(\dfrac{1+a_1 a_3}{1-a_1 a_3}\right) \mathrm{var}\,[N] + a_5^2 \,\mathrm{var}\,[\beta] + \left(\dfrac{1}{1+n}\right)^2 \mathrm{var}\,[B]}{\{[w\bar{N} + s_3 \bar{\beta}/(1+n)]/(1-a_3) + a_5 \bar{\beta}\}^2} \tag{9-25}
$$

In the case where $\bar{\beta} = 0$ and $a_5 = 1$, which we use particularly in the next section,

$$
V_{\bar{C}}^2 = V_{\bar{N}}^2 \frac{(1+a_1 a_3)(1-a_3)}{(1-a_1 a_3)(1+a_3)} + \frac{\mathrm{var}\,[\beta]}{(w\bar{N})^2} \frac{1-a_3}{1+a_3} \tag{9-26}
$$

where $V_{\bar{N}}^2$ is the coefficient of variation of earnings. The extent of inequality depends on the variation in N and β, magnified by the serial correlation induced by a_1 in the former case, but moderated by the term $(1-a_3)/(1+a_3)$.

The solution for the general case follows the same approach, and is left as an exercise.

Exercise 9-2 Examine the behaviour of the model where $a_2 > 0$, $s_2 > 0$. What is the indirect effect of parental wealth, via a_2, on the variance of bequests? How does forward-looking bequest behaviour ($s_2 > 0$) modify the distribution of lifetime consumption?

General Equilibrium Considerations

The model to this point has assumed fixed factor prices, an assumption that might apply to a small open economy (although even then constancy over time is unlikely), but that in a closed economy leaves out of account the general equilibrium effects discussed in earlier Lectures.

If we assume that aggregate output is a function of the mean inheritance and mean labour capacity,[13] and that the latter has converged to its equilibrium value (which we can then normalize at unity, $\bar{N} = 1$), then output per man at time u may be written as $f(\bar{B}_{u-1}/(1+n))$. We assume that the distribution of income to factors is such that $r(\bar{B}_{u-1})$ is a declining function and $w(\bar{B}_{u-1})$ is an increasing function. This allows for imperfect competition, e.g., with a constant monopoly mark-up. The development of the aggregate equilibrium is then governed by (from 9-17a)

$$
\bar{B}_u = \frac{s_1(r)}{1+n} \bar{B}_{u-1} + s_1(r)w + s_3(r)\bar{\beta} \tag{9-27}
$$

where r and w are functions of $\bar{B}_{u-1}$. A necessary condition, where $\bar{\beta} \geqslant 0$,

---

[13] The shortcomings of the aggregate production function have been discussed earlier. We may also note that a more satisfactory treatment would allow for life-cycle savings, so that the capital stock depends not just on inheritance—see Conlisk (1977) and Atkinson (1980).

for a steady state is that $s_1 < 1+n$. This then vindicates the use of this condition earlier, in that it must be satisfied at any steady-state equilibrium.

The aggregate behaviour in this model is independent of the distribution of inherited wealth or wages. This is a consequence of the linearity of the basic equations with respect to the variables that differ across individuals. As we have noted, the linearity assumption should be relaxed in a more general treatment. For example, the marginal propensity to make bequests out of lifetime income may rise with the level of income. In this case, the aggregate behaviour would depend on the distribution of wealth. The same applies where there are differences between individuals in the savings functions.

An Alternative Model

In the model described above, the distribution of income converges to an equilibrium state where inequality is attributable to differences in earning capacity, generated randomly by the genetic process, and to the stochastic element in income and bequests, interpreted either as entrepreneurial gains or uncertainty with regard to life expectancy. In this context, inheritance plays a rather different role from that usually envisaged in discussions of the distribution of wealth. In essence it "averages out" variations in incomes or consumption, as may be seen from the fact that in Eq. (9-26) V_C^2 is a declining function of the rate of saving a_3 (an aspect discussed further below).

In view of this, we present an alternative model where there is inequality in the equilibrium distribution resulting from the inheritance process. In order to focus attention on this, we assume that there is no variance in N or β, so that the model is deterministic. We replace however the equal division assumption by that of primogeniture, with estates being passed on intact to the eldest son (a model first analysed in Stiglitz, 1969a).

In steady state, with fixed factor prices, the equilibrium distribution may be characterized as follows (we have taken $s_2 = 0$ and assume $s_1 > 1.0$):

Proportion of population		Inherited wealth
$n/1+n$	younger children	0
$n/(1+n)^2$	first-generation older children	$s_1 w\bar{N} + s_3\bar{\beta} \equiv s^*$
$n/(1+n)^3$	second-generation older children	$s^* + s^*s_1$
$n/(1+n)^4$	third-generation older children	$s^*(1 + s_1 + s_1^2)$
$n/(1+n)^{j+1}$	jth-generation older children	$[s^*/(s_1 - 1)](s_1^j - 1) \equiv I^j$

The proportion with inherited wealth greater than or equal to I^j is then

$$\lambda(I_j) = \frac{n}{1+n} \sum_{k=j}^{\infty} \frac{1}{(1+n)^k} = (1+n)^{-j} \tag{9-28}$$

From the definition of I^j

$$\log\left[1 + \frac{(s_1-1)}{s^*} I^j\right] = j\log(s_1) \tag{9-29}$$

In the same way

$$\log \lambda = -j\log(1+n)$$

Eliminating j

$$\log \lambda = \log\left[1 + \frac{(s_1-1)}{s^*} I^j\right]\left[\frac{-\log(1+n)}{\log(s_1)}\right]$$

which gives

$$\lambda = \left[1 + \frac{(s_1-1)}{s^*} I^j\right]^{-\log(1+n)/\log(s_1)} \tag{9-30}$$

The equilibrium distribution is therefore of the Pareto type II form (Atkinson and Harrison, 1978), approaching the standard Pareto distribution for large wealth. The mean wealth per person is, as before in equilibrium,

$$\bar{I} = \frac{s^*}{1+n-s_1} = \frac{s_1 w \bar{N} + s_3 \bar{\beta}}{1+n-s_1} \tag{9-31}$$

and the condition $1+n > s_1$ is once more implied by the steady state of the general equilibrium. This condition means that the Pareto exponent $\mu \equiv \log(1+n)/\log s_1 > 1$, and we may note that a rise in s_1 reduces the Pareto exponent. For example, values of $n = 0.5$ and $s_1 = 1.1$ (for a 30-year generation) imply $\mu = 4.3$, whereas a rise to $s_1 = 1.2$ implies $\mu = 2.2$.

The main feature of this alternative model is that in equilibrium inequalities may be observed even though there are no differences in wages and no random influences on income. The implications for taxation are discussed at the end of the next section.

Exercise 9-3 Consider a model where people live for at most three periods and plan to spread their consumption equally over the three periods. Half the population die at the end of the third period, leaving no wealth; the other half die at the end of the second period, leaving an "unplanned" bequest. (There are no annuity markets.) Show that this can generate a steady-state distribution with a Pareto tail. (See Stiglitz 1978b, Section X.)

9-3 DISTRIBUTIONAL INCIDENCE

The model described in the last section provides a framework within which we can examine the effect of the government on the long-run development of wealth-holding. By considering the intergenerational transmission process, and by focusing on the equilibrium properties of the distribution, we are taking a long-term view. In practice, this equilibrium may well not be attained; since convergence may be slow, the parameters may shift in response to exogenous events, and government policy may be changing. The analysis should therefore be seen in the same way as the steady-state results of the previous Lecture—as an indicator of the effects rather than as a prediction. There is however an important difference, in that the *qualitative* properties of the steady state, and hence the comparative static conclusions, may depend critically on the assumptions of the model. In the main model of the previous section, based on equal division of estates, the equilibrium is characterized by inequality arising from differences in wages and random chance. In contrast, in the alternative model there is an equilibrium with inequality arising not from such differences but from the practice of primogeniture. The role of inheritance—and consequently of policies designed to influence inheritance—is quite different in the two models.

Intergenerational Transmission and Public Policy

Before investigating in detail particular tax measures, we consider some of the more general ways in which public policy may influence the intergenerational process.

First, the transmission of earning capacity is influenced by a number of social variables. We have already referred to marriage patterns. If social change leads to less random marriage, as may happen as a result of educational policy, then the rise in a_1 results in a smaller coefficient of variation of earnings, and from Eq. (9-26) we can see that the coefficient of variation of consumption would be decreased (in the case $a_5 = 1$, $\bar{\beta} = 0$). This somewhat paradoxical result illustrates one of the aspects of the model: that the variance and coefficient of variation may move in opposite directions. The rise in a_1 raises the variance by a factor $(1-a_1^2)^{-1}$, but the squared mean by $(1-a_1)^{-2}$, so that the latter dominates. Two qualifications to this result should be noted. The change in a_1 may well give rise to a change in savings behaviour (savings being influenced by the degree of regression to the mean), and this may modify the conclusions. Moreover, it has been assumed that the mean and variance of v is not affected, but this may not be the right normalization.

Second, it may be that earnings are not intrinsically related to capacity, N^i, but rather that there is a partially random screening process for a *given* earnings distribution. On this interpretation, one might see a_1 as a measure of the degree of inequality of opportunity. An equal opportunity policy, reducing a_1, would, for given earnings inequality V_N^2, reduce the inequality of consumption. From (9-26) we can see that V_C^2 would fall (in the case $\bar{\beta} = 0$ and $a_5 = 1$), and the same result holds more generally.

Third, the extent of inherited wealth influences the distribution. From Eq. (9-18) we can see that, where $\bar{\beta} = 0$ and $a_5 = 1$, the ratio of inherited wealth to wage income is $a_3/(1-a_3)$. The variance of lifetime consumption may be written:

$$\text{var}\,[C] = \frac{[1-a_3(1+n)/(1+r)]^2}{1-a_3^2}\left[(w^2\,\text{var}\,[N])\left(\frac{1+a_1a_3}{1-a_1a_3}\right) + \text{var}\,[\beta]\right]$$

$$(9\text{-}32)$$

If there were no inequality in wage income ($\text{var}\,[N] = 0$), then the condition for a rise in inheritance to magnify the variance of lifetime consumption is that $a_3 > (1+n)/(1+r)$. For example with $r = 1.5$, $n = 0.5$ (with a generation of 30 years), this means that $s_1 > 0.9$ (or a saving rate out of the present value of income of 36 per cent). On the other hand, if $n < r$ (and $\bar{\beta} = 0$) the mean consumption is reduced by a rise in a_3; and it may be seen from (9-26) that the coefficient of variation is decreased. In the opposite extreme, if $\text{var}[\beta] = 0$, a sufficient condition for the variance of lifetime consumption to increase with a_3 is that $a_1 > (1+n)/(1+r)$ and $r > n$. With the numbers taken before, this means $a_1 > 0.6$, which may or may not be satisfied (the degree of heredity is a controversial area). Even if it is satisfied, it may be seen that (with $a_1 < 1$) the coefficient of variation of consumption is a declining function of a_3 (from 9-26)).

The relationship between r and n brings out the role played by the "intrinsic" rate of capital accumulation, on one hand, and the division of estates (in this equal division model) on the other. If $r = n$, then it can be seen that the variance of lifetime consumption is definitely a decreasing function of a_3. A prohibitive tax on bequests would increase the variance.

These results follow from the fact that, as we have stressed earlier, inheritance serves the function in this model of averaging the random fluctuations in lifetime income. Where the savings rate is high, a large proportion of windfall gains is passed on to subsequent generations whose expected gains are lower.[14]

Finally, we may note the effect of the variance in β, which may again reflect policy measures. On the interpretation in terms of entrepreneurial or windfall gains, the variance may be reduced (e.g., by regulation of speculative activities or controls on land use) or increased (e.g., by zoning legislation, by frequent changes in policy or tax rates, etc.). On the

---

[14] Serial correlation in β should be considered here; the effect may be seen to be analogous to that of serial correlation in N via the parameter a_1.

"unplanned bequest" interpretation, the variance may be reduced by measures to improve the capital market (e.g., schemes for owner-occupiers to convert the equity in their houses into annuities) or by social security schemes. If $\bar{\beta} = 0$ and $a_5 = 1$, the coefficient of variation is increasing in var $[\beta]$. If $\bar{\beta} > 0$, the effect depends on the relative coefficients of variation in N and β, allowing for the serial correlation factor in the former case. We would probably expect the dispersion in β to be considerably larger than in N; on the other hand, this may be offset by its lower degree of serial correlation. In other words, the range of prizes is bigger in entrepreneurial activity but they are less likely to be repeated across generations.

Incidence of Taxation

From the preceding analysis, it is clear that taxation may influence the distribution of wealth, income and consumption in three distinct ways:

1. Redistributive taxation may directly affect the coefficient of variation of after-tax wages or after-tax windfall gains.
2. Behavioural coefficients, such as the savings rates, may be altered by taxation.
3. Relative factor returns, w and r, may be affected both directly and indirectly through the general equilibrium repercussions on the capital–labour ratio.

We illustrate the effects of taxation by considering several examples. Since the general equilibrium effects can be obtained from the earlier analysis, we leave these to the reader.

The first tax considered is a proportional tax on lifetime income at rate t, with the proceeds being used to finance current government spending. The coefficient of variation of wage income is unchanged. If we suppose initially that the savings propensity is unaffected, then the coefficient of variation of consumption (where $a_5 = 1$, $\bar{\beta} = 0$) depends on var $[\beta]/w^2$. If the income tax is levied on β, this term is unaltered, and the proportional tax has no effect on inequality (this is the analogue of the case discussed in Section 9-1). On the other hand, a tax that exempts all or part of β (e.g., because it consists of capital gains) leads to an increase in inequality. If we now allow for variation in the savings proportions, then we can apply the earlier results. In the case where s_1 (assumed equal to s_3) is reduced by the tax, then we have seen earlier that (with $\bar{\beta} = 0$) the inequality of lifetime consumption is increased. Conversely, if the tax encourages savings, then inequality is reduced.

Exercise 9-4 Examine the effect of a proportional lifetime income tax, where the proceeds are used to make a uniform payment to all. What would be the effect if the tax were levied solely on wage income?

The second tax considered is an estate (and gift) tax, which reduces the amount inherited from $B/(1+n)$ to $T_e B/(1+n)$, where $T_e < 1$, with the proceeds being used to pay a uniform capital grant (G). The basic difference equations may be written (where we have set $a_2 = 0$, $s_2 = 0$ and $s_3 = s_1$):

$$B_u^i = \frac{s_1}{1+n}[(T_e)B_{u-1}^i + (1 - T_e)\bar{B}_{u-1}] + s_1 w N_u^i + s_1 \beta_u^i$$

$$N_u^i = a_1 N_{u-1}^i + v_u^i \qquad\qquad (9\text{-}33)$$

The tax term does not enter the equations for the mean values of B and N. The equations for the variances become:

$$\operatorname{var}[B_u] = a_3^2 T_e^2 \operatorname{var}[B_{u-1}] + a_4^2 \operatorname{var}[N_u] + s_1^2 \operatorname{var}[\beta]$$
$$+ 2a_1 a_3 a_4 T_e \operatorname{cov}[B_{u-1}, N_{u-1}] \qquad (9\text{-}34)$$

$$\operatorname{cov}[B_u, N_u] = a_1 a_3 T_e \operatorname{cov}[B_{u-1}, N_{u-1}] + a_4 \operatorname{var}[N_u] \qquad (9\text{-}35)$$

(that for $\operatorname{var}[N]$ is unchanged). Suppose that, when the tax is introduced, the economy is in equilibrium. When the first tax is paid, this reduces the variance of B (via the first term). At the next time of passing, the first term is smaller again (since $\operatorname{var}[B_{u-1}]$ is lower) and the covariance is reduced, reinforcing the first effect. There is therefore a steady approach to a new equilibrium, with

$$\operatorname{var}[B] = \frac{1}{1 - a_3^2 T_e^2}\left[s_1^2 \operatorname{var}[\beta] + a_4^2 \frac{1 + a_1 a_3 T_e}{1 - a_1 a_3 T_e}\operatorname{var}[N] \right] \qquad (9\text{-}36a)$$

and

$$\operatorname{cov}[B, N] = \frac{a_4 \operatorname{var}[N]}{1 - a_1 a_3 T_e} \qquad (9\text{-}36b)$$

which are decreasing functions of the tax rate (increasing functions of T_e). The coefficient of variation of lifetime consumption is given by (with $\bar{\beta} = 0$):

$$V_C^2 = \frac{(1 - a_3)^2}{1 - a_3^2 T_e^2}\left[V_N^2 \frac{1 + a_1 a_3 T_e}{1 - a_1 a_3 T_e} + \frac{\operatorname{var}[\beta]}{(w\bar{N})^2} \right] \qquad (9\text{-}37)$$

It is clear that the tax reduces the coefficient of variation of lifetime consumption. In the limiting case where $T_e = 0$ (i.e., a 100 per cent tax on bequests), the inequality is that due to the variation in the income of the current generation (V_N^2 and $\operatorname{var}[\beta]$), moderated by saving (if $s_1 > 0$). Moreover, expression (9-37) is similar to (9-32), when multiplied by $(w\bar{N})^2$, with $a_3 T_e$ replacing a_3. Using the results obtained on page 279, we can examine the effect of changes in a_3 induced by the tax.[15] As we saw in Lecture 3, the effect on savings could go either way; this could strengthen or diminish the equalizing effect on the coefficient of variation of lifetime consumption.

The second-round effects of the estate tax may be seen in other areas. In particular, a tax on the transfer of material wealth may well make other forms of transfer more attractive. Thus, parents may seek to provide advantages for their children via increased earning power rather than direct transfers of capital. (In order to analyse this, we need to go back to the general model with $a_2 > 0$.) It is also possible that it leads to a change in the pattern of bequests.

Taxation in the Alternative Model

By way of contrast, we now consider the effects of taxation in the alternative model, where inheritance, and the unequal division of estates, leads to concentration of wealth. In the equilibrium state of the primogeniture model, the distribution of inherited wealth is given by Eq. (9-30). The first point we may note is that the coefficient of variation of lifetime consumption is (where finite) an increasing function of the extent of inheritance. The coefficient is given (where $s_3 = s_1$) by

$$V_C^2 = \frac{\text{var}\,[I]}{(w\bar{N} + \bar{\beta} + \bar{I})^2} = \frac{(1 - a_3)^2\,\text{var}\,[I]}{(w\bar{N} + \bar{\beta})^2} \tag{9-38}$$

(where we have used (9-31)). For ease of analysis, let us approximate the distribution (9-30) by the continuous version:

$$\lambda = \left(1 + \frac{s_1 - 1}{s^*}I\right)^{-n/(s_1 - 1)} \tag{9-30'}$$

(where we have replaced $\log(1 + x)$ by x). The variance may then be calculated as:[16]

$$\text{var}\,[I] = \frac{2s_1^2(w\bar{N} + \bar{\beta})^2}{(s_1 - 1)^2[n/(s_1 - 1)][n/(s_1 - 1) - 2]} \tag{9-39}$$

where we have assumed that the Pareto exponent exceeds 2, so that the variance is finite. Substituting into (9-38) shows that V_C^2 is proportional to

$$\frac{a_3^2}{(2 + n)/(2 + 2n) - a_3} \tag{9-40}$$

[15] Writing $a_3^* = a_3 T_e$, the expression is as (9-32) with $a_3 = a_3^*$ except that the first squared term is $(1 - a_3^*/T_e)$, so $1/T_e$ corresponds to $(1 + n)/(1 + r)$. Thus, where for example var $[N] = 0$, an increase in a_3 reduces V_C^2 where $a_3^* < (1 + n)/(1 + r)$ or $a_3 T_e < 1/T_e$, which is clearly satisfied for $T_e \leqslant 1$.

[16] To obtain the moments of the distribution, change the variable to $1/z = \{1 + [(s_1 - 1)/s^*]I\}$. The resulting integral is the Beta function, which can be evaluated straightforwardly.

where the denominator is positive by assumption. The coefficient of variation is an increasing function of a_3, and when $s_1 = 1 + n/2$ it becomes infinite.

The impact of a redistributive tax in this model may be seen directly. The youngest sons now receive the lump-sum capital payment, and the bequest is moderated at each stage by a factor T_e, where $T_e < 1$.

> **Exercise 9-6** Examine the effect of the redistributive estate tax on the equilibrium distribution of wealth in the alternative model, and on the coefficient of variation of lifetime consumption.

9-4 EMPIRICAL STUDIES OF THE REDISTRIBUTIVE IMPACT OF THE GOVERNMENT BUDGET

The theoretical models discussed so far provide insights into the distributional impact of policy measures; but for practical implementation the analytical skeleton needs to be clothed with empirical evidence on the actual distribution of endowments and on individual behaviour. This is far from easy. In this section, we outline the main methods and findings in the United States. We then draw attention to the strong assumptions underlying the studies that have been made, the limitations in the sources employed, and the problems in interpreting the results. These in turn indicate some of the ways in which the work may be developed.

Empirical Studies of Fiscal Redistribution

In the United States there have been a number of major studies of the redistributive impact of the government budget, including in recent years that by Musgrave and associates (1974) and *Who Bears the Tax Burden?* by Pechman and Okner (1974).[17] The latter, as the title suggests, deals solely with taxation, and we concentrate here on the Musgrave study, which covers both taxes and public spending. Musgrave *et al.* start from a distribution of income by ranges, and then allocate taxes and expenditures to these ranges. Thus, if the range \$12 500–\$17 500 receives total income of \$200 billion and is allocated \$70 billion of taxes and \$60 billion of expenditure, its tax rate is 35 per cent and its "net" position is −5 per cent. The income distribution by ranges is derived by Musgrave *et al.* from the Brookings MERGE file, in turn based on tax data and the Survey of Economic Opportunity. The distribution of taxes depends on the assumptions about the incidence, discussed below, and on the allocation

---

[17] Earlier studies in the United States include Colm and Tarasov (1940), Musgrave *et al.* (1951), and that by Gillespie (1965) of public expenditure. In the United Kingdom, major investigations have been undertaken by Lord Samuel (1919), Barna (1945), Cartter (1955) and Nicholson (1964).

series. The latter are taken from a variety of sources, including tax data and surveys on consumer expenditure. Thus, the excise tax on tobacco is allocated according to average expenditure by income range (from survey data), and the gift, estate, and death taxes are allocated to households with capital income whose total income exceeded $25 000 (in 1968). The Pechman and Okner study is more refined in that it uses individual observations from the MERGE file[18] rather than income ranges, but similar procedures are applied (for example, excises are allocated using consumer expenditure survey data).

The expenditure side is more complicated, and two classes of spending are identified. The first consists of goods where particular beneficiaries can (in theory) be identified—"allocable expenditures"—or of broadly publicly provided private goods (e.g., highways and education). The second group consists of "public goods" that cannot be directly allocated to particular individuals (e.g., defence). For allocable goods, the procedure adopted by Musgrave *et al.* is similar to that for taxes. For example, unemployment insurance benefits are allocated according to receipts from that source (given in MERGE file), education expenditure is allocated to the families of students, using data from the Census of Population. The second group of public goods are simply allocated on three assumptions: (1) in proportion to total income, (2) in proportion to taxes, and (3) equally to all persons.

The results of this exercise for 1968 are shown in Table 9-1, which is based on the "benchmark" assumptions (see below) about incidence and assumption (1) about public goods. Taxes paid as a percentage of total income (pre-tax but including transfers) vary little over the income range. The pattern is not greatly different from that reported by Jevons for Victorian Britain—the family on $35 000 paying, if anything, a lower percentage than the household on $10 000 a year. For the two-thirds of families between $5700 and $35 500, the tax ratio varies only in the range 32.4–33.9 per cent. In contrast, the effect of expenditure appears to be progressive, with cash transfers being sizeable at the lower end. The allocated benefit from public spending for the lowest group is more than 100 per cent of total income (including cash transfers), and the percentage falls quite sharply with income, the median family benefiting to the extent of some 20 per cent. The final row shows total spending, including the "public goods" category, allocated in proportion to income (i.e., adding a constant percentage).

Similar studies have been carried out for other countries, although the methods vary, reflecting the differences in availability of data and in fiscal systems. In the United Kingdom, the estimates published annually in

---

[18] The construction of the MERGE file, and that used by the Office of Tax Analysis, involves the matching of data sets relating to different populations. For discussion of the rationale of such matching, see Kadane (1975), and the references there.

Table 9-1 Tax burden/benefits as a percentage of total income—United States, 1968

Taxation	Lower limit of brackets ($) total income (including transfers)										
	under $4000	$4000–	$5700–	$7900–	$10 400–	$12 500–	$17 500–	$22 600–	$35 500–	$92 000–	Average
Federal											
Total	15.2	17.9	20.9	21.6	21.6	23.4	22.6	23.8	24.5	29.1	22.7
Income and estate tax*	2.0	2.8	5.9	7.1	7.9	10.1	10.6	13.3	16.8	21.2	10.3
Excise and customs	2.5	2.8	3.1	3.0	2.9	2.7	2.1	1.1	0.9	0.6	2.3
Corporation income tax	5.1	6.1	5.0	4.6	4.3	4.6	4.8	5.1	5.3	6.6	5.0
Social security payroll tax	5.5	6.3	7.0	6.9	6.7	6.1	5.2	4.2	1.5	0.6	5.2
State and local											
Total	13.4	12.6	11.9	11.6	11.1	10.6	9.7	9.1	7.1	6.9	10.3
Total	28.5	30.5	32.8	33.1	32.8	33.9	32.4	32.9	31.6	35.9	33.0
Expenditure											
Allocable											
Federal total	83.5	25.7	13.3	7.6	5.3	4.7	4.3	5.3	5.5	7.5	10.0
State and local total	27.1	18.7	15.8	12.2	9.4	7.4	4.8	3.6	2.2	0.9	8.4
Education ⎱ Federal	6.1	11.0	11.5	9.7	7.4	6.0	3.5	3.0	1.7	0.6	5.8
Highways ⎰ and	1.8	2.4	2.8	2.6	2.5	2.2	1.8	0.9	0.7	0.4	1.9
Medical ⎱ state and	7.6	7.4	3.9	2.0	1.2	0.7	0.5	0.3	0.1	0.0	1.5
Transfers ⎰ local	92.8	21.4	9.4	4.5	2.7	2.1	1.5	1.2	0.2	0.2	6.9
Total allocable	110.6	44.4	29.1	19.8	14.7	12.0	9.1	8.9	7.7	8.4	18.4
Total including non-allocable	127.3	61.1	45.8	36.5	31.4	28.8	25.8	25.6	24.4	25.1	35.1

Source: Musgrave, Case and Leonard (1974, Tables 2, 6, 7) based on "benchmark" assumptions and assumption (a) about public goods allocation. Reproduced by courtesy of Sage Publications. Inc.
* Including gift tax.

Economic Trends use individual data, rather than income ranges, from the Family Expenditure Survey, but the coverage of public spending is less extensive. The results are broadly the same.[19]

Limitations of Redistributional Studies

There is clearly a wide gap between the indicators of redistribution implemented in the studies described above and the theoretical concepts outlined in Section 9-1. First, the studies are based on a *current* measure of economic status. They therefore take no account of the considerable lifetime—and intergenerational—redistribution effected by the government, notably through social security. The impact of a state pension scheme in terms of current income is predominantly to transfer income to lower-income people from the better-off working population. The implications for lifetime income may however be quite different, and a pension scheme may involve no redistribution. The analysis of the lifetime impact is however far from straightforward, and may depend critically on the assumptions made about the degree of imperfection in the capital market (Polinsky, 1974). The analysis of intergenerational redistribution (whether, for example, the generation now retired has had a better or worse deal over their lifetime than those currently in the labour force) poses still more severe problems. Second, the studies adopt income as a measure of resources. This may be a quite defensible choice, but alternatives such as current expenditure need to be considered. Third, the studies are based on families, and take rather limited account of differences in needs. As we have noted earlier, the lack of any data on transfers within the family means that we cannot look at some of the interesting questions concerning the distribution between individuals (e.g., between men and women).

The empirical investigations relate to the current income of families, but even accepting these terms of reference there are substantial difficulties. This may be seen if we compare the definition of income with the comprehensive, or Haig–Simons, approach. First, there are matters of principle. These include the treatment of capital transfers, of charitable contributions, and of capital gains arising from interest rate changes. Arguments can be made for excluding or including these. Second, there are those types of receipt that are intrinsically unobservable because they do not correspond to market transactions—such as capital gains that are accrued but not realized, and home production. These should in theory be included in the measure of current income. Third, there are items that are not measured because of shortcomings of the data sources. Thus, the use of tax records means that

---

[19] Studies for other countries include Dodge (1975) and Gillespie (1976) for Canada, Cazenave and Morrisson (1974) for France, Franzén, Lövgren and Rosenberg (1975) for Sweden, and National Economic and Social Council (1975) for Eire.

income may be missing because it is not taxable or not declared (the adjustments made to reported income are discussed by Pechman and Okner, 1974). Finally, there is the important question of inflation. If the Haig–Simons definition relates to *real* income, then adjustments need to be made to the return to all assets and to the interest paid on all liabilities (i.e., the real cost of borrowing is $r - \rho$, where ρ is the rate of inflation)—see Diamond (1975a) and Aaron (1976).

The measure of income employed is therefore an imperfect indicator of comprehensive income, and this in turn is not truly equivalent to "ability to pay". This does not in itself mean that the analysis is invalid, and some of the deficiencies may be of little quantitative significance. It is however important to assess the possible magnitude of the different factors and the sensitivity of the results to alternative assumptions (e.g., about the adjustment for inflation).

The next set of problems concerns the nature of the comparative statics exercise implicit in the redistributive studies. In effect, they involve a comparison of the general equilibrium of the economy with and without the government budget. As we have noted in Lecture 1, the "no government" economy is a purely hypothetical construct, and several writers (e.g., Prest, 1968) have argued that the global comparison is for this reason of little interest. This is not entirely fair, since the hypothetical alternative state may provide a useful reference point—as in the theoretical discussion. On the other hand, this should be clearly stated by those using this approach, and it should be recognized that for policy purposes it is marginal changes in taxes or expenditure that are of most interest.

Even with marginal changes, assumptions about incidence are crucial and these are discussed in more detail below. Having decided on the incidence assumptions, the procedure adopted is to select an indicator of the effective tax liability or benefit, which is then used to allocate taxes and expenditure. Thus, Musgrave *et al.* assume in their benchmark case that the corporate income tax is borne half by consumers, allocated proportionately to consumption, and half by capital income recipients, allocated proportionately to capital income. This allocation poses empirical problems in that the necessary data may not be available in the original source or may be unreliable. Thus, capital income is typically less accurately reported than other items of income (such as earnings), and consumption is not reported in the tax data, so an extraneous source (the consumption survey) has to be employed.[20] Public expenditure poses particular difficulties. With publicly provided private goods it may not be easy to identify the beneficiaries (who visits museums?) and the correct allocation may be open

---

[20] Obtaining reliable data on certain aspects of consumption, notably alcohol and tobacco, may be difficult. In the United Kingdom, the reported expenditure on alcoholic drink in budget surveys is some 60 per cent of the known total.

to debate (what benefit should be allowed in the case of education?) Pure public goods raise in acute form the question of valuation. The three procedures outlined above are *ad hoc*. Aaron and McGuire (1970) derived from assumptions about individual utility functions and the procedure determining public goods supply an explicit allocation formula, which values the ith person's consumption of the public good at his marginal rate of substitution between the public good and income (using the conditions for the optimum supply of the public good—discussed in Lecture 16). The underlying assumptions (e.g., those concerning the level of supply of the public good) are however open to question (see Peacock, 1974; Brennan, 1976; and Ulph, 1979).

Finally, there is the assessment of the results. Typically, these involve the comparison of the pre- and post-distributions of incomes, sometimes summarized by a statistic such as the Gini coefficient. The limitations of summary statistics are well known, but less attention has been paid to the changes in ranking between the two distributions. Thus, we need to know not just the shape of the pre- and post-distributions but also the location of families within the distributions. This may be viewed as a transition matrix mapping pre-tax income positions into post-tax positions (Atkinson, 1979), and it is unlikely that this matrix is diagonal. For example, differences in consumption patterns coupled with differences in excises are likely to lead to changes in ranking, as is the differential treatment under the income tax of different sources. One of the few studies to take account of this is Pechman and Okner, who give the variance of tax rates within deciles (1974, Ch.5).

Assumptions about Incidence

The empirical work may be seen broadly as implementing the simple framework set out in Section 9-1 (applied to current rather than lifetime income). The endowments and behaviour of households are taken as given, as are all pre-tax factor prices and producer prices. The effect of the income tax is assumed to be to reduce post-tax income; the effect of indirect taxes is assumed to be an increase in the consumer price. These assumptions have been criticized as being unrealistic, not recognizing the mechanisms by which taxes are shifted (for example, the possibility that higher rates of income tax are merely reflected in higher gross salaries). Some writers have argued that they are inconsistent. Thus, Prest has claimed that the assumption about indirect taxes can be justified only where the supply is perfectly elastic (leaving aside the case of totally inelastic demand), whereas the assumption about income tax can be justified only when factor supplies are completely inelastic. He concludes that "calculations of the incidence of direct and indirect taxes are based on conflicting and contradictory assumptions" (Prest, 1955, p. 242).

These criticisms may be evaluated in two ways. First, we can investigate empirically the consequences of alternative assumptions about incidence, and this has been a feature of the work of Musgrave *et al.* (1974) and of Pechman and Okner (1974). Thus Musgrave *et al.* contrast the "benchmark" assumptions used in measuring tax incidence in Table 9-1 with "progressive" and "regressive" variants. These are defined in Table 9-2. The results are illustrated in Fig. 9-2. With the progressive assumption, the percentage paid in tax rises quite sharply—from 20.3 to 63.2 per cent—whereas with the regressive assumption it falls slightly—from 31.9 to 26.9 per cent. On the other hand, over the range of middle incomes, the percentages again remain broadly constant. Alternative incidence assumptions appear, on this basis, to be most crucial at the top and the bottom of the income scale. Rather similar conclusions are reached by Pechman and Okner (1974).

Table 9-2 Incidence assumptions made by Musgrave *et al.*

	"Progressive"	"Benchmark"	"Regressive"
Corporate income tax	Falls on dividend recipients	Half falls on all capital income receivers; half passed on to consumers	Passed on to all consumers
Property tax	Falls on all capital income receivers	Residential —occupants Commercial —half on all capital receivers —half on consumers	Residential —occupants Commercial —on consumers
Employers social insurance contributions	Falls on employee	Passed on to consumers	Passed on to consumers

Such empirical studies of the sensitivity of results will no doubt be further developed. Indeed, almost any investigation is likely to lead to results conditional on a range of alternative assumptions. At the same time, the second approach—via theoretical considerations—is also valuable in assessing the question of incidence. Thus, we may use the models discussed in previous sections to evaluate the possible consequences of alternative assumptions and to suggest different approaches.

The standard incidence assumptions may be related to the simple fixed-factor, two-sector model discussed in Lecture 6 (Section 6-5), where there

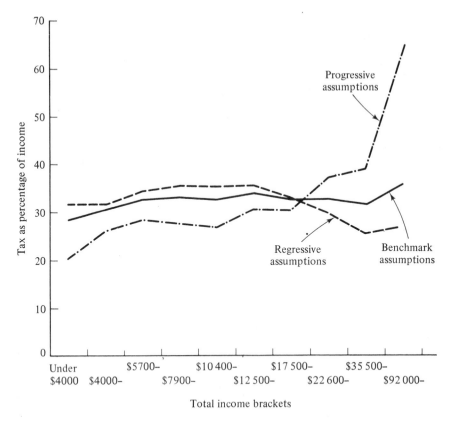

Figure 9-2 Redistributive effect of taxation under different assumptions about incidence: United States. (*Source:* Based on estimates given in Musgrave *et al.* (1974, p. 264.)

are two classes of consumer (with homothetic utility functions). This allows us in particular to consider the criticisms made by Prest.[21] Suppose that we consider an infinitesimal excise tax, T_X, on sector X; the other sector, Y, is untaxed and there are no other taxes. (The assumptions about government revenue are those in Lecture 6.) In general, the tax leads to a change in relative consumer prices (q_X/q_Y). From the analysis of Lecture 6, this is given by (from Eq. (6-11''))

$$\hat{q}_X - \hat{q}_Y = \theta^*(\hat{w} - \hat{r}) + \hat{T}_X \tag{9-41}$$

[21] In part these are directed at the use of the approach to calculate the effects of large changes in taxes and spending. Thus, Prest (1968, p. 84) refers to the index number problem of choosing between original and final prices. Although the studies described above have been concerned with the total effect of the budget, it is marginal changes that are of particular relevance in policy-making, and it is on these that we focus.

where θ^* is a measure of capital intensity defined in terms of the factor shares. Whether there is any induced change in factor prices depends on the demand effect, which from the earlier analysis (Eqs (6-42) and (6-43)) is

$$\hat{X} - \hat{Y} = -\sigma_D(\hat{q}_X - \hat{q}_Y) - \left[\left(\frac{X_1}{X} - \frac{Y_1}{Y}\right)(\kappa_1 - \kappa_1)\right](\hat{w} - \hat{r}) \qquad (9\text{-}42)$$

where X/Y is the ratio of the two outputs, σ_D is the elasticity of substitution in demand, X_i/X is the relative consumption of class i and κ_i is the share of capital in the income of group i. The supply side equation (from (6-16)) is

$$\lambda^*(\hat{X} - \hat{Y}) = (a_X\sigma_X + a_Y\sigma_Y)(\hat{w} - \hat{r}) \qquad (9\text{-}43)$$

where λ^* is a measure of capital intensity defined in terms of physical factor inputs.

The assumption made in empirical studies is that a selective excise is passed on fully, and that there is no change in factor incomes, which in the present context means $\hat{q}_X - \hat{q}_Y = \hat{T}_X$, and $\hat{w} - \hat{r} = 0$. The change in factor incomes is given by

$$(\sigma_D\lambda^*\theta^* + a_X\sigma_X + a_Y\sigma_Y + \lambda^*\Gamma)(\hat{w} - \hat{r}) = -\sigma_D\lambda^*\hat{T}_X \qquad (9\text{-}44)$$

where Γ denotes the coefficient of the distributional term in square brackets in (9-42). Unless $\lambda^* = 0$, factor prices in general change. This in turn causes the change in relative prices to depart from $\hat{T}_X$ unless $\theta^* = 0$.[22] It appears that the error introduced by the conventional assumption depends on the extent of differences in factor intensities across sectors. From the data presented for 19 industries in the United States by Fullerton, Shoven and Whalley (1978), the value shares appear to vary markedly.

These changes may be related to the indicator of the differential effect on the welfare of the two classes introduced in Lecture 6 (Eq. 6-45):

$$= -[(\kappa_1 - \kappa_2) + \theta^*(m_1 - m_2)](\hat{w} - \hat{r}) - (m_1 - m_2)\hat{T}_X \qquad (9\text{-}45)$$

where m_i is the marginal propensity of group i to consume good X. The conventional approach may be taken, as far as changes in welfare are concerned, as assuming either $\lambda^* = 0$ (no factor price changes) or that the square bracket in (9-45) is zero. These appear to be the assumptions that Musgrave had in mind: "that the size distribution of income originating in various industries is the same [or] there is a random relationship between the distributional origin of expenditures on any particular product and the distributional destination of factor payments" (Musgrave, *et al.*, 1964, p. 201). The condition on endowments and consumption patterns (that in the square bracket, generalized to n goods) may be more plausible than that on

---

[22] $\lambda^* = 0$ does not necessarily imply $\theta^* = 0$ (and vice-versa) when there are partial factor taxes—see Lecture 6.

physical factor intensities, but it needs to be investigated empirically to assess the likely magnitude of the error involved.

As a second example, we take a general tax on labour in both sectors, T_L. The first effect is parallel to the excise tax:

$$\hat{q}_X - \hat{q}_Y = \theta^*(\hat{w} + \hat{T}_L - \hat{r}) \tag{9-46}$$

The second effect is on the supply side:

$$\lambda^*(\hat{X} - \hat{Y}) = (a_X \sigma_X + a_Y \sigma_Y)(\hat{w} + \hat{T}_L - \hat{r}) \tag{9-47}$$

The assumption made in the empirical literature is that $\hat{q}_X - \hat{q}_Y = 0$ (no effect on consumer prices) and $\hat{w} - \hat{r} = -\hat{T}_L$ (tax borne in full by labour). The traditional justification is that the supply of factors is totally inelastic, and—in contrast to the previous case—this is consistent with the assumptions made here. On the other hand, this treatment is correct only if there are no redistributive effects on demand: for example, if $\kappa_1 \neq \kappa_2$, $m_1 \neq m_2$, $\lambda^* \neq 0$, then there is a change in the gross factor price ratio (wT_L/r), and the standard assumption is not correct. If labour income is disproportionately spent on a good that is labour-intensive, then some part of the tax is shifted via the rise in (w/r); conversely, if it is spent on the capital-intensive good, the initial impact is magnified.

This discussion brings out the care that is necessary in specifying assumptions about incidence, and the need for an explicit rather than an implicit model. We have however considered only a highly simplified view of the economy. The earlier Lectures have shown how the conclusions need to be modified to allow for market distortions, imperfect competition, unemployment, the accumulation of capital over time, etc. Thus, the effects of taxation may be seen only in future periods, as where they affect the accumulation of capital (see the discussion of the national debt in the previous Lecture). Conversely, future taxes and government expenditure may influence current incomes, as where they are capitalized in asset values. In the theoretical sections of this Lecture, we have described how taxation may affect the development of endowments over generations, taking account of the transmission of earning capacity and the inheritance of wealth. There is however a very large distance between these long-run theoretical considerations and empirical implementation. Not only is there the question of the availability of data on lifetime income, but also we know little about key relationships of the model such as the bequest function and the intergenerational association of earnings.

9-5 CONCLUDING COMMENTS

We have stressed the considerable gap between theory and empirical work. On the one hand, the empirical work has yet to incorporate many of the concerns that arise in the theoretical literature, as illustrated by the treatment of incidence; on the other hand, many of the theoretical models are far removed from being empirically implementable, and leave out of account important factors (such as the implications for production of the heterogeneity of labour). This leads one to ask how the gap can be narrowed. One obvious development is for the empirical studies to incorporate behavioural relationships. The analysis of the impact of taxes on households should allow for the labour supply responses and for changes in the pattern of consumption. This can draw on the kind of research we have described in earlier Lectures, although it is likely to be easier in some areas than in others. For example, the modelling of the corporate sector, particularly allowing for imperfect competition, is likely to pose formidable problems. Moreover, the attempt to build-in behavioural response highlights the need for taking a more fully integrated view; for instance, in the personal sector, saving, housing tenure, and labour supply decisions need to be considered in conjunction.

When extending the analysis to model the response of households and firms, we need also to consider how fiscal policy itself is determined. The redistributive impact of the state has been analysed in terms of the effect of a specified set of taxes and expenditures, but no attempt has been made to examine how particular types of policy came to be adopted. If it is true that, today as in 1869, low-income families pay broadly the same percentage of their income in tax as do middle-income groups, then one needs to explain why a supposedly "progressive" tax system has had this result.

READING

The theoretical sections draw particularly on Stiglitz (1969b, 1978b), Meade (1964, 1976), Conlisk (1977) and Atkinson (1980). Important references on the empirical studies in the United States are Musgrave *et al.* (1974) and Pechman and Okner (1974). For a general criticism of the approach, see Prest (1955, 1968).

TEN

THEORIES OF THE STATE AND PUBLIC ECONOMICS

10-1 INTRODUCTION

Throughout the previous Lectures we have stressed the importance of the assumptions made concerning the structure of the economy. We have presented different models of household behaviour, discussed the implications of different forms of corporate structure, and devoted considerable attention to the general equilibrium incidence of taxation. We have however said little about the behaviour of the state. Public decisions have been treated as exogenous variables, with the government able to alter tax rates and public expenditure at will. Yet such a view is contrary to the spirit of much of the rest of this work, where we emphasize the limited control that the government has over the private sector. Just as the response of households to a tax increase has to be taken into account, so too one needs to consider what political constraints the government faces in making such decisions and what machinery is necessary in order to put them into effect.

This Lecture may be seen as seeking to "close" the system, by incorporating explicitly the behaviour of the state. The need for this has been argued strongly by economists critical of mainstream public finance, notably in the work of Buchanan. He contrasts the "highly developed theory of market interaction" with the simplistic treatment of the public sector: "the 'public choices' that define the constraints within which market behaviour is allowed to take place are assumed to be made externally or exogenously, presumably by others than those who participate in market transactions" (Buchanan, 1972, p. 11). We need to consider how people respond to tax changes in terms not just of their labour supply and savings decisions but also of their actions as voters. How far are government decisions influenced by the preferences of the electorate? What constraints are imposed by representative democracy? How do people behave as voters, legislators, or bureaucrats?

The study of the state has a long history in the social sciences. Indeed, by comparison with the central place accorded to the subject by political theorists, philosophers and sociologists, the contributions of modern economists have been remarkably limited. In certain fields, such as voting theory, there have been significant advances, but the broader questions have tended to be left on one side. This Lecture is open to the same objection in that it focuses on a very limited range of issues. Our concern is primarily with the government's fiscal activities, and—as emphasized in Lecture 1— this is only part of its impact on the economic system. Perhaps more fundamentally, we take as given the basic framework of political institutions. We do not attempt to examine the economics of political constitutions, how certain political machinery came into existence, or the rationale for particular processes for political decision-making.[1] Rather, we assume that the characteristics of the political system are those typically found in Western democracies, and examine within the context of those assumptions (e.g., majority voting) the behaviour of the electorate, the government, and the bureaucracy.

As the title of the Lecture indicates, we are primarily concerned with the *economic* aspects of government behaviour, and there is a multiplicity of such theories. A number of different models have been developed (with varying degrees of thoroughness), and we have chosen to describe three main approaches:

1. voting models, viewing public choices as the outcome of an explicitly specified political process, typically majority voting;
2. bureaucratic models, emphasizing the limited control of the electorate over many aspects of public decision-making and the goals of those who administer government policies;
3. interest group models, including as an important special case Marxist models based on class interests.

Many readers will find some degree of truth in all three of these views, and, as we comment later, there is no real test of their validity. On the other hand, one's belief as to which provides the "best model" may be critical in determining the view taken about government policy. Suppose, for example, that the indirect tax structure could be reformed by introducing differential rates of tax on different commodities (so that, say, necessities bear a lower percentage), and that this could be done so as to make everyone better off

---

[1] In the next Lecture we discuss some aspects of the "contract" theories of the state.

(or no worse off). With a pure majority vote, this would presumably be enacted. Suppose however that there is a representative democracy, with political parties the providers of much of the information available to the electorate. Will the parties have an incentive to provide the information that this policy option exists? Suppose that the administration of the policy is in the hands of a government agency. Would the Bureau of Indirect Taxes resist such an addition to the complexity of their task? Suppose that interest groups are influential in the enactment and administration of the legislation. Would this lead to the principle of differentiation being accepted but used for different purposes, so that the goals of interest groups, rather than social welfare, dictate which commodities are taxed at a lower rate?

It is clear that the view of the state has profound implications for the normative analysis of Part Two, and this Lecture, together with Lecture 11, should be seen as a bridge between the two parts of the book.

Structure of the Lecture

In examining the behaviour of the state, we consider individuals as playing three main roles: as voters, as legislators and as administrators. The relationship between the roles is set out schematically in Fig. 10-1. Depending on the form of government, the voters express their preferences with regard to public decisions. These preferences may or may not weigh with the legislators who take decisions. The decisions are put into effect by administrators, who may be more or less effective in their execution. Thus, A. Smith may vote for, or lobby, Senator D. Ricardo to pass a bill reducing the income tax, since he would prefer a lower tax rate with the lower associated level of public goods. Senator Ricardo may enact such a bill so as to increase his chance of re-election, or he may oppose it because he favours public spending on ideological grounds. J. Mill of the Internal Revenue Service is instructed to collect the income tax at the lower rate but

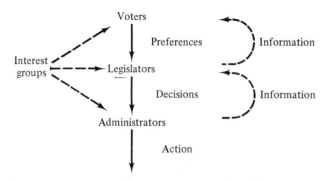

Figure 10-1 Political roles.

he may seek to maintain revenue, and hence the status of his agency, by closing loopholes.

In what follows we consider these links in turn. Section 10-2 is concerned with the relationship between preferences and decisions. It begins with a direct expression of preferences, as in Athenian democracy, where legislators play no role, and examines the nature of a majority voting equilibrium. It examines the conditions under which a voting equilibrium exists; and then goes on to representative democracy. Overall, we attempt in this section to give some flavour of the results that have been obtained in the field of mathematical politics, by political scientists as well as economists.

Section 10-3 is concerned with the process by which decisions get translated into actions. Here we start from the parallel between public and private institutions. This can be pursued at two levels. First there is the degree of decentralization. As in Musgrave's theory of the "public household", one can consider the division of functions between different government agencies, and the operation of these agencies as units playing the same role as firms do in the market. Second, there is the internal organization of the agency, typically hierarchical in structure, and the ways in which the incentives faced by individuals within that organization influence their behaviour. What latitude exists for bureaucrats to exercise discretion? These are issues that are discussed more in the literature on administrative science than in economics, but that are clearly of considerable importance to understanding the working of the government.

The same applies to the subject of Section 10-4: the impact of special interest groups and class conflict. The discussion so far has treated the analysis as being conducted in terms of individuals. Individuals decide how to vote, and the objectives of the individual bureaucrat guide his behaviour in carrying out decisions. Group action may however be highly significant. Pressure, or special interest, groups may seek to influence voter behaviour, to win over legislators, and to modify the administration of public policy. Classic examples would be consumer movements and welfare rights activists. In this section we discuss the role of such interest groups, and particularly that of class interests emphasized in Marxist theories of the state.

These three approaches to the theory of the state (which are summarized at the end of Section 10-4) have rather different origins and have tended to be formulated in quite different terms. The precise mathematical formulation of voting models may be compared with the historical approach of much Marxist writing. We do not try to put them into a common framework, and it is difficult to conceive of any satisfactory empirical tests. We do however consider in Section 10-5 the implications of the different approaches for the size of the public sector, and discuss some of the econometric investigations that have been made of the determinants of public spending.

Conflicts of Interest and the Role of Information

Since the three theories are rather different, it may be helpful to bring out here two common themes. The first is the conflict of interests. We have emphasized in earlier Lectures the importance of differences between individuals. If everyone had identical tastes and endowments, then many public finance questions would lose their significance, and this is particularly true of the behaviour of the state. If the interests of the members of society could be treated as those of a "representative" individual, then the role of the state would be reduced to that of efficiently carrying out agreed decisions.

The existence of differences is therefore essential to the analysis of the public sector. Only by explicitly modelling such differences can we treat the state in its key role of a mechanism by which conflicting interests are resolved in collective decisions. This is most apparent in the Marxist theories, which see the state as part of the arena in which class conflict takes place, different interests reflecting different positions in the process of production. Equally, the function of the electoral mechanism is the resolution of conflict (if there were unanimity, no vote would ever be necessary). Where voters have different tastes (e.g., with respect to public goods) or different endowments, then their preferred fiscal policies are likely to differ, and voting is a procedure for arriving at a collective decision. Whether it is successful depends on whether there exists an equilibrium of the particular voting process, and on whether the outcome is accepted. The voter may of course reject the outcome; e.g., with local public goods he may migrate to another community (in this sense, the minority may have an element of veto power—see Lecture 17). Finally, there are conflicts of interests between individuals in different roles. The legislator may be constrained by the preferences of the electorate (e.g., through the need for re-election), but his goals may differ from those of his constituents. In the bureaucratic models, the objectives of those who administer legislation may diverge from those of voters or politicians. The aim of such models is to explain how the constraints and incentives implied by the institutional structure affect the working out of divergent objectives.

The second theme is the role of information. We have stressed the need to set out explicitly the assumptions made about the information available to decision-makers. Thus, in Lecture 2 we discussed the extent of knowledge about the budget constraint and individual perceptions of marginal tax rates. In discussing the theory of the firm, we referred to the differential information available to shareholders and managers. In the case of public decisions, imperfect information is even more significant. With the simple voting framework, the voter has to form a judgement about the trade-offs between different objectives, for example, the level of taxes needed to finance a proposed spending programme. To obtain such information is costly and there are people or groups with an incentive to provide only partial or distorted information.

In the bureaucratic model, there is a close analogy with the theory of the firm. Those who administer a programme inevitably have more information than the legislative branch, and this is institutionalized in such procedures as congressional hearings. The differential information limits the ability of legislators or voters to take decisions or to monitor the performance of government agencies. (Moreover, since it is costly to acquire information, it may be socially desirable to allow an element of slack.)

These two aspects—conflicts of interest and imperfect information —take us into areas that are far from fully treated in the case of the private economy. We cannot therefore appeal to a widely accepted body of theory, and much of the discussion is qualitative in nature.

10-2 VOTING AND DECISIONS

This section is concerned with the electoral process and its relationship with decision-making in a constitutional democracy. The most straightforward version of this process is that of direct democracy, as in New England town meetings or Swiss municipalities, where decisions are taken directly by individual voters rather than indirectly via elected representatives. Although of limited relevance to modern societies, it serves to introduce some of the crucial questions.

Direct Democracy

We consider initially a single decision, which we take to be the level of government spending, G. This is financed by a pre-specified tax system, assumed to be a uniform poll tax, T. If the utility of individual i depends only on G and disposable income $Y^i - T$, then the preferences of i can be depicted as in Fig. 10-2. The effective budget constraint generated by different values of G is such that each extra unit of public spending costs $\$1/P$ where P is the size of the population. If the indifference curves are strictly convex to the origin, then there is a single preferred value of G for individual i, denoted by G^i and given by the tangency at Q. If the quantity of public goods were smaller, then the individual would be on a lower indifference curve, and the same applies at higher quantities (see the dashed indifference curve and points R and S). The individual utility is, given convexity, a function of G which is $\cap$-shaped. There is a single peak. (As drawn, the peak is interior to the interval $[0, PY^i]$, but it could be located at the endpoint.)

If everyone had the same preferences as individual i, the same pre-tax income Y^i, and the same perception of the tax required, then there would be

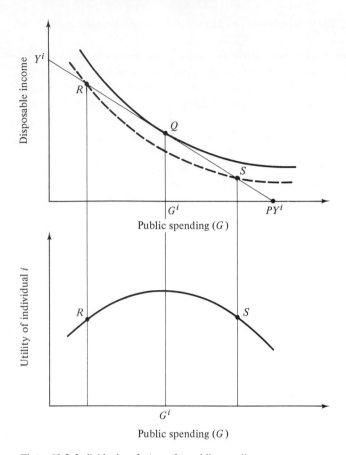

Figure 10-2 Individual preferences for public spending.

no disagreement over the level of public spending. Where these conditions do not hold, then the preferred levels differ—see Fig. 10-3, for the case of three individuals, h, i, j. In the case of private goods, the existence of differences in preferred quantities poses no problems; each person can choose his desired quantity. The essence of the public choice problem is that only a single decision can be made and the conflicting preferences have to be reconciled. One obvious solution is to let a single individual make the decision. The public decision is then the level of G preferred by this (enlightened or unenlightened) despot. This is however of limited interest in a positive theory of the state. Of greater relevance is majority voting.

Suppose first that we have pure majority voting—one man, one vote. We also assume that there is an odd number of individuals and that they vote "sincerely"; i.e., they do not strategically misrepresent their preferences. In the model of a single decision described above there is a majority voting equilibrium, which is the level of public goods preferred by the median individual. This may be seen heuristically by considering a vote between G and $G + \Delta G$, where ΔG is an infinitesimal positive increment. All those whose pieferred value of G is strictly to the right of G support such an increase (given the preferences shown). If we begin with $G = 0$, everyone votes for an increase, but the majority falls successively until we reach G^m, the most preferred point of the median individual. Any further increase would be opposed by a majority. In this case we have the simple result that the preferences of the median voter are decisive.

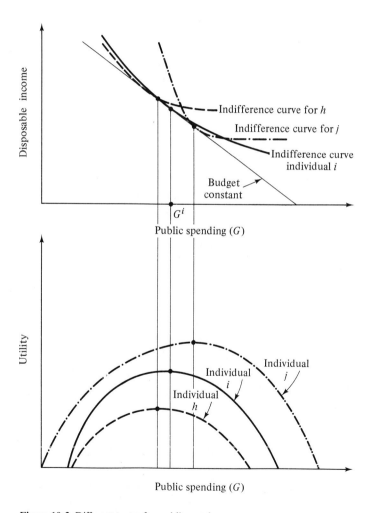

Figure 10-3 Different tastes for public goods.

The median voter model can be applied directly to yield predictions about the determinants of public expenditure. Suppose for example that people differ only in pre-tax income, and that the preferred level of public goods is a monotonic (say, increasing) function of income. The majority voting equilibrium is then the public goods quantity demanded by the person with median income, and—if tastes are unchanged—we should expect the level of spending to vary with median income. It is clear that the equilibrium depends on the method of finance. If, for example, the poll tax were to be replaced by a proportional income tax, this would in general change the tax burden on the median person, and hence—assuming that he remains decisive—change the voting outcome. There is of course no reason to expect the same person to be the median voter as policy changes; the identity of the median voter may alter.

> **Exercise 10-1** Suppose that everyone has a utility function $U = (1-a)\log(Y^i - T^i) + a\log G$, where T^i denotes taxes paid. Show that the majority voting equilibrium with a poll tax is such that $G/P = aY^m$, where Y^m is the median pre-tax income. Show that if the tax employed is proportional, there is unanimous agreement on $G/P = a\bar{Y}$, where $\bar{Y}$ denotes the mean. What happens if the tax is progressive?

The median voter model provides strong predictions; it does so however at the expense of strong assumptions (including that voting is sincere and that there is a single dimension to the decisions being taken, aspects discussed later). We should stress in particular the very considerable informational requirements. The voter has to be able to assess the benefits from public spending (typically *ex ante*) and to form a view of the implications for taxation. For example, the increase in the income tax rate needed to finance an expansion of government spending can be predicted only on the basis of the assumed response of households. Given the costs to the individual voter of acquiring this kind of information, it is not surprising that intermediaries have emerged. Direct democracy has tended to be replaced by representative democracy, and political parties, pressure groups and others have sought to provide the information needed by the electorate.

Existence of Voting Equilibrium

The median voter model has been widely used in both theoretical and empirical (see Section 10-5) work; it does, however, rest on the assumption that a majority voting equilibrium exists. This depends on the pattern of preferences. In particular, those shown in Fig. 10-3 have the "single-peaked" property. Where this condition (or slightly weaker versions—see Kramer,

1973) fails to hold, the celebrated voting paradox may arise. To illustrate this, we modify the model and suppose that the public good is an *alternative* to a private good. An obvious example is education, where a child attends either a state school or a private school. In the latter case the family is still liable to the tax, but may choose the private school because the level of expenditure is closer to that preferred. The pattern of preferences is now illustrated by Fig. 10-4. For levels of government expenditure below G_0, individual i chooses private provision (see Stiglitz, 1974a, for further discussion of this example).

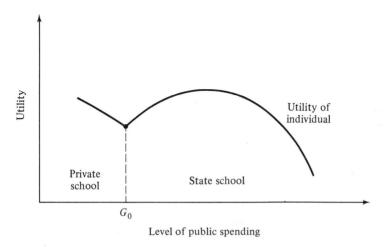

Figure 10-4 Non-single-peaked preferences.

Suppose now that there are three (equal-sized) groups, rich, average and poor, and that there are three possible levels of expenditure, high (H), medium (M) and low (L). The rich in this range always prefer private provision, so that their ranking is as shown in Fig. 10-5. The only effect of an increase in government spending is to increase their taxes and they are opposed. The poor do not choose private provision, and their ranking is assumed to be M preferred to H preferred to L (see Fig. 10-5). The average group however choose private provision when G is low or medium, hence preferring the lower level of state spending, but switch to public provision when G is high, this being their overall preferred level. It is then clear that there is no determinate outcome to majority voting; it depends on the order of voting between high (H), medium (M) and low (L). In a vote of L versus M, L wins (preferred by rich and average); in a vote of L versus H, H wins (preferred by average and poor); in a vote of H versus M, M wins (preferred by rich and poor).

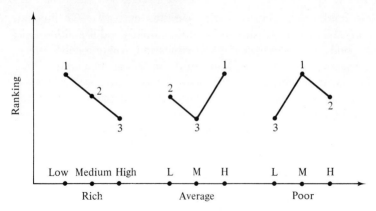

Figure 10-5 Cyclical voting.

In the situation we have just depicted, there is no majority voting equilibrium: there is no decision that can win a majority against *all* other options.[2] This famous voting paradox, noted as early as the eighteenth century by Borda and Condorcet, has given rise to a voluminous literature. In particular, it has been asked whether there are political mechanisms, other than dictatorship, that, without restricting the nature of the preferences of voters and the choices that they can make, do not give rise to the non-existence problem. It is the very considerable achievement of Arrow (1951) to have shown that under fairly weak conditions no such alternative political mechanism exists. These conditions may be summarized as follows:[3]

(U) the mechanism must work for all logically possible individual preference orderings;

(P) if everyone prefers x to y, then society must also prefer x to y (the weak Pareto principle);

(I) social choice over a set of alternatives must depend on the orderings of the individuals only over these alternatives and not on "irrelevant alternatives";

(D) there should be no individual such that, whenever he prefers x to y, society prefers x to y irrespective of the preferences of everyone else (no-dictatorship).

---

[2] Such situations are sometimes described as "cycling", or as exhibiting intransitivities. A transitive ranking is one in which A preferred to B and B preferred to C implies A preferred to C. In our example, we can see that the ordering is not transitive.

[3] We do not attempt to give a full or rigorous account. See, among others, Sen (1970b, 1977a) and Pattanaik (1971).

The Arrow Impossibility theorem showed in effect that there exists no social ordering (social welfare function) satisfying these conditions, where there are at least three alternatives. Translated into the context of positive political decision-making, this can be shown to mean that the only voting methods that can guarantee the existence of an equilibrium under every possible pattern of individual preferences are dictatorial (for a precise statement, see for example Wilson, 1970, and Kramer, 1977b).

Majority voting satisfies conditions P, I and D. Where it breaks down is that it does not satisfy U, as we have seen with the example of the voting paradox given earlier. Suppose therefore that we consider one of the alternatives: "rank order" voting. This yields a determinate outcome. For example, with the case shown in Fig. 10-5, we have:

			Rank	
	Poor	Average	Rich	Total
Low	3 (3)	2	1	6 (6)
Medium	1 (2)	3	2	6 (7)
High	2 (1)	1	3	6 (5)

The outcome is a tie (not depending on the order of voting). However, it does not satisfy condition I. Suppose that we consider the choice between L and M, ranked equally with the preferences shown, but that poor individuals decide that they prefer H to M (see ranks in brackets). Their ranking of L and M is unchanged, but low is now preferred by the rank order voting method. (With sincere majority voting the choice between L and M would be unaffected.)

The burden of the Arrow theorem is, therefore, that there exists no mechanism for making social choices that satisfy the four specified conditions simultaneously. This has naturally led to the search for ways in which they can be relaxed. In the case of majority voting, we have already seen one line of approach—to restrict the range of preferences. The property of single-peakedness exhibited by the first model has been shown (Black, 1948) to ensure existence of a voting equilibrium. However, the example of private education demonstrates that absence of single-peakedness is far from pathological,[4] and once we move to two dimensions the corresponding conditions are extremely restrictive: they are "probably not significantly less restrictive than the condition of complete unanimity" (Kramer, 1973, p. 296). The source of the difficulty is illustrated by the case

---

[4] The condition of single-peakedness is a restriction excluding certain preferences. Weaker exclusion conditions may be imposed (see Kramer, 1973), but they are still highly restrictive.

of two public goods in Fig. 10-6.[5] The indifference maps there generate the voting paradox. Individual i with a peak (preferred combination of G_1 and G_2) at Q_i ranks the three policies w, y, z in that order. Individual j with peak Q_j ranks them in order z, w, y, and individual h has ranking y, z, w. There is therefore no determinate outcome to majority voting. The conditions equivalent to single-peakedness essentially fail to hold if the marginal rates of substitution of any three voters differ (Kramer, 1973). Since it seems quite apparent that social decisions are likely to involve many dimensions (e.g., multiple expenditure programmes, different parameters of the tax system), this is an important result.

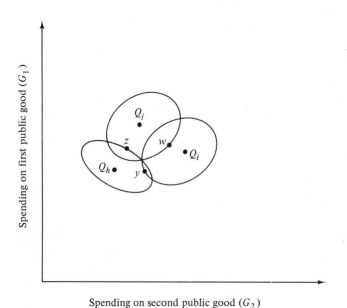

Spending on second public good (G_2)

Figure 10-6 Preferences over two public goods—example of non-single-peakedness.

Other attempts to restrict preferences of voters seem equally to have had limited success. Thus, conditions have been put forward limiting the distribution of voters' preferences (e.g., Plott, 1967), but these are also very restrictive. Similarly, it has been assumed that voters consider only alternatives in a small neighbourhood of the current position. Under fairly

[5] Suppose that public goods are financed by a uniform poll tax and that the utility function of individual i is

$$U^i[Y^i - (G_1 + G_2)/P, G_1, G_2]$$

where the first argument is income net of the necessary tax. Holding G_2 constant, utility first increases with G_1 and then falls; this generates the closed contours shown in Fig. 10-6.

weak conditions, with only one decision variable, such a "local" equilibrium can be shown to exist (Kramer and Klevorick, 1974), but whether it provides a persuasive resolution to the "majority voting paradox" depends on the extent to which choices are limited to small perturbations of the existing situation. (Many would argue that, since the fixed costs of change are large, it is only significant departures that are usually considered within the political process.) Finally, a set of restrictions that ensures existence in the case with several public goods is provided by Slutsky (1977). Basically, he reduces the multi-dimensional case to one dimension by imposing a linear restriction on the levels of the different public goods. Again it is not clear how far this is a relevant restriction.

What happens when a majority voting equilibrium does not exist has been explored in a number of studies. These have emphasized the importance of controlling the agenda (i.e., determining the order in which votes are taken) and of strategic voting (i.e., voting that may not represent one's true preferences). Thus, it may be argued that, after all the potential policies have appeared in at least one vote, then the outcome of the last vote will be accepted. There is therefore a determinate outcome (ruling out ties); e.g., in the education example, with the order of voting (L against M, winner against H), the outcome is H. In this case, the determination of the order of voting—and the termination rule—is clearly crucial, and the indeterminacy may simply be pushed one stage further back.

Strategic voting may be a way of altering the agenda. If we go back to the education example, and suppose that the first vote is between L and M, then if the rich vote sincerely L wins, and in the second round H defeats L. On the other hand, if the rich had voted for M in the first round, then M would have gone on to win in the second round. The rich group can therefore secure a preferred outcome (M rather than H) by misrepresenting their preferences.[6] Such strategic voting has been examined by Farquharson (1969), Gibbard (1973), Satterthwaite (1975), and others. In particular, it has been shown that the conditions for a voting procedure to be strategy-proof (i.e., no one has an incentive to vote strategically) are equivalent to the Arrow conditions. Hence there exists no (non-dictatorial) voting procedure that is strategy-proof. (The reader should also consider the possibility of "log-rolling" or "vote trading"—see Buchanan and Tullock, 1962; Wilson, 1969; and Tullock, 1970.)

Representative Democracy

To this juncture, we have discussed the aggregation of individual preferences directly into a public decision. With few exceptions, almost all

---

[6] Borda is said to have retorted, when the scope for manipulation was pointed out, that "my scheme is only intended for honest men!" (Black, 1958, p. 182).

decisions in the public sector are taken by elected representatives or civil servants. Occasionally, a referendum imposes direct constraints on the actions of the representatives, but this tends to be the exception in most countries.

Let us suppose that representatives belong to political parties. If party competition may be represented along a single spectrum (e.g., "left–right"), if individual preferences are single-peaked, and they vote sincerely, then as before a majority voting equilibrium exists. On the other hand, the behaviour of the political parties is itself endogenous and we have to explain the way in which each chooses its position on the political spectrum. Suppose first that parties are interested solely in winning elections, not in policies as such. Thus, in the Hotelling–Downs (see Downs, 1957) model of two party competition, the parties—just as in the case of spatial competition—choose the midpoint, i.e., the preferred point of the median. A party that did not choose this platform (e.g., for ideological reasons preferring less government spending) would be defeated if the other did. In the determination of government spending we would not expect—in this simple model—the replacement of direct by representative democracy to change the results. An empirical study based on the preferences of the median would still be valid; and there would not be any need in equilibrium situations to introduce party political dummy variables (a party whose ideology took it away from the median would not be victorious in an election and its policies would not be observed).

The result described does however depend on strong assumptions. Although the move to representative democracy may reduce the dimensionality, there may remain more than one dimension (e.g., "liberal–non-liberal" as well as "left–right"). In this case no pure strategy equilibrium in general exists for parties; i.e., there is no vector of strategies such that, given the strategies of others, no party wishes to change its platform. Various approaches have been suggested, including *mixed* strategies, for example where there is a set of policies each played with strictly positive probability (Shubik, 1970), or where there are stochastic abstentions (Hinich, Ledyard and Ordeshook, 1972). Alternatively, one can seek to model disequilibrium behaviour. For example, Kramer (1977a) assumes that in each election the incumbent party defends its established policy, whereas the opposition chooses its policy freely to maximize its vote. (The hypothesis supposes that voters have a short memory: they expect continuity only from the incumbent.)

The view of political parties as simply organizations for winning political power is clearly only a caricature. Party platforms are influenced by "ideology". A socialist party supports government provision; a big business party opposes taxation. Alternatively, parties may be dominated more by individuals than by issues, and the process may be one of competition for political leadership (Schumpeter, 1954). On a third view, parties may be seen as alternative "managerial teams" for running the economy and providing public services. In such a case, it is not so much differences in values as differences in judgements about managerial competence that are the main determinants of elections.

The representative democracy model also raises a number of questions concerning the behaviour of voters. In particular, how does the voter obtain information about the likely performance of the parties, and what determines whether or not he votes? These issues have been extensively discussed by Downs, who identifies several key steps in a "rational" voting process, including gathering information relevant to each issue, forming factual conclusions about alternative policies, appraising the consequences in the light of voters' goals, and aggregating over issues into a net evaluation of each party. In this process, there is an asymmetry between the incumbent and the opposition parties: "the incumbent's policies and personnel have been put to the test of very recent practice at the time of election, while the oppositions' probable performance can be inferred only from its statements of intention and its previous performance in office" (Kramer, 1977b, p. 699).

This representation makes clear that the activity of voting may involve the individual in non-trivial costs. If he acts solely from self-interest, then there are good reasons for expecting him not to participate in the democratic process. Suppose first that he has clearly formed preferences and all necessary information. Then he may still not vote for his preferred alternative if there are positive net costs to voting. This may be seen as a special case of the "free-rider" problem, discussed later in conjunction with public goods. In that situation, a person may choose not to contribute to a public facility on the grounds that others will pay enough to cover its finance (and he can have a "free ride"). In the voting case, he may choose not to vote because he calculates that he is unlikely to be decisive (i.e., there will be a majority for one outcome independently of his vote). The infinitesimal probability of being the decisive vote, coupled with the significant costs of voting, may indeed mean that no individual has an incentive to vote, even on issues of considerable importance.

The assumption of individual self-interest also applies to the acquisition of information. For the reasons just described, people may not have an incentive to assemble the information required to vote intelligently. At the same time, it is clear that the information provided by the parties is not purely informative, and that the transfer of the process of providing information to the parties does not mean that it is costless. Those financing the advertising of parties expect to receive a return on their outlay. The benefits do not have to be of a strictly pecuniary kind; individuals may enjoy the status of high office, even if they do not benefit financially from it, and advertising is a method of purchasing the status. (The cost of providing the information is then financed by the "rents" from political office.)

Nevertheless, there is a widespread view that much of the benefit accruing from the support of a party are of a strictly financial kind; this is particularly true of industry lobby support. In such cases, the payment of supporters may involve measures that distort the operation of the economy. For example, the enactment of import quotas, designed to compensate particular industrial supporters, may impose substantial additional costs. The elected government is unlikely to be fully "efficient" in its pursuit of the national interest.

There is therefore a quandary. If individuals are motivated by self-interest, then they have no incentive to acquire information, and this has to be supplied by the political parties and other interested organizations. On the other hand, the latter may require enough "slack" in the political system to allow vested interests to obtain a return for their investment, implying that certain decisions may be contrary to the national interest. This clearly has implications for the design of the political structure.

The assumption that individuals act out of self-interest, narrowly defined, is of course open to question, and Downs himself sought to explain electoral participation as the basis of "each citizen's realization that democracy cannot function unless many people vote" (Downs, 1957, p. 274). There may be a variety of social sanctions which lead to a high level of participation. Similarly, for political parties ideology may play a significant role (it is also a means of reducing information costs, allowing voters to predict party response). The incorporation of such behavioural considerations is clearly a necessary development of this approach.

Finally, we have not discussed the way in which elected representatives themselves reach decisions in the legislature and its committees. In part this involves issues similar to those discussed with regard to direct democracy; in part it is concerned with the control of the legislative branch over the bureaucracy, to which we now turn.

10-3 ADMINISTRATION AND BUREAUCRACIES

The administration of legislation is typically entrusted to a bureaucracy (where the term is used more in its Weberian, rather than its common, perjorative, sense). Expenditure programmes may be executed by the Department of Defense, by the State Highways Board or by agencies such as the Office of Economic Opportunity or the National Institutes of Health. Many different approaches can be adopted to the analysis of bureaucratic behaviour, and much can be learned from the work on administrative science and political sociology. For economists, who came late to the study of bureaucracy, it has been natural to start from the parallel with the private sector of the economy.

Public and Private Organizations

Public and private bodies are often regarded as quite different; they are commonly regarded as polar solutions to the problems of designing economic organizations. For instance, a distinction may be drawn in terms of the nature of objectives. In a private firm, it may be argued, the problem of executing policy involves only that the individual concerned takes the actions that maximize (expected) profits. In public administration, on the other hand, objectives are more complicated, with the intentions of legislators being much less straightforward and those in charge having discretion in implementing policy. Although governments may attempt to avoid these problems by framing legislation more specifically, the cost of doing so is not only greater complexity but also less adaptability, both for coping with new situations and for unforeseen cases. A contrast is also drawn with respect to the internal structure of the firm and the incentives faced by individuals. It is argued that within the private sector the method by which the firm ensures that individuals behave so as to maximize profits is to pay workers the value of marginal product. In contrast, in the public sector workers are instructed to perform certain tasks under direct control, and their performance has to be monitored to ensure compliance.

This polarization gives an over-simplified picture. As we have emphasized earlier, the objectives of the firm become much more complex once we allow for incomplete markets and for differences between shareholders in their beliefs and objectives. In such circumstances one cannot assume that there is a single goal, such as profit maximization, that represents the interests of the firm. There may be conflicts of interest between managers and shareholders, and the managers may have latitude to interpret the wishes of the owners and to pursue their own objectives. The same applies to the incentive structure within the firm. Many workers in the private sector receive some payment as a fixed fee independent of the value of their marginal product. As in the public sector, it is often difficult to ascertain the value of the individual's marginal product (e.g., on an assembly line). For this reason private firms may not be able to rely on implicit control systems based on observed output but may have to monitor performance directly.

We should therefore see private firms and public agencies as enjoying certain common features. Both are responsible to ultimate decision-makers (shareholders and legislators), but there is a degree of ambiguity about objectives which allows latitude to those managing the firm/agency. Both have an internal structure of direction and supervision, which affects the degree of control exercised by the managers. These similarities mean that in analysing the behaviour of bureaucracies we can draw on the parallels with the theory of the firm—notably on the separation of ownership and control, and on the economics of internal organization.

At the same time, there are critical differences, notably in the "market structure". In the public sector there is likely to be decentralization, and this is discussed below; but typically, within any government jurisdiction, there is only one department engaged in a particular activity (e.g., issuing automobile licences). This has several implications. First, it means that, viewing citizens as customers, they do not usually have a choice of alternative suppliers. In Hirschman's terminology (1970), if they do not like what they see, they cannot "exit"—they can only use "voice"; while in the market, both options are available. In this respect, local public goods represent an intermediate case where exit is indeed possible via migration. Second, the legislative branch has a weaker basis of comparison (than shareholders in a market firm) on which to judge the efficiency of the present administration. In the market, shareholders in one automobile firm can observe the profitability of the competitors to obtain at least a rough idea about the managerial quality of the given firm. (However, this may also apply in the public sector if there are overlapping agencies—see below.)

Closely related to this is the difficulty of entry. If Mr X believes he can produce a better automobile, and is willing to risk his funds, he can start producing them; he may or may not succeed, but the decision about whether he should have the opportunity to produce them is personal. But if he believes he can manage a licence bureau better, he must convince those within the bureaucratic channels. Similarly, there is no scope for take-over bids. In the market, a person who can perform certain activities more efficiently may be able to take over a firm and capture the rent accruing as a result of greater efficiency. On the other hand, the creation of new agencies is a possible move by the legislature, and the establishment of agencies with overlapping functions may be a mechanism of control. Thus, social work agencies may be a check on the efficiency of the social security department; the Fleet Air Arm and the Royal Air Force may perform similar functions.

We can therefore in analysing the public institutions make use of the parallel with the private sector, but it must be tempered by consideration of the monopoly position of the government agency and the limitations on entry. In what follows, we first consider the behaviour of the agency as an entity, parallel to the firm; then we examine the implications of its internal structure.

The Public Household and the Individual Agency

The view of the state described by Musgrave is that of the public sector as a "household", with different members of the household assigned different tasks. He identifies three major branches of the household sector: the redistribution branch, the allocative branch, and the stabilization branch. This division of the functions of the public sector has proved extremely useful as an analytical device, and it is indeed one that we have followed in this book (by abstracting from stabilization policy). From a normative point of view, of course, the separation of function is debatable as a principle. As we show in Part Two, there are likely to be many cases where we need to consider jointly two or more objectives. For instance, it may be possible only under very special conditions to consider separately the optimal supply of public goods and the redistribution of income.

From a positive standpoint, however, the view of the state as decentralizing its functions captures an important feature of reality. State agencies do act with a considerable degree of autonomy, and take limited account of their interaction with other branches of the government. We have therefore to consider the motives of those in charge of the decentralized units, and the control that can be exercised by the central executive.

In examining the motives of those in charge of government agencies, the analogy with the private sector has been influential. Just as modern theories of the firm have suggested that the managerial utility function may include the size and rate of growth of output, so too it has been argued (notably by Niskanen) that bureaucrats seek to maximize the size of their agency:

> Among the several variables that may enter the bureaucrat's utility function are the following: salary, perquisites of the office, public reputation, power, patronage, output of the bureau, ease of making changes, and ease of managing the bureau. All of these variables except the last two, I contend, are a positive monotonic function of the total *budget* of the bureau. [Niskanen, 1971, p. 38]

The argument is open to question. For example, there appears to be considerably more mobility between agencies than there is of managers between private firms, so that their interests are less closely linked. None the less, the Niskanen model provides a suggestive starting point.

The implications of size maximization depend on the control mechanisms open to the central executive. Niskanen assumes that the agency possesses a monopoly advantage: "although the nominal relation of a bureau and its sponsor is that of a bilateral monopoly, the relative incentives and available information, under most conditions, give the bureau the overwhelmingly dominant monopoly power" (Niskanen, 1971, p. 30). This is clearly too sharply drawn, since a number of control devices can be established (at a cost), including direct monitoring, establishment of overlapping agencies and transfer of personnel.

These features may be formalized in a number of ways (one is illustrated in Exercise 10-2 below). Here we simply give some examples of the ways in which independent agency objectives, coupled with limited control, may affect the behaviour of the government. First, the agency may seek to expand a given government programme by systematically overstating the benefits or understating the costs. If the executive attempt in turn to monitor budget requests, this adds control expenditure to the cost of provision. Second, if the agency has an overall budget, used as the instrument of control, but enjoys some discretion within that budget, then the pattern of expenditure may reflect the preferences of the agency rather than those of the legislators (for an empirical study, see McFadden, 1975, 1976). As a result, to achieve a given level of spending on a particular public good, it may be necessary to expand the budget above the minimum level required if there were complete control. Finally, if agencies are able to "control the agenda" by offering only one expenditure programme as an alternative to the "reversion level" if the plan is not accepted, then variations in the reversion level may have a perverse effect on spending. In particular, the adoption of zero-base budgeting, so that the reversion level becomes zero spending rather than that previously agreed, may lead to an *increase* in the agency's ability to pursue its own objectives—rather than the decrease commonly supposed.

> **Exercise 10-2** A government programme is administered by an agency that aims to maximize the scale of provision. The agency's plan has to be approved by a majority of the electorate. If the plan is not carried, then expenditure reverts to a pre-specified reversion level. Analyse how the agency determines the level of spending. What are the implications of a reduction in the reversion level? (Reference: Romer and Rosenthal, 1977.)

Hierarchical Agencies and Individual Incentives

Many public sector agencies are hierarchical in form with each "front-line" worker being responsible to a supervisor, who in turn reports to a superior, and so on. This form of internal organization arises from the need to maintain direct control of the activity of employees, indirect control via incentive schemes not being possible (we refer below to some of the issues that arise in the attempt to devise such incentive structures).

The simplest assumptions about the hierarchical organization are that there is a fixed span of control, ϕ, and a fixed salary differential, η, between grades. If the agency has $(h+1)$ grades, then there is 1 director, ϕ assistant directors, ϕ^2 department heads,..., and ϕ^h front-line workers. If the output of a spending agency is proportional to the number of front-line workers (for convenience we take the factor of proportionality as unity), an output of G requires an organization with $(h+1)$ grades where

$$h = \log G / \log \phi \qquad (10\text{-}1)$$

If the salary of the front-line worker is denoted by w, then the total labour cost involved in administering the output G is

$$wG \sum_{i=0}^{h} (\eta/\phi)^i = wG \left[\frac{1 - (\eta/\phi)^{h+1}}{1 - \eta/\phi} \right] \qquad (10\text{-}2)$$

where h is given by (10-1). If we assume, as seems reasonable, that the total salary bill declines with the grade in the organization, this implies that $\eta/\phi < 1$; in turn this means that the average cost approaches

$$\frac{w}{(1-\eta/\phi)} \tag{10-3}$$

as G tends to infinity. With a span of control of 5 and a salary differential of 25 per cent, this implies a "mark-up" over the front-line costs of $\frac{1}{3}$ to allow for the hierarchical "overhead". This provides a measure of the cost of control.

The existence of a vertical hierarchy arises from the need for supervision, and this raises issues about the design of organizational structures and the role of incentives.[7] These all illustrate the general problem of indirect control. The head of an agency cannot typically ensure that his subordinates behave in a way that is exactly specified; he can only design a policy to which they respond, and his perception of their response shapes the design. Thus, the efficiency of workers may be a function of the degree of supervision and of the salary differential (promotion being assumed to be a reward for efficiency). Similarly, the payment schedule has been assumed to be independent of efficiency, but incentive schemes can be introduced where there are observable measures of output. The individual's behaviour is a function of the incentive schedule, and the schedule must be designed with this taken into account. (Moreover, the behaviour of the agency director in designing the schedule is itself a function of the incentives he faces.)

This leads on to some general considerations about decision-making in a bureaucracy. Much of the activity of government officials appears to be directed at avoiding "mistakes". To the extent that they are thus led to perform well this is obviously desirable; the problem is that, in attempting to avoid noticeable mistakes, they ignore the costs that must be borne by the public. Thus, the red tape that so often seems to characterize bureaucracies need not be a manifestation of bureaucrats' love for due process. It reflects the fact that the private costs are not borne by them, and the red tape ensures that, if a mistake occurs, blame is not borne by any particular individual but is shared among the bureaucracy.

Second, what appear *ex post* to the legislators, or electors, to be "mistakes" are often associated with taking large risks; that is, it is usually difficult, if not impossible, to distinguish a "good" decision, which in the end turns out to be a failure, from a bad decision. One cannot know completely either the information that was available or the value that should have to be associated with obtaining more information prior to the decision being taken. Thus, since it is large "failures" that are easily detected and that, as a consequence, reap penalties, methods are sought to ensure that large risks

---

[7] For a rather different view of hierarchical organizations, see Marglin (1975).

that entail high probabilities of failure are not undertaken or, if undertaken, that responsibility does not rest on any single individual, for example by requiring consultation among a number of individuals. Those forces that make agencies fail to generate change also make them slow to respond to changes that are thrust upon them from the outside. Indeed, viewing society as a whole as an organization, we see that bureaucratic structures may generate a self-confirming equilibrium. That is, since the various parts of the bureaucracy fail to generate innovations, other parts are less often faced with the need to respond to changes. Hence the need for adaptability is reduced.

Finally, an important aspect of administering legislation is the application of the same provisions to a variety of people with different characteristics and the consequent need to use "discretion". This has a number of consequences. One is that it provides scope for corruption; e.g., in the placing of government purchases, the allocation of commodities in excess demand, and in regulatory activities. A second consequence is that malperformance is particularly likely to be revealed by differential treatment (in the case of corruption it is of course assumed that it is not revealed). There may therefore be internal pressures within the administration to secure horizontal equity.

10-4 POWER, INTEREST GROUPS AND MARXIST THEORIES

To this point we have assumed that people have equal weights in the decision-making process and that in seeking to influence the operation of the state they act individually. This section examines some of the ways in which one can model differences in power and the behaviour of interest groups, paying particular attention to the class interest view of the state which has received a great deal of attention in the Marxist literature.

Differential Power

We begin with the electoral process and the case of direct democracy. Earlier we assumed that there is one man, one vote. However, even though this is typically constitutionally prescribed, differential registration of voters and differential participation may significantly reduce the effective electorate. Moreover, participation is likely to be correlated with economic position. Upper-income groups "can impose a variety of restrictions upon voters which decreases the voter participation of other income classes. In particular, upper income classes increase their share of votes if they impose literacy requirements, poll taxes, and residence requirements" (Stigler, 1970, pp. 6–7). In this situation, we have to consider "differential" voting, where the effective voting power depends on economic and other variables. To the extent that eligibility and participation are correlated with endowments, the median of the effective voting population is likely to be at a higher level of income than the true median. This tends to bring the majority voting outcome, when it exists, up towards the mean of a positively skewed distribution.

The argument relating income to voting outcomes raises two issues. The first is the extent to which individuals combine to manipulate the electoral process (Stigler refers to a "dominant coalition"), and this is discussed below. The second is that voting behaviour may itself be endogenous to the model if the ability of upper-income groups to restrict the franchise depends on their incomes after tax and other state action. For a given structure of participation, we can determine the voting equilibrium G^* (again assuming existence), but the participation rates are in turn influenced by G^*. This introduces a further level of analysis: we have to consider not just how the electorate vote but also how public decisions themselves affect voting participation. What we have to look for is an equilibrium that is the outcome of majority voting at the participation rates that it implies (see Klevorick and Kramer, 1973). It is quite possible that there may be multiple equilibria with differential voting. Thus, there may be an equilibrium where upper income groups pay low taxes and their economic dominance allows them to shift the effective median vote to a position that ensures the continuance of these policies; at the same time, there may be another equilibrium where policy is more redistributive, and this is supported by an unrestricted franchise. Which of these two (or more) equilibria are attained depends on the dynamic process and on the history of the society.

The power discussed above is that of the purse. Public policy has been directed at limiting the role of such "monetary" influence, and the process of electoral reform may have reduced the dominance of upper income groups. On the other hand, this policy has been less successful in limiting the influence that arises from differential information. Expertise in particular (complex) questions may have a greater impact, and this brings us to special interest groups.

Interest Groups

The role of interest groups in influencing the behaviour of voters, the passage of legislation, and the operation of the bureaucracy has been widely documented. We do not attempt here to provide a detailed account of the operation of such bodies; our aim is rather to examine briefly some of the factors influencing the formation of interest groups.

The traditional view of interest groups regarded it as natural that individuals with common goals would tend to form groups to further these common interests. The American Medical Association may be seen as a vehicle for achieving the objectives common to the medical profession, and doctors join the Association so that they can collectively lobby Congress or government agencies and seek to influence public opinion. This view is however challenged in the work of Olson (1965) and others, who question whether it is in the individual interest of members to join such an interest group. Arguing that much of the gains achieved by the AMA are a collective good for the medical profession, they suggest that individual members do not have an incentive to contribute (via membership fees). The individual doctor enjoys the benefits whether or not he belongs, and would not therefore join on the basis of self-interest. If all doctors were similarly placed, then they would all react in the same way, and the Association would not have come into existence. (This is again a "free-rider" argument.)

In seeking to explain why interest groups *do* come into existence, Olson emphasizes several factors, including small group size, the asymmetry of interests of different individuals, and the role of sanctions.[8] The significance of small size is readily apparent and is a situation that applies particularly in certain spheres—notably groups of producers. Trade associations, typically with small memberships, play a significant role in many countries. This case also draws attention to the asymmetry of individual interests. The high degree of concentration in many industries increases, under certain conditions, the probability that a group is established (Stigler, 1974).[9] It is also likely that in these cases co-operative action (e.g., lobbying Congress) will be especially profitable.

The assumptions about strategic behaviour raise the issue of sanctions. The Olson analysis treats the decision as a single event, whereas there may be a sequence of choices—or, in game theoretic terminology, a "supergame" (a sequence of games). In such a supergame, the static non-co-operative strategy may not be optimal, and the existence of the interest group may therefore be related to the recurrence of an issue. The essence of the supergame strategy is that the future behaviour of other agents acts as a threat: the individual assumes that any departure from the co-operative solution will be followed in subsequent periods (the distinction between finite and infinite sequences clearly being important). The plausibility of this assumption may be questioned, but the general question of "sanctions" has to be considered. Suppose, for example, that Firm A does not join the trade association. Is it in the interest of Firm B to "punish" him by transferring its

---

[8] Olson also suggests that bodies such as the AMA provide as a "by-product" services for its members such as professional journals or malpractice insurance, and hence use the "profit" on these activities to finance collective action. This leaves open the question as to why a rival trade association cannot enter to provide these benefits at reduced cost (and no collective action).

[9] The sharing of the costs within an asymmetric group is discussed by Olson (1965), who argues that larger members bear a disproportionate share of the costs.

business to a higher-cost supplier? In terms of self-interest, such sanctions are not typically desirable. On the other hand, Firm B's failure to enforce sanctions may itself cause Firm C to "punish" B by transferring business. With an infinite regress of such sanctions, an equilibrium of enforced membership may exist.

The theory of interest group formation described above is founded on individual self-interest, but alternative views of political motives may lead to quite different results. We have emphasized the self-interest approach, in part because it relates closely to the discussion of public goods in Lectures 16 and 17, but we do not suppose that it provides the full picture. Just as the act of voting may be based on considerations other than rational calculation of expected net benefit, so too group activity may arise from a wider social context. This is well illustrated by the class conflict theories of the state.

Class Theories of the State

Despite the emphasis placed by Marx on the pursuit of self-interest, the concept of class has a wider significance in Marxist theories of the state. The membership of a class does not arise from individual calculation of net benefit but is determined by a person's role in the productive process. A person's interests are taken as being defined by his social class, rather than his membership of that class being influenced by his interest, with the key features of the definition of classes lying in the relationship to the ownership of capital. Moreover, it is typically assumed (at least implicitly) that the commonality of class interests is such that the problems of collective decision-making discussed earlier do not arise.[10]

This perspective of the role of class marks out the Marxist theories from the mainstream of public finance; at the same time, such thinking has tended to develop in several different directions. We make no attempt here to summarize the very substantial literature, and confine ourselves to sketching some of the main features.

At one extreme there is the view of the state as an extension of the capitalist class. The state is simply a reflection of the power of the class elsewhere in the economy, and fiscal decisions are made in such a way as to further the interests of capital. This may be modified to allow for certain constraints—for example, concessions to the working class to preserve the stability of the system—but basically the public sector is dominated by the needs of accumulation. This view has led writers to claim that "tax systems are simply particular forms of class systems" (O'Connor, 1973, p. 203), and to predict that taxes on capital are largely shifted on to workers. The fiscal

---

[10] The relationship between the class interests of a person, and his individual interest, and the mechanism that leads to his pursuing the former, clearly needs fuller specification.

structure therefore reflects the interests of capital (and beliefs about final incidence). This "instrumentalist" view of the state is however open to a number of criticisms. In particular, it does not explain how this form of social organization emerged, or the role played by the state in establishing the dominance of the capitalist class.

An alternative view is that the capitalist class is not sufficiently powerful either to dominate an exogenously created state or to have led to the state's emergence as part of the process of capitalist development. On the other hand, the state is largely shaped by the conflict between the interests of workers and capital. In this conflict the power of capital is typically great but it is not all pervasive:

> The agenda for State action and the major pressures on State policy grow out of the conflict between the capitalist and working classes over the appropriation of surplus value, and out of conflicts within the capitalist class over the distribution of surplus value. While capitalists in general and large capital in particular have a generally decisive advantage in these struggles, there is no reason to reduce the State and its policies to a simple expression of the dominance of the capitalist class or one fraction of it in modern society. [Foley, 1978, p. 225]

On this view, fiscal decisions will reflect the balance of power (in which electoral competition may have some role), with levels and patterns of taxation and spending depending on the success of workers in resisting offensive actions by capital.

Some of the implications of these different Marxist interpretations may be seen from considering the causes of the growth of public spending over the first three-quarters of this century. On the class struggle theory, the growth results from increased power in the hands of the working class, with the expansion of social security, public housing, public education, etc., representing the partial attainment of socialism within the capitalist state. On the other hand, it could be argued that the extension of state activity is necessary for the maintenance of the capitalist system — and hence in the capitalist interest. An extensive literature (e.g., O'Connor, 1973) treats the growth of the state as a response to crises of capitalism, with the government having to act to secure profitable capitalist production. The conditions necessary for the reproduction of capital being inherently contradictory, this means that state policy has to change with altering conditions. Thus the embrace of Keynesian fiscal measures to maintain demand has been succeeded by concern in the capitalist class about the effect of long periods of high employment on the bargaining power of labour. In this case the growth of public spending would not be steady and there would be periods when cuts in expenditure appeared in the interest of capital.

The difficulties with the theories that we have just described are not only that they do not usually fully articulate the mechanisms by which the system operates, but that they are usually presented in a way in which it is difficult to test the conclusions against competing hypotheses. This is, of course, also true of a number of the theories we presented earlier. In the next section, we discuss a selection of the empirical work in testing alternative theories.

Summary of Theoretical Approaches

The first model considered in this Lecture was that of direct democracy, where under certain conditions public decisions are determined by the preferences of the median voter. The conditions required are strong, and it is quite possible that no majority voting equilibrium exists, but the median voter case provides a useful benchmark—and is examined empirically in the next section.

The median voter model has been successively modified to allow for important features of the actual political process. In a representative democracy we have to consider the motives and behaviour of voters, parties and legislators. Among the factors we have identified as particularly important are the costs of acquiring information and the interests of political parties in supplying such information. In considering the relations between legislators and government administration, one can follow the parallel with private organizations, considering initially the behaviour of the government agency as a unit and then taking account of its internal structure. The motives of those who direct government agencies may well depart from those of the legislative branch, and, although control mechanisms are employed, they are typically not sufficient to ensure complete compliance. Within the agency itself, the need for control commonly gives rise to a hierarchical structure, which imposes additional administrative "overheads".

Finally, the operation of both the electoral process and administrative procedure is likely to be affected by special interest groups and by differential power. The ability of those with resources (either money or information) to influence the outcome of voting may secure a self-sustaining equilibrium. The pursuit of self-interest may lead to the formation of pressure groups, particularly where the numbers involved are small (e.g., trade associations) and where sanctions can be applied to ensure cohesion. Alternative versions of the class interest theory see the state as acting as the instrument of one class (capital), or as reflecting the balance of power between capital and labour.

10-5 EMPIRICAL STUDIES OF PUBLIC EXPENDITURE

As we have seen, there are a number of theories of the operation of the public sector, developed to varying degrees, which are at varying distances from being empirically testable. In this section, we first consider in detail the median voter model, which is that most easily translated into an empirically verifiable form, and then consider the other theories in more general terms.

Testing the Median Voter Model

Let us suppose that we are seeking to explain the cross-section differences in public spending, for example, between states or communities. In principle, the application of the median voter model is straightforward. If, for example, the demand function is taken to be log-linear, the level of public spending may be written as

$$\log G = a + b \log Y_m + c \log p_m \tag{10-4}$$

where Y_m denotes the after-tax income of the median voter and p_m the marginal "price" of public goods to him. It would then be possible to estimate the coefficients econometrically and to test the median voter hypothesis against alternatives, such as that the decisive voter is at the mean (e.g., with differential voting) or other quantiles of the income distribution.

There are however several difficulties. First, there is the problem of identifying the median voter. With identical tastes, uniform turnout in voting, and a monotonic relationship between income and desired public spending (taking account of the method of finance—see below), the median voter has the median income. If however the quantity demanded is not a monotonic function of income, or if there are differences in tastes, then we cannot necessarily identify the median voter in this way. This question is discussed by Bergstrom and Goodman (1973), who provide sufficient conditions under which the median income remains relevant. These conditions, which restrict the form of variation in the incomes of the subpopulations and in differences in tastes, are quite strong; and the issue becomes even more problematic if differential voting means that the decisive elector is not necessarily the median.

Second, the form of the demand function depends on the method of finance and the voter's perception of the tax system. The empirical studies have varied considerably in approach. Borcherding and Deacon (1972) simply assume that the tax share of the median voter is $1/P$, where P is the size of the population. In contrast, Bergstrom and Goodman (1973) discuss in detail the tax share of the median voter. They assume that perceived shares are randomly distributed around the share of property tax paid at the median income. There are however reasons why there may be *systematic* misperception. It is frequently argued that citizens tend to understate the cost of public services, since part of the taxation is concealed. Conversely, it may be argued (Gevers and Proost, 1978) that voters take a more sophisticated view of the trade-off between taxation and the level of public spending, allowing for the general equilibrium effects of tax changes.

Third, the cost of public spending varies across observations, as discussed for example by Borcherding and Deacon, depending on differences in factor prices. It also reflects the degree of "publicness" of the good and the economies or diseconomies of scale in its production. To represent the former, let us suppose that a total quantity of public good G generates benefits to the individual of

$$G^* = GP^{-\alpha} \tag{10-5}$$

so that $\alpha = 1$ may be taken as corresponding to a private good, and $\alpha = 0$ to a pure public good. The cost of G is assumed to be given by

$$qGP^\gamma \tag{10-6}$$

with $\gamma > 0$ representing increased per unit costs in a large population, and $\gamma < 0$ economies of scale in production in large populations. The median voter then chooses G^* subject to an effective cost per unit

$$p_m = t_m q P^{\alpha+\gamma} \tag{10-7}$$

where t_m denotes the tax share of the median voter, and q the price per unit. The desired level of G^* is given by (10-4):

$$\log G^* = a + b \log Y_m + c \log(t_m q P^{\alpha+\gamma}) \tag{10-8}$$

and the expenditure in *per capita* terms (denoted by E/P) is, from (10-5) and (10-6):

$$\log(E/P) = a + b \log Y_m + c \log t_m + (1+c) \log q$$
$$- [1 - (1+c)(\alpha+\gamma)] \log P \tag{10-9}$$

Fourth, we need to consider the precise sense in which the estimation of the equation represents a "test" of the median voter model. As noted by Romer and Rosenthal (1979), the model is rarely set against an explicit alternative, and in a number of cases it is not possible to reject the competing hypothesis that the spending is some multiple of that desired by the median voter or that another percentile (rather than the median) is decisive.

In order to illustrate these issues we have taken one of the many studies that have been carried out, that by Pommerehne and Schneider (1978), based on data for 110 Swiss cities in 1970.[11] They begin by estimating an equation similar to (10-9), where E represents aggregate municipal public expenditure, Y_m median net of tax income in the city, t_m the median tax share (assumed to be equal to the share in income tax), and P the residential population. The cost variable, q, is assumed constant across

---

[11] Studies for the United States include Bergstrom and Goodman (1973), Borcherding and Deacon (1972), Inman (1978), Lovell (1978) and Rubinfeld (1977).

cities. The resulting equation in *per capita* terms is

$$\log_e(E/P) = -11.90 + 1.29 \log_e Y_m - 0.70 \log_e t_m$$
$$ (6.97) \qquad (10.84)$$
$$-0.63 \log_e P$$
$$(7.93) \qquad\qquad \bar{R}^2 = 0.535$$

(the figures in brackets are t-statistics). It is possible to test this equation against alternatives, and this has been done by Pommerehne and Frey (1976) for the case where the mean, rather than the median, is decisive.[12] However, no test is possible of the hypothesis that E is *proportional* to that desired (the model yields no prediction of the size of the constant term—see Romer and Rosenthal, 1979). The individual coefficients imply an income elasticity of around unity, and that $0.3(\alpha + \gamma) = 0.37$. Since the maximum value for α is 1.0, this implies that γ is positive.

Pommerehne and Schneider go on to elaborate the model in two major respects. The first concerns the perceptions of tax burdens by the electorate. We have referred in Lecture 2 to attempts to calculate the perceived tax rate implicit in labour supply decisions; the approach of Pommerehne and Schneider is to postulate that the degree of under-estimation of the tax rate increases with the degree of complexity of the tax system and that under-estimation leads to a higher desired level of spending (as they note, both assumptions are debatable). As an index of the degree of complexity, they take the Herfindahl concentration index of tax revenues from different sources,[13] which is assumed to multiply the actual tax price. The index is unity when there is only one source of revenue, and less than 1.0 when there are multiple sources. A negative coefficient is predicted; and, as shown by row 2 in Table 10-1, this is found empirically. The choice of index is clearly arbitrary, but similar results are obtained for other measures, such as the share of highly "visible" taxes (personal income and wealth taxes).

The second development of the model is to allow for the differences in democratic institutions. Pommerehne and Schneider divide their sample into direct democracies (where decisions are taken in general assemblies open to all voters), representative democracies with referenda, and representative democracies without referenda. It seems reasonable to assume that the median voter model would become less relevant as we move from direct democracies to representative democracies without referenda, and this is indeed suggested by rows 3, 5 and 7 in Table 10-1 (although no formal framework for testing this hypothesis is provided).

---

[12] The overall level of explanation, as measured by R^2, is similar in the two equations estimated by Pommerehne and Frey, but the coefficient of the tax share is insignificant in the version with mean income, and the parameters generally are less plausible.

[13] The index is ΣR_i^2 where R_i is the share of tax revenue for the ith revenue category. The distinctions between categories are to some degree arbitrary, and obviously the index does not capture all aspects of complexity.

Table 10-1 Local public spending regression equations: results for Swiss cities, 1970

Equation	Demand elasticities with respect to:				$\bar{R}^2$
	Income	Tax share	Population	Complexity of tax system	
1. All 110 cities	1.29 (6.97)	−0.70 (10.84)	−0.63 (7.93)	—	0.535
2. All 110 cities	1.32 (7.34)	−0.64 (9.59)	−0.58 (7.31)	−0.33 (2.72)	0.561
3. 48 direct democracies	1.27 (6.39)	−0.72 (9.89)	−0.65 (5.48)	—	0.682
4. 48 direct democracies	1.26 (6.22)	−0.72 (9.67)	−0.64 (5.41)	−0.07 (0.66)	0.678
5. 35 representative democracies with referenda	0.88 (1.64)	−0.47 (3.72)	−0.33 (2.26)	—	0.372
6. 35 representative democracies with referenda	0.89 (1.80)	−0.17 (1.05)	−0.10 (0.60)	−0.67 (2.55)	0.467
7. 27 representative democracies without referenda	0.44 (0.97)	−0.43 (2.78)	−0.51 (2.34)	—	0.149
8. 27 representative democracies without referenda	1.28 (3.59)	−0.28 (2.55)	−0.28 (1.77)	−1.43 (5.00)	0.584

Figures in brackets are *t*-values. Equations estimated by ordinary least squares.
Source: Pommerehne and Schneider (1978, Tables 1 and 2).

Conversely, one might expect that the effect of "fiscal illusion" (measured by the index of complexity) would be greater in the representative democracy than in direct democracies, and this is again borne out by rows 4, 6, and 8 in the table. (The differences according to type of political institution are discussed further in Pommerehne, 1978.)

As in other areas of econometric work on public finance, the results of estimating median voter models are not conclusive. The models provide insight into a number of aspects, but are open to a number of criticisms. In part, these are qualifications that apply quite generally, for example, the use of single equation methods,[14] the specification of the functional form, and the treatment of the individual budget constraint. There are two aspects however that should be stressed. First, the heterogeneity of the population needs more explicit treatment, as recognized by Bergstrom and Goodman, allowing, for example, for the differences between Swiss citizens and other taxpayers, between owner-occupiers and tenants, or families with and without children. Second, the results should not be seen as constituting a test of the median voter model without a full specification of the range of competing hypotheses. Even where the median model provides a reasonable level of statistical explanation, as with direct democracies in Swiss cities, we cannot conclude that this is the only theory of public spending consistent with the evidence.

The Growth of Public Spending

The second major source of evidence about the determinants of public spending is that based on time series. As we have seen in Lecture 1, there has been a long-run tendency for the public sector to rise as a proportion of national income. Although there is no reason to extrapolate this into the future, the past secular trend provides a convenient "stylized fact" against which to compare different views of public spending.

The median voter model suggests at once a number of possible explanations. Rewriting Eq. (10-9) to give *per capita* spending (in real terms) relative to average incomes,

$$a_1 + a_2 \log(Y_m/\bar{Y}) + a_3 \log t_m + a_3 \log q$$
$$+ a_4 \log P + (a_2 - 1) \log \bar{Y} \quad (10\text{-}10)$$

We can identify the following possible explanations of a rising share for government spending:

1. rising *per capita* incomes, with public expenditure having an income elasticity greater than unity;

---

[14] For example, it would be preferable to consider the simultaneous determination of expenditures and tax rates.

2. redistribution of income, raising the median relative to the mean (where $a_2 > 0$);
3. decrease in (perceived) tax burden of median voter (where $a_3 < 0$), which may result from changes in fiscal structure or increased fiscal illusion;
4. decrease in relative price of public sector output (where $a_3 < 0$);
5. increase in population, where rising costs and low degree of "publicness" $(a_4 > 0)$.

It should be emphasized that we are not saying that these factors *have* operated in the direction indicated; indeed, it has been argued by Baumol (1967) and others that the relative price of the public sector has risen, as a result of an inherently lower rate of productivity increase. (Depending on the price elasticity, this may imply a rising share in terms of *expenditure*.)

Extending the model to include important aspects of political institutions not captured in the simple median voting model, there are other factors that may have intensified or moderated the growth of government spending:

6. extension of the franchise and increased participation of lower-income groups (e.g., via increased voter registration);
7. expansion of interest group activity (e.g., formation of trade associations pressing for aid to industry);
8. changing ideology of political parties, and shifts in the sources of financial support.

The "political" factors listed above may either supplement or replace the median voter model. Thus, one may view parties in a representative democracy as constrained by the electoral process but enjoying certain room for manoeuvre (on account of the issues concerning information, etc., discussed earlier). This line of argument is similar to that given prominence in Peacock and Wiseman's seminal study (1961). They were particularly concerned to explain why increases in public spending in the United Kingdom had tended to occur in discrete steps. The explanation advanced for these "displacement effects" is that the ability of governments to increase expenditure is limited, on the supply side, by the revenue that can be raised, and that people's ideas about the "tolerable" level of taxation tend to be relatively stable. Thus, in normal periods the growth of public expenditure tends to be relatively steady. On the other hand, there are periodic "social disturbances", during which people tolerate methods of financing previously considered unacceptable and the acceptance remains when the disturbance has disappeared. As a result, "expenditures which the government may have thought desirable before the disturbance, but which it did not then dare to implement, consequently become possible" (Peacock and Wiseman, 1967, p. xxxiv). Moreover, the kind of social disturbances considered by them, notably wars, may impose new obligations on the government and reveal new needs (an "inspection effect"). The mechanisms by which these processes operate are not fully spelled out (although see Breton, 1974).

The electoral/political explanations must be supplemented by consideration of the interests of the bureaucracy, and this suggests two further factors:

9. the aim of government agencies to expand provision, coupled with incomplete control by the legislature;
10. increasing costs of administrative hierarchies.

These factors operate independently of those discussed earlier, and it has indeed been argued that expenditure behaviour can be explained entirely in this way. Thus, Davis, Dempster and Wildavsky (1966) argue that the budgetary process can be represented by two straightforward relationships. In the simplest form, the requests by an agency are a fixed multiple of the previous appropriation made by the legislature (more generally, a linear function of the previous appropriation and previous request) plus a random component; in turn, the appropriation is a fixed proportion of the request plus a random component. The conditions under which this "rule of thumb" behaviour is likely to emerge from more basic assumptions clearly need to be examined.

Finally, the class interest theories would see the expansion of public spending as resulting from either:

11. the transfer of power to the working class, and the expansion of redistributive expenditure; or
12. the need for government intervention to secure the conditions for profitable accumulation of capital.

It is clear that any attempt to estimate empirically these different models, and to test the different hypotheses, is likely to encounter substantial difficulties. First, there is the definition of the public sector. As brought out in Lecture 1, there is no precise boundary, and theoretical constructs are not immediately matched in the national income accounts. The different hypotheses apply to varying extent to different concepts. Should we consider total spending, or only spending on goods and services? Should we consider the expenditure of individual agencies? Second, the hypotheses need to be put in a form where they can be empirically tested. Thus, in the case of the Peacock and Wiseman theories, we need to specify the circumstances in which the displacement effect takes place (even if we are only testing for structural breaks). The theories based on class interest require that one can use a non-tautological indicator of relative power.

Third, as with other econometric work, one has to consider the rest of the model in which the equation is embedded. In the past, inadequate attention has been paid to the simultaneous nature of the relationships. Typically, equations have been estimated with G, taken here as government spending on goods and services, as the dependent variable, and national income as one of the explanatory variables. However, this is a reversal of the usual macroeconomic treatment, where G is regarded as exogenous and income as the dependent variable. It is possible that the system is recursive, but in general the model should be treated as a simultaneous system.

Concluding Comments

The natural development of the work described in this section is the construction of full-scale models of politico-economic interactions, combining the explanation of government decisions as functions of economic (and political) circumstances with the modelling of the influence of government actions on the behaviour of the economy. At a theoretical level, there are models of the "political business cycle", where governments are assumed to design macro-policy to secure electoral advantage, given a set of economic constraints (see, for example, Nordhaus, 1975, Ben-Porath, 1975, MacRae, 1977, and Frey, 1978). At an empirical level, Frey and Schneider have estimated models for the United States (1978c), United Kingdom (1978a) and West Germany (1978b), in which the choice of instruments by the government depends on its electoral popularity (and ideological goals) and popularity depends on economic indicators.

In principle, these developments are most important. In seeking to make the activities of the government endogenous rather than exogenous, they are very much in the spirit of this Lecture. At the same time, it appears over-optimistic to expect that the empirical implementation will yield immediate, definitive findings. Experience with the estimation of individual relationships, such as labour supply functions or investment equations, has shown the problems in providing an unambiguous interpretation of the evidence or in testing alternative specifications. The history of the construction of macroeconomic models points to the many difficulties likely to arise in the estimation of a fully satisfactory simultaneous model integrating political and economic considerations.

READING

This Lecture is based on a wide range of material, and only a brief guide to reading can be given. For further discussion of the results on voting, see Sen (1970b) and Pattanaik (1971); for a review of the recent theoretical results on political mechanisms, see Kramer (1977b). For assessments from rather different perspectives, see Barry (1970) and Mueller (1976). On bureaucracy, see Niskanen (1971), Breton (1974) and the papers in Borcherding (1977). Marxist views of the state are discussed in surveys by Foley (1978) and Jessop (1977). Our review of the empirical literature has drawn on Romer and Rosenthal (1979) and Alt and Chrystal (1977).

THE DESIGN OF POLICY

ELEVEN

INTRODUCTION TO PART TWO— NORMATIVE ANALYSIS

11-1 INTRODUCTION

In Part One we examined the behaviour of households and firms in response to changes in fiscal policy, and in the last Lecture we recognized the endogeneity of the government itself. We described how different models of the economic activities of the state could be used to "close" the system. The levels of taxation and spending were influenced by the preferences of the electorate, by the objectives of political parties, by the degree of latitude allowed to the bureaucracy, and by the strengths of different interest groups. On an extreme view, the closing of the system in that way would mean that there were no normative questions to be answered. The behaviour would be completely determined; one could merely describe the laws of motion of the economy—private and public sector together—and work out their implications.

This deterministic view goes too far and overlooks an important role for the public finance economist. The process by which voters make choices, by which decisions get taken, by which policies are put into effect, is influenced by the arguments conducted by economists and by the evidence that they bring to bear. We have earlier stressed the consequences of imperfect information, and one of the functions of the economist is as a supplier of information. In part this is information of the "positive" kind discussed in Part One. The evidence on the disincentive effect of income taxation may influence voters, congressmen or civil servants in their attitudes to tax reform. But in part the information involves issues of a kind usually described as "normative", and these are the subject of Part Two.

333

Since the status of the economist in discussing normative questions has generated considerable controversy, it is important to make clear from the outset the position adopted here. The aim of the Lectures that follow is *not* to argue the case for particular policies; it is not their intention to provide an answer to the question, "what ought the government to do?" It is not that we believe there to be no role for polemical writing; indeed, public finance has produced some of the finest examples (Lord Kaldor's *An Expenditure Tax* being noteworthy in this century). Rather, it is that our concern here is with the *structure* of arguments rather than with the arguments themselves. The aim is to explore the relationship between specified objectives and the policy recommendations to which these objectives lead; it is to examine the way in which the recommendations vary with changing objectives or changing views as to how the economy works. We seek here to expound "the grammar of arguments about policy" (Hahn, 1973, p. 106), not to advocate policies themselves.

The interpretation of the role of normative public finance adopted here may be illustrated by the particular issue that forms the subject of Lecture 12: the design of the indirect tax system. Should we have a single rate of indirect tax on all commodities, or should the rates be differentiated? If the rates are differentiated, what should guide the choice of rates on different goods? A variety of arguments can be made. One, which we discuss in Lecture 12, is that indirect taxation should be designed to minimize distortion and that this involves a uniform rate of tax. What we set out to do in examining this argument is to see whether the recommendation follows from the specified objective (minimizing distortion), and how this depends on the assumptions made about the underlying model of the economy. In other words, we solve the minimization problem in the context of an explicit model, and assess the sensitivity of the solution to the specification of that model. A second argument that can be made is that indirect taxation should be designed for redistributive purposes and that luxuries should therefore be taxed more heavily. This illustrates another feature of the analysis—the way in which the argument depends on the objectives postulated. In Lecture 12 we examine how the introduction of distributional goals modifies the solution.

To sum up, our aim is not to conclude that the tax structure should be differentiated, still less that the optimal tax rate on bicycles is 16 per cent, but rather to illuminate the relationship between objectives and conclusions. This may reveal that the conclusions follow only under restrictive conditions (as turns out to be the case with the minimization of distortion), and that they need to be modified in other circumstances. The function of the analysis is then to identify these conditions and the nature of the modifications. The investigation may reveal weakness in the underlying model of economic behaviour or ignorance about key parameters of that model. Thus, we may conclude that the design of tax policy depends on obtaining more precise estimates of, for example, the elasticity of demand for different commodities. The normative analysis may in this case be seen as a laboratory for evaluating the value of additional information. We need to know, for example, whether inaccurate estimates of these parameters could lead to large losses (measured according to a specified criterion) or, more generally, where research effort is best directed. Should we allocate more effort to studying company rather than household behaviour?

Alternatively, the exploration of the structure of arguments may lead to the revision of attitudes to certain objectives. If it transpires that principle A leads consistently to policies that are unattractive, then this may make acceptance of this principle less likely or may lead to its being revised. This kind of iterative procedure between objectives and policies may be more appealing to intuitionists than to other philosophers, but there can be little doubt that public finance has been an important "testing ground" for principles of economic justice in recent years. The exploration of the implications for tax policy of the Rawlsian difference principle, for example, has helped to clarify the nature of that principle, and has influenced the degree to which it has been accepted as a basis for redistributive policy.

Part Two of the Lectures is, therefore, concerned with studying arguments that have been advanced in connection with the design of tax and expenditure policy. The treatment is selective in several respects. First, the particular public finance questions discussed are only a few out of those that could have been covered. In the choice we have tended to emphasize aspects that have been the subject of the recent literature on optimal taxation and that seem to us of especial policy interest, although undoubtedly the selection is biased towards the authors' own interests. Second, the treatment is selective in the range of objectives considered. Just as there are many views of the state as a positive entity, so too there are many approaches to its normative behaviour, and we cannot be exhaustive. Those considered reflect the dominant traditions in public finance, and all that we can claim is that we have been explicit in our formulation of the problem (explicitness with respect to assumed objectives not always being a characteristic of writing on public finance). ·

Purpose of this Lecture

In view of the key role played by the objectives of government policy, we have devoted much of this Lecture (Sections 11-2–11-4) to a discussion of the principles that underlie the main arguments discussed in subsequent Lectures. We do not try to assess the merits of these principles; the book is not a treatise in moral philosophy. Rather, we seek to formulate the principles in terms in which they can be applied to economic problems (in the process doing less than justice to a number of philosophical difficulties), and to illustrate some of their implications for public finance. The discussion in Section 11-2 is developed in terms of an increasing degree of emphasis on the role of the government, from the "minimal state", through arguments for the state to ensure Pareto efficiency and the maximization of social welfare, to the opposite extreme of the centrally planned economy. As explained at the end of that section, it is the intermediate views, attributing a significant, but not dominant, role to the state, that receive most attention here.

In the next two sections we consider the relationship of the different approaches to welfare economics and standard public finance objectives. As we have noted in Lecture 1, the basic theorems of welfare economics have commonly been used as a framework for analysing different reasons for government intervention, and in Section 11-3 we examine the ways in which fiscal policy may be necessary to secure Pareto efficiency. In Section 11-4, we explore the relationship between the formulation of government objectives in terms of social welfare maximization and the more usual public finance criteria, such as vertical and horizontal equity.

Finally, we have to consider the range of instruments at the disposal of the government, and this is a major aspect which has received insufficient notice. All too frequently arguments for a particular policy are conditional on the infeasibility of certain measures and the feasibility of others. This feasibility may be in administrative terms. Here, the role of information is again crucial. Whether the government could levy a tax based on intelligence depends on whether it is possible to measure intelligence in an accurate manner and to collect this information from all individuals. (Even where it is feasible, the costs of administration may be too great.) The feasibility may be in political terms. This brings us back to the positive theory of the state. The political process may constrain the range of instruments and the extent to which they can be levied. A tax related to IQ scores may be deemed politically unacceptable. The question of the range of feasible instruments is discussed in Section 11-5.

11-2 NORMATIVE THEORIES OF THE STATE

This section draws heavily on recent writing on political philosophy, without claiming in any way to provide an adequate account of the literature. The aim is to identify certain broad approaches to the prescription of the role of the state, to sketch briefly the kind of justification that has typically been advanced, and to draw out some of the ways in which they can be applied to public economics.

The "Minimal" State

To illustrate the minimalist approach to the functions of the state, we take the widely discussed work of Nozick, whose views are summarized in the Preface to *Anarchy, State, and Utopia*: "a minimal state, limited to the narrow functions of protection against force, theft, fraud, enforcement of contracts, and so on, is justified; that any more extensive state will violate persons' rights not to be forced to do certain things, and is unjustified" (Nozick, 1974, p. ix).

The support for this position provided by Nozick is in terms of the process by which a given outcome emerges. He rejects the notion that principles can be based on "end-states", and replaces this by a "historical" principle. Justice is defined not with respect to a particular distribution of incomes, but in terms of the process that generated those incomes. The initial position taken by Nozick, in the tradition of Hobbes and Locke, is a state of nature or anarchy. In this anarchic situation, there is a limited recognition of the rights of others, insufficient to allow peaceful co-existence, and Nozick argues that a dominant agency supplying protective services will emerge. This agency, because of free-rider problems, has to adopt coercive taxation to finance its operation. Hence the minimal or "night-watchman" justification for the state.[1]

On this view many of the functions of the state are not justified. The minimal state, in Nozick's conception, offers only one public good—protection against violence, theft and fraud—and the enforcement of contracts. Redistributive activity (as commonly understood—Nozick uses the term in a different sense) is limited to the financing of this minimal collective outlay. In these terms, the scope for discussing public finance issues is highly circumscribed, and this approach rules out of court many of the issues discussed in Part Two. (It may be noted that it is not clear from Nozick's argument why more widespread provision of public goods, in circumstances where it is Pareto-improving, cannot be allowed.)

Unanimity and Pareto Efficiency

The first step beyond the minimal state described by Nozick is to allow the government to carry out *unanimously approved* activities (Buchanan and Tullock, 1962). This opens the way for taxation and spending to achieve Pareto improvements, i.e., to make at least one person better off and no one worse off. Individuals acting in their self-interest will agree to such measures and, since they need no coercion, it can be argued that no violation of individual rights is involved.

The scope for intervention to secure Pareto efficiency[2] depends on a

---

[1] There are clearly a number of features of this argument that can be questioned (for example, the conditions under which original entitlements are just)—see Gordon (1976).

[2] A Pareto-efficient allocation is one where no Pareto-improving move can be made. Popular usage refers to Pareto *optimality*, but, as Koopmans pointed out long ago, the term is a misnomer.

number of factors. Indeed, the purpose of one of the basic theorems of welfare economics is to delineate situations in which Pareto efficiency is achieved by a competitive economy. This theorem, discussed in more detail in the next section, provides a basis for categorizing circumstances in which government action may be unanimously preferred. There may moreover be arguments for Pareto-improving redistribution based on interdependencies between utility functions, along the lines of the model of Hochman and Rodgers (1969) in its *n*-person variant (i.e., where redistribution would not necessarily occur voluntarily).

The force of the unanimity extension may be seen with the aid of Fig. 11-1 (based in part on Fig. 1 in Buchanan, 1976b). Suppose that there are

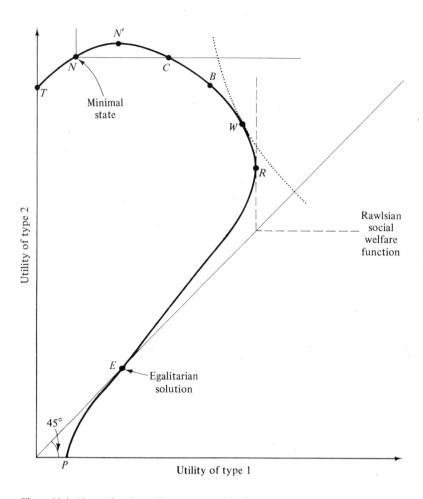

Figure 11-1 Alternative views of government objectives.

two classes of individuals, types 1 and 2, whose utilities are plotted on the axes.[3] With the minimal, night-watchman state, the outcome—given the initial entitlements—is, say, at point N. The feasible frontier, given the instruments at the government's disposal, is PT, and any point on NC represents a potential Pareto improvement. A move from N to any point on this section would be unanimously supported. (In contrast, if the minimal state had been at N', no Pareto improvement would have been possible.) The diagram also serves to bring out the standard problem with Pareto efficiency as a criterion: it provides only a partial ordering. All points on the section $N'C$ are unanimously preferred to N, and none of them commands a unanimous vote over the others.

Social Welfare Functions

The standard procedure for arriving at a complete ordering is to postulate a Paretian social welfare function. This function, which may be written as $\Gamma(U^1, U^2, U^3, \ldots, U^H)$ where U^h denotes the utility of individual h, is Paretian in the sense of respecting individual valuations. It is therefore consistent with the Pareto criterion, but goes beyond it in assuming that gains and losses can be compared (for discussion of the degree of comparability required, see Sen, 1970a, 1977a).

With an arbitrary social welfare function, we can draw social indifference contours, such as the dotted curve shown, and the resulting optimum is W. The argument would then be that taxation or expenditure should be carried to the point W, and we can explore—as we do in Lectures 12–17—the characteristics of the policy that achieves this welfare optimum. These characteristics depend on the shape of the social welfare function, that is, on the weights attached to individual utilities. To illustrate this, we may consider the two cases that have received most attention:

1. the Benthamite objective of maximizing the sum of individual utilities, i.e., any positive linear transformation of

$$\Gamma = U^1 + U^2 \ldots + U^H \qquad (11\text{-}1)$$

2. the Rawlsian objective of maximizing the welfare of the worst-off individual ("maxi-min"):[4]

$$\Gamma = \min_h (U^h) \qquad (11\text{-}2)$$

---

[3] The utilities are denoted by U^1, U^2 where the superscript identifies the type and does not denote an exponent.

[4] The principle is extended in the lexicographic form, so that if two policies are equivalent for the worst-off person, the maximand is then the utility of the next worst-off person, and so on (Sen, 1970a, p. 138).

These may be seen as special cases of the isoelastic formulation used in examples in later Lectures:

$$\Gamma = \frac{1}{1-v}\sum_h [(U^h)^{1-v} - 1] \qquad (11\text{-}3)$$

where the Benthamite case is $v = 0$ and the Rawlsian case is the limit as $v \to \infty$. In the two-person example shown in Fig. 11-1, the Benthamite social welfare function is a straight line with slope -1, giving the optimum indicated by B, and the Rawlsian contours have shape $\llcorner$ centred on the 45° line, so that the optimum is at R.

The ethical justification for the adoption of the social welfare function approach, and the use of the utilitarian or Rawlsian special cases, has been the subject of a long literature. That most fully articulated in recent years is the social contract theory of Rawls (1971). This again considers the choices made in an initial position, but this is now defined to be a state ("original position") such that people have no knowledge of their social position or preferences. This "veil of ignorance" is assumed to ensure that the choice of moral principles is impartial or just; it is asserted that the decisions made by people in that hypothetical position are an acceptable basis for a theory of justice.

Before describing the conclusions drawn by Rawls, we may note that a similar approach has been employed to rationalize the utilitarian objective. Drawing on a long tradition, one can consider a person who is uncertain of his position in a community where there is a given distribution of endowments and all individuals have identical preferences. It can then be argued (e.g., Vickrey, 1960) that in these conditions, if individual preferences satisfy the von Neumann–Morgenstern axioms, then the social maximand should be expected utility $(\sum_1^H U^h/H)$. The assumption of identical preferences is of course a strong one, and the more general case has been treated by Harsanyi (1955). The ensuing difficulties are discussed in Pattanaik (1971).

The utilitarian conclusion drawn from this formulation may be contrasted with the derivation by Rawls of the difference principle, or maxi-min, from consideration of behaviour behind the veil of ignorance. The conclusion of his argument may be seen as arising from the different assumption about attitude to risk, the maxi-min corresponding to infinite risk aversion. Rawls himself is not happy with this interpretation, objecting to a representation in which "we can shift smoothly from one moral conception to another simply by varying the parameter [v]" (Rawls, 1973, p. 644). In this respect we part company from Rawls, and have employed the parameterization in terms of v as a useful device to explore the sensitivity of the findings to changing views about the social welfare function. At the same time, there is much more to Rawls' *A Theory of Justice* than is captured in the maxi-min objective (11-2) or its lexicographic extension.

Non-Individualistic Social Welfare Functions

The discussion to this point has been individualistic. This applies as much to Rawls' rational egoist in the original position as to Nozick's anarchist. Moreover, it has been assumed that social welfare responds positively to individual welfare. The first departure from this is where the social welfare function still takes individual utilities as its arguments but is no longer monotonically increasing—it is individualistic but non-Paretian.

The implications of a non-Paretian objective may be seen by considering the principle of equalizing utilities, which we shall refer to as the egalitarian principle. Although the Rawlsian objective is frequently supposed to be egalitarian in this sense,[5] this is clearly not the case, as Fig. 11-1 demonstrates (the point R does not lie on the 45° line). The egalitarian objective, achieved at point E, is concerned with the distance between individuals, and where $U^2 > U^1$, the social welfare function is decreasing in U^2. Intermediate objectives may involve some trade-off between "distance" and the "level" of utilities: for example, following Nozick (1974, pp. 410–11), we may consider the case in which social welfare is measured (where $U^2 > U^1$) by $U^1 - \theta(U^2 - U^1)$. In terms of the social indifference map this involves contours that slope upwards, as illustrated in Fig. 11-2,[6] and the social optimum lies on the segment ER. Depending on the slope of the utility possibility function, and the weight θ attached to "distance", the egalitarian solution may be optimal.

The second departure is where the social valuation placed on an individual's welfare is no longer related to individual utilities U^h. Thus, social preferences may take a different, "paternalist", view of the consumption of certain items. This kind of argument may lie behind the taxation of commodities such as alcohol or tobacco, or the provision of merit wants. One example of the way in which it can be developed is the principle of "specific egalitarianism" of Tobin (1970), who discusses the argument that society is concerned not only with "general" inequality but also with the allocation of particular goods. A polar case is provided by items such as civil rights, the vote, essential foods in wartime, and possibly medical care, where strict equality of distribution is regarded as of crucial importance. There are also, however, commodities "where the egalitarian objective is "one-sided, not a strictly equal distribution but an assured universal minimum" (Tobin, 1970, p. 266). Examples may be food (in peacetime), education and housing.

---

[5] See, for example, Meade: "this we may call the 'egalitarian' criterion. We reckon social welfare solely by the utility of the poorest member of society" (1976, p. 49). Similarly, Okun: "Rawls has a clear, crisp answer: 'Give priority to equality'" (1975, p. 92).

[6] Social welfare functions of this kind are discussed by Meade (1976, Ch. 4), but he refers to them as "super-egalitarian". As we have already noted, this choice of terminology is confusing, and it seems more natural to refer to the case $\theta \to \infty$ as egalitarian.

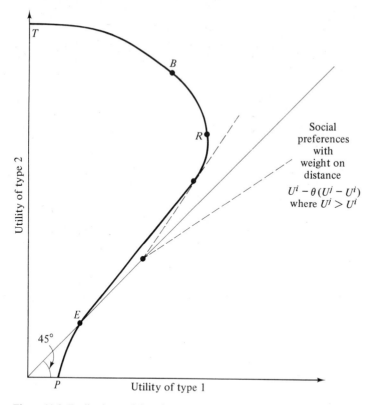

Figure 11-2 Egalitarian social preferences.

Centrally Planned Economies and Public Finance

The opposite extreme from the minimal state theories, with their emphasis on individual freedom to engage in economic activity, are those that regard it as a matter of principle that economic activity should be under collective or communal control. (Whether this is an ultimate or intermediate objective is not discussed here.)

In such a socialist economy, operated on centralized or decentralized lines, the formal status of public finance measures is rather different from that in a market or mixed economy. Although taxation typically plays a smaller role, the problem of determining the relation between after-tax wages and marginal products is equivalent to the problem of taxation in a market economy. The significance of public spending may be greater (see Musgrave, 1969, Ch. 1). (It is also the case that public finance may be able to learn from the literature on economic planning: for example in the design of procedures for tax reform or mechanisms for determining the optimal provision of public goods.)

Summing Up

In this section we have considered a range of views about the role of the state, and these imply varying importance for the use of public finance instruments. The minimal state would limit state activity to the provision of a very limited range of public goods; the controlled economy has other instruments that can be employed. In view of this we concentrate in Part Two on the middle cases on the spectrum of state intervention, where taxation and expenditure can play a significant part in securing Pareto improvements or the maximization of a specified social welfare function.

The different views of the function of the government make very different assumptions about the degree of interpersonal comparability of utilities—they have quite different informational requirements. Some (e.g., the minimal state of Nozick) make no assumptions, whereas others (e.g., the utilitarian objective) have strong requirements. Moreover, the nature of the information needed differs with different principles; for instance, the Rawlsian objective requires comparability of levels of welfare, but the Benthamite does not. We return to this question later.

11-3 PARETO EFFICIENCY AND WELFARE ECONOMICS

The standard approach to identifying situations where state intervention may lead to Pareto improvements is via the basic theorems of welfare economics. As we have noted in Lecture 1, the reference point adopted—of a perfectly competitive market economy in equilibrium—cannot be regarded as ethically neutral. It does however allow us to relate the analysis to the mainstream of welfare theory.

Basic Theorems of Welfare Economics

The basic theorems may be stated in the following way (this account is not intended to be rigorous, and the reader is referred to Arrow and Hahn, 1971, or Malinvaud, 1972, for a more complete statement and proofs).

First Theorem If (1) households and firms act perfectly competitively, taking prices as parametric, (2) there is a full set of markets, and (3) there is perfect information, *then* a competitive equilibrium, if it exists, is Pareto-efficient.

Second Theorem If household indifference maps and firm production sets are convex, if there is a full set of markets, if there is perfect information, and if lump-sum transfers and taxes may be carried out costlessly, *then* any Pareto-efficient allocation can be achieved as a competitive equilibrium with appropriate lump-sum transfers and taxes.

The implications of the conditions of these theorems, and their not being fulfilled, are discussed in detail below. For example, we explain what is entailed in there being a full set of markets (this rules out, for example, externalities). At this point we should note that the first theorem does not require convexity, but unless further assumptions are made beyond those listed a competitive equilibrium may fail to exist—at least, in an economy where there is a finite number of agents. (On the other hand, where there is an infinite number of agents, a competitive equilibrium may be attained, and its optimality properties hold, even when there are certain types of non-convexity.)

An Example

It may be helpful to give a concrete example, which is simple but which leads naturally to the models used in later lectures. Suppose that households supply labour (L) and consume a single good (X); and that there are equal numbers of two types of household. The two types differ in their earning power, so that for each hour they produce w_1 and w_2, respectively. On the other hand, they have the same tastes and maximize a utility function (which satisfies the convexity hypothesis):

$$\log U = a \log X + (1-a) \log (1-L) \quad \text{where } 0 < a < 1 \qquad (11\text{-}4)$$

The production constraint is of the simple form (which again satisfies convexity)

$$X_1 + X_2 = w_1 L_1 + w_2 L_2 \qquad (11\text{-}5)$$

The utility possibility frontier, giving the maximum level of utility for one group, for a specified level of utility for the other, may be obtained by considering the stationary points of[7]

$$\mathscr{L} = \eta_1 \log U^1 + \eta_2 \log U^2 + \lambda(w_1 L_1 + w_2 L_2 - X_1 - X_2) \qquad (11\text{-}6)$$

where η_i, λ are Lagrangean multipliers. The first-order conditions are, differentiating with respect to X_i,

$$\frac{\eta_1 a}{X_1} = \lambda = \frac{\eta_2 a}{X_2} \qquad (11\text{-}7a)$$

and with respect to L_i

$$\lambda w_i - \frac{\eta_i (1-a)}{1-L_i} \leqslant 0 \quad \text{with } L_i = 0 \text{ if strict inequality} \qquad (11\text{-}7b)$$

If both groups supply positive amounts of labour, (11-7b) implies

$$w_i L_i = w_i - \frac{\eta_i (1-a)}{\lambda}$$

---

[7] For clarification of this formulation of the conditions for Pareto efficiency, see Dorfman (1975) and Panzar and Willig (1976).

so

$$w_1 L_1 + w_2 L_2 = w_1 + w_2 - \frac{(1-a)}{\lambda}(\eta_1 + \eta_2)$$

But from (11-7a),

$$X_1 + X_2 = \frac{a}{\lambda}(\eta_1 + \eta_2)$$

so, from (11-5)

$$\frac{\eta_1 + \eta_2}{\lambda} = w_1 + w_2 \tag{11-8a}$$

Substituting from (11-7a and 11-7b) into (11-4),

$$U^i = \frac{\eta_i}{\lambda} A w_i^{-(1-a)} \quad \text{where } A = a^a (1-a)^{1-a} \tag{11-8b}$$

Hence (11-8a) gives

$$U^1 w_1^{1-a} + U^2 w_2^{1-a} = A(w_1 + w_2) \tag{11-8c}$$

This straight line segment (for the given cardinalization) of the utility possibility frontier is plotted as PQ in Fig. 11-3, where we adopt the convention that $w_2 > w_1$, so that the slope is less than $45°$. A corner solution with, say, $L_1 = 0$ implies

$$U^1 = X_1^a$$

Hence

$$w_2 L_2 = X_1 + X_2$$

$$w_2 - \frac{\eta_2}{\lambda}(1-a) = (U^1)^{1/a} + \frac{\eta_2 a}{\lambda}$$

Using (11-8b)

$$A(U^1)^{1/a} + U^2 w_2^{1-a} = A w_2 \tag{11-8d}$$

This strictly concave segment is shown in the lower right-hand part of the figure as QM (it intersects the axis where $U^1 = w_2^a$); the segment KP is defined similarly.[8]

---

[8] In drawing the figure, and in the discussion of the example, we assume that

$$\frac{w_1}{w_2} > \frac{a}{1-a}$$

and that (w_2/w_1) is less than x, where x is the solution to

$$x^a[1 - a(1 + 1/x)] = 1$$

The first condition ensures that U^2 (respectively U^1) is strictly positive at Q (respectively P); the second condition ensures Q lies below E.

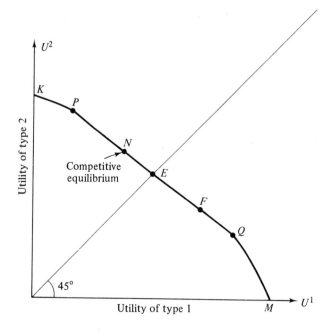

Figure 11-3 Utility possibility frontier for two-class example.

Figure 11-3 may be used to illustrate the two optimality theorems. First, in a competitive equilibrium with wage rates w_1 and w_2 (and the consumption good as the *numeraire*) without lump-sum redistributions, the first-order conditions for a person of type i to maximize U^i subject to $X_i = w_i L_i$ are

$$\frac{a}{X_i} = \alpha_i, \quad -\left(\frac{1-a}{1-L_i}\right) + w_i \alpha_i \leqslant 0 \qquad (11\text{-}9\text{a})$$

with $L_i = 0$ if strict inequality, where α_i is the Lagrangean multiplier associated with the ith person's budget constraint. From the budget constraint, $L_i > 0$ and we can eliminate α_i, giving

$$U^i = A w_i^a, \quad i = 1, 2 \qquad (11\text{-}9\text{b})$$

From (11-8c) we can check that this no-intervention equilibrium N lies on the utility possibility frontier (above the 45° line since $w_2 > w_1$).

Suppose now that we wish to attain another point on the utility possibility frontier, say F on the straight line segment. From the second optimality theorem it follows that this can be achieved by appropriate lump-sum transfers. Define the transfer to individual type i as T_i, so the individual budget constraint is $X_i = w_i L_i + T_i$. Solving, the utility is now

$$U^i = A(w_i + T_i)w_i^{-(1-a)} \tag{11-10}$$

Comparing with (11-8), we can see that $T_i = \eta_i/\lambda - w_i$ achieves the desired Pareto-efficient allocation, and that from (11-8a) $T_1 + T_2 = 0$.

> **Exercise 11-1** Show that it is possible to attain points on the nonlinear segments KP and QM in Fig. 11-3 by the use of appropriate lump-sum taxes and transfers.

In this example, as in any case covered by the conditions of the First Theorem, the no-intervention situation is Pareto-efficient. In terms of the discussion of Section 11-2, the point N with minimal government does not allow Pareto-improving moves. Any government activity—such as moving from N to a point F—must involve a ranking of Pareto-efficient points. On the other hand, where the conditions for the First Theorem do not hold, then N may lie inside the utility possibility frontier, and to this we now turn.

Breakdown of the Efficiency Conditions

The first assumption is perfect competition. That this may well fail to hold is suggested both by casual empiricism and by the fact that, with a finite number of agents, competitive behaviour is not "incentive-compatible"; i.e., a person may have an individual incentive to depart from the prescribed price-taking behaviour (the competitive response is not the Nash equilibrium for the non-co-operative game). Hurwicz (1972) demonstrates in fact that no process that selects Pareto-efficient allocations, and allows a no-trade option to each individual, can be both incentive-compatible and decentralized. The lack of incentive compatibility ceases to apply in an economy with an infinite number of agents (Roberts and Postlewaite, 1976). Where, in loose terms, the economy is not "large" enough for the incentives towards imperfect competition to be held in check, government intervention may be necessary to establish the conditions for perfect competition. This is particularly relevant to branches of policy-making not discussed here, such as anti-monopoly and merger legislation, but we take account at several points the implications of the existence of imperfect competition.

Perhaps the most important reason for there being a limited number of firms is the existence of non-convexities in production. It is clear that, for certain industries, increasing returns to scale are sufficiently large to lead, if not to monopoly, at least to a sufficiently high degree of concentration to make the perfectly competitive hypothesis invalid. (As we noted earlier, the convexity requirement may enter the conditions for the First Theorem via the *existence* of competitive equilibrium.) Thus, non-convexities may lead to the kind of monopolistically competitive equilibrium described in Lecture 7; although the economy is competitive, there being many products that are substitutes, firms do not take prices parametrically and the market equilibrium is not necessarily Pareto-efficient.

Market Failure

The second condition for the First Theorem is that there exists a full set of markets. The strength of this assumption is well known to economic theorists, although it is less frequently recognized in popular writing. It requires, for example, a full set of futures markets and a full set of markets for risk-bearing. There is an extensive literature enquiring into the consequences of the absence of markets—the analysis of "market failure"—but it is important to ask why such failure arises. This latter question is critically related to the costs associated with information and carrying out transactions (we discuss these below).

An important example of market failure, which arises even in a static economy with no uncertainty, is that of externalities. In a pure exchange economy, such externalities may be represented by supposing that the utility of the hth household is a function of the consumption of other households:

$$U^h = U^h(\mathbf{X}^1, \mathbf{X}^2, \dots, \mathbf{X}^h, \mathbf{X}^H) \tag{11-11}$$

(where $\mathbf{X}^h$ is the n-dimensional vector of goods consumed by household h). It is clear that in such cases the competitive equilibrium may not be Pareto-efficient (suppose, for example, that in the example given earlier U^2 depends on L_1 and U^1 on L_2). A case of considerable significance is where the utility functions depend, not on individual consumptions, but on the aggregate $\mathbf{X} = \Sigma_h \mathbf{X}_h$:

$$U^h = U^h(\mathbf{X}^h, \mathbf{X}) \tag{11-11a}$$

Thus, whereas in (11-11) the person is annoyed by his neighbour's car, in the case of (11-11a) it is the total volume of traffic that disturbs him. A still more special case is that of a public good. In this case there is a class of goods for which there is no individual consumption, and which enters the utility function only in the form of an aggregate. We have then a partition into n private goods and m public goods $G_1, \dots, G_m$, and the utility function is written

$$U^h = U^h(\mathbf{X}^h, \mathbf{G}) \tag{11-12}$$

As noted by Starrett (1974), the definition of an externality is conditional on a specified market structure. In a barter economy, with restricted trading, one individual's utility may well depend on another's offer. In a competitive market economy such interdependencies are eliminated, and it is those that remain that are typically characterized as external effects. On the other hand, if, following Arrow (1971a), we introduce new commodities $\mathbf{X}_{ik}^h$ (consumption of good k by i as it enters the utility function of h), there correspond prices p_{ik}^h such that a competitive equilibrium with standard optimality properties exists. Thus, there is a formal sense in which it is the failure of such markets that leads to the problem of externalities.

A second illustration of the consequences of market failure is provided by the case of an intertemporal economy where only spot markets exist—no future contracts can be entered into.[9] In this situation it is possible that the competitive economy may follow a path that is Pareto-inefficient. An example is provided by the model of Stiglitz (1974c) of an economy in which a single good is produced by capital and natural resources. At each point in time the condition for asset market equilibrium (holdings of capital and natural resources) and the rules for expectation formation determine the rate of change of relative prices. There is however an infinity of paths corresponding to different initial prices, and it is quite possible, with short-run perfect foresight, that the economy may follow forever a path that is inefficient, with the total stock of resources never being used up (the initial price being "too high").[10]

Imperfect Information

The third condition for the First Theorem is that of perfect information. This assumption is so ingrained in the standard way of thinking that it is usually not even listed as an assumption. Yet we have repeatedly seen the important role that it plays. Indeed, all the fundamental results of competitive analysis—the existence theorem, the optimality theorem, and the characterization results (e.g., the Law of the Single Price) are invalid if information is imperfect and costly to acquire.

The costs of information are closely related to the other conditions. Two of the major causes of the absence of insurance markets are moral hazard (the existence of insurance leads individuals to take less care than they otherwise would; if information were costless, the insurer could specify the actions to be taken by the insured); and adverse selection (only the worse risks apply for the insurance; again, if information were costless, the firm could screen good from bad prospects). It has indeed been shown recently that, with costly information, the assumption of a full set of

---

[9] One important reason for the non-existence of futures markets is that the agents potentially involved may not be alive.

[10] This is an example of the difficulties that arise with heterogeneous capital in dynamic models—see Hahn (1966).

markets is *inconsistent* with market equilibrium (Grossman and Stiglitz, 1976). For were there a full set of markets, all information would be revealed by the prices established on those markets, in which case individuals would have no incentive to obtain the information. In the same way, imperfect information is likely to be related to market imperfections; for example, there are fundamental non-convexities associated with the use and production of knowledge.

Finally, there is the assumption implicit in our earlier discussion that a competitive equilibrium is attained. As we have seen in Lecture 7, this may be problematical, and much of macroeconomic policy is directed at disequilibrium in factor markets, in the balance of payments, etc. Although stabilization policy is not our concern in this book, the existence of these obviously serious problems, problems that do not arise within the competitive equilibrium framework, serves again to alert us to the inadequacy of that framework.

11-4 STANDARD PUBLIC FINANCE OBJECTIVES

In this section we examine the relationship between the social welfare function approach to the choice of policies for the efficient frontier and the way in which the trade-off has typically been represented in the public finance literature.

Vertical Equity

It is conventional to distinguish between vertical and horizontal equity, the latter being concerned with the treatment of people who are in all relevant respects identical, and the former with the treatment of unequals. We begin with vertical equity.

The treatment of vertical equity objectives here is in the "ability to pay" tradition.[11] A wide variety of concepts of ability to pay have been advanced but of these the utilitarian approach, translated into a theory of marginal sacrifice, was particularly influential, as illustrated by the writing of Edgeworth (1897), Carver (1904) and later Pigou (1947). Applied to the problem of raising a specified revenue by taxation where pre-tax incomes were assumed fixed, maximization of the Benthamite social welfare function $\Gamma_B = U_1 + U_2 + \ldots + U_H$ led to striking conclusion that after-tax incomes should be equalized.

---

[11] For a detailed historical review of this, and the "benefit", approach, see Musgrave (1959), Chs 4 and 5.

This application of the utilitarian principle has often been regarded as an argument for pursuing egalitarian policies, and there is still a widespread belief that utilitarianism is synonymous with the egalitarian principle described earlier. This impression is however quite misleading. There is nothing inherent in the Benthamite social welfare function, Γ_B, that leads to equal utilities. This is brought out clearly by the example of the last section.[12] In Fig. 11-3 the social welfare function Γ_B is maximized on the segment QM (note that the downward slope of the straight line segment is less than 1).

The utilitarian solution is not only away from the egalitarian 45° line, but actually involves a reversal of ranking. The people of type 1 are worse off than type 2 in the competitive equilibrium (i.e. at N), but in the Benthamite solution they are better off than type 2. The reason for this is straightforward. Since they are both equally efficient "consumers", they receive exactly the same consumption level in the Benthamite solution; but it costs the more productive individual less loss in leisure to produce a given quantity of output, and he is required to work more. In this situation there would be an incentive for people of type 2 to disguise their higher earning capacity. People with the ability to earn w_2 ($> w_1$) would gain in terms of after-tax utility from taking the less well paid (before tax) jobs. If they act strategically in that way, then the utilitarian point is not attainable. It may therefore be necessary to formulate the problem as constrained by the condition that such strategic behaviour will not be advantageous.

It is clear that if the social welfare function is a symmetric and strictly quasi-concave function of individual utilities, this leads to a social optimum between the Benthamite solution and E (again, strategic considerations are relevant). In a loose sense, increasing the "concavity" of the function brings the welfare optimum closer to the egalitarian position. This may be represented by taking higher values of v in the isoelastic function (11-3), with $v \to \infty$ yielding the Rawlsian case. The latter coincides in this example with the equal utility outcome, but, as we have noted in relation to Fig. 11-1, this is not necessarily the case.

Public Policy and Interpersonal Comparability

Some readers will no doubt object strongly to much of the normative analysis of Part Two on the grounds that it makes unwarranted assumptions about the comparability of individual welfares. The great contribution of the New Welfare Economics over the earlier utilitarian analysis of Bentham, Mill, Sidgwick, and Edgeworth was to examine the

---

[12] This aspect of the utilitarian principle is frequently obscured in textbooks by the practice of drawing the utility possibility frontier as symmetric. In that case, of course, the frontier has slope -1 at $U_1 = U_2$ and the utilitarian solution is egalitarian.

consequences of not being able to make interpersonal utility comparisons. The New Welfare Economics was concerned with what economists could say without making such comparisons. Thus, in this view, the "New Public Economics", as represented by Part Two of this book, is a reversion to original sin.

The analysis of Part Two can be looked at in two different ways. On the one hand, the New Welfare Economics does not provide sufficient guidance for public policy decisions—it does not allow a complete ranking of all policies. In practice, governments have to choose between Pareto-efficient outcomes, and only the most die-hard conservative would reject all policies that made any one worse off. As Dalton recognized, "this is a difficult calculus, but statesmen must handle it as best they can, since there is no practical alternative" (1954, p. 142).

If public policy analysis has to take account of the fact that any project (tax) will benefit some people and make others worse off, then a natural procedure is to present the effects on different groups. Thus, policy may be debated in terms of the effect on "the poor" or "the rich". This is usually, however, far from systematic, and often involves inessential discontinuities, e.g., employing an arbitrary cut-off when measuring the extent of poverty. The treatment in Part Two in terms of social welfare may be viewed as an attempt to examine systematically the effects on different groups, relating the "weight" attached to individuals to their income (or other indicator). At the same time, this highlights the importance of ascertaining the sensitivity of the "optimum" policy to the choice of weights, and of the comparison of the conclusions reached with different social welfare functions.

The second way in which the analysis of Part Two may be viewed is as an extension of the incidence analysis of Part One; in particular, the analysis of taxation on the distribution of income. As we commented there, a complete incidence analysis would specify the effect of any tax policy on every individual in the economy, but such an approach, even were it practicable, would not be of much use for public policy purposes, and the information, once obtained, would undoubtedly be reduced to some summary statistics. The social welfare functions we employ in Part Two can be seen as forms of summary statistics, embedding both judgements about the distribution of income and trade-offs between "mean income" and inequality. Again, a complete ranking can be achieved only at the cost of specifying a particular form of the function, and different views about social welfare may lead to different conclusions. (For discussion in the context of measuring the inequality of income, see the Note at the end of this Lecture.)

In brief, the purpose of these Lectures is to contribute to the understanding of the arguments made concerning public policy; for better or worse, these arguments are commonly framed (either explicitly or implicitly) in terms of social welfare maximization.

Horizontal Equity

The approach adopted to the interpersonal comparability issue involves the assumption that individuals with the same observed characteristics, such as income, can be deemed to have the same level of welfare. Where people have the same indifference curves, this is—given the basic premise —relatively straightforward. It is natural to assign the same utility level to the same indifference curve for each person. In much of the analysis of Part Two this will be the case. We should however recognize the difficulties that arise when individuals differ in their preferences, so that their indifference curves cross. There is then no clear way of relating the indifference curves of individual 1 to those of individual 2, but the normalization adopted may have a significant effect on the desired pattern of government intervention.

This brings us to the question of horizontal equity. The principle of horizontal equity states that those who are in all relevant senses identical should be treated identically. The implementation of this principle raises several issues. The first is the definition of "relevant". The spirit of the principle can be illustrated by examples where agreement is clear; e.g., taxes should not be discriminatory according to hair colour or religion. However, there is undoubtedly scope for differences of opinion, and historically standards have altered. For instance, views are changing as to whether marital status should be an admissible distinguishing characteristic. Second, the meaning of equal treatment may need careful definition. There is widespread agreement that taxation should not differ according to sex. Yet, in their social security provisions—a special type of taxation—almost all governments engage in sex discrimination. Should women receive a pension equal to that for men (per year)? The typical response to this question is that they should, but if they do, then the actuarial benefits are unequal. (This raises the issue of *ex ante* and *ex post* welfare, taken up below.)

Let us now seek to make the principle more concrete. Suppose that individual welfare may be written as an indirect utility function, V, dependent on the taxes levied, $\mathbf{t}$, on expenditures, $\mathbf{G}$, and on characteristics. The latter are divided into those that are not regarded as admissible, γ, and those that are, $\boldsymbol{\theta}$. The implications of horizontal equity are now twofold. First, for any $\boldsymbol{\theta}$, with zero taxes and expenditure, there is a normalization for the indifference map:

$$V(\mathbf{0},\mathbf{0},\boldsymbol{\theta},\gamma) = \bar{V}(\mathbf{0},\mathbf{0},\boldsymbol{\theta}) \quad \text{all } \gamma \qquad (11\text{-}13)$$

Second, the government is constrained in levying taxes and allocating expenditure to maintain for all $\boldsymbol{\theta}$:

$$V(\mathbf{t},\mathbf{G},\boldsymbol{\theta},\gamma) = \bar{V}(\mathbf{t},\mathbf{G},\boldsymbol{\theta}) \quad \text{all } \gamma \qquad (11\text{-}14)$$

The application to indirect taxation is discussed in Lecture 12.

Relationship Between Horizontal and Vertical Equity

The formulation given above of the horizontal equity objective leads one to ask how this relates to the goal of vertical equity. There are in fact several interpretations of the relationship.

The first is that horizontal equity is simply an implication of the more general principle of welfare maximization. This was stated explicitly by Pigou: "tax arrangements that conform to the principle of least sacrifice always and necessarily conform also to the principle of equal sacrifice among similar and similarly situated persons" (1947, p. 45). A more recent example is provided by Musgrave and Musgrave: "both equity rules [horizontal and vertical] follow from the same principle" (1976, p. 216n).

The reasoning underlying this view has been set out by Feldstein:

> With the assumption that individuals all have the same utility function, the principle of horizontal equity requires nothing more than that individuals with the same consumption bundle (including leisure) should pay the same tax....*Since violation of this condition would reduce aggregate social welfare*, the equal taxation of equals is implied directly by utilitarianism and does not require a separate principle of horizontal equity. [Feldstein, 1976d, p. 82—our italics]

Feldstein goes on to argue that this breaks down when there is diversity of tastes, but even without introducing this complication the argument may be

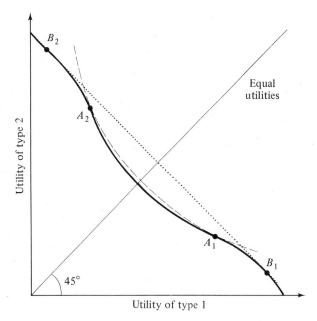

Figure 11-4 Differential treatment of identical individuals.

shown to be incorrect. If tastes are identical, the equal treatment of equals is still not necessarily implied by welfare maximization—the italicized statement in the quotation does not always hold. In particular, where the feasible set is non-convex, treating otherwise identical individuals differently may increase social welfare (Atkinson and Stiglitz, 1976). Diagrammatically, this is illustrated by the case shown in Fig. 11-4. If the feasible set has the (symmetric) shape drawn, and the social welfare contour is as indicated (again symmetric), then differential treatment raises aggregate social welfare. Moreover, it is possible to show that, with excise taxes, the feasible set may indeed have the shape shown, even when the utility functions and production functions are well behaved.

This brings us to the second view of horizontal equity—that it is an independent principle of justice, which has to be set into the balance alongside maximization of welfare. Although not usually made explicit, this appears to be what lies behind many treatments of the subject. The translation of the principle into an explicit measure has not however been widely attempted. Johnson and Mayer (1962), for example, discuss a number of possibilities, as does Feldstein (1976d), but the measures proposed lack a clear-cut rationale. Moreover, we have to recognize that the principle of horizontal equity accords a particular ethical status to the pre-intervention distribution. The principle is thus in harmony with the minimal state and unanimity approaches, but less acceptable to those who see the end-state as being the sole matter for concern. If government policy is evaluated by a social welfare function, this depends solely on post-intervention welfares.

The third interpretation casts the principle in a rather different form, viewing it as a restriction on instruments rather than as based on a comparison of distributions. This treats horizontal equity as "a safeguard against capricious discrimination" (Musgrave, 1959, p. 160). Taxation related to irrelevant characteristics, such as race or religion, is thereby precluded, as is the allocation of expenditure on such a basis. On this interpretation, the relationship between horizontal and vertical equity is lexicographic. The former imposes certain restrictions on the instruments open to the government, and vertical equity is then pursued subject to these prior constraints.

These three interpretations of horizontal equity are rather different. The first and second are concerned with the *results* of policy; the third is concerned with the *means* used to achieve the results. The first has the same informational requirements as the social welfare function of the vertical equity objective; the second requires at least the measurement of welfare differences; the third—in contrast—does not require any knowledge of individual welfares. Thus, the third interpretation is one that remains open even if one rejects any form of comparison (between people or between states).

Ex Ante and *Ex Post* **Considerations**

In the presence of uncertainty, the question arises as to whether we are concerned with *ex ante* or *ex post* optimality. This is clearly illustrated by the example shown in Fig. 11-4. Suppose that the government set the instruments of policy such that either A_1 or A_2 would be attained, each with a probability of one-half. This "randomization" of government policy means that, if both types of individual have a correct perception of the probabilities, then they have equal expected utility. In terms of expected utility, we have secured horizontal equity. Geometrically, with the axes measuring expected utility, we are at the point on A_1A_2 where it crosses the 45° line. Furthermore, expected utility could be increased by taking the common tangent to the frontier with slope -1, i.e., choosing one of B_1 or B_2 with probability with one-half (see the dotted line in Fig. 11-4). The policy that maximizes expected social welfare is therefore different from the one that measures welfare *ex post* (i.e., after the policy is decided).

In some writing on welfare economics, it has been assumed that *ex ante* welfare is the natural objective function; others would argue that the *ex ante* criterion is unacceptable and even, indeed, unconstitutional as a basis for taxation. The position adopted clearly depends on the extent to which one is willing to respect individual (1) attitudes to risk and (2) subjective probabilities. Thus, there may be someone who expects with certainty (but wrongly) that the world will end on 1 January next year, and therefore plans to have no consumption in that year. An *ex ante* criterion may appear in this case rather harsh.

In what follows, these problems will be side-stepped. The models employed do not typically include intrinsic uncertainty (a feature that is not of course satisfactory, but reflects the state of the art). The generation of uncertainty via "random" government policy is assumed to be ruled out on the grounds that this violates the third interpretation of horizontal equity ("capricious discrimination").

11-5 RANGE OF GOVERNMENT INSTRUMENTS

Limits on Lump-sum Taxes and Transfers

In the Second Theorem set out in Section 11-3, a key role is played by lump-sum taxes and transfers. The ability to attain a chosen point on the utility possibility frontier depends on the capacity to make lump-sum redistributions (as the example shows). Yet it is generally agreed that such taxes and transfers are extremely difficult to devise. Graaff, for example, argues that lump-sum measures are:

> not very helpful in securing desired redistributions unless we tax different men differently. But on what criteria should we discriminate between different men?... If we start taxing

the poor less than the rich, we are simply reintroducing an income-tax. If we tax able men more than dunderheads, we open the door to all forms of falsification: we make stupidity seem profitable—and any able man can make himself seem stupid. [Graaff, 1957, p. 78]

This last point is illustrated by the example given earlier. Suppose that the government tries to tax those doing type 2 jobs to make transfer payments to those doing type 1, so as to attain F in Fig. 11-3. Since at that point $U_1 > U_2$, all type 2 people would seek the lower paying type 1 job. (This strategic aspect has already been discussed in relation to the utilitarian objective.)

The basic difficulty is again that the information on which we would like to base differential lump-sum taxes is not observable, or is observable only at great cost, and individuals have an incentive not to reveal it. For these reasons, lump-sum taxes and transfers are widely assumed not to be available.[13]

This is a position that has to be adopted with caution. First, it is necessary to make explicit the reasons for ruling out lump-sum measures, and the view that this implies about the information available to the government. Thus, in the example given earlier we may assume that the government cannot levy a lump-sum tax related to earning capacity (w_i). Is it then inconsistent to suppose that it can levy an income tax on $w_i L_i$ (as we do in Lectures 13 and 14)? It can be argued that, with knowledge of the labour supply function, earning capacity can be deduced from income, and hence that observability of income implies that lump-sum taxes could be employed. The resolution of this apparent inconsistency lies in the status of different kinds of information. In particular, information concerning the labour supply function is typically based on statistical evidence (e.g., from sample surveys), and not on direct observation for the individual. Whereas the design of tax policy may make use of such evidence (ideally treating it as a statistical observation), it is generally accepted that the operation of the tax system must be framed in terms of variables observed for the individual; i.e., the tax function must be a function (in our example) of ($w_i L_i$). This may

---

[13] The assumption that lump-sum taxes are infeasible has been criticized by Hahn:

Somehow the belief has grown up amongst economists that lump-sum taxes and fees, etc., are simply impractical for unexplained reasons. But this is both unsatisfactory and hasty. The Poll Tax Act of 1660 taxed dukes at £100, earls at £60, baronets at £30, squires at £10....It levied a fee of £100 on archbishops and of £40 on dons. It taxed every £100 worth of land, money or stock at £2...the government has no less information than the 17th century legislators; indeed, it has a good deal more. What is stopping them from using appropriate instruments? [Hahn, 1973, p. 106]

His historical interpretation is not however totally convincing, since many elements of the Poll Tax were not lump-sum. This is illustrated by the tax on land, money or stock referred to in the quotation, and by such facts as that the payment by clergy was subject to a minimum income qualification and that hackney coach-keepers paid a certain amount for each coach and pair (Kennedy, 1913).

be regarded as a prior horizontal equity constraint which, in the absence of observations of L_i (or w_i) for all individuals, precludes the use of lump-sum taxes. This assumption may be questioned, but in the Lectures that follow we assume that it holds.

The second reason why the exclusion of lump-sum measures needs to be treated cautiously is that it may be possible to levy some kinds of lump-sum tax or transfer. There is a significant difference between limiting the freedom to levy any arbitrary pattern of taxes and ruling out *all* lump-sum measures.[14] In the example, we may preclude taxes based on w_i, but allow for a uniform lump-sum tax or transfer. Indeed, one of the major points made in our discussion of the optimal tax problem is that, by arbitrarily omitting the possibility of a poll tax, much of the literature is concerned with an artificial problem. The introduction of the poll tax, which is effectively embodied in nearly all income tax schedules, leads to substantial changes in the results.

Design of Policy as a Second-Best Problem

The solution that can be achieved where lump-sum taxes and transfers are freely variable is usually referred to as the *first-best*. In contrast, the solution where there are binding constraints on the use of lump-sum measures is referred to as the *second-best*. These second-best problems can be viewed as problems of indirect control. The government might like to control directly the levels of consumption and labour supply of each individual, but it cannot. It must resort to a variety of instruments that affect individual behaviour; i.e., it attempts to control behaviour indirectly. But these instruments are not perfect substitutes for direct control, and the equilibrium attained will thus necessarily be different.

The second-best utility possibility frontier depends on the instruments available, but typically it lies inside that for the first-best (except at the no intervention point N). This is illustrated in Fig. 11-5 for the case where the government may employ a linear income tax, with tax rate t and uniform grant per person G. The details of the construction are left as an exercise.

Exercise 11-2 Where the government levies a linear income tax, the budget constraint for a person of type i becomes

$$X_i = w_i(1-t)L_i + G \qquad (11\text{-}14a)$$

Describe the utility possibility frontier in the model of page 344 as the tax rate is varied ($0 \leqslant t < 1$), subject to the revenue constraint

$$t(w_1 L_1 + w_2 L_2) = 2G \qquad (11\text{-}15)$$

---

[14] Conversely, the demonstration that some lump-sum taxes have been employed (as in Hahn's argument in fn.[13]) does not imply that any combination of taxes could be effected.

Sketch the frontier for the values $a = 1/3$, $w_1 = 1$, $w_2 = 3/2$. Does the frontier intersect the 45° line?

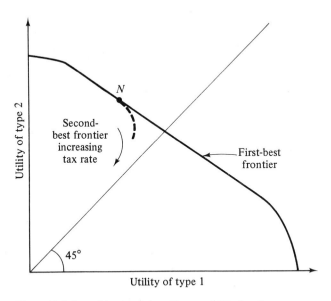

Figure 11-5 Second-best and the utility possibility frontier.

Where first-best instruments are not available, the government has to decide on the policies that can attain a second-best solution. Thus, it may use income taxation to redistribute according to unobserved endowments, or it may seek to design mechanisms to elicit unobserved preferences concerning public goods. The problem is in general terms one of selecting observable characteristics to which taxation and spending may be related in such a way as to achieve as far as possible the desired relation with the unobservable characteristics in which we are really interested. It may thus be seen as part of what has come to be called the "theory of screening" (for example, Spence, 1973, and Stiglitz, 1975a). The literature on screening has identified the following problems, all of which have their counterparts in the field of public economics:

1. the characteristics used for screening are to some extent under the control of the individual (e.g., wage rates, where the individual may choose his job);
2. the surrogate characteristics employed for screening are not perfectly correlated with the characteristics with which we are concerned;
3. there are costs (e.g., of administration) in observing characteristics.

The last of these considerations is one that we discuss relatively little in these Lectures. It is not that we feel that it is unimportant—quite the contrary—but little formal analysis has been undertaken (exceptions are Heller and Shell, 1974, and Stern, 1977). At an informal level we may note that there are likely to be substantial set-up costs in administration, and this is likely to lead to specialization in a subset of screening devices. On the other hand, the distortionary effect may increase rapidly with the size of the programme, arguing for diversification (this is the Kaldor argument for a large number of taxes each at a low rate). Moreover, the employment of additional devices may improve the correlation with the underlying unobserved characteristic. There may well be a trade-off between more accurate screening and the costs of observation.

It is the first and second problems that receive most attention in these Lectures. These may be seen, in loose terms, as concerned with achieving as far as possible the redistributional goals (consideration (2)) with the least distortionary effect on behaviour (consideration (1)). Thus, the government may be seen as designing the income tax schedule to balance the gain in distributional equity against the costs in terms of distorted decisions about work effort, the allocation of effort, savings, risk-taking, etc. The distinction between equity and efficiency is in a sense artificial, since both are subsumed in the objective of maximizing social welfare. None the less, the two concepts do feature prominently in public discussions of policy, the separation being exemplified by Musgrave's allocation and distribution branches (1959). We shall therefore refer to these concepts in later Lectures, and provide a more precise interpretation.

Choice of Instruments

Much of the literature has been concerned with the structure of a particular policy measure (for purposes of exposition, we concentrate on taxation), for example, the choice of rates for indirect taxes or the degree of progression for the income tax. However, it is helpful to employ a more general framework, which starts with the choice *between instruments*.

In order to explore this, let us suppose that the utility of households is a function of their consumption vector, $\mathbf{X}$, their labour supply, L, and their characteristics, γ. They maximize

$$U(\mathbf{X}, L, \gamma)$$

subject to the budget constraint:

$$\mathbf{p} \cdot \mathbf{X} = Y(L, w) - T \tag{11-16}$$

where $\mathbf{p}$ denotes the prices of goods, T is the tax levied, and Y gives their income as a function of labour supplied and endowments, w.

The tax instruments open to the government depend on what it can observe. Suppose first that it observes the amounts *consumed* of **X**. It can then impose a complicated nonlinear indirect tax schedule, where the tax function, $T(\mathbf{X})$, need not even be separable, i.e., so that the marginal tax rate on cigarettes might depend on the amount of alcohol consumed. More commonly, we observe the amounts purchased in the market but not the amounts consumed. If transfers between individuals outside the market are easily conducted, then we are effectively restricted to employing taxes with a constant marginal rate (otherwise the individual facing the lowest marginal tax rate will do all the purchasing).[15] In the special case where lump-sum taxes are not allowed ($T(\mathbf{0}) = 0$), this reduces to the classic Ramsey tax problem discussed in Lecture 12. Where a uniform lump-sum tax is allowed ($T(\mathbf{0})$ = constant for all w, γ), this is equivalent to the problem of an optimal excise tax in the presence of a linear income tax.

From this formulation, one can see naturally the choice between indirect and direct taxation. If the solution to the optimal indirect tax problem entails a uniform rate on all commodities, this is equivalent to a proportional expenditure tax. In this model, with no savings, this is in turn equivalent to a proportional income tax. On the other hand, if there are differential tax rates, the government will wish to impose both an income tax and indirect taxes, since the latter add an effective screening device.

When the direct tax is non-proportional, the position may change. The first stage is the introduction of a poll tax or subsidy element, so that the tax is linear but not proportional. This, as we see in Lecture 14, may lead to quite different conclusions. The second stage is the introduction of a nonlinear schedule, with varying marginal tax rates. This increases the effectiveness of the direct tax, and there is a significant class of situations where indirect taxation proves to be unnecessary. On the other hand, the scope for varying marginal rates depends again on observability. In particular, where the tax rates become very different, there exist strong incentives to rearrange incomes among members of a family or close friends. The scope for this is especially great for self-employed individuals and closely held firms, which are important in the upper ranges of the income distribution. Thus, if a wife's earnings are taxed independently, it pays a husband to employ his wife; if a child's income is taxed separately, transfer from the parent may avoid high marginal tax rates.

Income and expenditure are not the only possible screening devices; there are others that might be used either in conjunction with or instead of these taxes. Thus, in the framework used in Lecture 13, we assume that income, Y, can be written (before tax) as the product of the wage, w, and the number of hours, L. But the wage itself is a function of the individual's

---

[15] The scope for observing consumption (as opposed to purchase) depends very much on the character of the good; a nonlinear tax on cigarettes is probably infeasible; a nonlinear tax or subsidy on housing seems possible (although if the marginal tax rate differentials are large, there is the possibility of non-market transactions here too).

ability and effort, and may therefore be a better surrogate for ability than is income, when it is observable (for self-employed individuals, it clearly is not).[16] A rather different set of screening devices are individual characteristics that are relatively costless to observe, such as age and sex. These provide non-distortionary tax bases; there are other characteristics, such as marital status and family size, that are probably unaltered by taxation when the differentiation is low but that, when tax differentials are high, may become both distorted and costly to observe and monitor. In what follows we do not give particular attention to these characteristics, although they raise a number of important issues (e.g., the tax treatment of family size).

For a complete theory of the choice of tax base, a fully articulated model is necessary of the information available to the government and of the costs of observing the different characteristics. We do not try to develop such a theory here—there are a number of evident difficulties in doing so—and in subsequent Lectures we assume that only particular classes of instruments are available. At the same time, we hope that the discussion above has indicated qualitatively some of the features likely to emerge from a more complete treatment.

Political Constraints on the Choice of Policies

The feasibility of instruments has been discussed so far in terms of the costs of obtaining information; a second aspect, and one that is closely related, is that of political feasibility. As we have emphasized, the design of policy must be discussed within the context of the actual machinery of government. Not only are the arguments concerning different policies themselves a component of the political process, but also, in assessing them we must recognize the existence of constraints:

> "Optimal taxes" will only be put into practice if they are acceptable within the politico-economic process. This aspect must be analysed explicitly...because otherwise one may end up with the "optimal tax" proposals being completely distorted in the democratic process, or, even more likely, to remain a discussion topic among some academic economists. [Frey, 1976, p. 32]

These considerations have not played a major role in the mainstream of public finance, and for this reason the work discussed in the following Lectures (including that of the authors) is open to criticism. There are several ways however in which we can introduce the constraints imposed by the positive theories of the state. First, attaching weight to the electoral

---

[16] If we assumed that the wage is just a function of ability, then the observability of the wage would imply that we could obtain a first-best solution. As noted earlier, in the second-best case we are in effect assuming that L is not observed for each individual (although there is statistical information), so that w cannot be deduced from Y.

theories of government behaviour, we may consider the preferences of voters (majority voting over tax rates is discussed briefly in Lecture 13). Such preferences may reflect not just the impact of the tax system on the person's budget constraint, but also his attitudes to different kinds of taxation; i.e., the tax variables may enter the *direct* utility function. For example, it has been suggested that taxpayers or politicians may prefer "invisible" indirect taxes to direct taxes.[17] Dalton distinguished between "the subjective and the objective burden of taxation" (1954, p. 34), although he argued, with the authority of having been Chancellor of the Exchequer, that "the primary consideration is the objective burden, as measured by a given loss of resources to a taxpayer" (1954, p. 35).[18] (The awareness of taxes may also affect the speed of response to different kinds of tax structure.)

The view of the state as a bureaucracy pursuing its own objectives, with only limited control by the electorate or legislature, leads to a different formulation of the social decision. The determination of fiscal policy may then be seen as a two-stage process. Society (the electorate or Congress) determines the broad structure of the tax and expenditure system; it is then put into effect by the administrative agencies which determine the detailed operation.[19] The pursuit of social welfare is therefore constrained by the assumption that a programme will be administered in such a way as to further the goals of the agency, subject to certain (incomplete) controls. The government may then determine that there should be a broad based tax, such as the value added tax, but that the revenue raised will reflect the objectives of the collecting agencies. Alternatively, the government may agree to the principle of differentiation of indirect taxes, but the resulting pattern of tax rates may reflect the relative power of different interest groups rather than welfare maximization. This line of approach has not been very fully articulated to date, although the work of Brennan and Buchanan (1977, 1978) on the revenue-maximizing Leviathan is suggestive.

Consideration of the constraints on policy changes may lead to a more modest objective than social welfare maximization. The arguments may be made, not in terms of optimality, but in terms of welfare improvements. The

---

[17] As it is rather nicely put by the Marquis Garnier in his introduction to the French translation of *The Wealth of Nations*:

> C'est au milieu de la profusion des repas que se paient les taxes sur le vin, la bière, la sucre, le sel, et les articles de ce genre, et le trésor public trouve un source de gain dans les provocations à la dépense qui sont excitées par l'abandon et la gaieté des fêtes. [Garnier, 1822, CXV]

[18] For discussion of taxpayer attitudes, see, among others, Strümpel (1969) and Schmölders (1977).

[19] The social optimization in fact involves *three* levels of analysis: the choice by the government, the administrative decision of the agency, and the response of the private sector.

aim is to characterize changes that are in the right direction. This approach, which involves a relatively straightforward modification of the analysis, is discussed in the next Lecture.

Finally, it should be noted that, in concentrating on the uses of *distributional* incidence, we ignore many of the questions of incidence in terms of factor prices which were central to the discussion of Part One. Thus, in order to focus on certain aspects, such as the effect on the distribution of after-tax welfare, we employ simple general equilibrium models where, for example, before-tax wages are unaffected by taxation. In any complete assessment of the desirability of particular policies, the two parts of the analysis need to be brought together.

NOTE ON THE MEASUREMENT OF INCOME INEQUALITY

In empirical work on the redistributive impact of government policy (as discussed in Lecture 9), summary measures of income inequality, such as the Gini coefficient, have been widely used. In such applications, it is typically assumed that income may be taken as an indicator of individual welfare (although in theory any single dimensioned indicator, cardinal up to a linear transformation, could be employed). We are in effect concerned therefore with a welfare function $\Gamma(Y^1, \ldots, Y^H)$, where Y^h denotes the income of household h, and it is assumed that Γ is symmetric and strictly quasi-concave (in fact this can be weakened to s-concavity—see Sen, 1973). Suppose further that we are considering pure redistributions of a given total of income. Then the results of Kolm (1969) and Atkinson (1970) allow us to characterize the class of distributions that can be ranked without specifying further the form of Γ: a distribution **Y** is preferred to a distribution **Y*** (with the same mean) according to all symmetric and strictly quasi-concave social welfare functions if and only if the Lorenz curve for **Y** lies inside. that of **Y***. Thus, if distributional values are not sufficiently well formulated to allow us to take a single social welfare function, and any function (subject to symmetry and quasi-concavity) might find support, then we can only reach unambiguous conclusions where the Lorenz curves do not intersect.

This result provides some insight into the implications of using summary measures, like the coefficient of variation employed in Lecture 9, but it is limited in two respects that are important here. First, the Lorenz condition provides only a partial ordering of outcomes, whereas for many purposes a complete ordering is required. Second, the assumptions about the class of redistributions considered imply that social welfare is maximized where incomes are equalized. Where the possibility frontier does not have this property, then the approach needs reconsideration.

The analysis of the measurement of inequality has perhaps been most useful in suggesting ways in which attitudes towards redistribution may be parameterized, as has been done with the social welfare function (11-3) with the parameter v.

READING

The basic theorems of welfare economics are covered in textbooks on general equilibrium, including Arrow and Hahn (1971), Malinvaud (1972), Varian (1978). The role of imperfect information is discussed in Stiglitz (1975b, 1980). On economic inequality and its relation to concepts of justice, see Sen (1973). An interesting treatment of the formulation of government fiscal policy is provided (in French) by Kolm (1971).

TWELVE

THE STRUCTURE OF INDIRECT TAXATION

12-1 INTRODUCTION

In most countries excise taxes are levied on commodities at different rates. This is certainly true in the United States, where the rates of taxation vary widely. In European countries there has been a move towards uniformity of tax rates with the introduction of a value added tax (VAT). In the United Kingdom, VAT replaced a purchase tax which had rates varying from 50 per cent on items such as jewellery and cameras to $12\frac{1}{2}$ per cent on clothing, footwear and furniture. Even with VAT, however, differential rates have been maintained in most countries, and typically quite a wide range of goods have a zero rate. The rationale for these systems of indirect taxation, and for the changes made, needs however to be examined. Are there good reasons for taxing goods at different rates? Is the move in European countries towards a more uniform structure of indirect taxation desirable on efficiency or distributional grounds?

According to conventional wisdom, there is a definite preference for a uniform rate structure, and this view appears to influence government policy-making. The British Government, when announcing the introduction of a value added tax, claimed that:

> a more broadly-based structure..., by discriminating less between different types of goods and services, would reduce the distortion of consumer choice.... Selective taxation gives rise to distortion of trade and of personal consumption patterns, and can lead to the inefficient allocation of resources. [HMSO, 1971, p. 3]

This case is based on efficiency considerations; i.e., that a differentiated structure has greater distortionary effects. A second, and quite different, argument for a uniform system of taxation is that of equity between consumers: "a general sales tax or added-value tax on all expenditure at a single rate...would be fair as everyone would pay the same tax on all their expenditure" (Wheatcroft, 1969, p. 26). Similarly, "non-uniformity results in discrimination against those people having particular preference for the more heavily taxed goods" (Due, 1963, p. 285).

In assessing these arguments for uniform taxation, it is helpful to discuss the efficiency and equity aspects separately, since the considerations involved are different. For this reason we focus in the first part (Sections 12-1–12-4) of this lecture on a model where all individuals are identical, and are assumed to be treated identically.[1] No redistributional issues therefore arise, and we concentrate on the efficiency question as to whether, from the allocational standpoint, a uniform tax is preferable to a differentiated structure. This question is first discussed in the context of the partial equilibrium framework used in most textbooks and then extended to a general equilibrium treatment in Sections 12-2–12-4. In Section 12-5, distributional considerations are introduced and the balance between equity and efficiency considered.

Partial Equilibrium Analysis

In contrast to the view of the British Government, the standard textbook analysis of the structure of indirect taxation suggests that uniform rates are not in fact necessarily desirable from an efficiency standpoint. In this section, we show how this can be demonstrated by a simple partial equilibrium analysis,[2] where there are no cross-price effects and relevant income derivatives are zero.

Let us assume that the supply of good k is perfectly elastic at price p_k, so that the equilibrium in the absence of taxation is at point E in Fig. 12-1. The effect of an *ad valorem* tax at rate t_k is to raise the consumer price from p_k to $p_k(1+t_k)$. The after-tax equilibrium is at point B. In this partial equilibrium framework the distortion caused by the tax is often measured by the loss of consumer surplus over and above the revenue raised, the "excess burden". If we take the area $ABECD$ as a measure of the loss of consumer surplus, the excess burden is represented by the shaded area BCE. Let us denote the consumer price by q_k and write the demand curve, following Marshall, as $q_k(X_k)$. The excess burden caused by the tax on good k may then be seen from Fig. 12-1 to equal:

$$B_k \equiv \int_{X_k^t}^{X_k^0} q_k \, dX_k - p_k(X_k^0 - X_k^t) \tag{12-1}$$

Area $BEFGC$ − area $CEFG$

---

[1] The reason why this is an assumption and not an implication is explained below in the section on horizontal equity.

[2] See, for example, Hicks (1947, Ch. X). For a more formal argument, which draws attention to the limitation of her analysis, see Bishop (1968).

where X_k^0 denotes the equilibrium quantity before the tax is introduced, X_k^t that after the tax is introduced. From this it follows that

$$\frac{\partial B_k}{\partial t_k} = -q_k \frac{\partial X_k^t}{\partial t_k} + p_k \frac{\partial X_k^t}{\partial t_k} = -p_k t_k \frac{\partial X_k^t}{\partial t_k} \tag{12-2}$$

where the term in q_k arises from differentiating the lower limit of integration and the second step follows from the fact that $q_k = p_k(1 + t_k)$. The excess burden is therefore zero for infinitesimal taxes (i.e., evaluating at $t_k = 0$). As noted by Samuelson (1964a), all consumer surplus terms are of second order.

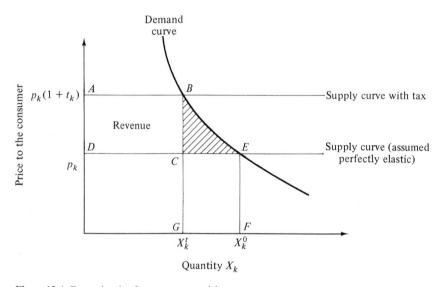

Figure 12-1 Excess burden from tax on good k.

Suppose now that the government chooses the tax rates on different goods $(t_1, \ldots, t_n)$ in such a way as to raise a specified revenue with the minimum total excess burden. The revenue condition is properly seen in terms of the government's purchasing a fixed amount of real commodities (government spending), but with fixed producer prices we can treat it as a financial constraint:

$$R \equiv \sum_{k=1}^{n} t_k p_k X_k^t = R_0 \tag{12-3}$$

where R_0 is the required level. This constrained maximization problem may be formulated in terms of the Lagrangean:

$$\mathscr{L} = -\sum_{k=1}^{n} B_k + \lambda(R - R_0) \tag{12-4}$$

The first-order conditions for the choice of t_k are therefore

$$\frac{\partial B_k}{\partial t_k} = \lambda \frac{\partial R}{\partial t_k} = \lambda p_k X_k^t + \lambda p_k t_k \frac{\partial X_k^t}{\partial t_k} \quad \text{for all } k \qquad (12\text{-}5)$$

Combining this with Eq. (12-2), we obtain

$$\frac{-t_k}{X_k^t} \frac{\partial X_k^t}{\partial t_k} = \frac{\lambda}{1+\lambda} \qquad (12\text{-}6)$$

or[3]

$$\frac{t_k}{1+t_k} = \frac{\theta}{\varepsilon_k^d} \qquad (12\text{-}7)$$

where θ is equal to $\lambda/(1+\lambda)$ and ε_k^d is the elasticity of demand for good k.

A solution satisfying these first-order conditions (the precise status of these conditions is discussed in Section 12-2) involves therefore the tax rate on good k being in inverse proportion to the price elasticity of demand. In the extreme case of a good demanded completely inelastically (or a factor supplied by households completely inelastically), the excess burden is zero and all revenue, or as much as feasible, should be raised by taxing this commodity. Apart from this, the optimal tax structure can be uniform only where all goods have the same elasticity of demand. In general, "the best way of raising a given revenue...is by a system of taxes, under which the rates become progressively higher as we pass from uses of very elastic demand or supply to uses where demand or supply are progressively less elastic" (Pigou, 1947, p. 105) (although we have not discussed the case where *supply* is less than perfectly elastic—see Lecture 15).[4]

This finding, although typically reported in public finance texts, is often regarded with considerable scepticism. Musgrave relegates it to a footnote

---

[3] This step may be seen if we rewrite the left-hand side as

$$\left(\frac{t_k}{1+t_k}\right)\left[\frac{p_k(1+t_k)}{X_k^t}\right]\left[-\frac{\partial X_k^t}{\partial p_k(1+t_k)}\right]$$

which equals $t_k/(1+t_k)$ times the elasticity of demand. The reader may like to compare this condition with the choice of $(1-\alpha)$, which is equivalent to a tax rate, in the capitalist's revenue-maximizing problem of Lecture 4 (cf. Eq. (4-29)), and to the price-setting condition for a monopolist, where the excess of price over marginal cost may be seen as equivalent to a tax.

[4] A further feature of the optimal tax structure may be noted in the case where the demand curve is linear: $X = a - bq$. Then

$$X_k^t - X_k^0 = -bp_k t_k$$

From (12-6), this gives

$$X_k^t - X_k^0 = -\theta X_k^t = \frac{-\theta}{1+\theta} X_k^0$$

i.e., the proportionate reduction in demand is the same for all commodities. As shown in the next section, this carries over in a weaker form to more general models.

and comments that "the theorem is arrived at within the framework of the old welfare economics of inter personal utility comparison. It belongs in the welfare view of the ability-to-pay approach and does not fit the context of the present argument" (Musgrave, 1959, p. 149n). However, Musgrave's own analysis is a special case of that described above. As pointed out by Bishop (1968, p. 212n), Musgrave's conclusion that "a general *ad valorem* tax is preferable to a system of selective excises imposed at differential rates" (Musgrave, 1959, p. 148) assumes a fixed supply of labour. The argument of the previous paragraph indicates that in this case all revenue should be raised by taxing labour; and, ignoring saving, this is equivalent to a uniform excise tax. Other writers have expressed reservations about the strength of the assumptions. Prest, for example, dismisses the results with the comment that "such restrictive assumptions have to be made in order to derive a solution, that they would appear to have little practical significance" (Prest, 1975, p. 53). However, he offers nothing in their place.

The assumptions underlying the partial equilibrium framework are indeed restrictive, requiring in effect that there be no income effects and that cross-price elasticities be zero. In the remainder of this Lecture, we adopt a general equilibrium approach, beginning with the classic paper by F. P. Ramsey, "A Contribution to the Theory of Taxation", published in the *Economic Journal* in 1927. This article provided the foundation for Pigou's discussion of the question in his textbook, and for the partial equilibrium treatment we have described.

12-2 THE RAMSEY TAX PROBLEM

The opening paragraph of Ramsey's article is worth quoting in full, since it sets out clearly the problem that had been posed to him by Pigou, and the framework within which he set about answering it:

> The problem I propose to tackle is this: a given revenue is to be raised by proportionate taxes on some or all uses of income, the taxes on different uses being possibly at different rates; how should these rates be adjusted in order that the decrement of utility may be a minimum? I propose to neglect altogether questions of distribution and considerations arising from the differences in the marginal utility of money to different people; and I shall deal only with a purely competitive system with no foreign trade. Further I shall suppose that, in Professor Pigou's terminology, private and social net products are always equal or have been made so by State interference not included in the taxation we are considering. I thus exclude the case discussed in Marshall's *Principles* in which a bounty on increasing-return commodities is advisable. Nevertheless we shall find that the obvious solution that there should be no differentiation is entirely erroneous. [Ramsey, 1927, p. 47]

The treatment here differs from that of Ramsey in certain respects, and we relax the assumptions about distribution (Section 12-5) and allow for externalities (Lecture 14). However, in this section we keep the specification as simple as possible.

The Model

Since the initial aim is to focus on efficiency considerations, it is assumed that all consumers are identical, and face identical tax rates, and that the objective of the government is to maximize the welfare of a "representative" individual. On the production side, it is assumed that there are fixed producer prices for all goods and a fixed wage rate w for labour. Labour is to be the only factor supplied by households, and they have no other source of income. Since the producer prices are fixed, we can without loss of generality set them at unity, so that the consumer price of good k is given by $q_k = 1 + t_k$.

The structure of the problem is that the government is maximizing subject to the demand and supply functions of individuals, which are themselves based on solving a constrained maximization problem. The representative consumer supplies L units of labour (where L is measured as a fraction of the working day) and consumes X_i of good i $(i = 1, \dots, n)$. He is assumed to maximize $U(\mathbf{X}, L)$ subject to the budget constraint

$$\sum_{i=1}^{n} q_i X_i = wL \tag{12-8}$$

It may be noted that there is assumed to be no tax on wage income, but if there is no other source of income for the consumer this involves no loss of generality. Suppose that a tax of τ is imposed on wage income. The consumer's budget constraint becomes

$$\sum_i q_i X_i = w(1 - \tau)L \tag{12-8'}$$

(the summation runs from 1 to n unless otherwise indicated). As far as the consumer is concerned, this is equivalent to a situation where there is no wage tax and q_i is increased to $q/(1-\tau)$; i.e., for the tax rate to become

$$t_i' = \frac{1 + t_i}{1 - \tau} - 1 = \frac{\tau + t_i}{1 - \tau} \tag{12-9}$$

The government revenue in the latter case is

$$\sum_i t_i' X_i = \sum_i \left(\frac{\tau + t_i}{1 - \tau}\right) X_i \tag{12-10}$$

which may be compared with that in the case of the wage tax:

$$\sum_i t_i X_i + \tau wL = \sum_i t_i X_i + \frac{\tau}{(1 - \tau)} \sum_i (1 + t_i) X_i = \sum_i \left(\frac{\tau + t_i}{1 - \tau}\right) X_i \tag{12-11}$$

where we have substituted for wL from (12-8′). The government revenue is also unaffected. A tax on wage income is therefore equivalent in this model to a uniform tax on all goods. This depends on the fact that there is no other source of income (such as profit income) and that we cannot tax the consumer's labour endowment (i.e., leisure).[5]

The government aims then to maximize individual welfare subject to the revenue constraint and the individual conditions for utility maximization. Following Diamond and Mirrlees (1971), the problem may conveniently be treated in terms of the indirect utility function $V(\mathbf{q}, w)$. Forming the Lagrangean

$$\mathcal{L} = V(\mathbf{q}, w) + \lambda \left(\sum_i t_i X_i - R_0 \right) \tag{12-12}$$

gives first-order conditions for the tax rate t_k

$$\frac{\partial V}{\partial q_k} = -\lambda \left(X_k + \sum_i t_i \frac{\partial X_i}{\partial q_k} \right) \quad \text{for } k = 1, \ldots, n \tag{12-13}$$

Writing α for the marginal utility of income to the consumer, and using the properties of the indirect utility function $(\partial V / \partial q_k = -\alpha X_k)$,

$$\sum_i t_i \frac{\partial X_i}{\partial q_k} = -\frac{(\lambda - \alpha)}{\lambda} X_k \quad \text{for } k = 1, \ldots, n \tag{12-14}$$

These equations may be transformed using the Slutsky relationship

$$\frac{\partial X_i}{\partial q_k} = S_{ik} - X_k \frac{\partial X_i}{\partial M} \quad \text{for all } i, k \tag{12-15}$$

where S_{ik} is the derivative of the compensated demand curve and $\partial X_i / \partial M$ denotes the income effect (evaluated at $M = 0$). Substituting, we obtain

$$\sum_i t_i S_{ik} = -\left(1 - \sum_i t_i \frac{\partial X_i}{\partial M} - \frac{\alpha}{\lambda} \right) X_k \quad \text{for } k = 1, \ldots, n \tag{12-16}$$

Using the symmetry of the Slutsky terms $(S_{ik} = S_{ki})$, and introducing θ for the coefficient of X_k in (12-16),[6]

$$\sum_i t_i S_{ki} = -\theta X_k \quad \text{for } k = 1, \ldots, n \tag{12-17}$$

---

[5] What is required is that the demand functions be homogeneous of degree zero in consumer prices. The demand functions do not have this property if the consumer receives lump-sum transfers (pays lump-sum taxes) in nominal units, or where there are profits from the production sector. See Dixit and Munk (1977).

[6] From this expression, one can see the relation with the partial equilibrium formula (12-6). If there are no income effects $(\partial X_i / \partial M = 0)$, and if $S_{ik} = 0$ for $i \neq k$, then Eq. (12-17) becomes $t_k(-S_{kk}) = \theta X_k$.

Discussion of the Results

The formulation (12-17) is due to Samuelson (1951), who gave the following interpretation: the left-hand side is the change in the demand for good k that would result if the consumer were compensated to stay on the same indifference curve and the derivatives of the compensated demand curves were constant. In fact, it is not possible for the latter condition to be satisfied for all commodities, but for small taxes it is approximately true that the optimal tax structure involves an equal proportionate movement along the compensated demand curve for all goods (since θ is independent of k).[7] The importance in this formula of the *compensated* derivatives accords with intuition: the income effect would arise with any form of taxation, and the distortion stems from the substitution effect. We may note that multiplying (12-17) by t_k and summing gives

$$\sum_k \sum_i t_k S_{ki} t_i = -\theta R_0 \qquad (12\text{-}18)$$

The left-hand side can be shown to be negative (using the negative semi-definiteness of the Slutsky matrix), so that θ has the same sign as government revenue.

A further interpretation may be given for θ by examining the effect of allowing the government to levy a lump-sum tax T. The Lagrangean then becomes

$$\mathscr{L} = V(\mathbf{q}, T) + \lambda \left(T + \sum_i t_i X_i - R_0 \right) \qquad (12\text{-}19)$$

From this we can see that, using the definition of θ,

$$\frac{\partial \mathscr{L}}{\partial T} = -\alpha + \lambda \left(1 - \sum_i t_i \frac{\partial X_i}{\partial M} \right) = \theta \lambda \qquad (12\text{-}20)$$

(since $\partial V / \partial T = -\alpha$ and $\partial X_i / \partial T = -\partial X_i / \partial M$). Now suppose that the government were allowed to make a small increase dT in the lump-sum tax (moving away from the optimum described above), where the commodity taxes are adjusted so that the revenue constraint continues to hold. Then $d\mathscr{L}/dT = \partial \mathscr{L}/\partial T$ (since $\partial \mathscr{L}/\partial t_k = 0$ for all k from the first-order conditions) and, since the revenue constraint continues to hold, $d\mathscr{L} = dV = \lambda \theta dT$. Welfare rises and θ measures the benefit *expressed in terms of revenue* from being able to switch from the (optimal) indirect tax system to lump-sum taxation.

At this point we may note the consequences of relaxing the assumption of fixed producer prices. Suppose that production takes place under constant returns to scale (as in Diamond and Mirrlees, 1971). The

---

[7] It has not been demonstrated that (12-17) holds for labour, but this can readily be shown.

government revenue constraint is replaced by a production constraint:

$$wL = F(X_1, \ldots, X_n) + R_0 \tag{12-21}$$

where w is fixed (labour is again the *numeraire*) and the right-hand side gives the labour requirements of the private sector, $F(X)$, and government revenue, R_0, expressed in terms of labour. The first-order conditions become

$$\frac{\partial V}{\partial q_k} = -\lambda \left(w \frac{\partial L}{\partial q_k} - \sum_i F_i \frac{\partial X_i}{\partial q_k} \right) \tag{12-22}$$

Since there are constant returns to scale, there is no pure profit income, so that differentiating the consumer's budget constraint yields

$$\frac{w \partial L}{\partial q_k} = X_k + \sum_i q_i \frac{\partial X_i}{\partial q_k} \tag{12-23}$$

Profit maximization in the private sector implies $F_i = p_i$, where p_i are producer prices,[8] so it follows that

$$\frac{\partial V}{\partial q_k} = -\lambda \left(X_k + \sum_i t_i \frac{\partial X_i}{\partial t_k} \right)$$

(noting that $q_i - p_i = t_i$). We are therefore back with condition (12-13). The *form* of the first-order conditions is therefore unaffected in the case of constant returns to scale (non-constant returns are discussed in Lecture 15); on the other hand, the producer prices in general vary with changes in the tax rates.

The analysis so far has been based on the first-order conditions, and we should note that their necessity has been asserted, not demonstrated. This point is discussed in detail by Diamond and Mirrlees (1971, Section X), who set out a constraint qualification such that the use of Lagrange multipliers is indeed valid, and the formulae given earlier are necessary for optimality. They also provide a valuable discussion of the question of uniqueness. There are two problems. First, the specification of the tax rates may not uniquely determine the behaviour of the system. Second, there may be more than one solution to the first-order conditions:

> if lump-sum transfers are excluded as a feasible policy, this problem may arise even when the production set is convex. There is no reason why the demand functions should have any of the nice convexity properties which ensure that first-order conditions imply global maximization. [Diamond and Mirrlees, 1971, p. 276]

It is possible to construct examples where more than one value of t_k satisfies the first-order conditions.[9] Moreover, it is quite possible that there are two

---

[8] The private sector maximizes $\sum p_i X_i - F(X_1, \ldots, X_n)$.

[9] For further discussion, see Harris (1975), Atkinson and Stiglitz (1976), and Atkinson (1977b).

goods, j and k, with identical demand conditions, leading to identical first-order conditions, where the global optimum involves an asymmetric solution $(t_j \neq t_k)$. For this reason, one needs to be careful in drawing conclusions about uniformity of taxes from the first-order conditions. The mere fact that the conditions for t_j and t_k are identical in form does not imply that they should be set equal. (There are also important implications for horizontal equity, taken up later.)

An Example

In order to illustrate the results, let us take the case where there are two goods and labour, and a non-negative revenue requirement. The conditions (12-17) then become:

$$t_1 S_{11} + t_2 S_{12} = -\theta X_1$$
$$t_1 S_{21} + t_2 S_{22} = -\theta X_2 \tag{12-24}$$

Solving,

$$t_1 = (\theta/S)(S_{12} X_2 - S_{22} X_1)$$
$$t_2 = (\theta/S)(S_{21} X_1 - S_{11} X_2)$$

where $S = S_{11} S_{22} - S_{12}^2$ and is positive by the properties of the Slutsky matrix. Defining the elasticities of compensated demand, and setting $p_i = 1$,

$$\varepsilon_{ij} = q_j S_{ij}/X_i \tag{12-25}$$

we have

$$\frac{t_1}{1+t_1} = \frac{t_2}{1+t_2} \left(\frac{\varepsilon_{12} - \varepsilon_{22}}{\varepsilon_{21} - \varepsilon_{11}} \right) \tag{12-26}$$

Let us introduce the notation that good 0 is leisure (i.e., minus leisure). From the properties of the Slutsky terms, we know that:[10]

$$\sum_{j=0}^{2} q_j S_{ij} = 0 \tag{12-27}$$

(where $q_0 = w$). So that:

$$\varepsilon_{10} + \varepsilon_{11} + \varepsilon_{12} = 0$$
$$\varepsilon_{20} + \varepsilon_{21} + \varepsilon_{22} = 0 \tag{12-28}$$

Hence, substituting in (12-26),

$$\frac{t_1}{1+t_1} = \frac{t_2}{1+t_2} \left[\frac{-(\varepsilon_{11} + \varepsilon_{22}) - \varepsilon_{10}}{-(\varepsilon_{11} + \varepsilon_{22}) - \varepsilon_{20}} \right] \tag{12-29}$$

---

[10] This may be seen from the fact that $S_{ij} = E_{ij}$, where E is the expenditure function, and E_i is homogeneous of degree zero in prices.

It follows that $\varepsilon_{10} > \varepsilon_{20}$ implies $t_1 < t_2$ (ε_{ii} being negative). At the optimum, the good with the larger cross-elasticity of compensated demand with the price of labour (leisure) has the smaller tax rate.[11] This is the basis of the result reached by Corlett and Hague (1953), Meade (1955, p. 30), Harberger (1964) and others that we should tax more heavily goods that are complementary with leisure.

Exercise 12-1 Derive the optimal tax structure where the utility functions have the Cobb–Douglas form

$$U = \sum_{i=1}^{n} a_i \log X_i + A \log(1 - L) \qquad (12\text{-}30\text{a})$$

where $A + \Sigma_i a_i = 1$ and $n = 2$.

Exercise 12-2 For the utility function

$$U = \sum_{i=1}^{n} A_i \frac{X_i^{1-1/\varepsilon_i}}{1 - 1/\varepsilon_i} - vL \qquad (12\text{-}30\text{b})$$

show that the income terms $(\partial X_i / \partial M)$ and cross-price terms are zero. Derive the optimal tax structure where ε_i are (positive) constants.

12-3 APPLICATION OF THE RAMSEY RESULTS

The general formulation given in the previous section provides important insights into the nature of the solution, but does not yield much in the way of concrete results. Equation (12-17) does not, for example, suggest which goods should be taxed more heavily, and the two-good example cannot readily be extended. In order to obtain more definite results, Ramsey himself made a number of special assumptions on the demand side equivalent to the partial equilibrium analysis described in Section 12-1. From this it might appear that we have to choose between definite results based on highly restrictive assumptions and more general models yielding only limited conclusions. However, it is possible by adopting an alternative approach to derive results midway in generality, and these are discussed in this section, together with some of the numerical applications. We retain for the present the assumption of identical individuals.

Alternative Formulation

The analysis in the previous section used the "dual" price variables as controls open to the government and exploited the properties of the indirect

---

[11] The elasticities are typically functions of the prices, and hence the tax rates, and there may be multiple solutions to (12-24).

utility function. (In the next section, we show how this relates to the expenditure function.) For many purposes, the dual approach provides a neat and compact treatment, and it has been widely adopted. On the other hand, in some cases the "primal" approach, using the quantities as controls, may aid understanding. In this section, we show how formulating the model in this way leads to an alternative form of the optimal tax conditions. We are in fact returning to Ramsey's original way of setting up the problem, since he worked with the direct utility function.

Let us therefore take as control variables for the government the quantities $X_1,\ldots,X_n$ and L, with the tax rates being obtained as functions of the control variables from the conditions for individual utility maximization. With this "primal" approach, we have to ensure that the consumer budget constraint is satisfied (see Atkinson and Stiglitz, 1972). For this purpose, we make use of the individual utility maximization conditions

$$U_i = \alpha q_i \quad i = 1,\ldots,n$$
$$-U_L = \alpha w \tag{12-31}$$

From these, the condition that the individual be on his offer curve may be written (substituting in the budget constraint and eliminating α),

$$\sum_i U_i X_i + U_L L = 0 \tag{12-32}$$

The Lagrangean then becomes[12]

$$\mathscr{L} = U(\mathbf{X},L) + \lambda\left(wL - \sum_i X_i - R_0\right) + \mu\left(\sum_i U_i X_i + U_L L\right) \tag{12-33}$$

and the first-order conditions

$$U_k = \lambda - \mu U_k\left(1 + \sum_i \frac{U_{ik}X_i}{U_k} + \frac{U_{Lk}L}{U_k}\right) \quad \text{for } k = 1,\ldots,n \tag{12-34}$$

Let us now define

$$H^k \equiv -\left(\sum_i \frac{U_{ik}X_i}{U_k} + \frac{U_{Lk}L}{U_k}\right) \quad \text{for } k = 1,\ldots,n \tag{12-35}$$

and substitute for $U_k = \alpha(1+t_k)$. This yields

$$(1+t_k)[1 - \mu(H^k - 1)] = \lambda/\alpha \tag{12-36} \cdot$$

There is in addition the condition with respect to L

$$U_L = -\lambda w - \mu U_L\left(1 + \sum_i \frac{U_{iL}X_i}{U_L} + \frac{U_{LL}L}{U_L}\right) \tag{12-34'}$$

---

[12] In the revenue constraint we have used the fact that

$$\sum_i t_i X_i = \sum_i (q_i - 1)X_i = wL - \sum_i X_i$$

If we define the corresponding expression

$$H^L \equiv -\left(\sum_i \frac{U_{iL} X_i}{U_L} + \frac{U_{LL} L}{U_L} \right) \tag{12-35'}$$

and substitute $U_L = -\alpha w$, we obtain

$$\mu(1 - H^L) = \frac{\lambda - \alpha}{\alpha} \tag{12-36'}$$

Eliminating μ between (12-36) and (12-36') gives[13]

$$\frac{t_k}{1 + t_k} = \frac{\lambda - \alpha}{\lambda} \left(\frac{H^k - H^L}{1 - H^L} \right) \tag{12-37}$$

While this equation does not in general provide an explicit formula for the optimal tax rate (since the terms H^k depend on the tax rates), it does allow us to draw a number of conclusions about the optimal structure. First, the partial equilibrium results can be seen as polar cases of this formula. Suppose on the one hand that $(-H^L)$ tends to infinity, which corresponds to a completely inelastic supply of labour $(-U_{LL} \to \infty)$; then the limit of (12-37) is a uniform tax on all goods at rate $(\lambda - \alpha)/\alpha$. Since we have seen that a uniform rate of tax on all goods is equivalent to a tax on labour alone, this corresponds to the conventional prescription that a factor in completely inelastic supply should bear all the tax. On the other hand, if H^L tends to zero, we have the case of a completely elastic supply of labour (constant marginal utility of income). If in addition we assume that $U_{ij} = 0$ for $i \neq j$ we have the conditions required for the validity of partial equilibrium analysis (no income effects and independent demands). Since[14]

$$U_{kk} \frac{\partial X_k}{\partial q_k} = \alpha \quad \text{implies} \quad H^k = \frac{1}{\varepsilon_k^d}$$

the optimal tax

$$\frac{t_k}{1 + t_k} = \frac{\lambda - \alpha}{\lambda} H^k = \frac{\lambda - \alpha}{\lambda} \frac{1}{\varepsilon_k^d} \tag{12-38}$$

as obtained in Section 12-1. This shows that the formula (12-37) may be seen as a "weighted average" of two polar tax systems: the uniform tax and taxes proportional to H^k. Where between these two extremes the optimal tax system depends on H^L.

Secondly, the formulation (12-37) suggests one case where the results may be particularly simple—that where the utility function is directly

---

[13] Equation (12-37) can also be obtained from the results of the previous section by inverting Eq. (12-17)—see Atkinson and Stiglitz (1972). For an alternative approach using the Antonelli matrix, see Deaton (1979).

[14] Differentiating $U_k = \alpha q_k$ where α is by assumption constant, and dividing by α.

additive. This implies that there exists some monotonic transformation of the utility function such that $U_{ij} = 0$ for $i \neq j$. Since H^k is invariant with respect to such transformations,[15] this means that

$$H^k = \frac{-U_{kk}X_k}{U_k}$$

But by differentiating the first-order conditions for utility maximization, we can see that this is inversely proportional to the income elasticity of demand for k:

$$U_{kk}\frac{\partial X_k}{\partial M} = q_k\frac{\partial \alpha}{\partial M} = U_k\frac{1}{\alpha}\frac{\partial \alpha}{\partial M}$$

or

$$H^k\frac{1}{X_k}\frac{\partial X_k}{\partial M} = \frac{-1}{\alpha}\frac{\partial \alpha}{\partial M} \qquad (12\text{-}39)$$

We have therefore the interesting result that *when the utility function is directly additive, the optimal tax rate depends inversely on the income elasticity of demand.* Necessities should be taxed more heavily than luxuries. This has important implications for the conflict between equity and efficiency, which are discussed further below. Direct additivity is a restrictive assumption; it is however considerably less restrictive than the assumptions required for partial equilibrium analysis to be valid (for $H^L \neq 0$, direct additivity does not imply zero cross-price effects). Moreover, direct additivity is assumed in many demand studies, e.g., the linear expenditure system discussed below.

Finally, the primal approach adopted in this section has been used by Deaton (1979) to discuss the conditions under which the optimal structure is uniform. He shows that the optimal tax conditions are identical for all goods if there is implicit separability between leisure and goods; i.e., where the expenditure function can be written $e[w, f(\mathbf{q}, U), U]$. Combined with weak separability between goods and leisure, this implies unitary expenditure elasticities (Sandmo, 1974a).[16] In considering these results, the earlier qualification concerning non-uniqueness of the first-order conditions should be borne in mind: the fact that the right-hand sides of (12-37) may be equal for two goods does not necessarily imply uniformity.

---

[15] Suppose U is replaced by $G(U)$; then $G_i = G'U_i$, $G_{ij} = G'U_{ij} + G''U_iU_j$. This means that

$$H^k = \sum_i\left(\frac{-G_{ik}X_i}{G_k}\right) = \sum_i\left(\frac{-U_{ik}X_i}{U_k}\right) - \frac{G''}{G'}\sum_i U_iX_i$$

but the second term disappears (using the budget constraint) establishing that H^k is invariant.

[16] Sandmo shows that it implies equal compensated elasticities with respect to the wage. See also Sadka (1977). The earlier statement in Atkinson and Stiglitz (1972, p. 105) was unclear, although it was not intended to carry the interpretation placed on it by Sadka.

Example of Linear Expenditure System

One function widely used in the empirical study of demand is the Stone–Geary function which generates the linear expenditure system:

$$U(\mathbf{X}, L) = \left\{ \delta^{1-\rho} \left[\prod_{i=1}^{n} \left(\frac{X_i - \gamma_i}{a_i} \right)^{a_i} \right]^{\rho} + (1-\delta)^{1-\rho}(L_0 - L)^{\rho} \right\}^{1/\rho} \quad (12\text{-}40)$$

where $\Sigma a_i = 1$. The parameters γ_i correspond to "committed" consumption, the a_i are share parameters, and ρ measures the ease of substitution between goods and leisure ($\sigma \equiv 1/(1-\rho)$ is the elasticity of substitution). From the first-order conditions for utility maximization and the budget constraint, we obtain the demand functions and the labour supply function:

$$q_k X_k = q_k \gamma_k + a_k \left(w L_0 - \sum_i q_i \gamma_i \right) Z \quad k = 1, \dots, n \quad (12\text{-}41\text{a})$$

$$wL = Z w L_0 + (1-Z) \sum_i q_i \gamma_i \quad (12\text{-}41\text{b})$$

where

$$Z \equiv 1 - \frac{(1-\delta)^{1-\rho}(L_0 - L)^{\rho}}{U^{\rho}} \quad (12\text{-}41\text{c})$$

(i.e., Z is a measure of the contribution of "goods" to total utility). The expenditure on good k consists of the committed expenditure ($q_k \gamma_k$) plus a fraction, $a_k Z$, of the remaining income, where the latter is defined as "full income", $w L_0$.

In order to apply the optimal tax formula (12-37), we need to calculate H^k and H^L. It is left as an exercise to the reader to show that

$$H^L = -(1-\rho)\frac{L}{L_0 - L}$$

$$H^k = \frac{X_k}{X_k - \gamma_k} - \rho \xi$$

where

$$\xi \equiv \sum_i \frac{a_i X_i}{X_i - \gamma_i} = 1 + \frac{1}{Z} \frac{\Sigma q_i \gamma_i}{w L_0 - \Sigma q_i \gamma_i}$$

(the last step substitutes for U_i and uses the fact that $\Sigma U_i X_i = \alpha w L$). Substituting in the condition (12-37) for optimal tax rates,

$$\frac{t_k}{1+t_k} = \frac{\lambda - \alpha}{\lambda} \frac{X_k/(X_k - \gamma_k) + (1-\rho)[L/(L_0 - L)] - \rho \xi}{1 + (1-\rho)[L/(L_0 - L)]} \quad (12\text{-}42)$$

In applying this formula so as to arrive at some illustrative calculations of the optimal tax rates, there are two difficulties. First, we require estimates of both commodity demand functions and the labour supply function.

Simultaneous estimation of both is relatively rare, and where it has been undertaken, for example by Abbott and Ashenfelter (1976), it has been on the basis of prior assumptions about the value of ρ (they set $\rho = 0$). In view of this, the calculations below are based on assumed values of ρ. Second, Eq. (12-42) is not an explicit formula for t_k, since X_k, Z and L depend on t_k. These problems are taken up in turn.

Let us first consider the influence of ρ. A useful benchmark is the case of unitary elasticity of substitution ($\sigma = 1$, $\rho = 0$). The relative tax rates on goods k and j are then

$$\frac{t_k/(1+t_k)}{t_j/(1+t_j)} = \frac{X_k/(X_k-\gamma_k)+L/(L_0-L)}{X_j/(X_j-\gamma_j)+L/(L_0-L)} \qquad (12\text{-}43)$$

In order to get some feel for this, let us suppose that γ varies from 0 (luxury) to $\frac{2}{3}X$ (necessity) and that $L = \frac{1}{2}L_0$. This implies a range of taxes such that the rate on the necessity is double that on the luxury. For elasticities of substitution less than unity ($\rho < 0$), the weight on the term $L/(L_0-L)$ tends to rise, and the effect of this is increased by the third term in the numerator of the right-hand side of (12-42). Where $\rho > 0$, we would expect the behaviour to depend more critically on its value. Moreover, it is important to note the sensitivity to the precise specification of the substitutability between goods and leisure. If in (12-40) the product Π were replaced by its logarithm, then the term $-\rho\xi$ would not appear on the right-hand side of (12-42). This in turn would imply that, as $\rho \to 1$ (i.e. $\sigma \to \infty$), which is the limiting case of a perfectly elastic labour supply, the relative tax rates would depend on the ratio of $X_k/(X_k-\gamma_k)$. This is the case considered by Atkinson and Stiglitz (1972), where we solve the resulting equations for t_k, using data for the United Kingdom.[17]

The "back of the envelope" calculations above give some feeling for the considerations likely to be important. An alternative approach, leading to precise computations, is that based on algorithms similar to those discussed in Lecture 6. Harris and MacKinnon (1979), for example, make use of demand parameters a_i and γ_i estimated for Canada and postulated values of L_0 and δ. Producer prices are fixed, labour is taken as the untaxed good, and the government has a fixed revenue requirement in labour units. The solution to the first-order conditions is then calculated for different values of σ. The results show, for example, a range of 19.6 per cent (transport) to 21.2 per cent (food) when $\sigma = 0.3$, widening to 18.9 to 26.5 per cent when $\sigma = 1.1$, and 13.9 to 57.5 per cent when $\sigma = 3.0$. For a larger revenue requirement, the range is even wider.

Where analytical conclusions are difficult to obtain, numerical results are undoubtedly valuable. At the same time, it would be a mistake to read

---

[17] Thus, although the results are a limiting case in the sense that $H^L = 0$, the form chosen for the utility derived from *goods* can be varied to give greater divergencies from uniform taxes.

too much into them, not least because the linear expenditure system is a rather restrictive specification. The main point of calculations of optimal tax rates is to throw light on the role of different considerations and what appear to be the sensitive features. In particular, it has allowed us to illustrative the role of labour supply, and the fact that the results may depend crucially on the specification. It does not however follow that there would be a substantial welfare loss if the function were incorrectly specified (and hence a sub-optimal tax policy chosen). For this, and other reasons, we need to explore the position away from the optimum, and this is the subject of the next section.

12-4 PARTIAL WELFARE IMPROVEMENTS AND TAX REFORM

The literature on optimal taxation has been criticized for directing too much attention at characterizing the optimum and not considering the process by which it can be attained. Feldstein, for example, has distinguished between tax *design*, or "tax laws being written *de novo* on 'a clean sheet of paper'" (quoting Woodrow Wilson), and tax *reform*, which takes "as its starting point the existing tax system and the fact that actual changes are slow and piecemeal" (Feldstein, 1976d, p. 77). We now consider therefore whether we can identify changes in tax rates that represent a partial welfare improvement in that, although falling short of the optimum, they represent a step in the right direction.

Partial Welfare Improvements

As is now well known from the literature on second-best, this is a difficult area. Reforms that may appear to move in the correct direction can turn out on closer inspection to reduce welfare. Intuition can be very misleading. None the less, the optimum tax results discussed in the previous sections provide some insights. For this purpose, we go back to the dual formulation of Section 12-2. In that case we were in effect evaluating possible changes in policy in terms of their effect on the indirect utility function. If we denote a possible variation in tax rates by the vector $\mathbf{dt}$, then, by the properties of the indirect utility function,

$$dV = -\alpha \mathbf{X}' \cdot \mathbf{dt} \tag{12-44}$$

The effect of this variation on the revenue is

$$dR = \mathbf{t}' \cdot \mathbf{dX} + \mathbf{X}' \cdot \mathbf{dt} \tag{12-45}$$

The solution involves identifying conditions under which variations satisfying (12-45) could not achieve an increase in welfare. In geometric terms, the condition for optimality is that the half-space of welfare-improving changes ($dV > 0$) be disjoint from the closed half-space of changes that satisfy the revenue constraint ($dR \geqslant 0$). This interpretation, due to Dixit (1975), is illustrated in Fig. 12-2a. This also brings out why a move towards lump-sum taxes from the distortionary tax optimum raises welfare (in effect $dR < 0$)—as shown by Atkinson and Stern (1974).

What happens however if we are not at the optimum? Is it possible to reach straightforward conclusions about directions for welfare improvement? We consider first a shift from distortionary taxation. Suppose that the government is able to raise revenue by other means and as a result R can be reduced ($dR \leqslant 0$). Does it follow that $dV > 0$? The answer is not necessarily affirmative. This may be seen geometrically in the two-tax case from Fig. 12-2b. The condition $dR \leqslant 0$ defines a closed half-space of *local* revenue-reducing changes, defined by $dR = 0$ in the diagram, with revenue being greater above this line. Correspondingly, we can define the open half-space of local strictly welfare-improving changes ($dV > 0$), with welfare higher below the line $dV = 0$. In the case shown in Fig. 12-2b, it is clearly possible to move from the point P to a new set of taxes where revenue is lower but welfare is lower. This is illustrated by PA. Even though it may appear intuitive that a switch from distortionary to lump-sum taxation raises welfare, this is not everywhere the case. (A formal treatment, using the properties of the expenditure function and allowing for more general assumptions about production is provided by Dixit, 1975. See also Dixit and Munk, 1977.)

The negative result just described is illustrative of those in the second-best literature which led to a general pessimism. As Dixit notes, "some particular rules that were at one time thought to be intuitively plausible by some economists turned out to be wrong, and this failure received a great deal of publicity" (Dixit, 1975, p. 122). On the other hand, this pessimism does not seem warranted. Even though it is not true, as we have seen, that any move to lump-sum taxation is necessarily welfare-improving, there are many directions in which tax changes may be welfare-improving—the hatched area in Fig. 12-2b. The issue is one of characterizing the directions of feasible welfare-improving change.

In order to illustrate the possibility of constructive rather than negative second-best results, we may note that it can be shown that under rather general conditions a proportionate reduction in the distortion raises welfare (Foster and Sonnenschein, 1970, and Bruno, 1972). To see this intuitively, suppose that all taxes are reduced proportionately with a compensating adjustment in lump-sum taxation, T, to maintain overall revenue. If the proportionate reduction is $db(>0)$, then

$$\mathbf{dt} = -(\mathbf{q}-\mathbf{p})db = -\mathbf{t}db \qquad (12\text{-}46)$$

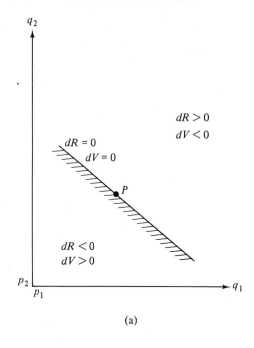

(a)

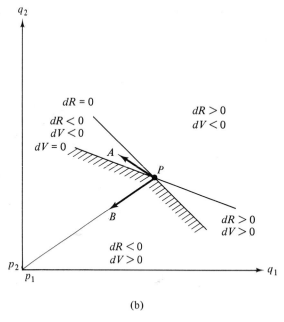

(b)

Figure 12-2 Directions of welfare improvement: (a) existing taxes optimal; (b) existing taxes non-optimal.

The change in lump-sum tax is

$$dT = -\mathbf{t'}\,\mathbf{dX} - \mathbf{X'}\,\mathbf{dt} \tag{12-47}$$

The change in welfare is

$$dV = -\alpha\mathbf{X'}\,\mathbf{dt} - \alpha dT \tag{12-48}$$
$$= \alpha\mathbf{t'}\,\mathbf{dX}$$

(using (12-47)). Now the change in demands consists of a substitution term and an income term. The substitution component is given by

$$\alpha\mathbf{t'}\,S\,\mathbf{dt} = -\alpha\mathbf{t'}\,St\,db \tag{12-49}$$

where S is the Slutsky matrix. From the negative semi-definiteness of S, it follows that this component is non-negative. If the income effect were such that the individual became worse off, which could only happen if T rises, this implies that the excise revenue collected from him goes up as his level of welfare falls. If we rule out this apparently perverse case, then the individual must be better off. (For a precise statement of the condition, see Dixit, 1975, p. 107.) Geometrically, the effect is that a move in the direction PB raises welfare (the origin being drawn at $t_1 = t_2 = 0$).

Another example of a "constructive" second-best result is that given by Corlett and Hague (1953). In the context of a simple model, with two consumption goods and labour, the latter being the untaxed *numeraire*, they show that, subject to one qualification, beginning with an initial situation of uniform taxes, welfare can be increased by raising the tax on the good "more complementary" with leisure, while lowering the other tax so that revenue is unchanged. From the earlier condition for an optimum (page 375), this represents a move "towards" the optimum. The qualification is to rule out what they call the "crazy" case, where an increase in the tax rate on one good lowers total revenue. The extension to n goods is left as an exercise.

> **Exercise 12-3** In a model with n goods and (untaxed) labour, derive the conditions under which a small revenue-neutral departure from uniform taxation increases welfare if all commodities whose prices are lowered are better substitutes for the *numeraire* than all those whose prices are raised. Illustrate geometrically for the case $n = 2$. (See Dixit, 1975, Theorem 6.)

The relation between optimal taxation and tax reform can be considered further. For a number of reasons policy-makers may be unwilling, or unable, to make large changes in the tax structure. The reasons include the fact that our knowledge of the relevant production and demand parameters is typically limited to the neighbourhood of the current position, and even here there may be considerable uncertainty. (A factor working in the opposite direction is that there are fixed costs to tax reform—which would point to infrequent changes.) In view of this, a number of writers have characterized the problem as one of choosing from neighbouring equilibria—or of designing the optimal tax change subject to a constraint on their overall magnitude. Thus Diewert (1978) imposes in effect the constraint

$$\sum_i (\Delta t_i)^2 \leqslant 1 \tag{12-50a}$$

and Dixit (1979) considers

$$\sum_i |\Delta t_i| \leqslant 1 \tag{12-50b}$$

This raises the question of the *process* of tax reform, where there is a clear parallel with the literature on planning algorithms (e.g. Heal, 1973). At each point we need to ask whether there is a feasible, welfare-improving step which can be made; and we need to ask whether the sequence of "tax reforms" converges and, if so, what are the characteristics of the limiting solution. These issues have been discussed by, among others, Guesnerie (1977) and Fogelman, Quinzii and Guesnerie (1978), in the context of a many-consumer model. Among the general features of their results are the difficulties posed by the basic non-convexity of the set of equilibria (already discussed in Section 12-2) and the demonstration that inefficiency in the production sector may be necessary *temporarily* in the process of tax reform. If the process of tax reform is subject to a constraint of the kind described, and is required to be welfare-improving, then the condition of production efficiency that characterizes the full optimum (under certain conditions—see Lecture 15) may not apply on the route to the optimum.

12-5 OPTIMAL TAXATION IN A MANY-PERSON ECONOMY

To this point we have assumed that all individuals are identical, and, as will be argued in Lecture 14, the Ramsey analysis is of limited policy relevance in this context. The extension to a many-consumer economy by Diamond and Mirrlees (1971), developed in Diamond (1975b), Mirrlees (1975) and Atkinson and Stiglitz (1976), is therefore of considerable importance.

Taxation and Redistribution

We now assume that there are H households, denoted by a superscript h, so that the indirect utility function of the hth household is V^h. The objectives of the government are assumed to be represented by maximizing the social welfare function

$$\psi(V^1, V^2, V^3, \ldots, V^H)$$

where ψ is increasing in all arguments. The government's maximization problem may be formulated in terms of the Lagrangean:

$$\mathscr{L} = \psi(\mathbf{V}(\mathbf{q})) + \lambda \left[\sum_{i=1}^{n} t_i \left(\sum_{h=1}^{H} X_i^h \right) - R_0 \right] \qquad (12\text{-}51)$$

This gives first-order conditions

$$\sum_h \frac{\partial \psi}{\partial V^h} \alpha^h X_k^h = \lambda \left[H \bar{X}_k + \sum_i t_i \left(\sum_h \frac{\partial X_i^h}{\partial t_k} \right) \right] \qquad (12\text{-}52)$$

where $\bar{X}_k = \sum_h X_k^h / H$. Denoting $(\partial \psi / \partial V^h) \alpha^h$ by β^h (the social marginal utility of income accruing to household h), and using the Slutsky relationship, this may be written as

$$\sum_i t_i \left(\sum_h S_{ik}^h \right) = -\left[H \bar{X}_k - \sum_h \frac{\beta^h}{\lambda} X_k^h - \sum_i t_i \left(\sum_h X_k^h \frac{\partial X_i^h}{\partial M^h} \right) \right] \qquad (12\text{-}53)$$

In order to help interpret this, let us define

$$b^h = \frac{\beta^h}{\lambda} + \sum_i t_i \frac{\partial X_i^h}{\partial M^h} \qquad (12\text{-}54a)$$

$$\bar{b} = \sum_h \frac{b^h}{H} \qquad (12\text{-}54b)$$

b^h is the net social marginal valuation of income, measured in terms of government revenue. It is *net* in the sense of measuring the benefit of transferring \$1 to household h *allowing* for the marginal tax paid on receiving this extra \$1. Equation (12-53) may then be written:

$$\frac{\sum_i t_i \sum_h (S_{ik}^h / H)}{\bar{X}_k} = -\left[1 - \sum_h \frac{b^h}{H} \left(\frac{X_k^h}{\bar{X}_k} \right) \right] \qquad k = 1, \ldots, n \qquad (12\text{-}55)$$

The left-hand side has the same interpretation as before: it is a proportional reduction in the consumption of the kth commodity along the compensated demand schedule. In contrast, the right-hand side is no longer necessarily the same for all commodities. It is independent of k if b^h is the same for all h or if $X_k^h / \bar{X}_k$ is the same for all commodities (there are no goods that are consumed disproportionately by rich or poor). In general, the compensated reduction in demand with the optimal tax structure is smaller:[18]

1. the more the good is consumed by individuals with a high social marginal valuation of income;
2. the more the good is consumed by households with a high marginal propensity to consume taxed goods.

Equation (12-55) can be rewritten in two ways which prove useful in the subsequent discussion:

$$\frac{\sum_i t_i \sum_h S_{ik}^h}{H} = -\bar{X}_k(1-\bar{b}r_k) \quad \text{for } k = 1,\ldots,n \tag{12-56}$$

where

$$r_k = \frac{\sum_h \left(\frac{X_k^h}{\bar{X}_k}\right)\left(\frac{b^h}{\bar{b}}\right)}{H} \tag{12-57}$$

and

$$\frac{\sum_i t_i \sum_h S_{ik}^h}{H} = -\bar{X}_k[(1-\bar{b})-\bar{b}\phi_k] \quad \text{for } k = 1,\ldots,n \tag{12-58}$$

where $\phi_k = r_k - 1$ is the normalized covariance between the consumption of the kth commodity and the net social marginal valuation of income. In the first of these formulae, r_k is a generalization of the distributional characteristic of Feldstein (1972a, 1972b). It shows that, if the average value of the net social marginal valuation, $\bar{b}$, is large, that is there would be large gains from a uniform lump-sum payment, then distributional considerations are to be weighted more heavily.

The extension of the Ramsey formula given above is relatively general. In particular, it allows individuals to differ with respect to both tastes and endowments; other taxes (e.g., a lump-sum tax) may be imposed; and not all commodities need be taxed. (As in the earlier Ramsey analysis, the result depends on there being either constant returns to scale in production or 100 per cent profits taxes—see Lecture 15.) However, to obtain detailed results on the optimal tax structure, we need to make more specific assumptions about the nature of differences between individuals and the form of the

---

[18] Diamond and Mirrlees (1971) derive the analogous expression for the uncompensated changes. Since the uncompensated reductions in demand with the optimal tax structure are not the same even without distributional considerations, to make the comparison with the Ramsey results more direct, we have employed compensated derivatives.

utility function. In order to facilitate this, we assume now that everyone has the same tastes, and that individuals differ solely with respect to their wage rate, w.

The easiest utility function to consider is the Cobb–Douglas given in Eq. (12-30a). In this case, however, with identical tastes, the optimal tax system is uniform, since $X_k^h/\bar{X}_k$ is the same for all k. Where individuals consume goods in the same proportions, it is not possible to use indirect taxes to redistribute income—they impose the same percentage burden on everyone. In view of this, we consider the more interesting situation of non-unitary expenditure elasticities. This is more complicated, and in order to simplify the analysis we assume that all individuals have identical utility functions:

$$U = \sum_i G_i(X_i) - L \tag{12-59}$$

(N.B. Exercise 12-2 is the constant elasticity version of this form), so that the first-order conditions give

$$\alpha = 1/w^h \quad \text{and} \quad G_i' = (q_i/w^h) \tag{12-60}$$

It follows that there are no income effects on the demand for goods and that the demand schedules are independent. The model is therefore equivalent to the partial equilibrium analysis of Section 12-1. While highly restrictive, it does allow us to examine the consequences of incorporating redistributional goals.

With this special assumption, the condition for optimality becomes

$$\frac{t_k}{1+t_k} = \frac{1-\bar{b}-\bar{b}\phi_k}{\bar{\varepsilon}_k} \quad \text{for all } k = 1,\ldots,n \tag{12-61}$$

where $\bar{\varepsilon}_k$ is the elasticity of the aggregate demand. In the situation where everyone is identical, this reduces to the familiar formula that the taxes should be inversely proportional to demand elasticities. Equation (12-61) provides a simple adjustment to this formula for distributional considerations. The term ϕ_k depends on the social marginal valuation of income received by different households and on the proportion of total consumption that goes to them. In particular, it depends on the degree of aversion to inequality. If β is constant, that is, if society is indifferent with regard to the distribution, then the optimal tax formula is the familiar one. But if the social marginal valuation of income falls with w, this tends to increase the tax rate on goods that are primarily consumed by those at the top of the scale.

A formula similar to (12-61) was given by Feldstein (1972a, 1972b), but he did not bring out the inherent conflict between equity and efficiency considerations. With this utility function, the demands depend on the ratio of the commodity price to the wage (see (12-60)). This means that a commodity with a low elasticity of demand appears from an efficiency standpoint to be a good candidate for taxation, but that, since the consumption of such a commodity rises only slowly with the wage, this points to low tax rates for equity reasons. Which of these factors predominates depends on the government's objectives and on the shape of the distribution of abilities. This is illustrated by the simple example where the government maximizes the sum of utilities, the demand curves have constant elasticity, and wage rates are distributed (continuously) according to the Pareto distribution; i.e.,

$$b^h = \alpha^h/\lambda, \quad X_k^h = A_k(w^h/q_k)^{\varepsilon_k} \tag{12-62}$$

and the density function of wage rates is

$$dF = \mu \mathbf{w}^\mu w^{-(1+\mu)} dw \quad \text{for } w \geqslant \mathbf{w} \tag{12-63}$$

On the assumption that $\mu > \varepsilon_k$ all k, it may be calculated that

$$r_k = \int_\mathbf{w}^\infty \left(\frac{X_k^h}{\bar{X}_k}\right)\left(\frac{b^h}{\bar{b}}\right) dF = \frac{\int_\mathbf{w}^\infty w^{\varepsilon_k - 1} dF}{\left(\int_\mathbf{w}^\infty w^{\varepsilon_k} dF\right)\left(\int_\mathbf{w}^\infty w^{-1} dF\right)} \tag{12-64}$$

Hence

$$\frac{t_k}{1+t_k} = -\frac{\bar{b}-1}{\varepsilon_k} + \frac{\bar{b}}{\mu(1+\mu-\varepsilon_k)} \tag{12-65}$$

It follows that, where the government would like to make a uniform lump-sum transfer to everyone ($\bar{b} > 1$), the tax rate rises with the elasticity of demand; this is therefore a sufficient condition for equity to outweigh efficiency considerations, and for goods with a high price elasticity to be taxed more heavily. It may also be noted that the magnitude of the distributional term falls with μ, or as the distribution of abilities becomes less unequal (for the same mean, see Chipman, 1974).

Exercise 12-4 Examine the optimal structure of taxation where wage rates are distributed lognormally and the demand functions are of the form given in Exercise 12-2. (See Feldstein, 1972a, and Atkinson and Stiglitz, 1976).

The special case considered above is not of course intended to be realistic, its purpose being to illustrate some of the factors at work. In any actual application, more general demand functions need to be employed, coupled with realistic assumptions about the distribution of endowments and a range of assumptions about the form of the social welfare function. For examples of such empirical calculations, see Deaton (1977), Heady and Mitra (1977), and Harris and MacKinnon (1979).

Horizontal Equity

As noted in Lecture 11, much of the literature on optimal taxation has assumed that the redistributive goals of the government may be represented by maximizing a social welfare function, such as $\psi(\mathbf{V})$ defined above, and has not discussed the relationship between this and the concept of horizontal equity. In the kind of second-best problem we are considering, horizontal inequity is not ruled out by the maximization of a social welfare function. This is a further example of the problems caused by the non-convexities referred to in Section 12-2, and, as shown in general terms in Lecture 11, it may be possible to raise social welfare by taxing identical individuals at different rates. This is discussed with particular reference to indirect taxes in Atkinson and Stiglitz (1976).

It is for this reason that the specification of the problem in terms of each individual facing identical tax rates is an assumption, not an implication of welfare maximization. On the other hand, it may not be an unreasonable assumption. As argued in Lecture 11, the most appealing interpretation of horizontal equity may be that it imposes certain prior constraints on the instruments the government can employ. The constraint that all individuals face the same rates of indirect tax may well appear reasonable in this context, and thus provide a justification for the assumption made (implicitly) in much of the literature.

The introduction of differences in tastes makes the problem even more severe. This is because the social welfare function approach evaluates taxes in terms of the individual's ability to derive utility from goods and leisure, in contrast to the criterion of "ability to pay", which bases taxation on opportunity sets. When the only differences are those in ability to produce, then maximizing ψ leads to redistribution from those with "better" opportunity sets to those with "poorer". There is no conflict between it and the ability-to-pay approach. But this may arise as soon as tastes differ. Suppose individual 1 has a higher productivity, so that his budget constraint lies outside that of individual 2. The ability to pay criterion would indicate that individual 1 paid more tax, but there are obviously numberings of their indifference curves which lead to the opposite result with the social welfare function ψ.

In order to illustrate the relationship between these objectives, let us suppose, as in Lecture 11, that tastes may be represented by a single parameter γ, so that the indirect utility function may be written as $V(\mathbf{q}, w, \gamma)$. The social welfare function approach recognizes such taste differences as a legitimate basis for discrimination, and the government maximizes $\psi(\mathbf{V}(\mathbf{q}, w, \gamma))$. On the other hand, if we introduce the concept of horizontal equity and interpret this as meaning that differences in tastes are not "relevant" characteristics for discrimination, then this has two implications. First, it introduces a cardinalization, $V(\mathbf{p}, w, \gamma) = \bar{V}(\mathbf{p}, w)$, so that only endowments (w) and consumer prices (normalized at before-tax levels) are relevant. Second, it constrains the government in levying taxes ($\mathbf{q} \neq \mathbf{p}$) to maintain

$$V(\mathbf{q}, w, \gamma) = \bar{V}(\mathbf{q}, w) \tag{12-66}$$

Suppose that the government were to adopt this version of horizontal equity; what would be the implications for the optimal tax structure? It is popularly believed that it would require uniform taxation. If two individuals are identical in all respects except that one likes chocolate ice cream and the other likes vanilla, a system that taxes chocolate ice cream at a higher rate is felt to be horizontally inequitable.[19] This is not however necessarily correct. In Atkinson and Stiglitz (1976), we give an example, based on the independent compensated demands–no income effect case considered earlier, that shows that horizontal equity does not imply uniform taxation where the elasticity of demand differs between the goods in question. The horizontal equity condition (12-66) implies in fact

$$q_1^{1-\varepsilon_1} = q_2^{1-\varepsilon_2} \tag{12-67}$$

where ε_i denotes the (constant) elasticity of demand for good i, and the taste differences are multiplicative (affecting X_1 and X_2 only). The condition for horizontal equity is not necessarily, therefore, uniform taxation; only if the price elasticity is the same—as of course it may be in the chocolate–vanilla ice cream case—would uniform tax rates be horizontally equitable.

Finally, we may note that this example also brings out the conflict between horizontal equity and maximization of a social welfare function. The condition (12-66) is not in general consistent with the maximization of $\Psi(V)$. On the other hand, on the interpretation of horizontal equity as a constraint on instruments—what we have identified as the "means", rather than "ends", approach—there is no necessary conflict. The horizontal equity criterion is logically prior, imposing constraints on the choice of tax policy. On this basis, discrimination against chocolate ice cream lovers would be ruled out *a priori*.

12-6 CONCLUDING COMMENTS

One of the main functions of the second-best literature has been to show that certain common preconceptions about the desirable policy changes are not necessarily correct, and that intuitive arguments based on first-best

---

[19] Pigou (1947) gives a nice example: "When England and Ireland were united under the same taxing authority it was strongly argued that, owing to the divergent tastes of Englishmen and Irishmen, it was improper to subject them to the same tax formulae in respect of beer and whiskey." The tax on spirits, more generally consumed in Ireland, was more than two-thirds of the price, whereas the tax rate on beer was only about one-sixth of the price.

considerations may be misleading. This is well illustrated by the arguments for a uniform structure of indirect taxation. As we have seen, the efficiency argument is far from convincing; nor does horizontal equity necessarily imply a general sales tax.

These counter-examples to conventional wisdom have led to a degree of pessimism about second-best tax policy. This is however unwarranted in the sense that, starting from an arbitrary initial tax structure, there is likely to be a large number of tax reforms that potentially raise welfare. Moreover, it is possible to obtain some insight into the role of different factors, particularly efficiency and equity considerations. At the same time, the characterization of an optimal tax structure, and of the process by which it can be attained, requires detailed investigation of the appropriate model. There are not typically simple rules with wide applicability.

READING

The classic articles are Ramsey (1927) and Samuelson (1951). A basic reference is Diamond and Mirrlees (1971), which stimulated much of the recent interest. A clear introduction to the literature is provided by Sandmo (1976b). The reader may also like to consult, on the material of Section 12-3, Atkinson and Stiglitz (1972); on Section 12-4, Dixit (1975); and on 12-5, Atkinson and Stiglitz (1976).

THIRTEEN

THE STRUCTURE OF INCOME TAXATION

13-1 INTRODUCTION

In both Britain and the United States the income tax has had a controversial history. In Britain the tax was introduced by Pitt in 1799 to help finance the Napoleonic Wars but was abolished in 1816 when the electorate felt that the tax was "hostile to every sense of freedom, revolting to the feelings of Englishmen" (Sabine, 1966, p. 43). The tax was revived in 1842 on a "temporary" basis and the debate about its continuance was not finally settled until the 1880s. In the United States Civil War there was experimentation with income taxation on both sides (the schedule being more steeply progressive for the Confederates), but the later tax introduced in 1894 was declared unconstitutional and the present income tax only came into being with the ratification of the Sixteenth Amendment in 1913.

One of the issues on which controversy concentrated in the early days of income taxation was whether the rate of tax should be graduated with income. For McCulloch, "graduation is not an evil to be paltered with. Adopt it and you will effectually paralyse industry....The savages described by Montesquieu, who to get at the fruit cut down the tree, are about as good financiers as the advocates of this sort of taxes" (McCulloch, 1845, Part I, Ch. IV). While the principle of graduation is probably now widely accepted, equally strong statements are made about the effect of high marginal tax rates on "incentives". In most advanced countries there are pressures to change the rate structure. In Britain, for example, the number of steps has been decreased, so that many people face the same basic rate of tax at the margin, and the top rate on earned income has been reduced. In Canada, the Carter Commission proposed in the 1960s a reduction in top marginal rates (accompanied by a broadening of the tax base). The arguments for and against such changes have not, however, been presented in any very precise way; and, although the design of the tax schedule must balance equity against disincentives, it is not clear exactly how these considerations interact.

The aim of this Lecture is to explore some of the considerations that enter the determination of the extent of redistributive income taxation. In particular, how it is influenced by differences in distributional objectives, by the responsiveness of labour supply to taxation (we are solely concerned in this Lecture with earned income), and by the magnitude of differences in pre-taxation incomes? Answers to these questions are implicit in government decisions, but are rarely discussed. The treatment here is necessarily based on strong simplifying assumptions. For example, no systematic analysis is provided of the administrative costs of different tax schedules. None the less, we hope that it serves to illuminate the kinds of argument that can be made for changes in the structure of income tax rates.

Traditional "Sacrifice" Theories

As an introduction to some of the main considerations, we describe briefly the traditional "equal sacrifice" approach to the determination of the optimal structure of tax rates. The statements by Adam Smith that "subjects should contribute in proportion to their respective abilities' and by John Stuart Mill that "whatever sacrifices the [government] requires...should be made to bear as nearly as possible with the same pressure upon all" were translated by later writers into more precise principles. These took a number of different forms, but the concept of equal marginal sacrifice put forward by Edgeworth, Carver, Pigou and others had the clearest rationale, being derived from the utilitarian objective of the maximization of the sum of individual utilities.[1]

The implications of the equal marginal sacrifice doctrine may be seen from the following simple model. Suppose that individuals differ in their earning ability, denoted by w. The before-tax earnings of a person of type w are denoted by $Z(w)$ and the tax paid, by $T(w)$. The utility derived from after-tax income is given by $U_w(Z(w) - T(w))$, so that if $F(w)$ is the cumulative distribution of people of type w, the integral of individual utilities is denoted by

$$\int_0^\infty U_w(Z(w) - T(w))\,dF \qquad (13\text{-}1)$$

The government determines the taxes paid (where $T(w)$ may be positive or negative) so as to maximize total utility subject to raising the required

---

[1] For an extensive discussion, see Musgrave (1959, Ch. 5), who describes the alternative concepts of equal absolute sacrifice and equal proportional sacrifice.

revenue R_0:

$$\int_0^\infty T(w)\,dF = R_0 \tag{13-2}$$

On the assumption that the functions U_w are such that $U_w' >$, $U_w'' < 0$, the solution involves

$$U_w' = \text{constant all } w \tag{13-3}$$

If the marginal utility of income schedule is assumed to be identical for everyone, the tax structure is such that after-tax incomes are equalized, "A system of equimarginal sacrifice fully carried out would involve lopping off the tops of all incomes above [a certain] income and leaving everybody, after taxation, with equal incomes' (Pigou, 1947, pp. 57–8). If $T(w)$ were constrained to be non-negative, we would have the solution described by Dalton: "taxing only the largest incomes, cutting down all above a certain level to that level, and exempting all below that level" (Dalton, 1954, p. 59). The recommendations appear therefore to be highly radical, and this may be one of the reasons for the widespread belief that pursuit of a utilitarian objective was synonymous with egalitarianism—a belief that we have already seen to be misguided (and further counter-examples are provided by the analysis of this Lecture).

Possibly because of its radical implications, the least sacrifice theory came under a great deal of attack. Three main lines of criticism may be distinguished:

1. that the minimum sacrifice theory takes no account of the possible disincentive effect of taxation (that $Z(w)$ may be influenced by the tax structure);
2. that the underlying utilitarian framework is inadequate;
3. that account must be taken of the restrictions on the types of taxes that may be levied.

The first of these was clearly recognized by those writing in the utilitarian tradition. Edgeworth describes Sidgwick as contemplating "the crowning height of the utilitarian first principle", but also as discerning "the enormous interposing chasms which deter practical wisdom from moving directly towards that ideal" (Edgeworth, 1925, p. 104). In particular, Sidgwick was concerned lest "a greater equality in the distribution of produce would lead ultimately to a reduction in the total amount to be distributed in consequence of a general preference of leisure" (quoted by Edgeworth, 1925).

In the second line of criticism one can distinguish a number of strands. One is the attack on the interpersonal comparability of utilities. This is, for example, the main ground for the rejection of the sacrifice approach by Prest:

> It seems reasonable to conclude that sacrifice is not only unmeasurable and incapable of quantification for any one individual but also not comparable as between individuals. With such fundamental objections it would seem to be impossible to accept the conclusions derived from the theories of sacrifice. [Prest, 1975, p. 122]

A rather different approach is that of Rawls (1971), who would accept comparability but reject the view that the sum of individual utilities is the appropriate maximand. As we have seen in Lecture 11, his theory of justice has been interpreted as saying that the guiding principle should be the maximization of the welfare of the least fortunate person (the "maxi-min" criterion).

Finally, it is possible that the social welfare function is non-Paretian, i.e., that it is not an increasing function of individual utilities. Thus an "egalitarian" social welfare function may be concerned about the distance between individuals. In the simple model discussed above, with no disincentive effects, the results would be unchanged (and the same applies to a Rawlsian objective), but in more realistic models, with a trade-off between equity and efficiency, differences in the social welfare function become significant.

The third criticism concerns the range of instruments at the government's disposal. This has been discussed in general terms in Lecture 11, but is well illustrated by the present case. Suppose that income is generated by working $L(w)$ hours so that $Z(w) = wL(w)$. The assumption made above is that $L(w)$ is unaffected by taxation. This means that the least sacrifice solution may be achieved by a lump-sum tax $(Z - \tau(w))$, by a wage tax $([w - t(w)]L)$, or by an income tax $(Z - T(Z))$. In a more general model, however, allowing for the response of individuals to taxation, these taxes may not be perfect substitutes, and we need to distinguish carefully between them. Our focus in what follows is on the income tax, but we also in Section 13-4 compare this with the first-best lump-sum tax.

The analysis in this Lecture may be seen as attempting to meet these criticisms of the earlier literature. In particular, it is centred on the conflict between efficiency and redistribution. The models used to represent this conflict are developed in order of increasing generality. In Section 13-2 we set out a simple illustrative model, intended to illuminate some of the main features, particularly the role of different distributional goals. The model is simple in its representation of individual decision-making and in being based on a linear income tax (with a constant marginal rate of tax). In Section 13-3, we present a less restrictive model of work–leisure choice but retain the assumption that the tax schedule is linear. Finally, in Section 13-4 we analyse a general income tax where the marginal rate of tax may vary freely with the level of income.

13-2 A SIMPLE MODEL

The analysis in this section is designed to illustrate the balancing of efficiency and equity considerations in the simplest of circumstances. To this end, we describe a model where gross earnings depend on ability and on decisions about education, and where the government levies a redistributive, linear income tax.

The Model

The individual's earnings are assumed to depend only on earning ability (w) and on the number of years of education received (D); i.e., hours of work (effort) are assumed to be fixed. While undergoing education the individual has zero earnings. At work he earns a constant amount $Z(w, D)$ and he retires after working Q years.[2] He maximizes the present value of his lifetime income, discounted at interest rate r back to the start of his education.

$$\int_{D}^{D+Q} [Z - T(Z)] e^{-ru} \, du$$

Since Z is constant over time, this is proportional to

$$\chi = [Z - T(Z)] e^{-rD} \tag{13-4}$$

(where the factor of proportionality is $(1 - e^{-rQ})/r$). The only difference between individuals is in earning ability, and in the consequent choice of D.

The tax schedule is assumed to be linear, so that, as in earlier lectures, there is a guaranteed income G and a constant marginal tax rate, denoted by t:

$$T(Z) = tZ - G \tag{13-5}$$

where there is a negative tax supplement ($T < 0$) for $Z < G/t$. The tax is assumed to be levied solely on wage income, and interest is tax-free (the tax treatment of savings is discussed in Lecture 14). The guaranteed income G is not paid during the period of education. If we assume that there is an equal number of people, with the same distribution of w, in each age group, and that revenue R_0 is required per cohort, the government budget constraint is

$$\int_{w}^{\infty} T(Z) \, dF = R_0 \tag{13-6}$$

---

[2] Thus, he retires $D+Q$ years after starting education. This means that people with more education retire at an older age. This could be modified to a common retirement age at the cost of slight additional complexity.

where the cumulative distribution of people with different ability is $F(w)$, and **w** denotes the lowest ability level.

As in the case of the Ramsey tax problem, there is a two-stage maximization process. The individual, faced with tax parameters t and G, chooses the level of education D to maximize χ. The government then chooses t and G in the light of this response. We begin with the individual's problem, and simplify this still further by assuming $Z(w, D) = wD$; i.e., earnings are proportional to years of education. The objective is then to maximize

$$\chi = [G + (1 - t)wD] e^{-rD} \qquad (13\text{-}7)$$

subject to $D \geqslant 0$. Taking logarithms, and differentiating with respect to D,

$$\frac{1}{\chi} \frac{\partial \chi}{\partial D} = \frac{(1 - t)w}{G + (1 - t)wD} - r$$

Re-arranging, the solution may be seen to be

$$D = \frac{1}{r} - \frac{G}{(1 - t)w} \quad \text{for } w \geqslant \frac{rG}{1 - t} (\equiv w_0) \qquad (13\text{-}8\text{a})$$

$$D = 0 \quad \text{for } w \leqslant w_0 \qquad (13\text{-}8\text{b})$$

The resulting level of χ is given by

$$\log \chi = \frac{rG}{(1 - t)w} - 1 + \log\left[\frac{(1 - t)w}{r}\right] \quad \text{for } w \geqslant w_0 \qquad (13\text{-}9\text{a})$$

$$= \log G \quad \text{for } w \leqslant w_0 \qquad (13\text{-}9\text{b})$$

It may be noted that in the absence of taxation everyone would choose the same level of D; the effect of taxation is to widen pre-tax income differentials while narrowing after-tax differentials.

Choice Open to Government

If we now consider the implications of individual behaviour for the government's choice of t and G, we can see that the revenue constraint may take one of two forms. In the first (case A), the level of w_0 is set such that all individuals have $D > 0$ (i.e. $\mathbf{w} > w_0$). We can then substitute from (13-8a) into the revenue constraint. If we normalize such that $\int_{\mathbf{w}}^{\infty} dF = 1$, then

$$G + R_0 = t \int_{\mathbf{w}}^{\infty} \left(\frac{w}{r} - \frac{G}{1 - t}\right) dF \qquad (13\text{-}10)$$

Writing $\bar{w}$ for the mean value of w, and re-arranging,

$$\frac{G}{1 - t} + R_0 = \frac{t\bar{w}}{r} \qquad (13\text{-}11)$$

In the second case (B), some individuals choose $D = 0$ ($w \leqslant w_0$). The revenue constraint is then:

$$G + R_0 = t \int_{w_0}^{\infty} \left(\frac{w}{r} - \frac{G}{1-t} \right) dF \qquad (13\text{-}12)$$

Introducing the notation for the incomplete mean,

$$\Phi(w_0) = \int_{\mathbf{w}}^{w_0} \frac{w}{\bar{w}} \, dF \qquad (13\text{-}13)$$

this expression may be rewritten as:

$$R_0 + \frac{G}{1-t} [1 - t F(w_0)] = \frac{t\bar{w}}{r} [1 - \Phi(w_0)] \qquad (13\text{-}14)$$

This is not an explicit expression for G (which enters via w_0), and is clearly more complicated than case A. In view of this, we give the results when the tax rates are such that case A applies, leaving the other case to the reader.

From the revenue constraint faced by the government in case A, the menu of choice may be plotted—as in Fig. 13-1. With $t = 0$, the revenue has to be raised by a poll-tax ($G < 0$). The slope of the constraint is given by

$$\frac{dG}{dt} = R_0 + (1 - 2t) \frac{\bar{w}}{r} \qquad (13\text{-}15)$$

so that it is first positive and then negative, G reaching a maximum at a tax rate in excess of 50 per cent. In order for case A to apply we require that $w_0 \leqslant \mathbf{w}$, which is satisfied for

$$t \leqslant \mathbf{w}/\bar{w} + r R_0/\bar{w}$$

(where we have used (13-8a) and (13-11)). Thus, if the revenue requirement is 20 per cent of mean income in the absence of taxation, and the lowest ability is 50 per cent of the mean, then case A applies for tax rates up to 70 per cent.

As an introduction to the government's decision, let us suppose first that it acts to maximize the lifetime income of a "representative" individual with wage w^*. From (13-9) we can see that, where the individual has $D > 0$, he would rank combinations of G and t according to:[3]

$$\chi^* \equiv \log \chi - \log \frac{w^*}{r} + 1 = \frac{rG}{(1-t)w^*} + \log(1-t) \qquad (13\text{-}16)$$

This gives indifference curves of the type illustrated in Fig. 13-1. In particular, the slope of the curve $\chi^* = $ constant is given by

$$\frac{dG}{dt} = \frac{w^*}{r} - \frac{G}{1-t} \qquad (13\text{-}17)$$

---

[3] The term $1 - \log(w^*/r)$ can be subtracted since it is independent of G and t.

Evaluating at $t = 0$, where $G = -R_0$, we can see that the slope is greater than that of the revenue constraint (given by Eq. (13-15)) where $w^* > \bar{w}$. It follows that, if the representative individual were above the mean, he would not favour the use of income taxation. If the representative man is below the mean, we have the situation illustrated in Fig. 13-1, where he has a preferred tax rate that is strictly positive. The preferred tax rate is that

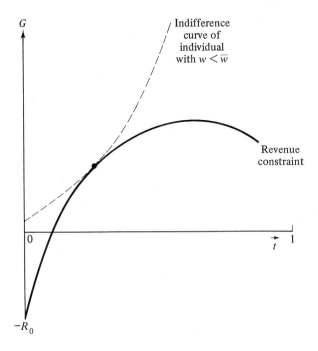

Figure 13-1 Feasible tax systems and individual preferences.

where the indifference curve is tangent to the constraint; i.e., from (13-15) and (13-17)

$$R_0 + (1 - 2t)\frac{\bar{w}}{r} = \frac{w^*}{r} - \frac{G}{1-t} = \frac{w^*}{r} + R_0 - \frac{t\bar{w}}{r} \qquad (13\text{-}18)$$

where the second step uses (13-11). It follows that the chosen $t^* = 1 - w^*/\bar{w}$, so that as the wage falls below the mean, the tax rate chosen rises linearly. In the limit, a person with the lowest wage $\mathbf{w}$ chooses $t^* = 1 - \mathbf{w}/\bar{w}$ (where this is feasible in case A). This is not the same as maximizing G, since, as is clear from (13-16), the lowest person also has an interest in keeping the tax rate down and trades off one against the other. In case B, the lowest person has no pre-tax income and is interested solely in maximizing G.

Social Welfare Maximization

The conflict of interests in choosing G and t is apparent from this discussion, and any decision rule for the government implies a weighting of these interests. As a starting point, let us take the Benthamite utilitarian objective of maximizing the sum of utilities derived from after-tax lifetime income, which is proportional to χ. For ease of exposition, we take the isoelastic form[4]

$$\frac{1}{1-v}\int_{\mathbf{w}}^{\infty}(\chi^{1-v}-1)\,dF \quad \text{where } v \geqslant 0 \text{ and } v \neq 1 \qquad (13\text{-}19a)$$

$$\int_{\mathbf{w}}^{\infty}\log\chi\,dF \qquad\qquad \text{where } v = 1 \qquad (13\text{-}19b)$$

The parameter v is the elasticity of the marginal utility of income. For $v = 0$, the objective function becomes mean income, and it can be shown that this is maximized by $t = 0$. Where $v > 0$, the tax rate chosen is strictly positive. The solution (in case A) may be found by substituting the expression for G from the revenue constraint (13-11) into the expression for (13-9a). This gives an unconstrained maximization problem, and the first-order conditions are derived by differentiating with respect to t (Atkinson, 1973).

> **Exercise 13-1** Show that, where $v = 1$ and $R_0 = 0$, the first-order conditions require
>
> $$\frac{1}{1-t} = \int_{\mathbf{w}}^{\infty}\frac{\bar{w}}{w}\,dF \qquad (13\text{-}20)$$
>
> Show that the right-hand side is strictly greater than unity for a distribution where there exist some differences in w.

In order to illustrate the solution, let us take the case where $R_0 = 0$ and the distribution $F(w)$ is Pareto in form (it should be emphasized that this is merely illustrative and not intended to be realistic):

$$dF = \mu\mathbf{w}^{\mu}w^{-\mu-1}\,dw \qquad (13\text{-}21)$$

It may be noted that $\bar{w} = (\mu/(\mu-1))\mathbf{w}$, so that case A applies for $t \leqslant 1 - 1/\mu$. The solutions to the problem of choosing t to maximize total utility subject to the revenue constraint for different values of v and μ are shown in Table 13-1. (Details of the calculations are given in Atkinson, 1973, pp. 102–3.) The value of μ reflects the degree of dispersion of abilities (see previous Lecture), and a lower value indicates greater inequality (for a constant mean). As might be expected, the tax rate rises as μ falls. The value of v

---

[4] That $v \to 1$ gives the logarithmic case may be seen by applying L'Hôpital's rule (and the fact that $\partial/\partial v(\chi^{1-v}) = -\chi^{1-v}\log\chi$). (We have written $\chi^{1-v}-1$, so that the limit is correct in this case.)

Table 13-1 Calculations of tax rates for Pareto distribution

Value of v	Value of μ		
	2.0	3.0	4.0
	%	%	%
1.0	25	11	6
2.0	33	18	9
4.0	36	21	14
6.0	39	24	15
8.0	40	25	18
16.0	43	28	21

reflects the cardinalization of the utility function and the results suggest that the optimal rate of income taxation may depend quite sensitively on the particular cardinalization adopted. (For $\mu = 3.0$, the tax rate doubles as v rises from 1.0 to 4.0.) This is likely to be a matter for concern if we cannot obtain any firm estimate from individual behaviour of the value that is likely to be taken by v. Moreover, we have to consider the possibility that v may reflect social values as well as individual utility—a point to which we now turn.

Exercise 13-2 Show that where $v = 1$, and case A applies, the Pareto case involves $t = 1/\mu^2$.

The objective function has so far been treated as the sum of individual utilities, but one standard objection to utilitarianism is that it fails to take account of the *distribution* of utilities. A more general formulation is the social welfare function:

$$\int_w^\infty \Psi[U(\chi)]\,dF \qquad (13\text{-}22)$$

where Ψ is an increasing, concave function. First, we may note that in the formulation of the minimum sacrifice theory this redefinition of the objective would have made no difference. The first-order conditions become

$$\Psi' \cdot U' \quad \text{equal all } w$$

giving the same solution. In the present case, this is no longer true. This may be illustrated by the situation where increasing the concavity of Ψ has the effect of increasing v. The consequences for the Pareto example may then be read directly from Table 13-1. The parameter v is now the elasticity of the *social* marginal utility of income, and its value depends on the attitudes of the government towards redistribution. A government that is more concerned about the distribution will, other things equal, apply a higher value of v and hence choose a higher tax rate.

The limiting case of the isoelastic function is that where $v \to \infty$, when we have the Rawlsian objective. The government then chooses the tax rate preferred by the person with the lowest ability. Where there is a solution with case A, we have seen that this involves

$$t = 1 - \mathbf{w}/\bar{w} \tag{13-23a}$$

In the Pareto case

$$\mathbf{w}/\bar{w} = 1 - 1/\mu \tag{13-23b}$$

so that the optimal tax rate is $1/\mu$ (which satisfies the condition for case A where $\mu \geqslant 2$). The rate of tax is higher than that likely to be obtained with the Benthamite objective, but none the less falls considerably short of the egalitarian prescriptions of Pigou and Edgeworth, which led to 100 per cent marginal rate of tax. In the present case this does not happen for two reasons. First, we have to take account of the effects on the decisions of the better-off groups. It is in the interests of the worst-off person to reduce the rate below 100 per cent to increase the revenue raised from those higher up the scale. Second, as stressed in Lecture 11, the Rawlsian objective is the most egalitarian of the Paretian social welfare functions, but does not coincide with the egalitarian principle in the sense of seeking to equalize utilities.

It is indeed possible that the social welfare function is non-Paretian. Some people may feel that the size of the gap between the top and the bottom should influence the choice of tax rate. Fair (1971) refers to the belief of Plato that no one should be more than four times richer than the poorest member of society. If this is so, we may well choose tax rates higher than the maxi-min solution. Although this would reduce the lifetime income of the poorest man, it would narrow the gap between him and those at the top. In the present model with the Pareto distribution, the after-tax income of the lowest man as a percentage of the average is (for $w_0 < \mathbf{w}$ and $R_0 = 0$)

$$(1 - 1/\mu)e^{t/(\mu - 1)} \tag{13-24}$$

The values of this ratio for different values of t (where $\mu = 3$) is given below:

$t = 0$	Ratio = 66 per cent
$t = 33\frac{1}{3}$ per cent (maxi-min solution)	Ratio = 79 per cent
$t = 50$ per cent	Ratio = 86 per cent
$t = 66\frac{2}{3}$ per cent (maximum feasible in case A)	Ratio = 93 per cent

Finally, the earlier presentation in terms of individual preferences about taxation allows us to relate the analysis to majority voting. Although it is unlikely that the precise details of the tax structure would be subject to voting, issues of broad policy regarding the degree of progression may well be settled by appeal to the electorate. This question has been discussed by Foley (1967), who considers the stability of different tax structures under majority rule (i.e., whether there is a tax schedule that is always supported by a majority against any alternative). As he points out, where the class of tax schedules under consideration is unrestricted, there is no majority voting equilibrium, but if, for example, attention is restricted to the class of linear tax schedules, this contains a stable element. Foley does not allow for the effect of taxation on the earnings of the individual, but his results can readily be extended to that case. In terms of the model set out above (with case A), an increase in t is opposed by all those with w greater than $\bar{w}(1-t)$ and favoured by those below this value.[5] Preferences are single-peaked, and the tax rate chosen as a result of majority voting will be $t = 1 - w_m/\bar{w}$ where w_m is the median. For positively skew distributions, $w_m < \bar{w}$, and voting leads to a positive tax rate. In the Pareto example, we obtain tax rates of 16 per cent (with $\mu = 3$) and 29 per cent (with $\mu = 2$). For further discussion of majority voting, see Romer (1975) and Roberts (1977). The latter shows that, if preferences are such that the ordering of people by income is independent of the tax schedule, then a most preferred outcome will exist for a wide class of voting mechanisms—even where single-peakedness does not apply.

13-3 LINEAR INCOME TAX

The model considered in the previous section was intended only to be illustrative. In this section we describe the treatment of individual labour supply decisions that has been employed in much of the literature on optimal income taxation, and which is closer to the empirical work on labour supply discussed in Lecture 2. We continue however to retain the assumption of a linear tax. This means that we can examine the degree of progression in terms of the behaviour of the average rate of tax ($G > 0$ implies that the tax is progressive in this sense), but that we can throw no light on the way in which the marginal rate should vary with income. This latter question is taken up in Section 13-4.

The Government's Problem

The model of individual behaviour is that used extensively in Lecture 2. An individual maximizes a utility function $U(Y,L)$ where Y is after-tax income and L is labour supplied. It is assumed that U is quasi-concave, continuously differentiable, strictly increasing in Y, and strictly decreasing

---

[5] This follows from the condition that the tax rate chosen by w^* is $t^* = 1 - w^*/\bar{w}$, and the fact that there are no other turning points.

in L. The individual maximizes utility subject to

$$Y = Z - T = (1-t)wL + G \tag{13-25}$$

since pre-tax income $Z = wL$ where w is the wage rate. The first-order conditions give

$$(1-t)wU_Y + U_L = 0 \tag{13-26a}$$

or

$$(1-t)wU_Y(G,0) + U_L(G,0) \leqslant 0 \quad \text{and} \quad L = 0 \tag{13-26b}$$

In the population as a whole, individuals are assumed to be identical in all respects except their wage rate (earning ability). (The implications of other differences are discussed below.) It can then be shown that there is a critical wage w_0 such that:

$$L(w) > 0 \quad \text{for} \quad w > w_0$$
$$L(w) = 0 \quad \text{for} \quad w \leqslant w_0 \tag{13-27}$$

(This is parallel to the model of the previous section.[6]) To see this, we may note that the left-hand side of (13-26b) is strictly negative at $w = 0$, and that it is a strictly increasing function of w. There is therefore a value w_0 such that this condition holds with equality, and for $w > w_0$ the left-hand side must be strictly positive (hence $L > 0$). If on the production side we assume constant producer prices and no profits, and if the revenue requirement is R_0, then the production constraint is

$$\int_{\mathbf{w}}^{\infty} Y\, dF + R_0 = \int_{w_0}^{\infty} wL\, dF \tag{13-28}$$

We normalize again by setting $\int_{\mathbf{w}}^{\infty} dF = 1$; and, using the individual budget constraint (13-25), this may be rewritten as a revenue constraint

$$G + R_0 = t \int_{w_0}^{\infty} wL\, dF \tag{13-29}$$

The government is assumed to maximize the social welfare function:

$$\int_{\mathbf{w}}^{\infty} \Psi(U)\, dF \tag{13-30}$$

where different assumptions about Ψ yield, for example, the utilitarian ($\Psi' = 1$) and Rawlsian objectives. Forming the Lagrangean:

$$\mathscr{L} = \int_{\mathbf{w}}^{\infty} [\Psi + \lambda(twL - G - R_0)]\, dF \tag{13-31}$$

---

[6] The model of the previous section may in fact be obtained as a special case where $U(Y,L) = \log Y - rL$.

we may derive the first-order conditions with respect to G and t (Sheshinski, 1972):

$$\int_{w}^{\infty}\left[\Psi'\frac{\partial U}{\partial G}+\lambda\left(tw\frac{\partial L}{\partial G}-1\right)\right]dF=0 \qquad (13\text{-}32a)$$

$$\int_{w}^{\infty}\left[\Psi'\frac{\partial U}{\partial t}+\lambda\left(wL+tw\frac{\partial L}{\partial t}\right)\right]dF=0 \qquad (13\text{-}32b)$$

where it should be noted that $L=0$ and $\partial L/\partial G=\partial L/\partial t=0$ for $w<w_0$.

The Optimum Linear Income Tax

The problem is parallel in several respects to the Ramsey tax model. In particular, there is no reason to expect the problem to be well-behaved, and we have to be careful in employing the first-order conditions. There may be more than one solution to the first-order conditions, so that satisfying (13-32a) and (13-32b) is not sufficient. Where more than one solution exists, a global comparison must be made of the levels of welfare.

Bearing these qualifications in mind, we may examine the implications. Our earlier experience with the Ramsey problem suggests that it may be illuminating to use the Slutsky relationship

$$\frac{\partial L}{\partial t}=-wS_{LL}-wL\frac{\partial L}{\partial M} \qquad (13\text{-}33)$$

where S_{LL} is the substitution term (compensated response of labour to the marginal net wage) and is non-negative. Using this, and the fact that $\partial U/\partial t=-\alpha wL$, where α is the private marginal utility of income, we can rearrange (13-32):

$$\int\left(\Psi'\frac{\alpha}{\lambda}+tw\frac{\partial L}{\partial M}-1\right)dF=0 \qquad (13\text{-}34a)$$

$$\int wL\left(\Psi'\frac{\alpha}{\lambda}+tw\frac{\partial L}{\partial M}-1+\frac{twS_{LL}}{L}\right)dF=0 \qquad (13\text{-}34b)$$

If we now define, as in the previous Lecture, the net social marginal valuation of income,

$$b=\Psi'\frac{\alpha}{\lambda}+tw\frac{\partial L}{\partial M} \qquad (13\text{-}35)$$

the conditions reduce to (Dixit and Sandmo, 1977; Stiglitz, 1976a):

$$\bar{b}=1 \qquad (13\text{-}36a)$$

$$\frac{t}{1-t}=\frac{-\operatorname{cov}[b,Z]}{\int Z\varepsilon_{LL}\,dF} \qquad (13\text{-}36b)$$

In the second equation, cov [   ] denotes the covariance, and ε_{LL} is the compensated elasticity ($[w(1-t)/L]S_{LL}$).[7] In interpreting these conditions we assume that Z is a non-decreasing function of w, so that the covariance is non-positive if the social marginal valuation of income is non-increasing with w. The covariance may be seen as a marginal measure of inequality (Stiglitz, 1976c).

The conditions (13-36a) and (13-36b) have a very natural interpretation. The first says that the lump-sum element should be adjusted such that b, the net social marginal valuation of the transfer of \$1 of income (measured in terms of government revenue), should on average be equal to the cost (\$1). The second indicates that the tax depends on the compensated labour supply elasticity and the way in which the marginal social valuation of income varies with w. These two factors are just what we would have expected on the basis of Lecture 12. In interpreting the condition (13-36b), the denominator is positive (since $S_{LL} > 0$), but the numerator could be negative. In particular it depends on $\partial L/\partial M$, and if leisure were to become an inferior good at high wages, then it is possible that b and Z could be positively correlated.

An Example

In order to illustrate the analysis, let us take the case of the Cobb–Douglas utility function:

$$U(Y, L) = a \log Y + (1-a) \log (1-L) \qquad (13\text{-}37)$$

where $0 < a < 1$. The labour supply may be derived from the first-order conditions for utility maximization. From (13-26), using the budget constraint to substitute for Y,

$$\frac{aw(1-t)}{w(1-t)L+G} = \frac{1-a}{1-L} \quad \text{or} \quad \frac{aw(1-t)}{G} \leqslant 1-a \quad \text{and} \quad L = 0$$

Hence

$$L = a - \frac{(1-a)G}{w(1-t)} \quad \text{for} \quad w \geqslant \frac{1-a}{a}\frac{G}{1-t}(\equiv w_0)$$

$$L = 0 \qquad\qquad\qquad \text{otherwise} \qquad\qquad (13\text{-}38)$$

---

[7] The derivation may be seen by re-arranging (13-34b)

$$\int Z\left(b - \bar{b} + \frac{t}{1-t}\varepsilon_{LL}\right)dF = 0$$

where we have used the fact that $\bar{b} = 1$.

It follows that the net social marginal valuation of income is given by

$$b = \Psi' \frac{\alpha}{\lambda} - \frac{t}{1-t}(1-a) \qquad \text{for} \quad w > w_0$$

$$= \Psi' \frac{\alpha}{\lambda} \qquad\qquad \text{for} \quad w \leqslant w_0 \qquad (13\text{-}39)$$

so that b jumps discontinuously downwards at w_0. We may also note that $\alpha = U_Y = a/Y$, which is a non-increasing function of w. It follows that $\Psi'' < 0$ is sufficient for b to fall with w, and for the covariance between b and Z to be negative (since Z increases with w). Hence the optimal tax is strictly positive.

The influence of different distributional objectives may be seen from the term $\Psi'\alpha$, with differing degrees of concavity for Ψ. In the extreme case of the Rawlsian objective, the solution is relatively simple. If we assume that the distribution has strictly positive density at all non-negative w (so that there are always some individuals not working), then the problem reduces to maximizing G. Forming the Lagrangean

$$\mathcal{L} = G + \lambda \int_0^\infty (twL - G - R_0)\, dF \qquad (13\text{-}40)$$

The first-order condition with respect to t yields

$$\int_{w_0}^\infty \left(wL + tw\frac{\partial L}{\partial t}\right) dF = 0 \qquad (13\text{-}41)$$

(this follows directly from (13-32b) by noting that $\partial U/\partial t = 0$ for all w for which $\Psi' \neq 0$). Using the government revenue constraint,

$$t^2 \int_{w_0}^\infty \left(\frac{-w\partial L}{\partial t}\right) dF = t \int_{w_0}^\infty wL\, dF = G + R_0 \qquad (13\text{-}42)$$

In the Cobb–Douglas case, from (13-38),

$$\frac{-w\partial L}{\partial t} = \frac{(1-a)G}{(1-t)^2}$$

Hence

$$\frac{t^2}{(1-t)^2} = \frac{(1+R_0/G)}{1-a}\frac{1}{1-F(w_0)} \qquad (13\text{-}43)$$

Where the revenue to be raised is non-negative ($R_0 \geqslant 0$), the right-hand side is greater than unity. There may be multiple solutions to this equation (N.B. w_0 depends on G and t), but all must be such that the tax rate is at least 50 per cent. With this Rawlsian objective the optimal marginal tax rates *may* therefore be quite high.

Exercise 13-3 Examine the optimal linear tax where $R_0 = 0$ and the distribution is of the Pareto form (13-21). Derive conditions such that there is a solution where everyone works ($w_0 < \mathbf{w}$) in the Rawlsian case, and calculate the optimum tax.

Numerical Calculations

The model just described is no more than illustrative. Among other things, the Cobb–Douglas utility function may give a misleading impression of the elasticity of labour supply. This aspect has been investigated by Stern (1976), who sought to relate the optimum tax literature to estimated labour supply functions of the type discussed in Lecture 2. He took for this purpose the constant elasticity function

$$U = [\delta^{1-\rho}Y^\rho + (1-\delta)^{1-\rho}(1-L)^\rho]^{1/\rho} \quad \text{where} \quad \rho \leqslant 1 \quad (13\text{-}44)$$

This may be seen to be a special case of the function considered in Lecture 12 (Y is a composite of all goods and there is zero committed expenditure). As there, $\sigma = 1/(1-\rho)$ is the elasticity of substitution, and the Cobb–Douglas case just considered has $\rho = 0$. On the basis of the empirical results of Ashenfelter and Heckman (1973), Stern estimates that $\sigma = 0.408$. This is a point estimate from one study, and relates to the hours of work of male heads of families in the United States. His discussion of the sensitivity of the estimate, based on the standard errors and on other studies for similar populations, indicates that a range of 0.2–0.6 may not be unreasonable.[8]

Stern formulates the problem in terms of the government choosing G and t to maximize

$$\frac{1}{1-v} \int_0^\infty (U^{1-v} - 1)dF \quad \text{where} \quad v \geqslant 0 \quad (13\text{-}45)$$

(again, the limit as $v \to 1$ is the logarithmic case), subject to the revenue constraint. The distribution is assumed to be lognormal with the standard deviation of logarithms equal to 0.39 (in the main set of results). This would imply, for $\sigma = 1$, a lognormal distribution of earnings with a Gini coefficient of 0.22. The maxima for different values of σ, v, and R_0 were obtained by a grid search procedure.[9]

A selection of results is shown in Table 13-2. These bear out our earlier findings about different forms of the social welfare function. With $v = 0$, we have the Benthamite utilitarian objective. For higher values of v the function is more concave, and the optimum tax rate rises markedly for all values of σ. For $v \to \infty$, the Rawlsian case, the tax rates are all in excess of

---

[8] The parameter δ is chosen such that $L = \frac{2}{3}$ for $G = 0$, $t = 0$ in the case $\sigma = \frac{1}{2}$.

[9] Evaluation suggested that there was at most one local maximum (Stern, 1976, p. 148).

Table 13-2 Stern's calculations of optimal linear tax rates (%)

σ	$v = 0$	$v = 2$	$v = 3$	$v \to \infty$
$R_0 = 0$ (Purely redistributive tax)				
0.2	36.2	62.7	67.0	92.6
0.4	22.3	47.7	52.7	83.9
0.6	17.0	38.9	43.8	75.6
0.8	14.1	33.1	37.6	68.2
1.0	12.7	29.1	33.4	62.1
$R_0 = 0.05$				
0.2	40.6	68.1	72.0	93.8
0.4	25.4	54.0	58.8	86.7
0.6	18.9	45.0	50.1	79.8
0.8	19.7	38.9	43.8	73.6
1.0	20.6	34.7	39.5	68.5
$R_0 = 0.10$				
0.2	45.6	73.3	76.7	95.0+
0.4	35.1	60.5	65.1	89.3
0.6	36.6	52.0	57.1	83.9
0.8	38.6	46.0	51.3	79.2
1.0	40.9	41.7	47.0	75.6

Source: Stern (1976, Table 3).
Note: The case 1.0 actually refers to $\sigma = 0.99$, and we have defined v differently from Stern.

50 per cent. Turning to Stern's particular concern—the role of the elasticity of substitution—we can see that the relationship between σ and the tax rate is not monotonic. However, it is noticeable that the tax for his preferred value, $\sigma = 0.4$, is (with one exception) higher than in the Cobb–Douglas case ($\sigma = 1.0$), and that, for all but the first column, the differences are quite substantial. With $v = 2$ and $R_0 = 0$, for example, the tax rate is 29 per cent for $\sigma = 1$ but 48 per cent for $\sigma = 0.4$ (and 39–63 per cent for the range $\sigma = 0.2$–0.6). As the author notes, this approach "gives taxation rates which are rather high without any appeal to extreme social welfare functions" (Stern, 1976, p. 152). A further feature is the effect of increasing revenue requirements. With $R_0 = 0.05$, which corresponds to the government absorbing about 20 per cent of GNP, the tax rates rise by some 5 per cent.

These calculations are valuable in assessing the likely sensitivity of the results to the formulation of the model, and in indicating the parameters that are likely to be of central importance. They are not however intended to be realistic, and Stern is careful to qualify the conclusions drawn. The results may change substantially with different assumptions about the demand for labour. The interpretation of labour supply in terms of hours worked is open to question. To the extent that it makes no allowance for other dimensions of work effort (discussed in Lecture 2), it may well mean that $\sigma = 0.4$ is an understatement of the true elasticity.

This leads to one final observation—that policy is designed in the face of considerable uncertainty about key parameters. The uncertainty surrounding σ, and other parameters, should be explicitly incorporated into the analysis of optimal tax rates. This has not been done in the research described above, but some light is provided by Stern's calculations of the welfare gains from redistributive taxation, measured in equivalent equally distributed consumption. Expressed as a function of the tax rate, the level of welfare is relatively flat for $v = 0$ but becomes much more peaked as v increases (Stern, 1976, Figs 3a, b). This suggests that reducing uncertainty about σ may be more important when the government is more concerned about redistribution, but this needs to be examined more fully.

13-4 GENERAL INCOME TAX

The assumption of a linear tax schedule has precluded any discussion of whether it is desirable for marginal tax rates to rise or to fall with income. We turn now to this question, considering a general income tax schedule $T(Z)$. The classic paper in this area is that by Mirrlees (1971).[10] It is not, however, easy reading. In what follows, we summarize the main features of the article, and of subsequent literature, without providing a rigorous treatment. We begin with a geometric exposition; we then set out an heuristic derivation of the basic solution and discuss its interpretation. The results at a general level are rather limited (although they yield interesting counter-examples to certain beliefs), and in the last part of the section we describe numerical results obtained in the special Cobb–Douglas case.

Geometric Exposition

In order to see qualitatively the considerations likely to influence the choice of the marginal tax rate, we draw in Fig. 13-2 the simple leisure–net income diagram used in Lecture 2, which we now modify by introducing different households with discretely different wage rates $w_1, w_2 ..., w_H$ (in increasing order), and by measuring along the horizontal axis gross earnings $Z = wL$ (for any household this is proportional to L), rather than labour (as in Mirrlees, 1977). To set the scene, let us suppose that the tax schedule has been fixed up to the point P (gross income Z_{i-1}) chosen by household $(i-1)$, and that we are deciding how to extend it beyond P. The indifference curve for $(i-1)$ is shown (for P to be chosen by him, the schedule at higher

---

[10] See also Zeckhauser (1969) for an early treatment, employing a quadratic tax function, and Wesson (1972).

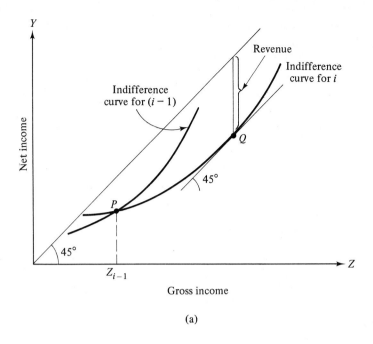

(a)

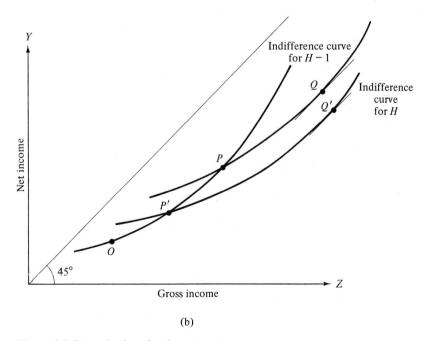

(b)

Figure 13-2 Determination of optimum tax rates.

Z must lie beneath this indifference curve), as is the indifference curve for the next household (i). By assumption (see below) the curve for a person with higher w is flatter at every point (Mirrlees, 1971, Seade, 1977).

Let us suppose first that the government attaches no value to the utility of households i and higher, and it aims simply to maximize revenue. Now if the marginal tax rate above Z_{i-1} were 100 per cent, the household i would choose $[Y(Z_{i-1}), Z_{i-1}/w_i]$.[11] This does not however maximize the revenue from household i, which is measured by the distance between the 45° line and the tax schedule. If the government were to maximize revenue subject to the consumer being no worse off than at P, then the solution is at the point Q in Fig. 13-2a, where the indifference curve through P has a slope of 45°. In other words, the marginal tax rate would be zero (the slope being 45°). If $i = H$ (the top household), then this would be the end of the story. Where there is a finite upper bound to the distribution, the marginal tax rate at the top should be zero. This result, which applies *a fortiori* to the case where the government places a positive value on the utility of the top household (see Seade, 1977), is in striking contrast to actual tax schedules. It does however need to be interpreted with caution, and we discuss this further below.

Where the household is not at the top of the distribution, we have to consider the implications for $i+1,\ldots,H$. Suppose, for example, $i = H-1$. We know that the household above is going to face a zero marginal tax rate and lie on the indifference curve passing through the point chosen for household $H-1$. Similarly, the household $H-1$ can be no worse off than at the point O, which is the gross income chosen by household $H-2$. Now if the government ignored the interdependence, it would maximize the revenue from $H-1$ by setting P at the point indicated in Fig. 13-2b where the slope is 45°. This maximizes the revenue from $H-1$ (subject to his being on the indifference curve through O). However, this would then imply that household H is at the point Q. It is clear (with leisure normal) that the revenue from H could be increased if the point P were lowered (for example, to P'). There is therefore a trade-off between the revenue from the two groups (H and $H-1$), which depends on the number of people in the two groups and on the extent to which labour supply responds to changes in the marginal tax rate. This last point however illustrates the value of a formal analysis. Although it is intuitive that the supply elasticity is relevant to calculating the optimum tax schedule, it is not clear in what form it should enter, or how it interacts with other considerations.

Heuristic Solution

In order to give an explicit solution, and to explore the consequences of the

---

[11] Note that this gives him a higher level of utility than a person of type $(i-1)$, so that there is no incentive for him to conceal his superior earning ability.

government's being concerned about the welfare of the households affected, we turn now to the formal analysis.[12] This is not particularly technical, but does assume familiarity with the Maximum principle; readers willing to take this on trust are advised to go straight to the sub-section headed "Interpretation".

The basic formulation is parallel to that in earlier sections. A person of type w maximizes $U(Y(w), L(w))$ where $Y(w) = Z - T(Z)$ and $Z = wL(w)$. There is again a value w_0 such that

$$L(w) = 0 \quad \text{for} \quad w \leqslant w_0$$
$$L(w) > 0 \quad \text{for} \quad w > w_0$$

In the latter case the conditions for utility maximization give

$$U_Y(1 - T')w + U_L = 0 \tag{13-46}$$

where it is assumed that the tax function is differentiable and that $T' < 1$ (see Mirrlees, 1971, p. 177). The government chooses the function $T(Z)$ to maximize the social welfare function (13-30) subject to the production constraint (13-28); i.e., we have retained the simplifying assumptions of constant producer prices and no profits.

The problem may be solved in an heuristic fashion by use of the Maximum principle (for a rigorous treatment of the problem, see Mirrlees, 1971, 1979). The objective function may be written (with λ as the multiplier associated with the production constraint):

$$\int_w^\infty [\Psi(U) + \lambda(Z - Y - R_0)]\, dF \tag{13-47}$$

In this maximization, $U(w)$ is treated as a state variable, and we need to derive the differential equation governing its behaviour. Differentiation of the utility function and the individual budget constraint, together with the first-order condition for utility maximization (13-46), yields

$$\frac{dU}{dw} = U_Y\frac{\partial Y}{\partial w} + U_L\frac{\partial L}{\partial w} = U_Y(1 - T')w\frac{\partial L}{\partial w} + U_L\frac{\partial L}{\partial w} + U_Y L(1 - T')$$

$$= U_Y L(1 - T') = -\frac{LU_L}{w} \tag{13-48}$$

---

[12] It should be noted that, in general, optimization problems of this type (optimizing subject to individual maximization) raise a number of difficult issues. In particular, it may not be legitimate to substitute first-order conditions for the maximization constraint. This may work under particular assumptions—as below—but an optimum may, for example, leave consumers indifferent over a range. For examples, and a clear discussion of the underlying mathematical structure, see Mirrlees (1979).

The control variable is taken to be $L(w)$, with $Y(w)$ being determined from $L(w)$ and $U(w)$.[13]

In applying the Maximum principle (see, for example, Intriligator, 1971), we introduce the multiplier $\zeta(w)$ associated with the differential equation (13-48) and writing the Hamiltonian as (where f is the density of the distribution of w)

$$\mathcal{H} = [\Psi(U) + \lambda(Z - Y)]f + \zeta\frac{dU}{dw} \qquad (13\text{-}49)$$

where ζ satisfies

$$\frac{-d\zeta}{dw} = \frac{\partial\mathcal{H}}{\partial U} = \left(\Psi' - \lambda\frac{\partial Y}{\partial U}\right)f - \zeta\frac{L}{w}U_{LY}\frac{\partial Y}{\partial U} \qquad (13\text{-}50)$$

The last term in this expression is obtained by differentiating dU/dw with respect to U, holding L constant but allowing for the dependence of Y on U. The control variable is then chosen to maximize $\mathcal{H}$, and the first-order condition is

$$\frac{\partial\mathcal{H}}{\partial L} = \lambda\left(w - \frac{dY}{dL}\Big|_{\bar{U}}\right)f + \zeta\frac{\partial}{\partial L}\left(\frac{dU}{dw}\right) = 0 \qquad (13\text{-}51)$$

where this is only necessary where Z is strictly increasing (see Mirrlees, 1971, p. 183). This expression may be re-arranged as

$$1 + \frac{U_L}{wU_Y} = \left[\frac{-\zeta(w)}{\lambda fw}\right]\left[\frac{\partial}{\partial L}\left(\frac{dU}{dw}\right)\right] \qquad (13\text{-}52)$$

From the first-order condition for utility maximization, the left-hand side is T', i.e., the marginal tax rate. This is beginning to look like the kind of formula we are seeking; in particular, the right-hand side may be seen as the implications of moving to the right in the diagram (increasing Z for a given w)—why, for groups below the top, we may want a non-zero marginal tax rate.

In order to simplify the ensuing discussion, we assume that $U_{LY} = 0$; i.e., with this representation U_L is independent of Y. This allows us to integrate (13-50) to obtain

$$\frac{-\zeta(w)}{\lambda} = \int_w^\infty \left(\frac{1}{U_Y} - \frac{\Psi'}{\lambda}\right)dF \qquad (13\text{-}53)$$

where we have used the transversality condition that $\zeta(\infty) = 0$.

The key conditions (13-52) and (13-53) may be combined to yield

---

[13] It is clearly necessary to consider the range of permissible variations in $L(w)$. It is assumed (Mirrlees, 1971, Assumption B) that (in the absence of taxation) consumption is an increasing function of w. In terms of the indifference curve diagram (Fig. 13-2b), it implies that the indifference curve of H through P (where the slope of the curve for $H-1$ is 45°) cuts as shown (so that the tangency with a slope of 45°, and the same lump-sum income, is to the right of P).

(where we have exploited the fact that $U_{LY} = 0$ in differentiating within the square bracket on the right-hand side of the former and the individual first-order condition has again been used):[14]

$$\frac{T'}{1-T'} = U_Y(w)\left[\int_w^\infty \left(\frac{1}{U_Y} - \frac{\Psi'}{\lambda}\right)dF\right]\left(\frac{\varepsilon^*}{wf}\right) \qquad (13\text{-}54)$$

where

$$\varepsilon^* = 1 + \frac{LU_{LL}}{U_L}$$

Interpretation

In interpreting this condition, let us begin with the integral on the right-hand side. The meaning may be seen from the following mental experiment. Suppose that we reduce the utility of everyone above w by a marginal unit (this is reminiscent of Fig. 13-2). The gain in increased revenue is $1/U_Y$ per person; the cost is a loss of welfare, measured in units of revenue, Ψ'/λ. The integral therefore represents the net effect of a marginal reduction in U above w. It depends on the number of people above w and on the social valuation, Ψ'. Where the latter declines, with w, we should expect a picture similar to that shown by the solid lines in Fig. 13-3, where the loss of welfare outweighs the gain from increased revenue at low values of w, but is less at high values. Indeed, at the top we have $\Psi' \to 0$. As a result, the integral on the right-hand side of (13-54) first rises and then falls—see the lower part of Fig. 13-3 (it rises where $1/U_Y < \Psi'/\lambda$). At the bottom, we are assuming $w_0 > \mathbf{w}$, so that some people have $L = 0$. Moreover, it can be shown that the integral evaluated at that point is positive.[15]

The integral therefore incorporates the effect on those with higher w in terms of revenue (as in the diagrammatic exposition) and of utility (not taken into account in the diagrams). Moreover, it tends to rise then fall, leading to the tax rate being higher in the middle ranges. For lower values of w the integral is small, since there are many "deserving" above; the integral reaches a maximum at the point where the net gain from a transfer is zero; and for high values of w it is low because of the small numbers involved. This property does however depend on the form of the social

[14] The differential of dU/dw is $-(1/w)(U_L + LU_{LL})$; we then divide by $-U_L/wU_Y(=1-T')$.

[15] The integral over the whole range, including those with $L = 0$, measures the net benefit from a unit increase in utility for everyone. Since this is a permissible variation, at the optimum the net effect must be zero; i.e.,

$$F(w_0)\left[\frac{1}{U_Y(w_0)} - \frac{\Psi'(w_0)}{\lambda}\right] + \int_{w_0}^\infty \left(\frac{1}{U_Y} - \frac{\Psi'}{\lambda}\right)dF = 0$$

The first term is negative, hence the second is positive.

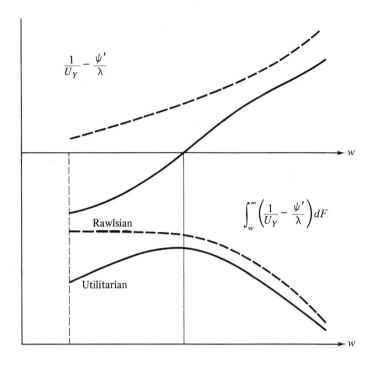

Figure 13-3 Interpretation of optimum income tax conditions.

welfare function. In the Rawlsian case (with $w_0 > \mathbf{w}$), the government maximizes $U(w_0)$ and $\Psi' = 0$ for $w > w_0$, so that the integral declines throughout the range (broken lines in Fig. 13-3). In this case, we are interested solely, as far as the higher groups are concerned, in the revenue raised—we have the situation discussed diagrammatically.

The earlier exposition suggested that these considerations need to be balanced against the effect on the labour supplied by those at w. This latter effect is represented by (ε^*/wf). From this we can see that the effect depends on:

1. ε^*, which is a measure of the elasticity of labour supply. It is not however the conventional definition of the elasticity, $\varepsilon^* - 1$ being in fact the response of L to a change in w, holding α constant.[16] The value of ε^* is

[16] The relationship with the compensated elasticity ε_{LL} in the additive case may be seen as follows. Let $U = u_1(Y) + u_2(L)$. Then in the absence of taxation

$$\varepsilon_{LL} = \frac{u_2'}{(u_2'' + w^2 u_1'')L} \quad \text{or} \quad \frac{1}{\varepsilon_{LL}} = \varepsilon^* - 1 + \left(\frac{-wLu_1''}{u_1'}\right)$$

equal to 1 if there is a constant marginal disutility of effort, and ε^* rises as the supply becomes less elastic.
2. The number of work units affected (wf). If the potential labour affected is low, then the marginal tax rate can be high. This suggests that the rate would be high at the lower and (to a lesser extent) the upper tails of the distribution.

The tax formula (13-54) provides considerable insight into the factors influencing the marginal tax rate, and the way in which they interact. Moreover, Sadka (1976) and Seade (1977) demonstrate conditions under which zero marginal rates are desirable at the top (with a bounded distribution) and bottom of the scale. These latter results have received considerable attention; and they do provide a striking counter-example to the widespread belief that the marginal tax rate should rise with income. It is however dangerous to use these results to argue, as some people have done, that tax rates on high incomes should be lower than they are at present in the United Kingdom or United States. The actual tax rates apply to a range of people, and if we consider the optimum tax rate for a range including more than one person it is no longer necessarily zero. Moreover, the limiting tax rates may be a bad approximation even for the top groups: "calculations suggest to me that these end results are of little practical value ... it is usually true that zero is a bad approximation to the marginal tax rate even within most of the top and bottom percentiles" (Mirrlees, 1976, p. 340). Finally, the result does not remain valid where the highest wage person is not a perfect substitute for the labour supplied by others (Allen, 1979).

Numerical Calculations

General results from the optimal tax formula are hard to obtain and need careful interpretation. Numerical calculations may therefore be helpful. This approach was used by Mirrlees (1971), who considered in particular the case where the utility function is Cobb–Douglas (Eq. (13-37) with $a = \frac{1}{2}$, and F is the lognormal distribution. On the basis of these calculations, Mirrlees drew a number of (qualified) conclusions. The most important for policy purposes include:

1. the optimal tax structure is approximately linear, i.e., a constant marginal tax rate, with an exemption level below which negative tax supplements are payable;
2. the marginal tax rates are rather low ("I must confess that I had expected the rigorous analysis of income-taxation in the utilitarian manner to provide arguments for high tax rates. It has not done so". (Mirrlees, 1971, p. 207));

3. "the income tax is a much less effective tool for reducing inequalities than has often been thought" (Mirrlees, 1971, p. 208).

The numerical results obtained by Mirrlees are illustrated by the column headed "Utilitarian" in Table 13-3. The marginal tax rates vary little over the range of w and are relatively low. However, as we have seen in the case of the linear tax, the results are likely to be sensitive to the assumptions made about the labour supply function, the level of revenue, and the form of the social welfare function. The work of Stern (1976) suggests that a lower elasticity of substitution between leisure and consumption than the unitary value implicit in the Cobb–Douglas may lead to higher tax rates (and the same is indicated by Eq. (13-54)).

The aspect on which we focus here is the form of the social welfare function. The results of Mirrlees given in Table 13-3 correspond to the case where $\Psi' = $ constant, i.e., the utilitarian case.[17] For contrast, we present in the right-hand part of the table the Rawlsian maxi-min case. This may be solved using the same approach as above (Atkinson, 1972; Phelps, 1973). The marginal tax rates are considerably higher for most of the income range. Only for the top 1 per cent and above are the marginal tax rates at all close to those obtained by Mirrlees. Moreover, the approximate linearity of the optimal tax schedule, which Mirrlees regarded as "perhaps the most striking features" of his results, does not carry over to the maxi-min case. The tax schedule departs significantly from linearity in the range that covers the majority of the population. Finally, in the cases considered by Mirrlees, the proportion of the population choosing not to work was close to zero. In the maxi-min case, about 16–20 per cent of the population would be in this position.

This suggests that conclusions (1) and (2) drawn by Mirrlees may depend rather sensitively on the formulation of the social welfare function; his third conclusion—that income tax is not a particularly effective weapon for redistributing income—is based in part on a comparison of the optimal income tax with the first-best attainable through lump-sum taxation, i.e., where the tax may be related directly to w. In the Cobb–Douglas case, with $a = \frac{1}{2}$, the individual then maximizes

$$\log[wL - T(w)] + \log(1 - L)$$

where we have substituted the budget constraint. The first-order condition is

$$w(1 - L) - (wL - T) = 0$$

---

[17] Mirrlees also gives results for the social welfare function $\Psi = -e^{-U}$. This may be compared with Stern's case $v = 2$. (N.B. Mirrlees' form of the Cobb–Douglas is the logarithm of that obtained from (13-44) by letting $\rho \to 0$, so that e^U corresponds to U in Stern's formulation.)

Table 13-3 Utilitarian and maxi-min solutions of optimal income tax

Level of w	"Utilitarian" Tax rates			Maxi-min Tax rates		
	Average	Marginal	Utility*	Average	Marginal	Utility*
Case I						
w_0	—	—	0.03	—	—	0.068
Median	6	21	0.08	10	52	0.074
Top decile	14	20	0.13	28	34	0.11
Top percentile	16	17	0.19	28	26	0.16
Case II						
w_0	—	—	0.05	—	—	0.079
Median	−13	19	0.10	−6	50	0.085
Top decile	4	19	0.15	22	33	0.12
Top percentile	7	17	0.21	25	25	0.17

Source: Atkinson (1972, Table 3).

Notes: * Y^0 (i.e., equivalent consumption at $L = 0$).

In Case I the revenue requirement is positive, in Case II it is negative (the government disposing of the profits of public sector production).

or

$$w + T(w) < 0 \quad \text{and} \quad L = 0$$

Hence the level of utility for a person with ability w is given by

$$V(w, T) = 2 \log\left(\frac{w - T}{2}\right) - \log w \quad \text{for} \quad T \geq -w \left(\text{where } Y = \frac{w - T}{2}\right)$$

$$= \log(-T) \qquad\qquad \text{for} \quad T \leq -w \left(\text{where } Y = -T\right)$$

The government chooses $T(w)$ subject to the revenue constraint. Since $T(w)$ can be varied independently, the first-order condition for the utilitarian objective is that $\partial V/\partial T = \lambda$, where λ is the multiplier associated with the revenue constraint. Since $\partial V/\partial T = -1/Y$, it follows that incomes are equalized, but not utilities:

$$-T = w_0 = Y, \quad L = 0, \quad V = \log w_0 \quad \text{for} \quad w \leq w_0$$

$$T = w - 2w_0, \quad Y = w_0, \quad L = 1 - \frac{w_0}{w}, \quad V < \log w_0 \quad \text{for} \quad w > w_0$$

Mirrlees comments that "it is an interesting curiosity" that V falls with w. There is however nothing pathological about this example. In Lecture 11, we showed how this reversal of ranking could arise with a utilitarian objective—and drew attention to the obvious incentive problems. In contrast, the maxi-min full optimum involves an equal level of utility.

Exercise 13-4 Describe the lump-sum tax optimum where the government maximizes a Rawlsian objective function.

The features of the first-best solution, coupled with the greater "progressivity" (in terms of utility) of the income tax in the maxi-min case, mean that the difference between the income tax and the first-best is much less marked with a maxi-min objective than in the utilitarian case.

13-5 CONCLUDING COMMENTS

The models considered in this Lecture are highly simplified and leave out many considerations. Some have been incorporated into the literature. This is true of the taxation of interest income, which is taken up in the next Lecture. It is true of interdependencies between utility functions, where Boskin and Sheshinski (1978) have examined how the optimum tax policy is changed when welfare depends on relative income. Similarly, the model may be elaborated to allow for differences in the utility functions of individuals (e.g., preferences with respect to work). As we have noted in Lecture 11, the approach here adopts a particular cardinalization of individual utilities, focusing on differences in ability to pay. If the social welfare function takes account of the possibility that some individuals are more "productive" in consumption, then the results may be quite different.

There are a number of developments that remain to be carried out. Thus, it is important to relax the highly simplified assumptions made about the production side (constant wage rates and prices). Feldstein (1973b) has investigated a model where there are two classes of worker and output is a Cobb–Douglas function of the two types of labour; but this does not allow sufficiently for the possible degrees of complementarity and substitutability between different kinds of labour. We should expect the results to depend, for example, on whether low-skilled labour is complementary to, or a substitute for, high-skilled labour, and on the relative elasticities of labour supply. A second example is the extension of the model to more than one dimension of differences between individuals. Not only are endowments likely to be multi-dimensioned, but also we need to allow for the simultaneous variation of endowments and tastes. This does however pose substantial difficulties (Mirrlees, 1979). Third, the formulation of the government's problems should allow for the uncertainty surrounding the model employed. We have referred in passing to uncertainty surrounding the elasticity of labour supply, and to the interpretation of F as a probability distribution, but this needs to be built in explicitly. Finally, administrative costs are of crucial importance when considering alternative schedules—and different tax bases—and must be incorporated.

In deciding on the direction of such research, one must bear firmly in mind the purpose of this kind of literature. The aim is not to provide a definite numerical answer to the question, "how progressive should the income tax be?" As Broome's parody (1975) shows, it is easy to take the analysis too literally. The purpose is rather to explore the implications of different beliefs about how the world works or about how governments should behave. Thus, the literature developed at much the same time as the Rawlsian theory of justice was being widely discussed. It both drew on that discussion, and contributed to it, in that seeing such principles in action helps understand how reasonable they are as a distributive standard (Rawls, 1974, p. 141). In the same way, the properties of utilitarianism have been exhibited much more clearly in this class of second-best problems.

The results are therefore qualitative, rather than quantitative. At the same time they serve to identify the key factors, and to provide counter-examples to certain popular views. In the case of the linear tax, the formula (13-36b) shows that the critical considerations are the weighted compensated elasticity and the marginal social valuation of income defined net of revenue. Although the former may have been clear intuitively, the form of the latter was not immediately apparent. With the general tax schedule, the results have shown that—with the assumptions made—there is no necessary reason for marginal tax rates to rise with income. This is often assumed to be an essential feature of a redistributional tax system, but lower income groups may gain from reducing the marginal tax rate at the top. More generally, the formula (13-54) brings out the interaction between distributional and efficiency issues, identifying in each case the characteristics relevant to the determination of the marginal tax rate.

READING

The key paper on optimal income taxation is Mirrlees (1971), although the reader might find it easier to start with Sheshinski (1972) and Atkinson (1973) on the linear income tax, Phelps (1973) on the Rawlsian solution, or Fair (1971) with numerical calculations.

LECTURE
FOURTEEN

A MORE GENERAL TREATMENT OF THE OPTIMAL TAX PROBLEM

14-1 INTRODUCTION

The aim of this Lecture is to widen the discussion of optimal taxation beyond the Ramsey and income tax problems examined in the previous two Lectures. Two principal themes are emphasized. The first is the importance of developing a broader framework for investigating the optimal tax structure, and the fact that the results may depend sensitively on the range of instruments assumed to be available to the government. The second is the need to consider the design of taxation outside the standard equilibrium model assumed in Lectures 12 and 13, and the implications of situations where the no-tax position is not necessarily Pareto-efficient.

In Sections 14-2 and 14-3, we show how the analysis of the previous two Lectures can be brought together within a single framework. This allows us to define more precisely the role of income taxation and of indirect taxes, and to analyse the optimal income tax rate and the optimal commodity tax structure *simultaneously*. It turns out that the interaction between the two is critical: the optimal structure of commodity taxes when there is an optimal income tax is markedly different from that when there is no income tax. This analysis is used to throw light on the longstanding controversy concerning "direct" and "indirect" taxation—which of the two is preferable, or, if both should be used, the role that each should play. The results are also relevant to the issue of the optimal provision of deductions from the tax base for certain items of expenditure (such as housing or medical expenses).

In Sections 14-4 and 14-5 we consider two directions in which the analysis can be extended beyond the model of earlier Lectures. These do not exhaust by any means the developments that are required (for example, it is still assumed that markets are perfectly competitive), but indicate some

424

of the ways in which the results may need to be modified. Section 14-4 investigates the tax treatment of savings in the context of an explicit intertemporal model, and examines how far the results from a static economy can be applied. Under what conditions is a zero rate of interest income tax likely to be optimal? Section 14-5 takes a different departure from the standard model, allowing for the existence of externalities in consumption, and studies the relation between the Ramsey tax structure and the pattern of Pigovian corrective taxes.

A More General Specification of the Tax Structure

In order to see how the tax structure may be viewed in more general terms than in Lectures 12 and 13, let us write L^h for the number of hours of labour supplied by individual h (we assume for simplicity that he has only one job), w^h for his wage rate, $\mathbf{X^h}$ for his consumption vector (of n goods), and γ^h for a vector of observable characteristics, such as age, or number of children, which may be relevant for tax purposes. The tax levied on individual h may then be written as

$$T^h = T(L^h, w^h, \mathbf{X^h}, \gamma^h) \tag{14-1}$$

where w^h and L^h can be observed separately. Where, as assumed below, only $Y^h = w^h L^h$ is observed, then those variables must enter in this form.

Suppose that we begin with the linear income tax discussed in the previous Lecture, in the static model with no savings or investment income. We then have

$$T^h = \tau Y^h - G \tag{14-2}$$

where τ is the tax rate and G the poll subsidy (effectively a guaranteed minimum income). In the absence of savings, it is clear that the tax on income is equivalent to a uniform expenditure tax (at the appropriate rate, see Lecture 12), so that a linear income tax is equivalent to a proportional indirect tax plus a uniform lump-sum payment (if $G > 0$). In other words, such a tax structure could be administered either as an income tax or as an indirect tax system (e.g., a value added tax) with a poll subsidy. The only distinction between the two would be in the mechanics of administration. (The element G, and indeed τ, may depend on γ, as discussed briefly below.)

From this, one can see that the only modification required to extend the analysis of the Ramsey tax problem of Lecture 12 to the case of the linear income tax of Lecture 13 is to introduce G. This however leads to a major change in the conclusions, since such a lump-sum measure is clearly preferred on efficiency grounds. Indeed, we have to ask on what grounds commodity taxes would still be employed when the range of instruments is extended in this way. Under what conditions does the optimal tax structure simply entail an income tax? To put the question another way, suppose that in addition to the instruments included in (14-2) the government is able to levy commodity taxes:

$$T^h = \tau Y^h + \sum_i t_i X_i^h - G \tag{14-3}$$

where t_i denotes the tax rate on the ith commodity. In what circumstances does the use of t_i allow a higher level of social welfare to be achieved?

When we allow for nonlinear tax schedules, the same questions arise—although the answers may well be different, as we show later. If the government's tax possibilities are extended to include nonlinear income tax schedules,

$$T^h = T(Y^h) + \sum_i t_i X_i^h \tag{14-4}$$

then this may widen the conditions under which a social optimum may be achieved by income taxation alone. We should however allow for the possibility that the commodity tax schedules be nonlinear:

$$T^h = T(Y^h) + \sum_i \tilde{t}_i(X_i^h) \tag{14-5}$$

although there are limitations on the use of such schedules, arising from the non-observability of individual consumption. Moreover, it is possible that the tax rates may depend on more than one variable. This is illustrated by the case of tax deductions discussed in Section 14-3, where the argument of T may be $Y^h - \kappa q_n \cdot X_n^h$ where n is a commodity such as medical care and κ is the fraction of expenditure on this commodity which may be set against income tax.

Finally, the tax schedules may be related to personal characteristics (γ). This may apply to the personal exemption or tax credit with the income tax (i.e., via G), as with the number of dependents, or to the tax rates, as where the government subsidizes the purchase of certain items for families with children. We do not here examine the factors influencing the optimal design of such provisions. In the case of family size, the reader is referred to Mirrlees (1972b).

Direct versus Indirect Taxation

The framework described above is used in Sections 14-2 and 14-3 to examine some of the arguments lying behind the debate on direct versus indirect taxation. First, however, the precise nature of this distinction must be clarified. In one usage, it is based on the method of administration. The taxpayer pays his income tax directly to the revenue authorities, but pays sales taxes only indirectly via the purchase of goods. This approach, which probably explains the terminology, has a long history, but most writers have felt that there is no reason to expect such an administrative classification to have economic significance.[1] For example, does it make any difference whether an individual or his employer pays the tax on earnings?

If we turn to definitions based on the economic effects of different types of taxation, that most commonly found in the public finance literature is based on some presumption about the ultimate incidence of the tax. For example, according to Due and Friedlaender, "Some taxes—often called *direct* taxes—reduce the real incomes of the persons who pay them to the government.... Other taxes may be shifted from some persons to others, [those] believed to be shifted in this fashion are called *indirect* taxes" (Due and Friedlaender, 1973, p. 229). Such a definition, however, leads to difficulties where the degree of shifting is neither zero, as assumed for direct taxes, nor 100 per cent, as assumed for indirect taxes. Moreover, it seems unsatisfactory to relate the classification of taxes to assumptions about shifting which may not in the event be realized; e.g., income tax may be shifted via wage bargaining.

In view of this, we focus here on what seems to be the essential aspect of the distinction: the fact that direct taxes may be adjusted to the individual characteristics of the taxpayer, whereas indirect taxes are levied on transactions irrespective of the circumstances of buyer or seller. Such a definition makes no assumption about shifting and in our view corresponds to the feature that most people have in mind when discussing the choice between direct and indirect taxation. The key feature of the indirect tax is that no characteristic of the individual, other than the amount that he purchases in this particular market, is relevant for the determination of his tax liability. In other words, it is the introduction of G that makes the income tax a direct tax, since each taxpayer is entitled to only one such exemption.

Arguments for Direct or Indirect Taxation

One can, in the literature, distinguish two main lines of argument. The first is that there should be a broad balance between direct and indirect taxation, a view that appears to find favour with many politicians, as is illustrated by the following piece of Gladstonian rhetoric:

> I never can think of direct and indirect taxation except as I should think of two attractive sisters,... differing only as sisters may differ. I cannot conceive any reason why there should be unfriendly rivalry between the admirers of these two damsels. I have always thought it not only allowable, but even an act of duty, to pay my addresses to them both. [House of Commons, 1861]

[1] This applies with even more force to definitions based on legal decisions, which may alter without any change in the effect of the taxes in question. For example, at one time the US Supreme Court, to avoid the requirement of the apportionment rule that all direct taxes be head taxes, declared the income tax to be an indirect tax. As Dalton remarked, this was merely "the economics of clever lawyers in a tight place" (Dalton, 1954, p. 24).

His reasons for holding such a view are not apparent, but in much popular discussion one can discern a form of assignment of *instruments* to *targets*: direct taxation is assigned to the equity objective, and indirect taxation is assigned to the goal of raising revenue efficiently. The rationale typically given for the first assignment is that indirect taxation, even differentiated according to luxuries and necessities, is a poor redistributive instrument: "taxes on transactions can only distribute the burden differentially between persons, according to some notion of equity, in a very clumsy and uncertain fashion" (Kaldor, 1955, pp. 21–2). There is less clear support for the assignment of indirect taxation to the goal of efficiency, although it is commonly felt to be a less "painful" way of raising revenue.

The second broad view is that direct taxation is superior on all counts to indirect taxation, and that it is only the administrative infeasibility of income taxation that had led to indirect taxes being widely adopted: "taxes upon commodities...are objectionable in principle...the important place which they occupy in our tax system can only be defended on the ground that they are survivals from a period when the administration of direct taxation was much more difficult than it is today" (Colwyn Committee, 1927, p. 372). A more recent statement of this view is that by Fromm and Taubman, who after examining the arguments based on equity, costs of administration, and excess burden, conclude that "a direct tax system is 'better' from an economic viewpoint" (Fromm and Taubman, 1973, p. 139).

One of the aims of the discussion in Sections 14-2 and 14-3 is to see how far, and under what conditions, these views can be related to the optimal taxation arguments.

14-2 INDIRECT TAXES AND LINEAR DIRECT TAXATION

In this section we examine the role of commodity taxation in a model where there is an (optimal) linear direct tax. We use the framework of the previous Lecture, letting G be the uniform lump-sum subsidy and q_i the consumer price of good i. Normalizing all producer prices to unity, we have $q_i = 1 + t_i$. As explained earlier, a uniform commodity tax is equivalent in this model to a tax on wage income. We therefore normalize by setting the tax rate on wages to be zero. This means that, if it turns out that the optimal tax structure involves $t_i = t$ for all i, then we have established that no commodity taxes need be employed (the optimum can be achieved by a tax on wage income alone).

Identical Individuals

We consider first the case where all individuals are identical, so that we are concerned solely with efficiency. The government chooses t_i $(i = 1, \ldots, n)$

and G to maximize the welfare of the typical individual, represented by the indirect utility function (we assume all individuals are treated identically):

$$V(\mathbf{q}, w, G) \tag{14-6}$$

subject to the revenue constraint (per person)

$$R \equiv \sum_i t_i X_i - G = R_0 \tag{14-7}$$

where for the present we drop the household superscripts. Writing the Lagrangean

$$\mathcal{L} = V(\mathbf{q}, w, G) + \lambda \left(\sum_i t_i X_i - G - R_0 \right) \tag{14-8}$$

the first-order conditions are

$$\frac{\partial \mathcal{L}}{\partial t_k} = \frac{\partial V}{\partial q_k} + \lambda \left(X_k + \sum_i t_i \frac{\partial X_i}{\partial q_k} \right) = 0 \quad \text{for} \quad k = 1, \ldots, n \tag{14-9a}$$

$$\frac{\partial \mathcal{L}}{\partial G} = \frac{\partial V}{\partial G} + \lambda \left(\sum_i t_i \frac{\partial X_i}{\partial M} - 1 \right) = 0 \tag{14-9b}$$

where $\partial X_i / \partial M$ denotes the income derivative of demand for good i. Using the properties of the indirect utility function ($\partial V / \partial q_k = -\alpha X_k$, and $\partial V / \partial G = \alpha$, where α is the private marginal utility of income), and the Slutsky equation

$$\frac{\partial X_i}{\partial q_k} = S_{ik} - X_k \frac{\partial X_i}{\partial M}$$

the first-order conditions may be re-arranged as (from (14-9a))

$$\sum_i \frac{t_i S_{ki}}{X_k} = -\left(1 - \frac{\alpha}{\lambda} - \sum_i t_i \frac{\partial X_i}{\partial M} \right) \equiv -\theta \quad \text{for} \quad k = 1, \ldots, n \tag{14-10a}$$

and (from (14-9b))

$$\theta = 1 - \frac{\alpha}{\lambda} - \Sigma t_i \frac{\partial X_i}{\partial M} = 0 \tag{14-10b}$$

The new element in the problem is the uniform subsidy G and the associated first-order condition (14-10b). It is immediately clear that this has a dramatic effect on the solution. In this model, if the government can vary G freely (so that it can be negative as well as positive), then the only solution satisfying the first-order conditions has $t_i = 0$. The poll tax is superior on efficiency grounds to any distortionary tax, and where individuals are identical there is no equity argument against a poll tax.

This straightforward, and intuitive, observation has two important implications. First, it casts doubt on the standard formulation of the

Ramsey problem with identical individuals. In effect this problem arises only because the constraint of no poll taxation is imposed, and there seems no clear rationale for ruling out this simple lump-sum tax. The analysis of the first part of Lecture 12 should be seen therefore as an intermediate step rather than of intrinsic interest. Second, it suggests that there is something wrong with the target–instrument view described earlier. A government concerned solely with efficiency should use the simplest of direct taxes and not use indirect taxes. As was recognized by Adam Smith, "in countries where the ease, comfort and security of the inferior ranks of people are little attended to, capitation taxes are very common" (Smith, 1776, p. 482).

Distributional Objectives

We have seen that the simplest of direct taxes is superior to indirect taxation from the standpoint of minimizing excess burden. How is this conclusion modified when we bring in distributional objectives? In order to simplify the discussion, it is assumed that the differences between people take the form of varying wage rates (w) and that tastes are assumed identical. As in Lecture 12, there are in all H households, and household h maximizes $U(\mathbf{X}^h, L^h)$ subject to

$$\sum_i q_i X_i^h = w^h L^h + G \tag{14-11}$$

The government maximizes the social welfare function, which is assumed to be a function of the individual indirect utility functions:

$$\Psi[V^1(\mathbf{q}, w, G), \ldots, V^h(\mathbf{q}, w, G), \ldots] \tag{14-12}$$

subject to the revenue constraint:

$$R \equiv \sum_i t_i \sum_h X_i^h - HG = R_0 \tag{14-13}$$

Forming the Lagrangean

$$\mathscr{L} = \Psi + \lambda(R - R_0) \tag{14-14}$$

we obtain the first-order conditions

$$\frac{\partial \mathscr{L}}{\partial t_k} = \sum_h \left[(\lambda - \beta^h) X_k^h + \lambda \sum_i t_i \frac{\partial X_i^h}{\partial t_k} \right] = 0 \quad k = 1, \ldots, n \tag{14-15a}$$

$$-\frac{\partial \mathscr{L}}{\partial G} = \sum_h \left[(\lambda - \beta^h) - \lambda \sum_i t_i \frac{\partial X_i^h}{\partial G} \right] = 0 \tag{14-15b}$$

where

$$\beta^h \equiv \frac{\partial \Psi}{\partial V^h} \frac{\partial V^h}{\partial M^h} \tag{14-16}$$

is the social marginal utility of income accruing to household h.

As in the previous Lectures, we introduce the concept of the net social marginal valuation of income, measured in terms of government revenue:

$$b^h \equiv \beta^h/\lambda + \partial R/\partial M^h \qquad (14\text{-}17)$$

This reflects both the direct benefit of transferring \$1 to household h and the indirect benefit from the increased tax revenue generated. Using this definition, and the Slutsky equation, the first-order conditions (14-15) may be rewritten:[2]

$$\frac{\sum_i \sum_h t_i S_{ik}^h}{H\bar{X}_k} = -\left[1 - \sum_h \left(b^h \frac{X_k^h}{H\bar{X}_k}\right)\right] \quad \text{for} \quad k = 1,\ldots,n \qquad (14\text{-}18a)$$

$$\bar{b} = 1 \qquad (14\text{-}18b)$$

where $\bar{X}_k$ denotes $(\sum_h X_k^h/H)$ and $\bar{b} = \sum_h b^h/H$.

These expressions are the generalization of (14-10) to the many-taxpayer case. Moreover, Eq. (14-18a) is that given in Lecture 12 (Eq. (12-55)), and we can see that the existence of (linear) income taxation modifies the results through the introduction of (14-18b). Approaching it the other way, condition (14-18b) is that found in the discussion of the optimal linear income tax in Lecture 13 (Eq. (13-36a)); it is now Eq. (14-18a) that replaces the previous one-commodity condition (Eq. (13-36b) in Lecture 13).

In the case of identical individuals, the combination of both direct and indirect taxation led to rather different results; in the present case the effect can also be far-reaching. In order to see this, let us introduce, as in Lecture 12:

$$\phi_k \equiv \sum_h \frac{1}{H}\left(\frac{X_k^h}{\bar{X}_k}\right)\left(\frac{b^h}{\bar{b}}\right) - 1 \qquad (14\text{-}19)$$

the normalized covariance between X_k^h and b^h. ϕ_k is the "distributional characteristic" of good k, and depends on the pattern of demand for k, and on the behaviour of the net social marginal valuation of income. If, for example, we interpret pursuit of the efficiency objective as the government being indifferent about the recipient of a marginal \$1, then this implies $b^h = \bar{b}$ all h and $\phi_k = 0$. For ϕ_k to be non-zero, b^h must vary with h; i.e., the government must have, in this sense, distributional objectives.

From Eq. (14-18a), and the definition of ϕ_k,

$$\sum_i \sum_h t_i \frac{S_{ik}^h}{H\bar{X}_k} = \bar{b}\phi_k - (1 - \bar{b}) \quad k = 1,\ldots,n \qquad (14\text{-}20)$$

If $\phi_k = 0$, then this gives the standard Samuelson formula that there should be a uniform percentage reduction in compensated demands; on the other

[2] Substituting $\partial X_i^h/\partial t_k = S_{ik}^h - X_k^h \partial X_i^h/\partial M^h$ into (14-15a) and dividing by $\lambda H\bar{X}_k$ gives (14-18a).

hand, where the uniform tax/subsidy G may be freely varied, the factor of proportionality $(1 - \bar{b})$ is zero. This leads to the rather surprising conclusion that the use of indirect taxes is associated with the equity objective. If efficiency were the only concern ($\phi_k = 0$ all k), then the government should employ the poll tax element of direct taxation; only if this is felt to be inequitable should indirect taxes be brought into play. In other words, the view of targets and instruments described earlier is turned precisely on its head.[3]

The distributional characteristic ϕ_k depends on how the net social marginal valuation of income b^h changes with w. In general there is a presumption that it is a declining function, and hence that the compensated reduction in demand (on the Samuelson interpretation) is greater for goods whose consumption increases more with w. (Note that it is variation *with w*, and not M, that is relevant, and that the changes in X_k^h may reflect substitutability for leisure or, in a more general model, variation in tastes.) Where there are no income effects, the behaviour of b^h depends solely on the social marginal utility of income, but where $\partial R / \partial M^h \neq 0$, it is possible (as noted in Lecture 13) that b^h rises with w. If the pattern of demand is such that it is goods with a high income elasticity that are consumed by the well-off, then it might turn out that it is goods consumed by people with a low wage rate that tend to be taxed more (in the sense of having a larger reduction in compensated demand). The important point brought out by this is that the relevant characteristic is not the social marginal utility of income (β^h), but the net social marginal valuation (b^h), which allows for the effect on revenue.

> **Exercise 14-1** Suppose that there are two classes of identical consumers, with n_i people in each ($i = 1, 2$). Write out the first-order conditions for this special case. Does $b^1 > 1$ imply that class 1 pays a smaller average tax payment at the optimum? Examine the conditions under which $b^1 - b^2$ and $\beta^1 - \beta^2$ may have opposite signs (the superscripts denote households). (Note: This example is due to Mirrlees, 1975, which the reader may like to consult.)

The results are not therefore entirely intuitive; moreover, intuition may be a treacherous guide to second-best policy problems. This is illustrated by the model considered here. If we argue along the lines of the penultimate paragraph that the introduction of a poll subsidy G leaves only a redistributional role for indirect taxation, then it appears—intuitively—that it would involve heavier taxes on luxury goods (those with a high income

---

[3] Historically, the role of indirect taxes has often been redistributional: for example, in seventeenth-century England the taxation of silks, coffee, and newspapers may well have been more progressive than a one-shilling-a-head poll tax.

elasticity). However, when distributional objectives are relevant, indirect taxes play two roles. First, by taxing luxuries at a higher rate they may increase the progressivity of the tax system; second, they provide an alternative source of revenue, allowing the regressive poll tax to be reduced or converted into a lump-sum payment. In the latter case, the government wants to raise the revenue in the distortion-minimizing way, and the final tax structure balances the two sets of considerations. This is brought out in the linear expenditure system example given below.

Example of Linear Expenditure System

Suppose that the direct utility function has the special Stone–Geary form:

$$U = \sum_{i=1}^{n} B_i \log(X_i - X_i^0) + B_0 \log(L_0 - L) \tag{14-21}$$

where $\Sigma_{i=0}^n B_i = 1$. This corresponds to the function used in Lecture 12 (Eq. (12-40)), with a unitary elasticity of substitution between goods and leisure. This functional form allows goods to be luxuries or necessities depending on the parameter values. The characteristics of the demand equations relevant to the optimality conditions are that:

$$S_{ik}^h = \frac{1}{\alpha^h} \frac{B_i B_k}{q_i q_k} \quad (i \neq k) \quad S_{kk}^h = \frac{B_k(B_k - 1)}{\alpha^h q_k^2}$$

$$\frac{\partial X_k^h}{\partial M^h} = \frac{B_k}{q_k} \tag{14-22}$$

The left-hand side of the first-order conditions (14-20) (multiplied by $H\bar{X}_k$) reduces therefore to

$$\frac{B_k}{q_k} \sum_h \frac{1}{\alpha^h} \left(B^* - \frac{t_k}{q_k} \right) \tag{14-23}$$

where

$$B^* \equiv \sum_{i=1}^{n} \frac{t_i B_i}{q_i}$$

In evaluating the right-hand side of the first-order conditions we may note that $\bar{b} = 1$ implies (with $\Psi' = 1$)

$$(1/H) \sum_h \frac{\alpha^h}{\lambda} = 1 - B^* \tag{14-24}$$

The right-hand side $(\phi_k H \bar{X}_k)$ equals (using (14-24))

$$\frac{B_k}{q_k} \left[\frac{H}{\lambda} - (1 - B^*) \sum_h \frac{1}{\alpha^h} \right] \tag{14-25}$$

Equating (14-23) and (14-25),

$$\frac{t_k}{1+t_k} = 1 - \frac{H}{\sum\limits_{h} (\lambda/\alpha^h)} \tag{14-26}$$

The only solutions that satisfy the first-order conditions therefore involve $t_k = t$ all k. Whether or not certain goods are luxuries, the optimal indirect tax structure is a uniform tax—or in other words, no indirect taxation need be employed. This may well appear counter-intuitive. However, as we have seen, there are two offsetting forces, and in the case of the linear expenditure system they exactly balance each other. (Note: the analysis does not allow for the possibility that $L = 0$. The reader should check the implications of this arising.)

Optimal Tax Structure and the Properties of Demand Functions

Our thinking about what the tax structure might look like is aided by another special case, originally investigated by Ramsey, where we have constant marginal utility of income and separable demand functions (see Eq. (12-60)):

$$\begin{aligned} X_i^h &= x_i(q_i/w^h) \quad i = 1,\ldots,n \\ b^h &= 1/\lambda w^h \end{aligned} \tag{14-27}$$

Substituting into the first-order conditions (14-18),

$$t_k \sum_{h} \frac{x_k'}{w^h} = \sum_{h} (b^h - \bar{b})x_k$$

$$\sum_{h} b^h = H \tag{14-28}$$

Suppose now that x_k can be expanded as a Taylor series about the point of the wage distribution corresponding to mean social marginal valuation utility of income ($\bar{b}$):

$$x_k(\lambda b q_k) = x_k(\lambda \bar{b} q_k) + \lambda q_k (b - \bar{b}) x_k'(\lambda \bar{b} q_k) + 0(b - \bar{b})^2$$

If terms of order $(b - \bar{b})^3$ can be ignored (i.e., ignoring terms containing second and higher derivatives of the demand function), then the first-order condition can be rewritten:

$$\frac{t_k}{q_k}\left[\frac{\sum_h(x_k' b^h/H)}{x_k'(\lambda \bar{b} q_k)}\right] = \sum_{h} \frac{(b^h - 1)^2}{H} \tag{14-29}$$

From this we can see that, in the case of the quadratic utility function, yielding linear demand curves, the term in square brackets on the left-hand side is unity. The optimal tax structure is then uniform, and the tax rate is equal to the variance of the social marginal valuation of income (it is assumed that the variation in w is not such that some demands are zero). This special case is not in itself of great interest; it does however bring out the fact that the case for differential taxation depends on second- and higher-order derivatives of the demand functions (and on the higher moments of the distribution). The functional forms typically assumed (such as constant elasticity) impose strong restrictions on these derivatives, but we can have little confidence that—in an unconstrained estimation procedure—the available data would allow us to determine them with great precision. This suggests that considerable circumspection is necessary in applying the theoretical results: "it is likely that empirically calculated tax rates, based on econometric estimates of parameters, will be determined in structure, not by the measurements actually made, but by arbitrary, untested (and even unconscious) hypotheses chosen by the econometrician for practical convenience" (Deaton, 1978, p. 1).

14-3 NONLINEAR TAX SCHEDULES AND TAX EXEMPTIONS

The direct tax considered in the previous section has a particularly simple form. Although there may be strong administrative reasons for governments restricting themselves to a linear tax schedule, we should also consider the more general case of a schedule with variable marginal rates of tax. In this section, we examine the choice between direct and indirect taxes in this context, and discuss a further variation in the possible tax instruments: exemptions from the income tax base.

Nonlinear Tax Schedules

We now assume that the government can freely vary the direct tax schedule, so that the analysis corresponds on the income tax side to that of Section 13-4. As there, it is convenient to assume a continuum of individuals, replacing the summation signs by integrals. We let $F(w)$ represent the cumulative distribution and normalize such that $F(\infty) = 1$.

The person with wage w faces a budget constraint:

$$\sum_i q_i X_i(w) = wL - T(wL) \tag{14-30}$$

The first-order conditions for individual utility maximization are (for an interior solution):[4]

$$U_k = \frac{(1 + t_k)(-U_L)}{w(1 - T')} \quad k = 1, \dots, n \tag{14-31}$$

---

[4] A corner solution involves, for labour, $L = 0$, $U_L + \alpha w(1 - T') < 0$ and $U_k/U_j = (1 + t_k)/(1 + t_j)$.

The government maximizes the social welfare function,

$$\int_0^\infty \Psi(U)dF \tag{14-32}$$

subject to

$$\int_0^\infty \left[\sum_i t_i X_i + T(wL) \right] dF = R_0$$

or

$$\int_0^\infty \left[wL - \sum_i X_i - R_0 \right] dF = 0 \tag{14-33}$$

This problem is treated in the same way as in Lecture 13. Adopting an heuristic approach, we take $X_2, \dots, X_n$ and L as the control variables, treating U as a state variable, and making use of the fact that X_1 depends on $U, X_2, \dots, X_n$ and L. From Eq. (13-48),

$$\frac{dU}{dw} = -\frac{LU_L}{w} \tag{14-34}$$

The Hamiltonian may then be written:

$$\mathcal{H} = \left[\Psi(U) + \lambda \left(wL - \sum_i X_i - R_0 \right) \right] f - \frac{\zeta L U_L}{w} \tag{14-35}$$

where f is the density function and $\zeta(w)$ the multiplier associated with the differential Eq. (14-34). (Again, the conditions under which this formulation of the optimization problem is legitimate need careful consideration—see Mirrlees, 1979.) Necessary conditions for the X_k ($k = 2, \dots, n$) to maximize $\mathcal{H}$ are (where $f > 0$):

$$-\lambda \left[\left(\frac{\partial X_1}{\partial X_k} \right)_{\bar{U}} + 1 \right] - \frac{\zeta L}{wf} \left[U_{L1} \left(\frac{\partial X_1}{\partial X_k} \right)_{\bar{U}} + U_{Lk} \right] = 0 \quad k = 2, \dots, n \tag{14-36}$$

From the first-order conditions for individual utility maximization,

$$\left(\frac{\partial X_1}{\partial X_k} \right)_{\bar{U}} = -\frac{U_k}{U_1} = -\frac{(1+t_k)}{(1+t_1)} \tag{14-37}$$

Thus, we can rewrite (14-36) as

$$\left(\frac{1+t_k}{1+t_1} - 1 \right) = \frac{\zeta L U_k}{\lambda wf} \frac{d\log(U_k/U_1)}{dL} \quad \text{for } k = 2, \dots, n \tag{14-38}$$

Without loss of generality, we may set $t_1 = 0$. Hence

$$\frac{t_k}{1+t_k} = \frac{\zeta L \alpha}{\lambda wf} \left[\frac{d\log(U_k/U_1)}{dL} \right] \tag{14-39}$$

(It may be noted that the multiplier ζ depends on w and that, for example, at a finite end-point $\zeta = 0$—the counterpart of the income tax result.)

The necessary condition for optimality (14-39) is based on the normalization that the first good be untaxed (hence its asymmetric form). This means that any t_k non-zero corresponds to a differentiated indirect tax structure. From the right-hand side we can see that differentiation depends on the relationship between labour and the marginal rate of substitution between commodities k and 1. In particular, where the utility function is weakly separable between labour and all goods together (the marginal rate of substitution between i and j is independent of L for all i and j), the right-hand side is zero and hence $t_k = 0$ (with this normalization). With the greater flexibility provided by the nonlinear income tax schedule, the result found for the linear expenditure case (with a linear income tax) holds for a more general class of utility functions. The assumption of weak separability between consumption and labour may not appear particularly reasonable. It is however an assumption that has been made in nearly all studies of demand and labour supply functions, and it provides a useful benchmark case. Finally, it is interesting to note that relative tax rates are independent of the social welfare function, so that they may be viewed as conditions for constrained Pareto optimality (Mirrlees, 1976).

The way in which the separability result arises may be seen from the parallel with the literature on second-best. We have a situation where there are differences in endowments (w) which we should ideally like to correct through first-best taxation linked directly with w. In practice however we are constrained to employ income taxation, and the problem becomes a second-best one. As a result, the optimum involves in general a wedge between before- and after-tax returns to labour at the margin, but this leaves open the question whether we want to have the first-best conditions satisfied elsewhere. As it was put by Davis and Whinston,

> the second best is concerned with the usefulness of the usual Pareto conditions in a situation in which there are imperfections in areas of the economic system which are not the particular one of immediate concern. When and under what conditions does the existence of imperfections in these "other areas" cause it to be undesirable (from the point of view of efficiency) to design policies for the achievement of the Pareto conditions in the area of concern? [Davis and Whinston, 1967, p. 330]

Where the government is concerned with redistribution, the same kind of question arises. The result given earlier makes precise the separability required in order for no indirect taxation to be needed (i.e., the Pareto conditions for the allocation between *goods* not to be disturbed).

Implications for Direct and Indirect Taxation

In terms of our earlier discussion of differing views about the direct–indirect tax problem, the weak separability result provides some limited support for the second broad view—that direct taxes are superior on both efficiency

Table 14-1 Summary of optimum tax formulae

	Indirect taxation and identical individuals	Indirect taxation and redistribution	Indirect taxation and a linear income tax	Indirect taxation and a general income tax
Individual	All individuals identical $\max U$ subject to $\mathbf{q} \cdot \mathbf{X} = wL$	Individuals differ in w $\max U$ subject to $\mathbf{q} \cdot \mathbf{X}(w) = wL(w)$	Individuals differ in w $\max U$ subject to $\mathbf{q} \cdot \mathbf{X} = wL + G$	Individuals differ in w $\max U$ subject to $\mathbf{q} \cdot \mathbf{X} = wL - T(wL)$
Government	max social welfare function U subject to revenue requirement $\mathbf{t} \cdot \mathbf{X} = R_0$	$\max \int \Psi(U)dF$ subject to $\int(\mathbf{t} \cdot \mathbf{X})dF = R_0$	$\max \int \Psi(U)dF$ subject to $\int(\mathbf{t} \cdot \mathbf{X} - G)dF = R_0$	$\max \int \Psi(U)dF$ subject to $\int[T(wL) + \mathbf{t} \cdot \mathbf{X}]dF = R_0$
First-order conditions for optimality	$\sum_i t_i S_{ki} = -(1-b)X_k$ for $k = 1, \ldots, n$ where $b = \dfrac{\beta}{\lambda} + \sum_i t_i \dfrac{\partial X_i}{\partial M}$ is the net social marginal valuation of income	$\int(\sum_i t_i S_{ki})dF$ $= -\bar{X}_k[(1-b) - \overline{b\phi_k}]$ for $k = 1, \ldots, n$ where $\bar{b}\bar{X}_k\phi_k = \int(X_k - \bar{X}_k)(b - \bar{b})dF$ $\bar{X}_k = \int X_k dF$	$\int(\sum_i t_i S_{ki})dF$ $= \bar{X}_k \phi_k$ for $k = 1, \ldots, n$	$\dfrac{t_k}{1+t_k}$ $= \dfrac{\zeta L\alpha \, d\log(U_k/U_1)}{\lambda wf}\,dL$ $k = 2, \ldots, n$ where normalized such that $t_1 = 0$

Note: the distribution is normalized, so that F is a *proportion* (for comparison with the discrete distribution used in the text, set $H = 1$).

and equity counts. Not just in the case of the linear expenditure system, but in a much wider class of demand systems, there is no need to employ differentiated indirect taxation to achieve an optimum. This does not require separability between goods, just weak separability between labour and all goods. At the same time, it does not provide a blanket justification for the view that direct taxes are superior, and it is quite possible that this separability requirement may not in practice be met, for example, in the case of leisure goods. For this reason no such categorical assertion can be made as that by Fromm and Taubman quoted earlier.

For the convenience of the reader, we have summarized in Table 14-1 the optimal tax formulae for the different cases we have considered. (The formulae relate to the case where w is distributed continuously.) This shows the development of the analysis, and the way in which the results depend on the range of instruments at the disposal of the government. There are of course a number of aspects of the choice between direct and indirect taxation not incorporated in the analysis, and the model needs to be elaborated in several respects. In particular, individuals are assumed to differ only in wages, and we have seen that this is a critical feature in explaining the results. Where people differ in tastes or in the prices faced for commodities, then the results do not necessarily apply. In the discussion of tax deductions below we refer to some of the implications of differences apart from those in w.

Nonlinear Indirect Taxes and Tax Deductions

The analysis can readily be extended to nonlinear indirect tax schedules, and it can be seen that weak separability leads to the same conclusions. The reason for the asymmetry between goods and labour is not that the latter was assumed above to be taxed in a nonlinear fashion; it is that the differences between people are in their wages, not in the commodity prices. The same applies to the tax deductibility of certain expenditures. It has been argued that items such as housing or medical expenses should be deducted from the income tax base. The result given above can be used however to show that—with the assumptions made—deductibility is not desirable where the weak separability condition applies.

In order to illustrate this, let us take the case of housing. To begin with, we treat it simply like any other commodity; the only difference is that we allow for the possibility that the after-tax price schedule may be nonlinear, reflecting housing assistance schemes, and that a fraction, κ, may be deductible from the income tax base. If good n denotes housing, then the individual budget constraint becomes

$$Q_n(X_n) + \sum_{1}^{n-1} q_i X_i = wL - T(wL - \kappa Q_n) \qquad (14\text{-}40)$$

where Q_n denotes the expenditure on housing (the pre-tax price is unity). The first-order condition for individual utility maximization is:

$$U_n = \left[\frac{-U_L}{w(1-T')} \right] Q'_n(1 - \kappa T') \tag{14-41}$$

(the other conditions are unchanged). Substituting from this, (14-31) and (14-37) into (14-36), with $t_1 = 0$, we can see that, where the weak separability condition holds between housing and labour,

$$Q'_n(1 - \kappa T') = 1 \tag{14-42}$$

The net price, allowing for the tax deductibility, should be equal to the pre-tax price; in other words, there should at the margin be no housing assistance or tax deduction.

From this, we can see that the case for subsidy or tax deduction must depend (1) on the weak separability condition not applying, (2) on there being restrictions on the use of nonlinear income tax schedules; or (3) on there being features of housing that are not captured by the model. The second of these is explored in Exercise 14-2 below. The third aspect raises the question whether it is right to treat housing as similar to other commodities. Here opinions diverge, and differences in policy recommendations can often be traced to differing views on the nature of the housing market. One can distinguish between situations where, in the long run, everyone faces the same housing cost per unit, and situations where there are long-run inequalities in the access to housing. The former view is that assumed above. Although it is held by a wide variety of writers,[5] there are good grounds for considering the alternative, that individuals differ not only in the wage but also in the price of housing that they face. The resulting multi-dimensioned control problem is however of considerable complexity (Mirrlees, 1979), although some explicit results can be obtained for special cases (Atkinson, 1977a).

Exercise 14-2 In a model with two goods (housing and other consumption) and labour, with individuals having identical utility functions, differing only in their wage per hour, and with fixed producer prices, examine the case for a proportional housing subsidy where the government can levy only a linear income tax.

A second example of the relationship between expenditures and the direct tax base is provided by medical expenses. The arguments here depend on the form of medical provision (private versus National Health Service) and on the extent of insurance. Here we suppose simply that sickness leads

---

[5] From Friedrich Engels to Milton Friedman. The former, in *The Housing Question*, wrote "The rent agreement is quite an ordinary commodity transaction which is... of no greater and no lesser interest to the worker than any other commodity transaction".

to private expenses (after insurance) of m, and that the population differs in the characteristics m and w. It is commonly argued that the higher is m, the lower is taxable capacity, and hence that there should be a tax deduction for medical expenses. Against this, it is suggested that deductibility is undesirable because it means (with a nonlinear income tax) that different people face different effective prices for medical care and it is inequitable that the price is lowered more for the rich than for the poor. For these reasons it is often proposed that a tax credit would be preferable to a tax deduction.

If there were no differences in m, or if an *ex ante* view were adopted (and all individuals had the same risk of illness), then the earlier analysis could be applied. Where there is a freely variable nonlinear income tax, and the weak separability result holds, then neither tax deductibility nor a tax credit would be desirable. The argument for special provisions must therefore rest on (in addition to the assumptions of separability and that there are no restrictions on income taxation) the recognition of individual differences with respect to medical needs. Where these exist, the optimal provision depends on the distortionary costs that may be imposed by a subsidy at the margin. (We are abstracting here from externalities.) The provision of a tax credit is just like partial insurance for medical expenses, and the considerations that lead to co-insurance in conventional insurance policies may restrict the credit below 100 per cent.

In order to see how this question can be formulated, we take a simplified representation where there are two goods (consumption and medical care), denoted by c and m, and the utility function

$$U \equiv u(c) + z(m, \eta) - v(\eta)L \qquad (14\text{-}43)$$

where η denotes the health needs of the individual. If a fraction κ_1 of medical expenditure is tax-deductible, and if there is a tax credit of value equal to a fraction κ_2, then with a nonlinear tax schedule the budget constraint is

$$c = wL - T(wL - \kappa_1 m) - (1 - \kappa_2)m \qquad (14\text{-}44)$$

The individual first-order conditions are (for an interior solution)

$$u'w(1 - T') = v \qquad (14\text{-}45\text{a})$$
$$u'(1 - \kappa_2 - \kappa_1 T') = z_m \qquad (14\text{-}45\text{b})$$

(the consumption pattern depending on health needs, η, via z_m and v). The government is concerned with maximizing social welfare:

$$\iint U dF(w, \eta) \qquad (14\text{-}46)$$

subject to the revenue constraint:

$$\iint [T(wL - \kappa_1 m) - \kappa_2 m] dF(w, \eta) = R_0 \qquad (14\text{-}47)$$

Introducing a Lagrangean multiplier for the revenue constraint, we may then write down the first-order conditions for the choice of κ_1 and κ_2. This is left as an exercise for the reader.

> **Exercise 14-3** Derive the first-order conditions in the problem described above for the choice of κ_1 and κ_2. In the case where individuals differ only in η (so that there is only one dimension), examine whether there are situations in which only a tax credit or a tax exemption should be employed. (Note: for further discussion of this model, see Stiglitz and Boskin, 1977.)

14-4 TAXATION OF SAVINGS

In the foregoing analysis income and expenditure have been treated as interchangeable, but much of the literature on direct versus indirect taxes has been concerned with the proper treatment of savings, or the choice between an expenditure and income tax. This raises the issue of whether income or consumption is the appropriate basis for assessing equity, as discussed in Lecture 9. Here we simply assume for the purposes of argument that, ignoring differences in tastes, the government is concerned with individual lifetime welfare derived from consumption and leisure. This in itself creates—at least in a perfect capital market—a presumption in favour of consumption as the appropriate base, and hence the total exemption of savings. However, this presumption needs to be qualified by the efficiency and redistributive considerations, with which we are here concerned.

A number of authors have suggested that the optimal tax results derived for a timeless economy may be applied directly to the tax treatment of savings. Indeed, the original Ramsey article included a brief section on savings.[6] In Atkinson and Stiglitz (1972), we discussed the case where a person lives for n periods, consumes X_i in period i, supplies labour L in period 1, and has a utility function that is additively separable. Application of the standard Ramsey results, with a proportional tax schedule, leads then to the conclusion that the optimal tax is a consumption tax where there are unitary expenditure elasticities (as, for example, with the Cobb–Douglas utility function). Where individuals differ in their wage rates, and there is a nonlinear tax on wage income, a sufficient condition for the consumption tax to be optimal is that there be weak separability between consumption and leisure. This result, based on the analysis given earlier in this Lecture,

---

[6] Interestingly, little reference has been made in recent papers to his treatment of savings. On the basis of an assumed infinite elasticity of demand for savings and a finite supply elasticity, he argues that "income-tax should be partially but not wholly remitted on savings" (Ramsey, 1927, p. 59).

has been used by Feldstein (1978b) and others, in discussion of the welfare gains from reducing the rates of taxation on capital income.

Since the static general equilibrium model used in earlier sections can be given a straightforward intertemporal interpretation, with commodities being distinguished according to their dates, it may seem that the previous results can be applied directly in this way. This does not however take account of the possibility that the government may wish to intervene to change the allocation of consumption over time—to achieve a socially desired intertemporal distribution. In view of this, we feel that it is preferable to formulate an explicit intertemporal model, and to use this to examine the conditions under which the optimal tax results can be applied to the treatment of savings.

The Intertemporal Model

The model is that of overlapping generations and life-cycle savings described in Lectures 3 and 8. People live for two periods, generation u born in period u consuming c_1^u in the first period and supplying labour L^u, and consuming c_2^u in the second period. They maximize identical utility functions:

$$U(c_1^u, c_2^u, L^u) \tag{14-48}$$

and face identical factor prices, r and w (i.e., no differences in wages). The total capital available in period $(u+1)$, K_{u+1}, is the savings of the preceding generation, denoted by A_u per head. Since the population is assumed to grow at rate $(1+n)$, the capital per worker is therefore

$$k_{u+1} = \frac{A_u}{1+n} \tag{14-49}$$

Net output per worker is assumed to be given by the production function

$$y_u = L^u g\left(\frac{k_u}{L^u}\right) \quad \text{where } g' > 0, g'' < 0 \tag{14-50}$$

(there is no technical progress or depreciation). This model has been used to examine the optimal tax treatment of savings by Ordover and Phelps (1975), Phelps (1977) and Ordover (1976).

As in the static model, the nature of the solution may depend critically on the range of instruments assumed to be at the disposal of the government. We therefore begin with a wide class of taxes, and by allowing for the possibility of debt policy. The taxes incorporated are those on consumption at time u, t_u, on interest income received by generation u, t_u^r; on wage income, t_u^w; and lump-sum taxes paid by those in the first generation (i.e., a lump-sum element to the wage tax), T_u. It is possible to include a further lump-sum element in the consumption tax, payable by both generations, but this can be shown to be equivalent to the issue of government debt (see Lecture 8, p. 248). The government debt, issued at time u, which pays the same interest as other capital, is denoted by B_u per worker. The individual budget constraint for generation u becomes therefore, where w and r denote the pre-tax wage and interest rate,

$$c_1^u(1+t_u) + \frac{c_2^u(1+t_{u+1})}{[1+r_{u+1}(1-t_u^r)]} = w_u(1-t_u^w)L^u - T_u \tag{14-51}$$

Everyone is assumed to have perfect foresight regarding r_{u+1} (see Lecture 8) and the future tax rates. We can write the consumption functions and labour supply functions for generation u as depending on t_u, t_{u+1}, p_u, ω_u, T_u, where

$$p_u = \frac{1}{1+r_{u+1}(1-t_u^r)} \quad \text{and} \quad \omega_u = w_u(1-t_u^w) \tag{14-52}$$

Finally, the capital market equation must now allow for government debt:

$$(1+n)k_{u+1} = A_u - B_u \tag{14-53}$$
$$= \omega_u L^u - T_u - c_1^u(1+t_u) - B_u \tag{14-54}$$

and from the production constraint (per worker):

$$L^u g = c_1^u + \frac{c_2^{u-1}}{1+n} + \frac{K_{u+1} - K_u}{P_u} + R_0$$

where P_u denotes the number of workers and R_0 the revenue requirement per worker. Rearranged, this gives

$$(1+n)k_{u+1} = k_u + L^u g - c_1^u - \frac{c_2^{u-1}}{1+n} - R_0 \tag{14-55}$$

Characterization of Optimum

How should the government choose the instruments at its disposal? In particular, should there be an interest income tax? The answers depend on the objective pursued by the government. This we take for the purposes of the analysis to be the sum of lifetime utilities over generations discounted by a factor γ, or, in terms of the indirect utility function,

$$\sum_{i=u}^{\infty} \gamma^i V^i \tag{14-56}$$

where we assume $\gamma < 1$. Suppose that the government starts planning at time u, having inherited a capital stock (per worker) k_u, and with the parameters that determine the welfare of the preceding generation being fixed. We can then introduce the state valuation function

$$\Gamma(k_u, t_{u-1}, t_u, p_{u-1}, \omega_{u-1}, T_{u-1})$$

to represent the maximal level of social welfare (discounted to time u) obtainable given those initial conditions. The government maximizes by choosing k_{u+1}, t_{u+1}, p_u, ω_u, T_u, and B_u subject to the constraints (14-54) and (14-55). Eliminating k_{u+1}, and introducing the multiplier λ_u for the remaining constraint, we can apply the principle of optimality of dynamic programming (as, for example, in Diamond (1973b), Pestieau (1974) and Mitra (1975)):

$$\Gamma(u) \equiv \max\left\{V^u + \lambda_u\left[k_u + t_u c_1^u + L^u(g - \omega_u) + T_u + B_u - R_0 - \frac{c_2^{u-1}}{1+n}\right]\right.$$

$$\left. + \gamma\Gamma(k_{u+1}, t_u, t_{u+1}, p_u, \omega_u, T_u)\right\} \quad (14\text{-}57)$$

where k_{u+1} is given by (14-55).

The simplest case to consider is that where B_u is freely variable. Since B_u does not enter V^u, the condition for optimality is that $\lambda_u = 0$. This accords with intuition. The debt policy allows the government to influence the relations between the savings by individuals and the level of capital formation; i.e., varying B_u ensures that a level of k_{u+1} that is feasible according to the production constraint (14-55) can be achieved by individual decisions subject to their lifetime budget constraints (i.e., (14-54)). Moreover, we can without loss of generality set the consumption tax at zero ($t_u = 0$ all u). We can then write the first-order conditions with respect to p_u, ω_u and T_u (using (14-55) to obtain the effect on k_{u+1}):

$$-V_p = \frac{\gamma}{1+n}\Gamma_1\left[\left(g - \frac{g'k_u}{L^u}\right)L_p^u - c_{1p}^u\right] + \gamma\Gamma_4 \quad (14\text{-}58\text{a})$$

$$-V_\omega = \frac{\gamma}{1+n}\Gamma_1\left[\left(g - \frac{g'k_u}{L^u}\right)L_\omega^u - c_{1\omega}^u\right] + \gamma\Gamma_5 \quad (14\text{-}58\text{b})$$

$$-V_T = \frac{\gamma}{1+n}\Gamma_1\left[\left(g - \frac{g'k_u}{L^u}\right)L_T^u - c_{1T}^u\right] + \gamma\Gamma_6 \quad (14\text{-}58\text{c})$$

where Γ_i denotes the derivative of i with respect to the ith argument, and L_p^u denotes the derivative with respect to p, etc. We can in addition obtain the difference equations governing Γ_i. Differentiating with respect to k_u, p_{u-1}, ω_{u-1}, T_{u-1}:

$$\Gamma_1(u) = \frac{\gamma}{1+n}\Gamma_1(u+1)(1+g') \quad (14\text{-}59\text{a})$$

$$\Gamma_4(u) = -\frac{\gamma}{(1+n)^2}\Gamma_1(u+1)c_{2p}^{u-1} \quad (14\text{-}59\text{b})$$

$$\Gamma_5(u) = -\frac{\gamma}{(1+n)^2}\Gamma_1(u+1)c_{2\omega}^{u-1} \quad (14\text{-}59\text{c})$$

$$\Gamma_6(u) = -\frac{\gamma}{(1+n)^2}\Gamma_1(u+1)c_{2T}^{u-1} \quad (14\text{-}59\text{d})$$

Interpretation of the Results

In interpreting the results, we assume that an optimum policy exists and that it converges to a steady state. In that steady state, from (14-59a),

$$1+g' = \frac{1+n}{\gamma} \tag{14-60}$$

Moreover, we can solve for the steady-state values of Γ_i/Γ_1 from (14-59b–14-59d). Substituting into the first-order conditions (14-58b and 14-58a),

$$-\frac{(1+n)V_\omega}{\gamma\Gamma_1} = -L + c_{2\omega}\left(p - \frac{1}{1+g'}\right) + t^w w L_\omega \tag{14-61a}$$

$$-\frac{(1+n)V_p}{\gamma\Gamma_1} = c_2 + c_{2p}\left(p - \frac{1}{1+g'}\right) + t^w w L_p \tag{14-61b}$$

where we have used the individual budget constraint, and the time variable has been omitted. From the properties of the indirect utility function, we know that $V_\omega = \alpha L$, $V_p = -\alpha c_2$. If we define

$$\tau \equiv p - \frac{1}{1+g'} = \frac{1}{1+r(1-t^r)} - \frac{1}{1+g'} = \frac{pt^r g'}{1+g'} \tag{14-62}$$

and

$$\theta = 1 - t^w w L_M - \tau c_{2M} - \frac{1+n}{\gamma}\frac{\alpha}{\Gamma_1} \tag{14-63}$$

where M denotes net lump-sum income, then the first-order conditions may be written in the familiar form:

$$-t^w w S_{LL} - \tau S_{2L} = -\theta L$$
$$t^w w S_{L2} + \tau S_{22} = -\theta c_2 \tag{14-64}$$

where S_{ij} denote the Slutsky terms.

Suppose first that the government cannot use lump-sum taxation, so $T_u = 0$. The condition (14-58c) is not then relevant, and we have the standard Ramsey results. Thus, where there are unitary expenditure elasticities (as with the Cobb–Douglas utility function), it can be shown that $\tau = 0$, which means that there should be no tax on interest income (see (14-62)). For other forms of the utility function, an interest income tax (or subsidy) may be optimal. It should be noted that $\tau > 0$ does not imply the superiority of an income tax; this would be the case only where the tax rate on interest income equalled that on wages. In order to see the relationship between the two, we may define the compensated elasticities:

$$\sigma_{LL} = \frac{\omega}{L} S_{LL} \quad \sigma_{2L} = \frac{\omega}{c_2} S_{2L}$$

$$\sigma_{L2} = \frac{p}{L} S_{L2} \quad \sigma_{22} = \frac{p}{c_2} S_{22} \tag{14-65}$$

and write the first-order conditions (eliminating θ and using $S_{2L} = -S_{L2}$):

$$\frac{t^w}{1-t^w}(\sigma_{LL}-\sigma_{2L}) = \frac{\tau}{p}(\sigma_{L2}-\sigma_{22}) \qquad (14\text{-}66)$$

The reader may like to experiment with possible values for the elasticities σ_{ij}. It is readily seen that the results are highly sensitive to parameters about which there is at present little empirical evidence, such as the elasticity of labour supply with respect to the interest rate.

The condition on the rate of interest (14-60) may be interpreted as ensuring a "first-best" intertemporal allocation—it characterizes the level of capital per worker hour that would be chosen in a fully controlled economy. Thus, where the objective function is the sum of total utility discounted at rate δ, we have $\gamma = (1+n)/(1+\delta)$, and (14-60) implies that $g' = \delta$. If, as in much of the optimal growth literature, the objective is the sum of average utility, discounted at rate δ, then $1+g' = (1+n)(1+\delta)$, which is often referred to as the "modified golden rule" (Cass, 1965). Where $\delta = 0$, this yields the golden rule itself, with $g' = n$ (here, since $\gamma = 1$, a different argument is necessary to characterize the optimum).

The Range of Instruments and a Constrained Optimum

The application of the Ramsey results described above can be criticized both for assuming too limited a degree of control and for assuming too great a scope for government intervention. First, as we have argued in the static Ramsey model, there is no reason, in a world of identical individuals, to rule out uniform lump-sum taxes. If the government can use T_u, then this implies that no distortionary taxes should be employed. (The first-order condition (14-58c) may be seen to imply $\theta = 0$.) As in the static model, the reason why the government may wish to use instruments other than the poll tax lie in its distributional objectives. These may relate to distribution at a point in time, and the analysis may be extended to differences between individuals. By analogy with the earlier results, where people differ only in wages, the weak separability condition (Section 14-3) implies that, with a fully flexible tax on wage income, no differential taxation of consumption is necessary (i.e., there is no interest income tax). (This is developed by Ordover and Phelps, 1979.)

The second aspect of equity concerns the distribution between different generations, and the choice of the path of capital stock. Here the assumption about debt policy has been seen to be crucial, and it may be argued that we have supposed too great a degree of control. It has in effect been assumed that the capital stock per worker can be set at its first-best level (with $1+g' = (1+n)/\gamma$). However, in the real world the attainment of this first-best condition does not appear to be especially straightforward, and the rate of capital accumulation is commonly thought to be too low. We should therefore consider the implications of the capital stock being in the absence of taxation below the socially optimal level (in steady state) given by (14-60).[7] At the same time, we should note that the existence of restrictions on B_u is not in itself enough to cause this problem to arise. As already noted, the capacity to levy differential lump-sum taxes in the two periods is equivalent to issuing debt, and we have to ask what it is that stops the government from employing a uniform lump-sum tax T_u in the first period and T_u^* in the second. The reason for this must lie in considerations not explicitly incorporated into the model, particularly redistributional objectives within a generation. Where individuals differ in, say, wages, the uniform lump-sum element in the tax plays an important role (as we have seen); moreover, there may be constraints on treating two generations at the same date differently. On the other hand, the generations may be treated differently via a social security scheme (Samuelson, 1975), and we have to ask whether this allows enough flexibility to achieve the desired intertemporal distribution. Finally, from the capital market equilibrium condition (with $B_u = 0$), it is clear that an equal proportionate rise in $1+t_u$, $1+t_{u+1}$, $(1-t_u^w)$, and T_u, which leaves the consumer budget constraint unaffected, raises private savings. The normalization of the tax is not in this case an arbitrary matter: a wage tax is not equivalent to a consumption tax (with appropriate adjustments in T_u). This can be seen another way: because of restrictions on debt policy, the government is not indifferent regarding receipts at different dates (cf. Lecture 3).

In order to see what happens when there are constraints that limit the scope for intertemporal reallocation, we consider the case where $B_u = 0$, $t_u = t_{u+1} = 0$ and $T_u = 0$ (as in Atkinson and Sandmo, 1977). These constraints are specified in an *ad hoc* manner; however, they may be seen as being derived from a balance of intertemporal and intratemporal distributional considerations (the latter are not modelled explicitly, but see Ordover and Phelps, 1979). Where these restrictions apply, it may be shown that in steady state the necessary conditions for optimality are that

$$\frac{\lambda}{\Gamma_1} = \frac{1}{1+g'} - \frac{\gamma}{1+n} \tag{14-67}$$

and that

$$-t^w w S_{LL} - \frac{\gamma(1+g')}{1+n}\tau S_{2L} = -\theta^* L$$

$$t^w w S_{L2} + \frac{\gamma(1+g')}{1+n}\tau S_{22} = -\left[\theta^* - (1+g')\frac{\lambda}{\Gamma_1}\right]c_2 \tag{14-68}$$

where

$$\theta^* = 1 - t^w w L_M - \frac{\gamma(1+g')}{1+n}\tau c_{2M} - \frac{\alpha(1+g')}{\Gamma_1}$$

[7] Current concern about capital formation does of course relate to the level *given the existence of* substantial taxes.

Let us examine the case where $\gamma = (1+n)/(1+\delta)$, i.e., the objective is the sum of total utility. If in the optimum $g' > \delta$, i.e., the capital stock is below the first-best level, then, from (14-67),

$$\zeta \equiv -(1+g')\frac{\lambda}{\Gamma_1} = \frac{g'-\delta}{(1+\delta)} > 0 \qquad (14\text{-}69)$$

and the condition for the tax rates may be written using the definitions of the compensated elasticities:

$$\frac{t^w}{1-t^w}(\sigma_{LL} - \sigma_{2L}) = \frac{\tau}{p}(\sigma_{L2} - \sigma_{22})(1+\zeta) - \zeta \qquad (14\text{-}70)$$

This differs from the standard formula (14-66) in the presence of the term in ζ (see Atkinson and Sandmo, 1977).

The implications of this result may be illustrated by the example where both utility and production functions are of the Cobb–Douglas form: in particular

$$U = a_1 \log c_1 + a_2 \log c_2 + (1 - a_1 - a_2)\log(1 - L) \qquad (14\text{-}71)$$

The Cobb–Douglas is a useful benchmark, as we know that in this case the standard Ramsey formulation involves no tax on interest income ($\tau = 0$), since there are unitary expenditure elasticities. Any non-zero tax on capital income in the present case must arise because of departures from the standard framework.

The central properties of the Cobb–Douglas case (their derivation is left as an exercise) are:

$$L = a_1 + a_2 \quad c_1 = a_1 w(1 - t^w) \quad pc_2 = a_2 w(1 - t^w)$$

$$\sigma_{LL} = \sigma_{2L} \quad \sigma_{22} = a_2 - 1 \qquad (14\text{-}72)$$

$$\sigma_{L2} = -a_2 \frac{(1 - a_1 - a_2)}{a_1 + a_2}$$

Substituting into the optimal tax formula (14-70), we may see that coefficient of t^w is zero, and it confirms that where $\zeta = 0$ the optimal tax on capital income is zero. In the same way, it may be calculated that

$$\frac{\tau}{p} = 1 - \frac{1}{p(1+g')} = \frac{\zeta}{1+\zeta}\frac{a_1 + a_2}{a_1} = \frac{g'-\delta}{1+g'}\frac{a_1 + a_2}{a_1} \qquad (14\text{-}73)$$

so that $g' > \delta$ implies a positive tax on capital income. The value of g' depends however on the other conditions. From the capital market equation (14-54) and the production constraint (14-55), it may be calculated, using the properties of the production function, that (Atkinson and Sandmo, 1977)

$$\left(\frac{1}{a_3} + \frac{a_2}{a_1}\right)(g' - \delta) = \frac{1-a_3}{a_3}(g'_{\text{no tax}} - \delta) + \frac{R_0}{k} \qquad (14\text{-}74)$$

where a_3 is the share of capital. It then follows that, if $g' > \delta$ at the no-tax equilibrium, and if the revenue requirement is non-negative, then at the optimum $g' > \delta$. Where $R_0 = 0$, the "distance" between g' and δ is reduced by the tax system, but the gap is not completely closed. If, for example, in the no-tax situation $g' = 2$, $\delta = 1.2$ (note that the period is a generation), and if $a_3 = \frac{1}{3}$, $a_1 = a_2$, then in the optimum $g' = 1.6$, the tax rate on capital income is $\frac{1}{2}$, and the ratio c_2/c_1 falls 40 per cent. As before, it should be noted that a positive rate of capital income tax does not imply that an income tax (with $t^w = t^r$) is superior to a wage tax.

The solution of the Cobb–Douglas case is shown in Fig. 14-1, using a diagram similar to that in Fig. 8-3. The no-tax equilibrium is shown at P, and at that point $g' > \delta$. The first-best solution is shown at B, where it is assumed that $\delta > n$. The constrained solution at Q involves an intermediate level of k, and a lower ratio of c_2/c_1 than at P. These two elements are

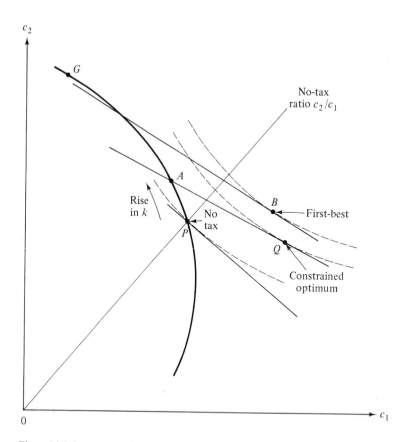

Figure 14-1 Intertemporal allocation in steady state: Cobb–Douglas example.

shown in Fig. 14-1 in terms of a rise in k (g' falls), indicated by the movement from P to A along the frontier, and a fall in (c_2/c_1) as a result of the fall in the net interest rate, indicated by the movement along the budget line AQ.

It may appear paradoxical that, where the no-tax capital stock is below the first-best level, there should be a positive tax rate on capital income (in the Cobb–Douglas example). However, the reason for intervention is the level of capital formation, and—with the particular savings function—private savings are increased by a (revenue-neutral) switch from t^w to τ. As it stands this is a special feature of the Cobb–Douglas, but the important point is that—where the government is concerned to change the intertemporal allocation of consumption—it is the absolute effect on savings that is relevant. We are interested in the *uncompensated* response of savings, rather than *compensated* responses which have received most attention in the optimal tax literature.

14-5 EXTERNALITIES IN CONSUMPTION AND CORRECTIVE TAXES

To this point we have, like Ramsey, abstracted from the presence of external effects in consumption. Where external economies or diseconomies affect decisions at the margin, then even in a static context the competitive equilibrium is not necessarily Pareto-efficient, and government intervention may be warranted on grounds of efficiency. The standard Pigovian approach to externalities is indeed via corrective taxes and subsidies; and it may be shown that, under certain conditions, a Pareto-efficient allocation can be achieved by these means (see, for example, Malinvaud, 1972, Ch. 9).[8]

It is not our intention here to discuss at any length the Pigovian approach, or the objections to it; rather, we are interested in the implications for the design of tax structure. How does the existence of external effects in consumption (for convenience, we talk about *dis*economies) affect the earlier results? How in turn are the Pigovian policy prescriptions affected when we take account of other objectives of government policy, such as raising revenue in an efficient and equitable manner?

Corrective Indirect Taxes

Returning to the framework of Section 14-2, let us suppose that the nth

---

[8] Starrett (1972) has emphasized the non-convexities associated with many situations where externalities are important on the production side; when there are non-convexities, it may not be possible to achieve a Pareto-efficient allocation by means of corrective taxes and subsidies. (We focus here on consumption externalities.)

good generates external diseconomies. The individual utility functions become

$$U^h(\mathbf{X}^h, N^h(X_n^1, \dots, X_n^h, \dots, X_n^H))$$

where the last term represents the effect of the external diseconomy "congestion" ($U_N^h \leqslant 0, N_i^h \geqslant 0$). The individual is assumed not to take account of his own contribution to congestion, so that the first-order conditions for individual utility maximization are

$$U_i^h = \alpha^h q_i \quad i = 1, \dots, n \tag{14-75}$$

where U_n^h denotes the derivative with respect to X_n^h, holding N^h constant. The instruments at the government's disposal are assumed to be the linear income tax, represented by G, and the commodity taxes, t_i. The government maximizes the social welfare function (14-12) subject to the revenue constraint (14-13). Forming the Lagrangean

$$\mathscr{L} = \Psi(\mathbf{V}) + \lambda(R - R_0) \tag{14-76}$$

the first-order conditions may be written:[9]

$$\frac{\partial \mathscr{L}}{\partial t_k} = \sum_h \left[\left(\lambda X_k^h + \Psi_h \frac{\partial V^h}{\partial t_k} \right) + \lambda \sum_i t_i \frac{\partial X_i^h}{\partial t_k} \right] = 0 \quad k = 1, \dots, n \tag{14-77a}$$

$$\frac{\partial \mathscr{L}}{\partial G} = -\left[\sum_h (\lambda - \beta^h) - \lambda \sum_i t_i \frac{\partial X_i^h}{\partial G} \right] \tag{14-77b}$$

where β^h is the social marginal utility of income.

The way in which externalities affect the optimal tax structure may be seen clearly in the special case where there are no cross-price or income effects.[10] In that case (14-77a) reduces to

$$\bar{X}_k + t_k \frac{\partial \bar{X}_k}{\partial q_k} + \frac{1}{H} \sum_h \frac{\Psi_h}{\lambda} \frac{\partial V^h}{\partial q_k} = 0 \quad \text{for } k = 1, \dots, n \tag{14-78}$$

Now

$$\frac{\partial V^h}{\partial q_k} = -\alpha^h X_k^h \quad \text{for } k = 1, \dots, n-1$$

but

$$\frac{\partial V^h}{\partial q_n} = -\alpha^h X_n^h + U_N^h \sum_j \left(\frac{\partial N^h}{\partial X_n^j} \frac{\partial X_n^j}{\partial q_n} \right) \tag{14-79}$$

Writing $b^h = \Psi_h(\alpha^h/\lambda)$, this gives, after re-arrangement, the same condition

---

[9] It should be noted that the demand derivatives include the effect on the individual demands of changes in N.

[10] This requires, in addition to the conditions discussed earlier, that X_i^h be independent of N for $i \neq n$.

as before for goods $1, \ldots, n-1$:

$$\frac{t_k}{1+t_k} = \frac{1}{\varepsilon_k}(1-\bar{b}-\bar{b}\phi_k) \tag{14-80}$$

(compare Eq. (12-61)) where ε_k is the elasticity of mean demand and ϕ_k the distributional characteristic (see (14-19)). In contrast, with the good generating the external effect, there is a further term (Sandmo, 1975):

$$\frac{t_n}{1+t_n} = \frac{1}{\varepsilon_n}(1-\bar{b}-\bar{b}\phi_n+\bar{b}D) \tag{14-81}$$

where

$$D \equiv \frac{\Sigma_h\{(b^h/\bar{b})(U_N^h/\alpha^h)\Sigma_j[(\partial N^h/\partial X_n^j)(\partial X_n^j/\partial q_n)]\}}{H\bar{X}_k} \tag{14-82}$$

Interpretation of the Results

Comparing (14-81) with (14-80), we can see that the difference in the form of the equation lies in the introduction of the term D. Where $D > 0$, the tax on good n is, other things equal, higher than indicated by the formula given earlier. Can we say anything about this term and in particular about the conditions under which it is positive or negative? Let us suppose first that all demands X_n^h are strictly decreasing functions of the price, and that at least some goods generate congestion ($N_i^h > 0$); it is then clear that, for a good that generates external diseconomies ($U_N^h < 0$), the term D is strictly positive, and the tax on this account positive. We can see in fact that the magnitude depends on the price responsiveness of the nth good weighted by its marginal social damage, where the latter depends in turn on its contribution to congestion and on which households are affected.[11] Reversing the order of summation in (14-82),

$$(H\bar{X}_k)D = \sum_j\left[\left(\frac{\partial X_n^j}{\partial q_n}\right)\sum_h\underline{\left(\frac{b^h}{\bar{b}}\frac{U_N^h}{\alpha^h}\frac{\partial N^h}{\partial X_n^j}\right)}\right] \equiv \sum_j\left(\frac{\partial X_n^j}{\partial q_n}\right)\Omega^j \tag{14-82a}$$

The underlined term is the loss of utility (converted to lump-sum income by dividing by α^h) to household h caused by the increase in X_n^j, weighted by the relative social valuation of household h. The expression Ω^j is the sum of this damage over all households. A further interpretation may be noted from the fact that, in an otherwise first-best world, where the government is indifferent about the distribution of income ($b^h = \bar{b}$ all h), the implied corrective tax for individual j is Ω^j. The term D may be seen therefore as a

---

[11] It may be noted that D has dimension H; this reflects the fact that the social damage is summed over households. There is a close relationship between this analysis and that of public goods in Lecture 16.

weighted average (with weights summing to unity) of the individual first-best corrective taxes.

The differences between the solution described here and the first-best corrective tax is that here we have assumed that all individuals face the same price. It is this that leads to the very natural weighted average result. It should however be noted that this constraint may lead to apparently paradoxical results, illustrating the general point that straightforward reasoning may become difficult once we leave the first-best. It may be the case that the demand derivatives are positive for some households (allowing for the indirect effect via N), and if these are individuals for whom Ω^j is large, then D may overall be zero or negative. In other words, D is a weighted average, but the weights may be negative. This is illustrated by the example contained in Exercise 14-4 (due to Diamond, 1973).

Exercise 14-4 The economy consists of equal numbers of two kinds of person with utility functions:

$$U^1 = \sqrt{X_1^1} - \tfrac{1}{3}X_1^2 - vL$$
$$U^2 = 0.3\log(X_1^2 + 0.9X_1^1) - X_1^1 - vL$$

(the superscripts denote households, not exponents). Show that the demand of household 2 increases with price up to 1.5, but that aggregate demand is a declining function of price. Calculate the corrective tax (levied at equal rate on both types of household) that maximizes the sum of utilities. Can such paradoxical results be ruled out by imposing stability conditions?

Finally, the example we have used has ruled out cross-price effects. Where one allows for complementarity and substitutability, then the question arises as to whether the "social damage" terms should also enter the conditions for other tax rates (via $\partial X_n^j/\partial q_k$ for $k \neq n$). This has been examined by Green and Sheshinski (1976) and Sandmo (1976a). They show that such "indirect" corrective taxes may be desirable, and indeed that there may be situations where only indirect measures are required. This challenge to the conventional presumption that direct measures are superior arises because the direct instruments that are assumed to be feasible do not allow attainment of the first-best.

14-6 CONCLUDING COMMENTS

From this Lecture it is clear that one needs to be careful in specifying the range of policy instruments at the disposal of the government, and that the conclusions may depend sensitively on this specification. This is well illustrated by the standard formulation of the Ramsey problem with identical individuals, which is of little ultimate interest when one can levy the uniform poll tax implied by virtually any direct tax schedule. It is brought out by the change in the results when we allow for a non-linear tax on wage income—the widening of the class of cases where no indirect taxation is necessary. It underlies the treatment of the taxation of savings in Section 14-4. Where the government is able to secure, by debt policy, lump-sum taxes or social security, the first-best relationship between the interest rate and the rate of time discount, the static optimal tax results can be applied to the issue of an expenditure versus an income tax. Where however the government is constrained, and the first-best condition is not ensured, then the tax formulae need to be modified. There is a further consideration—that of intertemporal distribution—which enters the optimal design of taxation.

There remains a great deal to be done in extending the analysis. The model needs to incorporate imperfectly competitive behaviour (discussed briefly in the next Lecture) and disequilibrium in labour and product markets. The treatment of savings has taken no account of differences between individuals in inherited wealth or in the rates of return received on their capital. The analysis ignores the costs of administration, or more generally the problems of limited information. As emphasized in Lecture 11, the costs of acquiring information (of "screening") is one of the main reasons why the government cannot attain the first-best allocation; but this is not explicitly introduced into the analysis. Much of the optimum tax literature has in effect been concerned with the balancing of efficiency and vertical equity, but policy-makers may feel that other considerations are relevant. Thus, the discussion of direct versus indirect taxation has been concerned primarily with vertical rather than horizontal equity, which many people regard as grounds for preferring direct taxes. (As may be seen from earlier arguments, this is not necessarily the case, and the implications of horizontal equity are less obvious than sometimes assumed.) A rather different factor, but one that politicians may feel to be particularly important, is the supposed preference of taxpayers for indirect taxation on the grounds that it is less visible. This requires a re-examination of the concept of the "burden" of taxation.

Before however the analysis is extended in these kinds of directions, one needs to ask what can be learned from this kind of literature. One common objection is that the analysis yields no results that could not have been ascertained by an intuitive argument without the need for a formal mathematical treatment. This clearly applies, for example, to the argument concerning the superiority of a poll tax in a model with identical individuals. However, experience suggests that intuition becomes an unreliable guide once one leaves the territory of the first-best. Consider, for example, the intuitively plausible arguments that:

> "If the role of indirect taxes is to achieve equity goals, then it is luxuries that should be taxed more heavily."

and

> "If the level of the capital stock is too low, then interest income should be subsidized."

Alternatively, we may take the weak separability condition concerning the role of indirect taxes in the presence of nonlinear income taxation (where individuals differ only in w). Intuition might have suggested that some kind of separability was required, but the precise form would not have been apparent without the mathematics.

A second objection is that the optimal tax literature does not lead to unambiguous policy conclusions and that the results depend sensitively on parameters about which we have little empirical knowledge, such as the second derivative of the demand function or the elasticity of the labour supply with respect to the rate of interest. This is a reasonable statement of the position (and indeed we have sought to bring this out), but it is a misunderstanding of the purpose of the literature to suppose that it can yield definite policy recommendations. As we emphasized at the outset, the aim is rather to explore the "grammar of arguments".

READING

Much of the discussion of the first part of this Lecture is based on Atkinson and Stiglitz (1976) and Atkinson (1977b). The discussion of the optimal tax treatment of savings draws on Diamond (1973b), Pestieau (1974), a series of papers by Ordover, Phelps and Riley (see references in Ordover and Phelps, 1979), and on Atkinson and Sandmo (1977). Public policy towards externalities is discussed in general in Mishan (1971) and Baumol and Oates (1975), among others. The treatment of corrective taxation given here draws on Sandmo (1975).

FIFTEEN

PUBLIC SECTOR PRICING AND PRODUCTION

15-1 INTRODUCTION

Countries differ in the extent to which output is supplied by the public or nationalized sector, but in nearly all Western countries there has been a great deal of interest in the policies to be pursued by the state sector, and the relationship between these policies and the behaviour of the private sector. Many managers of state enterprises seem to act in an identical way to the managers of private firms. Is such behaviour socially desirable? We focus in particular on the pricing and production decisions. Should public sector prices be equal to marginal cost, and, if not, how should they deviate? In choosing the technique of production, should state enterprises use market prices or should they be instructed to use shadow prices? If the latter, how should these shadow prices be calculated? What rate of discount should be employed in investment decisions?

This Lecture is addressed to these questions. We begin with pricing policy, taking as a reference point the first-best marginal cost pricing principle (described in more detail below). In Section 15-2 we examine some of the arguments that may be advanced to justify departures from marginal cost pricing. These include the problem of financing public enterprise deficits, the implications of monopoly elements in the private sector, and the impact on the distribution of income. In part, this treatment exploits the parallel between public sector prices and commodity taxation, and we do not repeat the earlier analysis (e.g., of the distributional effects). However, we also draw attention to the differences that may arise, and the fact that a simple translation of algebraic results may obscure significant features of the problem. We then consider the production decisions of the public enterprise, and in particular whether the shadow prices of inputs should be identical within the public sector and whether they should be equal to the market prices of inputs. Should British Steel use the same discount rate (for a given degree of risk) as British Gas, and should these rates be equal to an appropriate market rate? The questions of the desirability of "production efficiency", and the particular application to the social rate of discount, are the subjects of Sections 15-3 and 15-4.

Marginal Cost Pricing Principle

The principles of public enterprise pricing have long been the subject of discussion, and particular reference should be made to the tradition in France, dating back to the work of the Ecole des Ponts et Chaussées in the early nineteenth century (Ekelund, 1973). Much of this literature has argued in favour of marginal cost pricing, a case that was put forcefully by Hotelling in his classic paper:

> the optimum of the general welfare corresponds to the sale of everything at marginal cost. This means that toll bridges…are inefficient reversions; [that taxes on incomes, inheritances, and site values] might well be applied to cover the fixed costs of electric power plants, waterworks, railroads and other industries in which the fixed costs are large, so as to reduce to the level of marginal cost the prices charged for the services and products of these industries. The common assumption…that "every tub must stand on its own bottom" [is thus] inconsistent with the maximum of social efficiency. [Hotelling, 1938, p. 242]

In short, Hotelling argued that prices should be set at marginal cost and that any resulting deficit, in decreasing cost industries, should be financed by taxation. Moreover, as discussed later in the article, Hotelling assumes that such taxation would be lump-sum. This case for marginal cost pricing must be seen therefore as a first-best argument. As we have emphasized in earlier Lectures, there are reasons why there may be limits on the use of lump-sum taxes and why the government may have to rely on distortionary taxation (indeed, the taxes actually referred to by Hotelling are likely to be distortionary). The inability to impose fully variable lump-sum taxes may lead to deviation for marginal cost pricing. If the revenue necessary to finance deficits has to be raised in a way that is distortionary—so that for those economic activities price does not equal marginal cost—then there is no presumption that optimal pricing within the state enterprise will entail marginal cost pricing. If the desired redistribution cannot be achieved by lump-sum means, then public sector prices may have to be used as an instrument for this purpose.

The departures from marginal cost pricing in a second-best world have been the subject of much of the postwar literature. Thus, the behaviour of the public enterprise subject to a revenue constraint (e.g., that they should break even) was investigated by Boiteux (1956). He derived a formula for optimal pricing (see Section 15-2) that appears to be virtually identical to those derived in the treatment of the Ramsey tax problem (Lecture 12), e.g., that there should be an equi-proportionate reduction in consumption, along the compensated demand curve, from the level that would have ruled if price had been equal to marginal cost. That the formulae appear similar should not come as a surprise; indeed, the formal similarity was recognized by Hotelling. There is however the significant difference that each state enterprise may face a budget constraint that is separate from that faced by others.[1] So while we can exploit the earlier results, we need to bear in mind the special features of the position of the state enterprise and its relations with the government—to which we now turn.

Control over Public Enterprises

The formal similarity between the problems of taxation and public enterprise pricing provides considerable insight, but fails to do justice to the complexity of the questions arising from the relationship between the state enterprise and the government, and before presenting the analysis we should comment briefly on some of the relevant issues.

One central question is the nature of the "directives" from the government to the "state enterprises", and the degree of autonomy of the latter. There are varying degrees of autonomy. At one extreme, the enterprise may be run like a government department (as is sometimes the case with the Post Office); at the other, the enterprise may be an autonomous corporation like IBM or ICI, with the state receiving the profits like any other shareholder (this is true, for example, of certain joint ventures). More common is the intermediate case, where the public enterprise has independent management, but is set objectives by the state and is subject to specified constraints. The formal organizational relations may, however, imperfectly reflect the degree of autonomy. The civil servants running the Post Office may have more freedom of action than the head of the state steel corporation, who may be directed to locate his plants in certain areas, to build certain types of plants, etc.

In the design of the administrative structure, a key role is played by the incentive and informational problems to which we have alluded on several occasions. The interesting questions raised are not ones that we have space to explore here, and we simply assume that the structure is of the following two-stage nature. First, the *government* specifies the objectives of the enterprise and the constraints. For example, it decides on the target rate of return on capital that has to be achieved by the industry and the magnitude

---

[1] In a formal sense (as we note below) the taxation problem discussed earlier is a special case of the more general problem that Boiteux analysed: where there is a single budget constraint for the whole public sector, and the level of revenue raised for the public sector is set optimally (not, as in the Boiteux formulation, arbitrarily).

of the state subsidy (if any). Second, the *enterprise* determines its pricing policy so as to maximize its objective function subject to the constraints. For example, given that the National Electricity Corporation has to make profits of x, how should it determine the relative prices to households and industrial users? The efficiency and equity properties of the outcome depend on decisions made at both stages.

With this kind of structure, there is no direct link between public enterprises. The National Electricity Corporation does not take account of the effect of its policy on the National Coal Corporation. Such interactions—affecting such matters as transfer pricing—need to be taken into consideration by the government in laying down the guidelines for individual enterprises, e.g., to allow for the fact that they may be producing closely competing products (e.g., long distance train and air services).

The two-level structure is one reason why the parallel with the literature on optimum taxation is not complete. In that case, there was a one-stage problem. If we apply the Ramsey results directly at the level of the individual enterprise, then we are ignoring the fact that the constraints are themselves the subject of choice. The profit targets for different industries are set by the government, and take account of the interdependencies. On the other hand, if we collapse the problem into one stage, and treat all public enterprises as a single entity, we are ignoring the fact that the design of decentralized guidelines is an important institutional feature of the public sector.

In what follows, we pay particular attention to the relationship between the two levels of decision-making, and the wider question of the links with other instruments of policy. Do we, for example, want to keep public sector prices low for redistributional reasons, and how does that depend on the scope for redistribution via the tax system? In the analysis we of necessity have to leave on one side many important issues. We do not discuss the definition of marginal costs and related questions such as peak load pricing. We do not, in the models investigated, allow for uncertainty. The issue of incentives for the managers of public enterprises is not addressed directly, nor do we consider the information that is available to the government in its decision-making. We assume, for instance, that it knows the technologies and demand curves facing various industries, if this information is relevant for the directives it gives to different firms. (Of course, if it had this information, there would be less need for decentralization.)

The analysis here is concerned with the publicly owned enterprise. In a number of countries, particularly the United States, industries such as telephones, electricity, and railroads, are typically privately owned but publicly regulated. There is again a two-tier structure. The government imposes constraints on the operation of the industry, and the enterprise maximizes subject to the constraints. The difference is, however, that the enterprise objectives are now *private* objectives, such as the maximization of profits or sales. There has been an extensive literature on regulation (see, for example, Baumol and Klevorick, 1970; Bailey, 1973). We make no attempt to review this literature; we do however note *en passant* some of the main results. Finally, we shall have nothing to say about the relative merits of private ownership, with and without regulation, and direct public ownership and control. These issues are critical, but a full discussion is beyond the scope of these Lectures.

15-2 DEPARTURES FROM MARGINAL COST PRICING

In this section we consider the departures from marginal cost pricing that may be implied by the need to finance deficits, by the existence of monopoly elsewhere, and by redistributive goals. We assume initially that all individuals are identical, relaxing this when we refer to redistribution.

The Enterprise with a Profit Target

The simplest situation is that of a single public enterprise, producing one final product in quantity Z (in *per capita* terms), in an otherwise competitive economy (where the vector of *per capita* private outputs is denoted by $\mathbf{X}$). All individuals have identical utility functions $U(\mathbf{X}, Z, L)$, where L is the quantity of labour supplied per person. Labour is taken to be the *numeraire*. We denote by $\mathbf{q}$ the vector of prices of private sector products and by p the price of the public output. The production constraint is assumed to be of the form

$$\Omega \equiv F(\mathbf{X}) + C(Z) - L = 0 \tag{15-1}$$

where $F(\mathbf{X})$ gives the labour requirement in the private sector, and $C(Z)$ that in the public sector. It is assumed that the production set is convex. The condition for profit maximization in the private sector implies that private sector profit,

$$\Pi \equiv \mathbf{q} \cdot \mathbf{X} - F(X) \tag{15-2}$$

(i.e., value of net output minus labour costs), is maximized, a necessary condition for which is that $q_i = F_i$, where the latter denotes the derivative of F with respect to X_i. It is assumed at this stage that there are constant returns to scale in the private sector, so $\Pi = 0$. The implications of pure profits are discussed later.

The public enterprise is assumed to determine its price, p, to maximize social welfare, as measured by the indirect utility function of the representative consumer, denoted by $V(\mathbf{q}, p)$. The enterprise is constrained by the profit condition (per person)

$$pZ - C(Z) + T \geqslant \Pi^0 \tag{15-3}$$

where T denotes the subsidy provided by the government and Π^0 the profit target. The subsidy is assumed to be financed by lump-sum taxation, so that T enters the indirect utility function. There are assumed to be no other taxes at this stage. The solution to the pricing problem may be seen by forming the Lagrangean

$$\mathscr{L} = V(\mathbf{q}, p, T) + \lambda[pZ - C(Z) + T - \Pi^0] \tag{15-4}$$

The first-order condition with respect to p may be written using the properties of the indirect utility function (the assumption of constant returns to scale in the private sector means that the only change in V is that arising directly from p):

$$-\alpha Z + \lambda \left[Z + (p - C') \frac{\partial Z}{\partial p} \right] = 0 \tag{15-5}$$

where α is the private marginal utility of income.

Suppose first that T is freely variable, so that lump-sum taxation can be employed to finance any deficit. The first-order condition with respect to T (using the fact that $\partial V / \partial T = -\alpha$) is that

$$-\alpha + \lambda = 0 \tag{15-6}$$

From (15-5) it follows that (provided $\partial Z / \partial p \neq 0$) a necessary condition for optimality is that

$$p = C'(Z) \tag{15-7}$$

i.e., price equals marginal cost. This is an illustration of the standard argument for marginal cost pricing.

Where there are constraints on the use of T, and the enterprise has an effective profit target, then the pricing rule must be modified. Suppose that $T \leqslant 0$, and that with marginal cost pricing this is not sufficient to allow the enterprise to satisfy (15-3). This situation is illustrated in Fig. 15-1, where the profit target is taken to be that of breaking even. At the level of output where price equals marginal cost, there is the deficit indicated by the hatched area. In order to meet the profit target, the firm has to reduce output to Z_B, where price exceeds marginal cost. As drawn in that diagram, the instruction to the enterprise to break even completely determines its pricing policy. It sets prices above marginal cost to the extent necessary to avoid a deficit.

In practice, public enterprises produce more than one product, and this introduces degrees of freedom into the choice of pricing policy. Suppose that there are two products Z_1, Z_2. There are typically many combinations of the prices p_1, p_2 that will satisfy the profit constraint. How should the

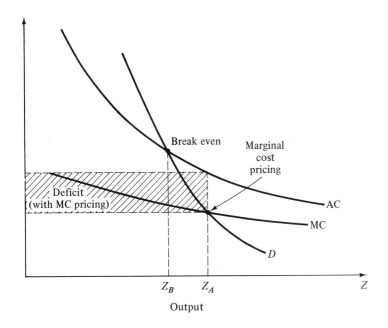

Figure 15-1 Public enterprise with break-even constraint.

firm depart from the marginal cost principle? There have been two main schools of thought. One view is that the mark-up over marginal cost should vary according to "what the market will bear", i.e., inversely with the elasticity of demand. Opposed is the position that prices should be *proportional* to marginal costs, advanced by, among others, Frisch (1939) and Allais (1948).

In order to consider the merits of these rival views, we may modify the earlier analysis, so that the maximization problem is now represented by the Lagrangean:

$$\mathscr{L} = V(\mathbf{q}, p_1, p_2, T) + \lambda[p_1 Z_1 + p_2 Z_2 - C(Z_1, Z_2) + T - \Pi_0] \quad (15\text{-}8)$$

We are assuming that the level of the lump-sum tax is fixed. The first-order conditions with respect to the prices, p_1 and p_2, are:

$$-\alpha Z_1 + \lambda \left[(p_1 - C_1) \frac{\partial Z_1}{\partial p_1} + (p_2 - C_2) \frac{\partial Z_2}{\partial p_1} + Z_1 \right] = 0$$

$$-\alpha Z_2 + \lambda \left[(p_1 - C_1) \frac{\partial Z_1}{\partial p_2} + (p_2 - C_2) \frac{\partial Z_2}{\partial p_2} + Z_2 \right] = 0 \quad (15\text{-}9)$$

where C_i denotes $\partial C / \partial Z_i$. The parallel with the Ramsey problem should at this point be clear. If we write $p_i - C_i \equiv t_i$, then these conditions are the same as those in Lecture 12 (see Eq. (12-13)).

If we consider the special case where demands are independent and there are no income effects, then, re-arranging, we have for good 1

$$\frac{p_1 - C_1}{p_1}\left(-\frac{p_1}{Z_1}\frac{\partial Z_1}{\partial p_1}\right) = \frac{\lambda - \alpha}{\lambda} \qquad (15\text{-}10)$$

This familiar Ramsey result, that the "tax" should be inversely related to the elasticity of demand, supports therefore the "what the market will bear" view rather than the Frisch–Allais proportionality rule. This, and other implications, were brought out by Boiteux (1956). The extent of deviations from marginal cost pricing depends on the budget constraint. Where this is not binding (e.g., because lump-sum taxes can be employed) $\lambda = \alpha$ and $p_i = C_i$. At the other extreme, as the required profit approaches the maximum possible, $\lambda \to \infty$, and the right-hand side of (15-10) tends to unity. This yields as a limiting case the price-discriminating monopolist, since marginal revenue equals marginal cost implies

$$\frac{p_1 - C_1}{p_1}(\varepsilon_1^d) = 1 \qquad (15\text{-}11)$$

where ε_1^d is the elasticity of demand.

As in the optimum tax literature, the analysis can be extended to interdependent demands. This is left as an exercise.

Exercise 15-1 Examine the optimal pricing policy where there are two goods with interdependent demands. How does the excess of price over marginal cost depend on the cross-elasticities? Are there circumstances in which a price less than marginal cost may be justified?

Profits in the Private Sector

The assumptions made to date (both here and in the earlier treatment of optimum taxation) do not allow for pure profits in the private sector, which arise in the competitive case where there are decreasing returns to scale. We now consider the implications of the existence of profits for public enterprise pricing and the relation to the optimum tax formulae.

With the introduction of pure profits, we have to be careful about the normalization of producer and consumer prices (Munk, 1978). We write $\mathbf{q}$ for consumer prices, $\mathbf{s}$ for producer prices, and for the present treat labour as commodity zero. Since the supply functions are homogeneous of degree zero in producer prices, and the demand functions are homogeneous of degree zero in consumer prices (including those of the public sector), in the absence of lump-sum income, one can in that case normalize by fixing one producer price and one consumer price. There is no loss of generality in assuming one good to be untaxed (as in the analysis to this point). This is however no longer true where the consumer receives profit income, since multiplying all producer prices by ζ implies that the profit income is also multiplied by ζ. The effect can be offset only by multiplying all consumer prices by ζ. The assumption of an untaxed good is not in this case innocuous. We can normalize one producer price *or* one consumer price.

The restrictions on commodity taxation are particularly important when considered in conjunction with restrictions on the tax rate on pure profit. Suppose that we set at unity one producer price (that of labour). The profit of the private sector is (*per capita*)

$$\Pi = s\,X - F(X) \tag{15-2'}$$

This is assumed to be taxed at a rate τ, so that the lump-sum income received by households is $(1-\tau)\Pi(\equiv I)$. Such a tax can be seen to be equivalent to a rise in all consumer prices by a factor of $1/(1-\tau)$, since demand functions are homogeneous of degree zero in consumer prices and I.[2] The taxing of pure profit can therefore be achieved by a uniform tax on all goods (and labour).[3] As a result, any restriction on profits taxation must limit both τ and the ability to tax all goods at a uniform rate. In what follows we assume that τ is fixed, and that there is one untaxed good, which is taken to be labour. The individual budget constraint is then, with a vector $\mathbf{Z}$ of public sector outputs,

$$\mathbf{q}\,X + \mathbf{p}\,Z = L + (1-\tau)\Pi \tag{15-12}$$

Combined with the production constraint and (15-2'), this yields the public sector budget constraint (*per capita*):

$$\mathbf{p}\,Z - C(Z) + (\mathbf{q} - \mathbf{s})\,X + \tau\Pi = 0 \tag{15-13}$$

or

$$\mathbf{p}\,Z - C(Z) + \mathbf{q}\,X - F(X) - (1-\tau)\Pi = 0 \tag{15-13'}$$

Let us now consider the position of the public sector as a whole, determining the prices to be charged where all goods can be taxed except labour (and there is no poll tax or subsidy). The maximization problem may then be formulated in terms of the Lagrangean:

$$\mathscr{L} = V(\mathbf{q},\mathbf{p},I) + \lambda[\mathbf{p}\,Z - C(Z) + \mathbf{q}\,X - F(X) - (1-\tau)\Pi] \tag{15-14}$$

---

[2] That is, the demand of the household for good i is

$$X_i[q_0,\ldots,q_n,p,(1-\tau)\Pi] = X_i\!\left(\frac{q_0}{1-\tau},\ldots,\frac{q_n}{1-\tau},\frac{p}{1-\tau},\Pi\right)$$

[3] This means in the optimal tax problem that, where the value of private profit exceeds the government requirement, denominated appropriately, a first-best solution can be attained either by a pure profits tax or by taxing all goods and factors. See Munk (1978).

The first-order condition for the choice of p_k is

$$\frac{\partial V}{\partial p_k} + \frac{\partial V}{\partial I}\frac{\partial I}{\partial p_k} + \lambda\left[Z_k + \sum_i (p_i - C_i)\frac{\partial Z_i}{\partial p_k} + \sum_j (q_j - F_j)\frac{\partial X_j}{\partial p_k}\right.$$

$$\left. - (1-\tau)\frac{\partial \Pi}{\partial p_k}\right] = 0 \quad (15\text{-}15)$$

The effect on profit is given by (from (15-2'))

$$\frac{\partial \Pi}{\partial p_k} = \sum_j (s_j - F_j)\frac{\partial X_j}{\partial p_k} + \sum_j \left(\sum_m X_m \frac{\partial s_m}{\partial X_j}\right)\frac{\partial X_j}{\partial p_k} \quad (15\text{-}16)$$

From competitive profit maximization, $s_i = F_i$, so that the first term on the right-hand side is zero, and we can replace $q_j - F_j$ by $q_j - s_j$ in (15-15). We may also make use of the properties of the indirect utility function, and observe that

$$\frac{\partial Z_i}{\partial p_k} = \left(\frac{\partial Z_i}{\partial p_k}\right)_{\bar{U}} - \frac{\partial Z_i}{\partial M}\left(Z_k - \frac{\partial I}{\partial p_k}\right) \quad (15\text{-}17)$$

where $(\ )_{\bar{U}}$ denotes the compensated demand derivative and $\partial Z_i/\partial M$ the income term (and there is a corresponding expression for private good demands). The first-order condition (15-15) can then be re-written as

$$\sum_i (p_i - C_i)\left(\frac{-\partial Z_i}{\partial p_k}\right)_{\bar{U}} + \sum_j (q_j - s_j)\left(\frac{-\partial X_j}{\partial p_k}\right)_{\bar{U}}$$

$$. = \left[1 - \frac{\alpha}{\lambda} - \sum_i (p_i - C_i)\frac{\partial Z_i}{\partial M} - \sum_j (q_j - s_j)\frac{\partial X_j}{\partial M}\right]\left(Z_k - \frac{\partial I}{\partial p_k}\right) \quad (15\text{-}18)$$

$$\equiv \theta\left(Z_k - \frac{\partial I}{\partial p_k}\right) \quad (15\text{-}19)$$

This formula allows one to see the role played by profits. The percentage reduction of consumption along the compensated demand schedule is no longer proportional for all commodities; there is an additional term representing the effect of profits. If raising the price of the kth commodity reduces profits by more than the lth commodity, then the consumption of the kth commodity should be reduced by less than the lth commodity.[4]

The derivation of the first-order conditions follows in the same way for the choice of indirect taxes (i.e., differentiating with respect to q_k). There is however a significant difference between the case of public sector pricing and that of optimal taxation. This is brought out clearly in the special case where there are independent demands, no income effects, and no joint production. In this case, a change in the public sector price has no effect on

---

[4] In the formulation given, it has been assumed that all goods (except labour) can be taxed; the effect of the restriction that good j cannot be taxed may be seen by adding the constraint $q_j = s_j$ to the Lagrangean (15-14).

private sector profit, and the first-order condition reduces to the familiar inverse elasticity form (as in (15-10)). In contrast, in the case of a tax on a private sector product, the effect on profits is given by (where $\partial s_m/\partial X_k = 0$ for $m \neq k$)

$$\frac{\partial \Pi}{\partial q_k} = X_k \frac{\partial s_k}{\partial X_k} \frac{\partial X_k}{\partial q_k} \qquad (15\text{-}20)$$

Substituting into (15-19), with the cross-price and income derivatives set to zero (and replacing Z_k by X_k),

$$(q_k - s_k)\left(\frac{-\partial X_k}{\partial q_k}\right)_{\bar{U}} = X_k\left(1 - \frac{\alpha}{\lambda}\right)\left[1 - (1-\tau)\frac{\partial s_k}{\partial X_k} \frac{\partial X_k}{\partial q_k}\right] \qquad (15\text{-}21)$$

This differs from the results given earlier for the no-profit case in the appearance of the term in $(1-\tau)$. Defining ε_k^d as before for the elasticity of demand, and

$$\varepsilon_k^s \equiv \frac{s_k}{X_k} \frac{\partial X_k}{\partial s_k} \qquad (15\text{-}22)$$

as the elasticity of supply, we can re-arrange (15-21) as (where $\theta = 1 - \alpha/\lambda$):

$$\frac{q_k - s_k}{q_k} = \frac{1/\varepsilon_k^d + (1-\tau)/\varepsilon_k^s}{1/\theta + (1-\tau)/\varepsilon_k^s} \qquad (15\text{-}23)$$

This is a generalization of the result originally derived by Ramsey (1927), in which the elasticity of supply now enters the determination of the optimum tax rate (he implicitly assumed that $\tau = 0$), and other things being equal the tax rate should be higher on goods supplied inelastically.[5] The difference between public sector pricing and the optimal tax case is brought out by the term $(1-\tau)$. In the public sector, τ is in effect unity, all profits being returned to the government, so that no supply considerations enter. In the case of private goods, where the rate of tax on profits is less than 100 per cent, the supply side has to be taken into account.

A natural question at this juncture is why governments do not impose 100 per cent profits taxes. Earlier we provided some explanation as to why lump-sum taxes should not be the only source of revenue. But, if profits taxes are non-distortionary, surely they should be set at 100 per cent, and thus the questions with which we have been concerned cease to be relevant? In practice, governments have not followed this Henry George-like policy. Although in wartime a few countries have imposed 100 per cent surtax rates, they typically do not levy on a regular basis 100 per cent taxes on profits and the incomes of fixed factors. The reason for this goes back to the lack of information at the disposal of the government. Most importantly, it

---

[5] Most textbooks refer to the formula that taxes should be proportional to $1/\varepsilon^d + 1/\varepsilon^s$ (e.g., Pigou, 1947, p. 108). For further discussion, see Stiglitz and Dasgupta (1971, p. 170).

finds considerable difficulty in distinguishing pure profits from the return to capital, or the return to entrepreneurship. This is seen most clearly in the case of unincorporated enterprises. If there were a 100 per cent profits tax, no such enterprise would ever declare a profit; it would always distribute the "pure profits" as wages to the entrepreneurs.

Monopoly and Second-Best

The existence of monopoly profits in the private sector gives rise to effects similar to those just discussed, but also raises other significant issues. Should the pattern of indirect taxes take account of the existence of monopoly and attempt to offset its effect? Do departures from marginal cost pricing in the private sector provide grounds for deviating from marginal cost in the public sector? In order to concentrate on this kind of question, we abstract from the effects of profits by assuming a 100 per cent profits tax ($\tau = 1$). For the reasons just outlined this is not realistic; it does however help separate the issues.

Suppose that we consider the choice of public enterprise pricing policy where there are no indirect taxes and the private sector monopolists have fixed prices, s_j, where $s_j > F_j$. Since $\tau = 1$, we can write down the first-order condition by analogy with earlier results:

$$\sum_i (p_i - C_i)\left(\frac{-\partial Z_i}{\partial p_k}\right)_{\bar{U}} = \theta Z_k + \underline{\sum_j (s_j - F_j)\frac{\partial X_j}{\partial p_k}} \tag{15-24}$$

The pricing rule in the absence of monopoly is now augmented by the term underlined in (15-24). This may be seen as the change in revenue from the profits tax arising from changes in private sector outputs induced by a rise in p_k (holding s_j and F_j constant for all j). To see the implications, let us take the case of a single public enterprise, producing goods whose demands are independent and where there are no income effects. The usual elasticity formula is augmented by the underlined term. If private firms price above marginal cost, and if their output is an increasing function of the public price, then we shall on this account want to raise the price above marginal cost. Conversely, if their output is a declining function of the public price, then the underlined term is negative. If $\theta = 0$, which is effectively the case taken by Green (1961), the deviation from marginal cost depends solely on the divergences $(s_j - F_j)$ in the private sector. In Lipsey and Lancaster (1956–7), these were taken as given. Intuitively, it might be felt that the corrective p_i/C_i ratio for the public sector should lie somewhere between the maximum and minimum values of s_j/F_j in the private sector, but Lipsey and Lancaster showed that this was not necessarily so. It is indeed possible that price could be below marginal cost if "monopolistic pricing of commodities complementary to it produce negative terms in the above sum [greater] than all the positive terms arising from...monopolistic pricing of substitutes" (Farrell, 1968, p. 48).

The treatment just given is rather special, relating to an "irreducible" distortion, where indirect taxes cannot be employed to correct the deviant behaviour. The analysis needs to be extended to allow for the use of indirect taxation—see Guesnerie (1975, 1978). We should also note that lying behind this treatment of the implications of market imperfections for public sector pricing is a view of the behaviour of the monopolist that is clearly not appropriate to oligopolistic markets, where strategic elements are likely to be important. Further development of the pricing rules requires a more soundly based general equilibrium theory of imperfect competition, and—as we have seen in Lecture 7—this is at present at a rather early stage.

> **Exercise 15-2** In the context of the model of imperfect competition described in Lecture 7 (pages 208–217), we examine the optimal policy of a state enterprise supplying the output Y. Should it charge more than marginal cost, on account of the mark-up in the private sector? Suppose that one of the firms in the X sector is taken over by the public enterprise. What should be its pricing policy?

Redistribution and Public Sector Prices

There has been considerable debate about the role of public sector prices in redistribution, as illustrated by the following quotations:

> By far the simplest way of securing the distribution...we desire is *through the price system*...the only price a public enterprise or nationalised industry can be expected to set is what we may as well call a *just price—a price which is set with some regard for its effect on the distribution of wealth* as well as for its effect on the allocation of resources. [Graaff, 1957, p. 155, his italics]

and:

> subsidies to the consumption of commodities are a particularly inefficient way of redistributing income.... The best way of making a particular individual better off is to give him an appropriate sum of money.... *It is thus unlikely that consideration of the distribution of income should lead to an optimal price below marginal cost.* [Farrell, 1958, pp. 113–14, our italics]

In attempting to assess the merits of these views, we can apply the same analysis as in earlier Lectures, introducing the distributional characteristic of the public sector good, ϕ_k (Feldstein, 1972a). The application is straightforward, following the same lines as in Lecture 12, and is left to the reader as an exercise:

> **Exercise 15-3** Suppose that individuals differ, being identified by

superscript h. There is a single public enterprise producing two products subject to a break-even constraint. Derive the first-order conditions corresponding to (15-9). For the special case where demands are independent and there are no income effects, show that the first-order condition reduces to

$$\frac{p_k - C_k}{p_k} = \frac{1 - \bar{b}(1 + \phi_k)}{\varepsilon_k^d} \qquad (15\text{-}25)$$

where b is the social marginal valuation of income and ϕ_k the covariance between $b^h/\bar{b}$ and $X_k^h/\bar{X}_k$.

From the example just given, it is clear that there may be situations where redistributional reasons dominate in the determination of the structure of prices (e.g., where $\bar{b} \geqslant 1$ and $\phi_k \geqslant 0$). In this sense, Graaff is correct. But the results depend critically on the extent to which other measures can be employed to redistribute income. If the government can vary the poll tax/subsidy element of direct taxation in such a way that $\bar{b} = 1$, then price is set below marginal cost only where $\phi_k > 0$. If the social marginal valuation of income falls with income, then ϕ_k is positive only for an inferior good. If the good is normal Farrell's conclusion is borne out.

We can go on to consider the range of pricing schedules open to the public enterprise. One commonly employed is the two-part tariff, involving a fixed payment coupled with a price per unit. This departs from a single price plus poll tax in that consumers choosing zero consumption are not liable for the fixed element.[6] More generally, the marginal price may vary with the quantity. The feasibility of such a nonlinear schedule depends on total consumption being observable. If resale or repeat purchasing is possible, then quantity discounts or premia can, respectively, be undone. For discussion of the optimal nonlinear schedule, the reader is referred to Spence (1977), Willig (1978), Goldman, Leland, and Sibley (1977), Roberts (1979), and Seade (1979).

15-3 CHOICE OF TECHNIQUE AND PRODUCTION EFFICIENCY

In this section we consider the choice of inputs for the public sector. The questions discussed may be posed—in a somewhat over-simplified form—in the following way. If there are a number of state enterprises, what should be the mix of inputs used by each enterprise? Put another way, suppose that the government sets shadow prices for inputs and tells enterprises to

---

[6] This feature of the two-part tariff is not captured in the empirical application by Feldstein (1972b), who treats the fixed payment as a uniform lump-sum tax.

minimize costs at those prices. Should these prices be the same for all enterprises and all sub-units of enterprises? What should be the relationship between these shadow prices and market prices?

Production Efficiency

The questions just described are equivalent to asking whether there should be *production efficiency*. Should the public sector be productively efficient in the sense that the marginal rate of technical substitution between any two inputs should be the same in different enterprises? Or should the railways make the choice between coal and oil on a different basis from that faced by the electricity industry? Should the economy as a whole be productively efficient in that the marginal rates of substitution are the same in both public and private sectors?[7]

Intuitively, it seems plausible that production efficiency is desirable. The literature on second-best has however led one to be suspicious of such intuitive arguments. Does, for example, the need to meet a profit target lead to input choices being different from those made on the basis of market prices? Are distributional considerations relevant in the choice of technique?

Our earlier discussions indicate that the most one can hope for is a result of the "separation" kind obtained in the Lectures on optimal taxation. Where there are departures from the first-best in one area, can we identify a set of "separable" decisions where the first-best conditions should none the less continue to hold? In the second-best models of the kind we have been analysing, if the government can impose 100 per cent profits taxation and tax all commodities and factors, if the budget constraints of enterprises are optimally chosen, then we will want to have production efficiency in the economy as a whole. On the other hand, where these conditions do not hold, the presumption in favour of production efficiency no longer obtains. Where, for example, the budget constraints are arbitrarily fixed, we will want to have efficiency within each enterprise, but there may be different shadow prices in different enterprises.

The issue of production efficiency was originally addressed in the classic paper by Boiteux (1956); he established the basic efficiency theorem for an arbitrarily given constraint. Diamond and Mirrlees (1971) examined the question, using more general techniques, for the case of unrestricted taxation and no pure profits, and established the desirability of production efficiency under fairly weak conditions. They require only that the social welfare function be individualistic and that there exist some good (with

[7] There is a closely related question, which we should more properly have asked in the Lectures on optimal taxation. Should the government impose differential factor taxes on different industries within the private sector; i.e., should the private sector of the economy be production efficient? See Stiglitz and Dasgupta (1971).

positive price) that is a "good" for all individuals.[8] The argument runs broadly as follows. If the optimum were in the interior of the production set, small changes in prices would still result in technically feasible demands. On the other hand, lowering the price of the good consumed by everyone (strictly, a good that no consumer supplies), or raising the price of the good supplied by everyone (strictly, one that no consumer purchases), raises welfare (given non-satiation and positive response of the welfare function). Therefore, given this condition, at an optimum, production must occur on the production frontier.

The extension of the analysis to economies where there are pure profits and restrictions on the set of admissible taxes is studied in Stiglitz and Dasgupta (1971), Dasgupta and Stiglitz (1972), Mirrlees (1972a) and Hahn (1973). The results show that, if there are enough instruments at the government's disposal, and in particular if the government is free to set any rates of tax (including 100 per cent) on the pure profits of different producers, then production efficiency is desirable even with decreasing returns to scale in the private sector (giving rise to pure profits). On the other hand, restrictions on the taxing possibilities of the government, for example, limits on taxing pure profits or when a tax cannot be levied on certain commodities or factors, may mean that production efficiency is not desirable.[9]

We do not attempt to provide a rigorous account of production efficiency; instead, we take an example that brings out the role of several factors. We consider a set of public enterprises, identified by an index j, each of which produces an output Z_j using inputs of two primary factors (types of labour) L^j_1 and L^j_2, according to the production function:

$$Z_j = Q^j(L^j_1, L^j_2) \qquad (15\text{-}26)$$

where Q^j is assumed to be a differentiable, well-behaved production function exhibiting constant returns to scale (an assumption that can be relaxed). For each enterprise there is a profit constraint

$$p_j Z_j - w_1 L^j_1 - w_2 L^j_2 = \Pi^0_j \qquad (15\text{-}27)$$

where w_i denote the producer input prices. On the assumption that the government can vary freely the taxes on all goods and factors, but is restricted to taxing pure profits at rate τ, we may derive the following first-order condition for the choice of inputs in the jth enterprise (where λ^j is the multiplier associated with the constraint (15-27) and μ a multiplier

---

[8] Even this restriction may be dropped if we allow trade taxes, i.e., taxes that are differentiated on the basis of whether the individual is buying or selling a commodity.

[9] Also, we noted in Lecture 12 that, in the course of a process of tax reform, where only limited steps may be made, there may be situations in which *temporary* inefficiencies are desirable even when the full optimum is characterized by production efficiency—Guesnerie (1977).

associated with an overall revenue constraint)—see Stiglitz and Dasgupta (1971):

$$\frac{Q_1^j}{Q_2^j} = \frac{w_1 + (1-\tau)\left[(\mu-\alpha)/\lambda^j\right]\dfrac{\partial\Pi}{\partial L_1^j}}{w_2 + (1-\tau)\left[(\mu-\alpha)/\lambda^j\right]\dfrac{\partial\Pi}{\partial L_2^j}} \tag{15-28}$$

From this result we can see at once that there are several sufficient conditions for production efficiency. If there are no profits in the private sector, then the marginal rate of substitution between L_1 and L_2 in the jth public enterprise should be equal to w_1/w_2. It is therefore the same in all public enterprises and equal to the private sector rate of substitution. Where $\partial\Pi/\partial L_k^j \neq 0$, then the same result can be ensured by 100 per cent profits taxes ($\tau = 1$), or if there is lump-sum taxation such that $\mu = \alpha$. Thus, if the government's revenue requirements can be met by a partial profits tax, we may have $\tau < 1$ but $\mu = \alpha$. Where these do not hold, but the profit targets Π_j^0 are set optimally, then λ^j will be equated for all j. In this case, the marginal rates of substitution are equal *within* the public sector (since $\partial\Pi/\partial L_m^j$ is equal for all j). All public enterprises use the same shadow prices.

It should be noted that the analysis assumes that the government can levy a full set of commodity taxes and that it can tax all factors in all uses. Otherwise, we may want to use distortionary factor taxes, in some industry, as a partial substitute for the absent commodity taxes. Similarly, the fact that we cannot tax labour in one use (e.g., household production) does not mean that we do not want to tax it in other uses. Many of the important instances of distortionary factor taxes can be related to these conditions; for instance, the differential tax treatment of capital in the unincorporated and incorporated sector may arise from the *impossibility* within the unincorporated sector of distinguishing between capital and wage income; hence, within that sector, the two factors must be treated the same.

Finally, we have taken no account so far of distributional considerations, but they may also provide a reason for productive inefficiency.[10]

Implications of Production Efficiency/Inefficiency

The efficiency/inefficiency result has several important implications; and it serves to integrate the discussion of a number of different policy problems.

First, production efficiency within the public sector implies that the transfer prices used by public enterprises for sales *within* the public sector should be marginal cost prices, and hence not necessarily equal to those charged to final consumers. The profit target should be met on sales outside

[10] See Dasgupta and Stiglitz (1972) and Mirrlees (1972a).

the public sector; to charge a mark-up on the transfer of electricity to the public steel industry would lead to production inefficiency (as would taxes on any intermediate transactions).

The second implication of the efficiency result concerns the setting of enterprise objectives related to input use. This applies particularly to the requirement of a minimum rate of return on capital or the imposition of a maximum rate of return (as with regulated industries). Such rate of return constraints may be compared with the absolute profit target considered above. It can be shown that for a given output a cost-minimizing firm subject to a binding *minimum* rate of return constraint produces its output using a more (less) capital-intensive method of production than with an absolute constraint if the minimum rate is less than (exceeds) the market rate (Gravelle, 1976). By contrast, a regulated private firm subject to a binding *maximum* rate of return constraint (in excess of the market rate) chooses a more capital-intensive technique than the one that minimizes costs for the output level produced (Baumol and Klevorick, 1970, Proposition 3). Where the conditions for production efficiency do not hold, then it may well be desirable for the shadow price of capital to differ from the market rate of interest, but such departures need to be derived from an explicit analysis of the kind described above, with full account taken of the instruments that the government has at its disposal.

In an open economy, the possibilities for international trade can be treated as private sector industries, and the efficiency result implies that in evaluating public sector decisions the international prices should be employed. This result holds not only when commodity taxes are chosen optimally, but also when they are fixed arbitrarily (Dasgupta and Stiglitz, 1974).

Finally, in the context of intertemporal decisions, the efficiency result implies that the correct shadow price of capital (the social rate of discount) is the producer rate of interest. This is in contrast to a substantial literature arguing that the social discount rate should be the rate of time preference, or some weighted average of this rate and the private rate of return on capital. In the next section we take up this application in more detail.

15-4 COST–BENEFIT ANALYSIS AND SOCIAL RATE OF DISCOUNT

The choice of the social rate of discount plays a critical role in cost–benefit analysis, and we begin with a more general review of the issues involved.[11]

---

[11] The situations with which we are concerned in this section are those where the government directly undertakes the project; there are other circumstances in which the government is called upon to *license* some private projects (particularly in less developed countries) or to provide some critical input (capital). Although many of the same considerations arise, one must bear in mind the distinction between these circumstances. In general, the criteria for evaluating projects in these two situations will be different.

Cost–Benefit Analysis

In principle, cost–benefit analysis is straightforward. Any investment project can be viewed as representing a perturbation of the economy from what it would have been had the project not been undertaken. To evaluate whether the project should be undertaken, we need to look at the levels of consumption of all individuals of all commodities at all dates, under the two different situations. If all individuals are better off with the project than without it, then it should be adopted (if there is an individualistic social welfare function); if all individuals are worse off, then it should be rejected. If some individuals are better off, and some worse off, whether we should adopt it depends on how we weight the gains and losses of different individuals.

Although this is obviously the "correct" procedure to follow in evaluating projects, it is not a practical one; the problem of cost–benefit analysis is simply whether we can find reasonable short cuts. In particular, we are presumed to have good information concerning the *direct* costs and benefits of a project (its inputs and its outputs);[12] the question is whether there is any simple way of relating the *total* effects (the total changes in the vectors of consumption) to the direct effects. Thus, in the case of the choice of discount rate, there is a trivial sense in which we would always wish to use the social rate of time preference for evaluating benefits and costs accruing in different periods. This however applies to *total* effects, and there is no reason to believe that these are simply proportional to the direct effects that are observed. If the ratio of total effects to direct effects changes systematically over time, then we would not wish to use the social rate of time discount in evaluating a project when looking only at direct costs and benefits.

In a first-best world, with no distortions and full scope for lump-sum redistributive taxation, if a project is "profitable" on the basis of its direct effects using market prices, then—with an individualistic social welfare function—it is socially desirable. The problem of finding the correct shadow prices for cost–benefit analysis arises from the existence of market imperfections and failures; it is concerned with situations where one cannot necessarily infer social desirability on the basis of the profitability of the project. In the case of the social rate of discount, the difficulties stem from differences between the private rate of return and the rate at which society can transfer resources between periods. The former is equal, in a competitive model, to the marginal *physical* rate of transformation of output in one period into output in the next. The latter is the rate at which the government can make the transfer, or what we refer to as the marginal *economic* rate of transformation.

---

[12] In practice, these are seldom known with accuracy, and obtaining good estimates may be critical. To some observers, it appears that the major lessons in project selection have more to do with this than with the use of incorrect prices.

In applying this approach, we need to begin with the reasons why a first-best cannot be attained. This depends on the initial sources of market failure, and on the extent to which government policy instruments can be employed to approach the first-best. As we have seen in earlier Lectures, there is no more reason to believe that the intertemporal allocation generated in the absence of government intervention is socially optimal than there is that the distribution of income is socially optimal at any point in time. Savings may be too low, e.g., where individuals give less weight to succeeding generations than they would collectively. Savings may be too high, e.g., because people can give as much to their descendants as they would like but are constrained in giving to antecedents. The direction of the misallocation may not therefore be clear, but there is certainly no presumption that the market solution is socially optimal.

Social Discount Rate in the Overlapping Generations Model

In order to explore this in more depth, we make use of the overlapping generations model described in earlier Lectures and which provided the basis for the treatment of the optimum taxation of savings in Lecture 14. The main modification is that there is now assumed to be a government capital good—the social discount rate being the return on public capital. Total government capital is denoted by G and enters the determination of aggregate output in period u, which is assumed to be given by a constant returns to scale production function:

$$Y_u = F(K_u, G_u, L_u P_u) \qquad (15\text{-}29)$$

where P_u denotes the total population, L_u hours of work, and K_u the private capital stock, at time u. The return to public capital accrues to the government. Output can be used interchangeably as either a consumption or a capital good:

$$Y_u = C_u + (K_{u+1} - K_u) + (G_{u+1} - G_u) \qquad (15\text{-}30)$$

where there is assumed to be no depreciation and no current government spending, and where C_u denotes total consumption.

Initially we assume that all individuals are identical; this is a critical assumption which is later relaxed. They live for two periods, working in the first, and the lifetime utility of a representative member of the generation born at u is $U(c_1^u, c_2^u, L_u)$, where c_i^u denotes consumption in period i. Total consumption at date u is therefore, per worker,

$$c_1^u + \frac{c_2^{u-1}}{1+n} \qquad (15\text{-}31)$$

where n is the rate of growth of the population. The wage rate is w_u before tax and ω_u after tax, and the price of second period consumption to generation u is p_u. The indirect utility function, V^u, is a function of ω_u and p_u (there are assumed to be no lump-sum taxes—although see below).

The level of capital goods at date u is related to the savings of the older generation, and the capital market equation may be written (see Eq. (14-53))

$$(1+n)k_{u+1} = A_u - B_u \qquad (15\text{-}32)$$

where k_{u+1} is capital per worker, A_u savings per worker, and B_u the level of government bonds per worker. It is assumed that there are only two assets in the economy—bonds and real capital. In particular, there is at this stage no equity investment in firms. There are no "pure" profits. Again, this is a critical assumption. From the individual budget constraint,

$$(1+n)k_{u+1} = \omega_u L_u - c_1^u - B_u \qquad (15\text{-}33)$$

Finally, the production constraint may be expressed in per worker terms and re-arranged to yield

$$(1+n)k_{u+1} = k_u + L_u f\left(\frac{k_u}{L_u}, \frac{g_u}{L_u}\right) - c_1^u - \frac{c_2^{u-1}}{1+n} - (1+n)g_{u+1} + g_u \qquad (15\text{-}34)$$

where g_u is government capital per worker (and we revert to f for the production function).

As in the previous Lecture, we assume that the government maximizes the sum of lifetime utilities over generations discounted by a factor γ (where $\gamma \leqslant 1$):

$$\sum_{i=1}^{\infty} \gamma^i V^i \qquad (15\text{-}35)$$

We introduce as before the state valuation function:

$$\Gamma(u) \equiv \Gamma(k_u, g_u, p_{u-1}, \omega_u)$$

$$= \max\left\{ V^u + \lambda_u \left[k_u + L_u(f - \omega_u) + B_u - \frac{c_2^{u-1}}{1+n} \right. \right.$$

$$\left. \left. - (1+n)g_{u+1} + g_u \right] + \gamma\Gamma(u+1) \right\} \qquad (15\text{-}36)$$

where we have eliminated k_{u+1} between (15-33) and (15-34), and k_{u+1} in $\Gamma(u+1)$ is given by the latter. The analysis of the optimal wage tax (ω) and interest tax (p) follows the same lines as in Lecture 14. Here we concentrate on the effects of government capital. The first-order condition for the choice of g_{u+1} is:

$$-\gamma\Gamma_k(u+1) + \gamma\Gamma_g(u+1) - \lambda_u(1+n) = 0 \qquad (15\text{-}37)$$

The difference equations governing Γ_i are:

$$\Gamma_k(u) = \gamma \Gamma_k(u+1)\left(\frac{1+f_k}{1+n}\right) + \lambda_u(1+f_k) \qquad (15\text{-}38)$$

$$\Gamma_g(u) = \gamma \Gamma_k(u+1)\left(\frac{1+f_g}{1+n}\right) + \lambda_u(1+f_g) \qquad (15\text{-}39)$$

where f_k, f_g denote the marginal products of private and government capital respectively. As before, we assume that an optimal policy exists.

Implications of Results

We begin by considering the case where the government has full control over debt policy. Since B_u does not affect V^u, the first-order condition is that $\lambda_u = 0$. It then follows from (15-37)–(15-39) that

$$\Gamma_g(u) = \Gamma_k(u)$$

and

$$\frac{1+f_g}{1+f_k} = \frac{\Gamma_g(u)}{\Gamma_k(u)} = 1 \qquad (15\text{-}40)$$

It is immediate therefore that in this model, with identical individuals, all pure profits taxed away and a completely flexible debt policy, the rate of return on public capital must equal that on private capital. The social rate of discount is the private rate of return. The intuitive reason for this is that, with optimally chosen taxes and debt policies, aggregate savings are fixed, and a unit of public capital displaces precisely one unit of private capital, and has no further repercussions. From the difference equation (15-38), with $\lambda_u = 0$, the steady-state value of f_k is given by (in steady state k, g, L and all other *per capita* variables are constant):[13]

$$1+f_k = \frac{1+n}{\gamma} \qquad (15\text{-}41)$$

If the objective function is the total sum of utilities (so $\gamma = (1+n)/(1+\delta)$), the steady-state rate of return is equal to the social rate of time preference. This does not in general hold outside the steady state.[14]

These results give a straightforward answer to the question of the choice of social discount rate. The assumptions required are, however, of dubious validity. The government does not use debt policy primarily for purposes of intertemporal redistribution, as the above analysis requires, and does not impose 100 per cent pure profits taxes; finally, individuals are not identical.

---

[13] As in Lecture 14, we assume that an optimum, if it exists, converges to a steady state.

[14] It should be noted that the discount factor relates to *utilities*, not consumption—see Pestieau (1974).

The assumption about debt policy can be interpreted more generally as applying to monetary policy: the issue of money can have the same effect as B_u. Moreover, as noted in earlier Lectures, the use of differential lump-sum taxes on the two generations is equivalent to the use of debt. Thus a combination of lump-sum taxes with zero present value has no impact on the individual budget constraint, and does not affect behaviour, but may allow the government to shift resources through time. Nevertheless, even when debt policy is viewed more broadly, there may be situations where the government does not have complete freedom to achieve intertemporal redistribution. Where this is so, $\lambda_u \neq 0$, and we have (from (15-37)–(15-39)):

$$\frac{1+f_g}{1+f_k} = \frac{\Gamma_g(u)}{\Gamma_k(u)} = 1 + \left(\frac{1+n}{\gamma}\right)\lambda_{u-1}\Big/\Gamma_k(u) \qquad (15\text{-}42)$$

If the government cannot use debt/monetary policy freely for purposes of intertemporal redistribution, the social rate of discount is not necessarily equal to the producer rate of interest. In steady state, it is still true that $f_g = \delta$, the social rate of time preference, but $\lambda < 0$ implies $f_k > \delta$. The value of λ depends on the choice of tax instruments—see the following exercise (based on Pestieau, 1974).

Exercise 15-4 Derive the first-order conditions for the choice of p_u and ω_u (by differentiating (15-36)), and examine their interpretation in steady state (making use of the difference equations in Γ_p and Γ_ω). Use these results to express the rate of return on public capital as a function of the private return and the consumer rate of interest. Show that where there is no tax on wages f_g is a weighted average of the two rates, but that the weights need not lie in the interval $[0, 1]$.

The model discussed above is parallel to that of Diamond and Mirrlees (1971), assuming constant returns to scale and hence no pure profits.[15] We have seen however that production efficiency may not be desirable: the social discount rate is not necessarily equal to the private rate of return. The reason for this is that the government cannot—because of the assumption of restricted debt/monetary policy—transfer resources at will between periods. It cannot in effect trade freely on all markets. Where this restriction is present, and $\lambda > 0$, then the marginal physical rate of transformation of output in one period into output in the next $(1+f_k)$ is not

---

[15] The assumption of constant returns to scale ensures that in steady state all relevant variables are constant in *per capita* terms. It also means that, if the return to the public capital (δg per worker in steady state) accrues to the government, it is sufficient to finance the new public capital formation (ng per worker), since the assumption $\gamma \leqslant 1$ implies that $\delta \geqslant n$. If therefore the return to public capital is appropriated by the state, or 100 per cent pure profits taxation is possible, then there is no need for distortionary taxes to finance public capital formation.

necessarily equal to the rate of transformation that can be achieved by the government using a restricted class of instruments (the marginal economic rate of transformation). This can be viewed another way. Private savings are only channelled into private capital accumulation; the government on the other hand is constrained in its ability to influence private capital formation (where B_u is fixed).

Finally, we allow for differences between people. If the government is constrained in its ability to levy differential taxation, then, even with 100 per cent profits taxes and complete control of debt policy, the social rate of discount may deviate from the private rate of return for distributional reasons. Moreover, if the distributional impact differs across capital goods, then different social rates of discount ought to be employed for different types of investment.

15-5 CONCLUDING COMMENTS

Our treatment of decisions in the public sector has been highly selective, and there are many issues that have been left on one side. We have not considered peak load pricing or the interrelation between pricing and investment decisions. No account has been taken of uncertainty or of rationed demand. The discussion of cost–benefit analysis has been very circumscribed. There is however one shortcoming that we should emphasize: the lack of any explicit analysis of the information available to the government and of the process by which it is obtained.

This may be illustrated by reference to the setting of guidelines to public enterprises. Suppose that the government possesses the same information as the producers (in both private and public sectors). Then, clearly, it could solve the problem of optimal pricing for the entire economy. Having done this, it could calculate the deficit associated with each enterprise and then face the enterprise with the constraint of not exceeding this level. The government does not however possess this quantity of information; and if it did, it would hardly need to decentralize. We have therefore to consider the mechanisms available to the government that enable it to elicit the necessary information, and the motives of those in charge of the enterprises. The latter will depend on the kind of considerations discussed in Lecture 10 and on the specific incentive structures that are in effect. Thus, there is an extensive literature in the field of economic planning concerned with the effect of different incentive schemes (for a recent review, see Johansen, 1978, Ch. 5). The problem is moreover close to that of the revelation of preferences for public goods. In the next Lecture, we examine some of the procedures that have been proposed.

READING

The Anglo-Saxon literature on marginal cost pricing is usefully collected in Turvey (1968); for an extensive account of the French literature, see Drèze (1964). Recent discussions of public enterprise pricing include Bergson (1972), Kolm (1968, 1971), Rees (1968, 1976) and Turvey (1971). For discussion of the distributional aspect, see Feldstein (1972a, 1972b). On the regulation of public utilities, see the original article by Averch and Johnson (1962), and surveys of the field by Baumol and Klevorick (1970) and Bailey (1973). The results on production efficiency are discussed in Diamond and Mirrlees (1971); for a broader treatment of the results in relation to second-best theory, see Guesnerie (1978). There is an extensive literature on cost—benefit and the choice of the social discount rate—see Little and Mirrlees (1974) and the references given there.

SIXTEEN

PUBLIC GOODS AND PUBLICLY PROVIDED PRIVATE GOODS

16-1 INTRODUCTION

This Lecture deals with the public provision of goods and services. We are concerned with four basic questions:

1. How do we characterize those goods that are, or ought to be, provided publicly?
2. If the government knew the preferences of all members of society, how ought the supply of each of the public goods to be determined?
3. How are the supplies of public goods in fact determined, and how does this contrast with the optimal provision?
4. How can the government ascertain the preferences of the members of society regarding the provision of public goods?

These questions are of considerable importance and have generated a great deal of controversy. There are those who claim that the government is engaged in supplying goods that ought to be privately marketed, for instance, that education ought to be privately rather than publicly provided. There are others who claim that public programmes receive insufficient funds and that there are activities at present privately supplied that ought to be provided by the government. What we shall have to say here does not resolve these controversies, but we believe that a careful consideration of the kinds of issue treated in this Lecture will help focus the debate.

At the outset we need to make an important distinction, between public *production* and public *provision*. The two are often confused, though both logically and in practice they are distinct. The government provides for the

National Defence, yet much of the production of the goods purchased for national defence is within the private sector. The government has, in many countries, a monopoly of the mail service, yet it charges for the use of mail in a manner little different from that of private enterprise. In the previous Lecture we dealt with the pricing of publicly produced commodities; here we are concerned with goods and services that are provided freely, perhaps in rationed amounts, to all members of society. (We are also at this stage concerned with public goods for the whole society; local public goods are discussed in the next Lecture.)

Characteristics of Publicly Provided Goods

The free provision of goods may be seen as the limiting case of subsidization, i.e., the delivery to consumers of commodities at a price below the cost of production. In this sense, the analysis of this Lecture, and that of public sector pricing, are aspects of the same subject. There is however a distinct feature of public provision which this approach does not capture and which is the focus of much of our discussion: with public provision there is not necessarily any monitoring of usage, whereas with any price, positive or negative, usage must be recorded.

The issue of monitoring usage introduces the first aspect that is relevant to characterizing those goods that are, or ought to be, publicly provided: it may be impossible, or extremely costly, to charge for the use of a specified commodity. In other words, it may not be possible to *exclude* non-contributors. This is essentially a technical question, and depends on the available technology. In the case of television, calculation of the extent of use depends on it being possible to determine from outside whether the receiver is in operation or on the employment of scrambling devices. It has been suggested that automatic metering devices could be installed to record the passage of vehicles through the highways system and that with large-scale computer networks it would be feasible to charge for actual usage. For some goods, such as national defence, it is hard to imagine that even future developments in information processing will allow individual benefit to be determined; so that for these exclusion is indeed impossible.[1]

Where exclusion is not technically impossible, it may still be decided to supply the good publicly, for reasons parallel to those discussed earlier in other contexts. The first is that it may not be desirable on *efficiency* grounds to use prices to govern the usage of a commodity. The effects of charging

---

[1] It should be noted that the term "exclusion" is being used in a slightly different sense from, for example, that employed by Musgrave. He refers to the exclusion principle as indicating that a person "is excluded from the enjoyment of any particular commodity or service unless he is willing to pay the stipulated price" (1959, p. 9). This however reflects a *choice* about the method by which the good is to be allocated. Our definition relates solely to the technical possibilities.

depend on (1) the conditions of demand and (2) the conditions on which the good can be supplied *to an additional individual*. If the demand is highly inelastic, then pricing has little effect on usage. In the extreme case, if demand is completely inelastic, there is no efficiency loss from not charging for the commodity (although there may be other arguments, such as raising revenue, as we have seen). Many places do not charge for the quantity of water used, because it is judged that the benefits for metering would be relatively small, demands not being very elastic, and insufficient to warrant the installation of metering devices. (There may also be external economies in consumption—at least, that was an important historical reason for public provision.)

Standard discussions tend in effect to focus on the second aspect—that usage by one person does not reduce the amount that others can consume. In other words, the cost of supplying a fixed quantity to another *individual* is zero. Examples typically given include television programmes (my listening to a TV programme transmitted over the airwaves does not detract from others listening); information (my knowing something does not detract from others knowing the same thing); and national defence. These are extreme cases, and are referred to as *pure* public goods, where "each individual's consumption of such a good leads to no subtraction from any other individual's consumption" (Samuelson, 1954, p. 387). More generally, there is a range of commodities that have the property that an increase in one person's consumption (keeping aggregate expenditure on the commodity constant) may not decrease the consumption of other people by the same amount. If one person travels on a little-used highway, the benefits of the road to others are reduced only slightly.

On this view, private goods are at one extreme of a spectrum, where an increase of one unit in the consumption by Mr X reduces the consumption available to others by one unit; and pure public goods at the other extreme, where an increase in Mr X's consumption leads to no reduction for others. These polar cases are sometimes characterized in the following way. Let X_i^h be the consumption by household h of the ith commodity. Then for private goods,

$$\sum_h X_i^h = X_i \tag{16-1}$$

where X_i is the aggregate supply. In contrast, for a pure public good,

$$X_i^h = X_i \quad \text{all } h \tag{16-2}$$

It may be noted that this assumes no *free disposal*. For many public goods, such as defence, this may not be an unreasonable assumption; on the other hand, for goods such as television, free disposal is possible, and (16-2) should be replaced by

$$X_i^h \leqslant X_i \quad \text{all } h \tag{16-2'}$$

The intermediate cases are somewhat harder to characterize, and various approaches have been suggested in the literature. One is to write the consumption possibility frontier for the economy as being for good i:

$$\chi(X_i^1,\ldots,X_i^h,\ldots,X_i^H,X_i) = 0 \tag{16-3}$$

with

$$\frac{\partial\chi}{\partial X_i^h} = 0 \quad \text{(for all } h\text{) for pure public goods,}$$

$$\frac{\partial\chi/\partial X_i^h}{\partial\chi/\partial X_i^k} = 1 \quad \text{(for all } h, k\text{) for pure private goods}$$

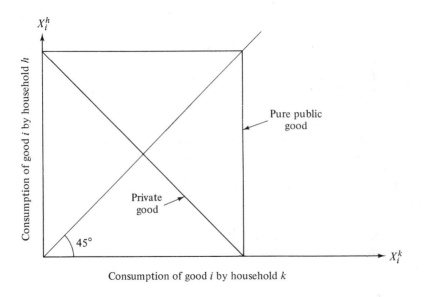

Figure 16-1 Public and private goods.

These are illustrated in Fig. 16-1 and the reader is invited to consider how intermediate cases can be handled. An alternative approach is in terms of consumption externalities (as discussed in Lecture 14), and this has been developed by Samuelson (1969). In this case the purchase of good i by household h may enter the utility function of other individuals.

In both cases, we have a problem of defining what it is that is being consumed, and how it is to be measured. For instance, for television and radio broadcasts, the obvious unit to measure consumption is "programmes listened to". In this case, the first approach seems more natural. On the other hand, if individuals privately purchase protective services (e.g., police guards), utility may be a function of the level of "safety" in the community, which may be a function of the aggregate expenditure on protective services, as well as on the private level of protection. Individuals, in providing protection for themselves (and thus lowering the return to crime), are providing a public good (safety), and the consumption externalities representation seems natural. This problem can however be reformulated in terms of our first approach, although one must be careful how this is done. For instance, if P represents the total number of policemen available, and P^h represents the number of policemen assigned to ("consumed by") the household h, then $\Sigma_h P^h = P$, and police appear to be a private good, yielding consumption externalities. If however what is consumed (negatively) is the expected number of crimes suffered by household h, denoted by C^h, then we have a consumption possibilities curve

$$\chi(C^1, \ldots, C^h, \ldots, C_1^H; P) = 0 \qquad (16\text{-}4)$$

where an increase in the number of policemen reduces the crimes committed.

The third set of reasons for public provision relates to distributional objectives. This may stem either from a general distributional goal, for example embodied in a social welfare function, or from principles of specific egalitarianism as discussed in Lecture 11. Thus, distributional reasons are probably the primary rationale for the public provision of education—either because it reduces inequality of endowments, or because access to at least a minimum level of education is an objective in itself. This may be put another way. As in earlier Lectures, we may derive for each commodity an optimal nonlinear price function. For certain goods, that function may have the characteristic that no price is charged for consumption below a specified minimum.

We have tried to bring out some of the features that characterize goods that may be publicly provided. In determining whether or not they are supplied in this way, the various factors are likely to be of differing importance. In Table 16-1 we have listed some of the goods that are commonly, but not necessarily universally, publicly provided. In each case, one can ask whether exclusion is feasible (at reasonable cost), what are the properties of demand, what are the costs of supplying to the individual, and whether there are likely to be distributional arguments. For the first six, we have suggested our own judgement; the reader may like to consider how far he agrees, and to complete the remainder.

In what follows, we concentrate particularly on the cases that are at the extreme ends of the spectrum for the cost of individual supply. In Sections 16-2 and 16-3, we consider the provision of pure public goods; in 16-4 we take the opposite extreme of publicly provided private goods. These sections are concerned with the arguments regarding the optimum level of

Table 16-1 Characteristics of publicly supplied goods

	Costly exclusion ?	Demand irresponsive ?	Low cost of individual supply ?	Distributional arguments ?
National defence	Yes	Yes	Yes	
Roads and bridges	Yes		Yes ?	
TV and radio	Yes ?		Yes	
Education				Yes
Water		Yes		Yes ?
Police	Yes		Yes	Yes

Medical care
Fire protection
Legal system—criminal cases
           —civil cases
Sewerage and rubbish
National parks

provision, and—in the case of publicly provided private goods—its allocation among individuals, on the assumption that the government has full information about individual preferences and endowments. The actual procedures by which public spending decisions may be effected, and preferences revealed, are the subject of Sections 16-5 and 16-6.

16-2 OPTIMUM PROVISION OF PURE PUBLIC GOODS— EFFICIENCY

In this section we consider the optimum level of provision of a single, pure public good, consumed in quantity G by everyone. There is an aggregate production relationship:

$$F(\mathbf{X}, G) = 0 \qquad (16\text{-}5)$$

where $\mathbf{X}$ denotes the vector of total private good production.

First-Best Allocation

The government of a fully controlled economy is assumed to choose the level of G, and the allocation of private goods $\mathbf{X^h}$ to household h (where $h = 1, \ldots, H$) to maximize an individualistic social welfare function.[2] If the

---

[2] The modern general equilibrium treatment of the optimum provision of public goods dates from Samuelson (1954); he has returned to the subject in Samuelson (1955, 1958b, 1969).

individual utility function is $U^h(\mathbf{X^h}, G)$, then the social welfare function may be written as

$$\Psi[U^1, \ldots, U^h, \ldots, U^H] \qquad (16\text{-}6)$$

where Ψ is assumed to be a twice differentiable, concave function and to be increasing in all arguments. If we form the Lagrangean

$$\mathscr{L} = \Psi - \lambda F(\mathbf{X}, G) \qquad (16\text{-}7)$$

the first-order conditions are

$$\frac{\partial \mathscr{L}}{\partial X_i^h} = \Psi_h U_i^h - \lambda F_i = 0 \quad \text{for all } i, h \qquad (16\text{-}8a)$$

$$\frac{\partial \mathscr{L}}{\partial G} = \sum_h \Psi_h U_G^h - \lambda F_G = 0 \qquad (16\text{-}8b)$$

The condition (16-8a) yields the standard first-best welfare conditions (equality of marginal rates of substitution and transformation). The new condition is (16-8b).

From (16-8a) we can see that $\Psi_h U_i^h = \lambda F_i$ (i.e., the left-hand side is the same for all h). We can then divide the hth term in the sum on the left-hand side of (16-8b) by $\Psi_h U_i^h$, giving

$$\sum_h (U_G^h / U_i^h) = F_G / F_i \quad \text{for all } i \qquad (16\text{-}9)$$

This is the basic condition for the optimum supply of public goods: *the sum of the marginal rates of substitution* between the public good (and some private good) must equal the marginal rate of transformation ($\Sigma MRS = MRT$). There is a clear intuitive interpretation of these conditions for a full optimum. The marginal benefit of an extra unit of a public good is the benefit that person 1 gets, plus the benefit that person 2 gets, etc. In contrast, an extra unit of a private good is *either* given to person 1 *or* given to person 2.

The solution may be illustrated diagrammatically for the case where there are two individuals and two goods (X = private good, G = pure public good). Figure 16-2 shows in the upper part the indifference curves for citizen I and the production constraint AB. Suppose we fix citizen I on the indifference curve U^I. The possibilities for citizen II are shown in the lower part of Fig. 16-2 by CD (the difference between AB and U^I). Clearly, Pareto efficiency requires the marginal rate of substitution of the second individual be equal to the slope of the curve CD (i.e., at point E). But this is just the difference between the marginal rate of transformation (the slope of the production possibilities schedule) and the marginal rate of substitution of the first individual (the slope of his indifference curve). Thus, we have

$$MRS^{II} = MRT - MRS^I$$

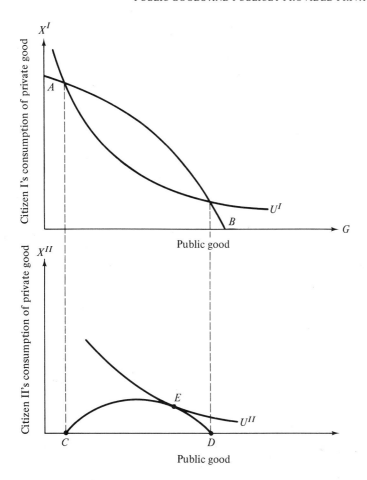

Figure 16-2 Optimum provision of public goods—two-person example.

i.e.,

$$MRS^I + MRS^{II} = MRT$$

the sum of the marginal rates of substitution must equal the marginal rate of transformation.[3]

---

[3] As recognized by Samuelson (1954), his treatment was a general equilibrium version of the earlier partial equilibrium analysis of Lindahl (1919) and Bowen (1943). In that case, the "total demand" is found by adding up the demand curves; but unlike private goods, where we add horizontally (the total demand at a given price), for public goods we add vertically (the total amount that all individuals are willing to pay for the given amount of the public good).

The analysis so far has been conducted in terms of a fully controlled economy. It is however equivalent to the situation in a competitive economy where the government is able to levy first-best lump-sum taxes, both to finance the expenditure and to redistribute income. As in earlier Lectures, we need to ask what happens when first-best taxation is not possible. In the remainder of this section, we consider the efficiency aspects, taking for this purpose the case where individuals are all identical; in the next section, we take up the issue of redistribution.

Financing of Public Goods by Distortionary Taxation

When the public expenditure is financed by taxes that generate an excess burden, it appears likely on intuitive grounds that the rule of equating ΣMRS with MRT will lead to too high a level of spending. As it was put by Pigou,

> The raising of an additional £ of revenue...inflicts indirect damage on the taxpayers as a body over and above the loss they suffer in actual money payment. Where there is indirect damage, it ought to be added to the direct loss of satisfaction involved in the withdrawal of the marginal unit of resources by taxation, before this is balanced against the satisfaction yielded by the marginal expenditure. [Pigou, 1947, pp. 33–4]

Pigou's intuitive argument is not, however, necessarily correct.

In order to explore this, let us take the case of two private goods—consumption (X) and labour (L)—and one public good. We take leisure ($=$ minus labour) as the *numeraire*, and denote the producer price of the consumption good by p, that of the public good by p_G. For convenience, we assume a linear production constraint:

$$p \sum_h X^h + p_G G = \sum_h L^h \qquad (16\text{-}10)$$

If all individuals are identical, and are treated identically, this can be written

$$pHX + p_G G = HL \qquad (16\text{-}11)$$

(where X, L now denote the *individual* level of consumption).

In order to examine the effect of different methods of financing, we assume that the public good is financed partly by a uniform lump-sum tax T on all individuals and partly by a specific tax at rate t on the consumption good. The individual budget constraint is therefore (there is no profit income)

$$(p+t)X = L - T \qquad (16\text{-}12)$$

and the first-order conditions for individual utility maximization,

$$U_X = \alpha(p+t) \qquad (16\text{-}13\text{a})$$
$$(-U_L) = \alpha \qquad (16\text{-}13\text{b})$$

where α denotes the private marginal utility of income. From these we can derive the individual demand and labour supply functions of p, t, T, and G.

The government aims to maximize welfare measured by HU, subject to the production constraint. The Lagrangean can therefore be written:

$$\mathscr{L} = HU(X, L, G) - \lambda(pHX + p_G G - HL) \tag{16-14}$$

The necessary conditions for optimality involve

$$\frac{\partial \mathscr{L}}{\partial G} = HU_G - \lambda\left(pH\frac{\partial X}{\partial G} + p_G - H\frac{\partial L}{\partial G}\right) = 0 \tag{16-15}$$

From this it follows that government expenditure should be carried to the point where:[4]

$$\frac{HU_G}{\alpha} = \frac{\lambda}{\alpha}\left(p_G - tH\frac{\partial X}{\partial G}\right) \tag{16-16}$$

The left-hand side represents the sum of the marginal rates of substitution between G and the *numeraire* good (leisure), while on the right-hand side p_G corresponds to the marginal rate of transformation.

From this expression we can see that the existence of indirect taxes modifies the conventional $\Sigma MRS = MRT$ formula in two ways:

1. To the extent that an increase in G leads to an increase in the consumption of taxed goods ($\partial X/\partial G > 0$), this reduces the revenue to be raised (through the term $tH(\partial X/\partial G)$). The right-hand side is therefore lower than with the conventional formula, or vice-versa if $\partial X/\partial G < 0$. If, for example, the provision of a further television channel increases the demand for television sets, and these are subject to an indirect tax, it may be socially optimal to carry provision to a point where the sum of the marginal rates of substitution is less than the marginal rate of transformation, even though the expenditure has to be financed by distortionary taxation.
2. The conventional formula is based on the assumption that raising \$1 extra revenue would have a social cost equal to the marginal utility of income. However, where there are non-lump-sum taxes this is no longer true. The social cost of raising \$1 (λ) may in fact be greater or less than the private marginal utility of income (α).

The intuition behind these results is that the government wishes to set the sum of the marginal rates of substitution equal to the marginal *economic* rate of transformation (as in earlier Lectures). With taxes that are not lump-sum, the marginal economic rate of transformation is in general

---

[4] Using the fact that $(p+t)\partial X/\partial G = \partial L/\partial G$ obtained from differentiating the individual budget constraint (16-12).

different from the marginal physical rate of transformation. The difference arises from the fact that, when there is distortionary taxation, the changes in taxes required to raise the extra revenue to finance the addition to public expenditure affect the deadweight loss (Stiglitz and Dasgupta, 1971). The relationship between λ and α may be seen from the condition for the choice of t:

$$\frac{\partial \mathscr{L}}{\partial t} = H \frac{\partial U}{\partial t} - \lambda \left(pH \frac{\partial X}{\partial t} - H \frac{\partial L}{\partial t} \right) = 0 \qquad (16\text{-}17)$$

Using the fact that $\partial U / \partial t = -\alpha X$, we obtain

$$\alpha X = -\lambda \left(p \frac{\partial X}{\partial t} - \frac{\partial L}{\partial t} \right) = \lambda \left(X + t \frac{\partial X}{\partial t} \right) \equiv \lambda \frac{\partial R}{\partial t} \qquad (16\text{-}18)$$

(the second step following from differentiating the individual budget constraint). Where $t \neq 0$, we have to allow for the effect on revenue (R) of the change in X. Substituting into (16-16), we obtain

$$\Sigma MRS = \frac{p_G - tH(\partial X / \partial G)}{1 + (t/X)(\partial X / \partial t)} \qquad (16\text{-}19)$$

Exercise 16-1 Carry out the same analysis where there is a tax on wage income and no indirect tax. What differences are there in the results and how can they be explained? (See Atkinson and Stern, 1974.)

Comparison with Lump-sum Taxation

The analysis so far has considered the effect of non-lump-sum taxation on the $\Sigma MRS = MRT$ *rule*; it is important to emphasize that the results do not tell us anything about the optimum *level* of provision for public goods—whether the optimum provision in the case of distortionary taxation is larger or smaller than where lump-sum taxation can be employed. One cannot in general make deductions from the first-order conditions about the behaviour of the optimum quantities—a point that is often confused. (For example, the form of the first-order conditions depends on the choice of the untaxed good, but this has no implications for the optimum level of G.)

In order to investigate how the optimal quantity of the public good may be affected by the method of financing, we assume that the utility function is additively separable between "private utility" $u(X, L)$, and the public good:

$$U = u(X, L) + g(G) \qquad (16\text{-}20)$$

where $g' > 0$, $g'' < 0$ and u is strictly concave. The government constraint is

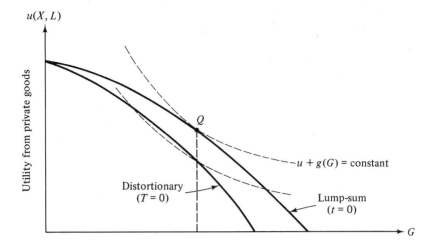

$u(X, L)$

Utility from private goods

Q

$u + g(G) = $ constant

Distortionary
$(T = 0)$

Lump-sum
$(t = 0)$

G

Figure 16-3 Provision of public goods with distortionary taxation.

given by:[5]

$$H(tX + T) = p_G G \qquad (16\text{-}21)$$

In the case $t = 0$ (lump-sum financing), we can trace out the transformation curve between $u(X, L)$ and G, with slope given by $-\alpha p_G/H$ (see Fig. 16-3).[6] The optimum level of provision is found by maximizing the welfare of a representative individual, which with contours as shown in Fig. 16-3 gives the point Q. The concavity of u implies that α is a declining function of lump-sum income, and hence that the frontier is concave to the origin.

Let us now consider the case of the indirect tax, with $T = 0$. The level of private utility is given by

$$u^{**}(G) = \max_{L} u\left(\frac{L}{p+t}, L\right) \qquad (16\text{-}22)$$

and the government budget constraint

$$HtX = p_G G \qquad (16\text{-}23)$$

---

[5] This can be obtained by summing the individual budget constraints $(p+t)HX = HL - HT$ and subtracting the aggregate production constraint (16-11).

[6] Define

$$u^*(G) = \max_{L} u[(L - p_G G/H)/p, L]$$

then

$$\frac{du^*}{dG} = -\alpha p_G/H$$

The slope of the transformation frontier is therefore

$$\frac{du^{**}}{dG} = \frac{-Xu_X}{p+t}\frac{dt}{dG} = -\alpha\left(\frac{p_G}{H}\right)\frac{1}{1+(d\log X/d\log t)} \qquad (16\text{-}24)$$

This frontier is illustrated by the curve nearer the origin in Fig. 16-3, although it should be noted that there is no necessary reason why it should be concave.

Optimality again requires a tangency between the social welfare function and the transformation curve. The slope of the social welfare function is $-g'$ and is a function simply of G. If the distortionary tax transformation curve is steeper than the no-distortionary tax transformation curve, then this implies that at the level of G that was optimal with lump-sum taxation, the distortionary transformation curve cuts the indifference curve from below; i.e., optimality requires a smaller level of production of public goods. This situation is illustrated in Fig. 16-3. However, while "on average" the distortionary curve is steeper, and hence there may be a presumption that expenditure will be reduced, it is not necessarily so and global results cannot be deduced. At the same time, sufficient conditions can be given for the level of G with indirect taxation to be lower than that with lump-sum taxation, for example, for small levels of t and G. (N.B.: the transformation frontiers have identical slope at $G = 0$.) It is also possible to establish that a small reduction in the possibilities for lump-sum taxation from the first-best optimum ($t = 0$) leads to a fall in the optimum quantity of the public good (Atkinson and Stern, 1974, p. 124).

Exercise 16-2 For the Cobb–Douglas utility function

$$u(X,L) = a\log X + (1-a)\log(1-L) \qquad (16\text{-}25)$$

describe the transformation frontiers with $t = 0$ and $T = 0$. What conclusions can be drawn about the optimum quantity of G in the two situations?

16-3 OPTIMUM PROVISION OF PURE PUBLIC GOODS— DISTRIBUTION

In this section we examine how the conditions for the optimum supply of public goods are influenced by distributional considerations, paying particular attention to situations in which there are restrictions on the set of feasible taxes.

Redistribution and Non-Distortionary Taxation

In the previous section we derived the first-best allocation rule $\Sigma MRS = MRT$, where the optimum could be attained by the use of lump-sum taxes and transfers. Typically, the government does not enjoy complete freedom in its choice of lump-sum taxes, and indeed we have earlier argued that these may be restricted to a uniform poll tax or subsidy. Where this is so, the $\Sigma MRS = MRT$ condition is no longer necessarily applicable. To see this, let us suppose that the government can levy tax T^h on household h, where M^h is the (fixed) income. There is one private good (quantity $X^h = M^h - T^h$) and one public good (G). The government chooses G and T^h to maximize

$$\Psi[U^1(X^1, G), \ldots, U^H(X^H, G)]$$

subject to

$$\sum_h T^h = p_G G \qquad (16\text{-}26)$$

and a set of restrictions on feasible tax rates.

The solution depends on the nature of the restrictions. If T^h can be varied freely, the first-order conditions imply

$$\Psi_h U_X^h = \lambda \quad \text{all } h$$

$$\sum_h \Psi_h U_G^h = \lambda p_G \qquad (16\text{-}27)$$

which imply $\Sigma MRS = MRT$, the result used earlier. If the government is constrained to set $T^h = T$ all h, it follows that $T = p_G G/H$, and the first-order condition may be seen to be

$$\sum_h \Psi_h \left(\frac{p_G U_X^h}{H} - U_G^h \right) = 0 \qquad (16\text{-}28)$$

Writing

$$\beta^h \equiv \Psi_h U_X^h \qquad (16\text{-}29)$$

for the social marginal utility of income, we obtain

$$\sum_h \left(\frac{\beta^h}{\bar{\beta}} \right) MRS^h = p_G \qquad (16\text{-}30)$$

where $\bar{\beta}$ is the mean value. In other words, the appropriate measure of benefits is a weighted sum of marginal rates of substitution, the weights being proportional to the social marginal utility of income and summing to unity.

This corresponds to the distributional weights sometimes used in cost–benefit analysis (see, for example, Weisbrod, 1968). An alternative way of writing the rule is

$$\sum_h MRS^h + H \operatorname{cov}\left[\frac{\beta^h}{\bar{\beta}}, MRS^h \right] = p_G \qquad (16\text{-}31)$$

where $\text{cov}[A, B]$ denotes the covariance between A and B. The $\Sigma MRS = MRT$ rule is therefore modified by taking account of the covariance between the social marginal utility of income and the marginal rate of substitution. As in the earlier optimal tax discussion, this may be written in terms of the "distributional characteristic", ϕ (see Arnott, 1978):

$$\sum_h MRS^h(1+\phi_G) = p_G \qquad (16\text{-}31')$$

where

$$\phi_G \equiv \text{cov}\left[\frac{\beta^h}{\bar{\beta}}, \frac{MRS^h}{\overline{MRS}}\right]$$

If β^h falls with M^h, this means that for public goods that are valued more highly by the poor than by others the level of provision will be taken to a point where ΣMRS is less than MRT. (As before, one cannot draw conclusions about quantities from the first-order conditions.)

Distortionary Taxation and Redistribution

The taxes considered above are not distortionary; we now consider the combined implications of deadweight loss and distributional objectives. For this purpose, we take the case where there are two private goods (consumption, X, and labour, L) and one public good. Individuals have identical utility functions, but differ in their wage rate, denoted by w^h.

The government is assumed to determine the level of indirect taxation, t, and public goods, G, to maximize $\Psi[\mathbf{V}(t, T, G, w)]$, where $\mathbf{V}$ denotes the vector of indirect utility functions, and T denotes a uniform lump-sum tax (for the present assumed to be zero). We form the Lagrangean

$$\mathscr{L} = \Psi + \lambda\left(t \sum_h X^h + HT - p_G G\right) \qquad (16\text{-}32)$$

where the bracket gives the revenue constraint.

The first-order conditions are:[7]

$$\frac{\partial \mathscr{L}}{\partial t} = \sum_h (-\beta^h X^h) + \lambda H\left(\bar{X} + t\frac{\partial \bar{X}}{\partial t}\right) = 0 \qquad (16\text{-}33a)$$

$$\frac{\partial \mathscr{L}}{\partial G} = \sum_h \beta^h MRS^h - \lambda\left(p_G - tH\frac{\partial \bar{X}}{\partial G}\right) = 0 \qquad (16\text{-}33b)$$

where $\bar{X}$ denotes the mean consumption. Rearranging, this gives:

$$\sum_h MRS^h(1+\phi_G) = (1+\phi_X)\frac{p_G - tH\, \partial \bar{X}/\partial G}{1 + t/\bar{X}\, \partial \bar{X}/\partial t} \qquad (16\text{-}34)$$

[7] We have used the facts that $MRS^h = U_G^h/\alpha^h$ and $\beta^h = \Psi_h \alpha^h$.

where

$$\phi_X \equiv \text{cov}\left[\frac{\beta^h}{\bar{\beta}}, \frac{X^h}{\bar{X}}\right]$$

is the distributional characteristic for the private good. The $\Sigma MRS = MRT$ rule has therefore to be modified for the distributional effect of public goods (on left-hand side) and for the distributional effect of the indirect tax (distributional characteristic on right-hand side), in addition to the corrections for distortionary taxation (compare Eq. (16-19)). If provision of the public good is more progressive than consumption of the private good, in the sense that $\phi_G > \phi_X$, this raises the relative weighting of the benefit side.

Suppose now that the government can levy a uniform poll tax—as with the linear income tax. There is the further first-order condition:

$$\frac{\partial \mathcal{L}}{\partial T} = \sum_h (-\beta^h) + \lambda H\left(1 - t\frac{\partial \bar{X}}{\partial M}\right) = 0 \qquad (16\text{-}33\text{c})$$

Using this to substitute for λ, the right-hand side of (16-34) becomes

$$\frac{p_G - tH\,\partial\bar{X}/\partial G}{1 - t\,\partial\bar{X}/\partial M} \qquad (16\text{-}34')$$

The marginal economic rate of transformation exceeds p_G where $\partial\bar{X}/\partial G \leqslant 0$ and consumption is a normal good.

16-4 PUBLICLY PROVIDED PRIVATE GOODS

In this section we consider goods that, as far as cost of supply to an individual are concerned, are exactly like private goods, but are publicly provided. The examples most commonly given, such as education and medical care (in some countries), may not strictly have these properties (e.g., because of externalities). However, just as we considered an idealized version of public goods in the preceding sections, so here we take the pure case of a private good supplied at zero charge in a specified quantity. We begin with the situation where all individuals are identical and there is uniform provision of the good; we then extend the analysis to that where people differ, but the government is again required to provide an identical allocation to each individual. Finally, we consider the case where the government can provide for different individuals a different quantity of the good in question. We assume throughout that the good cannot be traded; the reader should consider the implications of this assumption.

Uniform Public Provision

With identical individuals, and financing via a poll tax (T), the optimum public provision of the private good, denoted by E, must satisfy a first-order condition identical to that implied by individual choice if we had used a price system.[8] Suppose that there is private consumption, X, and labour, L, in addition to the publicly provided good. The price of private consumption is p, that of E is p_E, and labour is the *numeraire*. The government maximizes:

$$HU(X, L, E)$$

subject to $T = p_E E$. The first-order condition is that

$$HU_E = Hp_E(-U_L) \tag{16-35}$$

or, where $MRS^h = U_E/(-U_L)$,

$$MRS^h = p_E \tag{16-36}$$

This is identical to the first-order condition for individual utility maximization when faced with a price p_E. As one would expect, there is in this case no summation of individual marginal rates of substitution.

Where the public provision is financed by distortionary taxation, the first-order conditions have to be modified in the same way as before. The marginal physical rate of transformation, represented in (16-36) by p_E, has to be replaced by the marginal economic rate of transformation. This is left as an exercise.

Exercise 16-3 Suppose that the method of financing is an indirect tax on X at rate t. Show that the first-order condition for public provision is

$$\frac{U_E}{-U_L} = \frac{p_E - t\partial X/\partial E}{1 + (t/X)\partial X/\partial t} \tag{16-37}$$

What conclusions can be drawn about the optimum public supply compared with that in a private market?

If people differ, then uniform public provision is closer to a public good in the sense that we have to determine a single level for all individuals. Suppose first that the government has complete freedom in the use of lump-sum taxes, T^h, on individual h. The government's problem may be formulated in terms of the Lagrangean:

$$\mathcal{L} = \Psi[U(X, L, E)] + \lambda\left(\sum_h T^h - Hp_E E\right) \tag{16-38}$$

---

[8] Note that we are *assuming* uniform provision. The reader should consider whether there can be situations where the government would want to allocate different amounts to identical people.

The first-order conditions may be written:

$$\frac{\partial \mathscr{L}}{\partial T^h} = -\Psi_h(-U_L^h) + \lambda = 0 \quad \text{all } h \tag{16-39a}$$

$$\frac{\partial \mathscr{L}}{\partial E} = \sum_h \Psi_h U_E^h - \lambda H p_E = 0 \tag{16-39b}$$

Hence

$$\frac{1}{H} \sum_h MRS^h = p_E \tag{16-40}$$

The *average MRS* should be equated to the *MRT*. Clearly, the success of public provision depends on the extent of divergence of tastes for consumption about this average. Where there is not full freedom to vary T^h, then there is a distributional adjustment; for example, with $T^h = T$ all h, there is an additional covariance term, $\text{cov}[\beta^h, MRS^h]$, as in the discussion of public goods.

Optimum Allocation of Publicly Provided Private Goods

In the model just discussed, the good is provided uniformly; we need however to ask whether this is socially optimal. This is a question that is frequently debated. Should educational resources be concentrated more heavily on gifted children, or should the emphasis primarily be on compensatory education? Should the government provide equal *inputs*, or should it aim to ensure equal *outputs* (e.g., as measured by earning ability)? If there were free use of lump-sum redistributive taxes and transfers, then—in an otherwise first-best world—the criterion would be straightforward: we allocate the good according to private demand. In other words, we would not have a uniform level, based on an average *MRS*, but would allocate so that individual *MRS* equal the cost of provision. However, in the absence of such freely flexible lump-sum taxes, the conditions for optimum public provision will, in general, be different from those arising from private allocation.

To illustrate the way in which public provision may differ, suppose that the social welfare function is the sum of identical individual utility functions which are additive in the publicly provided good. Then the optimal provision is uniform, and unless the tax policy equates the marginal utility of income, this involves differing marginal rates of substitution across individuals.

To set this out formally, and to see what happens when we relax the assumption of additivity of the utility and welfare functions, suppose that individuals differ only in health needs, η^h, where $\partial U^h/\partial \eta^h < 0$. The first-order condition for an optimum allocation, E^h, is (for an interior solution)

$$\Psi_h \cdot U_E^h = \lambda p_E \quad \text{all } h \tag{16-41}$$

where λ is the multiplier associated with the total expenditure constraint. This model is that examined by Arrow (1971a), who is concerned with the utilitarian objective ($\Psi_h = 1$ all h). He defines a policy as "input-progressive" where $dE^h/d\eta^h > 0$; i.e., people with greater health needs are allocated more expenditure. This may appear—in the health context—a natural conclusion; however, from (16-41) we can see that, differentiating totally with respect to η^h (where $\Psi_h = 1$),

$$U^h_{EE} \frac{dE^h}{d\eta^h} + U^h_{E\eta} = 0 \qquad (16\text{-}42)$$

If $U^h_{EE} < 0$, the optimum policy is input-progressive if and only if $U^h_{E\eta} > 0$. In other words, resources are allocated according to their effect at the margin. If a worsening of a person's medical condition makes health care less productive, then the optimal input may decline.

We can also ask whether the allocation is less than or more than fully compensatory. Since

$$\frac{dU^h}{d\eta^h} = U^h_\eta + U^h_E \frac{dE^h}{d\eta^h} \qquad (16\text{-}43)$$

it follows that an equal input policy is still not fully compensatory. In the light of our earlier discussions, it should not come as a surprise to see that a utilitarian policy does not ensure a fully compensatory policy. The role played by the form of the social welfare function may be seen by allowing for $\Psi_{hh} < 0$. Differentiating (16-41) and re-arranging then gives

$$\frac{dE^h}{d\eta^h} = \frac{U^h_{E\eta} + (-\Psi_{hh}/\Psi_h)(U^h_E)(-U^h_\eta)}{-U^h_{EE} + (-\Psi_{hh}/\Psi_h)(U^h_E)^2} \qquad (16\text{-}44)$$

The terms in $(-\Psi_{hh}/\Psi_h)$ are both positive, and tend to make it more likely that the optimum policy is input-progressive. (The reader may like to consider the implications of a Rawlsian objective function.)

Different Abilities and the Allocation of Education

We now examine the case where individuals differ in ability, as in earlier Lectures, but where this "raw" ability (a) is supplemented by education (E), so that the wage of an individual is given by $w = g(a, E)$. As in Lectures 12–14, we assume that ability is distributed continuously with density function $f(a)$ and this is the only characteristic in which people differ.

The government is assumed to determine the optimum allocation $E(a)$ and the optimum method of financing. If a lump-sum tax, $T(a)$, related to ability is not feasible,[9] then the allocation of education departs from that which would be made on grounds of allocative efficiency. To see this, let us compare the use of the lump-sum tax with a linear income tax, at rate t and with an income guarantee G^*. The government's problem may be formulated as maximizing

$$\int \Psi \{V[(1-t)g(a,E), G^* - T(a)]\} f da \qquad (16\text{-}45)$$

subject to

$$\int [G^* + E(a) - T(a) - tg(a,E)L] f da = 0 \qquad (16\text{-}46)$$

The first-order conditions for the choice of $E(a)$ and $T(a)$ are (introducing the multiplier λ for the constraint)

$$\Psi' V_\omega (1-t) \frac{\partial g}{\partial E} = \lambda \left[1 - t \left(L \frac{\partial g}{\partial E} + g \frac{\partial L}{\partial E} \right) \right] \qquad (16\text{-}47a)$$

$$\Psi' \alpha = \lambda \qquad (16\text{-}47b)$$

where V_ω denotes the derivative with respect to the after-tax wage. Since $V_\omega = \alpha L$, the use of lump-sum taxation, with $t = 0$, implies

$$\frac{\partial g}{\partial E} L = 1 \quad \text{all } a \qquad (16\text{-}48)$$

In other words, the first-order conditions imply that education should be allocated so that its marginal contribution to wages (weighted by L) is equalized. (A full treatment should consider the form of the function $g(a,E)$ and possible non-convexities.)

Where, however, there are restrictions on lump-sum taxation, this "efficiency" condition for the allocation of education ceases to apply. This can be seen from (16-47a), where we can no longer simplify by using (16-47b) and $t \neq 0$. In this situation one cannot in general treat the allocation of publicly provided goods separately from the redistributive tax policy, even when the latter parameters (t and G^*) are optimally chosen. (The reader may like to check that this is also true with a nonlinear income tax—see Ulph, 1977.) In determining the allocation, one has to balance the fact that—with the assumptions made here—the more able can use education more effectively, against the redistributive factors embodied in $\Psi' \cdot \alpha$, taking account of the contribution to government revenue.

---

[9] As in earlier Lectures, this assumes that information may be used by the government for certain purposes but not others. It is assumed that a is observed by the education authorities with sufficient accuracy to allocate E, but that this information either is not available to the tax officials or else is not acceptable as a basis for determining tax liabilities. Although a more complete treatment of information would be desirable, we feel that this captures an important feature of the problem.

Choice Between Public and Private Provision

Many goods can be allocated either publicly or privately (i.e., they can be supplied without charge, or they can be allocated on the private market); moreover, there are cases where there are private goods (e.g., security agencies) that are a close substitute for public goods (police). Thus, the required services can be supplied in either a public or a private mode, and we have to consider which goods are to be provided publicly.

The problem may be seen in general terms as that of designing the optimal price schedule, and the way in which it is likely to work may be described heuristically. Where public provision of a uniform quantity, E^*, is socially desirable, then the schedule has a zero price up to E^* and then rises vertically (i.e., there is an infinite price of further units). Where public provision of unlimited quantities is desirable, then the optimal price is zero throughout. Where private provision is preferable, then the optimal price of the first unit of public provision is infinite. In this way, we can see the relation to the earlier analysis of the optimal indirect tax and public sector price schedules.

There are two features of this general problem that should be noted. First, the solution may depend sensitively on the range of instruments at the government's disposal—as we have stressed earlier. Thus, consider the finding that a uniform allocation of the publicly provided good is socially optimal where the welfare function is utilitarian and the individual utility function additive (page 499). This appears to be in conflict with the earlier result (Lecture 14) that, where individuals differ in wages, and the utility function is locally separable in labour and commodities, the optimal price schedule is linear for commodities. However, we did not allow for the choice between public and private provision—it was *assumed* that the good was supplied by the government.

The second feature of the problem is that non-convexities are likely to be most important. We have seen in the discussion of optimum taxation that there is no reason to expect the maximization problem to be well behaved, and in the present case there are further reasons to expect serious non-convexities. A clear example is provided by administrative costs. There are good reasons to suppose that these are likely to be less in certain fields with public provision, for example, because of economies of scale or because monitoring of individual usage is not required. It may well be necessary therefore to make global comparisons, reliance on local optimality conditions not being sufficient.

In the comparison of public and private provision, several factors are likely to be influential. In addition to the administrative costs just mentioned, diversity of tastes and distributional objectives play a major role. To illustrate the effect of tastes, suppose that individuals differ in their preferences (denoted by η^h) concerning the good, but not otherwise, and that utility functions have the special form (as in Weitzman, 1977):

$$U^h = 2\eta^h E^h - (E^h)^2 + 2\alpha X^h \qquad (16\text{-}49)$$

where X^h is the (composite) consumption of other goods, taken as the *numeraire*. With private supply of the good at its production price, p, the demand by household h is

$$E^h = \eta^h - \alpha p \qquad (16\text{-}50)$$

and the resultant level of utility is (up to a constant):

$$U^h = (\eta^h - \alpha p)^2 \qquad (16\text{-}51)$$

If the good is supplied publicly in uniform quantity $\bar{E}$, financed by a poll tax $p\bar{E}$, the level of utility is (again dropping the constant)

$$\bar{E}[2(\eta^h - \alpha p) - \bar{E}] \qquad (16\text{-}52)$$

As we have seen earlier, $\bar{E}$ is optimally chosen according to the average of the marginal rates of substitution (in this case according to (16-50) with $\eta^h = \bar{\eta}$). The provision of a uniform quantity involves a loss of total utility, which may be calculated from (16-51) and (16-52), with $\bar{E} = \bar{\eta} - \alpha p$. The loss is

$$\sum_h (\eta^h - \alpha p)^2 - (\bar{\eta} - \alpha p) \sum_h (2\eta^h - \bar{\eta} - \alpha p) \qquad (16\text{-}53)$$

which can be shown to reduce to H times the variance of η. The loss in efficiency of allocation from public provision is therefore governed by the variance of the taste parameter.

In making the comparison between private supply and uniform public supply, the efficiency loss has to be balanced against any advantage in administrative costs on the side of public supply (and distributional factors). Suppose, for example, that the costs of administration are less in the public sector to the extent of $\theta\bar{E}$ units of the good per person; then the condition for private supply to be superior to public (with uniform provision) is that:[10]

$$\frac{\text{var}[\eta]}{\bar{\eta}^2} > 2\theta\gamma(1 - \gamma) \qquad (16\text{-}54)$$

where γ denotes $\alpha p/\bar{\eta}$. A sufficient condition for this to hold is that the coefficient of variation in the taste parameter is greater than $\sqrt{(\theta/2)}$. On the other hand, if we consider the case of public provision where individuals can consume unlimited quantities at a zero price (e.g., with water supply) and there is a uniform poll tax, then the condition for private supply to be

---

[10] The utility loss per person from the costs of administration is $2\alpha p\theta\bar{E}$.

superior is that:[11]

$$\gamma > 2\theta \qquad (16\text{-}55)$$

In this case, differences in tastes are provided for, and the efficiency loss arises on account of consumption in excess of that demanded at price equal to marginal cost. Where this excess consumption is relatively small (γ is small) it requires only a small advantage in terms of administrative costs for public provision to be justified.

The full-scale analysis of the choice between private and public provision in a general model is beyond the scope of these Lectures. The example of education may however serve to illustrate how the problem may be formulated in more general terms. People are supplied with a uniform level of public education (which may be zero), and may purchase private education in addition (they are not alternatives as assumed in Lecture 10). The government can impose a tax on the private purchase of education, in addition to an optimal linear income tax. The key questions for policy are whether the uniform level of public provision is strictly positive and whether or not the tax on private education should be set at a prohibitive level. The working out of the details of this analysis are left as an exercise, but it can be shown that, even with an optimally chosen income tax, free public provision of education may be desirable on distributional grounds. (This result can be demonstrated from local properties, but for a fuller characterization of the optimum, care needs to be taken to allow for possible non-convexities.)

> **Exercise 16-4** Consider the model set out on pages 500–501 and show how it can be extended to include individual purchase of additional education, so that a person's outlay on education is $(E - E_g)(1 + t_e)$, where E_g is the public provision, t_e is the tax rate on education, and $E \geqslant E_g$. The level of public provision is assumed uniform for all. The government can vary the tax rates t_e, t (on income) and the poll subsidy, G^*. Formulate the maximization problem and write down the first-order conditions. By examining the condition with respect to E_g, describe the conditions under which a strictly positive level of state provision is desirable. Show that under certain conditions it is optimal to levy a tax on education. In what circumstances should this tax be prohibitive?

The arguments discussed above are not intended to capture all important features of the case for public provision of education. It has for example been assumed implicitly that an individual has no constraints on the access to resources to finance education, whereas in practice capital markets are less than perfect, and parental wealth may be a major

---

[11] The welfare loss from public provision is then $H(\alpha p)^2$.

determinant of access to education. The scope for the expression of individual preferences and the extent of response of the school authorities may be important. These, and other broader considerations, need to be borne in mind in assessing the case for the public provision of education; and similar issues arise with other publicly provided private goods such as medical care.

16-5 EQUILIBRIUM LEVELS OF PUBLIC EXPENDITURE

The preceding sections have been concerned with the optimum provision of pure public, or publicly provided private, goods; we now ask how this compares with the levels of provision likely to emerge from actual procedures for determining public spending. We consider three classes of models. In the first, we ask, what would be the equilibrium supply if there were no government? This is sometimes referred to as a "subscription equilibrium", where each individual voluntarily contributes the amount he wishes to pay. In the second set of "political" models, we discuss the level of public expenditures that arises in a voting equilibrium. Is the public budget likely to be too small in a democracy? The third model is known as the "Lindahl" equilibrium. This represents an attempt to devise a mechanism that attains a Pareto-efficient allocation of public goods and has certain formal similarities to the competitive equilibrium model. We confine our attention to the case of pure public goods.

No-Government Equilibrium

Even in the absence of government, individuals may contribute to public goods; and indeed, in actual economies, with substantial public provision, there is still extensive private support for such items as medicine, education and research. The motives for this support are varied, and are perhaps not adequately captured by the kind of individualistic utility functions we have posited for most of the analysis. But it is worthwhile analysing what the economy might look like with such individualistic functions in the absence of government provision of the public good.

We take the conventional approach of analysing the Cournot–Nash equilibrium of the economy: each individual takes the others' supply of the public good as given, independent of his own purchase. For convenience, we assume that there is a single public good, which can be produced at constant marginal cost, p_G. There is a single private good, X, taken as the *numeraire*, of which individual h has endowment M^h. The individual purchases G^h of the public good, chosen to maximize

$$U^h\left(M^h - p_G G^h, G^h + \sum_{i \neq h} G^i\right) \tag{16-56}$$

Each individual treats the sum (over $i \neq h$) as fixed; we then obtain the first-order condition:

$$U_G^h / U_X^h = p_G \quad \text{all } h \tag{16-57}$$

In other words, he determines his expenditure such that his *own* MRS is equal to the marginal rate of transformation. The aggregate ΣMRS is therefore H times p_G, and hence greater than p_G at this level of public goods.

The solution is illustrated in Fig. 16-4. The upper part shows the choice of G^h given $\Sigma_{i \neq h} G^i$; i.e., the person chooses S on QR. By varying the sum, we can generate the reaction curve indicated. If we now assume that all individuals are identical, then it is a condition of overall equilibrium that $X = M - p_G G/H$. The intersection P with the reaction curve in the lower part of the diagram gives the Nash equilibrium. It is clear that the individual indifference curve cuts the line $X = M - p_G G/H$ at P, and that the maximization of social welfare (with lump-sum taxation) indicates a higher level of G. The condition $\Sigma MRS = MRT$ is in fact satisfied at P^*.

The comparison of the optimum with the no-government solution is less straightforward where individuals differ and where the government cannot levy freely variable lump-sum taxes. In that case, the level of public expenditure in the optimum depends on the social weights associated with different groups. It is clearly possible that the Nash equilibrium leads to greater spending if the welfare-maximizing solution attaches particular weight to people who do not like the public good in question. On the other hand, it is possible to make some statements. Suppose that the government provides a quantity G of the public good, financed by a uniform poll tax. The level of social welfare is given by

$$\Psi\left[U\left(M^h - p_G G^h - \frac{p_G G}{H}, G^h + \sum_{i \neq h} G^i + G \right) \right] \tag{16-58}$$

Differentiating with respect to G, and evaluating at $G = 0$, it may be seen that social welfare is locally increasing in the level of public provision, where (after some rearrangement)

$$(H-1)\left(1 + \frac{\partial}{\partial G} \sum_i G^i \right) > H \operatorname{cov}\left[\frac{\beta^h}{\bar{\beta}}, \frac{\partial G^h}{\partial G} \right] \tag{16-59}$$

(we have used the fact that $MRS^h = p_G$ at the Nash equilibrium, and have divided by $\bar{\beta} p_G$). The left-hand side is positive, where an increase in G increases the total provision of public goods, allowing for any offsetting reduction in private provision. Where this is the case, a sufficient condition for social welfare to be locally increasing in government spending is that the more "deserving" (according to β^h) individuals reduce the private provision by more.

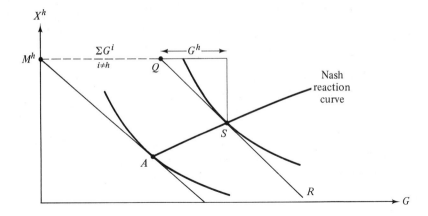

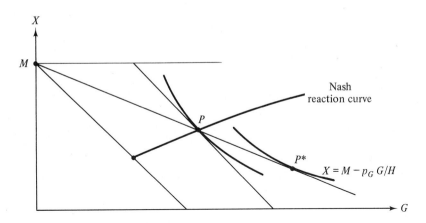

Figure 16-4 Nash equilibrium for public goods.

Voting over Public Goods

The determination of public spending by means of voting was discussed in Lecture 10, where we drew attention to a number of the problems that arise. In particular, no voting equilibrium may exist. When there is a single decision variable then restrictions on preferences of individuals such as single-peakedness ensure a determinate outcome. It is however debatable how reasonable such assumptions are (the example was given there of public and private education, where these are alternatives), and once we move to two or more dimensions the conditions on preferences necessary to ensure a voting equilibrium are extremely restrictive. On the other hand, a determinate outcome may be ensured if there are exogenously determined rules governing the agenda.

Here we simply make the comparison between the level of expenditure determined by majority voting under conditions in which an equilibrium exists. In particular, we assume that there is a single decision—that concerning the level of a public good financed by a uniform poll tax. It is assumed that individuals vote "sincerely" (see Lecture 10). The utility of the h-individual is

$$U^h\left(M^h - \frac{p_G G}{H}, G\right) \tag{16-60}$$

and, as we saw in Lecture 10, the individual valuation of different levels of G is a single-peaked function. The voting equilibrium is therefore characterized by the preferred level of the median voter (denoted by m):

$$\frac{U_G^m}{U_X^m} = \frac{p_G}{H} \tag{16-61}$$

Does the voting outcome lead to a higher or lower level of G than is socially optimal? Suppose that we consider a small increase in G above the level determined by the median voter. The effect on social welfare is given by (this tells us whether or not social welfare is *locally* increased by an increase in spending above the amount in the voting equilibrium)

$$\sum_h \Psi_h U_X^h (MRS^h - p_G/H) \tag{16-62}$$

It is clear that there is no presumption that·this is either positive or negative. If the government has no distributional preferences, the ΣMRS may be greater or less than p_G at the median voter equilibrium, as is illustrated by Exercise 16-5. If $\Psi_h \cdot U_X^h$ differs across individuals, then whether (16-62) is positive or negative depends on the weights attached to different individuals and their position relative to the median. If, for example, the preferred level of government spending is a strictly declining function of income, and the government is concerned solely with the welfare of the lowest income group, then the social optimum involves a higher level of public spending than in the voting equilibrium.

Exercise 16-5 For the special case of the utility function

$$U = X^{1-\alpha}/(1-\alpha) + g(G)$$

show that the social optimum may involve more or less government spending than the voting equilibrium where the government has no distributional preferences. What difference does it make if the public good is financed by a proportional tax on income? (See Stiglitz, 1974a.)

The analysis just given should be treated simply as a counter-example to the proposition that majority voting leads to a level of government spending that is below (conversely above) the social optimum. The example shows that there is no presumption either way. In order to reach more positive conclusions, it is necessary to specify more fully the political machinery and procedures lying behind public spending decisions. This would need to take account of the conditions that ensure a determinate outcome, and the role played by legislators and bureaucrats in addition to that of voters.

Lindahl Equilibrium

The inefficiency of the Nash equilibrium arises because each consumer is faced with a price equal to that of the public good, whereas some of the benefit accrues to others. By analogy with the case of consumption externalities, we can seek therefore a set of corrective subsidies, which will in general have to vary across individuals—we need "personalized" prices. This procedure was discussed by Samuelson (1969) as a "pseudo-demand algorithm" to calculate the optimal level of public goods supply, but was proposed as an actual allocation process by Lindahl (1919).

The essence of the Lindahl procedure is that individuals "demand" a total quantity of public goods on the basis of a specified distribution of the tax burden (see Johansen, 1965, Ch. 6). Thus each individual faces a tax *share* τ^h of the expenditure, where $\Sigma_h \tau^h = 1$, and these tax shares perform the function of personalized prices, referred to as "Lindahl prices". An equilibrium is a set of Lindahl prices such that at those prices everyone demands the same level of each public good. In the case of a single public and a single private good, individual h maximizes

$$U^h(M^h - \tau^h p_G G, G) \tag{16-63}$$

so that the first-order condition is

$$MRS^h = \frac{U^h_G}{U^h_X} = \tau^h p_G \tag{16-64}$$

Summing over h, we obtain

$$\sum_h MRS^h = p_G \sum_h \tau^h = p_G \tag{16-65}$$

The Lindahl equilibrium satisfies the necessary condition for a Pareto-efficient supply of public goods in a full optimum.

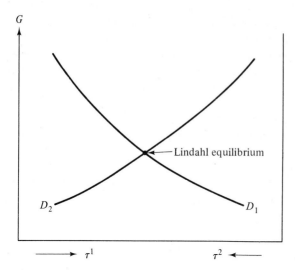

Figure 16-5 Lindahl equilibrium: two-person example.

The Lindahl equilibrium is illustrated in Fig. 16-5 for the case where there are two (types of) individuals. The share of the first is denoted by τ^1 and the demand is shown by D_1; the share of the second is given by $1-\tau^1$ and the demand is shown by D_2. The intersection is the Lindahl equilibrium.

The general properties of the Lindahl equilibrium have been extensively discussed in the literature. These include the Pareto efficiency referred to above, and the converse of this result that, under certain conditions, every Pareto-efficient allocation can be generated by a Lindahl equilibrium with suitable lump-sum taxes and transfers.[12] A particular question that has received considerable attention is the relationship between Lindahl equilibria and the *core*. An allocation (of goods among individuals) is said to be in the core if no coalition of individuals can together propose an alternative allocation of its *own* resources that makes at least one member better off and no member worse off—they cannot in this sense improve upon the allocation.[13] For a two-good, two-person economy, the core is simply the set of Pareto-efficient points that represent an improvement for both individuals over their no-trade position. It is shown, in the standard

---

[12] On this, see, for example, Foley (1970). For discussion of the existence of Lindahl equilibria, see Milleron (1972) and Roberts (1974b). Reference should also be made to the planning procedures for public goods, such as those proposed by Malinvaud (1971a, 1971b) and Drèze and de la Vallée Poussin (1971). A useful survey of work in this area is contained in Tulkens (1978).

[13] The reader should note that we have read Shapley (1973) and have resolved not to use the term "blocking".

Edgeworth box diagram, by the points on the contract curve between the indifference curves through the initial endowment.

In an exchange economy with no public goods, complete markets and full information, there are two basic theorems concerning the relationship between the core and the competitive economy:

1. the competitive economy is contained in the core;
2. the core "shrinks" to the competitive economy as the number of traders increases.

The first proposition is trivial. Since the competitive economy represents an improvement for all individuals (or at least no decrease in welfare) relative to the no-trade point, and since the competitive economy is Pareto-efficient, it is clearly contained in the core. The second proposition may be illustrated as follows. Suppose that there are two types of individual, but a large number of each type. The first step is to show that any allocation in the core must be symmetric; i.e., everyone of the same type gets the same consumption bundle.[14] The second step is to show that, if we can replicate the economy by any arbitrary factor, then the only possible core allocations are the competitive equilibria. For this, we need only to consider points on the contract curve. Suppose that we consider a point such as Q in Fig. 16-6, which is not a competitive equilibrium. A line from the initial endowment point to Q intersects at least one of the indifference curves through Q, and there exist points such as P where advantageous trades can be made. A group consisting of individuals of type I and II in appropriate ratio can improve on the allocation at Q, and replication ensures that this is feasible (with integral numbers of individuals).

When we introduce public goods, the natural parallel results would be for the Lindahl equilibrium to belong to the core, and for the core to shrink to the set of Lindahl equilibria as the number of traders increases. The latter would be particularly significant, since

> one could then argue that, no matter by what system [public] goods actually are allocated, if ... we assume that trade and production will take place among agents as long as it is advantageous, then any allocation that actually arose could have been achieved by the Lindahl price mechanism. [Roberts, 1974b, p. 38]

However, although the first result—that any Lindahl equilibrium is in the core—can be demonstrated under certain conditions (Milleron, 1972), the second result does not hold. For instance, Muench (1972) gives an example where the Lindahl equilibrium is unique but the core is very large (see also Milleron, 1972). The reason for this can be seen to lie in the requirement

---

[14] If not, the "underdogs" can form a coalition. For an exposition, see Hildenbrand and Kirman (1976, Ch. 1) or Varian (1978, p. 181–2).

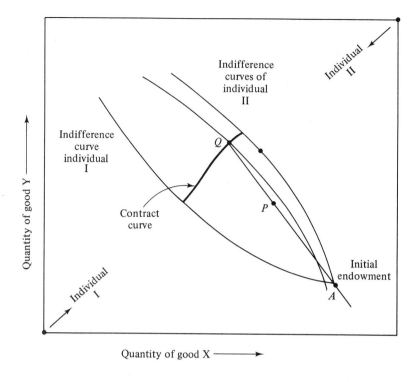

Figure 16-6 Competitive equilibrium and the core.

that the coalition must be able to make its members better off irrespective of the actions of the remaining group. In the context of public goods, this means that they must be better off even if the remaining individuals decide to produce *no* public goods. It thus becomes difficult for small groups to improve upon the proposed allocation; the core of the economy is likely to be bigger.[15]

Since much of the appeal of the concept of a Lindahl equilibrium stems from the parallel with competitive equilibrium, the results just described reduce the strength of the claims that can be made. We must therefore reconsider either the concept of the core as applied to a public goods economy, or the status of the Lindahl equilibrium. In any event the Lindahl equilibrium is probably best regarded as an analytical benchmark.

[15] The assumption that the cost of the public good is totally independent of the size of the economy may be questioned. For discussion of the question of "returns to group size", and "semi-public goods", see Roberts (1974b).

16-6 REVELATION OF PREFERENCES

Throughout the previous sections, we have assumed that the government knows the preferences of individuals (in the analysis of optimum provision of public goods) or (in the voting model) that individuals vote for their "true" preferences. This raises two closely related questions: how can the government learn the preferences of consumers, and how can we be sure that in any actual procedure for determining the provision of public goods, individuals will behave "honestly"? If we start from a presumption that individuals reveal the truth, unless it is in their interest not so to do, then this means examining the incentives for lying or for providing the government with false information.

That the demand for public goods may provide people with such incentives has been recognized for a long time. If the amount an individual has to pay for the public good is related in some way to his "revealed preference", then he has an incentive to understate his demand. As Samuelson expressed it in his classic paper, "it is in the selfish interest of each person to give *false* signals, to pretend to have less interest in a given collective consumption activity than he really has" (1954, pp. 888–9). This is sometimes referred to as the "free-rider problem"; and it arises in a variety of contexts apart from public goods. Unions claim that the reason that all individuals should be required to contribute dues is that there exists a free-rider problem. They provide a collective good (negotiating better terms with the management); and any individual disclaiming interest in the good has the advantage of enjoying the benefit without paying the cost. The general problem is the same as that of incentive compatibility in a (finite) competitive private economy, to which we referred in Lecture 11. In that case, the incentive for individuals to misrepresent their preferences disappears as the economy becomes "large". For public goods, however, the incentives do not improve as the number of people increases (see Roberts, 1976); and in this respect there is indeed a contrast between the allocation of public and private goods.[16]

Mechanisms for the Revelation of Preferences

A general class of mechanisms can be described as follows. The hth individual is asked to report a valuation of public goods, $z^h(G)$. The government announces that the tax shares of the hth individual and the

---

[16] The problem of incentive compatibility may arise quite widely where there is government intervention in the economy. For example, we have seen in Lecture 13 that the first-best redistributive tax may involve utility being a declining function of ability, and that this would give people an incentive to misrepresent their ability.

supply of public goods will be a function of all statements according to some rule:

$$\tau^h = \Gamma^h(\mathbf{z}(G))$$
$$G = \gamma(\mathbf{z}(G)) \qquad (16\text{-}66)$$

In designing the mechanism, the government may seek to secure properties such as the following:

1. The Nash equilibrium (where everyone takes the announcements of others as given) is Pareto-efficient where each person chooses his announcement to maximize his own welfare.
2. In the Nash equilibrium, everyone reports truthfully their valuation of public goods (for Pareto efficiency this is not necessary; all that is required is that the government can "translate" the announced valuations).
3. Truthful reporting is a dominant strategy (that is, it pays each individual to report $z^h(G)$ accurately regardless of the announcements of others).

There have been a number of attempts to devise mechanisms that have some or all of these properties. The earliest of these mechanisms was that of Vickrey (1961), who developed a procedure for a public marketing agency faced by monopolistic buyers and sellers. He showed that it would be possible to motivate individuals to give correct information by paying them the net increase in the sum of producer and consumer surpluses *of the other persons in the market* that resulted from the supply or demand curve revealed. This procedure was then independently discovered and developed by Clarke (1971, 1972) and Groves (1970, 1973; Groves and Loeb, 1975). (See also the discussion of elicitation functions in Kurz, 1974.)

The procedure may be described in a partial equilibrium model where utility functions are of the form

$$U^h = g^h(G) + M^h \qquad (16\text{-}67)$$

It is assumed that lump-sum transfers of income M^h can be made freely. The stated valuation function of individual h (note that it is a *function* and not simply a single value) is $z^h(G)$. The level of public provision, G^*, is chosen to maximize $\Sigma_h z^h - p_G G$, and individuals are taxed in a lump-sum way according to the schedule

$$p_G G^* - \sum_{i \neq h} z^i(G^*) + \kappa^h(\mathbf{z}^{-h}) \qquad (16\text{-}68)$$

where the last term is an arbitrary function of the vector $\mathbf{z}$, excluding z^h. The level of individual utility is

$$U = g^h(G^*) - z^h(G^*) + \sum_i z^i - p_G G^* - \kappa^h \qquad (16\text{-}69)$$

With this procedure, the dominant strategy is for each person to reveal the true marginal valuation. To see this, suppose that his response is a function of G and some variable ζ (so that we can think of his answer as being represented by the choice of ζ). A variation in ζ has no direct effect on U (since the terms in z^h in (16-69) cancel); it has an indirect effect via $dG^*/d\zeta$. By the conditions determining the choice of G^*, this has no effect on the underlined term in (16-69), and the variation is therefore proportional to $g^h_G - z^h_G$. With the optimal choice of ζ, this is zero, so $z^h(G)$ must equal $g^h(G)$ up to the addition of a constant.[17]

This preference revelation mechanism has therefore certain attractive properties, and Green and Laffont (1977a) have shown that this is the only class of mechanisms such that stating one's true preferences is a dominant strategy and that the outcome is Pareto-efficient. It is however limited, both by the assumptions made and by the fact that the mechanism does not guarantee a balanced budget for the government (on this, see Groves and Ledyard, 1977). It does not allow for collusion between individuals, and *coalition* incentive compatibility raises further issues (see Green and Laffont, 1979). Finally, no equity considerations are allowed for.

Empirical Significance of Free-Riding

Preference revelation and incentive compatibility is an active area of research. This is undoubtedly a valuable antidote to much of the earlier literature, which, with exceptions such as Samuelson (1954) and Buchanan (1968), has tended to ignore the problem—as in previous sections of this Lecture. On the other hand, there are those who argue that there is little evidence to suggest that the problem of correct revelation of preference has been of empirical significance:

> we have a lot of public goods around, probably more than we would expect on the basis of the theory of the free-rider tendency...and there are also many groups and individuals around who by no means appear to conceal their preferences for public goods. [Johansen, 1977, p. 148]

There are two principal reasons for questioning the importance of the free-rider problem. The first is that honesty may itself be a social norm, rather than simply the outcome of maximizing utility:

> economic theory, in this as well as in some other fields, tends to suggest that people are honest only to the extent that they have economic incentives for being so...the assumption can hardly be true in its most extreme form. [Johansen, 1977, p. 148]

---

[17] The Clarke procedure has a rather simpler form with the arbitrary functions κ^h being replaced by the valuation of public goods to the remaining $H-1$ people, at a level G^{**} chosen to maximize $\Sigma_{i \neq h} z^i(G) - p_G G$. See Tideman and Tullock (1976).

In societies where honesty is a social norm, one would not expect misrepresentation of preferences unless the pay-off to dishonesty reaches a threshold level. Where there is uncertainty about the pay-offs, individuals may feel that the choice of strategy is too complicated or time-consuming and resort to telling the truth: "since I cannot find a way to beat the system, I had just as well tell the truth" (Bohm, 1971, p. 56). The second reason why the revelation of preferences may be less important is that the decision is not made directly by individuals but typically through elected representatives. Johansen argues that in this case misrepresentation is unlikely to pay, either in terms of electoral success or in terms of decisions made by legislative assemblies. This brings us back to some of the issues discussed in Lecture 10.

There have in fact been experimental studies of individual preference revelation under different incentive schemes. For example, Bohm (1972) carried out an experiment at the Swedish Radio-TV Company, where 211 people were asked to express their willingness to pay to see a new programme, not yet shown to the public. They were paid on arrival 50 Kr (approximately $10) for taking part, and then asked to specify how much they would contribute to see the programme under a specified payments structure. They were told that the programme would be shown if the total sum stated exceeded the costs (500 Kr). The main results are set out in Table 16-2. Although there are some differences in the means and medians between the different incentive schemes, none of the differences are significant at the 5 per cent level. This experiment is clearly on a small scale, and intended more to assess the feasibility of the method, but it is none the less interesting that so little difference emerges.

Table 16-2 Experimental evidence on willingness to pay

Number of cases	Payment scheme	Amount willing to pay (Kr) Mean	Median
23	(I) The amount stated by respondent	7.61	5
29	(II) A percentage of the amount stated (so that total collected = total cost)	8.84	7
29	(III) One of four possibilities determined by a lottery (with equal probabilities)—designed to represent the case of "uncertainty"	7.29	5
37	(IV) Five Kr	7.73	6.50
39	(V) Nothing	8.78	7

Source: Bohm (1972, p. 121).

Decentralization and Information

The models employed in earlier sections assume that the government knows not only the preferences of the individuals, but also the production possibilities of all firms. In fact, the government does not have at its disposal all the requisite information, nor does it have the ability to solve all the problems of production and allocation simultaneously.

This is one of the main motivations for organizing governments in a decentralized manner, i.e., having branches responsible for different activities or functions. Thus, Musgrave's (1959) division of the branches of government into the stabilization, allocative and distribution branches may be thought of as more than just an analytical device. On the other hand, the sense in which the different branches can carry on their business separately from one another is not made clear in Musgrave (or in most of the subsequent literature), and the conditions under which various schemes of decentralization lead to a full optimum are not spelled out.

This may be illustrated by reference to the provision of public goods. Suppose first that lump-sum taxes may be freely used, and that public spending is decentralized to an agency that has a fixed budget and is instructed to maximize social welfare subject to the budget (public goods being charged for at the producer prices). The agency will then equate the ΣMRS to λMRT where λ is the multiplier associated with the budget constraint, and if λ is chosen correctly the social optimum is reached. (We are ignoring here the problem of revelation of preferences.) Where, however, there are non-lump-sum taxes, we have to allow both for the fact that varying G may affect government revenues and for the distributional effects of public goods. There is then a fundamental interdependence between decisions about the relative quantities supplied of various public goods and the structure of taxation for the finance of these goods. As a consequence, the marginal rate of substitution between two public goods is not in general equal at the optimum to their marginal rate of transformation (the ratio of the producer prices).[18] Moreover, the benefits for public goods need to be weighted according to the social marginal utility of income, and these weights depend on other aspects of distributional policy.

There is therefore a presumption that decentralization will entail certain costs, which have to be balanced against the administrative and informational advantages. The rigorous analysis of this problem, taking account of such factors as the motives of those who administer government programmes and of political power, is clearly a major task. In the next Lecture, we consider one particular form of decentralization—where individuals form local communities for the supply of local public goods.

---

[18] The conditions under which such decentralization remains possible despite the existence of non-lump-sum taxes has been examined by Lau, Sheshinski and Stiglitz (1978).

READING

Key references on the optimal provision of public goods are the papers by Samuelson (1954, 1955, 1958b, 1969). A valuable survey of the area is provided by Milleron (1972). On the public provision of private goods, see Arrow (1971a) and the subsequent literature. The discussion of voting on public goods draws on Stiglitz (1974b). A useful review of dynamic processes for the provision of public goods is provided by Tulkens (1978). The revelation of preferences is dealt with in depth by Green and Laffont (1979), and the references contained therein.

SEVENTEEN

LOCAL PUBLIC GOODS

17-1 INTRODUCTION

The theory of local public goods differs from the analysis of the previous Lecture in that goods are assumed to be specific to a particular geographical location, and consumers, in deciding on their location, can exercise choice with respect to the quantity and types of public goods provided. For some public goods there may be no spatial restriction (for example, the benefits from research and development); but for others the benefits, although available at no additional cost to new residents, are confined to one community (possibly with some spill-over to neighbouring communities). The construction of sea defences benefits those protected by the sea wall; the transmission of a television programme benefits those within a certain distance of the transmitter. In this Lecture we examine some of the implications of the local nature of such public goods and their provision by local communities. There is of course no necessary reason why they should be provided by local rather than central government; our focus is on the former, but in the final section we consider the fiscal relations between different levels of government.

Local Public Goods and the Market Analogy

The mobility of individuals between communities supplying local public goods has a number of major implications. It is in particular relevant to the problem of the revelation of preferences. Indeed, much of the interest in local public goods was stimulated by the intriguing suggestion of Tiebout (1956) that, if there were enough communities, individuals would reveal their true preference for public goods by the choice of community in which to live (in much the same way as individuals reveal their preferences for private goods by their choices). Where there is a wide range of choice, all those deciding to live in the same community would have essentially the same tastes, and there would be no problem of reconciling conflicting preferences. Moreover, it is often asserted that such a local public goods equilibrium would be Pareto-efficient.

This argument is based largely on the analogy with private goods:

> Just as the consumer may be visualised as walking to a private market place to buy his goods, ... we place him in the position of walking to a community where the prices (taxes) of community services are set. Both trips take the consumer to the market. There is no way in which the consumer can avoid revealing his preferences in a spatial economy. [Tiebout, 1956, p. 422]

This parallel ignores however certain key characteristics of local public goods. One of the most important of these is the essential non-convexity associated with the provision of such goods to individual citizens. In the conventional analysis of markets with only private goods, the assumption of convexity is critical in three ways· (1) as a result of non-convexities, there may exist no competitive equilibrium; (2) non-convexities in practice are likely to be associated with various kinds of non-competitive behaviour; and (3) where there are non-convexities, it is not necessarily the case that every Pareto-efficient allocation can be supported by a competitive equilibrium with appropriate lump-sum redistributions.

In the case of local public goods, non-convexities are inherent in that the cost of supplying a given quantity of a public good (e.g., a local radio programme) to an additional individual is zero (in the pure case). As we shall show, a local public goods equilibrium may not exist. Whether or not it does depends on the precise equilibrium notion employed, and, as we note below, several alternative concepts suggest themselves. Second, when there is a limited number of communities, they may attempt to make themselves more attractive to outsiders, acting in this way analogously to monopolistically competitive firms. On the one hand, this provides a motive for ensuring efficiency in the provision of public services; on the other, the mix and level of public goods provided may not be Pareto-efficient. Finally, not every Pareto-efficient allocation can be sustained by a local public goods equilibrium.

There are therefore reasons to doubt the usefulness of the competitive market analogy when considering the provision of local public goods and the claims that have been made for its efficiency. In a local public goods equilibrium, there may well be fewer communities than different types of individuals (it may indeed be socially optimal to have only one). The person may not therefore be able to find a community of individuals whose tastes are essentially identical to his own, and there may not be an optimum number and mix of people in a community.

Finally, there are the issues raised by redistribution. In the United

States at least, it would appear that the pattern of local community formation has much to do with the rich attempting to segregate themselves from the poor, in part because there is a large element of redistribution involved in the provision of education and other services of the local community. By moving to their own communities, the rich can avoid this redistribution. This phenomenon, which has no direct parallel with private goods, clearly must form part of the analysis.

Organization of the Lecture

In this Lecture we concentrate particularly on the optimum provision of local public goods and its relationship with the quantity provided under different market mechanisms. The analysis can become fairly complex, and the aim of the models presented here is to bring out the key points in the simplest possible context. In Section 17-2, we begin with the first-best allocation, where optimality is defined in terms of social welfare maximization. We first consider the case where individuals are identical, and then we extend the analysis to allow for differences in tastes and endowments.

In Sections 17-3 and 17-4 we examine the allocations attained under different market processes. It turns out that the analysis depends on a number of assumptions, and that we need to specify:

1. how the level of public goods supply is determined within a community (e.g., by simple majority voting);
2. what the decision-makers (voters) in each community take as given in deciding on the level of government expenditures (e.g., do they take into account the effects of different policies on migration?);
3. whether migration is restricted or unrestricted (for most of the analysis, we assume there are no restrictions on migration);
4. whether immigrants are treated differently from original residents with respect to taxes or the provision of government services (in the analysis that follows, we assume that there is no such differential treatment).

The existence, stability and efficiency of the market outcome is investigated under different assumptions about the process. Section 17-3 deals with the case where all individuals are identical; Section 17-4 is concerned with the implications of heterogeneity in tastes and endowments. These assumptions do not cover all possible cases; and their aim is to illustrate some of the possible problems that may arise. It is not the intention of this Lecture to provide a fully developed analysis of the decision-making machinery of local government.

The models discussed in Sections 17-3–17-4 treat the local communities as autonomous; in practice, in most countries there are higher level authorities (state, regional, federal). The higher tier may seek to influence or constrain the activities of local communities by direct regulation (local authorities may be forbidden from enacting certain restrictive legislation or compelled to provide a minimum standard of service), or by taxation and subsidies (e.g., matching grants). The motivation for the use of such controls by central authorities, as well as the design of the mechanisms by which this is done, is discussed in Section 17-5 on fiscal federalism.

17-2 OPTIMUM PROVISION OF LOCAL PUBLIC GOODS

For a pure public good that is not spatially limited (such as the benefits from research and development), the issue of the number and size of communities does not arise. Where however the benefits from a public good are spatially restricted, we have to consider these questions. As far as the public good is concerned, it is indeed natural to ask why there should be more than one community. If the addition of a person does not detract from the benefits enjoyed by others, then—from this point of view—the optimum allocation would involve everyone living in the same community. Against this, however, must be balanced the diminishing returns to labour with a fixed quantity of land, or the declining utility arising from congestion (e.g., as residential density increases). Moreover, for some public goods congestion may set in beyond a certain size of community (as emphasized in the treatment by Tiebout).[1]

In this section we focus on a single pure public good, considering the balance between the increasing returns inherent in its provision and the decreasing returns to labour as the population within a community is increased. We assume at this stage that all individuals are identical and examine the optimum allocation over a number of identical communities (i.e. with the same quantity and quality of land). One can envisage there being a large number of islands, and we want to know how many islands should be inhabited and what is the optimum level of public goods provision on each island. (This is essentially the optimum "club" problem formulated by Buchanan, 1965.)

Basic Framework

The model is a highly simplified one, in which total output, Y, in a community can be used either for private consumption (X per person) or for the public good, G, in that community. It is assumed that output is an

---

[1] An essential aspect of the analysis is that individuals belong to a single community; i.e., their place of residence, work and consumption coincide. Obviously, this is not strictly true, but the assumption seems a useful abstraction.

increasing, concave function of the number of workers in the community, N:

$$Y = f(N) \quad f' > 0, f'' < 0 \tag{17-1}$$

where $f \to 0$ as $N \to 0$ and as $N \to \infty$, $f \to \infty$ and $f' \to 0$. On the assumption that everyone in the community is identical and is treated the same, the aggregate production constraint gives:

$$Y = XN + G = f(N) \tag{17-2}$$

For fixed N, this defines the consumption opportunity set illustrated in Fig. 17-1.

We assume that individuals have identical preferences, represented by the utility function $U(X, G)$, where U is assumed to be quasi-concave. If the government chooses G to maximize U for a given level of N, this gives the point of tangency in Fig. 17-1. The condition for a maximum of U is that

$$U_X = NU_G$$

or

$$\frac{NU_G}{U_X} = 1 \tag{17-3}$$

which is the conventional result that the sum of the marginal rates of substitution equal the marginal rate of transformation ($\Sigma MRS = MRT$).

As we increase N, output, and hence the maximum level of public goods, increases (since $f'(N) > 0$) but the maximum level of consumption *per capita* ($f(N)/N$) decreases. The variable N opportunity locus is the

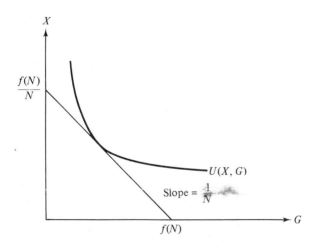

Figure 17-1 Opportunity set for fixed population.

outer envelope of the fixed N opportunity loci—see Fig. 17-2. This outer envelope may be characterized by taking a fixed value of G and then varying N to maximize X. Since

$$X = \frac{f(N) - G}{N} \qquad (17\text{-}4)$$

the first-order condition implies

$$f' = \frac{f(N) - G}{N} = X \qquad (17\text{-}5a)$$

or

$$G = f - Nf' \qquad (17\text{-}5b)$$

The second of these conditions has an interesting interpretation. Since f' is the marginal product of labour, $f - Nf'$ is output minus wage payments if workers are paid their marginal product. Thus, if the level of public

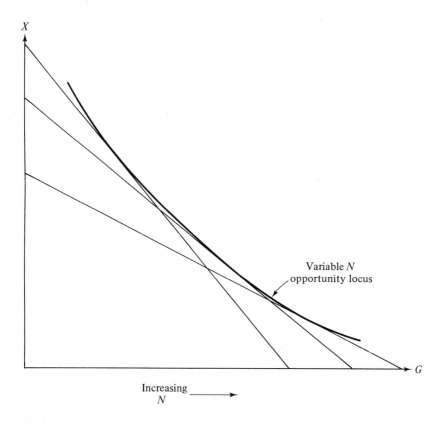

Figure 17-2 Opportunity set for variable population.

expenditure is fixed, but the population is variable, the population that maximizes consumption *per capita* is such that rents equal public goods expenditure. This has been dubbed the "Henry George" theorem (Stiglitz, 1977), since not only is the land tax non-distortionary, but also it is the "single tax" required to finance the public good.

Properties of the Social Optimum

If we now put these two elements together—variation in G and variation in N—then we immediately have to face the problem that the variable N opportunity locus is convex to the origin (rather than concave, as typically assumed with private goods in a conventional model). An explicit example is provided in Exercise 17-1. As a result, the community size that maximizes *per capita* utility may be zero, infinite or finite, as illustrated by Figs 17-3a–17-3c. If the indifference curve is more "curved" than the opportunity locus, then there is an "interior" solution. This is likely to be the case if public and private goods are strong complements so the indifference curve is very curved. Otherwise, utility is maximized with only private goods being produced and a "zero" population, or with only public goods being produced and an "infinite" population. (It is assumed that N may be treated as a continuous variable, and that we can ignore the problems that may arise if the total population is not a multiple of the optimum N; these aspects are discussed below.)

These findings may be related to the results on optimum population. If the objective is to maximize *per capita* utility, then with only private goods consumption is maximized with an infinitesimal population. On the other hand, if there were only public goods, utility would be maximized with the largest possible population—we would have a national public good. If individuals value both private and public goods, then there is a balancing of these two effects.

> **Exercise 17-1** Suppose that the production function is of the Cobb–Douglas form $f = N^\alpha$. Describe the variable N opportunity locus. Suppose that
>
> $$U(X, G) = X^{1-\gamma}G^\gamma \qquad (17\text{-}6)$$
>
> What can be said about the optimum in this case?

Even where there is an interior solution, it may not be unique, as is illustrated in Fig. 17-3d, where there are two combinations of X, G (and hence N) that give local maxima. In order to explore this further, let us define the maximum level of utility that can be attained for a given community size, N, by $V(N)$. In other words, it is the value of the

526

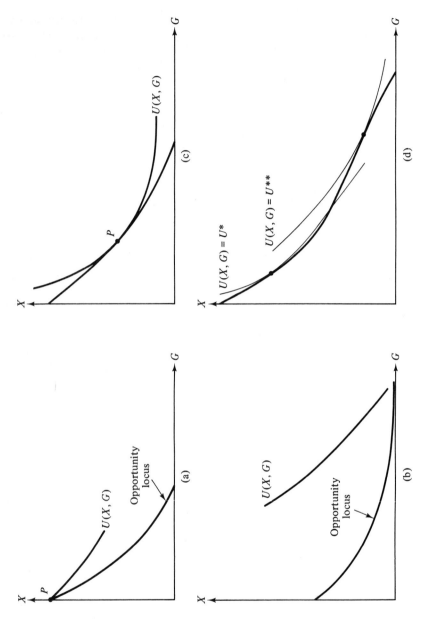

Figure 17-3 Optimal population: (a) optimal population is zero; (b) optimal population is infinite; (c) finite optimal population: single optimal N; (d) finite optimal population: multiple local optima.

maximand obtained from solving the fixed N problem with which we began:

$$V(N) \equiv \max_{X} [U(X, f(N) - XN)] \tag{17-7}$$

Differentiating with respect to N and using the envelope condition (i.e., that X is chosen optimally for any given N),

$$V'(N) = U_G(f' - X)$$
$$= \frac{U_G}{N}(Nf' - NX) \tag{17-8}$$

Using (17-2) and the first-order condition (17-3),

$$V'(N) = \frac{U_X}{N^2}[G - (f - Nf')] \tag{17-9}$$

At an interior optimum for N, where $U_X > 0$, the square bracket is zero, which gives Eq. (17-5b). If we now take the second derivative and evaluate at $V' = 0$,

$$V''(N)|_{V'=0} = \frac{U_X}{N^2}\left(\frac{dG}{dN} + Nf''\right) \tag{17-10}$$

The second term in the bracket is negative; its magnitude depends on the elasticity of substitution of the production function. From the definition of the elasticity (σ_p),

$$-Nf'' = \left(\frac{1}{\sigma_p}\right)\frac{f'(f - Nf')}{f} \tag{17-11}$$

If we define γ to be the share of government spending in total output, then at the optimum (from (17-5b))

$$\gamma = \frac{G}{f} = \frac{f - Nf'}{f} \tag{17-12}$$

On the other hand, from the indifference map (which we assume for convenience to be homothetic), the elasticity of substitution along an indifference curve is

$$\sigma_c \equiv \frac{d\log(G/X)}{d\log N} = \frac{d[\log\gamma - \log(1-\gamma) + \log N]}{d\log N} \tag{17-13}$$

So that (if $\gamma' \equiv d\gamma/dN$)

$$\sigma_c - 1 = \frac{\gamma'N}{\gamma(1-\gamma)} \tag{17-14}$$

Hence

$$\frac{dG}{dN} = \frac{d}{dN}(\gamma f) = \gamma f' + \gamma'f = \gamma f'\sigma_c \tag{17-15}$$

where the last step substitutes from (17-14) and (17-12). Assembling the pieces (Eqs (17-11), (17-12), and (17-15), and substituting into (17-10)),

$$V''|_{V'=0} = \frac{U_X}{N^2} \gamma f' \left(\sigma_c - \frac{1}{\sigma_p} \right) \qquad (17\text{-}16)$$

If $\sigma_c \sigma_p$ is everywhere less than 1, this rules out a local minimum, and hence cases such as that shown in Fig. 17-3d (where there is a local minimum between the two maxima). This confirms the earlier suggestion that strong complements in consumption (low σ_c) increase the curvature of the indifference map and tend to lead to a unique interior solution. It also brings out that strong complementarity in production (low σ_p) has the same effect, since this leads to a flat opportunity locus.[2]

In the analysis so far it has been assumed that labour is supplied inelastically, but the results can readily be extended and the Henry George theorem remains valid. This is left for the reader to consider (see Stiglitz, 1977, p. 281).

Fixed Population and Fixed Number of Communities

To this point we have assumed that there is no obstacle to the establishment of sufficient local communities of optimum size to accommodate the total population. One problem is that the total number of people may not be an integral multiple of N. This has been discussed in the literature on optimal club size (e.g., Pauly, 1967). More serious in the context of local governments is likely to be the limit on the number of potential communities. Although in a frontier society it may be possible to establish new towns, and thus reduce N, there is likely to be an end to this process. Settlement in most advanced countries is restricted to a fixed number of locations.

We now consider the implications of this feature of local jurisdictions. For ease of exposition, we assume that there are two communities, denoted by 1 and 2, with identical quantity and quality of land, and that a fixed population, $2N^*$, has to be divided between them. If the social optimum involves equal treatment, then the solution is relatively straightforward. There is however no necessary reason why equal treatment should be implied.

---

[2] Along the variable N opportunity locus

$$\frac{dX}{dG} = -\frac{1}{N}, \quad \frac{X}{G} = \frac{f'}{f - f'N}.$$

Hence

$$-\frac{d\log X/G}{d\log(-dX/dG)} = \frac{d\log f'/(f-f'N)}{d\log N} = \frac{ff''N}{f'(f-f'N)} = -\frac{1}{\sigma_p}$$

In order to examine the social optimum, let us denote by N_i the number of people in community i and by V_i the level of utility where G_i is chosen optimally in each community. Suppose that the government maximizes the Benthamite social welfare function

$$\Psi = N_1 V_1 + N_2 V_2 \qquad (17\text{-}17)$$

The first and second derivatives are (substituting $N_2 = 2N^* - N_1$)

$$\frac{d\Psi}{dN_1} = (V_1 - V_2) + N_1 V_1' - (2N^* - N_1)V_2' \qquad (17\text{-}18)$$

$$\frac{d^2\Psi}{dN_1^2} = 2(V_1' + V_2') + N_1 V_1'' + (2N^* - N_1)V_2'' \qquad (17\text{-}19)$$

Evaluating at $N_1 = N_2$, the equal treatment case is clearly a turning point, but there is no guarantee that it is a maximum, since at that solution

$$\frac{1}{2}\frac{d^2\Psi}{dN_1^2}\bigg|_{N_1 = N_2} = V'(N^*) + N^* V''(N^*) \qquad (17\text{-}20)$$

Suppose first that N^* coincides, by chance, with a value of N that, in the variable number of communities case, gives a local maximum. Then $V'(N^*) = 0$, $V''(N^*) < 0$, and we have a local maximum of the constrained case. If there is an "excess" population, so that $V'(N^*) < 0$, then it is sufficient for a local maximum that $V''(N^*) \leqslant 0$. On the other hand, it is quite possible that there is a population "shortage", so that $V'(N^*) > 0$. It can then happen that the equal treatment solution is a local minimum. This means that social welfare could be increased by moving to an asymmetric allocation, which in effect allows one community to get closer to the optimum and a larger fraction of the total population to enjoy the consequent higher level of V.

Some possible situations are illustrated in Figs 17-4a and b. In the first case, the social optimum involves all the population being in one jurisdiction; this is horizontally equitable in that all people are treated identically. On the other hand, if the possibility frontier has the shape illustrated in Fig. 14-4b, then the social optimum involves the asymmetric treatment of identical individuals. This may at first seem surprising, but it is only a further illustration of the point made in earlier Lectures—that welfare maximization does not necessarily imply equal treatment of equals. It is quite possible that we may want to constrain the government to choose only between policies that ensure equal utilities, but this must be introduced as a separate principle of horizontal equity.

The solution does of course depend on the instruments at the disposal of the government. We have not, for example, allowed for lump-sum subsidies between communities. It may be seen however that with a utilitarian objective this involves the equalization of the marginal utility of

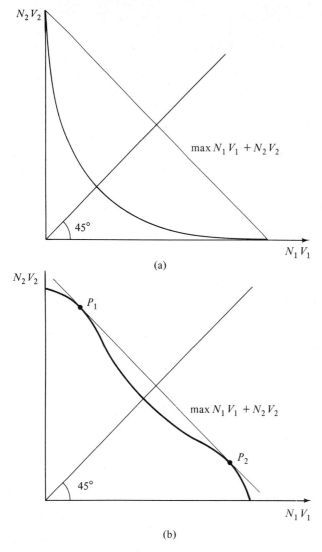

Figure 17-4 Social optimum: (a) all population in one jurisdiction; (b) asymmetric treatment.

consumption and that this does not necessarily imply equalization of utility if the level of public good provision differs.

Exercise 17-2 Suppose that the two potential communities differ in land quality, so that $V_1(N) > V_2(N)$ for all N. Show that maximization of Ψ entails that, if both are settled, the levels of utility at the optimum are not necessarily equalized.

Differences Among Individuals

The analysis of the case with identical individuals is mainly of interest because it provides the necessary background for the general theory where individuals differ. As we have seen, the hypothesis of Tiebout was that, where there are heterogeneous individuals, they would sort themselves out according to their preferences; communities would thus be homogeneous. We need to ask, however, under what conditions such complete sorting is optimal.

The first point concerns the production side of the economy. Such considerations were in effect assumed away by Tiebout: "restrictions due to employment opportunities are not considered. It may be assumed that all persons are living on dividend income" (1956, p. 419). This clearly ignores an important factor leading to mixed communities. If doctors and lawyers are not perfect substitutes, then it may pay to have communities in which there are both. Of course, if doctors and lawyers have the same preferences, then it is still possible that all individuals in the same community have the same tastes. But this seems unlikely. More generally, we would require that the distribution of tastes of lawyers and doctors be identical, and that they have the same incomes; but since the latter depends on their relative supplies, this could not be true in general unless they were perfect substitutes for each other.

Leaving aside the mixing due to interactions in production, it is not the case that individuals are always better off forming homogeneous communities with people of identical tastes. Suppose that there are two communities that could be settled, and equal numbers of two types of person, identical except for their preferences regarding public goods. There are three public goods, and the utility functions of the two types are

$$U(X, G_1 + \kappa G_3) \quad \text{and} \quad U(X, G_2 + \kappa G_3) \qquad (17\text{-}21)$$

where $0 < \kappa < 1$. In other words, group 1 prefers public good 1 (swimming pools), gets no utility at all out of public good 2 (ski lifts), but enjoys hiking trails (public good 3). Hiking and swimming are perfect substitutes, but at a trade-off of less than 1 to 1. Group 2 has symmetric preferences, preferring public good 2, getting no utility out of public good 1 and limited enjoyment from public good 3.

Clearly, if they form separate communities, each will produce the public good of its own preference: swimming pools in 1 and ski lifts in 2. We need however to compare this with the possibility of a merged community, where—as a compromise—good 3 is produced. In this case, they can enjoy the benefits of the economies of scale associated with public goods: if $\kappa > \frac{1}{2}$, then with the same tax payments the effective public goods supply to each person goes up. Against this must be balanced the diminishing returns to labour as the size of the community is doubled, but it is clear that there are circumstances in which everyone is better off. This is more likely to be the case, the closer κ is to 1 and the less is the extent of diminishing returns. (For a related discussion, see McGuire, 1974, and Berglas, 1976.)

The desirability of forming homogeneous or heterogeneous communities may depend on the ability to identify different groups. Assume, for instance, that there are two groups in the population, one of which has a low preference for the public good, the other of which has a high preference. Assume there are no diminishing returns to labour. Clearly, if a single community were formed, a supply of public goods equal to the original high level could be provided, and everyone's taxes cut. Hence, such a combination would be Pareto-improving. But if everyone in the mixed community has to be taxed identically, on the grounds that we cannot identify those who prefer the low quantity of public good, there might be no allocation that would improve the position for both types. This is illustrated in Fig. 17-5, where P_1 and P_2 denote the positions chosen when the two groups form separate communities. The mixed community with equal treatment involves a point on the line AB, and there is no such point that is preferred by both groups.

This provides one reason why benefit taxation may be desirable, even though it may reduce the consumption of a public good that has no marginal cost of usage (e.g., tolls on uncrowded bridges). Although such

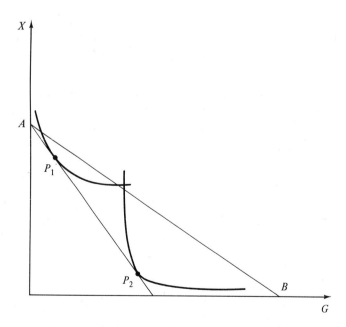

Figure 17-5 Pareto-inefficient community formation.

taxation may, with perfect information, be sub-optimal, it may be warranted if it allows the assignment of tax burdens in such a way as to permit the formation of larger communities than otherwise would be the case.

17-3 MARKET EQUILIBRIA AND OPTIMALITY: IDENTICAL INDIVIDUALS

To assess the claims made for the market provision of local public goods, we need to specify the way in which the mechanism is assumed to work and what is meant by a local public equilibrium. We must then ascertain under what conditions such an equilibrium exists (recall that in the presence of non-convexities, competitive equilibria often do not exist); finally, we need to determine whether, if equilibrium exists, it is Pareto-efficient.

We proceed in the same way as in the earlier analysis. We first assume, in this section, that people are identical. This means that the critical issue of matching people by communities does not arise, but we can still ask whether communities of the optimal size will be formed, and whether, within each community, the optimal supply of public goods will be provided. We then turn in 'Section 17-4 to the more difficult issue of analysing local public goods equilibria when individuals differ.

Basic Model

As explained in the Introduction, the behaviour of the market process depends on the conditions governing migration and the way in which the decisions are made regarding local public goods. Here we assume that there is free migration, and that in each community all individuals are treated identically.[3] It is then a condition of equilibrium that all individuals have the same level of utility. As far as local public good decisions are concerned, we assume initially that each community acts to maximize utility for a given population. In other words, decision-makers ignore the effect on migration. Alternatives to this myopic assumption are discussed below.

For ease of analysis, we make the same simplifying assumptions as earlier. There is a single private good and a single public good. There are two potential communities, both identical. The conditions for equilibrium may be given in terms of $V(N)$, which represents the maximum utility assuming N is constant (i.e., ignoring the effect on migration):

$$V(N_1) = V(N_2) \quad \text{if both communities settled}$$

$$V(2N^*) \geq V(0) \quad \text{if only one community settled} \qquad (17\text{-}22)$$

---

[3] That is, we assume there is no differential taxation of immigrants and original occupants. The analysis can be viewed as applying to a "socialist economy" in which all residents share equally in rents.

Some of the various possibilities are illustrated in Fig. 17-6. We may note that continuity of $V(N)$ is sufficient to ensure existence of at least one equilibrium.[4]

There are in fact quite possibly multiple equilibria. Let us take first the case shown in Fig. 17-6a, where $V' > 0$ for all N. In the market economy, there is an equal-population equilibrium at E, and two single-community equilibria at E_1 and E_2. Which of these is attained depends on the adjustment process. Suppose that migration takes place according to the difference in utility levels. If the population is disturbed from the equilibrium E in Fig. 17-6a, it will tend to diverge. If $N_1 = N^* + \varepsilon$, where $\varepsilon > 0$, then $V(N_1) > V(N_2)$ and people will move to community 1. The limit of this process is a locally stable equilibrium at E_1, with only community 1 inhabited. The case in Fig. 17-6b also has three equilibria, with the same stability pattern (although different welfare implications—see below). The third case, Fig. 17-6c, exhibits three interior equilibria, of which E_1 and E_2 are locally stable under the assumed adjustment process. The final case, 17-6d, has no fewer than five equilibria. The equal-size equilibrium E is locally (but not globally) stable, as are the one-community equilibria.

Turning to the efficiency properties of these equilibria, we can see that the case shown in Fig. 17-6a corresponds to that in Fig. 17-4a, where maximization of $N_1 V_1 + N_2 V_2$ involved only one community being populated. As we have seen, the only locally stable equilibria of the market process in this case are those with single communities, so that the migration of individuals does achieve an efficient allocation. On the other hand, there is no guarantee that this will come about. Figure 17-6b shows the case where the single-community equilibria are again locally stable, but there exist allocations at which everyone is strictly better off. For example, if the population were allocated equally (i.e., at E), this would make everyone strictly better off. The converse applies in Fig. 17-6d, where the equal-community equilibrium, which is locally stable, is clearly Pareto-inferior to the one-community equilibria.

This simple model demonstrates the lack of generality of Tiebout's hypothesis. Even in the absence of any problems of sorting individuals according to differences in tastes, the local public goods equilibrium may not be Pareto-efficient. Nor is the problem alleviated if we let the number of communities and the number of individuals increase (in proportion). The analysis has moreover ignored two problems that mean that it is even less likely that the equilibrium be efficient: the effect of migration on land values, and differences among communities.

---

[4] If $N_1 = 0$ is not an equilibrium, then V_1 must be above V_2; conversely V_2 is above V_1 at $N_1 = 2N^*$; hence by continuity there is an intersection.

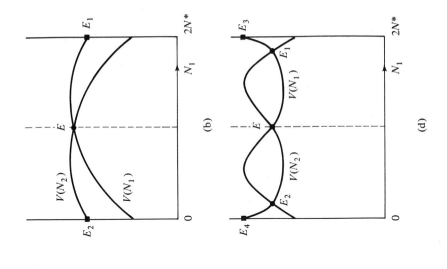

Key

■ Locally stable
equilibrium

● Unstable
equilibrium

Figure 17-6 Market equilibria.

535

Land Values and Capitalization

The previous analysis assumed that all individuals had identical claims; in effect, we modelled a state in which land is publicly owned and all migrants have equal access to the rents (after paying for the public goods). Equivalently, there is a 100 per cent rent tax, with the deficit or surplus between government revenue and expenditure being made up by lump-sum taxes or subsidies. Assume now, however, that we give all individuals one unit of land but for half of the population we concentrate δ of their ownership claims in one community $(1-\delta$ in the other); for the other half of the population, there is δ in the other community $(1-\delta$ in the first), where $\delta > \frac{1}{2}$. Moreover, we assume that the government is restricted in its imposition of rent taxes to a rate τ which is less than 100 per cent (reasons why this may be a reasonable restriction have been discussed in Lecture 15). The difference between government expenditure and the revenue from rent taxes is raised (or distributed) as before as a uniform lump-sum tax, T_i in community i.

In this situation, the citizens will take account of the effect of decisions about public goods on the rents they receive, and it is quite possible that this will entail an inefficient level of expenditure on local public goods. There is in effect "capitalization" of the benefits in land values. To see the considerations involved, consider a position where $N_1 > N_2$ but $N_2 > 0$. There are some people working in community 1 whose land is more (i.e., δ of it) in community 2; they are not however the majority. Majority voting means that the level of G_1 is chosen to maximize the utility of a person who owns δ of his land in community 1. The consumption of this person is given by

$$X^{11} = f'(N_1) + (1-\tau)[\delta R_1 + (1-\delta)R_2] - T_1 \qquad (17\text{-}23)$$

where R_i denotes the rent per unit of land:

$$R_i = \frac{f(N_i) - N_i f'}{N^*} \qquad (17\text{-}24)$$

and the tax required per worker in community i is

$$T_i = \frac{G_i}{N_i} - \frac{\tau N^* R_i}{N_i} \qquad (17\text{-}25)$$

In contrast to the earlier analysis, individuals are assumed to act non-myopically to the extent that they allow for the effect of migration. The total derivative of $U(X^{11}, G_1)$ with respect to G_1 is therefore given by

$$\frac{dU(X^{11}, G_1)}{dG_1} = U_G(X^{11}, G_1) - \frac{U_X(X^{11}, G_1)}{N_1}\left(1 - \frac{N_1 dX^{11}}{dN_1}\frac{dN_1}{dG_1}\right)$$

$$(17\text{-}26)$$

From this we can see that the level of public goods is influenced by two considerations not previously present: the difference in the interests of different community members and the effect of migration. To see the effect of the former, suppose that $dN_1/dG_1 = 0$. The level of public goods is then determined by equating the sum of the marginal rates of substitution to the MRT, but assuming that everyone places the same value on the public good as does the majority.

The effect of migration on the consumption of a member of the majority can be broken down into several components:

$$\frac{dX^{11}}{dN_1} = \underbrace{-[-f''(N_1)]}_{\text{wage effect}} + \frac{(1-\tau)}{N^*}\{\underbrace{\delta[-N_1 f''(N_1)] + (1-\delta)[N_2 f''(N_2)]}_{\text{rent effect}}\}$$

$$+ \underbrace{\frac{T_1}{N_1}}_{\substack{\text{spreading} \\ \text{tax burden}}} + \frac{\tau}{N_1}\underbrace{[-N_1 f''(N_1)]}_{\substack{\text{tax on} \\ \text{landowners}}} \quad (17\text{-}27)$$

The first term is the reduction in wages caused by the induced migration. This appears as in the earlier analysis, but the effect on rent is different (previously the rent R_1 accrued to all residents in community 1). Migration to 1 raises rents and hence land values in community 1 and lowers land values in community 2. The net effect depends on the pattern of ownership; and the benefit to the individual depends on the extent to which increases in land values are taxed. If $\delta = 1$, so that land holdings are concentrated, then the net result of the first two terms (wage and rent effects) is a rise in X^{11} if $\tau < 1 - N^*/N_1$. The third term arises from the spreading of the tax burden, as before, but the final effect allows for the fact that some of the increased land value is taxed away.

The level of migration depends on the equilibrium condition, and in this sense those whose land is predominantly in 2 but who live in 1 can exercise an influence, even though they are not decisive in the majority vote. In an equilibrium with $N_2 < N^* < N_1$, their utility must equal that of residents in community 2:

$$U(X^{21}, G_1) = U(X^{22}, G_2) \quad (17\text{-}28)$$

where

$$X^{21} = f'(N_1) + (1-\tau)[\delta R_2 + (1-\delta)R_1] - T_1$$
$$X^{22} = f'(N_2) + (1-\tau)[\delta R_2 + (1-\delta)R_1] - T_2 \quad (17\text{-}29)$$

Exercise 17-3 Derive the effect on migration (dN_1/dG_1), and examine the way in which this term modifies the first-order condition for the choice of G_1. How does the minority's option to leave or enter change the decision that would have been made by the majority if they could ignore migration?

Differences Among Communities

Returning to the basic model, with myopic decisions, we may consider the consequences of differences in land size or quality. The optimum allocation of population with a utilitarian social welfare function between two islands does not in general entail equal utility (see Exercise 17-2). Yet the market equilibrium always implies that all individuals have the same utility. The utilitarian optimum cannot therefore be achieved by a market solution. We can however go further and show that the market equilibrium is not in general Pareto-efficient.

To bring this out, consider the effect of allowing a lump-sum transfer subsidy from community 1 to community 2 at rate T. Can this transfer raise the common level of utility? This may be seen by taking the derivative of V at the equilibrium with respect to T and evaluating at $T = 0$. In the case where the communities are identical, then at the equal allocation equilibrium $N_1 = N_2$, and the transfer cannot raise utility. In contrast, where they are asymmetric, with (say) $V_1(N) > V_2(N)$ for all N, then the market equilibrium does not involve $N_1 = N_2$, and a transfer can raise the common level of utility. The market equilibrium is not then Pareto-efficient.

Where there are only two communities, it is reasonable to suppose that each would perceive this, and that the transfers would take place. But when we increase the number of communities and people proportionately, then any community from which a transfer is due will attempt to be a "free-rider". It would prefer all other donor islands to provide the subsidy, while it enjoys the benefits in terms of the allocation of the population. This may lead to arguments for a central authority to enforce transfers. It may also be noted that in the situation where certain communities have "excess" populations, if free mobility were permitted, there may be attempts to restrict migration. The implications depend on the initial distribution of the population, but it is clear that where no migration occurs the analysis of the determination of public spending in each community is parallel to that in Lecture 16.

An Alternative Equilibrium Concept: The Core

In our discussion of the market equilibrium we noted that there was, with respect to the allocation of population, no natural price-taking assumption, and we had to make assumptions concerning perceived responses to the migration of individuals. This makes the competitive model less persuasive than in the conventional private goods economy, and suggests that the implications of other equilibrium concepts ought to be pursued. One such concept was discussed in the preceding chapter: the core. We argued there that with public goods the core was, in a sense, quite large because the coalitions containing less than the entire population suffered from the loss of the contributions of the excluded individuals to the tax base. In contrast, in the case of local public goods, just the opposite may be true. The core may well be empty; i.e., there is no allocation that cannot be improved upon by some group (Stiglitz, 1977).

To illustrate this, we consider the case where there are two potential communities and a total population $2N^*$. Each person is assumed to have $1/N^*$ of the land on *one* of the islands. We assume that $V'(N) > 0$ for all $N \leqslant N^*$, but that $V(2N^*) < V(N^*)$. Both the public and private good are taken to be normal. These assumptions are somewhat special, but the intention is to exhibit the possibility that the core is empty rather than to prove a general result.[5]

An allocation is described by an assignment of individuals to communities, of private consumption goods to each individual, and a level of expenditure on public goods in each community. The set of individuals who live in community i are denoted by $\{N_1\}$. There are two situations that we need to consider: where the population is divided equally, and where one of the communities (taken to be the first) has a larger population. In the first case, we take it that individuals live in the community on which they own land; while in the second, there are some people who own land in community 2 who work in community 1. Feasibility requires that

$$G_1 + G_2 + \sum_j X^j \lessgtr f(N_1) + f(N_2) \tag{17-30}$$

The demonstration that the core is empty proceeds by a series of steps (further details are given in Stiglitz, 1977, pp. 295–7):

1. In any allocation in the core, there cannot be a subsidy by members of the larger of the two communities to the smaller:

$$\sum_{j \in \{N_1\}} X^j + G_1 \geqslant f(N_1) \tag{17-31}$$

If this were not so, the coalition consisting of the members of $\{N_1\}$ could improve upon the allocation. It follows immediately that, if the islands have the same population, one cannot subsidize the other.
2. In community 2, the worst-off person receives less than his marginal product; i.e.,

$$\min_{j \in \{N_2\}} X^j < f'(N_2) \tag{17-32}$$

This follows from the facts that any allocation in the core must be Pareto-efficient and that no subsidy is paid to community 2, combined

---

[5] A rather different example is that of Pauly (1970b), based on the case where there is a variable number of communities and the ratio of total population to the optimum community size is not an integer.

with the assumptions made earlier. Pareto efficiency requires that

$$\sum_{j \in \{N_2\}} \frac{U_G}{U_X} [X^j, f(N_2) - \Sigma X^j] = 1 \qquad (17\text{-}33)$$

On the other hand, since $N_2 \leqslant N^*$, there exists a value $\hat{X}$, such that

$$\sum_{j \in \{N_2\}} \frac{U_G}{U_X} [\hat{X}, f(N_2) - N_2 \hat{X}] = 1 \qquad (17\text{-}34)$$

and $\hat{X} < f'(N_2)$, since $V'(N) > 0$ by assumption. It may then be shown that min X^j is less than $\hat{X}$.[6]

3. One of the communities must be strictly smaller than the other. This may be seen by assuming that they are equal in size and that, without loss of generality, $G_1 \geqslant G_2$. Then a coalition consisting of all people in community 1 and the person with min X^j in community 2 can improve upon the allocation. By moving to community 1 he increases output by $f'(N^*)$ but requires no more than min X^j to stay on the same indifference curve, and this is less than $f'(N^*)$ by step 2.

4. The worst-off person in community 1 who owns land in community 2 (Mr A) must be worse off than the worst-off person in community 2 (Mr B). Otherwise, a coalition consisting of Mr B and all members of community 1 except Mr A could improve on the allocation.

5. The worst-off person in community 1 (Mr C) is at least as badly off as Mr A (indeed, C and A may be the same person), and hence is worse off than Mr B. Mr B receives strictly less than his marginal product (by step 2). It follows that a coalition of $\{N_2\}$ and Mr C can improve upon the allocation (e.g., by offering Mr C slightly less than his marginal product).

There is therefore no allocation that cannot be improved upon, i.e., the core is empty. This is not necessarily the case (see Stiglitz, 1977), but the important point is that one must be careful in extending conventional equilibrium notions to economies with public goods.

17-4 MARKET EQUILIBRIA AND OPTIMALITY: HETEROGENEOUS INDIVIDUALS

This section allows for differences between individuals in tastes and endowments. These do not in themselves mean that the Tiebout argument cannot be employed, and we begin with a model where communities are

---

[6] Suppose that it were not true, then $\Sigma_{j \in \{N_2\}} X^j \geqslant N_2 \hat{X}$ and the level of public goods is no higher than in the equal consumption allocation. Since the level of private good consumption is higher, the assumption of normality implies that U_G/U_X is higher and hence that the left-hand side of (17-33) would exceed unity.

mixed (by virtue of the assumptions made about production) but where there is unanimity about the level of public goods and this is Pareto-efficient. The model does however assume that individuals take account of the effects on migration (act non-myopically) and that the number of communities is freely variable. Where these assumptions do not hold, there may exist no local public goods equilibrium and there may be inefficiency—both in the level of public goods, and in the matching of types of people in communities.

The Tiebout Hypothesis in Mixed Communities

The model we employ initially is one in which the conditions of production are such that communities must be mixed. There are two groups, who interact in production, and both are essential to produce a strictly positive output. The two types are denoted by m and n, with number m_j, n_j in community j. Output in community j is

$$Y_j = f(m_j, n_j) \tag{17-35}$$

where

$$f(0, n_j) = f(m_j, 0) = 0. \tag{17-36}$$

Members of the two groups may have different tastes, and their utility in community j is written $U_j^i(X_j^i, G_j)$, where $i = m, n$. None the less, under certain assumptions it can be shown that, if each group acts in a utility-taking manner (the natural analogue of price-taking), then in an equilibrium, if it exists, there will be unanimity on the allocation of public goods and it will be Pareto-efficient. (For a more general statement of this result, see Stiglitz, 1979.)

The first condition for a local public goods equilibrium concerns migration. For equilibrium, all people of a given type must have the same utility in all communities in which they live, and must perceive themselves to obtain a lower utility in any other community.[7] Given that all communities contain people of both types,

$$U_i^m = U_*^m \quad \text{all } i, \text{ and} \quad U_i^n = U_*^n \quad \text{all } i \tag{17-37}$$

Now, any community is assumed to act as a *utility-taker*. In other words, it believes that, so long as it offers to people of type i a utility level U_*^i, it can attract an arbitrary number of such people. This is a natural extension of price-taking behaviour. There is assumed, for example, to be an international market for doctors, and if any community offers a lower utility

---

[7] We use the term "perceived" because the individual must form a conjecture about what his utility would be if there is no one of exactly his type within the community. For instance, if there are no doctors within a community, a doctor would have to conjecture the wages that a doctor would be paid (after tax). We assume that these conjectures are correct.

level (taking account of both private consumption and local public goods) then it cannot secure their services.

Now consider the characterization of a Pareto-efficient allocation, on the assumption that all people of a given type are treated symmetrically. This may be formulated in terms of maximizing for a given community (where we drop the subscript j):

$$U^m(X^m, G) \tag{17-38}$$

subject to

$$U^n(X^n, G) \geqslant U_*^n \tag{17-39}$$

and

$$G + mX^m + nX^n = f(m, n) \tag{17-40}$$

Forming the Lagrangean

$$\mathscr{L} = U^m + \lambda_1 U^n + \lambda_2[f(m, n) - G - mX^m - nX^n] \tag{17-41}$$

the first-order conditions are

$$U_X^m = \lambda_2 m \quad \text{and} \quad \lambda_1 U_X^n = \lambda_2 n \tag{17-42a}$$

$$f_m = X^m \quad \text{and} \quad f_n = X^n \tag{17-42b}$$

$$U_G^m + \lambda_1 U_G^n = \lambda_2 \tag{17-42c}$$

Dividing by λ_2 ($= U_X^m/m$ and $\lambda_1 U_X^n/n$ from (17-42a)), condition (17-42c) gives

$$\frac{mU_G^m}{U_X^m} + \frac{nU_G^n}{U_X^n} = 1 \tag{17-43}$$

This is the conventional $\Sigma MRS = MRT$ condition. Moreover, from (17-42b), the marginal product of each group equals its consumption, and

$$f - mf_m - nf_n = G \tag{17-44}$$

In other words, the Henry George theorem again holds.[8]

The nature of the solution may be seen in terms of the utility possibility curve generated by varying U_*^n, and this is shown in Fig. 17-7. For each value of U_*^n, there is a maximum value of U_*^m and the associated ratio of n to m. This n/m ratio may be thought of as reflecting the relative "demand" for the two types of person. We would normally expect that, as the level of utility we give people of type n is increased, the relative demand would be decreased, as shown in the lower part of the diagram.

---

[8] For a discussion of the conditions under which the theorem is valid, see Arnott and Stiglitz (1980).

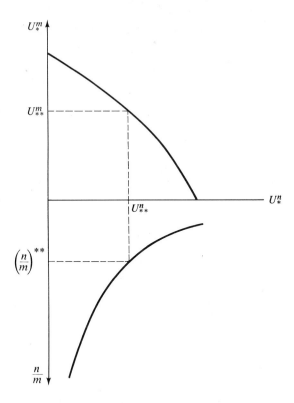

Figure 17-7 Utility-taking communities.

Exercise 17-4 Suppose that the production function is Cobb–Douglas, and that there is sharply diminishing returns:

$$Y = m^{\alpha_m} n^{\alpha_n} \tag{17-45}$$

where $\max(\alpha_m, \alpha_n) < 1 - \alpha_m - \alpha_n$, and that the utility function is Cobb–Douglas:

$$U = \log X + \log G$$

Describe the utility possibility frontier, and the associated ratios of n to m.

Let us now return to the characterization of the market equilibrium, where one exists. Suppose that the actual relative supplies are $(n/m)^{**}$, as indicated on Fig. 17-7. Then we can show that the Pareto-efficient allocation corresponding to this ratio is a market equilibrium, with utility-taking behaviour. Consider a community in that situation. The supply price of type n workers, in terms of utility, is U^n_{**}. If a group of type m workers got together, the best they could do is to attain the point on the utility possibility schedule U_{**}^m. They can reach this by forming a community with the optimum population size and supplying the Pareto-efficient level of public goods. Since everyone is then indifferent whether they live in this or another community, the given population size is attainable. Finally, when they all have the given population ratio, with an arbitrarily large number of islands and individuals, everyone will be within a community, and there is no incentive for anyone to move. Thus, under these highly idealized conditions, even though communities are mixed, there is unanimity. Given that each recognizes that there is a utility supply curve for individuals of a particular type, there is no longer any scope for political choice and the market equilibrium generates a Pareto-efficient level of public goods.

The conditions are very strong, however. We have assumed that there is an arbitrary number of communities, and that decisions take account of the effects on migration—the utility-taking assumption. Where these conditions do not hold, there is no guarantee of efficiency, or indeed that a market equilibrium exists.

Non-Existence of Local Public Goods Equilibrium

The possible non-existence of an equilibrium is illustrated by the example of Westhoff (1977), where there is a continuum of consumers with differing preferences and a limited number of communities. In each community the level of public goods is determined by myopic majority voting, this being a most important assumption. Here we give a rather simpler example.

There are three types of local public good, G_1, G_2, and G_3, and three types of person, m, n, and o. The preferences of the different types may be written

$$U^m = u(X^m) + v(G_1 + \kappa_m G_3) \tag{17-46a}$$

$$U^n = u(X^n) + v(G_2 + \kappa_n G_3 + \kappa_N G_1) \tag{17-46b}$$

$$U^o = u(X^o) + v(G_3 + \varepsilon G_1) \tag{17-46c}$$

where u is strictly increasing, $v(0) = 0$, $0 < \kappa_m < 1$, $0 < \kappa_n < \kappa_N < 1$, and ε is a small positive number. In other words, m gets no utility from good 2 and prefers 1 to 3, n prefers good 2 to good 1, and slightly prefers good 1 to good 3; o gets no utility from good 2, and almost none from good 1.[9] There are assumed to be an odd number P_i of each type, where

$$P_m < P_o < P_n \quad \text{and} \quad P_m + P_o > P_n \tag{17-47}$$

---

[9] It should be noted that the example is not based on cyclical voting. The preferences are (in decreasing order) (1, 3, 2), (2, 1, 3), and (3, 1, 2), so that, unless one of types n or o was in an absolute majority, public good 1 would always be selected by the population as a whole.

Everyone is assumed to have the same income, I, and the public good is financed by a uniform poll tax.

The technical conditions of production of the public good are such that it is either produced or not, and it has to be used exclusively for one of the three types (e.g., there can only be one television channel and it has to be used *either* for sport *or* for music *or* for news).[10] The cost is fixed at unity (independent of the type of use). Finally, we assume that

$$u(I - \tfrac{1}{2}) + v(1) > u(I) > u(I - 1) + v(1)$$

This means that a group of two people of the same type would choose to produce the preferred public good, but one person on his own would not.

Within each community, the decisions regarding public goods are made by a majority vote. Voters are myopic and take no account of the effect on migration. Migration takes place where a person can obtain a higher utility level in a different community, including the possibility of not joining. We consider in turn the possible equilibrium configurations, and indicate how a set of conditions can be derived under which no equilibrium exists:

1. *A single community* (which we denote by *MNO*). Majority voting leads to the choice of good 1, preferred to 2 by m and o (who form a majority), and preferred to 3 by m and n (who form a majority). However, if there is a strictly positive level of provision, then for small enough ε the benefit to a person of type o is insufficient to outweigh the cost of the poll tax. He therefore migrates to form a new community on his own; hence this is not an equilibrium.
2. *Two communities* (*MN* and *O*). In the former, type n is now in a majority, so that good 2 is produced. Type m obtains no utility from good 2, so that its members migrate.
3. *Two communities* (*N* and *MO*). If the type m members join with type o, then good 3 is produced (since o is in a majority). For a given quantity of the public good, the tax rate in *MO* is lower than in *N*, since the former has a bigger population. Type n prefers good 2 to good 3, but if the margin of preference is not too great, then members of type n migrate.
4. *Two communities* (*M* and *NO*). In the latter, good 2 is produced, since type n is in a majority. Type o migrates, since its members get no utility from the good.
5. *Three communities* (*M*, *N* and *O*). A person of type m considers joining the community with type *O*. In *O*, good 3 is produced rather than good 1, but the tax from a given quantity is lower (since $P_o > P_m$). If the relative preference for good 1 is sufficiently small, then type m migrates.
6. *Equilibria*, where there are people of type i in more than one community.

---

[10] This assumption is not essential; indeed, no one would vote (myopically at least) for a mixed programme.

The equilibrium condition is that the level of utility of people of type i must be the same in all communities in which they reside. Suppose, for example, that we have (MN and NO). For this to be an equilibrium, type n must be in a minority in both, so that the former produces G_1, and the latter G_3. If the relative preference of type n for good 1 is slight, then the total numbers in the two communities must be close (so as to equalize the tax burden). On the other hand, for P_m small, this involves type n being a majority in the first community. Hence it cannot be an equilibrium. Other cases of split populations can similarly be ruled out.

A crucial role in this example is played by the assumption of myopic voting. In each case, the majority ignores the possibility that the minority may leave. It is however the threat of "exit" that may allow minorities to exert an influence on the outcome. If, for instance, type n recognizes in the community (MNO) that a vote for good 1 will cause group o to leave, then they may vote for good 3, which can then be an equilibrium. It was this recognition of the effect on migration that lay behind the earlier utility-taking model, and it is developed further in the model of rich and poor communities below. Before that, however, we consider a model of capitalization in land values.

Land Values

We saw earlier that, with private land ownership, people voted for public goods not just on the basis of their direct utility but also allowing for the effect of any induced migration on the value of their land. In order to bring out the implications in the context of heterogeneous tastes, we now consider a model where land is owned by people whose only concern is with the effect of the choice of public goods on the land value. We have, for example, a lake in each community that can be used by the residents for two mutually exclusive activities (swimming and boating), and the public decision concerns the proportion, η, of the time for which the lake is devoted to the first of these activities. Individual preferences (which are otherwise independent of location) are given by the distance from their preferred value, η^h:

$$v^h(\eta) = |\eta^h - \eta| \qquad (17\text{-}48)$$

with η^h varying across individuals, with median η^*. This means that, if there are two communities, offering η_1 and η_2 respectively (where $\eta_2 > \eta_1$), then all people with $\eta^h < \frac{1}{2}(\eta_1 + \eta_2)$ live in community 1 and the remainder live in community 2.

The decision about η is made collectively by those owning land in the community, who are assumed to get no direct enjoyment from the public good, either because the local authority is a land development agency rather than a democratic body, or because decisions are made by a generation who are at a stage of the life cycle when they have acquired assets (land) but lost the taste for water sports. The majority voting outcome is to maximize land values, and this is taken to coincide with maximizing the number of people who wish to live in the community.[11] Moreover, it is assumed that each community takes land usage in the other as given. It can then be seen that the position $\eta_1 = \eta_2 = \eta^*$ is an equilibrium of the model. Where the land use is equal to that preferred by the median, neither community can raise land rents by departing from the median, taking the behaviour of the other community as given.

In this equilibrium, the two communities produce exactly the same public goods, in spite of the heterogeneity of tastes. Obviously, this is not a social welfare optimum; it is only the preferences of the marginal individual that are taken into account. The preferences of the intramarginal individuals—virtually the total population—are completely ignored. Any social welfare function that did not assign all the weight to the median individual in society would have the different communities produce different public goods. Moreover, it is quite possible to construct examples where the equilibrium is not only inconsistent with any social welfare function that does not give all weight to the median, but is actually Pareto-inefficient.

Exercise 17-5 Suppose that there are three groups in the population with $\eta^1 = 0$, $\eta^2 = \frac{1}{2}$, $\eta^3 = 1$ and that the numbers in groups 1 and 3 are equal and much larger than in group 2. There is an equilibrium with both communities producing the public good that maximizes the utility of type 2, and group 2 divides itself equally between the two communities. Examine what would be achieved if community 1 were to choose $\eta = 0$ but provide a subsidy to community 2.

The similarity between this model and the standard theories of product differentiation, in particular that derived from the seminal work of Hotelling (1929), should be clear. Indeed, the issues are closely parallel. The number of communities is limited by the returns to scale associated with public goods, while the number of commodities is limited by the returns to scale in production. The market solution involves firms maximizing profits and ignoring the effects of their actions on the profits of others. So too, here, communities do not pursue the correct objective function; they maximize the value of land, rather than social welfare, and ignore the effect on intramarginal individuals and on the other communities.[12]

---

[11] This can be obtained from a model of demands derived from utility maximization where the utility functions are Cobb–Douglas and on the basis of certain assumptions about the formation of expectations regarding future land prices.

[12] We should note that recent work has established the special nature of the Hotelling model, and the problems that arise when there is more than one dimension over which the firms can compete.

Rich and Poor Communities

Differences in tastes are no doubt significant, but probably much more important are differences in endowments. One of the most striking aspects of local government in the United States and other advanced countries is the marked difference in the wealth of local communities.

If the local public good is in fact a publicly provided private good, then there are clear reasons why the rich would be interested in excluding the poor.[13] With the case of pure public goods, with which we are concerned here, there is no additional cost to supplying a further individual within a geographical area: the consumption of the poor does not detract from that of the rich. On the other hand, the rich may be interested in excluding the poor because of differences in the levels of demand for the public goods and the redistribution implied in the method of financing. The poor may vote for a different combination of public goods and taxation, and if there is a specified method of financing (e.g., a property tax) then the taxes paid may not match benefits received.

In order to illustrate the way in which exclusion may be practised we assume, for simplicity, that there are only two groups in the population. The rich, referred to by a superscript R, have income (*per capita*) of M^R, while the poor, referred to by a superscript P, have *per capita* income M^P, where $M^P < M^R$. The income is assumed independent of the number of people living in the community—there are no costs of congestion in terms of diminishing returns. The utility functions are given by $U^P(X^P, G^P)$ and $U^R(X^R, G^R)$. With complete exclusion, the equilibrium for each group is given by maximizing $U^i(X^i, G^i)$ subject to $N^i X^i + G^i = N^i M^i$ where N^i is the number in each group. The solution values are denoted by an asterisk and are shown in Fig. 17-8a.

Now let us suppose first that direct (costless) exclusion can be practised by either group. Each community then compares the utility obtained in the exclusionary equilibrium with that obtainable if they merge. The production possibilities of the merged community are:

$$N^P X^P + N^R X^R + G = N^P M^P + N^R M^R \equiv G_{\text{max}} \qquad (17\text{-}49)$$

If we assume that the tax levied is a proportional income tax at rate t (an assumption that is critical to much of the analysis), then the merged community offers the poor person points along the line joining M^P to G_{max} in Fig. 17-8b, and the rich person points on the line joining M^R to G_{max}.

As drawn in Fig. 17-8b, there is scope for both groups to gain from a merged community. The poor gain if the level of public good is set between

---

[13] This may well be the case with education. The provision of a uniform level of education to all children regardless of the wealth of their parents, financed by a proportional wealth tax, involves in effect considerable redistribution; and this is still greater if taxation is progressive. For analysis of this case, see Stiglitz (1977).

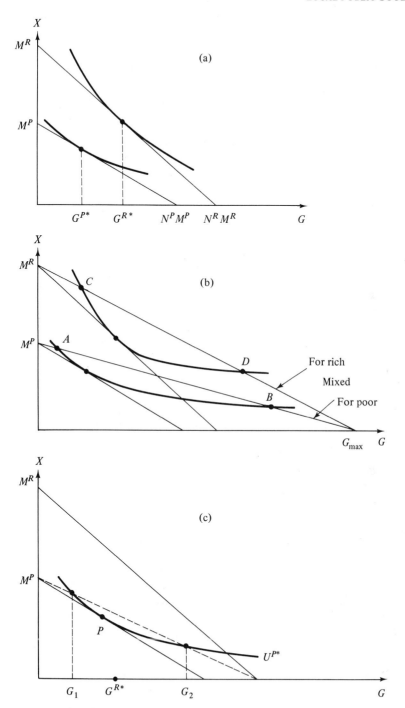

Figure 17-8 Rich and poor communities.

that corresponding to the points A and B, and the rich gain between C and D. However, the outcome depends on the process by which the conflicting interests of rich and poor in the mixed community are reconciled. Suppose that the poor are in a majority, and that they are able to exercise political control. The decision depends on the level of sophistication exercised in voting, and if they vote myopically, the resulting equilibrium may well be inefficient—as we have seen before. Suppose that the poor maximize U^P without regard to the position of the rich. If the resulting level of U^R is less than that obtainable at the exclusionary equilibrium (e.g., to the right of D in Fig. (17-8b)), the rich will opt out. There will be two separate communities, even though both could be better off with a single, integrated community. Since there are no diminishing returns, the social optimum is that where both groups live in one community—and share as fully as possible in the spill-overs from public goods.

How is this affected if direct exclusion is not possible? Suppose that a poor person can choose to live in a rich community if he wishes. In order to preserve a segregated community, the rich are restricted to choosing a tax rate and a level of public spending that do not attract the poor. We can then put the problem of the rich community as

$$\max U^R(X^R, G^R)$$

subject to

$$X^R = (1 - t^R)M^R$$

$$t^R = G^R/N^R M^R$$

$$U^P[(1 - t^R)M^P, G^R] \leqslant U^{P*} \tag{17-50}$$

where U^{P*} is the level that the poor achieve in the exclusionary case. Figure 17-8c shows the solution to this problem diagrammatically. The possibilities open to a single poor person joining the rich community are indicated by the dashed line. Consequently there are two *exclusionary points*. For levels of G^R below G_1 or above G_2 the poor person will not be attracted to the rich community; for other levels of G^R he will be. As shown, the exclusionary constraint is binding. The rich community, in order to exclude the poor, chooses either a higher or a lower level of public expenditure than it would have chosen in the equilibrium where direct exclusion was feasible.[14] Essentially, in the higher equilibrium, the tax rate is so high that the poor cannot afford to live in the community; the amount of private consumption that they are left with is "inadequate". In the lower equilibrium, the government expenditure is very low. The rich can purchase private goods that are "substitutes" for the public good; the poor, however, cannot do this, and thus they prefer to remain in their own communities.

---

[14] We need also to allow for the possibility that the rich do not act collusively and that it may pay individual members of the rich community to join the poor. The relevant budget line joins M^R to $N^P M^P$.

One can observe both extremes of behaviour in rich communities in the United States.

Concluding Comments

The analogy between local public goods that are competitively supplied by different communities and the conventional competitive equilibrium model for private goods is a suggestive one, but, for reasons that we noted in the introduction, the analogy is of more limited validity, and the analysis is of far greater complexity than Tiebout's original article suggested. There are certain circumstances in which communities and individuals exist in just the right proportions so that every community is at the optimal size, and where individuals act non-myopically, in which a local public goods equilibrium is Pareto-efficient. But in the more realistic case, where there is a limited number of jurisdictions, or where people act myopically, equilibrium may not exist, and when it does exist it may not be Pareto-efficient. The equilibria displayed inefficiencies in (1) the numbers of individuals within the community; (2) the level of public goods and the choice of public goods supplied within each community; (3) the number of communities formed; and (4) the matching of individuals together to form communities. Even, therefore, without introducing any social judgements as to the desirability of certain types of community (e.g., favouring integrated communities), there may be strong arguments for intervention by a central authority.

17-5 FISCAL FEDERALISM

In many countries, there are complicated relationships between the local and higher-level authorities (e.g., state and national). The higher-level governments may impose restrictions on the actions of those at the lower level, requiring them, for example, to provide a minimum level of services, placing a maximum on the expenditure on education, imposing a maximum tax rate, etc. The higher-level authorities may provide lump-sum grants (based, say, on the population of the local community); and they may provide grants that are conditional on the local authorities taking certain actions (e.g., they may provide matching grants for certain services).

This raises a complex set of descriptive and normative questions. Since the central authorities do not control the local authorities, the effects of federal programmes may not be those intended; and the central authority must take the reactions of the communities into account. This problem of indirect control is parallel to the design of tax and expenditure policy, where the government had to take into account the reaction functions of individuals. In just the same way, we need to ask what are the appropriate instruments for the central government to employ.

There are several reasons why the central authority may intervene:

1. *Redistribution.* Without central authority intervention, there may be a strong motivation for the formation of local communities of individuals with similar income or wealth, with direct or indirect exclusion of others.
2. *Externalities* (sometimes referred to as spill-overs). The actions of one community have an important effect on externalities for other communities. This is particularly important for education, in countries like the United States, where there is extensive migration between communities. The local government may pay for education, but some part of the benefit may be appropriated by the communities in which the individual resides after he is educated.
3. *Correcting inefficiencies in the local public goods equilibrium.* For instance, in our earlier analysis we have seen that the equilibrium may be Pareto-inefficient with respect to the size of communities, the level and choice of public goods, or the matching of individuals.

These reasons for central government intervention raise the fundamental question as to why there are local governments at all. Why does the central government use local authorities as intermediaries? If it is concerned about redistribution, why does it not attempt to redistribute directly to the individuals involved, rather than indirectly, by giving grants to poorer communities (which presumably also benefit the rich who live within that community)? If there are important spill-overs, as in education, why does not the central authority directly administer and pay for the programme itself? These are of course questions that have been the source of a great deal of political debate, and they are answered differently in each country.

We make no attempt here to resolve such basic questions of government structure. There are however a number of factors that may be seen from our analysis. Some are parallel to those discussed in earlier Lectures. The indirect control problem, with differential information at the centre and in the local units, the revelation of preferences, the consequences of externalities, are all relevant to determining the optimum degree of decentralization. Thus, there may be a trade-off between the desire to redistribute between communities and the degree of knowledge about individual needs (local communities being better informed about the true position of individuals); there may be conflict between provisions that respond to differential needs in different communities and the incentives given to local communities to misrepresent their needs.

In this respect, we can draw on earlier analysis; there are however certain features distinctive to the problem of intergenerational fiscal relations.

Can Local Governments be Treated as Individuals?

Much of the literature on central/local government relationships has treated the latter as if it were acting like an individual. Thus, Williams (1966a) views local communities as having indifference curves between private and public goods with familiar properties, and in the discussion on matching grants (for example, Wilde, 1968), similar assumptions have been made. This however ignores the political structure and the process by which collective decisions are made. There clearly are cases where a single person's preferences are decisive. This applies for example to the median voter model, if the identity of the median is not changed, or to city "bosses" (as in Boskin, 1973a). The structure does however warrant more careful attention.

Of particular concern is the effect of central financing on local government expenditure. Thus, in the United States, the State and Local Fiscal Assistance Act of 1972, based on earlier Heller–Pechman revenue-sharing proposals (Heller, 1966; Pechman, 1965), provided a system of unrestricted cash grants from the federal administration to the states, and then on to local communities. If the community is assumed to have preferences like an individual, the lump-sum grant has a pure income effect. Suppose however that we take account of the fact that the local government is a collectivity with decisions reached via a political process. Does the grant to the local body have the same effect as a set of lump-sum grants to the individual citizens? If it does, then revenue-sharing is simply equivalent to a reduction in federal (lump-sum) taxes with local taxes being increased to finance any rise in public spending.

The answer depends on the political machinery by which decisions are taken, but Bradford and Oates (1971b) argue that under a fairly wide range of conditions the equivalence holds. To illustrate this, they consider the Lindahl process and simple majority rule. In the latter case, with fixed tax shares, standard assumptions about individual preferences ensure single-peakedness and hence a majority voting equilibrium where the median voter's preferences are decisive. If the community receives a lump-sum grant, I, which allows taxes to be reduced for any given level of public goods, then the perceived budget constraint of the median voter shifts by $t_m I$, where t_m is his tax share. Assuming that he remains decisive (the reader is left to work out the case where the median shifts), there is the same effect on the decision about public goods as if he had received a grant direct from the federal government of that amount.

Bradford and Oates recognize that this result may need qualification. The equivalence may fail to hold where there are constraints on the decisions made by the local government. Suppose, to take the example of Bradford and Oates, that the local constitution requires a two-thirds majority for tax rates in excess of some specified level t^*, and that the constitution can be amended only by the same majority. If the tax rate implied by the median choice were in excess of t^*, there may be a constrained equilibrium where there is not a two-thirds majority in favour of increasing the tax rate, but a simple majority (all that is required) oppose any reduction. In this constrained case, a majority favour spending part at least of the federal cash grant on increased public goods, whereas with direct transfers to individuals the constraint on the local tax rate may remain binding and prevent any increase.

The equivalence may also need to be qualified if there are administrative obstacles to the distribution by the federal government of a lump-sum grant to individuals proportional to their tax shares in local spending. It may well be administratively less costly to make the grant to the local authority.

Perhaps most important is the fact that individuals as voters have only limited control over the local government. The authority may enjoy considerable room for manoeuvre, with the electorate responding vigorously only to substantial increases in the local tax rate or serious shortfalls in the provision of local services. Earlier, in Lecture 5, we noted a "corporate veil", such that individuals do not necessarily take fully into account the income accruing to firms in which they are shareholders. In the case of local government there may be a similar phenomenon. Central grants to local authorities may not be fully "integrated" into the income of voters, and revenue-sharing may provide greater scope for the expansion of local public services than otherwise would be possible.

Lump-sum Versus Matching Grants

Revenue-sharing via lump-sum grants has often been seen as an alternative to matching grants where the federal contribution (m) is some proportion of the total local outlay on public goods. This reduces the effective "price" faced by the local government. Analyses based on the local community acting like a single individual (for example, Wilde, 1968) suggest that a matching grant schedule, offering the same tax/expenditure possibility as under the lump-sum grant, will lead to a higher level of local spending. We are in effect considering a compensated change, and the substitution effect alone is relevant. Care does however need to be exercised in extending this result to actual political processes.

The argument is straightforwardly translated to any particular voter in a majority voting equilibrium, but we need to allow for the fact that the identity of the median voter may be changed by the tax (Bradford and Oates, 1971a). This is illustrated in Fig. 17-9, where P denotes the equilibrium under the lump-sum grant. The matching grant schedule that allows P to be chosen is shown by the less steep line, and it is clear that the choice of the person previously at the median shifts to a point such as Q. We need however to consider individuals who previously preferred higher spending than at P, for example with indifference curve $I'I'$. For them, it is conceivable that their preferred level of spending falls. If their preferences are rather different from those of the person previously at the median, it is possible that one of them replaces him as the median voter. None the less, it is clear from Fig. 17-9 that their choice cannot involve a level of the public good lower than that at P. It follows that there is a point on the matching grant schedule, with higher expenditure than under the lump-sum grant, which is preferred by a majority. The conclusion that expenditure will increase is therefore correct in this case, but the amount of the increase does not necessarily correspond to the desired increase of any single voter. It may be more or less than the increase in demand by the person who was previously at the median. (The changes considered are not revenue-neutral; for discussion of the relationship with the taxes necessary to finance the grant, see Sheshinski, 1977.)

Mobility and the Constraints on Taxation

The earlier analysis has demonstrated the importance of geographical mobility as a constraint on the actions of local governments. The local authority has to maximize its objective function (or the objective function of

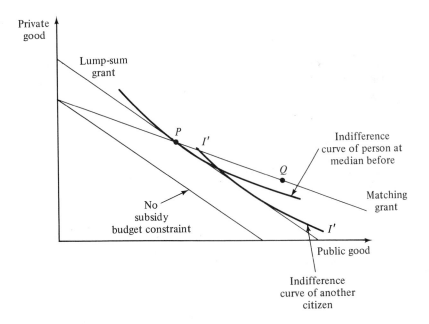

Figure 17-9 Lump-sum and matching grants.

the median voter, if that is the appropriate political model), subject not just to the standard revenue constraint, with fixed population, but also to the constraint that people may leave. This imposes important limitations on the set of taxes that the local authorities can impose.

Not only can individuals leave, but the supply of other factors (like capital) is affected by local taxation. Indeed, in a well functioning national capital market, a tax on capital within a single community will be entirely shifted unless restrictions are imposed on residents investing their capital in other communities. Although such restrictions have some limited efficacy across national borders, they are not allowed internally. Moreover, it may be extremely difficult if not infeasible to monitor some kinds of taxes locally. When production of a commodity occurs within several communities (at different stages) it may be impossible to ascertain how much of the profits generated was due to the activity within any particular community. (The problem is parallel to that of taxing multinational companies, where extensive use is made of transfer pricing to minimize the tax burden.)

At the central government level, the design of policy is now constrained by the reactions both of individuals and of lower-level governments. The positive theory of local decision-making is therefore of considerable importance, underlying one of the themes of earlier Lectures. In this Lecture, we have made strongly simplified assumptions about the decision-making process, relying particularly on the majority voting assumption. This is not, however, a particularly satisfactory basis, and a great deal remains to be done on the analysis of local government behaviour.

READING

The basic article, from which much of the literature starts, is Tiebout (1956); see also the discussion in Samuelson (1958b). Our discussion here draws extensively on Stiglitz (1977), Flatters, Henderson and Mieszkowski (1974), and Arnott and Stiglitz (1980). On the theory of clubs, see Buchanan (1965) and Pauly (1967). On fiscal federalism, see Oates (1972).

EIGHTEEN

PUBLIC ECONOMICS: THEORY AND POLICY

18-1 ON THE SOURCES OF DISAGREEMENT IN POLICY ANALYSIS

Concern with public economics is motivated largely by the major policy questions that face society at the present time and those that it is likely to face over the coming years. There is continuing debate over such issues as the reform of the tax system, the level of expenditure on national defence, the rationalization of social security, and the performance of public enterprises and agencies. This debate may well seem quite removed from the analysis we have presented, much of which has been conducted at a highly theoretical level. We have indeed emphasized that our intention has been to provide insights, not answers to current policy problems. We are not seeking to examine in detail proposals for reform, or to persuade the reader that particular changes would be desirable.[1]

At the same time, we hope that the analysis has provided tools that can be used—with due caution—to investigate the degree of success or failure of present fiscal policies and the desirability of proposed reforms. Although we cannot do more than illustrate this belief, we have given in Sections 18-2 and 18-3 some examples of how the analysis may be helpful in thinking about policy. For this purpose we have taken two issues in the reform of personal taxation (the case for an expenditure tax, and the extension of the tax base under a comprehensive income tax) and two major areas of public spending (income maintenance and state education). Before turning to

---

[1] Not least because of the very differing views we individually hold about the merits of different reforms.

these, we consider in more general terms the role which can be played by the analysis.

One of the most important functions of the analysis is to identify the source of disagreements. What, for example, are the essential elements in the case for an expenditure tax that distinguishes the proponents from the opponents? Is it disagreement about the consequences of the tax? Or is it disagreement about the purposes of taxation? We consider in turn the different sources of controversy, and how they are illustrated by the earlier analysis.

Failure to Trace the Full Consequences

Disagreements may arise because of the failure to trace the full consequences of a particular policy. We have repeatedly noted that there may be indirect or general equilibrium effects. These may reinforce the direct effect. Alternatively, they may work in the opposite direction and undermine the intended consequences. It may have been that the number of windows in a person's house was a good surrogate for his ability to pay, and the window tax (enacted in England in 1696 under the Act for Making Good the Deficiency of the Clipped Money) may have appeared an equitable basis for taxation. It was presumably not the intention of those who levied the tax that windows should be blocked up, but this consequential effect reduced the impact of the tax (and led to dark houses).

The assessment of policy must take account of the responses of individuals or firms, and this has been illustrated at numerous points in these Lectures. In Lectures 2 and 3 we noted that people may be led by the income tax to direct their economic activities into forms that are untaxed (such as home production) or taxed at a lower rate (capital gains). Even when economic activity is not significantly changed, efforts are made to alter the appearances in such a way as to lower the tax rate, e.g., converting ordinary income into capital gains, or changing the form of compensation for individuals. The responses may also show up in asset prices. Where a tax increase is confidently expected, asset prices may fall prior to its imposition, so that the effect is felt by those who owned assets then rather than when the tax is actually introduced.

The way in which the analysis goes most often astray however is in its failure to allow for the general equilibrium consequences (both short and long run) on which we have focused so much attention. As a result of these repercussions, the incidence of a tax or expenditure may be shifted on to people other than those on whom the tax is levied. In Lecture 6, we considered how a tax on capital in one sector may lower the return to capital in the rest of the economy, and lead to a reduction in wages. In Lecture 8 we showed how, as a result of changes in the supply of capital, a tax on capital might be borne entirely by workers, the after-tax rate of return being the same as before the tax. A tax that was apparently progressive, in terms of its effect on the distribution of income, might—as a result of changes in factor supplies and in their allocation—have the reverse effect.

One should not conclude from this that government action is inefficacious. While it is possible that ill-considered policy may have the reverse of its intended impact, this does not mean that these effects cannot be allowed for in the design of policy. What is needed is a clear recognition of the general equilibrium nature of the economy and an adequate model within which the second-round effects may be investigated. This however brings us to a second form of disagreement—about how the economic system operates.

Differences About the Correct Model of the Economy

Both sides in a debate may agree that it is necessary to consider the full implications of the policy and to have a full-scale general equilibrium model of the economy, but may disagree fundamentally about the correct nature of this model.

A major example of this kind of disagreement concerns the assumptions about the nature of competition. The predictions of the responses of firms to the corporate profits tax depend critically on the nature of the markets within which firms operate. We examined two main cases—perfect competition and monopolistic competition—and noted that the effects were markedly different. The behaviour of oligopolies is likely to be still different, and a fuller analysis of alternative assumptions is necessary. It should also be recognized that the degree of competition (the nature of the market structure) may itself be affected by tax policy and governmental regulation (e.g., the regulation of business may act to increase the fixed costs associated with production).

Differences concerning the correct model may arise in other respects. We have referred to controversies surrounding the use of an aggregate production function. It is our view that simplified assumptions may be adequate for demonstrating the potential range of effects, but a thorough analysis of a particular tax or expenditure requires a full-scale specification of the production technology and of the derived relationship between factor use and factor prices. The treatment of disequilibrium, particularly in the labour and commodity markets, is another example. Some people may feel that equilibrium models can provide no insights; others are of the opinion that they represent a useful abstraction for some purposes. Yet another instance is provided by the distributional models of Lecture 9, where one reaches quite different conclusions using a model where bequests moderate the forces of chance from those obtained in a model where bequests are a major force leading to the concentration of property.

Differing perspectives are also significant in assessing the literature on the optimal design of taxation. As we discussed in Lecture 11, the view of the state as pursuing the maximization of social welfare ignores the many factors influencing and constraining its activities. Indeed, some people would regard the behaviour of the state as fully determined by the specification of the objectives of voters, politicians and bureaucrats, with discussion of optimality being mere intellectual superstructure. Most people hold a position somewhere between these two extremes—of pure welfare maximization and complete determinism—and this choice of position determines the weight attached to the arguments discussed in Part Two.

Differences About Empirical Magnitudes

Disagreements may arise even when people agree about the theoretical model and about the possible patterns of response, because they differ about the magnitude of key parameters. Thus, it may be accepted that there are income and substitution effects of an income tax on work effort, but some people believe the substitution effect to be small relative to the income effect and others believe the converse. People may agree that a tax on savings could reduce savings but disagree as to whether it is empirically significant.

Such differences arise to a considerable extent because of the difficulty of obtaining reliable evidence. In Part One we have discussed a variety of sources of evidence on the behaviour of households (labour supply, savings and portfolio decisions) and of firms (investment and the cost of capital). None of the different sources—interview, cross-section, time-series or experimental—is without shortcomings. Many of the relevant effects are difficult, if not impossible, to observe directly. Those who believe that the income tax is a disincentive may argue that hours worked are relatively little affected, but that the effort put in while on the job is seriously reduced. Even where the relevant data are available, there are often problems of interpretation, e.g., identifying the extent to which observed variations in behaviour are due to differences in tax rates.

This raises questions concerning the allocation of resources to research. For example, the substantial programme of work on the New Jersey and other experiments was in direct response to the need for better evidence on labour supply elasticities when assessing proposals for a negative income tax. One of the aims of Part Two has been to draw attention to the parameters that appear to be critical in designing policy. In part, the conclusions are pessimistic. For example, the optimum indirect tax structure appeared (Lecture 14) to depend on properties of the demand functions, which are not readily estimated. In the same way, the optimum tax treatment of savings may be sensitive to the interest elasticity of labour supply, which has received very little notice. None the less, some of the findings are constructive and allow us to use available evidence. One example is the conclusion that, where the government is restricted in its ability to reallocate consumption over time, it may be concerned with the absolute level of savings, and hence it is the total rather than the compensated elasticity that is of concern.

Disagreements over Objectives

People obviously may differ in their recommendations about policy because they have different objectives or differing views about how economists should discuss normative issues. It is not the function of these Lectures to resolve such disagreements; however, the analysis may go some way towards clarifying the nature of objectives and their relationship to the proposed policies.

First, many popularly expressed goals are too ill defined to be applied in a meaningful way. In this case an important contribution is to make precise exactly what is entailed. For instance, it is sometimes stated that the government should do the "most good for the largest number of people". This, as it stands, is virtually meaningless. The official handbook on *The British System of Taxation* describes as a principle that "the burden should be fairly spread without impairing national prosperity". How should such a statement be interpreted?

Second, certain objectives of government policy are put forward because it is believed that their achievement will help secure a more basic goal. They are in effect "intermediate" objectives. In this case, analysis may help clarify the relationship with the true, underlying, objective. There is, for instance, a widespread belief that in tax policy the government ought to pursue a policy of "neutrality". This is a secondary objective; the primary objective, with which most people who ascribe to the neutrality objective would agree, is some notion of economic efficiency (say, Pareto efficiency). A tax that is not neutral is distortionary; it causes inefficiencies. This, as we have said repeatedly, is not correct. Even a lump-sum tax would have allocative effects. Yet (by definition) it is non-distortionary. Similarly, the fact that the income tax may lead to no changes in work effort, because the income and substitution effects cancel, does not mean that there is no loss in welfare. Nor can one demonstrate neutrality in terms of uniform rates of taxation. If lump-sum taxes are not feasible, then the policy that minimizes distortion may well involve taxing different commodities at different rates. Another example is provided by those who implicitly or explicitly argue that the tax structure should minimize the number of distortions, e.g., those who favour the consumption tax on the grounds that it only affects the work–leisure decision.

Third, there are objectives the nature of which cannot really be assessed without exploring their full consequences. By analysing their implications, sometimes in idealized situations, one can help to assess the extent to which they are likely to command support. If it turns out that a particular principle leads consistently to unacceptable conclusions, then this may lead to a revision of objectives. As we noted in Lecture 11, public economics has been an important test-bed for principles of economic justice in recent years. This is well illustrated by the Rawlsian objective which we have discussed on a number of occasions. It also applies to the utilitarian approach. The confrontation of these principles with particular policy trade-offs has, for example, clarified their relationship with egalitarianism. Similarly, the position of vertical and horizontal equity has been illuminated. In contrast to the claims sometimes made, horizontal equity is not simply a consequence of welfare maximization (for example, we noted several situations where a utilitarian objective would lead to identical people being treated differently). The principle of horizontal equity can in fact be given a number of different interpretations, and we distinguished between versions concerned with "ends" and versions concerned with "means".

Objectives differ in their informational requirements. This, we saw, lay at the heart of the debate about interpersonal comparability. Alternatively, there may be agreement on the basis of comparison, but uncertainty about the form of the social welfare function—the degree of aversion to inequality. There is a trade-off between the assumptions made about the objective function and the extent to which different policies can be ranked. One of the aims of the analysis is to clarify the relationship between the information the government is assumed to have concerning social objectives and the policy conclusions that can be reached. In certain circumstances, differing goals may still lead to the same policy. A utilitarian cake-cutter will arrive at the same division as a Rawlsian, if utility functions are identical. In other cases, the principles are likely to be in opposition, and the calibration of the sensitivity of the conclusions to the form of the objectives is an important exercise.

Role of Formal Analysis

In tracing the full consequences of policy, in exploring alternative models, in relating the theory to the empirical evidence, and in clarifying the nature of objectives and the relationship between them, public economics has an important role to play. In our view, this role can be fulfilled only if the analysis is based on a fully articulated theoretical framework and a precise statement of its implications. This view is reflected in the fact that this book has a ratio of equations to words well above the norm for public finance texts. Although we appreciate that this can be a barrier, we are quite convinced that there is a substantial gain in terms of clarity of argument and the avoidance of ambiguity.

The need for formal analysis is particularly apparent in two of the areas we have emphasized—the general equilibrium effects and the design of policy when the first-best cannot be attained. In both cases, intuition may help explain the results obtained mathematically but on its own may be an unreliable guide. Some of the findings are quite apparent, but others run counter to what appears to be intuitively obvious. At the end of a lengthy footnote seeking to explain in words a proof of Cournot, Edgeworth comments that "the general reader will perhaps be disappointed in his expectation of simplicity. I don't know that much has been effected by this cumbrous simplification, except to show the great superiority of the genuine mathematical method" (Edgeworth, 1925, p. 91).

18-2 THINKING ABOUT POLICY: TAXATION

Surveys in the United States have shown that the American public considers tax reform the third most pressing national problem, ranking only behind the control of inflation and reduction in the crime rate. In this section, we describe briefly how the analysis of these Lectures may be employed to discuss two important policy issues: the case for an expenditure tax, and the comprehensive income tax base. The treatment is necessarily very limited; the main purpose is to show the tools "in action", illustrating both strengths and weaknesses.

The Expenditure Tax

The idea that direct taxation should be based on expenditure, or consumption, rather than income has a long history and has had many distinguished supporters including J. S. Mill, Alfred Marshall, I. Fisher (1937) and Lord Kaldor (1955). Recently, the idea has received renewed attention in the United States (US Treasury, *Blueprints for Basic Tax Reform*, 1977), in the United Kingdom (report of the Meade Committee (Meade, 1978)), in Sweden (Lodin, 1976), and elsewhere.

The arguments made in support of the expenditure tax have shown an interesting shift over time. For Marshall and others the tax was taken to be self-evidently preferable in theory to an income tax, but it was felt to be incapable of practical implementation, a position that led Keynes to conclude that, although "perhaps theoretically sound, it is practically impossible" (quoted in Kaldor, 1955, p. 12). In contrast, the recent arguments "stand that conventional wisdom almost precisely on its head, [suggesting] that the theoretical arguments are, at best, rather indecisive and that the case for expenditure tax is essentially practical" (Kay, 1978).

The theoretical case is made on grounds of both efficiency and equity. The *efficiency* argument has commonly been based on the distortion associated with the taxation of savings under an income tax: "income tax lowers the rate of return on savings and thus distorts everyone's choice between consuming today and saving for a higher level of consumption in the future.... The consumption tax would eliminate this wasteful distortion" (Feldstein, 1976e, p. 16). However, an expenditure tax is not itself lump-sum, and affects, for example the work–leisure choice. One lesson that we have learnt from second-best welfare economics is that one cannot evaluate tax systems simply by comparing the *number* of distortions involved: one has to consider the magnitude of the various effects and their interaction, and there is no *prima facie* case that the exemption of the interest income is desirable.

The balancing of one source of deadweight loss against another is one of the central concerns of Lectures 12–14 on optimum taxation, and several authors have sought to apply these results in putting forward a case for an expenditure tax. Confining attention first to linear tax schedules, then if the Ramsey framework is applied directly, treating consumption at different dates as different commodities, the results of Lecture 12 can be interpreted as showing that the optimum tax is uniform where the wealth elasticities of consumption are unity (as with the Cobb–Douglas utility function). This argument is made by, among others, Bradford (1978). However, as we have shown in Lecture 14, it is necessary to formulate the problem in an explicit intertemporal framework in order to bring out fully the issues involved. Moreover, the optimum tax structure depends on the range of instruments at the disposal of the government.

The standard Ramsey formulation is in fact of limited interest, since with identical individuals a uniform lump-sum tax can attain the first-best solution. In an intertemporal economy, not only might the government use lump-sum taxation to raise any requisite revenue, but also, by varying the lump-sum tax (or payment) at different dates of a person's life, it can regulate the pattern of capital accumulation to achieve a first-best allocation of consumption over time. Even when individuals differ in their wage rates, so long as the government can impose an optimal nonlinear income tax, and through one instrument or another (e.g., debt policy) can control the growth path of the economy, then, applying the results of Lecture 14, we can find conditions under which an expenditure tax is optimal, in particular where labour is weakly separable from commodities (Ordover and Phelps, 1979).

This result provides theoretical support for the expenditure tax; on the other hand, it is based on strong assumptions. If (1) there are restrictions on the government's ability to control the intertemporal allocation of consumption, or (2) the government is not free to vary the nonlinear income tax schedule, or (3) the weak separability condition does not hold, or (4) individuals differ in other respects in addition to their wage rates, then we cannot appeal to the result. There is no necessary presumption that the expenditure tax is optimal. On the other hand, this does not mean that there is support for an income tax, which implies equality between the rates of tax on capital and other income. While a non-zero rate of tax on interest income may raise welfare, it does not follow that it would be desirable to set it at the same level as the tax on earned incomes.

A rather different kind of efficiency argument is that concerned with the absolute level of savings. This focuses on the possibility that a tax on interest income may change the *level* of savings, and not simply on the *distortion*; i.e., it is concerned with the uncompensated rather than simply the compensated effect. This indeed emerges from the welfare analysis. If the government is unable to achieve the desired intertemporal allocation of consumption, then it is the absolute change in savings that is relevant; e.g., does the tax move the steady-state capital stock nearer the modified golden rule? This highlights an important feature—that when the no-tax equilibrium is not necessarily first-best, then it is not just compensated elasticities that are relevant—and has implications for empirical work on the determinants of savings. On the other hand, one has to consider the use of other instruments. Why have they failed to achieve the desired level of savings? Cannot debt/monetary policy be adjusted to increase the savings rate? Can social security provisions be varied as an alternative to taxing/subsidizing capital income?

The first *equity* argument for an expenditure tax is that it is fairer to tax people on what they consume rather than on what they produce. This is frequently made in terms of emotive examples, such as the celebrated quotation from Hobbes: "what reason is there, that he which laboureth much, and sparing the fruits of his labour, consumeth little, should be more charged, than he that living idly, getteth little and spendeth all he gets" (*Leviathan*, Ch. xxx). As is noted by Kay and King (1978), this example is misleading, since much of its force comes from the differences in leisure, which are taxed under neither an income tax nor an expenditure tax. The expenditure tax does not allow us to base the tax on potential rather than actual flows; it does not get round the difficulties in incorporating unobservable elements relevant to the opportunity set such as leisure.[2]

The second equity argument is that in terms of the lifetime budget constraint developed in Lecture 9. According to this, the expenditure tax with lifetime cumulation, and an unchanging tax schedule, would correspond to the individual budget constraint in a perfect capital market. Equivalently, it could be achieved by a tax on all wage and other receipts apart from interest income. The assumptions of lifetime cumulation, of a stable tax schedule, and of a perfect capital market are however important.

---

[2] An example is provided by consumption within the firm. Both an expenditure tax and an income tax would have difficulty in determining the extent to which business expenses are concealed remuneration in kind.

A tax that levies increasing marginal tax rates on annual expenditure does not correspond to the lifetime concept; nor is this ensured when the tax rates vary over time. The imperfections in the capital market were emphasized in Lecture 9. Where, for example, individuals face differing possibilities for borrowing or lending, neither lifetime income nor lifetime expenditure provides a complete description of opportunity sets.

This brief discussion has, we hope, served to show that the earlier analysis provides definite insights into the efficiency and equity arguments but leads to no clear presumption in favour of either expenditure or income taxation. It may well be therefore that the administrative aspects are decisive. Although we have on occasion drawn attention to this subject, we cannot at present call on a well-developed body of analysis that deals with the administration of taxation. None the less, there are some points that can be made. Most important is the critical role played by observability in the design of tax structures. Distinctions that make clear economic sense may not be easily enforceable. For example, the distinction between wage and capital income is one that economists make regularly. On the other hand, in unincorporated enterprises, even if the entrepreneur could distinguish between the two, which is itself problematic, there is effectively no way that the government can.

The fact that certain variables are not easily observable means that one may have to make distinctions for administrative reasons (e.g., between capital in the corporate and non-corporate sectors) that one would not otherwise make and that generate both distortions and additional problems of equity. Much of the administrative burden is associated with these kinds of distinctions. We should note in particular those concerned with deferred compensation, depreciation, capital gains, and owner-occupation. For discussion of these, and other administrative problems, see Meade (1978), Kay and King (1978) and Mieszkowski (1977).

Comprehensive Income Tax

The comparison of the administrative characteristics of expenditure and income taxation must be based on a detailed investigation of how the pure concept is translated into actual tax legislation. In the case of the income tax, this has been the subject of considerable debate. In particular, it is argued that the tax base as operated falls short of the comprehensive ideal, and that the base should be broadened, thus allowing a reduction in tax rates.

The case for a comprehensive income tax base typically starts from the Haig–Simons definition of income (discussed in Lecture 9), accepting this as a measure of ability to pay. It then focuses on the way in which the tax codes depart from this ideal definition, including:

1. differential rates of tax on different types of income (e.g., capital gains);

2. total exemption of certain forms of income (e.g., fringe benefits, imputed rent on owner-occupied houses and other assets, interest on state and local bonds in the United States);
3. deduction of certain kinds of expenditure (e.g., medical expenses, interest payments, charitable contributions, state and local taxes);
4. tax credits for certain items (e.g., child care expenses).

The case for eliminating these provisions is based on equity and efficiency considerations. It is argued that horizontal equity requires that people with the same Haig–Simons income should face the same tax burden, and that vertical equity would be improved by the extension of the tax base, since the exemptions and deductions provide disproportionate benefit to the better off (see Fig. 2-1). On efficiency grounds, it is suggested that the specific provisions lead to a misdirection of resources (e.g., too great an allocation of savings to home ownership) and that in general the reduction in tax rates, facilitated by a broadening of the base, would reduce the welfare loss associated with the income tax.

In assessing the validity of these arguments, the earlier analysis is again useful. The status of horizontal equity is crucial. As we have seen, this is best interpreted as an independent principle, constraining the range of instruments open to the government. It may therefore be decided as a matter of principle that no departures from Haig–Simons can be justified.[3] But this assumes what is to be established—that the Haig–Simons basis is the appropriate one.

If such a position is not taken, then one can see that there may be arguments for departing from the comprehensive tax base. First, there may be efficiency gains, for example from treating different forms of income differently, and the trade-off between equity and efficiency may indicate that some differentiation is optimal. Second, where the government cannot vary tax rates freely with ability to pay, the exemption of certain items may improve the redistributive effectiveness of the tax; for example, exemption of housing outlays may increase the effective progression of the tax. Moreover, it may be argued from an equity standpoint that ability to pay ("enjoyable consumption" on a utilitarian approach) is not exactly captured by the Haig–Simons definition, and that adjustments are necessary, for example, for differences in needs (such as medical expenses). Third, the tax policy of a federal government may have to be devised taking the behaviour of lower-level governments as given, and special provisions for local taxes or borrowing may be desirable given these constraints.

The first of these is illustrated by the treatment of the earnings of different family members. There is empirical evidence (discussed in Lecture 2)

---

[3] A related, but different, argument is that, even though departures are in theory desirable, the working of the political machinery is such that the actual exemptions that emerge are socially undesirable. A blanket prohibition of exemptions may therefore be preferable.

that the elasticity of labour supply by married women is significantly greater than that for male heads of household (this may of course change with changing cultural mores). Arguments based on the optimum tax results (Lectures 12 and 13) suggest that we may therefore want to have lower rates of tax on the earnings of married women. (The treatment of married couples in most tax systems has the reverse effect of raising the marginal rate on the secondary worker while lowering that on the primary worker.) A similar illustration is provided by the tax treatment of savings. As we have seen, the optimum tax framework does not lead to conclusive results, but there is no presumption that capital and labour income should, on efficiency grounds, be taxed at the same rate.

The second argument concerns equity. Suppose initially that individuals differ only in earning power; then the results of Lecture 14 allow us to see the conditions under which the deductibility of certain expenditures, say housing, does not add to the redistributive effectiveness of government policy. Where there are no restrictions on the use of nonlinear schedules, and where there is weak separability between housing and labour, then the net price of housing should at the margin be equal to the pre-tax price. This again brings out the interdependence between the detailed design of policy and the range of instruments assumed to be at the government's disposal. If there were restrictions on the income tax schedules that could be levied—for administrative or other reasons—then deductibility might be desirable.

The case for deductibility may however be based on the view that the item is relevant to ability to pay. A good example is provided by medical expenses, where it may be argued that ability to pay should be measured by income net of "necessary" medical outlays (where these are not state-provided or covered by universal insurance). The difficulty clearly arises of identifying necessary expenditure, and the optimal treatment of deductions, discussed in Lecture 14, must balance the inequity of not accounting for differing need against the distortion that may be introduced by encouraging medical expenses.

Charitable contributions raise still further issues. On one view, they are transfers that should simply be deducted from income in assessing ability to pay. On an alternative view, they form part of endowments but may warrant special treatment on the grounds that they have externalities. The case for a tax deduction would then depend on the extent to which they contribute to social goals (e.g., the proportion of charitable giving that is redistributive or directed at the provision of public goods), and on the responsiveness of contributions to tax incentives. Clearly, part of the difficulty is administrative. In principle we would like to limit the provision for charitable contributions to the provision of public goods or redistributive payments, but it is often very difficult to distinguish between goods that are largely "public" from those with a substantial private element. There is an additional question concerning the desirability of allowing the private determination of the allocation of public goods/distributional payments (as tax deductibility essentially does). If the charitable contribution were limited to public goods, then—so long as the private charitable provision (e.g., of hospitals) did not exceed the level desired publicly—it would not appear to make any difference. However, there are likely to be divergences in the kind, if not the level, of provision from that desired socially—and these costs have to be balanced against any advantages from decentralized provision.

The treatment of local government taxes and borrowing introduces a number of questions related to those discussed in Lectures 16 and 17. Many of the services supplied by local authorities are really publicly provided private goods rather than pure public goods. To the extent that deductibility of state and local taxes used to finance such goods is equivalent to the deductibility of the expenditures themselves, we need to ask why they should be treated differently from other categories of spending. Why should outlays on refuse collection by local authorities be deductible, but not the purchase of garden incinerators? In Lecture 16 we suggested that there might be arguments for the public provision of education. It might, for example, be optimal to provide a basic level of education free to everyone, and to impose a tax on expenditures on education in excess of this amount. The provision of education by local authorities, coupled with the deductibility under the income tax of state and local taxes, effectively provides a subsidy (at the margin) for this category of expenditure. At the same time, it introduces a bias in favour of the collective provision of these services.[4]

Finally, arguments for departing from the comprehensive tax base may be seen as a variation on the standard second-best analysis. Where the first-best (Haig–Simons) tax base is not achievable, then it does not follow that we should try and approximate it as closely as possible (Bossons, 1965). If, for example, the true income base deducts necessary but unobservable health costs, then we may have to accept that the second-best tax base involves exempting some elements that strictly should not be deducted. If imputed rent (which should be included) is not observable, then it may be that the second-best tax base would involve a deduction for the housing

---

[4] Where the interest on state and local bonds is not taxable, this lowers the interest rate that has to be paid on such bonds, and therefore acts as an effective subsidy to state and local expenditures. The effects also depend on whether individuals can borrow without restriction. If individuals could borrow freely to finance purchases of state and local bonds, only those with the highest marginal tax rate would purchase such bonds, and the rate of interest would be such as to equalize rates of return for this group. (This is a "tax arbitrage" argument of the kind discussed in Lecture 5.) The restriction on borrowing imposed in the United States effectively raises the interest cost to the local communities.

costs of renters. In that sense, we would want to move away from the comprehensive definition.

This line of argument may be illustrated by reference to the treatment of local governments. Suppose that the federal government is required by the provisions of the constitution to exempt local taxes paid. There is then an incentive for the use of tax rather than bond finance at the local level. Reducing debt by \$1 costs the taxpayer with marginal tax rate, t, an amount \$$(1-t)$, on which he would have earned after-tax interest of \$$r(1-t)^2$ per year; this is less than the cost of financing the debt, which is \$$r(1-t)$ per year. On the other hand, if the interest on local bonds is exempt, and all individuals have the same marginal tax rate, then he is indifferent (the interest cost to the local government falls to $r(1-t)$). In this respect—and in these rather special circumstances—the *further* exemption ensures neutrality with respect to financing. This does not in itself suggest that full exemption is optimal, since we have to take account of the general subsidy provided to local government expenditure, but it shows how the different provisions may interact.

We have focused on the definition of the tax base; a closely related question is how exceptions from the comprehensive definition should be treated—as deductions or as tax credits. Many of the considerations discussed are also relevant to this issue. For example, with a tax deduction the implicit price of medical care falls with income, and this may affect the allocation of resources. It is often argued that deductions are vertically inequitable; on the other hand, this assumes the validity of the Haig–Simons definition, whereas an alternative view would deduct medical costs when assessing ability to pay. These arguments cannot however be considered in isolation, and we need to take account of the different interactions. The effective difference between credits and exemptions arises only where marginal rates of tax differ, and we have to place the choice between them in the context of the wider question of the design of the tax schedule. If it is then difficult to arrive at simple answers, that is one of the lessons of the analysis.

18-3 THINKING ABOUT POLICY: EXPENDITURES

The Lectures have paid rather more attention to taxation than to expenditure. At the same time, many of the same questions arise. The issue of incidence, for example, applies as much to expenditures as to taxes. And there are close interrelations between taxes and spending, as is illustrated by the examples of income maintenance and education taken here.

Income Maintenance

For much of the early history of social security, it was treated as quite separate from the tax system. It has however come to be realized that the two are closely interrelated, and that we need to adopt a consistent approach to the design of the two branches of government policy. It has indeed been proposed by many people, including Milton Friedman and James Meade in the 1940s and presidential candidates and chancellors of the Exchequer in the 1970s, that income maintenance be integrated with income taxation in a negative income tax or social dividend scheme.

The essence of such proposals is captured by considering a simple modification of the linear income tax examined at a number of stages in these Lectures. The simple straight line schedule incorporates a minimum income guarantee, G, and a tax rate t on all income, up to a break-even level of income, equal to G/t. Suppose now that we combine it with the standard "positive" income tax above the break-even level, with a marginal tax rate τ. The design of the tax schedule/income maintenance system then amounts to the choice of G, t and τ, subject to the condition that they be feasible. In particular, is it possible to improve on the existing system, which involves a high marginal tax rate for some low-income families and inadequate support for others?

The earlier analysis has indicated several critical issues. The first is the effect on pre-tax incomes, particularly the supply of labour (and savings). As we have seen, this is a complicated question, and individuals may be affected very differently. People at different levels of income may exhibit quite varied responses. The effect of a change in the income maintenance system would make some people better off, some worse off; it would raise the marginal tax rate for some, but lower it for others. The impact would depend on existing benefits received, on family circumstances, and other factors. This variation makes it difficult to interpret the empirical evidence—even in this relatively well researched area.

The investigation of the responses of pre-tax income may allow the government to trace out the feasible combinations of policies—to see what tax rate, τ, is implied for those above the break-even level by programmes of differing degrees of generosity. The balancing of the cost (in terms of τ) against the benefits (raising G and lowering t) clearly depends on the nature of social objectives. These do however interact with the factors entering the constraints, particularly the elasticity of labour supply. Thus, a Rawlsian objective may still lead to a relatively low tax rate, where this generates a higher revenue and hence a higher guaranteed income. The Rawlsian objective may indeed stop short of maximizing the guarantee, where the least-advantaged person is in employment.

The design of income maintenance illustrates again the need to take account of the other instruments at the disposal of the government. As we, noted in Lecture 11, the full range may include not just income-related taxes. and benefits but also wage-related taxes and benefits (depending on the information available to the government). We need to consider the relative merits of income subsidies and wage subsidies (Kesselman, 1973). More generally, there is the relationship with categorical social insurance programmes. The guarantee under the negative income tax is typically taken to be differentiated only in relation to family size, and possibly age. Suppose however that we can characterize different groups, who vary in earning capacity or needs or in other relevant respects. Should we treat them differently?

In effect, social insurance involves a payment to people who satisfy certain eligibility criteria unrelated to income (e.g., having retired, not having a job, certified ill, etc.), where the amount of the benefit may or may not be related to income (e.g., the retirement pension may have an earnings rule). If the people can be identified without error, then the use of such categorical programmes can be shown to raise welfare (Akerlof, 1978), and we can see from the earlier analysis the form that the programme is likely to take. We may, for example, want to have a higher guarantee and a lower tax rate for retired people than for the population of working age, on the grounds that the needs of the former are greater and that their labour supply (where non-zero) may be more elastic.

The use of categorical programmes depends on it being possible to identify people at reasonable cost and with an acceptable degree of error. This is one of the issues that attracts most public attention. Where the accuracy is less than 100 per cent, the effectiveness of the categorical approach is lessened, and its superiority may be called into question; in addition, there are questions of horizontal equity. The optimum design of taxation in the presence of such errors must balance the loss of welfare caused by errors in classification of taxation against the advantages from the differentiation (Stern, 1977). More broadly, considerations of administration must consider the costs to recipients. The experience with income-related benefits has shown (Atkinson, 1969) that the "take-up" rate is considerably less than 100 per cent, reflecting the pecuniary or psychic costs associated with claiming benefits.

In the assessment of proposals for income maintenance, the general equilibrium and longer-run effects may well be important, although they are frequently ignored. We have referred to the response of individual labour supply, but the implications for the general equilibrium need to be followed through. Such effects, undoubtedly important in historical debate on the relief of poverty, are of lesser significance when the group affected is relatively small, but concentration in particular occupations and regions may lead to a significant response. The long-run consequences may work through several different mechanisms, including those relating to education, to access to well-paying jobs, and to the accumulation and passing on of material wealth.

State Education

Public education has been the subject of considerable controversy, ranging over the financing of the school systems, the relationship between state and private schools, and the structure of the state school system. In the United Kingdom, attention has focused on the replacement of selective with comprehensive schools, the size of state support to higher education, and on whether restrictions should be imposed on private education. In the United States, discussion has centred on the marked inequality in educational expenditure between school districts, on the provision of compensatory education for disadvantaged groups within society, on public support (possibly through tax deductions or educational vouchers) of private education, and on the financing of higher education.

The analysis of alternative educational policies is seriously handicapped by our limited understanding of the relation between expenditure and outcome (for example, in terms of earning power). For instance, it is often asserted that large variation in state expenditure per child on education is a major factor leading to inequality in incomes. This is based on the view that differential spending is likely to lead to inequality in educational attainment, and this will exacerbate inequality of incomes. These empirical propositions have been the subject of considerable disagreement, and we cannot attempt to discuss them here. We therefore assume for the purposes of argument that the linkages hold to at least a limited extent.

On the assumption that educational expenditure provides economic advantage (it may also of course generate consumption benefits), we have to consider how this publicly provided private good should be supplied.[5] A straightforward application of the analysis of Lecture 16 suggests that the level should be centrally determined, with a balance of equity and efficiency considerations. On a utilitarian approach, expenditure would be allocated according to its effect at the margin. There is no reason why this should be expected to lead to compensatory education, and the policy may well involve a lower allocation of resources to the less able. In contrast, an objective that attaches weight to differences in outcome, such as the Rawlsian principle, is more likely to lead to a compensatory policy. In both cases, account needs to be taken of the interaction with the tax system. Part of the pecuniary return to education is collected in income tax; on the other hand, the government is typically limited in its ability to levy redistributive taxes.

The allocation of education deduced from the maximization of welfare may however conflict with other principles advanced in connection with education. The first of these is that of local autonomy: that communities ought to have the right to decide on the amount of education provided to their children. This means that if we wish to influence educational expenditure—e.g., to equalize it across communities (an input equal policy)—then we have to do it indirectly, through some system that leads

---

[5] There are clearly elements of pure publicness (externalities) about education, but for present purposes it appears adequate to treat it as a private good.

communities to choose different levels of education from those they currently do. One proposal that has received extensive discussion is that of a tax on the expenditures of rich communities and a subsidy on those of poor communities. The particular form that is sometimes suggested is the following: a community pays taxes tW, where W denotes its wealth *per capita* and t is its tax rate (chosen by the community) and receives educational resources $t\bar{W}$, where $\bar{W}$ is the mean over all communities.

The implication of this formula is that the rich communities face a higher effective price of education than do poorer communities. But rich communities also have a higher income. Suppose the major determinants of expenditures on education are simply "income" and "price". Then, if the price response is less than the income response, this will reduce inequality in expenditures but will not eliminate it; but if the price response is greater than the income response, the rich communities will actually spend less on education than the poor.

This suggests in turn a basic problem with this proposal, which is related to a second principle often invoked: the right of parents to send their children to private schools. It would pay parents in rich communities to close down their state schools and to have only private schools. (Since they may by law be required to provide some level of education, in practice this may amount to providing a bare minimum.)[6] The constraints imposed by this second principle—the ability of parents to opt out of state education—are even more important when we consider the *distribution* of educational expenditure. Consider, for instance, the extent of the provision of compensatory education for the disadvantaged. The existence of compensatory education effectively raises the cost to other children. This provides parents (voting selfishly) with an incentive to vote for less state education and, possibly, to opt out of the state school system altogether.

This brief discussion highlights how the introduction of prior constraints—local autonomy and parental choice—coupled with decentralized decision-making by majority voting leads to a problem considerably more complex than those treated in these Lectures. It does however have some of the same features of "indirect control" that have been emphasized in many applications.

---

[6] There may be some wedge, provided by deductibility of taxes from the income tax and the fact that local bonds are tax-exempt, that means that a person in a community with a per student wealth 25 per cent greater than the mean would be willing to vote for public education provided his marginal tax rate exceeded 25 per cent. Allowing tax deductibility of private education would, in this case, have dramatic effects on the viability of this kind of scheme.

18-4 POLICY REFORM AND POLITICAL ECONOMY

This Lecture has concentrated so far on the arguments for and against particular tax or expenditure policies; it has not considered the process of reform, i.e., the way in which a policy change is introduced and the political mechanism by which it is achieved.

As we have emphasized in Lecture 12, the results on the optimum design of policy can be applied to the more limited goal of characterizing *improvements* in policy, and this is possibly the most useful interpretation. The aim should be to describe conditions under which a step can be made in a welfare-improving direction—with specified objectives and constraints on policy. Thus, we may conclude that, if the labour supply of wives is sufficiently elastic, the partial exemption of their earnings would raise tax revenue and increase the transfer that can be made to disadvantaged groups. This does not require us to say that the exemption is optimal or to describe the optimum—which may be a considerable distance from the present position.

The recognition that policy change is likely to be gradual, or piecemeal, takes on particular significance when we allow for uncertainty about the parameters of the model and the acquisition of information. In the preceding Lectures, incomplete information has played a key role, but we have not allowed explicitly for the revision of the government's views in the light of further evidence. The process may however be better seen as one of continual refinement: of a groping towards a better set of policies. Thus, the enactment of the tax exemption for wives may provide further evidence about labour supply response, and may lead to revision of the previously estimated parameters. In turn, this may lead to policy reversals, where predicted effects have failed to materialize.

A second important feature of the partial reform process is that a step in one period may close options in later periods. It is conceivable that application of the principle of horizontal equity may prevent tax changes where the effects have been capitalized in asset values (Feldstein, 1976d) or where long-term decisions have been made on the assumption that they would continue. Suppose that the government grants a tax exemption to a particular firm, and this is capitalized in the value of its shares. If at a later date, the government wishes to abolish the exemption, this would impose a capital loss on the then shareholders, none of whom may have enjoyed the initial windfall gain. Having made the initial concession, as a partial step,[7] the government may be prevented from attaining the optimum by considerations of horizontal equity.

---

[7] In Lecture 15, we noted that the process of tax reform may involve temporary inefficiencies in production (Guesnerie, 1977).

The design of a process of policy reform must equally take account of political constraints. What are political constraints is of course a subject of considerable debate. What does it mean to say that policy X is "politically unfeasible"? It may mean little more than that it is not acceptable to those currently in power, whereas much of history consists of the politically impossible becoming possible.

In order to provide content to the concept of political feasibility, one needs to examine the relationship of policy to the structure of government and political institutions. Proposals have to be sold to those responsible for their adoption. Legislators must be convinced not only that the objective is desirable but also that it can be achieved by the means proposed and that there are no unacceptable side-effects. In this, experts and interest groups play a critical role—indeed, this is one of the main ways in which economists may seek to influence the course of events. Interest groups may not only attempt to sway public opinion but may also use the threat of political and economic power. This applies both to broad "principles" of policy and to its translation into legislation. At the administrative stage, the interests of bureaucrats may lead to policies being diverted from their intended functions, and special interests may again be influential.

These very real features of government behaviour—and the wider political structure—must be taken into account in any realistic assessment of the prospects for reform. In this return to "political economy", a great deal remains to be done.

BIBLIOGRAPHY

Aaron, H. J. (1975), "Cautionary notes on the experiment" in *Work Incentives and Income Guarantees*, J. A. Pechman and P. M. Timpane (eds), Brookings Institution, Washington DC.

—— (ed.) (1976), *Inflation and the Income Tax*, Brookings Institution, Washington DC.

Aaron, H. J. and M. C. McGuire (1969), "Efficiency and equity in the optimal supply of a public good", *Review of Economics and Statistics*, **51**, 31–39.

—— and —— (1970), "Public goods and income distribution", *Econometrica*, **38**, 907–920.

Abbott, M. and O. Ashenfelter (1976), "Labour supply, commodity demand and the allocation of time", *Review of Economic Studies*, **43**, 389–412.

Ahsan, S. M. (1974), "Progression and risk-taking", *Oxford Economic Papers*, **26**, 318–328.

—— (1976), "Taxation in a two-period temporal model of consumption and portfolio allocation", *Journal of Public Economics*, **5**, 337–352.

Akerlof, G. A. (1978), "The economics of 'tagging'", *American Economic Review*, **68**, 8–19.

Allais, M. (1948), "Le problème de la coordination des transports et la théorie économique", *Revue Economique Politique*, **58**, 212–271.

Allen, F. (1979), M.Phil. thesis, University of Oxford.

Allingham, M. G. (1972), "The measurement of inequality", *Journal of Economic Theory*, **5**, 163–169.

Allingham, M. G. and A. Sandmo (1972), "Income tax evasion: a theoretical analysis", *Journal of Public Economics*, **1**, 323–338.

Alt, J. and A. Chrystal (1977), "Endogenous government behaviour", University of Essex Discussion Paper.

Ando, A. and F. Modigliani (1963), "The 'life cycle' hypothesis of saving: aggregate implications and tests", *American Economic Review*, **53**, 55–84.

Arnott, R. (1978), unpublished paper, Queen's University.

Arnott, R. and J. E. Stiglitz (1980), "Aggregate land rents, aggregate transport costs and expenditure on public goods", *Quarterly Journal of Economics*, **97**,

Arrow, K. J. (1951), *Social Choice and Individual Values*, John Wiley, New York (2nd edn 1963).

—— (1962), "The economic implications of learning by doing", *Review of Economic Studies*, **29**, 155–173.

—— (1965), *Aspects of the Theory of Risk-Bearing*, Yrjö Jahnssonin Säätiö, Helsinki.

—— (1970a), *Essays in the Theory of Risk-Bearing*, North-Holland, Amsterdam.

—— (1970b), "The organisation of economic activity: issues pertinent to the choice of market versus non-market allocation" in *Public Expenditure and Policy Analysis*, R. H. Haveman and J. Margolis (eds), Markham, Chicago.

—— (1971a), "Equality in public expenditure", *Quarterly Journal of Economics*, **85**, 409–415.

—— (1971b), "Political and economic evaluation of social effects and externalities" in *Frontiers of Quantitative Economics*, M. D. Intriligator (ed.), North-Holland, Amsterdam.

—— (1973), "Some ordinalist–utilitarian notes on Rawls's theory of justice", *Journal of Philosophy*, **70**, 245–263.

Arrow, K. J. and F. H. Hahn (1971), *General Competitive Analysis*, Oliver and Boyd, Edinburgh.

Arrow, K. J. and R. C. Lind (1970), "Uncertainty and the evaluation of public investment decisions", *American Economic Review*, **60**, 364–378.

Ashenfelter, O. (1978), "The labour supply response of wage earners" in *Welfare in Rural Areas*, J. L. Palmer and J. A. Pechman (eds), Brookings Institution, Washington DC.

Ashenfelter, O. and J. Heckman (1973), "Estimating labor-supply functions" in *Income Maintenance and Labor Supply*, G. G. Cain and H. W. Watts (eds), Rand McNally, Chicago.

—— and —— (1974), "The estimation of income and substitution effects in a model of family labor supply", *Econometrica*, **42**, 73–85.

Ashworth, J. and D. T. Ulph (1977), "On the structure of family labour supply decisions", University of Stirling discussion paper.

Asimakopoulos, A. and J. B. Burbidge (1974), "The short-period incidence of taxation", *Economic Journal*, **84**, 267–288.

Atkinson, A. B. (1969), *Poverty in Britain and the Reform of Social Security*, Cambridge University Press, London.

—— (1970), "On the measurement of inequality", *Journal of Economic Theory*, **2**, 244–263.

—— (1971), "Capital taxes, the redistribution of wealth and individual savings", *Review of Economic Studies*, **38**, 209–228.

—— (1972), "Maxi min and optimal income taxation", paper presented at the Budapest Meeting of the Econometric Society.

—— (1973), "How progressive should income tax be?" in *Essays in Modern Economics*, M. Parkin and A. R. Nobay (eds), Longman, London.

—— (1975a), "La 'maxi-min' et l'imposition optimale des revenus", *Cahiers du Séminaire d'Econométrie*, Nr 16.

—— (1975b), *The Economics of Inequality*, Oxford University Press, Oxford.

—— (1976), "The income tax treatment of charitable contributions" in *Public and Urban Economics*, R. E. Grieson (ed.), Lexington Books, Lexington, Mass.

—— (1977a), "Housing allowances, income maintenance and income taxation" in *The Economics of Public Services*, M. S. Feldstein and R. P. Inman (eds), Macmillan, London.

—— (1977b), "Optimal taxation and the direct versus indirect tax controversy", *Canadian Journal of Economics*, **10**, 590–606.

—— (1979), "Horizontal equity and the distribution of the tax burden" in *The Economics of Taxation*, H. J. Aaron and M. J. Boskin (eds), Brookings Institution, Washington DC.

—— (1980), "The distribution of income and the taxation of inheritance" in *Essays in Honour of James Meade*, G. M. Heal and G. A. Hughes (eds), Allen and Unwin, London.

Atkinson, A. B. and A. J. Harrison (1978), *Distribution of Personal Wealth in Britain*, Cambridge University Press, London.

Atkinson, A. B. and A. Sandmo (1977), "The welfare implications of personal income and consumption taxes", University College London Discussion Series, revised 1979.

Atkinson, A. B. and N. H. Stern (1974), "Pigou, taxation and public goods", *Review of Economic Studies*, **41**, 119–128.

Atkinson, A. B. and N. H. Stern (1979), "On labour supply and commodity demands", SSRC Programme on Taxation, Incentives and the Distribution of Income, Discussion Paper.

Atkinson, A. B. and J. E. Stiglitz (1969), "A new view of technological change", *Economic Journal*, **79**, 573–578.

—— and —— (1972), "The structure of indirect taxation and economic efficiency", *Journal of Public Economics*, **1**, 97–119.

—— and —— (1976), "The design of tax structure: direct versus indirect taxation", *Journal of Public Economics*, **6**, 55–75.

Averch, H. and L. L. Johnson (1962), "Behavior of the firm under regulatory constraint", *American Economic Review*, **52**, 1052–1069.

Bailey, E. E. (1973), *Economic Theory of Regulatory Constraint*, Lexington Books, Lexington, Massachusetts.

Balasko, Y. (1978), "Economic equilibrium and catastrophe theory: an introduction", *Econometrica*, **46**, 557–569.

Ballentine, J. G. (1977), "Non-profit-maximising behavior and the short run incidence of the corporation income tax", *Journal of Public Economics*, **7**, 135–146.

Ballentine, J. G. and I. Eris (1975), "On the general equilibrium analysis of tax incidence", *Journal of Political Economy*, **83**, 633–644.

Barlow, R., H. E. Brazer and J. N. Morgan (1966), *Economic Behavior of the Affluent*, Brookings Institution, Washington DC.

Barlow, R. and G. R. Sparks (1964), "A note on progression and leisure", *American Economic Review*, **54**, 372–377.

Barna, T. (1945), *Redistribution of Income Through Public Finance in 1937*, Oxford University Press, Oxford.

Barr, N. A., S. R. James and A. R. Prest (1977), *Self-Assessment for Income Tax*, Heinemann, London.

Barro, R. J. (1974), "Are government bonds net wealth?", *Journal of Political Economy*, **82**, 1095–1117.

Barro, R. J. and H. I. Grossman (1976), *Money, Employment and Inflation*, Cambridge University Press, London.

Barry, B. M. (1970), *Sociologists, Economists and Democracy*, Collier Macmillan, London.

Baumol, W. J. (1958), "On the theory of oligopoly", *Economica*, **25**, 187–198.

—— (1967), "Macroeconomics of unbalanced growth: the anatomy of urban crisis", *American Economic Review*, **57**, 415–426.

Baumol, W. J. and D. F. Bradford (1970), "Optimal Departures from Marginal Cost Pricing", *American Economic Review*, **60**, 265–283.

Baumol, W. J. and A. K. Klevorick (1970), "Input choices and rate of return regulation: an overview of the discussion", *Bell Journal of Economics*, **1**, 162–190.

Baumol, W. J. and W. E. Oates (1975), *The Theory of Environmental Policy*, Prentice-Hall, Englewood Cliffs, NJ.

Becker, G. S. (1965), "A theory of the allocation of time", *Economic Journal*, **75**, 493–517.

—— (1974), "A theory of social interactions", *Journal of Political Economy*, **82**, 1063–1093.

Ben-Porath, Y. (1975), "The years of plenty and the years of famine: a political business cycle", *Kyklos*, **28**, 410–413.

Berglas, E. (1976), "Distribution of tastes and skills and the provision of local public goods", *Journal of Public Economics*, **6**, 409–423.

Bergson, A. (1972), "Optimal pricing for a public enterprise", *Quarterly Journal of Economics*, **86**, 519–544.

Bergstrom, T. C. and R. P. Goodman (1973), "Private demands for public goods", *American Economic Review*, **63**, 280–296.

Bevan, D. L. (1974), "Savings, inheritance and economic growth", unpublished paper, Oxford University.

Bhatia, K. B. (1979), "Corporate taxation, retained earnings and capital formation", *Journal of Public Economics*, **11**, 123–134.

Bierwag, G. O. and M. A. Grove (1967), "Portfolio selection and taxation", *Oxford Economic Papers*, **19**, 215–220.

Bierwag, G. O., M. A. Grove and C. Khang (1969), "National debt in a neoclassical growth model: comment", *American Economic Review*, **59**, 205–210.

Bischoff, C. W. (1969), "Hypothesis testing and the demand for capital goods", *Review of Economics and Statistics*, **51**, 354–368.

—— (1971), "The effect of alternative lag distributions" in *Tax Incentives and Capital Spending*, G. Fromm (ed.), North-Holland, Amsterdam.

Bishop, R. L. (1968), "The effects of specific and ad valorem taxes", *Quarterly Journal of Economics*, **82**, 198–218.

Black, D. (1948), "On the rationale of group decision-making", *Journal of Political Economy*, **56**, 23–34.

—— (1958), *The Theory of Committees and Elections*, Cambridge University Press, Cambridge.

Blinder, A. S. (1973), "A model of inherited wealth", *Quarterly Journal of Economics*, **87**, 608–626.

—— (1975), "Distribution effects and the aggregate consumption function", *Journal of Political Economy*, **83**, 447–475.

Bliss, C. J. (1975), *Capital Theory and the Distribution of Income*, North-Holland, Amsterdam.

Blum, W. J. and H. Kalven (1963), *The Uneasy Case for Progressive Taxation*, University of Chicago Press and Phoenix Books, London.

Boadway, R. W. and N. Bruce (1979), "Depreciation and interest deductions and the effect of the corporation income tax on investment", *Journal of Public Economics*, **11**, 93–105.

Bohm, P. (1971), "An approach to the problem of estimating the demand for public goods", *Swedish Journal of Economics*, **73**, 55–66.

—— (1972), "Estimating demand for public goods: an experiment", *European Economic Review*, **3**, 111–130.

Boiteux, M. (1956), "Sur la gestion des monopoles publics astreints à l'équilibre budgétaire", *Econometrica*, **24**, 22–40.

—— (1971), "On the management of public monopolies subject to budgetary constraints" (translation of Boiteux, 1956), *Journal of Economic Theory*, **3**, 219–240.

Borcherding, T. E. (ed.) (1977), *Budgets and Bureaucrats*, Duke University Press, Durham, North Carolina.

Borcherding, T. E. and R. T. Deacon (1972), "The demand for the services of non-federal governments", *American Economic Review*, **62**, 842–853.

Bös, D. (1978), "Cost of living indices and public prices", *Economica*, **45**, 59–69.

Boskin, M. J. (1967), "The negative income tax and the supply of work effort", *National Tax Journal*, **20**, 353–367.

—— (1973a), "Local government tax and product competition and the optimal provision of public goods", *Journal of Political Economy*, **81**, 203–210.

—— (1973b), "The economics of labor supply" in *Income Maintenance and Labour Supply*, G. G. Cain and H. W. Watts (eds), Rand McNally, Chicago.

—— (1975a), "Efficiency aspects of the differential tax treatment of market and household economic activity", *Journal of Public Economics*, **4**, 1–25.

—— (1975b), "Notes on the tax treatment of human capital" in *Conference on Tax Research 1975*, Department of the Treasury, Washington DC.

—— (1977), "Social security and retirement decisions", *Economic Inquiry*, **15**, 1–25.

——— (1978), "Taxation, saving, and the rate of interest", *Journal of Political Economy*, **86**, S3–S27.

Boskin, M. J. and M. D. Hurd (1978), "The effect of social security on early retirement", *Journal of Public Economics*, **10**, 361–377.

Boskin, M. J. and L. J. Lau (1978), "Taxation, and aggregate factor supply, preliminary estimates" in *Compendium of Tax Research 1978*, Department of the Treasury, Washington DC.

Boskin, M. J. and E. Sheshinski (1978), "Optimal income redistribution when individual welfare depends on relative income", *Quarterly Journal of Economics*, **92**, 589–602.

Bossons, J. (1965), "A comprehensive tax base as a tax reform goal", *Journal of Law and Economics*, **8**, 327–363.

Bosworth, B. (1975), "The stock market and the economy", *Brookings Papers on Economic Activity*, 257–290.

Bowen, H. R. (1943), "The interpretation of voting in the allocation of economic resources", *Quarterly Journal of Economics*, **58**, 27–48.

Bowen, W. G., R. G. Davis and D. H. Kopf (1960), "The public debt: a burden on future generations?", *American Economic Review*, **50**, 701–706.

Bradford, D. F. (1978), "The case for a personal consumption tax", paper presented to Brookings Conference.

Bradford, D. F. and W. E. Oates (1971a), "Towards a predictive theory of intergovernmental grants", *American Economic Review*, Papers and Proceedings, **61**, 440–448.

——— and ——— (1971b), "The analysis of revenue-sharing in a new approach to collective fiscal decisions", *Quarterly Journal of Economics*, **85**, 416–439.

Bradford, D. F. and H. S. Rosen (1976), "The optimal taxation of commodities and income", *American Economic Review*, Papers and Proceedings, **66**, 94–101.

Break, G. F. (1957), "Income taxes and incentives to work: an empirical study", *American Economic Review*, **47**, 529–549.

——— (1974), "The incidence and economic effects of taxation" in *The Economics of Public Finance*, A. Blinder *et al.*, Brookings Institution, Washington DC.

Brechling, F. P. R. (1975), *Investment and Employment Decisions*, Manchester University Press, Manchester.

Brennan, G. (1976), "The distributional implications of public goods", *Econometrica*, **44**, 391–399.

Brennan, G. and J. M. Buchanan (1977), "Towards a tax constitution for Leviathan", *Journal of Public Economics*, **8**, 255–274.

——— and ——— (1978), "Tax instruments as constraints on the disposition of public revenues", *Journal of Public Economics*, **9**, 301–318.

Breton, A. (1974), *The Economic Theory of Representative Government*, Macmillan, London.

Brittain, J. A. (1966), *Corporate Dividend Policy*, Brookings Institution, Washington DC.

——— (1972), *The Payroll Tax for Social Security*, Brookings Institution, Washington DC.

Broome, J. (1975), "An important theorem on income tax", *Review of Economic Studies*, **42**, 649–652.

Brown, C. V. and E. Levin (1974), "The effects of income taxation on overtime", *Economic Journal*, **84**, 833–848.

Brown, C. V., E. Levin and D. T. Ulph (1976), "Estimates of labour hours supplied by married male workers in Great Britain", *Scottish Journal of Political Economy*, **23**, 261–277.

Brown, E. C. (1948), "Business income taxation and investment incentives" in *Income, Employment and Public Policy, Essays in Honor of Alvin H. Hansen*, L. A. Metzler *et al.* (eds), Norton, New York.

Browning, E. K. (1971), "Incentive and disincentive experimentation for income maintenance policy purposes: note", *American Economic Review*, **61**, 709–712.

Bruno, M. (1972), "Market distortions and gradual reform", *Review of Economic Studies*, **39**, 373–383.

―――― (1976), "Equality, complementarity and the incidence of public expenditures", *Journal of Public Economics*, **6**, 395–407.

Buchanan, J. M. (1958), *Public Principles of Public Debt*, Irwin, Homewood, Illinois.

―――― (1960), *Fiscal Theory and Political Economy*, University of North Carolina Press, Chapel Hill, North Carolina.

―――― (1965), "An economic theory of clubs", *Economica*, **32**, 1–14.

―――― (1968), *The Demand and Supply of Public Goods*, Rand McNally, Chicago.

―――― (1969), "External diseconomies, corrective taxes and market structure", *American Economic Review*, **59**, 174–177.

―――― (1970), *The Public Finances* (3rd edn), Irwin, Homewood, Illinois.

―――― (1972), "Toward analysis of closed behavioral systems" in *Theory of Public Choice*, J. M. Buchanan and R. D. Tollison (eds), University of Michigan Press, Ann Arbor, Michigan.

―――― (1976a), "Barro on the Ricardian equivalence theorem", *Journal of Political Economy*, **84**, 337–342.

―――― (1976b), "A Hobbesian interpretation of the Rawlsian difference principle", *Kyklos*, **29**, 5–25.

Buchanan, J. M. and M. Z. Kafoglis (1963), "A note on public goods supply", *American Economic Review*, **53**, 403–414.

Buchanan, J. M. and G. Tullock (1962), *The Calculus of Consent*, University of Michigan Press, Ann Arbor, Michigan.

Burmeister, E. and A. R. Dobell (1970), *Mathematical Theories of Economic Growth*, Collier-Macmillan, New York.

Burtless, G. and J. A. Hausman (1978), "The effect of taxation on labor supply: evaluating the Gary negative income tax experiment", *Journal of Political Economy*, **86**, 1103–1130.

Cain, G. G. and M. D. Dooley (1976), "Estimation of a model of labor supply, fertility, and wages of married women", *Journal of Political Economy*, **84**, S179–199.

Cain, G. G. and H. W. Watts (eds) (1973), *Income Maintenance and Labour Supply*, Rand McNally, Chicago.

Cartter, A. M. (1955), *The Redistribution of Income in Postwar Britain*, Yale University Press, New Haven, Connecticut.

Carver, T. N. (1904), "The minimum sacrifice theory of taxation", *Political Science Quarterly*, **19**, 66–79.

Cass, D. (1965), "Optimum growth in an aggregative model of capital accumulation", *Review of Economic Studies*, **32**, 233–240.

Cass, D. and J. E. Stiglitz (1970), "The structure of investor preferences and asset returns, and separability in portfolio allocation", *Journal of Economic Theory*, **2**, 122–160.

―――― and ―――― (1972), "Risk aversion and wealth effects on portfolios with many assets", *Review of Economic Studies*, **39**, 331–354.

Caves, R. E. and R. W. Jones (1977), *World Trade and Payments*, Little, Brown, Boston.

Cazenave, P. and C. Morrisson (1974), "Income redistribution in France, Great Britain and United States", *Revue Economique*, **25**, 635–671.

Central Statistical Office (1979), "The effects of taxes and benefits on household income 1977", *Economic Trends*, **303**, 97–130.

Chipman, J. S. (1974), "The welfare ranking of Pareto distributions", *Journal of Economic Theory*, **9**, 275–282.

Clarke, E. H. (1971), "Multipart pricing of public goods", *Public Choice*, **11**, 17–33.

―――― (1972), "Multipart pricing of public goods: an example" in *Public Prices for Public Products*, S. Mushkin (ed.), Urban Institute, Washington DC.

Coen, R. M. (1971), "The effect of cash flow on the speed of adjustment" in *Tax Incentives and Capital Spending*, G. Fromm (ed.), North-Holland, Amsterdam.

Coen, R. M. and B. G. Hickman (1970), "Constrained joint estimation of factor demand and production functions", *Review of Economics and Statistics*, **52**, 287–310.

Colm, G. and H. Tarasov (1940), *Who Pays the Taxes?* Temporary National Economic Committee, Monograph 3, Washington DC.

Colwyn Committee (1927), *Report of the Committee on National Debt and Taxation*, HMSO, London.

Conlisk, J. (1977), "An exploratory model of the size distribution of income", *Economic Inquiry*, **15**, 345–366.

Cooper, G. (1952), "Taxation and incentive in mobilization", *Quarterly Journal of Economics*, **66**, 43–66.

Cootner, R. and E. Helpman (1974), "Optimal income taxation for transfer payments", *Quarterly Journal of Economics*, **88**, 656–670.

Corlett, W. J. and D. C. Hague (1953), "Complementarity and the excess burden of taxation", *Review of Economic Studies*, **21**, 21–30.

Dalton, H. (1954), *Principles of Public Finance*, Routledge and Kegan Paul, London.

Danziger, L. (1976), "A graphic representation of the Nash and Lindahl equilibria in an economy with a public good", *Journal of Public Economics*, **6**, 295–307.

Dasgupta, P. S. and J. E. Stiglitz (1972), "On optimal taxation and public production", *Review of Economic Studies*, **39**, 87–103.

—— and —— (1974), "Benefit–cost analysis and trade policies", *Journal of Political Economy*, **82**, 1–33.

David, M. (1968), *Alternative Approaches to Capital Gains Taxation*, Brookings Institution, Washington DC.

David, P. A. and J. L. Scadding (1974), "Private savings: ultrarationality, aggregation and 'Denison's law'", *Journal of Political Economy*, **82**, 225–249.

Davidson, J. E. H., D. F. Hendry, F. Srba and S. Yeo (1978), "Econometric modelling of the aggregate time-series relationship between consumers' expenditure and income in the United Kingdom", *Economic Journal*, **88**, 661–692.

Davis, O. A., M. A. H. Dempster and A. Wildavsky (1966), "A theory of the budgetary process", *American Political Science Review*, **60**, 529–547.

Davis, O. A. and A. B. Whinston (1967), "Piecemeal policy in the theory of second best", *Review of Economic Studies*, **34**, 323–331.

Deaton, A. S. (1977), "Equity, efficiency and the structure of indirect taxation", *Journal of Public Economics*, **8**, 299–312.

—— (1978), "Optimal taxes and the structure of preferences", mimeo, University of Bristol, 1978.

—— (1979), "The distance function in consumer behaviour with applications to index numbers and optimal taxation", *Review of Economic Studies*,

Debreu, G. (1959), *Theory of Value*, John Wiley, New York.

—— (1976), "Regular differentiable economics", *American Economic Review*, **66**, 280–287.

Diamond, P. A. (1965), "National debt in a neoclassical growth model", *American Economic Review*, **55**, 1125–1150.

—— (1968), "Negative taxes and the poverty problem: a review article", *National Tax Journal*, **31**, 288–303.

—— (1970), "Incidence of an interest income tax", *Journal of Economic Theory*, **2**, 211–224.

—— (1973a), "Consumption externalities and imperfect competitive pricing", *Bell Journal of Economics*, **4**, 526–538.

—— (1973b), "Taxation and public production in a growth setting" in *Models of Economic Growth*, J. A. Mirrlees and N. H. Stern (eds), Macmillan, London.

—— (1975a), "Inflation and the comprehensive tax base", *Journal of Public Economics*, **4**, 227–244.

—— (1975b), "A many-person Ramsey tax rule", *Journal of Public Economics*, **4**, 335–342.

—— (1978), "Tax incidence in a two good model", *Journal of Public Economics*, **9**, 283–299.

Diamond, P. A. and D. L. McFadden (1974), "Some uses of the expenditure function in public finance", *Journal of Public Economics*, **3**, 3–21.

Diamond, P. A. and J. A. Mirrlees (1971), "Optimal taxation and public production I: production efficiency and II: tax rules", *American Economic Review*, **61**, 8–27 and 261–278.

—— and —— (1973), "Aggregate production with consumption externalities", *Quarterly Journal of Economics*, **87**, 1–24.

Diamond, P. A. and J. E. Stiglitz (1974), "Increases in risk and in risk aversion", *Journal of Economic Theory*, **8**, 337–360.

Diamond, P. A. and M. Yaari (1972), "Implications of the theory of rationing for consumer choice under uncertainty", *American Economic Review*, **62**, 333–343.

Diewert, W. E. (1974), "Applications of duality theory" in *Frontiers of Quantitative Economics II*, M. D. Intriligator and D. Kendrick (eds), North-Holland, Amsterdam.

—— (1978), "Optimal tax perturbations", *Journal of Public Economics*, **10**, 139–177.

—— (1979), "Duality Approaches to Microeconomic Theory" in *Handbook of Mathematical Economics*, K. J. Arrow and M. Intriligator (eds), North-Holland, Amsterdam.

Dixit, A. K. (1970), "On the optimum structure of commodity taxes", *American Economic Review*, **60**, 295–301.

—— (1975), "Welfare effects of tax and price changes", *Journal of Public Economics*, **4**, 103–123.

—— (1976a), *Optimization in Economic Theory*, Oxford University Press, London.

—— (1976b), *The Theory of Equilibrium Growth*, Oxford University Press, Oxford.

—— (1976c), "Public finance in a Keynesian temporary equilibrium", *Journal of Economic Theory*, **12**, 242–258.

—— (1979), "The role of investment in entry-deterrence", Warwick Economic Research Paper 140.

Dixit, A. K. and K. J. Munk (1977), "Welfare effects of tax and price changes: a correction", *Journal of Public Economics*, **8**, 103–107.

Dixit, A. K. and A. Sandmo (1977), "Some simplified formulae for optimal income taxation", *Scandinavian Journal of Economics*, **79**, 417–423.

Dixit, A. K. and J. E. Stiglitz (1977), "Monopolistic competition and optimum product diversity", *American Economic Review*, **67**, 297–308.

Dodge, D. A. (1975), "Impact of tax, transfer, and expenditure policies of government on the distribution of personal income in Canada", *Review of Income and Wealth*, **21**, 1–52.

Domar, E. D. and R. A. Musgrave (1944), "Proportional income taxation and risk-taking", *Quarterly Journal of Economics*, **58**, 388–422.

Dorfman, R. (1975), "Note on a common mistake in welfare economics", *Journal of Political Economy*, **83**, 863–864.

Douglas, P. H. (1934), *The Theory of Wages*, Macmillan, New York.

Downs, A. (1957), *An Economic Theory of Democracy*, Harper and Row, New York.

Drèze, J. H. (1964), "Some postwar contributions of French economists to theory and public policy", *American Economic Review*, **54** (Supplement).

Drèze, J. H., J. Jaskold-Gabszewicz and A. Postlewaite (1977), "Disadvantageous monopolies and disadvantageous endowments", *Journal of Economic Theory*, **16**, 116–121.

Drèze, J. H. and F. Modigliani (1972), "Consumption decisions under uncertainty", *Journal of Economic Theory*, **5**, 308–335.

Drèze, J. H. and D. de la Vallée Poussin (1971), "A tâtonnement process for public goods", *Review of Economic Studies*, **38**, 133–150.

Due, J. F. (1963), *Government Finance* (3rd edn), Irwin, Homewood, Illinois.

Due, J. F. and A. F. Friedlaender (1973), *Government Finance* (5th edn), Irwin, Homewood, Illinois.

Eatwell, J. L. (1971), "On the proposed reform of corporation tax", *Bulletin of the Oxford University Institute of Economics and Statistics*, **33**, 267–274.

Edgeworth, F. Y. (1897), "The pure theory of taxation", *Economic Journal*, **7**, 46–70, 226–238 and 550–571 (reprinted in Edgeworth, 1925).

——— (1925), *Papers Relating to Political Economy*, Volume II, Royal Economic Society, Macmillan, London.

Eisner, R. and M. I. Nadiri (1968), "Investment behavior and neo-classical theory", *Review of Economics and Statistics*, **50**, 369–382.

Eisner, R. and R. Strotz (1963), "Determinants of business investment" in *Impacts of Monetary Policy: A Series of Research Studies Prepared for the Commission of Money and Credit*, D. B. Suits *et al.*, Prentice-Hall, Englewood Cliffs, New Jersey.

Ekelund, R. B. (1973), "Public economics at the Ecole des Ponts et Chaussées: 1830–1850", *Journal of Public Economics*, **2**, 241–256.

Ekern, S. (1971), "Taxation, political risk and portfolio selection", *Economica*, **38**, 421–430.

Ekern, S. and R. Wilson (1974), "On the theory of the firm in an economy with incomplete markets", *Bell Journal of Economics and Management Science*, **5**, 171–180.

Ellickson, B. (1973), "A generalization of the pure theory of public goods", *American Economic Review*, **63**, 417–432.

Fair, R. C. (1971), "The optimal distribution of income", *Quarterly Journal of Economics*, **85**, 551–579.

Farquharson, R. (1969), *Theory of Voting*, Yale University Press, New Haven, Connecticut.

Farrell, M. J. (1958), "In defence of public-utility price theory", *Oxford Economic Papers*, **10**, 109–123; amended version in R. Turvey (ed.) (1968), *Public Enterprise*, Penguin, Harmondsworth.

Feldstein, M. S. (1969), "The effects of taxation on risk-taking", *Journal of Political Economy*, **77**, 755–764.

——— (1970a), "Inflation, specification bias, and the impact of interest rates", *Journal of Political Economy*, **78**, 1325–1339.

——— (1970b), "Corporate taxation and dividend behaviour", *Review of Economic Studies*, **37**, 57–72.

——— (1972a), "Distributional equity and the optimal structure of public prices", *American Economic Review*, **62**, 32–36.

——— (1972b), "Equity and efficiency in public sector pricing: the optimal two-part tariff", *Quarterly Journal of Economics*, **86**, 175–187.

——— (1973a), "Tax incentives, corporate saving and capital accumulation in the United States", *Journal of Public Economics*, **2**, 159–171.

——— (1973b), "On the optimal progressivity of the income tax", *Journal of Public Economics*, **2**, 357–376.

——— (1974a), "Social security, induced retirement and aggregate capital accumulation", *Journal of Political Economy*, **82**, 905–926.

——— (1974b), "Tax incidence in a growing economy with variable factor supply", *Quarterly Journal of Economics*, **88**, 551–573.

——— (1974c), "Incidence of a capital income tax in a growing economy with variable savings rates", *Review of Economic Studies*, **41**, 505–513.

——— (1976a), "Social security and saving: the extended life cycle theory", *American Economic Review*, Papers and Proceedings, **66**, 77–86.

——— (1976b), "Personal taxation and portfolio composition: an econometric analysis", *Econometrica*, **44**, 631–650.

——— (1976c), "Perceived wealth in bonds and social security: a comment", *Journal of Political Economy*, **84**, 331–336.

——— (1976d), "On the theory of tax reform", *Journal of Public Economics*, **6**, 77–104.

——— (1976e), "Taxing consumption", *The New Republic*, 28 February.

——— (1977), "Social security and private savings: international evidence in an extended life cycle model" in *The Economics of Public Services*, M. S. Feldstein and R. P. Inman (eds), Macmillan, London.

——— (1978a), "The rate of return, taxation and personal savings", *Economic Journal*, **88**, 482–487.

—— (1978b), "The welfare cost of capital income taxation", *Journal of Political Economy*, **86**, S29–51.

Feldstein, M. S. and J. S. Flemming (1971), "Tax policy, corporate saving and investment behaviour in Britain", *Review of Economic Studies*, **38**, 415–434.

Feldstein, M. S., J. R. Green and E. Sheshinski (1977), "Corporate financial policy and taxation in a growing economy", Harvard Discussion Paper 556.

Feldstein, M. S. and R. P. Inman (eds) (1977), *The Economics of Public Services*, Macmillan, London.

Feldstein, M. S. and A. Pellechio (1977), "Social security and household wealth accumulation", NBER Paper No. 206.

Feldstein, M. S. and S. C. Tsiang (1968), "The interest rate, taxation, and the personal savings incentive", *Quarterly Journal of Economics*, **82**, 419–434.

Feldstein, M. S. and S. Yitzhaki (1978), "The effects of the capital gains tax on the selling and switching of common stock", *Journal of Public Economics*, **9**, 17–36.

Ferber, R. and W. Z. Hirsch (1978), "Social experimentation and economic policy: a survey", *Journal of Economic Literature*, **16**, 1379–1414.

Ferguson, J. M. (1964), *Public Debt and Future Generations*, University of North Carolina Press, Chapel Hill, North Carolina.

Fisher, F. M. (1971), "Discussion" in *Tax Incentives and Capital Spending*, G. Fromm (ed.), North-Holland, Amsterdam.

Fisher, I. (1937), "Income in theory and income taxation in practice", *Econometrica*, **5**, 1–55.

Flatters, F., V. Henderson and P. Mieszkowski (1974), "Public goods, efficiency, and regional fiscal equalisation", *Journal of Public Economics*, **3**, 99–112.

Fogelman, F., M. Quinzii and R. Guesnerie (1978), "Dynamic processes for tax reform theory", *Journal of Economic Theory*, **17**, 200–226.

Foley, D. K. (1967), "Resource allocation and the public sector", *Yale Economic Essays*, **7**, 45–98.

—— (1970), "Lindahl's solution and the core of an economy with public goods", *Econometrica*, **38**, 66–72.

—— (1978), "State expenditure from a Marxist perspective", *Journal of Public Economics*, **9**, 221–238.

Foster, E. and H. Sonnenschein (1970), "Price distortion and economic welfare", *Econometrica*, **38**, 281–297.

Franzén, P., K. Lövgren and I. Rosenberg (1975), "Redistribution effects of taxes and public expenditures in Sweden", *Swedish Journal of Economics*, **77**, 31–55.

Frey, B. S. (1976), "Taxation in fiscal exchange—a comment", *Journal of Public Economics*, **6**, 31–35.

—— (1978), "Politico-economic models and cycles", *Journal of Public Economics*, **9**, 203–220.

Frey, B. S. and F. Schneider (1978a), "A politico-economic model of the United Kingdom", *Economic Journal*, **88**, 243–253.

—— and —— (1978b), "An econometric model with an endogenous government sector", *Public Choice*.

—— and —— (1978c), "An empirical study of politico-economic interaction in the United States", *Review of Economics and Statistics*, **60**, 174–183.

Friedlaender, A. F. (1967), "Indirect taxes and relative prices", *Quarterly Journal of Economics*, **81**, 125–139.

Friedman, M. (1952), "The 'welfare' effects of an income tax and an excise tax", *Journal of Political Economy*, **60**, 25–33.

—— (1957), *A Theory of the Consumption Function*, Princeton University Press, Princeton, New Jersey.

Frisch, R. (1939), "The Dupuit taxation theorem", *Econometrica*, **7**, 145–150.

Fromm, G. and P. Taubman (1973), *Public Economic Theory and Policy*, Macmillan, New York.

Fullerton, D., J. B. Shoven and J. Whalley (1978), "General equilibrium analysis of U.S. taxation policy" in *Compendium of Tax Research 1978*, Department of the Treasury, Washington DC.

Garnier, Le Marquis (ed.) (1822), Introduction to *Recherches sur le Nature et les Causes de la Richesse de Nations*, Agasse, Paris.

Gevers, L. and S. Proost (1978), "Some effects of taxation and collective goods in postwar America: a tentative appraisal", *Journal of Public Economics*, **9**, 115–137.

Gibbard, A. (1973), "Manipulation of voting schemes: a general result", *Econometrica*, **41**, 587–601.

Gillespie, W. I. (1965), "Effect of public expenditure on the distribution of income" in *Essays in Fiscal Federalism*, R. A. Musgrave (ed.), Brookings Institution, Washington DC.

——— (1976), "On the redistribution of income in Canada", *Canadian Tax Journal*, **24**, 419–450.

Godfrey, L. (1975), *Theoretical and Empirical Aspects of the Effects of Taxation on the Supply of Labour*, OECD, Paris.

Goetz, C. G. (1977), "Fiscal illusion in state and local finance" in *Budgets and Bureaucrats*, T. E. Borcherding (ed.), Duke University Press, Durham, North Carolina.

Goldman, M. B., H. E. Leland and D. S. Sibley (1977), "Optimal non-uniform prices", Bell Laboratories Discussion Paper.

Golladay, F. L. and R. H. Haveman (1977), *The Economic Impacts of Tax-Transfer Policy*, Academic Press, New York.

Goode, R. (1949), "The income tax and the supply of labour", *Journal of Political Economy*, **57**, 428–437.

——— (1964), *The Individual Income Tax*, Brookings Institution, Washington DC (2nd edn 1976).

——— (1977), "The economic definition of income" in *Comprehensive Income Taxation*, J. A. Pechman (ed.), Brookings Institution, Washington DC.

Gordon, D. M. (1972), "Taxation of the poor and the normative theory of tax incidence", *American Economic Review*, Papers and Proceedings, **62**, 319–328.

Gordon, R. J. (1967), "The incidence of the corporation income tax in U.S. manufacturing 1925–62", *American Economic Review*, **57**, 731–758.

Gordon, S. (1976), "The new contractarians", *Journal of Political Economy*, **84**, 573–590.

Gorman, W. M. (1976), "Tricks with utility functions" in *Essays in Economic Analysis*, M. J. Artis and A. R. Nobay (eds), Cambridge University Press, London.

Graaff, J. de V. (1957), *Theoretical Welfare Economics*, Cambridge University Press, London.

Grandmont, J. M. (1977), "Temporary general equilibrium theory", *Econometrica*, **45**, 535–572.

Gravelle, H. S. E. (1976), "Public enterprises under rate of return financial targets", *Manchester School*, **44**, 1–16.

Green, H. A. J. (1961), "The social optimum in the presence of monopoly and taxation", *Review of Economic Studies*, **29**, 66–78.

——— (1976), *Consumer Theory* (2nd edn), Macmillan, London.

Green, J., E. Kohlberg and J-J. Laffont (1976), "Partial equilibrium approach to the free-rider problem", *Journal of Public Economics*, **6**, 375–394.

Green, J. and J-J. Laffont (1977a), "Characterisation of satisfactory mechanisms for the revelation of preferences for public goods", *Econometrica*, **45**, 427–438.

——— and ——— (1977b), "On the revelation of preferences for public goods", *Journal of Public Economics*, **8**, 79–93.

——— and ——— (1979), *Individual Incentives in Public Decision-Making*, North-Holland Amsterdam.

Green, J. and E. Sheshinski (1976), "Direct versus indirect remedies for externalities", *Journal of Political Economy*, **84**, 797–808.

────── and ────── (1978), "Optimal capital-gains taxation under limited information", *Journal of Political Economy*, **86**, 1143–1158.

Grieson, R. E. (1975), "The incidence of profits taxes in a neoclassical growth model", *Journal of Public Economics*, **4**, 75–85.

Gronau, R. (1973), "The effect of children on the housewife's value of time", *Journal of Political Economy*, **81**, S168–199.

Grossman, S. J. and J. E. Stiglitz (1976), "Information and competitive price systems", *American Economic Review*, Papers and Proceedings, **66**, 246–253.

────── and ────── (1977), "On value maximisation and alternative objectives of the firm", *Journal of Finance*, **32**, 389–402.

Groves, T. (1970), Ph.D. dissertation, University of California, Berkeley.

────── (1973), "Incentives in teams", *Econometrica*, **41**, 617–631.

Groves, T. and J. Ledyard (1977), "Optimal allocation of public goods: a solution to the 'free-rider' problem", *Econometrica*, **45**, 783–809.

Groves, T. and M. Loeb (1975), "Incentives and public inputs", *Journal of Public Economics*, **4**, 211–226.

Guesnerie, R. (1975), "Public production and taxation in a simple second best model", *Journal of Economic Theory*, **10**, 127–156.

────── (1977), "On the direction of tax reform", *Journal of Public Economics*, **7**, 179–202.

────── (1978), "General statements on second-best Pareto optimality", *Journal of Mathematical Economics*,

Hahn, F. H. (1965), "On two-sector growth models", *Review of Economic Studies*, **32**, 339–346.

────── (1966), "Equilibrium dynamics with heterogeneous capital goods, *Quarterly Journal of Economics*, **80**, 633–646.

────── (1973), "On optimum taxation", *Journal of Economic Theory*, **6**, 96–106.

────── (1977), "Keynesian economics and general equilibrium theory: reflections on some current debates" in *The Microeconomic Foundations of Macroeconomics*, G. C. Harcourt (ed.), Macmillan, London.

Hahn, F. H. and R. C. O. Matthews (1964), "The theory of economic growth: a survey", *Economic Journal*, **74**, 779–902.

Hakansson, N. H. (1970), "Optimal investment and consumption strategies under risk for a class of utility functions", *Econometrica*, **38**, 587–607.

Hall, R. E. (1969), "Consumption taxes versus income taxes: implications for economic growth", *Proceedings of the 61st National Tax Conference*, National Tax Association, Columbus, Ohio.

────── (1973), "Wages, income and hours of work in the US labor force" in *Income Maintenance and Labour Supply*, G. G. Cain and H. W. Watts (eds), Rand McNally, Chicago.

────── (1975), "Effects of the experimental negative income tax on labor supply" in *Work Incentives and Income Guarantees*, J. A. Pechman and P. M. Timpane (eds), Brookings Institution, Washington DC.

────── (1977), "Investment, interest rates, and the effects of stabilization policies", *Brookings Economic Papers*, 61–103.

Hall, R. E. and D. W. Jorgenson (1967), "Tax policy and investment behavior", *American Economic Review*, **57**, 391–414.

────── and ────── (1969), "Reply and further results", *American Economic Review*, **59**, 388–401.

────── and ────── (1971), "Application of the theory of optimum capital accumulation" in *Tax Incentives and Capital Spending*, G. Fromm (ed.), North-Holland, Amsterdam.

Hamada, K. (1972), "Lifetime equity and dynamic efficiency on the balanced growth path", *Journal of Public Economics*, **1**, 379–396.

Hannaway, J. (1979), unpublished paper, Columbia University.

Hanoch, G. and M. Honig (1978), "The labor supply curve under income maintenance programs", *Journal of Public Economics*, **9**, 1–16.

Hansen, B. (1958), *The Economic Theory of Fiscal Policy*, Allen and Unwin, London.

Harberger, A. C. (1962), "The incidence of the corporation income tax", *Journal of Political Economy*, **70**, 215–240.

—— (1964), "Taxation, resource allocation, and welfare" in *The Role of Direct and Indirect Taxes in the Federal Revenue System*, J. Due (ed.), Princeton University Press, Princeton, New Jersey.

—— (1968), "Taxation: corporation income taxes" in *International Encyclopedia of the Social Sciences*, D. L. Sills (ed.), Macmillan, New York.

—— (1974), "The corporation income tax: an empirical appraisal" in *Taxation and Welfare*, Little, Brown, Boston.

Harberger, A. C. and N. Bruce (1976), "The incidence and efficiency effects of taxes on income from capital: a reply", *Journal of Political Economy*, **84**, 1285–1292.

Harcourt, G. C. (1972), *Some Cambridge Controversies in the Theory of Capital*, Cambridge University Press, London.

—— (ed.) (1977), *The Microeconomic Foundations of Macroeconomics*, Macmillan, London.

Harris, R. G. (1975), "A note on convex–concave demand systems", Queen's University Discussion Paper No. 197.

Harris, R. G. and J. G. MacKinnon (1979), "Computing optimal tax equilibria", *Journal of Public Economics*, **11**, 197–212.

Harsanyi, J. C. (1955), "Cardinal welfare, individualistic ethics and interpersonal comparisons of utility", *Journal of Political Economy*, **73**, 309–321.

Hart, O. D. (1975), "Some negative results on the existence of comparative statics results in portfolio theory", *Review of Economic Studies*, **42**, 615–621.

—— (1977), "Take-over bids and stock market equilibrium", *Journal of Economic Theory*, **16**, 53–83.

Hatta, T. (1977), "A theory of piecemeal policy recommendations", *Review of Economic Studies*, **44**, 1–21.

Hausman, J. A. and D. A. Wise (1977), "Social experimentation, truncated distributions, and efficient estimation", *Econometrica*, **45**, 919–938.

Head, J. G. (1962), "Public goods and public policy", *Public Finance*, **17**, 197–219.

—— (1966), "A note on progression and leisure: comment", *American Economic Review*, **56**, 172–179.

Head, J. G. and C. S. Shoup (1969), "Public goods, private goods and ambiguous goods", *Economic Journal*, **79**, 567–572.

Heady, C. and P. Mitra (1977), "The computation of optimum linear taxation", University College London Discussion Papers in Public Economics, 1.

Heal, G. M. (1973), *The Theory of Economic Planning*, North-Holland, Amsterdam.

Heckman, J. J. (1974), "Shadow prices, market wages and labor supply", *Econometrica*, **42**, 679–694.

—— (1978), "A partial survey of recent research on the labour supply of women", *American Economic Review*, Papers and Proceedings, **68**, 200–207.

—— (1979), "Sample selection bias as a specification error", *Econometrica*, **47**, 153–161.

Heller, W. (1966), *New Dimensions of Political Economy*, Harvard University Press, Cambridge, Massachusetts.

Heller, W. P. and K. Shell (1974), "On optimal taxation with costly administration", *American Economic Review*, Papers and Proceedings, **64**, 338–345.

Helliwell, J. F. (1972), "Book review of Fromm (1971)", *Journal of Public Economics*, **1**, 159–161.

—— (ed.) (1976), *Aggregate Investment: Selected Readings*, Penguin, Harmondsworth.

Hemming, R. C. L. (1977), "The effect of state and private pensions on retirement behaviour and personal capital accumulation", *Review of Economic Studies*, **44**, 169–172.

Hicks, J. R. (1939), *Value and Capital*, Oxford University Press, London.

⸻ (1962), "Liquidity", *Economic Journal*, **72**, 787–802.

⸻ (1965), *Capital and Growth*, Oxford University Press, Oxford.

Hicks, U. K. (1947), *Public Finance*, Nisbet, London.

Hildenbrand, W. and A. P. Kirman (1976), *Introduction to Equilibrium Analysis*, North-Holland, Amsterdam.

Hinich, M. J., J. O. Ledyard and P. C. Ordeshook (1972), "Nonvoting and the existence of equilibrium under majority rule", *Journal of Economic Theory*, **4**, 144–153.

Hirschman, A. O. (1970), *Exit, Voice and Loyalty*, Harvard University Press, Cambridge, Massachusetts.

HMSO (1971), *Value-Added Tax*, Cmnd 4621, London, HMSO.

Hochman, H. M. and J. D. Rodgers (1969), "Pareto optimal redistribution", *American Economic Review*, **59**, 542–557.

Hoffman, R. F. (1972), "Disaggregation and calculations of the welfare cost of a tax", *Journal of Political Economy*, **80**, 409–417.

Holland, Daniel M. (1969), "The effect of taxation on effort: some results for business executives" in National Tax Association, *Proceedings of the Sixty-Second Annual Conference*, September 1969.

⸻ (1977), "Effect of taxation on incentives of higher income groups" in *Fiscal Policy and Labour Supply*, Institute for Fiscal Studies, London.

Hotelling, H. (1929), "Stability in competition", *Economic Journal*, **39**, 41–57.

⸻ (1938), "The general welfare in relation to problems of taxation and of railway and utility rates", *Econometrica*, **6**, 242–269.

Houthakker, H. S. (1960), "Additive preferences", *Econometrica*, **28**, 244–257.

Hurwicz, L. (1972), "On informationally decentralised systems" in *Decision and Organisation*, R. Radner and C. B. McGuire (eds), North-Holland, Amsterdam.

Inada, K. (1963), "On a two-sector model of economic growth: comments and a generalisation", *Review of Economic Studies*, **30**, 119–127.

Inman, R. P. (1978), "Testing political economy's 'As If' proposition: is the median income voter really decisive?", *Public Choice*, **33**.

Intriligator, M. D. (1971), *Mathematical Optimization and Economic Theory*, Prentice-Hall, Englewood Cliffs, New Jersey.

Itsumi, Y. (1974), "Distributional effects of linear income tax schedules", *Review of Economic Studies*, **41**, 371–382.

Jaffee, D. M. and T. Russell (1976), "Symposium. The economics of information: imperfect information, uncertainty, and credit rationing", *Quarterly Journal of Economics*, **90**, 651–666.

Jakobsson, U. (1976), "On the measurement of the degree of progression", *Journal of Public Economics*, **5**, 161–168.

Jessop, B. (1977), "Recent theories of the capitalist state", *Cambridge Journal of Economics*, **1**, 353–373.

Johansen, L. (1960), *A Multi-Sectoral Study of Economic Growth*, North-Holland, Amsterdam.

⸻ (1965), *Public Economics*, North-Holland, Amsterdam.

⸻ (1977), "The theory of public goods: misplaced emphasis?" *Journal of Public Economics*, **7**, 147–152.

⸻ (1978), *Lectures on Macroeconomic Planning*, Volume 2, North-Holland, Amsterdam.

Johnson, H. G. (1956), "General equilibrium analysis of excise taxes, comment", *American Economic Review*, **46**, 151–156.

⸻ (1959), "International trade, income distribution and the offer curve", *Manchester School*, **27**, 241–260.

Johnson, H. G. and P. M. Mieszkowski (1970), "The effects of unionization on the distribution of income: a general equilibrium approach", *Quarterly Journal of Economics*, **84**, 539–561.

Johnson, S. B. and T. Mayer (1962), "An extension of Sidgwick's equity principle", *Quarterly Journal of Economics*, **76**, 454–463.

Jones, H. G. (1975), *An Introduction to Modern Theories of Economic Growth*, Nelson, London.

Jones, R. W. (1965), "The structure of simple general equilibrium models", *Journal of Political Economy*, **73**, 557–572.

—— (1971a), "Distortions in factor markets and the general equilibrium model of production", *Journal of Political Economy*, **79**, 437–459.

—— (1971b), "A three-factor model in theory, trade and history" in *Trade, Balance of Payments and Growth*, J. Bhagwati *et al.* (eds), North-Holland, Amsterdam.

Jorgenson, D. W. (1963), "Capital theory and investment behavior", *American Economic Review*, **53**, 247–259.

—— (1971), "Econometric studies of investment behavior: a survey", *Journal of Economic Literature*, **9**, 1111–1147.

—— (1972), "Investment behavior and the production function", *Bell Journal of Economics*, **3**, 220–251.

Jorgenson, D. W. and J. A. Stephenson (1967), "Investment behavior in U.S. manufacturing 1947–1960", *Econometrica*, **35**, 169–220.

Junankar, P. N. (1972), *Investment: Theories and Evidence*, Macmillan, London.

Kadane, J. B. (1975), "Statistical problems of merged data files", Office of Tax Analysis Paper 6.

Kaizuka, K. (1965), "Public goods and decentralization of production", *Review of Economics and Statistics*, **47**, 118–120.

Kaldor, N. (1955), *An Expenditure Tax*, Allen and Unwin, London.

—— (1956), "Alternative theories of distribution", *Review of Economic Studies*, **23**, 83–100.

—— (1966), "Marginal productivity and the macro-economic theories of distribution", *Review of Economic Studies*, **33**, 309–320.

Kaldor, N. with J. A. Mirrlees (1962), "A new model of economic growth", *Review of Economic Studies*, **29**, 174–192.

Kalecki, M. (1937), "A theory of commodity, income and capital taxation", *Economic Journal*, **47**, 444–450.

Kay, J. A. (1977), "Inflation accounting: a review article", *Economic Journal*, **87**, 300–311.

—— (1978), "A lifetime expenditure tax", unpublished paper, St John's College, Oxford.

Kay, J. A. and M. A. King (1978), *The British Tax System*, Oxford University Press, London.

Kennedy, C. (1964), "Induced bias in innovation and the theory of distribution", *Economic Journal*, **74**, 541–547.

Kennedy, W. (1913), *English Taxation 1640–1799*, Bell, London.

Kesselman, J. R. (1973), "A comprehensive approach to income maintenance: SWIFT", *Journal of Public Economics*, **2**, 59–88.

—— (1976), "Tax effects on job search, training and work effort", *Journal of Public Economics*, **6**, 255–272.

King, M. A. (1972), "Taxation and investment incentives in a vintage investment model", *Journal of Public Economics*, **1**, 121–147.

—— (1974), "Taxation and the cost of capital", *Review of Economic Studies*, **41**, 21–35.

—— (1975), "Taxation, corporate financial policy and the cost of capital—a comment", *Journal of Public Economics*, **4**, 271–279.

—— (1977), *Public Policy and the Corporation*, Chapman and Hall, London.

Klevorick, A. K. and G. H. Kramer (1973), "Social choice on pollution management: the Genossenschaften", *Journal of Public Economics*, **2**, 101–146.

Kolm, S-Ch. (1968), *Prix Publics Optimaux*, CNRS, Paris.

—— (1969), "The optimal production of social justice" in *Public Economics*, J. Margolis and H. Guitton (eds), Macmillan, London.

—— (1971), *L'Etat et le système des prix, I: La Valeur Publique II: Prix publics optimaux, III: La théorie des contraintes de valeur et ses applications*, Dunod, Paris.

Kramer, G. H. (1973), "On a class of equilibrium conditions for majority rule", *Econometrica*, **41**, 285–297.

—— (1977a), "A dynamical model of political equilibrium", *Journal of Economic Theory*, **16**, 310–334.

—— (1977b), "Theories of political processes" in *Frontiers of Quantitative Economics III*, M. D. Intriligator (ed.), North-Holland, Amsterdam.

Kramer, G. H. and A. K. Klevorick (1974), "Existence of a 'local' co-operative equilibrium in a class of voting games", *Review of Economic Studies*, **41**, 539–547.

Krauss, M. B. (1971), "General equilibrium aspects of Canada's white paper on tax reform", *Canadian Journal of Economics*, **4**, 256–263.

—— (1972), "Differential tax incidence: large versus small tax changes", *Journal of Political Economy*, **80**, 193–197.

Krauss, M. B. and H. G. Johnson (1972), "The theory of tax incidence: a diagrammatic analysis", *Economica*, **39**, 357–382.

Krzyzaniak, M. (1967), "Long-run burden of a general tax on profits in a neoclassical world", *Public Finance*, **22**, 472–491.

Krzyzaniak, M. and R. A. Musgrave (1963), *The Shifting of the Corporation Income Tax*, Johns Hopkins Press, Baltimore.

Kuhn, H. W. (1968), "Simplicial approximations of fixed points", *Proceedings of the National Academy of Sciences*, **61**, 1238–1242.

—— (1976), "How to compute economic equilibria by pivotal methods" in *Computing Equilibria: How and Why*, J. Los and M. W. Los (eds), North-Holland, Amsterdam.

Kurz, M. (1974), "Experimental approach to the determination of the demand for public goods", *Journal of Public Economics*, **3**, 329–348.

Lancaster, K. J. (1966), "A new approach to consumer theory", *Journal of Political Economy*, **74**, 132–157.

Lau, L. J., E. Sheshinski and J. E. Stiglitz (1978), "Efficiency in the optimum supply of public goods", *Econometrica*, **46**, 269–284.

Leitman, G. (1966), *An Introduction to Optimal Control*, McGraw-Hill, New York.

Leland, H. E. (1974), "Production theory and the stock market", *Bell Journal of Economics and Management Science*, **5**, 125–144.

Lerner, A. P. (1944), *The Economics of Control*, Macmillan, New York.

—— (1948), "The burden of the National Debt" in *Income, Employment and Public Policy: Essays in Honor of Alvin H. Hansen*, L. A. Metzler *et al.* (eds), Norton, New York.

—— (1959), "Consumption loan interest and money", *Journal of Political Economy*, **67**, 523–525.

Leuthold, J. H. (1968), "An empirical study of formula income transfers and the work decision of the poor", *Journal of Human Resources*, **3**, 312–323.

Levhari, D. and T. N. Srinivasan (1969), "Optimal savings under uncertainty", *Review of Economic Studies*, **36**, 153–164.

Levitt, M. (1964), "Comparison of the equilibrium labor supply under proportional and progressive taxation", *Journal of Political Economy*, **72**, 496–497.

Lewis, W. A. (1941), "The two-part tariff", *Economica*, **8**, 249–270.

Lindahl, E. (1919), "Positive Lösung, Die Gerechtigkeit der Besteuerung", translated as "Just taxation—a positive solution" in *Classics in the Theory of Public Finance*, R. A. Musgrave and A. T. Peacock (eds), Macmillan, London.

Lipsey, R. G. and K. Lancaster (1956–7), "The General Theory of Second Best", *Review of Economic Studies*, **24**, 11–32.

Little, I. M. D. (1951), "Direct versus indirect taxes", *Economic Journal*, **61**, 577–584.

Little, I. M. D. and J. A. Mirrlees (1974), *Project Appraisal and Planning for Developing Countries*, Heinemann, London.

Liviatan, N. (1966), "Multiperiod future consumption as an aggregate", *American Economic Review*, **56**, 828–840.

Lluch, C., A. A. Powell and R. A. Williams (1977), *Patterns in Household Demand and Saving*, Oxford University Press, New York.

Lodin, S. O. (1976), *Progressive Utgiftsskatt-ett alternativ?*, Statens Offentliga Utredringa, Stockholm.

Loistl, O. (1976), "The erroneous approximation of expected utility by means of a Taylor's series expansion: analytic and computational results", *American Economic Review*, **66**, 904–910.

Lovell, M. C. (1978), "Spending for education: the exercise of public choice", *Review of Economics and Statistics*, **60**, 487–495.

Lucas, R. E. (1967), "Adjustment costs and the theory of supply", *Journal of Political Economy*, **75**, 321–335.

—— (1976), "Econometric policy evaluation: a critique" in *The Phillips Curve and Labor Markets*, K. Brunner and A. H. Meltzer (eds), North-Holland, Amsterdam.

McCulloch, J. R. (1845), *A Treatise on the Principles and Practical Influence of Taxation and the Funding System*, (Scottish Economic Society edn, 1975, ed. D. P. O'Brien, Scottish Academic Press, Edinburgh).

McFadden, D. (1975, 1976), "The revealed preferences of a government of bureaucracy", *Bell Journal of Economics*, **6**, 401–416; **7**, 55–72.

McGuire, M. C. (1974), "Group segregation and optimal jurisdictions", *Journal of Political Economy*, **82**, 112–132.

McLure, C. E. Jr. (1969), "The inter-regional incidence of general regional taxes, *Public Finance*, **24**, 457–483.

—— (1970), "Taxation, substitution, and industrial location", *Journal of Political Economy*, **78**, 112–132.

—— (1971), "The theory of tax incidence with imperfect factor mobility", *Finanzarchiv*, **30**, 27–48.

—— (1974), "A diagrammatic exposition of the Harberger model with one immobile factor", *Journal of Political Economy*, **82**, 56–82.

—— (1975), "General equilibrium incidence analysis: the Harberger model after ten years", *Journal of Public Economics*, **4**, 125–161.

McLure, C. E. and W. R. Thirsk (1975), "A simplified exposition of the Harberger model I: Tax incidence", *National Tax Journal*, **28**, 1–27.

MacRae, D. C. (1977), "A political model of the business cycle", *Journal of Political Economy*, **85**, 239–263.

Magee, S. P. (1971), "Factor market distortions, production, distribution and the pure theory of international trade", *Quarterly Journal of Economics*, **85**, 623–643.

—— (1973), "Factor market distortions, production and trade: a survey", *Oxford Economic Papers*, **25**, 1–43.

—— (1976), *International Trade and Distortions in Factor Markets*, Marcel Dekker, New York.

Malinvaud, E. (1971a), "Procedures for the determination of a program of collective consumption", *European Economic Review*, **2**, 187–217.

—— (1971b), "A planning approach to the public good problem", *Swedish Journal of Economics*, **11**, 96–112.

—— (1972), *Lectures on Microeconomic Theory*, North-Holland, Amsterdam.

—— (1977), *The Theory of Unemployment Reconsidered*, Basil Blackwell, Oxford.

Marglin, S. A. (1975), "What do bosses do?—Part II", *Review of Radical Political Economics*.

Markowitz, H. M. (1959), *Portfolio Selection: Efficient Diversification of Investments*, John Wiley, New York.

Marris, R. (1964), *The Economic Theory of "Managerial" Capitalism*, Macmillan, London.

Mayston, D. J. (1975), "Optimal licensing in public sector tariff structures" in *Contemporary Issues in Economics*, M. Parkin and A. R. Nobay (eds), Manchester University Press, Manchester.

Meade, J. E. (1951), *Balance of Payments*, Oxford University Press, Oxford.

—— (1955), *Trade and Welfare: Mathematical Supplement*, Oxford University Press, Oxford.

—— (1958, 1959), "Is the National Debt a burden?", *Oxford Economic Papers*, **10**, 163–183; **11**, 109–110.

—— (1961), *A Neo-Classical Theory of Economic Growth*, Allen and Unwin, London.

—— (1964), *Efficiency, Equality and the Ownership of Property*, Allen and Unwin, London.

—— (1966), "Life-cycle savings, inheritance and economic growth", *Review of Economic Studies*, **33**, 61–78.

—— (1975), *The Intelligent Radical's Guide to Economic Policy*, Allen and Unwin, London.

—— (1976), *The Just Economy*, Allen and Unwin, London.

—— (1978), *The Structure and Reform of Direct Taxation*, Allen and Unwin, London.

Meade, J. E. and J. M. Fleming (1944), "Price and output policy of state enterprise", *Economic Journal*, **54**, 321–339.

Meade, J. E. and F. H. Hahn (1965), "The rate of profit in a growing economy", *Economic Journal*, **75**, 445–448.

Metcalf, C. E. (1973), "Making inferences from controlled income maintenance experiments", *American Economic Review*, **63**, 478–483.

—— (1974), "Predicting the effects of permanent programs from a limited duration experiment", *Journal of Human Resources*, **9**, 530–555.

Metcalfe, J. E. and I. Steedman (1971), "Some effects of taxation in a linear model of production", *Manchester School*, **39**, 171–185.

Metzler, L. A. (1951), "Taxes and subsidies in Leontief's input–output model", *Quarterly Journal of Economics*, **65**, 433–438.

Mieszkowski, P. M. (1966), "The comparative efficiency of tariffs and other tax-subsidy schemes as a means of obtaining revenue or protecting domestic production", *Journal of Political Economy*, **74**, 587–599.

—— (1967), "On the theory of tax incidence", *Journal of Political Economy*, **75**, 250–262.

—— (1969), "Tax incidence theory: the effects of taxes on the distribution of income", *Journal of Economic Literature*, **7**, 1103–1124.

—— (1972), "The property tax: an excise tax or a profits tax?", *Journal of Public Economics*, **1**, 73–96.

—— (1977), "The cash flow version of an expenditure tax", Office of Tax Analysis Paper 26.

Milleron, J-C. (1968), "L'approche par dualité dans la théorie des effets externes et des consommations collectives", INSEE.

—— (1972), "Theory of value with public goods: a survey article", *Journal of Economic Theory*, **5**, 419–477.

Minarik, J. J. (1977), "The yield of a comprehensive income tax" in *Comprehensive Income Taxation*, J. A. Pechman (ed.), Brookings Institution, Washington DC.

Mirrlees, J. A. (1971), "An exploration in the theory of optimum income taxation", *Review of Economic Studies*, **38**, 175–208.

—— (1972a), "On producer taxation", *Review of Economic Studies*, **39**, 105–111.

—— (1972b), "Population policy and the taxation of family size", *Journal of Public Economics*, **1**, 169–198.

—— (1973), "Introduction", in *Models of Economic Growth*, J. A. Mirrlees and N. H. Stern (eds), Macmillan, London.

—— (1975), "Optimal commodity taxation in a two-class economy", *Journal of Public Economics*, **4**, 27–33.

—— (1976), "Optimal tax theory: a synthesis", *Journal of Public Economics*, **6**, 327–358.

—— (1977), "Labour supply behaviour and optimal taxes" in *Fiscal Policy and Labour Supply*, Institute for Fiscal Studies, London.

—— (1979), "The theory of optimal taxation" in *Handbook of Mathematical Economics*, K. J. Arrow and M. D. Intriligator (eds), North-Holland, Amsterdam.

Mishan, E. J. (1963), "How to make a burden of the public debt", *Journal of Political Economy*, **71**, 529–542.

—— (1971), "The post war literature on externalities: an interpretive essay", *Journal of Economic Literature*, **9**, 1–28.

Mitra, P. K. (1975), "Taxation and intergenerational equity", mimeo, University College London.

Modigliani, F. (1961), "Long-run implications of alternative fiscal policies and the burden of the national debt", *Economic Journal*, **71**, 730–755.

—— (1975), "The life cycle hypothesis twenty years later" in *Current Economic Problems*, M. Parkin and A. R. Nobay (eds), Cambridge University Press, Cambridge.

Modigliani, F. and R. Brumberg (1955), "Utility analysis and the consumption function: an interpretation of cross-section data" in *Post Keynesian Economics*, K. K. Kurihara (ed.), Allen and Unwin, London.

Modigliani, F. and M. H. Miller (1958), "The cost of capital, corporation finance, and the theory of investment", *American Economic Review*, **48**, 261–297.

Mossin, J. (1968), "Taxation and risk-taking: an expected utility approach", *Economica*, **35**, 74–82.

Muellbauer, J. N. J. (1975), "Aggregation, income distribution and consumer demand", *Review of Economic Studies*, **42**, 525–543.

—— (1976), "Community preferences and the representative consumer", *Econometrica*, **44**, 979–999.

Mueller, D. C. (1976), "Public choice: a survey", *Journal of Economic Literature*, **14**, 396–433.

Muench, T. J. (1972), "The core and the Lindahl equilibrium of an economy with a public good: an example", *Journal of Economic Theory*, **4**, 241–255.

Munk, K. J. (1975), "Optimal public sector pricing taking the distributional aspects into consideration", Aarhus Discussion Paper.

—— (1978), "Optimal taxation and pure profit", *Scandinavian Journal of Economics*, **80**, 1–19.

Munnell, A. H. (1976), "Private pensions and saving: new evidence", *Journal of Political Economy*, **84**, 1013–1032.

Musgrave, R. A. (1953a), "General equilibrium aspects of incidence theory", *American Economic Review*, **43**, 504–517.

—— (1953b), "On incidence", *Journal of Political Economy*, **61**, 306–323.

—— (1959), *The Theory of Public Finance*, McGraw-Hill, New York.

—— (1964), "Estimating the distribution of the tax burden" in *Income Redistribution and the Statistical Foundations of Economic Policy*, C. Clark and G. Stuvel (eds), Bowes and Bowes, London.

—— (1969), *Fiscal Systems*, Yale University Press, London.

—— (1976), "ET, OT and SBT", *Journal of Public Economics*, **6**, 3–16.

Musgrave, R. A., J. J. Carroll, L. D. Cook and L. Frane (1951), "Distribution of tax payments by income groups: a case study for 1948", *National Tax Journal*, **4**, 1–53.

Musgrave, R. A., K. E. Case and H. Leonard (1974), "The distribution of fiscal burdens and benefits", *Public Finance Quarterly*, **2**, 259–311.

Musgrave, R. A. and P. B. Musgrave (1976), *Public Finance in Theory and Practice*, 2nd edn, McGraw-Hill, New York.

Musgrave, R. A. and Tun Thin (1948), "Income tax progression 1929–1948", *Journal of Political Economy*, **56**, 498–514.

Mussa, M. (1974), "Tariffs and the distribution of income", *Journal of Political Economy*, **32**, 1191–1203.

Muth, R. (1966), "Household production and consumer demand functions", *Econometrica*, **34**, 699–708.

Nadiri, M. I. and S. Rosen (1969), "Interrelated factor demand functions", *American Economic Review*, **59**, 457–471.

National Economic and Social Council (1975), *Income Distribution: A Preliminary Report*, Prl 4575, The Stationary Office, Dublin.

Neary, J. P. (1976), B.Phil. Thesis, University of Oxford.

—— (1978), "Dynamic stability and the theory of factor-market distortions", *American Economic Review*, **68**, 671–682.

Negishi, T. (1967), "The perceived demand curve in the theory of Second Best", *Review of Economic Studies*, **34**, 315–321.

Newbery, D. M. G. and J. E. Stiglitz (1979), "Pareto inferior trade", Oxford University Discussion Paper.

Ng, Y. and M. Weisser (1974), "Optimal pricing with a budget constraint—the case of the two-part tariff', *Review of Economic Studies*, **41**, 337–345.

Nicholson, J. L. (1964), *Redistribution of Income in the United Kingdom in 1959, 1957 and 1953*, Bowes and Bowes, Cambridge.

Nickell, S. J. (1978), *The Investment Decisions of Firms*, J. Nisbet, Welwyn Garden City.

Niskanen, W. A. Jr. (1971), *Bureaucracy and Representative Government*, Aldine, Chicago.

Nordhaus, W. D. (1975), "The political business cycle", *Review of Economic Studies*, **42**, 169–190.

Nozick, R. (1974), *Anarchy, State and Utopia*, Basil Blackwell, Oxford.

Oates, W. E. (1972), *Fiscal Federalism*, Harcourt Brace Jovanovich, New York.

O'Connor, J. (1973), *The Fiscal Crisis of the State*, St Martin's Press, New York.

Okun, A. M. (1975), *Equality and Efficiency*, Brookings Institution, Washington DC.

Olson, M. (1965), *The Logic of Collective Action*, Harvard University Press, Cambridge, Massachusetts.

Orcutt, G. H. and A. G. Orcutt (1968), "Incentive and disincentive experimentation for income maintenance policy purposes", *American Economic Review*, **58**, 754–772.

Ordover, J. A. (1976), "Distributive justice and optimal taxation of wages and interest in a growing economy", *Journal of Public Economics*, **5**, 139–160.

Ordover, J. A. and E. S. Phelps (1975), "Linear taxation of wealth and wages for intragenerational lifetime justice: some steady-state cases", *American Economic Review*, **65**, 660–673.

—— and —— (1979), "The concept of optimal taxation in an over-lapping generations model of capital and wealth", *Journal of Public Economics*, **12**, 1–26.

Panzar, J. C. and R. D. Willig (1976), "Vindication of a 'common mistake' in welfare economics", *Journal of Political Economy*, **84**, 1361–1363.

Pasinetti, L. L. (1962), "Rate of profit and income distribution in relation to the rate of economic growth", *Review of Economic Studies*, **29**, 267–279.

Pattanaik, P. K. (1971), *Voting and Collective Choice*, Cambridge University Press. Cambridge.

Pauly, M. V. (1967), "Clubs, commonality, and the core", *Economica*, **34**, 314–324.

—— (1970a), "Optimality, 'public' goods, and local government: a general theoretical analysis", *Journal of Political Economy*, **78**, 572–585.

—— (1970b), "Cores and clubs", *Public Choice*, **9**, 53–65.

Peacock, A. T. (1974), "The treatment of government expenditure in studies of income redistribution" in *Public Finance and Stabilisation Policy*, W. L. Smith and J. M. Culbertson (eds), North-Holland, Amsterdam.

Peacock, A. T. and J. Wiseman (1967), *The Growth of Public Expenditure in the United Kingdom*, 2nd edn, Allen and Unwin, London.

Pechman, J. A. (1965), "Financing state and local government", *Proceedings of a Symposium on Federal Taxation*, American Bankers' Association, New York.

Pechman, J. A. and B. A. Okner (1972), "Individual income tax erosion by income classes" in Joint Economic Committee, *The Economics of Federal Subsidy Programs*, US Congress, Washington DC.

—— and —— (1974), *Who Bears the Tax Burden?*, Brookings Institution, Washington DC.

Pechman, J. A. and P. M. Timpane (eds) (1975), *Work Incentives and Income Guarantees*, Brookings Institution, Washington DC.

Pencavel, J. (1979), "Constant-Utility Index Numbers of Real Wages", *American Economic Review*, **69**, 240–243.

Pestieau, P. M. (1974), "Optimal taxation and discount rate for public investment in a growth setting", *Journal of Public Economics*, **3**, 217–235.

Phelps, E. S. (1973), "The taxation of wage income for economic justice", *Quarterly Journal of Economics*, **87**, 331–354.

—— (1977), "Linear 'maximin' taxation of wage and property income on a 'maximin' growth path", in *Economic Progress, Private Values and Public Policy*, B. Balassa and R. Nelson (eds), North-Holland, Amsterdam.

Phelps, E. S. and K. Shell (1969), "Public debt, taxation, and capital intensiveness", *Journal of Economic Theory*, **1**, 330–346.

Pigou, A. C. (1947), *A Study in Public Finance* (3rd edn), Macmillan, London.

Plott, C. R. (1967), "A notion of equilibrium and its possibility under majority rule", *American Economic Review*, **57**, 787–806.

Polinsky, A. M. (1973), "A note on the measurement of incidence", *Public Finance Quarterly*, **1**, 219–230.

—— (1974), "Imperfect capital markets, intertemporal redistribution and progressive taxation", in *Redistribution Through Public Choice*, H. M. Hochman and G. E. Peterson (eds), Columbia University Press, New York.

Pommerehne, W. W. (1978), "Institutional approaches to public expenditure: empirical evidence from Swiss municipalities", *Journal of Public Economics*, **9**, 255–280.

Pommerehne, W. W. and B. S. Frey (1976), "Two approaches to estimating public expenditures", *Public Finance Quarterly*, **4**, 395–407.

Pommerehne, W. W. and F. Schneider (1978), "Fiscal illusion, political institutions, and local public spending", *Kyklos*, **31**, 381–408.

Pratt, J. W. (1964), "Risk aversion in the small and in the large", *Econometrica*, **32**, 122–136.

Prest, A. R. (1955), "Statistical calculations of tax burdens", *Economica*, **22**, 234–245.

—— (1968), "The budget and interpersonal distribution", *Public Finance*, **23**, 80–98.

—— (1975), *Public Finance in Theory and Practice* (5th edn), Weidenfeld and Nicolson, London.

Projector, D. S. and G. S. Weiss (1966), *Survey of Financial Characteristics of Consumers*, Board of Governors of the Federal Reserve System, Washington, DC.

Quinn, J. F. (1977), "Microeconomic determinants of early retirement: a cross-sectional view of white married men", *Journal of Human Resources*, **12**, 329–346.

Ramsey, F. P. (1927), "A contribution to the theory of taxation", *Economic Journal*, **37**, 47–61.

Rawls, J. (1971), *A Theory of Justice*, Harvard University Press, Cambridge, Massachusetts.

—— (1973), "Reply to Alexander and Musgrave", *Quarterly Journal of Economics*, **87**, 633–655.

—— (1974), "Concepts of distributional equity: some reasons for the maximin criterion", *American Economic Review*, Papers and Proceedings, **64**, 141–146.

Rayner, A. C. (1969), "On the identification of the supply of working hours", *Oxford Economic Papers*, **21**, 293–298.

Reddaway, W. B. (1970), *Effects of the Selective Employment Tax, First Report, The Distributive Trades*, HMSO, London.

Rees, A. and H. W. Watts (1975), "An overview of the labor supply results" in *Work Incentives and Income Guarantees*, J. A. Pechman and P. M. Timpane, Brookings Institution, Washington DC.

Rees, R. (1968), "Second best rules for public enterprise pricing", *Economica*, **35**, 260–273.

—— (1976), *Public Enterprise Economics*, Weidenfeld and Nicolson, London.

Reynolds, M. and E. Smolensky (1976), *Public Expenditures, Taxes and the Distribution of Income*, Academic Press, New York.

Richter, D. K. (1978), "Existence and computation of a Tiebout general equilibrium", *Econometrica*, **46**, 779–805.

Richter, M. K. (1960), "Cardinal utility, portfolio selection and taxation", *Review of Economic Studies*, **27**, 152–166.

Robbins, L. (1930), "On the elasticity of demand for income in terms of effort", *Economica*, **10**, 123–129.

—— (1938), "Interpersonal comparisons of utility: a comment", *Economic Journal*, **48**, 635–641.

Roberts, D. J. (1973), "Existence of Lindahl equilibrium with a measure space of consumers", *Journal of Economic Theory*, **6**, 355–381.

—— (1974a), "A note on returns to group size and the core with public goods", *Journal of Economic Theory*, **9**, 350–356.

—— (1974b), "The Lindahl solution for economies with public goods", *Journal of Public Economics*, **3**, 23–42.

—— (1976), "The incentives for correct revelation of preferences and the number of consumers", *Journal of Public Economics*, **6**, 359–374.

Roberts, D. J. and A. Postlewaite (1976), "The incentives for price-taking behavior in large exchange economies", *Econometrica*, **44**, 115–128.

Roberts, D. J. and H. Sonnenschein (1977), "On the foundations of the theory of monopolistic competition", *Econometrica*, **45**, 101–113.

Roberts, K. W. S. (1977), "Voting Over income tax schedules", *Journal of Public Economics*, **8**, 329–340.

—— (1979), "Welfare considerations of nonlinear pricing", *Economic Journal*, **89**, 66–83.

Roberts, M. J. (1971), "Portfolio models and the impact of taxation on investment: a reconsideration", Harvard Discussion Paper.

Robertson, D. H. (1927), "The Colwyn Committee, the income tax and the price level", *Economic Journal*, **37**, 566–581.

Romer, T. (1975), "Individual welfare, majority voting and the properties of a linear income tax", *Journal of Public Economics*, **4**, 163–185.

Romer, T. and H. Rosenthal (1977), "Bureaucrats vs voters", unpublished paper, Carnegie-Mellon.

—— and —— (1979), "The elusive median voter", *Journal of Public Economics*, **12**, 143–170.

Rosen, H. S. (1976a), "Taxes in a labor supply model with joint wage-hours determination", *Econometrica*, **44**, 485–507.

—— (1976b), "Tax illusion and the labor supply of married women", *Review of Economics and Statistics*, **58**, 167–172.

Roseveare, H. (1973), *The Treasury*, Allen and Unwin, London.

Rossi, P. H. (1975), "A critical review of the analysis of nonlabour force responses" in *Work Incentives and Income Guarantees*, J. A. Pechman and P. M. Timpane (eds), Brookings Institution, Washington DC.

Rothschild, M. (1971), "On the cost of adjustment", *Quarterly Journal of Economics*, **85**, 605–622.

Rothschild, M. and J. E. Stiglitz (1970), "Increasing risk I: A definition", *Journal of Economic Theory*, **2**, 225–243.

—— and —— (1971), "Increasing risk II: Its economic consequences", *Journal of Economic Theory*, **3**, 66–84.

—— and —— (1976), "Equilibrium in competitive insurance markets", *Quarterly Journal of Economics*, **90**, 629–650.

Rubinfeld, D. L. (1977), "Voting in a local school election: a micro analysis", *Review of Economics and Statistics*, **59**, 30–42.

Russell, T. (1974), "The effect of improvements in the consumer loan market", *Journal of Economic Theory*, **9**, 327–339.

Sabine, B. E. V. (1966), *A History of Income Tax*, Allen and Unwin, London.

Sadka, E. (1976), "On income distribution, incentive effects and optimal income taxation", *Review of Economic Studies*, **43**, 261–268.

—— (1977), "A theorem on uniform taxation", *Journal of Public Economics*, **7**, 387–391.

Samuel, Lord (1919), "The taxation of the various classes of the people", *Journal of the Royal Statistical Society*, **82**, 143–182.

Samuelson, P. A. (1947), *Foundations of Economic Analysis*, Harvard University Press, Cambridge, Massachusetts.

—— (1951), Unpublished memorandum for the US Treasury.

—— (1954), "The pure theory of public expenditure", *Review of Economics and Statistics*, **36**, 387–389.

—— (1955), "Diagrammatic exposition of a theory of public expenditure", *Review of Economics and Statistics*, **37**, 350–356.

—— (1956), "Social indifference curves", *Quarterly Journal of Economics*, **70**, 1–22.

—— (1958a), "An exact consumption-loan model of interest with or without the social contrivance of money", *Journal of Political Economy*, **66**, 467–482.

—— (1958b), "Aspects of public expenditure theories", *Review of Economics and Statistics*, **40**, 332–338.

—— (1964a), "Discussion" in *American Economic Review*, Papers and Proceedings, **54**, 93–96.

—— (1964b), "Tax deductibility of economic depreciation to insure invariant valuations", *Journal of Political Economy*, **72**, 604–606.

—— (1965), "A theory of induced innovation along Kennedy–Weizsäcker lines", *Review of Economics and Statistics*, **47**, 343–356.

—— (1969), "Pure theory of public expenditures and taxation" in *Public Economics*, J. Margolis and H. Guitton (eds), Macmillan, London.

—— (1975), "Optimum social security in a life-cycle growth model", *International Economic Review*, **16**, 539–544.

Samuelson, P. A. and F. Modigliani (1966), "The Pasinetti paradox in neoclassical and more general models", *Review of Economic Studies*, **33**, 269–303.

Sandmo, A. (1969), "Capital, risk, consumption, and portfolio choice", *Econometrica*, **37**, 586–599.

—— (1970), "The effect of uncertainty on saving decisions", *Review of Economic Studies*, **37**, 353–360.

—— (1972), "Optimality rules for the provision of collective factors of production", *Journal of Public Economics*, **1**, 149–157.

—— (1973), "Public goods and the technology of consumption", *Review of Economic Studies*, **40**, 517–528.

—— (1974a), "A note on the structure of optimal taxation", *American Economic Review*, **64**, 701–706.

—— (1974b), "Investment incentives and the corporate income tax", *Journal of Political Economy*, **82**, 287–302.

—— (1975), "Optimal taxation in the presence of externalities", *Swedish Journal of Economics*, **77**, 86–98.

—— (1976a), "Direct versus indirect Pigovian taxation", *European Economic Review*, **7**, 337–349.

—— (1976b), "Optimal taxation—an introduction to the literature", *Journal of Public Economics*, **6**, 37–54.

Sato, R. and R. F. Hoffman (1974), "Tax incidence in a growing economy", in *Public Finance and Stabilisation Policy*, W. L. Smith and J. M. Culbertson (eds), North-Holland, Amsterdam.

Satterthwaite, M. A. (1975), "Strategy-proofness and Arrow's conditions", *Journal of Economic Theory*, **10**, 187–217.

Sawers, L. and H. M. Wachtel (1975), "Theory of the state, government tax and purchasing policy, and income distribution", *Review of Income and Wealth*, **21**, 111–124.

Scarf, H. E. (1967), "On the computation of equilibrium prices", in *Ten Economic Studies in the Tradition of Irving Fisher*, John Wiley, New York.

—— (1969), "An example of an algorithm for calculating general equilibrium prices", *American Economic Review*, **59**, 669–677.

Scarf, H. E. with the collaboration of T. Hansen (1973), *The Computation of Economic Equilibria*, Yale University Press, New Haven, Connecticut.

Schmölders, G. (1977), "Attitudes to taxation and their effects on work effort" in *Fiscal Policy and Labour Supply*, Institute for Fiscal Studies, London.

Schumpeter, J. A. (1954), *Capitalism, Socialism and Democracy*, Harper, New York.

Scitovsky, T. (1976), *The Joyless Economy*, Oxford University Press, New York.

Seade, J. K. (1977), "On the shape of optimal tax schedules", *Journal of Public Economics*, **7**, 203–236.

—— (1979), "Optimal nonlinear policies for non-utilitarian motives", Warwick Economic Research Paper.

Sen, A. K. (1966), "Labour allocation in a cooperative enterprise", *Review of Economic Studies*, **33**, 361–371.

—— (1970a), "Interpersonal aggregation and partial comparability", *Econometrica*, **38**, 393–409.

—— (1970b), *Collective Choice and Social Welfare*, Holden-Day, San Francisco.

—— (1973), *On Economic Inequality*, Oxford University Press, Oxford.

—— (1977a), "Social choice theory: a re-examination", *Econometrica*, **45**, 53–89.

—— (1977b), "On weights and measures: informational constraints in social welfare analysis", *Econometrica*, **45**, 1539–1572.

Shapley, L. S. (1973), "Lets block 'block'", *Econometrica*, **41**, 1201–1202.

Shapley, L. S. and M. Shubik (1977), "An example of a trading economy with three competitive equilibria", *Journal of Political Economy*, **85**, 873–875.

Shephard, R. W. (1944), "A mathematical theory of the incidence of taxation", *Econometrica*, **12**, 1–18.

Sheshinski, E. (1971a), "Welfare aspects of a regulatory constraint: note", *American Economic Review*, **61**, 175–178.

—— (1971b), "On the theory of optimal income taxation", HIER Discussion Paper No. 172.

—— (1972), "The optimal linear income tax", *Review of Economic Studies*, **39**, 297–302.

—— (1976), "Income taxation and capital accumulation", *Quarterly Journal of Economics*, **90**, 138–149.

—— (1977), "The supply of communal goods and revenue sharing" in *The Economics of Public Services*, M. S. Feldstein and R. P. Inman (eds), Macmillan, London.

Shorrocks, A. F. (1975), "On stochastic models of size distributions", *Review of Economic Studies*, **42**, 631–641.

—— (1979), "The structure of intergenerational transfers between families", *Economica*, **46**, (in press).

Shoup, C. S. (1969), *Public Finance*, Weidenfeld and Nicolson, London.

Shoven, J. B. (1974), "A proof of the existence of a general equilibrium with ad valorem commodity taxes", *Journal of Economic Theory*, **8**, 1–25.

—— (1976), "The incidence and efficiency effects of taxes on income from capital", *Journal of Political Economy*, **84**, 1261–1284.

Shoven, J. B. and J. Whalley (1972), "A general equilibrium calculation of the effects of differential taxation of income from capital in the U.S.", *Journal of Public Economics*, **1**, 281–321.

—— and —— (1973), "General equilibrium with taxes: a computational procedure and an existence proof", *Review of Economic Studies*, **60**, 475–490.

—— and —— (1977), "Equal yield tax alternatives: general equilibrium computational technique", *Journal of Public Economics*, **8**, 211–224.

Shubik, M. (1970), "Voting, or a price system in a competitive market structure", *American Political Science Review*, **64**, 179–181.

Sidgwick, H. (1883), *Principles of Political Economy*, Macmillan, London.

Simons, H. C. (1938), *Personal Income Taxation*, University of Chicago Press, Chicago.

Slutsky, S. M. (1975), "Abstentions and majority equilibrium", *Journal of Economic Theory*, **11**, 292–304.

—— (1977), "A voting model for the allocation of public goods: existence of an equilibrium", *Journal of Economic Theory*, **14**, 299–325.

Smith, Adam (1776), *An Inquiry into the Nature and Causes of the Wealth of Nations*, E. Cannan (ed.), Methuen, London, 1904.

Solow, R. M. (1956), "A contribution to the theory of economic growth", *Quarterly Journal of Economics*, **70**, 65–94.

—— (1961), "Note on Uzawa's two-sector model of economic growth", *Review of Economic Studies*, **29**, 48–50.

—— (1970), *Growth Theory: An Exposition*, Clarendon Press, Oxford.

—— (1971), "Some implications of alternative criteria for the firm", in *The Corporate Economy*, R. Marris and A. Wood (eds), Macmillan, London.

Spence, M. (1973), "Job market signaling", *Quarterly Journal of Economics*, **87**, 355–379.

—— (1977), "Non-linear prices and welfare", *Journal of Public Economics*, **8**, 1–18.

Starrett, D. A. (1972), "Fundamental non-convexities in the theory of externalities", *Journal of Economic Theory*, **4**, 180–199.

—— (1974), "On the nature of externalities", IMSSS Technical Report 129, Stanford University.

Stern, N. H. (1976), "On the specification of models of optimum income taxation", *Journal of Public Economics*, **6**, 123–162.

—— (1977), "Optimum taxation with errors in administration", University of Oxford (unpublished).

Stigler, G. J. (1967), "Imperfections in the capital market", *Journal of Political Economy*, **75**, 287–292.

—— (1970), "Director's law of public income redistribution", *Journal of Law and Economics*, **13**, 1–10.

—— (1974), "Free riders and collective action", *Bell Journal of Economics*, **5**, 359–365.

—— (1975), *The Citizen and the State*, University of Chicago Press, Chicago.

Stiglitz, J. E. (1969a), "A re-examination of the Modigliani–Miller theorem", *American Economic Review*, **59**, 784–793.

—— (1969b), "Distribution of income and wealth among individuals", *Econometrica*, **37**, 382–397.

—— (1969c), "The effects of income, wealth and capital gains taxation on risk-taking", *Quarterly Journal of Economics*, **83**, 262–283.

—— (1970a), "Factor price equalization in a dynamic economy", *Journal of Political Economy*, **78**, 456–488.

—— (1970b), "A consumption-oriented theory of the demand for financial assets and the term structure of interest rates", *Review of Economic Studies*, **37**, 321–351.

—— (1972), "Theory of finance", *Bell Journal of Economics and Management Science*, **3**, 458–482.

—— (1973), "Taxation, corporate financial policy, and the cost of capital", *Journal of Public Economics*, **2**, 1–34.

—— (1974a), "On the irrelevance of corporate financial policy", *American Economic Review*, **64**, 851–866.

—— (1974b), "The demand for education in public and private school systems", *Journal of Public Economics*, **3**, 349–385.

—— (1974c), "Growth with exhaustible natural resources: the competitive economy", *Review of Economic Studies*, **41**, 139–152.

—— (1975a), "The theory of 'screening', education, and the distribution of income", *American Economic Review*, **65**, 283–300.

—— (1975b), "Information and economic analysis" in *Current Economic Problems*, M. Parkin and A. R. Nobay (eds), Cambridge University Press, Cambridge.

—— (1976a), "The corporation tax", *Journal of Public Economics*, **5**, 303–311.

—— (1976b), "Estate taxes, growth and redistribution" in *Public and Urban Economics*, R. E. Grieson (ed.), Lexington Books, Lexington, Massachusetts.

—— (1976c), "Simple formulae for optimal income taxation and the measurement of inequality", mimeo.

—— (1977), "The theory of local public goods" in *The Economics of Public Services*, M. S. Feldstein and R. P. Inman (eds), Macmillan, London.

—— (1978a), "Notes on estate taxes, redistribution, and the concept of balanced growth path incidence", *Journal of Political Economy*, **86**, S137–150.

—— (1978b), "Equality, taxation and inheritance" in *Personal Income Distribution*, W. Krelle and A. F. Shorrocks (eds), North-Holland, Amsterdam.

—— (1979), "Local public goods and matching", unpublished, Oxford University.

—— (1980), *Information and Economic Analysis*, Oxford University Press, Oxford.

Stiglitz, J. E. and M. J. Boskin (1977), "Some lessons from the new public finance", *American Economic Review*, **67**, 295–301.

Stiglitz, J. E. and P. S. Dasgupta (1971), "Differential taxation, public goods, and economic efficiency", *Review of Economic Studies*, **38**, 151–174.

Stiglitz, J. E. and H. Uzawa (eds) (1969), *Readings in the Modern Theory of Economic Growth*, MIT Press, Cambridge, Massachusetts.

Stiglitz, J. E. and A. Weiss (1979), "Theory of credit rationing", unpublished discussion paper, Bell Laboratories.

Stone, J. R. N. (1954), "Linear Expenditure Systems and Demand Analysis", *Economic Journal*, **64**, 511–527.

—— (1964), "Private saving in Britain, past, present and future", *Manchester School*, **32**, 79–112.

Strümpel, B. (1969), "The contribution of survey research to public finance", in *Quantitative Analysis in Public Finance*, A. T. Peacock (ed.), Praeger, New York.

Sumner, M. T. (1975), "Neutrality of corporate taxation, or On not accounting for inflation", *Manchester School*, **43**, 353–361.

Thompson, E. A. (1967), "Debt instruments in macroeconomic and capital theory", *American Economic Review*, **57**, 1196–1210.

Tideman, T. N. and G. Tullock (1976), "A new and superior process for making social choices", *Journal of Political Economy*, **84**, 1145–1159.

Tiebout, C. M. (1956), "A pure theory of local expenditures", *Journal of Political Economy*, **64**, 416–424.

Tobin, J. (1955), "A dynamic aggregative model", *Journal of Political Economy*, **63**, 103–115.

—— (1958), "Liquidity preference as behavior towards risk", *Review of Economic Studies*, **25**, 65–86.

—— (1965), "The burden of the public debt: A review article", *Journal of Finance*, **20**, 679–682.

—— (1967), "Life cycle saving and balanced growth" in *Ten Economic Studies in the Tradition of Irving Fisher*, John Wiley, New York.

—— (1970), "On limiting the domain of inequality", *Journal of Law and Economics*, **13**, 263–277.

Townsend, P. B. (1968), "The difficulties of negative income tax" in *Social Services for All? Part Four*, Fabian Society, London.

Tulkens, H. (1978), "Dynamic processes for public goods: an institution-oriented survey", *Journal of Public Economics*, **9**, 163–201.

Tullock, G. (1970), "A simple algebraic logrolling model", *American Economic Review*, **60**, 419–426.

Turvey, R. (ed.), (1968), *Public Enterprise*, Penguin, Harmondsworth.

—— (1971), *Economic Analysis and Public Enterprises*, Allen and Unwin, London.

Ulph, D. T. (1976), "Income distribution and public goods", mimeo.

—— (1978), "On the optimal distribution of income and educational expenditure", *Journal of Economic Theory*, **19**, 492–512.

—— (1977), "On labour supply and the measurement of inequality", mimeo.

—— (1979), "Income distribution and public goods", *Econometrica*, **47**,

US Department of Health, Education and Welfare (1973), *Summary Report: New Jersey Graduated Work Incentive Experiment*, Government Printing Office, Washington DC.

US Treasury (1977), *Blueprints for Basic Tax Reform*, Government Printing Office, Washington DC.

Usher, D. (1977), "The welfare economics of the socialisation of commodities", *Journal of Public Economics*, **8**, 151–168.

Uzawa, H. (1961), "On a two-sector model of economic growth", *Review of Economic Studies*, **29**, 40–47.

Vandendorpe, A. L. and A. F. Friedlaender (1976), "Differential incidence in the presence of initial distorting taxes", *Journal of Public Economics*, **6**, 205–229.

Varian, H. R. (1978), *Microeconomic Analysis*, Norton, New York.

Vickrey, W. S. (1947), *Agenda for Progressive Taxation*, Ronald Press, New York.

—— (1960), "Utility, strategy and social decision rules", *Quarterly Journal of Economics*, **74**, 507–535.

—— (1961), "Counterspeculation, auctions and competitive sealed tenders", *Journal of Finance*, **16**, 8–37.

Viner, J. (1920), "Who paid for the war?", *Journal of Political Economy*, **28**, 46–76.

Wales, T. J. and A. D. Woodland (1979), "Labor supply and progressive taxes", *Review of Economic Studies*, **46**, 83–95.

Walker, D. (1955), "The direct–indirect tax problem: Fifteen years of controversy", *Public Finance*, **10**, 153–176.

Walters, A. A. (1967), "How to make a benefit of the burden of national debt", *National Tax Journal*, **20**, 316–318.

Wan, H. Y. (1971), *Economic Growth*, Harcourt Brace Jovanovich, New York.

Watts, H. W. *et al.* (1974), "The labor-supply response of husbands", *Journal of Human Resources*, **9**, 181–200.

Watts, H. W. and A. Rees (eds) (1977), *The New Jersey Income-Maintenance Experiment: Volume 2—Labor Supply Responses*, Academic Press, New York.

Weisbrod, B. A. (1968), "Income redistribution effects and benefit–cost analysis" in *Problems in Public Expenditure Analysis*, S. B. Chase (ed.), Brookings Institution, Washington DC.

Weitzman, M. L. (1974), "Prices vs quantities", *Review of Economic Studies*, **41**, 477–491.

—— (1977), "Is the price system or rationing more effective in getting a commodity to those who need it most?", *Bell Journal of Economics*, **8**, 517–524.

von Weizsäcker, C. C. (1966), "Tentative notes on a two sector model with induced technical progress", *Review of Economic Studies*, **33**, 245–251.

Wells, P. (1955), "General equilibrium analysis of excise taxes", *American Economic Review*, **45**, 345–359.

Wesson, J. (1972), "On the distribution of personal incomes", *Review of Economic Studies*, **39**, 77–86.

Westhoff, F. (1977), "Existence of equilibria in economies with a local public good", *Journal of Economic Theory*, **14**, 84–112.

Whalley, J. (1975), "A general equilibrium assessment of the 1973 United Kingdom tax reform", *Economica*, **42**, 139–161.

——— (1977), "The United Kingdom tax system 1968–1970: some fixed point indications of its economic impact", *Econometrica*, **45**, 1837–1858.

Whalley, J. and J. R. Piggott (1977), "General equilibrium investigations of U.K. tax-subsidy policy: a progress report" in *Studies in Modern Economic Analysis*, M. J. Artis and A. R. Nobay (eds), AUTE 1976 Conference Volume, Oxford.

Wheatcroft, G. S. A. (1969), "Inequity in Britain's tax structure", *Lloyds Bank Review*, **93**, 11–26.

Wilde, J. A. (1968), "The expenditure effects of grant-in-aid programs", *National Tax Journal*, **21**, 340–348.

Williams, A. (1966a), "The optimal provision of public goods in a system of local government", *Journal of Political Economy*, **74**, 18–33.

——— (1966b), *Tax Policy—Can Surveys Help?*, PEP Broadsheet.

Williamson, J. (1966), "Profit, growth and sales maximisation", *Economica*, **33**, 1–16.

Williamson, O. E. (1964), *The Economics of Discretionary Behavior*, Kershaw, London.

Willig, R. D. (1978), "Pareto-superior nonlinear outlay schedules", *Bell Journal of Economics*, **9**, 56–69.

Wilson, R. B. (1969), "An axiomatic model of logrolling", *American Economic Review*, **59**, 331–341.

——— (1970), "The game-theoretic structure of Arrow's General Possibility theorem", *Journal of Economic Theory*, **2**, 14–20.

Wright, C. (1967), "Some evidence on the interest elasticity of consumption", *American Economic Review*, **57**, 850–855.

——— (1969), "Saving and the rate of interest" in *The Taxation of Income from Capital*, A. C. Harberger and M. J. Bailey (eds), Brookings Institution, Washington DC.

Yaari, M. E. (1964), "On the consumer's lifetime allocation process", *International Economic Review*, **5**, 304–317.

——— (1965), "Uncertain lifetime, life insurance and the theory of the consumer", *Review of Economic Studies*, **32**, 137–150.

Zeckhauser, R. (1969), "Uncertainty and the need for collective action" in *The Analysis and Evaluation of Public Expenditures: The PPB System*, Joint Economic Committee, US Congress. Reprinted in R. Haveman and J. Margolis (eds) (1970), *Public Expenditures and Policy Analysis*, Markham, Chicago.

——— (1977), "Taxes in fantasy, or Most any tax on labor can turn out to help the laborers", *Journal of Public Economics*, **8**, 133–150.

AUTHOR INDEX

SUBJECT INDEX

610